The Song of Songs Through the Ages

Studies of the Bible and Its Reception

Edited by
Constance M. Furey, Brian Matz,
Joel Marcus LeMon, Thomas Römer,
Jens Schröter, Barry Dov Walfish,
and Eric Ziolkowski

Volume 8

The Song of Songs Through the Ages

―

Essays on the Song's Reception History
in Different Times, Contexts, and Genres

Edited by
Annette Schellenberg

DE GRUYTER

ISBN 978-3-11-162094-7
e-ISBN (PDF) 978-3-11-075079-9
e-ISBN (EPUB) 978-3-11-075082-9
ISSN 2195-450X

Library of Congress Control Number: 2022952374

Bibliographic information published by the Deutsche Nationalbibliothek
The Deutsche Nationalbibliothek lists this publication in the Deutsche Nationalbibliografie; detailed bibliographic data are available on the internet at http://dnb.dnb.de.

© 2024 Walter de Gruyter GmbH, Berlin/Boston
This volume is text- and page-identical with the hardback published in 2023.
Typesetting: Integra Software Services Pvt. Ltd.

www.degruyter.com

Contents

Annette Schellenberg
The Song of Songs Through the Ages: Introduction —— 1

Uta Heil
Between Hippolytus and Athanasius: The Variety of Patristic Song of Songs' Interpretations —— 11

Jonathan Kaplan
"Dripping from the Lips of Sleeping Ones": The Interpretation of the Song of Songs from Tannaitic Literature to the Palestinian Talmud —— 37

Tamar Kadari
The Exegesis of all Exegeses: The Uniqueness of Shir HaShirim Rabbah's Approach to the Song of Songs —— 55

Gerhard Langer
"I Slept but My Heart Was Awake": Rabbinic Interpretations of Song of Songs 5:2 —— 71

Erik Wade
Reading the Old English *Life of Saint Mary of Egypt* with Abbot Hadrian of Africa: The Influence of Byzantine Readings of the Song of Songs on Early Medieval England —— 89

Günter Stemberger
Targum Song of Songs, the History of Israel, and the Study of Torah —— 115

Elliot R. Wolfson
Do Not Wake or Arouse Love: Erotics of Time and the Dream of Messianic Waiting —— 129

Ariel Zinder
Of Songs and Sequels: The Song of Songs in the Hebrew Liturgical Poetry of Al-Andalus —— 145

Jonathan Vardi
A Vocabulary of Love: The Song of Songs in the Secular Hebrew Love Poetry from Muslim Spain —— 165

Ludger Schwienhorst-Schönberger
Bernard of Clairvaux: The Song of Songs as an Instruction on the Spiritual Life —— 177

Hannah W. Matis
Preaching the Song of Songs at Admont: A Minority Report from the Twelfth Century —— 199

Rabea Kohnen
Voices Shifting and Voices Layered: The Song of Songs in Medieval German Commentaries —— 213

Christopher Ocker
An Ecology of Desire: Pierre d'Ailly's First Theological Work, a Latin Commentary on the Song of Songs —— 241

Lieke Smits
Lovers, Gardens, and Wounds: An Exploration of the Medieval Iconographies of the Song of Songs —— 263

Stefan Gasch
Singing the Song of Songs in the Late Middle Ages and the Renaissance: The Evidence of the Alamire Manuscripts —— 287

Bernard McGinn
Early Modern Women Comment on the Song of Songs —— 311

Timothy H. Robinson
Varieties of Reformed and Puritan Reception of the Song of Songs, 1550–1730 —— 329

Yael Almog
The Song of Songs in Late Eighteenth-Century Germany: Theology and Desire —— 347

Elisabeth Birnbaum
The Song of Songs as a Drama: A Radical Change of Interpretation in the Eighteenth and Nineteenth Century —— 363

Caroline Sauter
Love and Language: The Song of Songs in Scholem and Rosenzweig —— 393

Michaela C. Hastetter
"Black and Beautiful" (Song 1:5): A Key Verse in the Exegesis of the Song of Songs from Origen to Dieter Salbert's *Schwarz—wie die Teppiche Salomos* (1971) —— 415

Ute Jung-Kaiser
"I Am Black *and* Comely": Literal and/or Allegorical Interpretations in Theology, Music, and Image, Especially in the Present Time —— 437

P. W. (Bill) Goodman
"The Time of Singing has Come": The Lure of the Song of Songs for Today's Composers and Songwriters —— 469

Contributors —— 483

Index —— 485

Annette Schellenberg
The Song of Songs Through the Ages
Introduction

The Song of Songs is a fascinating text. With its monologues and dialogues about desire and love, plot fragments, sensual descriptions, and metaphorical language, it triggers the imagination of its readers and draws them into its world. How they experience this world depends on their imagination. The text leaves many questions open; there is considerable ambiguity and ample room for diverse interpretations. According to the common understanding of modern biblical scholarship, the Song of Songs is a text (or collection of texts) about human love: it describes the desire and love between a man and a woman, and its only connection to the divine is the "divine" character of human love. Why such an erotic text was included in the collection of sacred writings in ancient Israel remains a question of dispute. Regardless, with the inclusion in the Hebrew Bible the Song became a biblical book, which increases its draw and is an essential factor to explain its popularity.

Both in the Jewish and the Christian traditions, it became common early on to read the Song allegorically, as a text on the relationship between the divine and humans. Consequently, the Song became one if not the most influential texts of the entire Bible—cherished because it was understood as a text that addresses the fundamental question of God's love for Israel, the church, and individual believers, respectively. Over the course of time, different variants of allegorical interpretation have been developed. Some of them stand in contrast with one another (cf. the polemics between Christians and Jews on the question of who is the beloved spouse of God), others were employed side by side (e.g., Marian and mystical interpretations). Throughout antiquity, the Middle Ages, the time of the Reformation, and the following century, allegorical interpretations of the Song were the norm; nonetheless, many of the allegorical interpreters still paid attention to the text's literal meaning. A fundamental change came only in the eighteenth century: from here on, literal interpretations of the Song are prevalent; nonetheless, some interpreters still ask about allegorical meanings and the Song's religious significance. Beyond the question of allegorical and literal understandings, the Song's reception history is exceedingly rich because it is not limited to interpretations in commentaries, sermons, and the like. Alongside with exegetical debates, the Song also had an enormous impact on spirituality, theological and intellectual debates, understandings of marriage and love, as well as the arts (literature, music, paintings, etc.).

With the increased general interest in the reception history of biblical books, in the last few decades also the reception history of the Song of Songs has gained attention. In addition to studies on particular works of reception, several volumes have been published that give more comprehensive overviews. Particularly notable are *The Song of Songs in the Middle Ages* by Ann W. Astell (1990), *A Two Thousand Year History of the Influence of the Song of Songs on Religion, Literature, Music, and Art* by Chaim T. Horovitz (2010), *The Song of Songs: A Biography* by Ilana Pardes (2019), and *A Companion to the Song of Songs in the History of Spirituality* by Timothy H. Robinson (2021). These volumes are most helpful to gain overviews, but of course they have to make choices and leave out many aspects that are interesting as well. The present volume does not aim at filling all the gaps, but the hope is to present another "bouquet" of essays on the Song of Songs' reception history that informs about major lines of interpretation, illustrates the diversity of forms of impact, and illuminates aspects that have not been dealt with before.

The volume originated from a conference that should have taken place in Vienna in 2020 but had to be cancelled due to the Corona pandemic. It includes twenty-three contributions of scholars in different fields, covering the Song's reception history through the ages, including not only interpretations in the narrow sense of the word but also literary adaptions and receptions in music and art, etc. The contributors have been asked to provide some general background information so that readers who are not experts in their field of specialization get the broader picture. Many followed the suggestion to address how the Song's eroticism was dealt with in its reception history and whether/how it was interpreted literally and/or allegorically. The articles are ordered chronologically. The following overview shall give a first impression of their breadth and depth.

The volume opens with an article by *Uta Heil* on Christian interpretations of the Song of Songs in the Patristic period. Heil first recalls that it was normal for Christian authors in Late Antiquity to understand the Song figuratively and interpret it spiritually, and then shows that even with this shared point of departure there was a huge variety of interpretations. To illustrate the variety and creativity of patristic interpretations of the Song, she first gives an overview of the different interpretations in Greek commentaries on the Song from the third to fifth century (Hippolytus, Origen, Gregory of Nyssa, Theodoret of Cyrus, Philo of Carpasia) and then presents two texts, which are less known. These two texts—the *Homilia in Canticum Canticorum* and the *Synopsis Scripturae Sacrae*—are attributed to Athanasius of Alexandria but they are pseudepigraphic. Heil shows that they offer a Christological interpretation of the Song in the narrower sense and thereby combine a collective allegory, related to the church, and an individual allegory, related to the Christian and his soul.

Jonathan Kaplan's article on rabbinic interpretations of the Song in the Tannaitic (ca. 70–220 CE) and Amoraic (ca. 220–500 CE) period is the volume's first article on Jewish interpretations of the Song. In both periods, the rabbis associated the

Song's male protagonist with God and the female protagonist with Israel, as is usual for Jewish interpretations. Their interpretations are neither erotic nor sensual but they read the Song typologically to characterize the relationship between God and Israel as one marked by deep love and mutual devotion. Kaplan shows that beyond this shared hermeneutical approach, the amoraic interpretations of the Song found scattered throughout the Palestinian Talmud also offer novel interpretations and reflect a shift from interpreting verses from the Song on an idealized vision of Israel's biblical history (exodus, Sinai, theophany, wanderings through the wilderness) to associating them with contemporary rabbinic society and practice.

Tamar Kadari presents Shir ha-Shirim Rabbah (Song of Songs Rabbah), the earliest and longest midrashic collection on the Song, which she has recently edited in a Synoptic edition. This important work, which is structured according to the biblical text, is a collection of interpretations by different sages from several centuries, redacted at the end of the sixth or beginning of the seventh century. Kadari points out the work's richness. For almost all verses, Shir ha-Shirim Rabbah offers interpretations attributed to different sages, reflecting a multiplicity of views and opinions. Sometimes the rabbis attempt to clarify the literal meanings of words, sometimes they touch on questions that concern the text's overall character, but in most cases they interpret the Song allegorically on the relationship between God and Israel, describing phases of both closeness and distance. One passage (on Song 1:6) offers a parable on the question of the identity of the chosen people, indicating that the allegorical interpretation of the Song might also have played a role in Jewish-Christian polemics.

Gerhard Langer focuses on three concrete examples of rabbinic interpretations of Song 5:2 ("I slept but my heart was awake . . .") and uses them to show how rabbinic exegesis works. The first two examples, explained in detail, are the midrash Pesiqta de Rab Kahana (fifth century) and the Song of Songs Rabbah; the third is the Targum of the Song of Songs (ninth century?), treated in an outlook. Langer shows how the rabbis interpret the Song allegorically on different phases in the history of God with Israel, bridging the past and the present and emphasizing the deep love of God, how they argue intertextually and linguistically, and how their interpretations are connected with their world view and theology.

Erik Wade presents two lesser-known examples of Christian receptions of the Song of Songs, namely the echoes of the Song in the Old English *Life of Saint Mary of Egypt* and the teachings (glosses) on the Song by Abbot Hadrian of Africa and (probably) Archbishop Theodore from Tarsus (present-day Turkey), who arrived in England in the second half of the seventh century and introduced the English to the Byzantine version of the legend of St. Mary of Egypt. Wade argues that the two monks of non-European origin defied the usual Christian exegesis and did not connect the blackness of the woman mentioned in Song 1:5 with sin and did not oppose it to beauty (thus Vulg. 1:4,[1] with the influential translation "black but beautiful"; cf. the articles by Michaela C. Hastetter and Ute Jung-Kaiser). His analysis further shows that Hadrian and Theodore understood the Song as a text with a spiritual message but did not contrast this spirituality with eroticism and the text's human level. In the appendix Wade provides Hadrian's glosses on the Song in Latin, with an English translation.

With the Targum Song of Songs, *Günter Stemberger* presents another important Jewish interpretation of the Song. Unlike the midrash Shir HaShirim Rabbah and other rabbinic texts, the Targum Song is not a compilation of different traditions but provides one coherent interpretation and probably is the work of one single author. Stemberger draws the attention to more recent discussions on the text's date (eight/ninth century? tenth/eleventh century?) and country of origin (Palestine? diaspora?) and then shows how the author of the Targum takes up and expands the rabbinic line of interpreting the Song allegorically on the history of God with Israel, thereby infusing it with religious meaning. Unlike the earlier rabbinic works, in the Targum this approach is applied not only to selected verses from the Song but to the entire text from its beginning to its end. The Targum offers a fully consistent reading of the Song on Israel's history from creation to final redemption, with a special focus on the study of the Torah under its rabbinic institutions.

Elliot R. Wolfson writes about the allegorical interpretations of the Song in the Jewish (and Christian) tradition and argues that they reflect awareness of the essentially metaphorical nature of eros and affirm the essentially erotic nature of metaphor (cf. the article by Caroline Sauter on similar ideas expressed by later Jewish interpreters). As an "iconographic" text the Song can serve as a portal through which readers get access to the realms of the transcendent and envision the invisible in its invisibility. Wolfson points out that in rabbinic interpretations the Song's eroticism is not undermined but on the contrary is amplified; the literal and the figurative converge. Important aspects are a non-linear understanding of time, the dreamlike character of the Song, and the oscillation between presence and absence, consummating and postponing desire. Particularly noteworthy is the Song's refrain "Do not wake or arouse love until it desire" (Song 2:7, etc.), which provided the rationale to read the Song messianically.

The volume's next two articles both deal with the Song's impact in medieval Muslim Spain (al-Andalus). *Ariel Zinder* presents the Hebrew liturgical poems (*piyyutim*) from al-Andalus, which date from the tenth and eleventh centuries.

---

[1] For three passages in the Song, the verse numbering in the Vulgate differs from the verse numbering in the Hebrew tradition (Hebr. 1:2–17 = Vulg. 1:1–16; Hebr. 6:2–12 = Vulg. 6:1–11; Hebr. 7:3–14 = Vulg. 7:2–13). If not noted otherwise, this volume gives the verse numbering of the Hebrew tradition.

Their Jewish authors continue the allegorical reading of the Song on the relationship of God and Israel, but they do so in a new way. Using the technique of narrative extension, they provide something like sequels to the Song, telling the story of the two lovers after their marriage and separation. In this interpretation, the female speaker represents the contemporary exiled Israel. Zinder explains this new interpretation with a bracketing of the Song's allegorical meaning and the interpretative gaze at the literal level of the lovers' story (cf. the secular love poems, treated in the article by Jonathan Vardi). In that the poets describe a later phase than the one described in the Song but still use the words exchanged in the Song, they also provoke to hear the Song in a new way.

Jonathan Vardi focuses on secular texts that are influenced by the Song, namely the Hebrew love poetry from Al-Andalus. Beginning in the tenth century, poets from the Jewish elite created a new school of poetry, imitating the masterpieces of Arabic poetry, strictly using biblical Hebrew. Vardi shows how in their love poems, which were always presented in the voice of a male speaker, expressing his love for either a female or male lover, the Jewish poets made use of the Song's vocabulary, metaphors, and motifs, constantly shifting between recitation, adaption, emendation, exegesis, and even parody. The process of transmuting the Song into "modern," Arabic-style love poetry was not unidirectional, but the new poetic ideal also had an influence on how the Jewish poets read the Song itself (cf. the article by Ariel Zinder).

Ludger Schwienhorst-Schönberger writes about Bernard of Clairvaux, the Cistercian abbot from the twelfth century, whose sermons on the Song of Songs had a huge impact on its reception for many centuries to come. Taking up the classification by medievalist Jean Leclercq, Schwienhorst-Schönberger describes Bernard as one of the main exponents of monastic theology, which unlike scholastic theology was less interested in asking critical questions and attaining knowledge, but first and foremost in spiritual experience. Thus, in Bernard's exegetical approach, one's own experience is vital in order to understand biblical texts. Accordingly, he interpreted the Song of Songs mystically, on the relationship between God and the soul of the individual believer, and read it as a guide for a spiritual life. An important verse for Bernhard was Song 1:2 ("let him kiss me with the kisses of his mouth!"). Like many mystics after him, he understood the woman's wish as expression of the soul's desire for a direct encounter with God.

Like Ludger Schwienhorst-Schönberger, *Hannah W. Matis* deals with the reception of the Song in the twelfth century and its role for monastic spirituality. But she delivers a "minority report" (as she formulates in the subtitle of her article), namely in writing about the Song's reception by women. More concretely, Matis investigates the Song's reception in the double monastery of Admont (present-day Austria), which since around 1120 also accepted nuns. Admont was known for biblical exegesis, and as usual in the Middle Ages, the Song was a favorite text. The dominant mode of how the Song was interpreted in Admont was Marian: neither ecclesiologically (God-church) nor mystically (God-soul) but as love song between Christ and Mary. Matis connects this observation with the thesis that most probably many of the sermons on the Song copied in Admont have been written (and heard) not by men but by women. For them, Mary was the preeminent personification for their own piety, and the Song thus important to understand their own bridal vocation.

Rabea Kohnen draws the attention to medieval receptions of the Song in the German vernacular and presents the *Expositio in Canticum Canticorum* by Williram of Ebersberg (eleventh century), the anonymous *Lehre der liebenden Gotteserkenntnis*, better known as *Das St. Trudperter Hohelied* (twelfth century; presumably written in Admont), and *Hohelied* by Brun of Schönebeck (thirteenth century). All three works are literary adaptions of the Song that at the same time are exegetical, aimed at a better understanding of the biblical text. Williram's *Expositio* interprets the Song as a dialogue between Christ and the church (and sometimes the synagogue and the church of the gentiles). *Das St. Trudperter Hohelied* includes mystic and Marian elements but also has a strong emphasis on the community. Schönebeck's *Hohelied* consists of a new version of a literal understanding of the Song and three different allegorical readings (Marian, tropological, ecclesiological). Kohnen analyzes the three works, paying particular attention to how they construct the dialogues between the voices of groom (*sponsus*) and bride (*sponsa*), the narrating voice (primary voice) and the (implied) recipients, and the voice of the text and the voices of older textual traditions.

Christopher Ocker deals with the interpretation of the Song in different works by Pierre d'Ailly, a French theologian from the fourteenth/fifteenth century. The youngest of these works is *Le Jardin amoureux de l'âme devote*, a well-known essay based on an allegorical reading of the Song, with which d'Ailly contributed to a debate on a popular romance novel from medieval France. The main focus of Ocker's article is on two texts that mark the beginning of d'Ailly's interest in the Song: an inaugural lecture and a commentary on the Song, which both have not been studied before. In the lecture, d'Ailly interprets the Song's garden imagery metaphorically on scripture, thereby emphasizing a sensuality that is fundamentally naturalistic. Similarly, in his commentary (1374), he reads the Song allegorically, thereby expanding the Song's natural associations and thus integrating the spiritual world into its setting, the entire life-world.

Lieke Smits draws the attention to the Song's huge impact on medieval visual culture. Focusing on Christianity in Western Europe in the Late Middle Ages, she provides a systematic overview of the different ways of how medieval images relate to the Song. Some images have a strong connection to the text. For example, many manuscripts contain illustrations in the "O" of *Osculetur me osculo oris sui* ("Let him kiss me with the kiss of his mouth"), the Song's opening verse. These images reflect different allegorical interpretations (esp. Christ-Ecclesia; Christ-Mary), but some also depict the text on the literal level (Solomon-queen of Sheba). Similarly, images related to the Song in biblical picture books (texts and images) and in the *Biblia pauperium* (solely images) provide "visual exegesis" (as Smits calls it). Other images are connected to the Song more indirectly. Smits discusses horticultural allusions (most famous the *hortus conclusus*), dramatizations of the narrative (often connected with the scene of the bride/soul searching the man/Christ), and images of Christ on the cross that can be perceived as representations of the heavenly bridegroom, evoking bridal desire.

Stefan Gasch investigates a group of musical manuscripts from the Late Middle Ages and the Renaissance, thus illuminating the Song's impact on music. This impact is closely connected with the Song's Marian interpretation and its inclusion in the Roman-Catholic Liturgy of the Hours (particularly linked with the Feast of the Assumption) in the ninth century. Connected with a growing importance of Marian devotion, during the fourteenth to sixteenth centuries many motets have been composed that are based on the Song. Gasch focuses on six manuscripts from the scribal workshop of Petrus Imhoff, also known as Alamire (fifteenth/sixteenth century). His selection is significant not only because it expands the overview of the development of the Song in liturgy and music by Jürg Stenzl (2008), which covers the ninth through the fifteenth centuries. It also documents a change that took place around 1500: Until then, polyphonic music with texts from the Song was almost exclusively used in liturgy. Connected with the growing importance of Mary in private devotion, however, from the end of the fifteenth century more and more musical works with texts from the Song were composed for individual needs.

Bernard McGinn takes up the topic of female interpreters of the Song (cf. the article by Hannah W. Matis). After mentioning the interesting phenomenon of gender-crossing (male mystics identify with the voice of the Bride), in the introduction he gives an overview on mystical literature by women from the twelfth through the seventeenth centuries. The Song was popular in mystical literature by women especially in the thirteenth, sixteenth, and seventeenth centuries. In the main bulk of the article, McGinn focuses on early modern (sixteenth and seventeenth centuries) female mystical exegetes and their practice of writing commentaries on the Song. More concretely, he presents commentaries and commentary-like works by Teresa of Avila, Jeanne de Cambry, Cecilia del Nacimiento, Marie de l'Incarnation, and Jeanne Guyon, and for each of them asks how the female mystics worked exegetically and how they understood the Song. His analysis shows that these commentaries are quite diverse: there is not *one* female mystical approach to the Song but a whole variety.

Timothy H. Robinson deals with Protestant interpretations of the Song and, more concretely, its reception among Reformed and Puritan theologians from the sixteenth through the eighteenth centuries. Correcting the wide-spread assumption that the Puritans avoided the Song because of its eroticism, he shows that it played an important role in their theology and spirituality. Puritans readers did not reject the Song's erotic language but appreciated it as part of the analogy between earthly marriage between man and woman and the spiritual marriage between Christ and the church/the soul. Unlike Catholic clergy, Protestant readers read the Song from their own experiences of marriage. Robinson differentiates three ways of how Reformed and Puritan readers appreciated the Song: as a historical-prophetic allegory on the relation of church and state; as nurturing an erotic-affective spirituality; and as an archetypal poem that inspires readers to initiate it in their own spiritual practice of writing.

Yael Almog analyzes the cultural background that in late eighteenth-century Germany (early Romanticism) led to an increasing interest in the Song of Songs and to its de-allegorization. With Johann Gottfried Herder, Johann Goethe, and Moses Mendelssohn, Almog presents three major German intellectuals from this period that each had a different approach to the Song. Most influential was Herder. He opposed an allegorical understanding of the Bible and instead advocated reading it as a human text. The Song was an ideal example because it addresses human sexuality so overtly. In addition, Herder was fascinated by the Song's poetry—for him a prime example of the untamed aesthetics of "the Orientals." Like Herder, Goethe was fascinated by the Song because it centers on human desire. But his main interest was not on the text's cultural background but on its qualities to elicit interpreters' inventiveness. Mendelssohn represents a third approach: As observant Jew, he emphasized the tenets of traditional Jewish scholarship. He was committed to the literal meaning of the Song (*peshat*) but nonetheless, against his Romantic contemporaries, insisted that its imagery concerns the divine-human relationship.

Elisabeth Birnbaum further illuminates the radical change in the interpretation of the Song in the eighteenth and nineteenth centuries. Emphasizing the strong connections between the intellectual, theological, and cultural elites of this period, she explains the change with three main trends: the development of the historical-critical method; a new concept of marriage and love; and the new enthusiasm for the Orient. Whereas Herder read the Song as a collection of folk songs, the dominant interpretation between 1820 und 1920 was the drama theory. In detailed analyses, Birnbaum shows how it was driven by the motivation to uncover the Song's historical setting and to "prove" its morality. In the last part of her article, she points out the drama-theory's long-lasting impacts: it inspired librettist and playwrights, so that at the end of the nineteenth century the Song had become a favorite subject of musical and nonmusical stage plays. And it led to the interpretation that Solomon had a harem, which (in the interpretation of 8:11–12) lives on until today.

Caroline Sauter analyses the Song's role in the thinking of German-Jewish language theory in the early twentieth century. More specifically, she focuses on the works of Gershom Scholem and Franz Rosenzweig and shows how for both of them the Song is at the core of their reflections on language and love. Scholem translated the text at the age of eighteen. This translation, as well as his reflections on it in his diary and in the correspondence with his friend Walter Benjamin, are illuminating for his early language philosophy. Important factors in Scholem's understanding of the Song are its Jewishness and greatness, which he connects with the ideas of severity, dignity, and veneration. According to Scholem, the Song possesses greatness in its pure literalness, but its language has the ability to accommodate elements that go beyond the literal expression. Better known is Rosenzweig's understanding of the Song. He deals with it in his famous work *The Star of Redemption* (1921), thereby displaying what he calls "speech-thinking": a thinking of language that combines poetry, theology, and philosophy, to capture the "cognition of the All." The Song is important in this thinking because of his "gleichnishaft" ("simile-like" or "allegorical") character, which is typical for both language (of love) and love.

The volume's next two articles deal both with Song 1:5, this famous verse which has attracted much attention because it mentions the woman's blackness and raised the question of whether to translate the Hebrew text as "black and beautiful" or "black but beautiful." Through the interpretation of the verse as a statement about the woman's natural skin color, the verse has also become important in view of race and racism. Both articles touch on these issues in that they discuss interpretations that convey negative views of blackness, but the problem of racist implications is not their main focus. *Michaela C. Hastetter* presents the composition *Schwarz— wie die Teppiche Salomos* by Dieter Salbert and connects the question of how to interpret it with the patristic dispute on allegorical vs. literal interpretations. In the first part of her article, she unfolds the allegorical interpretation of Origen of Alexandria (cf. the article by Uta Heil) and the literal interpretation of Theodore of Mopsuestia. This provides the background for the second part of the article, in which she interprets Salbert's composition from 1971 and points out aspects that suggest a eucharistic and a soteriological-baptismal interpretation.

Ute Jung-Kaiser discusses interpretations of Song 1:5 through the ages, both in theological writings as well as in film, literature, art, and music. After recalling different translations ("black and beautiful" vs. "black but beautiful") and different possibilities of how to interpret the woman's blackness (black skin color; sun tan; metaphor for sin, etc.), in the first part of the article she presents a significant selection of diverse interpretations of the verse from antiquity to the present, which illuminates the diversity of possible interpretations. In the second and third part of the article, she focuses on the twentieth and twenty-first centuries and presents musical compositions that quote or allude to Song 1:5 as well as visual representations of the (black) woman, pointing out reflections of both spiritual and humanitarian understandings of the verse.

The volume closes with an article by *P. W. (Bill) Goodman*. Fitting for the Song's superscription ("Song of Songs"), which highlights the text's musicality, he presents three contemporary musical appropriations of the Song: one classical ("Rise Up My Love" by Howard Skempton), one pop/rock ("Dark I am Yet Lovely" by Sinéad O'Connor), and one rock-style worship ("You Won't Relent" by Misty Edwards). For all three compositions, Goodman shows which texts they choose, what aspects they accentuate, and what messages they convey.

All the articles in this volume are rich and insightful on their own; and together they build a colorful "bouquet" that illuminates the richness of the Song's reception history, from antiquity up to today. Most of the articles were submitted in April 2021. For a variety of reasons, the publication process took longer as expected. I thank the authors for their patience. In addition, my thanks goes to Rebekka Rüger for assisting me with the formal editing of the articles, Sarah Shectman for improving the English in several articles, Elisabeth Oberleitner, Niklas von Hülsen, Leo Potyka, and Joe Pavlisko for help with the indexes and other tasks, and finally Alice Meroz, Aaron Sanborn-Overby, and Albrecht Döhnert from de Gruyter for their support in the publishing process.

Annette Schellenberg
Vienna, November 2022

Uta Heil

Between Hippolytus and Athanasius
The Variety of Patristic Song of Songs' Interpretations

1 Introduction

The Song of Songs in its Greek translation of the Septuagint was commented on with remarkable frequency by Christian authors of Late Antiquity. It was natural for almost all of them[1] to understand the text figuratively and to interpret it spiritually. This basic hermeneutic approach, however, should not lead us to overlook how different these interpretations can turn out to be. In fact, it is astonishing how diversely and creatively the songs were disclosed.

Of course, this cannot be demonstrated in detail in one essay. It is also impossible to present all of the transmitted works, so the following explanations will be limited to those works from Greek-speaking regions during the third to fifth century.[2] At the outset, however, major Greek commentaries on the Song of Songs will be briefly presented and their underlying main assumptions outlined. Therefore, the focus will first be on prefaces or prologues, where they have been transmitted (part 2). The main second section (parts 3 and 4), however, will present two texts on the Song of Songs that are attributed in the tradition to Athanasius of Alexandria, but are certainly pseudepigraphic. These two texts, which are otherwise rather on the margins of scholarly interest, enrich the exegesis of the Song of Songs and show once again the diversity of interpretations.

---

[1] See below, n. 17, on Theodore of Mopsuestia.
[2] See now also Cain, *Mystical Wounds*, the recently published overview on Greek commentaries, mainly concentrating on Origen and Gregory of Nyssa. For the Latin commentaries, see the study of Matter, *Voice of My Beloved*, with an excellent list of the Latin commentaries up to 1200 CE (204–210). See also Kannengiesser, *Handbook of Patristic Exegesis*, 303–304 and 310, and recently Shuve, *A Garden Enclosed*.

2 Major Greek Commentaries—a Survey

2.1 Hippolytus, *Interpretatio Cantici Canticorum* (CPG 1871)

The first extant Christian commentary on the Song of Songs is attributed to Hippolytus.[3] Here the research is confronted with two problems: First of all, who was this Hippolytus? There are doubts whether all the works attributed to Hippolytus were written by one person, and whether this person was the Roman presbyter who quarrelled with Calix of Rome (217–222 CE) and ultimately died in exile in Sardinia in 235 CE. Nevertheless, if one wants to distinguish an exegete Hippolytus from this presbyter Hippolytus, the dating of the work to the beginning of the third century remains probable, as does a location in Rome and not in Asia Minor or Arabia.[4] Second, what was the original Greek version of his commentary, which no longer survives? Regarding this question, however, the Georgian translation of a no longer extant Armenian translation of the Greek text, a Greek paraphrase, Slavonic florilegia, and further Armenian and Syrian fragments do provide a quite good impression of this work.[5]

Hippolytus introduces his commentary with the remark that Samuel, threefold inspired by the Father, Son, and Holy Spirit, composed the three works *Proverbia*, *Ecclesiastes*, and *Canticum Canticorum*. The third work of the Holy Spirit is a hymn

---

[3] See Chappuzeau, "Die Auslegung des Hohenliedes," 45–81, for possible Jewish predecessors. See on this in general Vulliaud, *Le Cantique des Cantiques*. There are, of course, further interpretations of the Song of Songs; from the early period one may refer to Methodius of Olympus, who in the seventh speech of his *Symposium* presents Prozilla, who justifies the special value of virginity with an exegesis of the Song of Songs.

[4] As suggested by Cerrato, "Hippolytus' *On the Song of Songs*," 268–273; idem, *Hippolytus between East and West*; Nautin, *Hippolyte et Josipe*; Simonetti, *Nuove Ricerche su Ippolito*. See, however, the statement of Eusebius of Caesarea in his *Church History* (6,22) about Hippolytus, namely, that he wrote a work on the Song of Songs (εἰς τὸ Ἆισμα) and that he was a church leader somewhere, without naming the place; see also Jerome, *De viris illustribus* 61. Cf. the review of Cerrato by Scholten in *Vigiliae Christianae*. See for the "Roman" hypothesis Brent, *Hippolytus and the Roman Church*; Frickel, *Das Dunkel um Hippolyt von Rom*.

[5] See Garitte, ed., *Traités d'Hippolyte*, 32–70 (edition of the Georgian version); Hippolytus, *Kommentar zum Hohenlied*, edited and translated by Bonwetsch (German translation of the Georgian version according to the older edition of Marr, published in St. Petersburg 1901); Richard, "Une paraphrase grecque," 140–154 (later Greek paraphrase of the commentary); Hippolytus, *Exegetische und homiletische Schriften*, edited and translated by Bonwetsch, 341–374 (translation of the Slavonic, Syriac, and Armenian fragments). See now Smith, *Mystery of Anointing* (a new translation and commentary of this work).

and a prophecy in praise of the Holy Spirit and serves for consolation.[6] It is in praise of the divine Sophia and Logos incarnate in the scripture and actually present in the church, according to God's plan and economy. Christ himself appears in the role of the bridegroom. As the divine Word, in him the Old Testament promise is fulfilled, in him God enters into humanity; he is the expected beloved. When, for example, Song 1:2–3 states that "your breasts are good beyond wine, and the fragrance of your anointing oils beyond any spice," Hippolytus asks what such a fragrant ointment might be if not the Word, which is rightly esteemed like incense. For as the dissolution of incense gives off fragrance, so the Word, proceeding from the Father, delights the hearers.[7] In sum, therefore, Hippolytus suggests that the beloved represents the church, that the lover is Christ, and that love defines the relationship between Christ and his followers.

Furthermore, Hippolytus outlines salvation history and describes the desire for the redeemer (as a desire for the ointment) in the course of Israel's history. Accordingly, he also interprets, for example, the two breasts as the two testaments.[8] Correspondingly, however, there is also, so to say, a negative salvation history, in which Christ is rejected and his call to repentance goes unheard.[9] Therefore, the church of the gentiles replaces the synagogue;[10] the gentiles are elected and the synagogue falls silent.

2.2 Origen's Commentaries and Homilies (CPG 1432–1434)

The most important and influential interpreter of the Song of Songs was undoubtedly Origen († 253/4 AD). He apparently commented on the work several times. An early work in two volumes (CPG 1434) that has not survived is mentioned by Jerome (*Epist.* 33,4; cf. the fragment in *Philoc.* 7,1[11]). His great commentary in ten books (CPG 1433) is a late work from the 240s (cf. Eusebius, *Hist. eccl.* 6,32,2), but it survives only in the Latin adaptation by Rufinus of Aquileia, who translated only the first three books, which extend to Song 2:15. The fragments from the catenary

---

[6] Smith interprets this commentary actually as a series of speeches designed to introduce newly baptized believers into certain mysteries of the faith in the context of Paschal or Easter initiation.
[7] See Hippolytus, *Interpretatio* in Cant. II on Song 1:2–3 (Bonwetsch, ed., trans., TU 23,2c, 26).
[8] See Hippolytus, *Interpretatio* in Cant. III on Song 1:2 (Bonwetsch, ed., trans., TU 23,2c, 34); XII on Song 1:13 (ibid., 45).
[9] Hippolytus, *Interpretatio* in Cant. VIII on Song 1:9 (Bonwetsch, ed., trans., TU 23,2c, 43–44); XIX on Song 2:10, 13 (ibid., 51).
[10] See Hippolytus, *Interpretatio* in Cant. XXV on Song 3:4 (Bonwetsch, ed., trans., TU 23,2c, 70).
[11] Origen, *Philocalie* 7,1 (Harl, ed., 356) about the necessity of distinguishing the speakers in biblical books.

manuscripts, therefore, are also valuable.[12] In addition, there are two homilies (on Song 1:1–12 and 1:12–2:14; CPG 1432) which Jerome translated during his time in Rome (383/384 CE) and dedicated to Pope Damasus.[13]

The basic assumption of Origen's interpretation is that this text is a wedding song in the form of a multi-role drama, which, employing the image of love between the bridegroom and the bride, explores the relationship of spiritual love between Christ and his church or between the Word of God and the individual believing soul. Therefore, Origen determines four roles: a) the bridegroom, b) the bride, c) the maidens who accompany the bride, and d) the crowd of companions of the groom. The bridegroom he understands to be Christ, the bride the immaculate church. The maidens, who appear to have already been granted salvation, are the souls of the faithful. Finally, the men with the bridegroom are the angels. Origen, unlike Hippolytus, thinks not only of a collective interpretation of the bride as Israel or the church, but also of the individual, or rather his soul, as the bride of Christ. However, the Song of Songs is a text for advanced readers, not least because of the possible misunderstandings of the eroticism of the text. Therefore, the Song of Songs offers a spiritual description of the mysticism of love, which, as a union of the soul with the Word of God, is actually accessible only to "perfected" Christians.

2.3 Gregory of Nyssa, *In Canticum Canticorum homiliae XV*

Gregory of Nyssa († after 394 CE) composed his fifteen homilies on the Song of the Songs (on Song 1:1–6:9) probably in the early 390s in Nyssa and republished them for Olympias[14] in Constantinople afterwards.[15] In his prologue to the homilies, he defends not only his reasons for supplementing Origin's commentary on this biblical text, but also its necessarily spiritual interpretation. The Song of Songs contains a hidden philosophy, which becomes recognizable after discarding the literal

---

12 On the catenary fragments, see Auwers, *L'interprétation*, 321–358.
13 The critical edition is Origen, *Homilien zu Samuel I, zum Hohelied und zu den Propheten*, translated and edited by W.A. Baehrens; an English translation is Origen, *Song of Songs: Commentary and Homilies*, translated and edited by Lawson; German translations are Origenes, *Der Kommentar zum Hohelied*; and Origenes, *Die Homilien und Fragmente zum Hohelied*, both volumes translated and edited by Fürst and Strutwolf and with very useful introductions and further literature. See on one homily also Deutsch, "Interpreter as Intertext."
14 On the famous deaconess in Constantinople, Olympias († 408 CE), see Grieser, "Olympias."
15 The critical edition is Gregory of Nyssa, *In Canticum Canticorum*, edited by Langerbeck; a German translation is Gregor von Nyssa, *In Canticum Canticorum Homiliae*, translated by Dünzl. See also Cahill, "Date and Setting"; Origen and Gregorio di Nissa, *Sul Cantico dei Cantici*, translated and edited by Limone and Moreschini; Maspero et al., eds., *Gregory of Nyssa: In Canticum Canticorum*.

meaning. Nevertheless, in contrast to Origen's opinion, the text is not only meant for advanced readers, but especially for beginners or simple Christians, who can be led here to a spiritual and immaterial state of the soul.[16] However, especially in answer to critics of spiritual exegesis, it must be maintained that a biblical text is to be interpreted in such a way that it is useful for faith and leads to the divine mysteries and to a purer way of life. A comparable example is the spiritual interpretation of water, bread, temple, way, and door from the Gospel of John, where Christ himself leads our thoughts towards that which is divine and incorporeal. The Song of Songs invites every human being to move towards the Divine—this ascent of the soul towards God is the main theme of the Song of Songs. It describes a mystical vision, and the soul is adorned here as a bride for an incorporeal, spiritual, and immaculate partnership with God, which should be pursued out of love and not fear.

Gregory's criticism of a literal interpretation of the Song of Songs is actually tangible only in one author: Theodore of Mopsuestia, in Cilicia (352–428 CE).[17] He belongs to the so-called Antiochene school, both in terms of his Christology and his exegesis.[18] However, only a brief fragment on the Song of Songs is available (probably from an otherwise unknown letter and not from a commentary), in which he rejects a figurative interpretation of this text: There is no prophecy of the blessings of the church that can be discerned, and God is not mentioned anywhere. For Theodore, the songs were composed by Solomon to win his wife's favor, and in defence of his desire for an Egyptian wife and against the reproaches to which his choice of her led.[19]

---

[16] See Dünzl, "Die Canticum-Exegese," 106–107: "Zwar kennt auch Gregor unterschiedliche Grade der Vollkommenheit, die er—wie Origenes—an den Gestalten der Braut und der Mädchen des Canticum demonstriert, doch ist die erstere bei ihm nicht 'vollkommen', sondern nur 'vollkommener' als jene, also weiter vorangekommen auf ihrem Weg, ohne an ein abschließendes Ziel gelangt zu sein. Im Gegenteil: Die bleibende Unfaßbarkeit Gottes (auch für die Vollkommeneren!) herauszustellen ist eines der durchgängigen Anliegen seiner hom. in. Cant., was sich für die Canticum-Exegese des Origenes nicht sagen läßt. Diese Differenz gründet in der veränderten theologiegeschichtlichen Situation: Die Unfaßbarkeit Gottes wird (erst) in der Kontroverse um den (Neo-)Arianismus zu einem der wichtigsten Argumente der nizänischen Partei."
[17] On Theodore of Mopsuestia, see the introduction by McLeod, *Theodore of Mopsuestia*, and on Theodor as exegete, see also Ondrey, *Minor Prophets as Christian Scripture*.
[18] About the so-called exegetical school of Antioch, see Hill, *Reading the Old Testament*; O'Keefe, "A Letter that Killeth"; Schäublin, "Zur paganen Prägung."
[19] Within the acts of the condemnation of Theodor at the Council in Constantinople in 553 CE, only a short quotation about the Song of Songs is transmitted: "Proclaim your blackness, my dusky and graceful bride, proclaim your race! They are disparaging a race that is cognate with the honourable origins of Israel. At the start of a reply to them begin [as follows]: from my hot kisses may they learn that we enjoy amorous discourse with one other." The quotation is from the records of the council

2.4 Theodoret of Cyrus, *Explanatio in Canticum Canticorum* (CPG 6203)

However, Theodor of Mopsuestia seems to have uttered here a quite isolated opinion, for Theodoret of Cyrus (393–ca. 460 CE),[20] who also belongs to the Antiochene school, apparently wrote a detailed commentary on the Song of Songs, as well as advocating a spiritual (πνευματικῶς PG 81, 37) or tropical (τροπικῶς PG 81, 33) interpretation here. He is directly criticising those who understand the songs as written by Solomon about himself and his Egyptian wife (PG 81, 29A). Unfortunately, this commentary has survived only in Catenae, of which, moreover, no new critical edition is available. The text printed in the *Patrologia Graeca* stems from the second volume of *Bibliotheca Veterum Patrum*[21] from 1624 and is based on a manuscript also from the seventeenth century (*Codex Vaticanus graecus* 621), which is one of the later witnesses to this type of Song of Songs Catena.[22] Interestingly, however, his dedicatory letter to John of Germanicia deals thoroughly with criticisms of this book as uncanonical and unworthy, and supports his pneumatic interpretation with earlier Christian commentators from Eusebius of Caesarea to John Chrysostom.[23] In addition, he discusses many biblical examples outside of the Songs of Songs for non-literal interpretation. In the end, he connects the Song with a statement of Paul in 2Cor 11:2 and with John 3:29, in order to clarify who the bride is here: She is the pious and virtuous souls, therefore the church (PG 81, 44–45). In sum, the three works of Solomon display a progression towards a climax: from ἠθικόν (about morality) to φυσιολογικόν (on understanding nature) to μυστικόν (mystic—on contemplating the divine; PG 81, 48).

---

from the fourth session (*Concilium Universale Constantinopolitanum sub Iustiniano habitum*, ACO IV, 1,69,28–31; Straub, ed.); the English translation is by Price (*The Acts of the Council of Constantinople of 553*; Price ed., trans., 266).

20 See Wesseling, "Theodoret von Kyros," *BBKL* 11:936–957.

21 *Bibliotheca Veterum Patrum*, 681–761.

22 See Theodoret of Cyrus, *Explanatio in Canticum Canticorum* (CPG 6203), PG 81, 28–213. An English translation is *Commentary on the Song of Songs*, translated and edited by Hill. See on this Catena Faulhaber, *Hohelied- Proverbien und Prediger-Catenen*, 6–15. On PG 81, 28–48 is a letter on the Song of Songs to John of Germanicia; PG 81, 49–53 is a kind of prologue to the commentary fragments by Theodoret.

23 See Eusebius, *Scholia in Canticum Canticorum* (CPG 3469: fr. 8), survived only in fragments in Catenae; see Faulhaber, *Hohelied- Proverbien und Prediger-Catenen*, 32–33 and 57–58. The so-called Catena of Eusebius is pseudepigraphic; this Catena is attributed to Eusebius because of the first prologue, also attributed to Eusebius (see n. 26)—however, this attribution originates from the *Synopsis Scripturae Sacrae*, a pseudepigraphic writing of Athanasius of Alexandria; see below, p. 21–31. A commentary of John Chrysostom is unknown.

Interestingly, therefore, Theodoret can state, like Origen, that this book is only for the perfected.[24]

2.5 Philo of Carpasia, *Ennarratio in Canticum Canticorum* and Further Greek Commentaries

Philo, bishop of Carpasia in Cyprus (around 385 CE), wrote the commentary[25] *Ennarratio in Canticum Canticorum* (CPG 3810), which closely follows this line of spiritual interpretation (πνευματικῶς). Only those whose thoughts are purified from all earthly things (τις τὸ ἑαυτοῦ φρόνημα τῶν σαρκικῶν ἀπαλλάξῃ παθῶν PG 40, 32B) can understand the Song of Songs correctly, for in the Song, for example, the church as the bride speaks profound and mystical words of faith to her bridegroom (οὕτω καὶ ἐν τοῖς ᾄσμασι τῶν ᾀσμάτων ἡ ἁγία νύμφη ἐκκλησία τὰ βαθέα καὶ μυστηριώδη τῆς πίστεως ῥήματα τῷ ἰδίῳ προσλαλεῖ νυμφίῳ PG 40, 32C). Therefore, it is not a matter of carnal love but of spiritual love (φίλημα πνευματικόν PG 40, 33A).

Also in Philo one finds, as in Hippolytus, a history of the replacement of the synagogue by the church of the gentiles, a theme which is repeatedly interwoven in the commentary. Both testaments affirm the same mind-set, proclaim the Christian faith, and are the foundation for the kingdom of heaven (PG 40, 44). Therefore, those Jews who believe are also invited (PG 40, 45; 40, 48C; 40, 52C–53A); otherwise, they are rebuked as heretics (PG 40, 49B; 40, 144CD). Accordingly, Song 2:17 ("Turn away, my beloved friend, like a gazelle"), for example, is interpreted thus: Turn to me, away from the synagogue of the Jews and to the church of the gentiles, since the former have not accepted the message of the doctrine of salvation. The bearers of this message are understood primarily as the apostles, an interpretation that is reinforced with a quotation from Paul's letter to the Romans (Rom 10:15), which in turn is a quotation from Isa 52:7: "How lovely are the feet of the messengers of joy who proclaim good" (PG 40, 76). Furthermore, Song 3:11 ("come out") is explained with Gal 3:11: Turn away from the curse of the Law, from the unbelief

---

24 Probably Origen also inspired Theodoret to list other biblical songs in his interpretation of the title of the book (PG 81, 49; see Origen, *Libri X in Canticum Canticorum*, prologue 4).
25 The Greek text is in PG 40, 27–154, which is a reprint of the edition of Giacomelli (Rome 1772). The commentary was translated into Latin by Epiphanius Scholasticus for Cassiodor in the sixth century, who thought the commentary was written by Epiphanius of Salamis (Ceresa-Gastaldo, ed., *Commentarium in Canticum Canticorum ex antiqua uersione latina Epiphanii Scholastici*). See on this commentary and its excerpts in the Catenae Faulhaber, *Hohelied- Proverbien und Prediger-Catenen*, 72, and Auwers, *L'interprétation*, 359–387. See also Sagot, "Une récente édition du *Commentaire*."

of the Jews. The mother addressed in this verse from Song 3, who crowns him is the synagogue, is interpreted as the human mother who put the crown of thorns on Christ (PG 40, 88).

To complete the picture, the following commentaries should at least be listed. Further interpretations are unfortunately only available in fragments that have survived in Catenae. This applies first to Didymus the Blind, *Fragmentum in Canticum Canticorum* (CPG 2554),[26] but also to Apollinaris of Laodicea, *Fragmenta in Canticum Canticorum* (CPG 3684),[27] Cyril of Alexandria, *Fragmenta in Canticum Canticorum* (CPG 5205.4),[28] and Nilus of Ancyra.[29] Unfortunately, no prologues to these commentaries have survived.

The situation is different with the two texts that will be the focus of the following sections, both of which have been handed down as writings of Athanasius of Alexandria. Here one finds another interesting approach to interpreting the Song of Songs spiritually, one which is uniquely Christological in a narrow sense. In addition, a unique statement about the Jews and Jerusalem can be read here.

3 (Ps.-)Athanasius of Alexandria, *Homilia in Canticum Canticorum* (CPG 2239)

The first text attributed to Athanasius of Alexandria is not a prologue or part of an entire commentary, but a single sermon. Here, a Christological interpretation in the narrower sense is recognizable only in rudimentary form, but nevertheless it is an interesting commentary on the text, which is worth mentioning.

This sermon[30] on Song 4:16–5:1 has been handed down in the manuscript *Codex Ambrosianus* D 51 sup. (Milano, fol. 180v–188v) as a work of Athanasius,

---

26 The one fragment of Didymus is transmitted in the so-called type C-Catena of Procopius of Gaza (CPG C82) and the type E-Catena of Pseudo-Eusebius (CPG C84; see nn. 23 and 42); see Faulhaber, *Hohelied- Proverbien und Prediger-Catenen*, 59, and the critical edition of Auwers and Guérard, *Procopii Gazaei Epitome*.
27 On the fragments of Apollinaris of Laodicea, see again the critical edition of the important Catena of Procopius of Gaza of Auwers and Guérard, *Procopii Gazaei Epitome*; see also the study Auwers, *L'interpretation*, 391–395.
28 Cyril of Alexandria in PG 69, 1277–1293; but see now the critical edition of the important Catena of Procopius of Gaza of Auwers and Guérard, *Procopii Gazaei Epitome*; see also Auwers, *L'interpretation*, 397–407.
29 Nilus of Ancyra, *Kommentar zum Hohelied*, translated and edited by Rosenbaum; Nilus of Ancyra, *Commentaire sur le Cantique des Cantiques*, edited by Guérard.
30 Greek text in PG 27, 1349–1361; there is no modern translation available.

and partially also in a dogmatic Catena with Athanasian texts as an excerpt (*Codex Laurentianus* plut. IV 23, Florenz, fol. 120v–122v). Its assessment by Bernard de Montfaucon (in the *Admonitio* in PG 27, 1349–1350) as a work of an unknown author from the eighth to tenth century, based on the fact that Manicheans are mentioned, can only be considered as a misinterpretation of one sentence at the end of the sermon (PG 27, 1360D). This has already been noted by Eduard Schwartz, who himself interpreted the sermon as preceding the Christological controversy because of its undifferentiated two-nature doctrine.[31] Marcel Richard suggested Markell of Ancyra as the author.[32] Since then, however, the sermon has remained unnoticed.

The sermon begins with a general reflection about the inspiring and elevating power of the divine scripture as "giving wings," that is, awakening a longing for the heavenly realm (πτεροποιοῦσι γὰρ ἀληθῶς αἱ θεῖαι γραφαὶ τοὺς πιστοὺς τῷ πόθῳ τῶν οὐρανίων; PG 27, 1349C; Ps 54:7 and Phil 3:14 are also quoted). Therefore, Song 4:16 is to be read as a request of the soul inspired by divine assurance: "Lift yourself away, north wind, and come here, south wind; pass through my garden, and my aromatics shall flow." The soul trusts in God and is confident, like a firmly grounded house on the rock that is Christ (1Cor 10:4), so that fierce winds cannot knock it down—it instead challenges these winds of temptation, persecution, tribulation, famine, war, or other struggles such as fleshly desires (PG 27, 1351BC). The soul is not afraid and does not fear the devil coming from the north with these temptations, but becomes like a eunuch for the sake of the kingdom of heaven (quoting Matt 19:12).[33] This is illustrated by the story of Susanna and with the quotation from Sir 25:2 (PG 27, 1352D–1353A).

The soul gains the greatest confidence from the crucifixion and resurrection of the Savior. At that time, the disciples, who at first hid in a room from the reviling Jews (cf. John 20:19) and laughing gentiles, also called out to the Lord with these words from Song 4:16. For the body of the Lord (τὸ σῶμα) lay in the north of Jerusalem, while the divine Word deprived Hades in the south—therefore, the Logos came from the south, while the body was raised in the north after three days, and, reunited with the body, went to the disciples. This was actually the moment in which the fragrances spread (PG 27, 1353CD).[34]

In sum, this is simultaneously a typological and Christological interpretation of Song 4:16. The author justifies this with his own geographical observations (ἡμεῖς,

---

31 See Schwartz, ed., *Der s.g. Sermo maior de fide des Athanasius*.
32 See Richard, "Bulletin," 128.
33 To become like a eunuch is repeated in PG 27, 1356C.
34 This passage is quoted in the Catena of dogmatic writings of Athanasius; see above.

ὅτε γεγόναμεν ἐν τῷ τόπῳ ἐκείνῳ ὅπου ἐσταυρώθη ὁ Χριστός [. . .] καὶ ἦν βορεινὸς ὁ τόπος ὅπου ἦν σταυρωθεὶς ὁ κύριος; PG 27, 1353D–1356A), namely, that the place where Jesus was crucified is in the north of Jerusalem. His unspecific use of the terms σῶμα and λόγος may indeed, as Eduard Schwartz suggested, hint at the end of the fourth or beginning of the fifth century.[35] Furthermore, Jerusalem already seems to be a pilgrimage center, even if the place where Christ was crucified is only mentioned generally and no church building is specified. However, the "we" in the quoted sentence remains unclear: Has the preacher just made a pilgrimage to Jerusalem with his congregation? Probably not. Rather, the preacher simply refers here to himself and to his topographical insights.

The Christological theme continues in the interpretation of the second half of Song 4:16, in which the verb "to descend" (καταβαίνω; PG 27, 1356C) is particularly used: The phrase "shall descend" into the garden refers to the world, to men, who are the fruit trees, and to their works, the fruit. In other words, the preacher says that if we are ready to offer the Lord the fruits of the Law, then we should call the Lord to come down and eat the fruits of his fruit trees, because we are the fruit trees he has made, created for good works.[36]

Song 5:1 also demonstrates that this song is not to be interpreted in the "fleshly" sense (διὰ τοῦτο μηδεὶς νομιζέτω σαρκικοὺς εἶναι τοὺς λόγους τούτους; PG 27, 1357C), because the woman is simultaneously called bride and sister—referring to both body or flesh and soul (PG 27, 1357C). This whole verse is spoken by the divine Word about his incarnation and passion. In addition, the foods named also demonstrate the unity of the Old and New Testament, or the Law and the Gospel, because milk and honey stand for the Law, bread and wine for the Gospel. Since it says, "I ate my bread with my honey, I drank my wine with my milk," this composition shows the unity of the Old and New Testaments.[37] The Jews—who consume

---

[35] However, see on this also below, p. 31.
[36] See PG 27, 1356D: Οὕτω καὶ ἡμεῖς εἰ ἔχομεν ἑτοίμους τοῦ νόμου ἀποδοῦναι τοὺς καρποὺς τῷ Κυρίῳ, παρακαλῶμεν καὶ ἡμεῖς τὸν Λόγον καταβῆναι καὶ φαγεῖν τὸν καρπὸν τῶν ἀκροδρύων αὐτοῦ· αὐτοῦ γάρ ἐσμεν ἀκρόδρυα καὶ ποιήματα κτισθέντες ἐπ' ἔργοις ἀγαθοῖς.
[37] PG 27, 1360CD: Διὰ τοῦτο καλῶς λέγει· Ἐτρύγησα σμύρναν μου μετὰ ἀρωμάτων μου· ἔφαγον ἄρτον μου μετὰ μέλιτός μου· ἔπιον οἶνόν μου μετὰ γάλακτός μου. (Song 5:1) Θεωρεῖς τὸν Λόγον τὸν πρὸς πᾶσαν ἡλικίαν γιγνόμενον; καὶ τοῖς Ἰουδαίοις νηπίοις οὖσιν διδοὺς τροφὴν μέλι καὶ γάλα· μέλι δὲ καὶ γάλα ἐὰν ἀκούσῃς, τὸν νόμον νόμιζε· ὡς γὰρ νηπίοις αὐτοῖς οὖσιν ἐδόθη τὸ γάλα· τοῖς δὲ τελείοις ὁ ἄρτος καὶ ὁ οἶνος δίδοται· στερεὰ γάρ ἐστι τροφὴ καὶ ὁ ἄρτος καὶ ὁ οἶνος, τουτέστι τὸ Εὐαγγέλιον. Διὰ τοῦτο τοίνυν καλῶς λέγει ὁ Σωτήρ· Ἔφαγον ἄρτον μου μετὰ μέλιτός μου, ἔπιον οἶνόν μου μετὰ γάλακτός μου. Θεωρεῖς πῶς πανταχοῦ λέγει; Αὐτοῦ γάρ ἐστι καὶ ἡ Καινὴ καὶ ἡ Παλαιά. Διὰ τοῦτο οὐαὶ τοῖς Ἰουδαίοις τοῖς τὸ μέλι καὶ γάλα ἐσθίουσιν. Ὡσαύτως δὲ καὶ οἱ Μανιχαῖοι τὸν ἄρτον καὶ τὸν οἶνον ἐσθίουσιν· ἡ δὲ Καθολικὴ Ἐκκλησία τὰ δύο ὁμοῦ ἐσθίει, τὸν ἄρτον μετὰ τοῦ

only milk and honey—are therefore to be rejected, as are the Manicheans[38]—who consume only bread and wine. The catholic church, however, consumes both foods. An invitation to the Eucharist ends this sermon.

This sermon stands alone, even though one might suspect that it belonged to a cycle of sermons on the Song of Songs. Gregory of Nyssa does not seem to have been the model, and a homily by Origen on these verses has not survived; even a short fragment by Origen from the Catena sets a different tone, as does a fragment from Theodoret. The mention of "body" and "Word" for Christ could suggest Apollinaris of Laodicea, however, the unspecific use of these terms could also be due to the sermon genre. The conspicuous reference to the disciples' behavior at the crucifixion and resurrection could be indicative of the Easter season as the context for this sermon.

4 (Ps.-)Athanasius of Alexandria, *Synopsis Scripturae Sacrae* (CPG 2249)

Two works comparable to typical biblical introductions nowadays and both called *Synopsis Scripturae Sacrae* have come down to us from late antiquity, one of which is attributed to John Chrysostom (CPG 4559[39]), the other to Athanasius of Alexandria. A modern critical edition of this work is still pending.[40] Probably the fact that the famous orthodox Nicene bishop of Alexandria, Athanasius, had also written the important *Festal Letter* (Ep. fest. 39) on canonical and non-canonical scriptures led to the attribution of this text to him. At least, the introductory remark about the

---

μέλιτος, καὶ πίνει τὸν οἶνον μετὰ τοῦ γάλακτος· καὶ ἐσθίοντες μὲν τὸν ἄρτον συναναλίσκομεν τῷ λόγῳ καὶ τὸ μέλι.

38 This short mention of the Manicheans—contrary to the introductory remark of Bernard de Montfaucon—does not allow any more exact dating. They are mentioned here only as heretics who reject the Old Testament.

39 PG 56, 313–386. The *Synopsis*, which is attributed to Chrysostom, does not refer to anything from Leviticus, 1 and 2 Chronicles, 1 and 2 Ezra, Psalms, Job, Proverbs, Ecclesiastes, Song of Songs, Wisdom of Solomon, Esther, Tobit, Judith, or the New Testament (see Klostermann, *Analecta zur Septuaginta*, 106).

40 Ps.-Athanasius, *Synopsis Scripturae Sacrae*, PG 28, 284–437, with PG 28, 349–357 on the Song of Songs. The one manuscript used for this edition is now lost. See Auwers, *L'interprétation*, 422 with n. 26.

canonized scriptures is very reminiscent of Athanasius' description in this *Festal Letter*.[41]

Within the *Synopsis*, the Song of Songs is introduced quite extensively, and this passage will be presented here. This interesting introduction to the Song has also been given an independent transmission, namely as one of the prologues to the Song of Songs in the Catena manuscripts, which is called the Catena of Eusebius (of Caesarea).[42] Meanwhile, Jean-Marie Auwers has provided a new edition of this version of the prologue and also offers the latest study on it.[43] This second text attributed to Athanasius offers as its main theme a clearly Christological interpretation of the Song of Songs and a specific view on the law and the Jews.

The presentation of the Song of Songs in the *Synopsis* is accomplished in two steps: First the leading theme, the coming of the Word, is presented; then the underlying scheme of the dialogue is analysed, which narrates salvation history. But before any of this, the work starts with an introductory remark: This book was composed by Solomon from beginning to end in a mystical manner full of enigmatic allegory (PG 28, 349: ἀπ' ἀρχῆς μέχρι τέλους μυστικῶς μετὰ ἀλληγορίας αἰνιγματώδους); its hidden meaning is only for those of perceptive mind.

The title "Song of Songs" demonstrates that it comes after other biblical songs. This reference is taken up again in the form of an *inclusio* at the end of the first part: "It is the Song of Songs, since there is none to be expected afterwards. For as there was a Holy Place under the Law, and after that the Holy of Holies (cf. Hebr 9:2f.), and after the Holy of Holies no more interior place, so also after the Song came the Song of Songs; and after this Song of Songs no further or newer Gospel is to be expected. For only once (cf. Hebr 7:27; 9:12) did the Word become flesh (cf. John 1:14) and complete the work (cf. John 4:34; 17:4)."[44] Similar remarks

---

[41] PG 28, 284A, 293D. About Athanasius, *Ep. fest.* 39, see Brakke, "Canon Formation and Social Conflict"; idem, "A New Fragment of Athanasius's Thirty-Ninth *Festal Letter*"; Athanasius, *Lettere festali*, translated and edited by Alberto Camplani, 498–518; Lucchesi, "Un nouveau complement"; Pedersen, "New Testament Canon."

[42] This Catena is only available in the edition from van Meurs, *Eusebii, Polychronii, Pselli in Canticum Canticoum*, 1–74, and together with a Latin translation from van Meurs, *Operum volumen octavum*, 129–212. See on the relevant seven manuscripts Faulhaber, *Hohelied- Proverbien und Prediger-Catenen*, 50–64. See above n. 26.

[43] See Auwers, *L'interprétation*, 411–426 and 465–467 (Greek text of the prologue with French translation). See also Harl, "Les trois livres de Salomon"; Klostermann, *Analecta zur Septuaginta*.

[44] PG 28, 352D: Ἄισμα οὖν ἀσμάτων, διὰ τὸ μετὰ τὰ ἐκ τούτου μηδὲν ἕτερον προσδοκᾶν. Καὶ ὥσπερ κατὰ τὸν νόμον Ἅγια ἦν, καὶ μετὰ τὰ Ἅγια Ἅγια ἁγίων, μετὰ δὲ τὰ Ἅγια τῶν ἁγίων οὐκ ἔτι ἦν ἐσώτερος τόπος· οὕτως μετὰ τὰ ᾄσματα τὸ Ἄισμα τῶν ἀσμάτων, μετὰ δὲ τὸ Ἄισμα τῶν ἀσμάτων οὐκ ἔτι προσδοκᾶν ἔστιν ἐσωτέραν καὶ καινοτέραν ἐπαγγελίαν. Ἅπαξ γὰρ ὁ Λόγος ἐγένετο σὰρξ καὶ τετελείωκε τὸ ἔργον.

are found in other interpretations of the Song, where, in addition to the comparison with the Holy of Holies, other examples such as the Sabbath of Sabbaths are offered.⁴⁵

So what is the theme of the Song of Songs? The author now claims that the whole of divine scripture prophesies the descent of the Word to us and his incarnation (Πᾶσα ἡ θεία Γραφὴ περὶ τῆς εἰς ἡμᾶς καθόδου τοῦ Λόγου καὶ ἐνσάρκου παρουσίας αὐτοῦ προφητεύει; PG 28, 349D). This is the outstanding theme of all biblical books, even if further passages mention other things: the incarnation remains the dominant topic. Compared to the, however, other scriptures only announce the coming of the Word (such as Deut 18:15; Isa 7:14; Mic 4:1). The Song of Songs, on the contrary, is not prophetic, not a foreshadowing, but shows the Word as having already come. Therefore, the Song sings of the marriage, that is, the union (συζυγίαν) of the Word with the flesh.⁴⁶ Interestingly, this first part of the introduction includes an anti-heretical demarcation: After the incarnation, there can be no further prophecy; furthermore, it is also said that the Law and the Prophets reach only to John (cf. Luke 16:16; Matt 11:13)—so what else could there be after the arrival of the redeemer but judgment and retribution? Therefore, the Phrygians, i.e., the Montanists,⁴⁷ were rightly condemned and ostracized as heretics.⁴⁸

Now, in the second part, the dialogic structure is demonstrated. The author states that the whole book is filled with dialogues between the ancient people of Israel or Jerusalem, the church of the gentiles, and the whole of humanity with the

---

45 See Origen, *Libri X in Canticum Canticorum*, prologue 4,1; *In Canticum Canticorum Homiliae* 1,1; Philo of Carpasia, *Enarratio in Canticum Canticorum* (PG 40, 49); Theodoret in his introductory remark.
46 PG 28, 352B: Τὸ δὲ Ἆισμα τῶν ᾀσμάτων οὐχ ὡς προφητεῦόν ἐστιν, οὐδὲ ὡς προσημαῖνον· ἀλλὰ ὃν ἄλλοι προαπήγγελλον, τοῦτον ὡς ἤδη ἐλθόντα δείκνυσι, καὶ ἤδη ἀναλαβόντα τὴν σάρκα· διὸ καὶ ὡς ἐπὶ συζυγίᾳ τοῦ Λόγου καὶ τῆς σαρκὸς ἐπιθαλάμιον ᾄδει τὸ Ἆισμα τῶν ᾀσμάτων.
47 On the "New Prophecy" or the so-called "Montanists" or "Phrygians," a prophetic movement in Asia Minor in the second century, see Tabbernee, *Montanist Inscriptions*; Trevett, *Montanism*; Tibbs, "'Do Not Believe.'"
48 PG 28, 352C: Ὥσπερ οὖν μετὰ τὴν οἰκονομίαν τὴν τοῦ Σωτῆρος οὐκ ἔτι προφήτην προσδοκῶμεν, οὕτως μετὰ τὰ ἐν τῷ Ἆισματι τῶν ᾀσμάτων σημαινόμενα οὐκ ἔστιν ἄλλο τι καινότερον προσδοκᾶν σημαινόμενον. Καὶ γὰρ τὰ ἐν τῷ Ἆισματι σημαινόμενα, ταῦτα καὶ ἐν τοῖς προφήταις καὶ ἐν ταῖς ἄλλαις Γραφαῖς ἐκ διαστημάτων λεγόμενα εὑρίσκεται. Πάλιν τε ὥσπερ δεικνύντος τοῦ Ἰωάννου τὸν Ἀμνόν, ἕως Ἰωάννου ὁ νόμος καὶ οἱ προφῆται εἰσίν· οὕτως τὰ ἐν τῷ Ἆισματι τῶν ᾀσμάτων σημαινόμενα τέλος ἐστὶ πάντων ἐν πάσῃ τῇ θείᾳ Γραφῇ σημαινομένων. Τί γὰρ ἄλλο μετὰ τὴν τοῦ Χριστοῦ παρουσίαν προσδοκᾶν δεῖ ἢ κρίσιν καὶ ἀνταπόδοσιν; Καὶ διὰ τοῦτο οἱ κατὰ Φρύγας παρεισάγοντες προφήτας μετὰ τὸν Κύριον, σφάλλονται, καὶ ὡς αἱρετικοὶ κατεκρίθησαν.

Word, and also between the ministering angels and the elect men.[49] Ten dialogues are held by the ancient and the new people with the Word; a last round of conversation is the proclamation of the angels. It begins with the request to the Word to descend and become man. Then follows the proclamation of the incarnate Word to the people, especially to the ancient people and also to the pagans. This is followed by a conversation between the ancient people and the new people composed of gentiles. At the end there are three calls to the gentiles, one from the Word, one from the ancient people, and finally one from the angels. All of these parts of the dialogue are assigned corresponding verses from the Song of Songs. The following overview illustrates this.

1   The ancient people beg him to come down and to take on flesh (Τοῦ μὲν οὖν παλαιοῦ λαοῦ ἀξιοῦντος αὐτὸν κατελθεῖν καὶ συναφθῆναι [ἑνωθῆναι in the prologue version] τῇ σαρκί – PG 28, 353A):
    – Song 1:2: Let him kiss me with the kisses of his mouth, because your breasts are good beyond wine (Φιλησάτω με ἀπὸ φιλημάτων στόματος αὐτοῦ· ὅτι ἀγαθοὶ μαστοί σου ὑπὲρ οἶνον).
    – Song 7:14: New and old things I have stored for you, my brotherkin (Νέα πρὸς παλαιὰ ἐτήρησά σοι, ἀδελφιδέ μου).
    – Song 8:1–2: Who might give you as my brotherkin, nursing at my mother's breasts? When I find you outside and love you, and nobody should despise me. I would take you and bring you in the house of my mother and into the chamber of her who conceived me (Τίς δῴη σε, ἀδελφιδέ μου, θηλάζοντα μαστοὺς μητρός μου; εὑροῦσά σε ἔξω, φιλήσω σε, καὶ οὐκ ἐξουδενήσουσί με. Παραλήψομαί σε, εἰσάξω σε εἰς οἶκον μητρός μου, καὶ εἰς τὸ ταμεῖον τῆς συλλαβούσης με).

This is briefly commented on with a remark about the incarnation, that the Word indeed took on a body like us human beings, namely from the virgin Mary, the human God-bearer.[50]

---

49 PG 28, 353A: Ἔστι δὲ ὅλον τὸ βιβλίον τοῦτο διαλόγων πλῆρες τοῦ παλαιοῦ πρὸς τὸν Λόγον, καὶ καθόλου τοῦ ἀνθρωπίνου γένους πρὸς τὸν Λόγον, καὶ τῆς ἐξ ἐθνῶν Ἐκκλησίας πρὸς αὐτόν, καὶ τοῦ Λόγου πάλιν πρὸς αὐτὴν καὶ πρὸς τὸ ἀνθρώπινον γένος· εἶτα τῶν ἐθνῶν πρὸς τὴν Ἰερουσαλήμ, καὶ τῆς Ἰερουσαλὴμ περὶ τῆς ἐξ ἐθνῶν καὶ περὶ αὐτῆς διάλογος· εἶτα καὶ τῶν διακονούντων ἀγγέλων πρὸς τοὺς κληθέντας ἀνθρώπους τὸ κήρυγμα. Cf. the completely different actors in the dialogue described by Origen above, p. 13–14.
50 PG 28, 353B: Οὐ γὰρ ἔξωθεν, ἀλλ' ἀφ' ἧς ἐγεννήθημεν μήτρας, ἀναλαβεῖν αὐτὸν ἠξίουν τὸ σῶμα, εἰ καὶ μὴ ὡς ἡμεῖς ἐξ ἀνδρὸς καὶ γυναικός. Ἐκ γὰρ μόνης Παρθένου, ὡς πλάστης, ἑαυτῷ ἔλαβε τὸ σῶμα, πλὴν ὅτι ἐξ ἀνθρώπου· ἄνθρωπος γὰρ ἡ Θεοτόκος Μαρία. / "For they begged him that he would take on a body not from another, but of that mother of which we are born, as well, although

2. The Word incarnate announces himself to those who begged him to come down and take flesh from the virgin (τοῦ Λόγου δὲ πρὸς τοὺς ἀξιώσαντας ἀναλαμβάνοντος ἤδη τὴν σάρκα ἐκ τῆς Παρθένου – PG 28, 353B):
   - Song 5:1: I have come into my garden, my sister and bride; I have collected my myrrh together with my spices, I have eaten my bread with my honey, I have drunk my wine with my milk (Εἰσῆλθον εἰς κῆπόν μου, ἀδελφή μου νύμφη, ἐτρύγησα σμύρναν μου μετὰ ἀρωμάτων μου, ἔφαγον ἄρτον μου μετὰ μέλιτός μου, ἔπιον οἶνόν μου μετὰ γάλακτός μου).[51]

This is again supplemented with a description of the incarnate Word: The body itself is mortal but united now with the Word. Therefore, he is both human and God, even as he consumes both milk and wine. So he accomplishes in the body the works of the Godhead.[52]

3. The Word incarnate calls the ancient people to whom the messages were first entrusted (ὁ Λόγος λοιπὸν ἐνδυσάμενος [λαβὼν in the version of the prologue] τὸ σῶμα προσκαλεῖται τὸν παλαιὸν λαὸν ὡς πρῶτον πιστευθέντα τὰ λόγια – PG 28, 353C):
   - Song 2:10–13: Rise, come, my dearest, my beauty, my dove; for look, the winter is gone, the rain is over, gone on its way. The blossoms appear on the earth, the time for pruning has come; the voice of the turtle dove is heard on our earth, the fig tree has put forth its figs, our vines bear fruit (Ἀνάστα, ἐλθὲ πλησίον μου, καλή μου, περιστερά μου· ὅτι ἰδοὺ ὁ χειμὼν παρῆλθεν, ὁ ὑετὸς ἀπῆλθεν, ἐπορεύθη ἑαυτῷ. Τὰ ἄνθη ὤφθη ἐν τῇ γῇ, καιρὸς τῆς τομῆς ἔφθακε, φωνὴ τοῦ τρυγόνος ἠκούσθη ἐν τῇ γῇ ἡμῶν, ἡ συκῆ ἐξήνεγκεν ὀλύνθους αὐτῆς, αἱ ἄμπελοι ἡμῶν κυπρίζουσιν).

---

not as we from a man and a woman. Because he, as creator, took on flesh only from a virgin but nevertheless from a human being, because Mary, Theotokos, was a human being."

51 See the similar passage in the sermon on Song 5:1 above, p. 20.

52 PG 28, 353BC: Εἰς γὰρ τὸν ἴδιον κῆπον εἰσελθών, τὴν κτίσιν, ἔλαβεν ἑαυτῷ ἐκ τῆς Παρθένου τὸ σῶμα, καὶ γέγονεν ἄνθρωπος. Θνητὸν μὲν ἦν τὸ σῶμα, ἀλλὰ μετὰ εὐωδίας τοῦ παναγίου Λόγου συνῆπτο (ἀλλὰ μετὰ εὐωδίας· τῷ γὰρ παναγίῳ καθ' ὑπόστασιν ἥνωτο λόγῳ in the version of the prologue). Καὶ εἰ γάλα, ὡς ἄνθρωπος, ἠφίει τὸ σῶμα φαγεῖν, ἀλλὰ μετεδίδου αὐτῷ καὶ οἴνου τῆς ἑαυτοῦ τελειότητος. Καὶ γὰρ ὥσπερ ἤσθιε γάλα, οὕτως ἐν αὐτῷ τὰ τῆς θεότητος ἐποίει ἔργα (οὕτως καὶ αὐτῷ καὶ ἅπαν τὸ ἴδιον ἐνειργάζετο in the version of the prologue). / "For having entered into his own garden, the creature, he took himself a body of the virgin and was made man. For the body was mortal, but joined the sweet savour of the most holy Word. And although, as man, he admitted milk for his body, yet he added to it also the wine of his own perfection. For as he drank milk, he himself did the work of divinity."

With these words, the Word instructs his first people, "Jerusalem," and reminds them of the Law, which they had received as a shadow of what was to come.[53]

4 After calling Jerusalem, the Word subsequently addresses the gentiles, as well (Προσκαλεσάμενος δὲ ὁ Λόγος τὴν Ἰερουσαλήμ, προσκαλεῖται λοιπὸν καὶ τοὺς ἀπὸ τῶν ἐθνῶν – PG 28, 353D):
  – Song 4:8: Come here, bride, from Lebanon; from Lebanon come and pass through from the beginning of the faith, from the top of Senir and Hermon, from the lions' dens, from the mountains of the leopards (Δεῦρο ἀπὸ Λιβάνου, νύμφη. Ἀπὸ Λιβάνου ἐλεύσῃ, καὶ διελεύσῃ ἀπ' ἀρχῆς πίστεως, ἀπὸ κεφαλῆς Σανεὶρ καὶ Ἀερμῶν, ἀπὸ μανδρῶν λεόντων, ἀπὸ ὀρέων παρδάλεων).

This call is supported with the statement that the Word is the one Lord of both the Jews and the pagans (εἷς γάρ ἐστι Κύριος καὶ Ἰουδαίων καὶ ἐθνῶν; PG 28, 353D).

5 After this call, the pagans confess to the Word (Κληθεῖσα τοίνυν ἐξ ἐθνῶν καὶ ἤδη κατανυγεῖσα, λέγει πρὸς τὸν Λόγον – PG 28, 353D):
  – Song 1:7: Tell me, you whom my soul came to love, where you pasture, where you make your flock to rest at noon, lest I become like one roaming among the herds of your companions (Ἀπάγγειλόν μοι, ὃν ἠγάπησεν ἡ ψυχή μου· ποῦ ποιμαίνεις, ποῦ κοιτάζεις ἐν μεσημβρίᾳ· μήποτε γένωμαι ὡς περιβαλλομένη ἐπ' ἀγέλαις ἑταίρων σου).

For after the gentiles had experienced many vicissitudes, they asked to be strengthened and affirmed from now on, so that they would not have to experience these uncertainties again.[54]

6 In response to this request, the Word gives the following instruction to the gentiles (Παρακληθεὶς ὁ Λόγος, διδάσκει λοιπὸν αὐτὴν – PG 28, 356A):
  – Song 1:8: If you do not know yourself, your beauty among women, go forth in the footsteps of the flocks, and pasture your kids beside the tents of the shepherds (Ἐὰν μὴ γνῷς ἑαυτήν, ἡ καλὴ ἐν γυναιξὶν, ἔξελθε ἐν πτέρναις τῶν ποιμνίων, καὶ ποίμαινε τὰς ἐρίφους σου ἐπὶ σκηνώμασι τῶν ποιμένων).

---

[53] PG 28, 353D: Ὡς γὰρ λαβόντος τοῦ πρώτου λαοῦ ἕως καιροῦ τὴν σκιὰν τὴν ἐν νόμῳ, διδάσκει, καὶ ὡς ἰδότα τὴν φωνὴν τοῦ τρυγόνος, ὑπομιμνήσκει. / "For thus He instructs his first people as having received temporarily the shadow of the law and as knowing the voice of the turtle." Cf. the similar statement of the catenary fragment on Song 3:11, attributed to Athanasius (PG 27, 1349AB).
[54] PG 28, 356A: Πεῖραν γὰρ ἔχουσα τῆς εἰς πολλὰ μεταβολῆς, ἠξίου στηριχθῆναι λοιπὸν καὶ βεβαιωθῆναι·μήποτε πάθῃ πάλιν τὸ αὐτό.

The following is a brief explanation of the connection between knowledge of God and knowledge of self. Self-knowledge is connected with piety, because it is a knowledge in the soul that is combined with faith.[55]

7   Now the ancient people, that is Jerusalem, when she saw the call to the Gentiles as it went out among the uncircumcised of the faith, turn to the gentiles in amazement (Ἡ Ἰερουσαλήμ, ὁρῶσα τὴν κλῆσιν τῶν ἐθνῶν γινομένην ἐν ἀκροβυστίᾳ πίστεως, θαυμάζουσα – PG 28, 356A):
    – Song 7:1: Why do you look upon the Shulamite, who comes like a group of dancers from the camps? (Τί ὄψεσθε ἐν τῇ Σουναμίτιδι, ἡ ἐρχομένη ὡς χοροὶ τῶν παρεμβολῶν).

The author adds: "For they came not from one, but from all nations, abandoning their own camps, crushing their weapons, and finally considering peace." (Οὐ γὰρ ἐξ ἑνός, ἀλλ' ἐκ παντὸς ἔθνους ἤρχοντο, ἀφέντες τὰς ἰδίας παρεμβολὰς καὶ συντρίψαντες τὰς μαχαίρας καὶ λοιπὸν εἰρηνικὰ φρονοῦντες- PG 28, 356A) This brings to mind the idea of the pilgrimage of the nations to Zion and the kingdom of peace as described in Mic 4:1–4. This passage is followed by the longest section about the dialogue, a kind of apology from the gentiles for also being invited or called by the Word:

8   The church of the gentiles, when she saw Jerusalem rebuking her, defends herself that she has not been called by the Word in vain (Ἡ ἐξ ἐθνῶν ὁρῶσα τὴν Ἰερουσαλήμ, ὥσπερ μεμφομένην, ἀπολογεῖται περὶ ἑαυτῆς· ὅτι μὴ ἀργὴ αὐτῆς ἐστιν ἡ κλῆσις – PG 28, 356B):
    – Song 1:5–6: I am black and beautiful, daughters of Jerusalem, like the tents of Kedar, like the curtains of Solomon. Do not look upon me because I am black, because the sun has looked down on me. The sons of my mother have fought against me; they have made me the keeper of the vineyards. My own vineyards I have not kept (Μέλαινά εἰμι καὶ καλή, θυγατέρες Ἰερουσαλήμ, ὡς σκηνώματα Κηδάρ, ὡς δέρρεις Σαλομῶν. Μὴ βλέψητέ με, ὅτι ἐγὼ μεμελανωμένη εἰμί, ὅτι παρέβλεψέ με ὁ ἥλιος. Υἱοὶ μητρός μου ἐμαχέσαντο ἐν ἐμοί· ἔθεντό με φυλάκισσαν ἐν ἀμπελῶσιν. Ἀμπελῶνα ἐμὸν οὐκ ἐφύλαξα).

---

55 PG 28, 356A: Οὐ δύναται γάρ τις γνῶναι Θεόν, μὴ πρότερον γνοὺς ἑαυτόν. Εὐσέβεια γὰρ εἰς Θεὸν ἀρχὴ αἰσθήσεως· αἴσθησις δὲ οὐχ ἡ ἔξωθεν, ἀλλ' ἡ κατὰ ψυχὴν διάνοια μετὰ πίστεως. / "No one is able to know God, before he knows himself. Because, piety towards God is the beginning of perception. But the perception not from outside, but a recognition of the soul with faith." See the similar statement of the catenary fragment on Song 1:7–8, attributed to Athanasius (PG 27, 1348D).

- Song 2:4–5: Bring me to the house of wine, set love over me, preserve me with ointments, overload me with apples because I am wounded with love (Εἰσάγαγέ με εἰς οἶκον τοῦ οἴνου, τάξατε ἐπ' ἐμὲ ἀγάπην, τηρήσατέ με ἐν μύροις, στοιβάσατέ με ἐν μήλοις· ὅτι τετρωμένη ἀγάπης ἐγώ).
- Song 2:7: I have adjured you, daughters of Jerusalem, by the powers and the might of the field that you do not stir up nor awaken love until he wishes (Ὥρκισα ὑμᾶς, θυγατέρες Ἰερουσαλήμ, ἐν ταῖς δυνάμεσι καὶ ταῖς ἰσχύσι τοῦ ἀγροῦ, ἐὰν ἐγείρητε, καὶ ἐξεγείρητε τὴν ἀγάπην, ἕως οὗ θελήσῃ).

The author interprets the first quotation such that the gentiles rejected idols, went forth like Abraham, and now also belong to the faith: "Even though I am uncircumcised, I have rejected idols, and I have moved out of my mother's house, as did Abraham, because I also belong to this faith."[56] Therefore, circumcision should be dispensed with, because love is more important than the Law and compensates for the lack of circumcision, which is what the second quotation refers to. So the gentiles ask for admission, since also Adam was uncircumcised. It is now about the renewal of paradise, where there was no circumcision.

9 The Word sees the faith of the gentiles and accepts them (Ὁ Λόγος ὁρῶν τὴν πίστιν τῶν ἐθνῶν, καὶ ἀποδεχόμενος – PG 28, 356C), stating:
- Song 6:4: You are beautiful, my nearest, as goodwill, graceful as Jerusalem, impressive like a phalanx (Καλὴ, ἡ πλησίον μου, ὡς εὐδοκία, ὡραία ὡς Ἰερουσαλήμ, θάμβος ὡς τεταγμέναι).

Here follows a resolute emphasis on the necessity of the gentiles becoming like the Jews, or like Jerusalem, by honoring the Law. Law and Gospel must come together, that is, reverence for the Law and faith in Christ. Only in this way can there be one people or one church. The author states: "There is no other way than this, that those of the Gentiles become like Jerusalem, so that there will be one people. This happens when they believe in Christ by also honoring the Law. After all, there is one God of both the Law and the Gospels. And if someone does not become like Jerusalem, he cannot come near the Word."[57]

---

56 PG 28, 356B: Εἰ γὰρ καὶ ἀκρόβυστός εἰμι, φησίν, ἀλλ' ἀπεταξάμην εἰδώλοις, καὶ ἐξῆλθον ἐκ τοῦ οἴκου τῆς μητρός μου, ὥσπερ καὶ ὁ Ἀβραάμ· ἐκείνης γάρ εἰμι τῆς πίστεως.
57 PG 28, 356D: Οὐ γὰρ ἄλλως, ἢ ὡς τὴν Ἰερουσαλὴμ δεῖ εἶναι τοὺς ἀπὸ τῶν ἐθνῶν, ἵνα εἷς λαὸς γένηται. Τοῦτο δὲ γίνεται, ὅταν μετὰ τοῦ τιμᾶν τὸν νόμον πιστεύωμεν τὸν Χριστόν. Εἷς γὰρ ὁ Θεὸς τοῦ νόμου καὶ τῶν Εὐαγγελίων. Καὶ ὁ μὴ ὡς Ἰερουσαλὴμ γενόμενος οὐ γίνεται πλησίον τοῦ Λόγου.

10 Last but not least, Jerusalem turns to the church of the gentiles after she recognizes their faith and also the philanthropy of the Word (Ἡ Ἱερουσαλὴμ ὁρῶσα τῶν τέκνων τὴν πίστιν, καὶ τὴν τοῦ Λόγου φιλανθρωπίαν – PG 28, 356D):
   – Song 6:11–12: I went down into the garden of nuts to see the fruits of the valley, whether the trees are blooming; there I will give you my breasts. My soul did not understand, it made me like the chariots of Aminadab (Εἰς κῆπον καρύας κατέβην ἰδεῖν ἐν γεννήματι τοῦ χειμάρρου, εἰ ἤνθησαν αἱ ῥοιαί· ἐκεῖ δώσω τοὺς μαστούς μου. Οὐκ ἔγνω ἡ ψυχή μου, ἔθετό με ἅρματα Ἀμιναδάβ).

The nut garden here, according to the author, refers to the biblical writings—hard on the outside but spiritual within. Jerusalem is sent to the nations, and Jews and gentiles together must be united under the same yoke. Jerusalem speaks: "And I have seen that I must be yoked as in a chariot to those called from among the gentiles. When the two peoples are united under the same yoke, the preaching is sent forth everywhere."[58]

11 Then the angels proclaim:
   – Song 3:11: Go forth and look at Solomon with the crown with which his mother crowned him on the day of his wedding and on the day of the gladness of his heart (Ἐξέλθετε καὶ ἴδετε ἐν τῷ Σαλωμὼν ἐν τῷ στεφάνῳ, ᾧ ἐστεφάνωσεν αὐτὸν ἡ μήτηρ αὐτοῦ ἐν ἡμέρᾳ νυμφεύσεως αὐτοῦ, καὶ ἐν ἡμέρᾳ εὐφροσύνης καρδίας αὐτοῦ).

With this last paragraph, the author returns to the theme of the incarnation of the Word. The union of the Word with a body brings victory over death and worldwide joy.[59] The final sentence once again affirms the necessarily spiritual interpretation of the Song of Songs and holds out this prospect to the reader: Whoever knows how to read the Song spiritually can hereby achieve his own spiritual perfection.

---

58 PG 28, 357A: Εἶδον, ὅτι ζευχθῆναί με δεῖ ὡς ἐν ἅρματι τῇ ἐξ ἐθνῶν κλήσει. Ζευχθέντων τοίνυν ἀμφοτέρων τῶν λαῶν, λοιπὸν πανταχοῦ τὸ κήρυγμα ἀπεστάλη.
59 PG 28, 357A: Ὁ γὰρ ἐξερχόμενος ἀπὸ τῆς κακίας ὄψεται καὶ τὴν τοῦ Λόγου πρὸς τὸ σῶμα ἄτρεπτον ἕνωσιν [συνάφειαν in the version of the prologue]. Ὅτε γὰρ γέγονε νύμφευσις τοῦ Λόγου πρὸς ἡμᾶς διὰ τῆς τοῦ σώματος ἑνώσεως [προσλήψεως in the version of the prologue], τότε καὶ τὴν κατὰ τοῦ θανάτου νίκην πεποίηκε, δι' ἣν εὐφροσύνης πάντα πεπλήρωκε. / "For he who goes forth from wickedness shall also see the immutable union of the Word with the body. For as the marriage of the Word with us happened through the union with the body, at that moment it also brought about the victory over death, through which it filled the whole world with joy."

This interpretation of the Song of Songs is also unique in this second part. The author presents the Jews and the gentiles in the dialogue as the circumcised and the uncircumcised, the ancient and the new people, Jerusalem and the world or all nations. Here, too, anti-heretical demarcations are evident, if only implicitly. While in the first part the Phrygians or Montanists are explicitly mentioned, here in the second part there seems to be an indirect rejection of docetic teachings, especially in dialogue parts one and two, where the body of the Incarnate and the humanity of Mary are emphasized. This seems to be a dissociation from ideas like Marcion's and thus anti-docetic, as well as being anti-gnostic, inasmuch as dualism is thoroughly rejected.[60]

Furthermore, the emphasis on the one church composed of both gentiles and Jews is remarkable. Veneration of the Law as well as of the faith is necessary; both peoples are united under one yoke, and there is one Lord of both Jews and gentiles. Perhaps the interpretation of the Song of Songs in the *Synopsis* can be assigned to a Judaeo-Christian environment like that of the *Pseudo-Clementines* and the *Apostolic Constitutions*.[61] If one compares this interpretation of the Song of Songs with that of Hippolytus or also of Philo, a clear difference becomes apparent once again. Whereas here the one church of the Jews and the gentiles is encountered in the union of Law and Gospel, in Hippolytus and Philo a replacement or substitution of the Jews by the gentiles in salvation history is recognizable: The call to repentance to the Jews goes unheard, so the Word turns to the gentiles. Here, however, the gentiles seek to join the Jewish people—the other peoples must, so to speak, come to Jerusalem and become like Jerusalem.

It could therefore be assumed that this short commentary on the Song of Songs also belongs to the third century, like Hippolytus, or that it is to be dated to the fourth century at the latest. This particular anti-heretical profile renders such a dating likely; there is little need for these emphases in later times. How this text then found its way into the *Synopsis Scripturae Sacrae* cannot be determined. It is also noteworthy that in the sermon presented above, attributed to Athanasius, there is also an emphasis on the unity of the two testaments and the necessity of following the law.[62] There are also parallels in the interpretation of Song 5:1, which have already been pointed out above.[63] Both relate this verse to the incarnation and juxtapose the Word with the body. This congruence may also explain the attri-

---

[60] Cf. on Marcion the special issue of the *Journal of Ancient Christianity / Zeitschrift für Antikes Christentum* (ZAC 21,1) from 2017.
[61] See on Jewish Christianity Skarsaune and Hvalvik, eds., *Jewish Believers*; Reed, "'Jewish Christianity.'"
[62] See above, nn. 8 and 37, and p. 32.
[63] See p. 20 and 25. See also the catenary fragments, mentioned at p. 22.

bution of the two texts to one author (Athanasius), without being able to clarify the connections more precisely.

The passage on the Song of Songs in the *Synopsis* was later also included as a prologue in manuscripts containing Catenae to the Song. In this tradition, minor corrections were made in the passages describing the incarnation, because in the meantime the Christological controversy had forced clarifications here. Earlier expressions had lost their neutrality. The statement about the descent of the Word and his coming in the flesh (Πᾶσα ἡ θεία Γραφὴ περὶ τῆς εἰς ἡμᾶς καθόδου τοῦ Λόγου καὶ ἐνσάρκου παρουσίας αὐτοῦ προφητεύει PG 28, 349D) remained unchanged, as well as "the Word has taken on flesh" (ἀναλαβόντα τὴν σάρκα / τὸ σῶμα PG 28, 352B and above part one). Two verbs, however, which were apparently too clearly to be associated with ideas of Nestorius, were replaced in the prologue version of the Catena. This concerns συνάπτειν (join together)[64] (see parts one and two in the dialogue above) and ἐνδύειν (put on; see part three), which was replaced by ἐνοῦν (unite), one time even in καθ' ὑπόστασιν ἥνωτο (unite according to the hypostasis; see part two).[65] But this is only a suggestion, because in the last part of the dialogue (part eleven) there is a contradictory finding: Here the version of the text of the *Synopsis* gives ἕνωσις (unity), while in this version of the prologue one actually reads συνάφεια (conjunction) and πρόσληψις (acquisition).[66] This inconsistency is difficult to explain, but it shows that it was precisely the exact terminology for the incarnation that was disputed in later times and required copyists to make corrections, although they did not achieve complete consistency.

---

[64] This is a preferred verb of Nestorius, see, e.g., from the quoted fragments of Nestorius at the Council of Ephesus in 431 AD: ἀσύγχυτον τοίνυν τῶν φύσεων τηρῶμεν συνάφειαν (ACO I 1,2, 48,12; Schwartz, ed.); ὡς σφοδρά τις τῆς θεότητος ὑπῆρχεν συνάφεια (48,21); ὡς τῷ λαβόντι συναφθείς (49,16).

[65] See here the text edited by Auwers, *L'interprétation*, 456–467, especially 461,77 for καθ' ὑπόστασιν ἥνωτο. See for Cyril of Alexandria his second letter to Nestorius (ACO I 1,1, 25,23–28,26; Schwartz, ed.), here, e.g.: σάρκα ἐμψυχωμένη ψυχῇ λογικῇ ἑνώσας ὁ λόγος ἑαυτῷ καθ' ὑπόστασιν ἀφράστως τε καὶ ἀπερινοήτως γέγονε ἄνθρωπος (26,27–28); also 27,11; see also his third letter to Nestorius (ACO I 1,1, 35,26; 36,24; and in anathema two and three [40,25.28]) and here also his rejection of συνάφεια (36,19–20).

[66] Auwers, *L'interprétation*, speaks of "un correcteur chalcédonien" (424), but probably "anti-nestorienne" would suit better—however, not for part 13.

5 A Short Conclusion

The two pseudepigraphic texts of Athanasius on the Song of Songs presented above expand the range of possible interpretations of this biblical book. There is, so to speak, a "collective allegory" of the Song of Songs related to the church, but also an individual one related to the Christian or his soul, which strives towards that which is heavenly. Some consider the Song of Songs to be a text suitable for beginners, others, on the contrary, for advanced readers. This is evidenced, for example, by the fact that the speakers of the Song of Songs are interpreted as corresponding to different people. Especially the dialogue presented in the *Synopsis* above turns out to be quite different from what Origen imagines. However, the various interpretations consistently concern the progress of the soul in its spiritual life and its approach to the heavenly life.

What is striking, however, is the reference to Christology in the narrower sense in the pseudathanasian texts as presented above. Also interesting are the differences in accounts of salvation history, especially regarding the role assigned to Israel or Jerusalem, or to the Jews and the synagogue—of course, only in the "collective allegory." Especially the inclusion of the Jews or the fulfillment of the Law for redemption, instead of a substitution theory, catches one's attention in the introductory text to the Song of Songs from the *Synopsis*. Accordingly, although this of course remains speculative, this passage from the *Synopsis* seems to be quite a bit older than first assumed. The recognizable discussions, as well as the explicit and implicit anti-heretical tendencies, are indications for this as well. There are also some connections to the aforementioned pseudepigraphic sermon, so that perhaps a single author can be surmised. How the affiliation with Athanasius of Alexandria came about, however, cannot be determined. In sum, due to the double tradition in the anthology *Synopsis Scripturae Sacrae* and in the Catena, this text was awarded greater importance in late antiquity than it has been in modern research.

Bibliography

Primary Works

(Ps.)-Athanasius. *Admonitio*. PG 27:1349–1350.
Athanasius of Alessandria. *Lettere festali*, introduced, translated, and commented by Alberto Camplani. Letture cristiane del primo millennio 34. Milano: Paoline, 2003.
Athanasius of Alexandria. *Homilia in Canticum Canticorum*. PG 27:1349–1361.
Ps.-Athanasius. *Synopsis Scripturae Sacrae*. PG 28:284–437.
Bibliothecae Veterum Patrum. Vol. 2. Paris, 1624.

Ps.-Chrysostom. *Synopsis Scripturae Sacrae.* PG 56:313–386.
Concilium Universale Constantinopolitanum sub Iustiniano habitum, edited by Johannes Straub. ACO 4. Berlin: de Gruyter, 1971.
The Acts of the Council of Constantinople of 553: With Related Texts on the Three Chapters Controversy, translated and edited by Richard Price. Vol. 1 and 2 of *Translated Texts for Historians* 51. Liverpool: Liverpool University Press, 2012.
Cyril of Alexandria. *Fragmenta in Canticum Canticorum.* PG 69:1277–1293.
Gregory of Nyssa. *In Canticum Canticorum Homiliae: Homilien zum Hohenlied*, edited and translated by Franz Dünzl. FC 16. Freiburg im Breisgau: Herder, 1994.
Gregory of Nyssa. *In Canticum Canticorum*, edited by Hermann Langerbeck. GNO 6. Leiden: Brill, 1986.
Hippolytus. *Exegetische und homiletische Schriften*, edited and translated by Gottlieb Nathanael Bonwetsch. Hippolyt Werke 1. GCS 1. Leipzig: Hinrichs, 1897.
Hippolytus. *Kommentar zum Hohenlied auf Grund von N. Marrs Ausgabe des grusinischen Textes*, edited and translated by Gottlieb Nathanael Bonwetsch. TU 23,2c. Leipzig: Hinrichs, 1902.
Meurs, Johannes van. *Eusebii, Polychronii, Pselli in Canticum Canticoum expositiones Graece.* Lyon: Basson, 1617.
Meurs, Johannes van. *Operum volumen octavum ex recensione Joannis Lami.* Florenz: Tartinium et Franchium, 1746.
Nilus of Ancyra. *Commentaire sur le Cantique des Cantiques*, translated and edited by Marie-Gabrielle Guérard. Vol. 1. SC 403. Paris: Cerf, 1994.
Nilus of Ancyra. *Kommentar zum Hohelied*, translated and edited by Hans-Udo Rosenbaum. Vol. 1 of *Nilus von Ancyra Schriften*. PTS 57. Berlin: de Gruyter, 2004.
Origen. *Der Kommentar zum Hohelied*, translated and edited by Alfons Fürst and Holger Strutwolf. Orig. WD 9,1. Berlin: de Gruyter, 2016.
Origen. *Die Homilien und Fragmente zum Hohelied*, translated and edited by Alfons Fürst and Holger Strutwolf. Orig.WD 9,2. Berlin: de Gruyter, 2016.
Origen and Gregorio di Nissa. *Sul Cantico dei Cantici*, translated and edited by Vito Limone and Claudio Moreschini. Milano: Bompiani, 2016.
Origen. *Homilien zu Samuel I, zum Hohelied und zu den Propheten: Kommentar zum Hohelied in Rufins und Hieronymus' Übersetzungen*, translated and edited by Wilhelm A. Baehrens. GCS 33: Origenes Werke VIII. Leipzig: Hinrichs, 1925.
Origen. *The Song of Songs: Commentary and Homilies*, translated and edited by R. P. Lawson. ACW 26. Westminster, MD: Newman Press, 1957.
Origin. *Philocalie*, edited by Marguerite Harl. SC 302. Paris: Cerf, 1983.
Philo of Carpasia. *Commentarium in Canticum Canticorum ex antiqua uersione latina Epiphanii Scholastici*, edited by Andreas Ceresa-Gastaldo. CorPat 6. Torino: Società editrice internazionale, 1979.
Philo of Carpasia. *Enarratio in Canticum Canticorum.* PG 40:27–154.
Philo of Carpasia. *Enarratio in Canticum Canticorum: Gaecum textum, adhuc ineditum, quamplurimis in locis depravatum emendavit, & nova interpretatione adjecta nunc primum in lucem profert*, edited by Michel'Angelo Giacomelli. Rome: Apud Benedictum Franzesi, 1772.
Procopius of Gaza. *Procopii Gazaei Epitome in Canticum Canticorum*, edited by Jean-Marie Auwers and Marie-Gabrielle Guérard. CCSG 67. Turnhout: Brepols, 2011.
Theodoret of Cyrus. *Commentary on the Song of Songs*, translated and edited by Robert C. Hill. Early Christian Studies 2. Brisbane: Australian Catholic University, 2001.
Theodoret of Cyrus. *Explanatio in Canticum Canticorum.* PG 81:28–214.

Secondary Works

Auwers, Jean-Marie. *L'interprétation du Cantique des cantiques à travers les chaînes exégétiques grecques.* IPM 56. Turnhout: Brepols, 2011.
Brakke, David. "A New Fragment of Athanasius's Thirty-Ninth *Festal Letter*: Heresy, Apocrypha, and the Canon." *HTR* 103 (2010): 47–66.
Brakke, David. "Canon Formation and Social Conflict in Fourth-Century Egypt: Athanasius of Alexandria's Thirty-Ninth *Festal Letter.*" *HTR* 87 (1994): 395–419.
Brent, Allen. *Hippolytus and the Roman Church in the Third Century: Communities in Tension before the Emergence of a Monarch-Bishop.* SVigChr 31. Leiden: Brill, 1995.
Cahill, J. B. "The Date and Setting of Gregory of Nyssa's Commentary on the Song of Songs." *JTS* 32 (1981): 447–460.
Cain, Emily R. "Mystical Wounds. Eastern Patristic Authors on the Song of Songs." in A Companion to the Song of Songs in the History of Spirituality, edited by Timothy H. Robinson. 18–41. Brill's Companion to the Christian Tradition 98. Leiden: Brill, 2021.
Cerrato, John A. *Hippolytus between East and West: The Commentaries and the Provenance of the Corpus.* OTM. Oxford: Oxford University Press, 2002.
Cerrato, John A. "'Hippolytus' *On the Song of Songs* and the New Prophecy." *StPatr* 31 (1997): 268–273.
Chappuzeau, Gertrud. "Die Auslegung des Hohenliedes durch Hippolyt von Rom." *JAC* 19 (1976): 45–81.
Deutsch, Celia M. "The Interpreter as Intertext: Origen's First Homily on the Canticle of Canticles." In *Crossing Boundaries in Early Judaism and Christianity: Ambiguities, Complexities, and Half-Forgotten Adversaries,* edited by Kimberly Stratton and Andrea Lieber, 221–254. JSJ.S 177. Leiden: Brill, 2016.
Dünzl, Franz. "Die Canticum-Exegese des Gregor von Nyssa und des Origenes im Vergleich." *JAC* 36 (1993): 94–109.
Faulhaber, Michael von. *Hohelied- Proverbien und Prediger-Catenen.* Theologische Studien der Leo-Gesellschaft 4. Vienna: Mayer, 1902.
Frickel, Josef. *Das Dunkel um Hippolyt von Rom: Ein Lösungsversuch; Die Schriften Elenchos und Contra Noëtum.* GrTS 13. Graz: Eigenverlag des Instituts für Ökumenische Theologie und Patrologie an der Universität Graz, 1988.
Garitte, Gérard, ed. *Traités d'Hippolyte sur David et Goliath, sur le Cantique des cantiques et sur l'Antéchrist.* CSCO 263. Leuven: Peeters, 1965.
Grieser, Heike. "Olympias." *RAC* 26:125–131.
Harl, Marguerite. "Les trois livres de Salomon et les trois parties de la philosophie dans les Prologues des Commentaires sur le *Cantique des Cantiques* (d'Origène aux Chaînes exégétiques grecques)." In *Texte und Textkritik: Eine Aufsatzsammlung,* edited by Jürgen Dummer, 249–269. TUGAL 133. Berlin: Akademieverlag, 1987.
Hill, Robert C. *Reading the Old Testament in Antioch.* Bible in Ancient Christianity 5. Leiden: Brill, 2005.
Kannengiesser, Charles. *Handbook of Patristic Exegesis: The Bible in Ancient Christianity.* Vol. 1. Leiden: Brill, 2004.
Klostermann, Erich. *Analecta zur Septuaginta, Hexapla und Patristik.* Leipzig: Deichert, 1895.
Lucchesi, Enzo. "Un nouveau complement aux Lettres festales d'Athanase." *AnBoll* 119 (2001): 255–260.
Maspero, Giulio, Miguel Brugarolas, and Ilaria Vigorelli, eds. *Gregory of Nyssa: In Canticum Canticorum; Analytical and Supporting Studies; Proceedings of the 13th International Colloquium on Gregory of Nyssa (Rome, 17–20 September 2014).* SVigChr 150. Leiden: Brill, 2018.
Matter, E. Ann. *The Voice of My Beloved: The Song of Songs in Western Medieval Christianity.* Middle Ages Series. Philadelphia: University of Pennsylvania Press, 1990.

McLeod, Frederick G. *Theodore of Mopsuestia*. The Early Church Fathers. London: Routledge, 2008.
Nautin, Pierre. *Hippolyte et Josipe: Contribution à l'histoire de la littérature chrétienne du troisième siècle*. Études et textes pour l'histoire du dogme de la Trinité 1. Paris: Cerf, 1947.
O'Keefe, John J. "A Letter that Killeth: Toward a Reassessment of Antiochene Exegesis, or Diodore, Theodore, and Theodoret on the Psalms." *JECS* 8 (2000): 83–104.
Ondrey, Hauna T. *The Minor Prophets as Christian Scripture in the Commentaries of Theodore of Mopsuestia and Cyril of Alexandria*. OECS. Oxford: Oxford University Press, 2018.
Pedersen, Nils A. "The New Testament Canon and Athanasius of Alexandria's 39th *Festal Letter*." In *The Discursive Fight over Religious Texts in Antiquity*, edited by Anders-Christian Jacobsen, 168–177. Vol. 1 of *Religion and Normativity*. AJut 23. Aarhus: Aarhus University Press, 2009.
Reed, Annette Yoshiko. "'Jewish Christianity' after the 'Parting of the Ways': Approaches to Historiography and Self-Definition in the Pseudo-Clementines." In *The Ways That Never Parted: Jews and Christians in Late Antiquity and the Early Middle Ages*, edited by Adam H. Becker, 189–231. Tübingen: Mohr, 2003.
Richard, Marcel. "Bulletin de Patrologie II." *MScRel* 6 (1949): 117–133.
Richard, Marcel. "Une paraphrase grecque résumée du commentaire d'Hippolyte sur le Cantique des cantiques." *Le Muséon* 77 (1964): 137–154.
Robinson, Timothy H. *A Companion to the Song of Songs in the History of Spirituality*. Brill's Companion to Christian Tradition 98. Leiden: Brill, 2021.
Sagot, Solange. "Une récente édition du *Commentaire sur le Cantique des Cantiques* de Philon de Carpasia." *VC* 35 (1981): 358–376.
Schäublin, Christoph. "Zur paganen Prägung der christlichen Exegese." In *Christliche Exegese zwischen Nicaea und Chalcedon*, edited by Johannes van Oort and Ulrich Wickert, 148–173. Kampen: Kok Pharos Publishing House, 1992.
Scholten, Clemens. "Review of J.A. Cerrato, Hippolytus between East and West: The Commentaries and the Provenance of the Corpus." *VC* 59 (2005): 85–92.
Schwartz, Eduard, ed. *Der s.g. Sermo maior de fide des Athanasius*. SBAW.PH 6. München: Bayerischen Akademie der Wissenschaften, 1925.
Shuve, Karl. "A Garden Enclosed. A Fountain Sealed." In *A Companion to the Song of Songs in the History of Spirituality*, edited by Timothy H. Robinson. 42–69. Brill's Companion to the Christian Tradition 98. Leiden: Brill, 2021.
Simonetti, Manlio. *Nuove Ricerche su Ippolito*. SEAug 30. Rome: Institutum Patristicum Augustinianum, 1989.
Skarsaune, Oskar and Reidar Hvalvik, eds. *Jewish Believers in Jesus: The Early Centuries*. Peabody, MA: Hendrickson, 2007.
Smith, Yancy. *The Mystery of Anointing: Hippolytus' Commentary on the Song of Songs in Social and Critical Contexts; Texts, Translations, and Comprehensive Study*. Gorgias Studies in Early Christianity and Patristics 62. Piscataway, NJ: Gorgias Press, 2015.
Tabbernee, William. *Montanist Inscriptions and Testimonia: Epigraphic Sources Illustrating the History of Montanism*. PatMS 16. Macon, GA: Mercer University Press, 1997.
Tibbs, Eugene C. "'Do Not Believe Every Spirit': Discerning the Ethics of Prophetic Agency in Early Christian Culture." *HTR* 114 (2021): 27–50.
Trevett, Christine. *Montanism: Gender, Authority and the New Prophecy*. Cambridge: Cambridge University Press, 2002.
Vulliaud, Paul. *Le Cantique des Cantiques d'après la traduction juive*. Paris: Les Presses Universitaires de France, 1925.
Wesseling, Klaus-Gunther. "Theodoret von Kyros." *BBKL* 11:936–957.

Jonathan Kaplan
"Dripping from the Lips of Sleeping Ones"
The Interpretation of the Song of Songs from Tannaitic Literature to the Palestinian Talmud

The rabbis in both the tannaitic (ca. 70–220 CE) and amoraic (ca. 220–500 CE) periods mapped their understanding of the relationship between God and Israel onto their interpretation of the Song of Songs.[1] They consistently correlated the female protagonist of the Song with the people of Israel and the male beloved with Israel's God. This particular rabbinic approach developed in the tannaitic period as the early rabbinic sages interpreted the Song typologically and correlated it to an idealized vision of Israel's history and practice found in the period of the exodus, Sinai Theophany, and wilderness wanderings. While this mode of interpretation is neither erotic or sensual, the rabbis employed the Song in order to characterize this relationship as one marked by deep affection and mutual devotion.[2] In this essay, after surveying the general shape of tannaitic interpretation of the Song and the state of scholarly discussion of this topic, I turn my attention to the development of this interpretive mode in the corpus of Amoraic interpretations of the Song scattered throughout the Palestinian Talmud (known alternately as the Jerusalem Talmud or Talmud Yerushalmi).[3] While these amoraic passages develop implicitly the earlier tannaitic mode of interpreting the Song, they display little interest in citing interpretive traditions found in the Tannaitic Midrashim. Rather, as I argue, these passages exhibit an increased emphasis on presenting new interpretations of the Song through which the Amoraim valorize contemporary rabbinic society and halachah, claim to esteem the position of the Jewish people within the Greco-Roman world, and embed these rabbinic ideals in the Song alongside other scriptural works as the intended meaning of these texts.

---

[1] On the tannaitic and amoraic periods, see Ben-Eliyahu et al., *Handbook*, xix, xxiii–xxiv.
[2] On tannaitic interpretation of the Song and whether or not it can be classed as erotic, see Kaplan, *My Perfect One*, 118–122.
[3] The majority of Palestinian Amoraic interpretations of the Song are found in Song of Songs Rabbah and the Pesiqta of Rav Kahana. On these works, see, for instance, Rapp-de Lange, "Rabbinische Liebe"; Kadari, "On the Redaction"; Anisfeld, *Sustain Me*. Note that there has been more limited work on the interpretation of biblical passages and books in the Palestinian and Babylonian Talmuds. See, for instance, Klein, "Anregungen."

Note: I would like to thank Jason Kalman and Gregg E. Gardner, who read earlier versions of this essay and offered helpful corrections and comments. All remaining deficiencies are my own.

1 The Song of Songs in Tannaitic Literature

Because the interpretations of the Song found in the Palestinian Talmud build on the interpretive approach to this scriptural work found in tannaitic literature, it is important to survey the general shape of this interpretative mode before turning to examine in detail the later material in the Palestinian Talmud. Tannaitic literature compiles interpretive traditions associated with the rabbinic sages from the first two centuries of the common era. While there are some limited citations of verses from the Song in the Mishnah and the Tosefta, the majority of passages that reference the Song are found in the Tannaitic Midrashim.[4] These works contain both halachic and aggadic material arranged according to the sequence of verses found in Exodus, Leviticus, Numbers, and Deuteronomy. The Mekilta of Rabbi Ishmael, one of the tannaitic commentaries on Exodus, contains the highest concentration of passages that cite verses from the Song. These passages are found principally in the section of the work that focuses on Exod 15. The midrashic work Sifre Deuteronomy also contains another significant concentration of interpretations of the Song. Notably, the majority of the interpretations of the Song found in the Tannaitic Midrashim are not attributed to any individual Tanna (the rabbinic sages of the period) but rather appear anonymously.[5]

The following passage is a typical example of tannaitic interpretation of the Song from the Mekilta of Rabbi Ishmael:

ויעמדו מרחוק, חוץ משנים עשר מיל; מגיד שהיו ישראל נרתעים לאחוריהם שנים עשר מיל וחוזרין לפניהם שנים עשר מיל, הרי עשרים וארבעה מיל על כל דיבור ודיבור, נמצאו מהלכים באותו היום מאתים וארבעים מיל. באותה שעה אמר הקב״ה למלאכי השרת רדו[6] וסייעו את אחיכם, שנ׳ מלכי צבאות ידודון ידודון, ידודון ידודון בהליכה וידודון בחזרה. ולא מלאכי השרת בלבד, אלא אף הקב״ה, שנ׳ שמאלו תחת לראשי וימינו תחבקני.

> "And they stood at a distance" [Exod 20:15]. Beyond twelve miles. This indicates that the Israelites were startled and moved backward twelve miles and then again, returning, moved forward twelve miles. This totals twenty-four miles at each commandment. Thus, they found

---

4 Passages in the Mishnah and the Tosefta that cite the Song include m. Avod. Zar. 2:5; m. Ta'an. 4:8; t. Hag. 2:3–4; t. Ketub. 5:10. Note also that the Song is referenced in both m. Yad. 3:5; t. Yad. 2:6; t. Sanh. 12:10, but verses from it are not specifically interpreted in these passages. Due to the fact that substantial portions of the Pentateuch contain legal material, the Tannaitic Midrashim are often also named the Halachic Midrashim. For detailed introductions to tannaitic literature, see Strack and Stemberger, *Introduction*, 108–163, 247–275; Ben-Eliyahu et al., *Handbook*, 23–28, 61–78.
5 On the distribution of interpretations of the Song in the Tannaitic Midrashim, see Kaplan, *My Perfect One*, 7–8.
6 Reading רדו instead of דדו as the former (more preferable) reading is attested in MS Oxford no. 151 (no. 2), MS Munich, Cod. Hebr. 117, the 1545 Venice edition of Mekilta, various printed editions, and Yalqut Shemoni.

themselves walking on that day two hundred and forty miles. During that time, the blessed Holy One said to the ministering angels: Go down and assist your brothers, as it is said, "Angels of hosts march, they march" [Ps 68:13]. I.e., "they march [with Israel]" in going and "they march [with Israel]" when returning. And not only the ministering angels but also the blessed Holy One, as it is said, "His left hand is under my head, and his right hand embraces me" [Song 2:6].[7]

In this passage, Song 2:6 is employed intertextually by the anonymous interpreter in order to elaborate on the statement in Exod 20:15 that Israel stood at a distance from the mountain during the Sinai Theophany. In this interpretation, Yhwh addresses Israel's fear in the face of this theophany. Yhwh, along with the whole host of heaven, accompanies and comforts Israel during their flight from Sinai. The interpreter cites Song 2:6 to describe this interaction and envisions it as Yhwh's intimate embrace of Israel. While this picture of Sinai as a union between Yhwh and Israel is characteristic of rabbinic interpretations of the Song, such a perspective is noticeably absent from the narrative in the book of Exodus. In this regard, this anonymous tradition seems to be relying on unspoken co-texts from prophetic works that describe the events of Sinai and the subsequent wilderness wanderings using the metaphor of divine betrothal of Israel (e.g., Jer 2:2).[8]

While the interpretive effect of the use of the Song in this passage is clear, describing this interpretive mode has been a subject of ongoing scholarly discussion. Scholars have generally termed this hermeneutical approach "allegorical," as Laura Lieber does in her important volume on the use of the Song in Jewish liturgical poetry (*piyyutim*) from Late Antiquity. Other scholars have pushed for a more specific description of this approach.[9] Daniel Boyarin contends that the Song is employed in rabbinic interpretation as a *mashal*, or parable, that enables the rabbis to unlock the "more complex, difficult, or hermetic text" of the Torah through "analogy."[10] In response to Boyarin's description, David Stern characterizes the tannaitic approach as an example of midrashic allegory, which is distinguished from philosophical allegory by its emphasis on connecting ahistorical verses from the Song with Israel's primary historical narrative. Stern also issues a challenge for scholars to attend to the specific practices of reading evidenced in ancient interpretations, with particular emphasis on whether a given interpreta-

---

[7] Mekilta of Rabbi Ishmael, Baḥodesh 9 (Horovitz and Rabin, eds., *Mechilta*, 236). For a fuller discussion of this passage, see Kaplan, *My Perfect One*, 18–19.
[8] On a discussion of the midrashic process underlying the idea of unspoken co-texts, see Boyarin, "Midrash and Martyrdom," 144–145.
[9] See Lieber, *Vocabulary of Desire*, esp. 28–30.
[10] Boyarin, *Intertextuality*, 106. See also Boyarin, *Tannaitic Midrash*, 169–184. An earlier and more extended version appears in Boyarin, "Two Introductions."

tion is exoteric or esoteric.[11] More recently, I have sharpened Stern's use of historical allegory to describe tannaitic interpretation of the Song. I contend that typology, or figural interpretation, is a more apt descriptor for the interpretive processes at work in tannaitic interpretation of the Song. As is characteristic of Christian figural interpretation, tannaitic interpretation exhibits a concern for interpreting a verse from the Song as having the same form as found in an ideal, historical personage, event, or practice described elsewhere in Israel's scriptures.[12]

In addition, there has also been a related discussion regarding the consistency of the rabbinic approach to the Song.[13] Saul Lieberman argued famously that the Tannaim employed a "consistent" and sustained interpretive approach to the Song, while the later Amoraim adopted a more eclectic approach to this work.[14] For Lieberman, this consistency is seen in the fact that in the tannaitic period Rabbi Akiva and his disciples correlated the Song to the events at Sinai while Rabbi Eliezer and his students connected it to the crossing of the Reed Sea.[15] More recently, Alon Goshen Gottstein has highlighted significant weaknesses in Lieberman's analysis. He argues that tannaitic interpretations of the Song cannot be so neatly divided between Rabbi Akiva and Rabbi Eliezer as "both sages can apply verses from the Song to different contexts."[16] Despite Goshen Gottstein's valid criticisms of Lieberman, there is a remarkable consistency in tannaitic interpretation of the Song at the level of their overall approach to the work. The passages found in the Tannaitic Midrashim consistently interpret verses from the Song as figurations of paradigmatic events and institutions of Israel's ideal national historical narrative.[17]

As Lieberman's work highlights, the specter of Rabbi Akiva, the Tanna famously martyred during the second Jewish revolt against Rome (132–135 CE), looms large in scholarly narratives regarding the origins of rabbinic interpretation of the Song.[18] Remarkably, very few interpretations of the Song found in tannaitic sources are attributed to Rabbi Akiva. The vast majority of these passages lack attribution to any named sage. In addition, many of the same interpretations of particular verses of the Song appear in parallel versions in works associated with both the schools of Rabbi Akiva and of Rabbi Ishmael. While works associated with these schools exhibit distinctive hermeneutical commitments, scholars have long noted that

---

11 See Stern, "Ancient Jewish Interpretation."
12 For a fuller discussion of this proposal, see Kaplan, *My Perfect One*, esp. 20–34.
13 For a fuller discussion of scholarly debate on this question, see Kaplan, *My Perfect One*, 47–48.
14 See Lieberman, "Mishnat Shir ha-Shirim."
15 See Lieberman, "Mishnat Shir ha-Shirim," 118, 121.
16 Goshen Gottstein, "Did the Tannaim Interpret," 271.
17 See Kaplan, *My Perfect One*, 47–93.
18 For a fuller discussion of Rabbi Akiva and the Song, see Kaplan, "Martyrdom."

they draw from a common body of aggadic material that likely predates the tannaitic period and stems from interpretive traditions with their roots in the Second Temple period.[19] In the case of the Song, that the work is cited most frequently in anonymous passages and is interpreted in a consistent fashion in works associated with both schools suggests that the works of tannaitic literature draw on an earlier common interpretive tradition. While no commentaries on the Song survive from before the third century CE, there are echoes and allusions to the work scattered throughout late Second Temple works such as the book of Revelation and 4Ezra.[20] These pre-rabbinic references to the Song support the contention that the Tannaim drew on earlier traditions as the basis for their engagement with the work rather than innovating this interpretive method.[21]

2 Recycled Interpretive Traditions about the Song of Songs in the Palestinian Talmud

In general, the Song is cited infrequently in the Palestinian Talmud. Citations appear in only twenty-four discrete passages by my count, with a broad distribution of these citations across the various tractates of the Palestinian Talmud. A significant number of these passages are parallel passages, and are primarily aggadic, as would be expected.[22] There is a minimal reuse of earlier tannaitic materials in which verses from the Song are cited in the Palestinian Talmud. Exceptions include passages from the Mishnah, the work on which the Palestinian Talmud comments and whose structure it follows (m. Ta'an 4:8; m. Avod. Zar. 2:5), and citations of material from the Tosefta (t. Hag. 2:3–4; t. Ketub. 5:10). The infrequency of citations of the Song in the Palestinian Talmud is not, however, a reason to write the Song off as insignificant. Rather, because the Palestinian Talmud is primarily a halachic work and is organized as a commentary on the Mishnah, the appearances of the Song are remarkable and are precisely the reason to pay attention to them. One way to cate-

---

19 On the schools and their interpretive assumptions, see most recently Yadin-Israel, *Scripture and Tradition*; idem, *Scripture as Logos*. On the sources of the aggadic material in the Tannaitic Midrashim, see Finkelstein, "Sources," 214–215. See also Horovitz, *Siphre ad Numeros*, xi.
20 E.g., Rev 1:13; 3:20; 4Ezra 4:36–37. The literature on this topic is vast. For recent treatments of the topic, see Kaplan, "Song"; Tomson, "Song"; Elgvin, *Literary Growth*, 172–182, and the bibliography contained therein.
21 For a fuller discussion of this topic, see Kaplan, *My Perfect One*, 185–187; idem, "Martyrdom," 293–294.
22 Repetition of material in the Palestinian Talmud is a long-recognized phenomenon. For a brief discussion of this critical issue, see Strack and Stemberger, *Introduction*, 168–169.

gorize these interpretations is to divide them between passages that revisit and represent earlier interpretative traditions, whether explicitly or implicitly, and those that build upon and expand earlier traditions or innovate new ones. It is in this latter category of passages that the Palestinian Talmud's use of the Song to valorize rabbinic textual and halachic culture and embed these rabbinic ideals in the Song alongside other scriptural works as the intended meaning of these texts can be seen most clearly. Before I turn to analyze those passages, I will examine first the recycling of earlier interpretive traditions about the Song in the Palestinian Talmud.

Because the Palestinian Talmud is organized as a commentary on the Mishnah and is primarily halachic in orientation, it only explicitly cites or references four tannaitic passages from the Mishnah and the Tosefta that contain interpretations of the Song. Of these four passages, only the discussion of the end of m. Avod. Zar. 2:5 found in y. Avod. Zar. 2:8, 41c–d develops further the interpretation of verses from the Song found in its tannaitic source. I will discuss the longer passage from y. Avod. Zar. in the later part of this essay. In contrast, the other three passages cite or reference their tannaitic sources with little interpretation or elaboration. First, the citation of m. Ta'an. 4:8 found in y. Ta'an. 4:10–11, 67b does not substantially develop the typological interpretation of Song 3:11 found in this mishnah, which links phrases from this verse to the giving of the Torah and the building of the Temple.[23] Second, y. Hag. 2:1, 77b retells the tradition describing the journey of four tannaitic sages (Rabbi Akiva, Ben Azzai, Ben Zoma, and Elisha ben Abuyah) to Pardes found first in t. Hag. 2:3–4.[24] While this version of the tradition of the mystical journey of the four tannaim is more developed than the one from the Tosefta, the use of Song 1:4 in both passages is the same. Third, y. Ketub. 5:13, 30b references, with little elaboration, an earlier tradition found in t. Ketub. 5:10 in which Rabbi Eleazar ben Rabbi Tsadok interprets Song 1:8 (along with Deut 28:56) as a figuration of a woman collecting barley grains from between horses' hooves at Akko.[25] In a parallel aggadic passage that appears in different works of the Tannaitic Midrashim, Rabbi Yoḥanan ben Zakkai is described similarly as using Song 1:8 to explain a girl picking barley grains out of the excrement of a horse or collecting it from under the feet of Arab cattle.[26] The choice of citing the version of this story found in t. Ketub.

---

[23] For fuller discussion of this mishnah, see Kaplan, *My Perfect One*, 67–68; Lieber, *Vocabulary*, 30–31; Samely, *Rabbinic Interpretation*, 131–132.
[24] For a recent discussion of this passage, see Kaplan, "Martyrdom," 305–306.
[25] For this passage, see Lieberman, *Tosefta*, 3:74.
[26] See Mekilta of Rabbi Ishmael, Baḥodesh 1 (Horovitz and Rabin, eds., *Mechilta*, 203) and Sifre Deuteronomy 305 (Finkelstein, *Siphre*, 325, lines 4–15). For a fuller discussion of these two passages, see Kaplan, *My Perfect One*, 68–71. For an examination of the various versions of this story and their interrelationships (including these versions and others), see Meir, "Story."

rather than from one of the Tannaitic Midrashim is to be expected given that this passage is found in the corresponding tractate in the Palestinian Talmud. However, that similar material also appears in the Tannaitic Midrashim brings into relief the absence of traditions from the Tannaitic Midrashim related to the Song in the Palestinian Talmud.

Despite the general absence in the Palestinian Talmud of specific citations of material from the Tannaitic Midrashim that contain interpretations of the Song, there is one passage that seems to build on an interpretation of a verse from the Song also found in the Tannaitic Midrashim. This passage is found in y. Hal. 4:8, 60a // y. Shev. 6:1, 36d and describes Rabbi Justus bar Shunem interpreting Song 4:8 as a figuration of the eschatological return of the Jewish people from the Diaspora.[27] The passage appears at the end of a long discussion regarding the borders of the Land of Israel. The following version of the passage is from y. Hal 4:8, 60a (MS Leiden, Scaliger 3): אמ' ר' יוסטא בר שונם. לכשיגיעו הגליות לטוורס אמנם[28] הן עתידות לומ' שירה. שנ' תשורי מראש אמנה. "Rabbi Justus bar Shunem said, 'When the people of the Diaspora arrive at Taurus Amanus, they will recite a song. As it is said, 'Sing from the top of Amanah [Song 4:8].'" In this tradition, Rabbi Justus employs Song 4:8 to describe the return of exiles from the Diaspora. When the returning exiles arrive at Taurus Amanus, the mountain range on the northern border of the Land of Israel according to the preceding discussion in this section of the Palestinian Talmud, they will sing. Two different, earlier anonymous traditions in the Mekilta of Rabbi Ishmael (found in Pisḥa 14 and Beshallaḥ 6) similarly employ Song 4:8 as a figuration of the actions of the returning exiles.[29] Only the passage from Beshallaḥ 7 focuses its use of Song 4:8 on the phrase תשורי מראש אמנה as in Rabbi Justus's interpretation. Rabbi Justus's interpretation differs from this earlier reading in two important ways. First, he understands the verbal form תשורי as coming from the root ש׳׳ר "to sing" rather than the root שו׳׳ר "to journey," as in the earlier tannaitic reading of this verse. Second, he correctly identifies the word אמנה as a toponym in reference to the Amanus Mountains in Lebanon whereas the passage from the Mekilta of Rabbi Ishmael understands the word as the biblical word meaning

---

27 In contrast to the Tannaitic Midrashim, in which a majority of interpretations of the Song are anonymous, the Palestinian Talmud regularly associates particular traditions with specific sages. On the shift away from anonymous interpretive traditions, see Kalman, "Rabbinic Interpretation," 31–32; Wyrick, *Ascension*, 31.

28 Note that לטוורס אמנם is written earlier as לטוורס אמנס in this section of MS Leiden, Scaliger 3. The final *mem* on אמנם here is likely a scribal error in place of the similarly shaped *samekh*.

29 See Mekilta of Rabbi Ishmael, Pisḥa 14 and Beshallaḥ 6 (Horovitz and Rabin, eds., *Mechilta*, 52, 115). For a fuller discussion of these passages, see Kaplan, *My Perfect One*, 65, 170–172.

"trust" or "support" (Neh 10:1; 11:23; see Song 4:8 LXX *pisteos*).[30] Rabbi Justus's interpretation thus shares affinities with the earlier typological reading of Song 4:8 in terms of his hermeneutical approach to the Song more generally and this verse specifically. However, his interpretation is indebted only to the general rabbinic (if not earlier Second Temple Jewish) approach to Song 4:8 rather than to the specific tannaitic version of the tradition.

3 Innovative Interpretive Traditions about the Song of Songs in the Palestinian Talmud

Despite the absence of specific citations in the Palestinian Talmud of passages from the Tannaitic Midrashim in which verses from the Song are cited, the Palestinian Talmud preserves a number of interpretations of the Song that build on the general typological approach to the Song found in tannaitic literature. These interpretations offer novel correlations of specific verses from the Song to events and personages in ideal and idyllic passages, events, and persons in Israel's scriptural history. These interpretations include:

1. In y. Ber. 9:1, 13a, Rabbi Yudan recites a tradition in the name of Rabbi Isaac that only God is capable of protecting a justly convicted person from capital punishment. He cites Exod 18:4 ("And [God] saved me from Pharaoh's sword") as proof of this conviction. In the next section of the passage, Rabbi Yannai proposes that Moses was only able to escape a death sentence for having killed an Egyptian (see Exod 2:15) because the sword slipped off his neck and broke when they were about to execute him. Rabbi Yannai employs Song 7:5 (צוארך כמגדל השן "Your neck is like an ivory tower") as a figuration of Moses to support this interpretation.

2. In y. Sukkah 4:8, 54d, Rabbi Shimon employs the second half of Song 7:2 (חמוקי ירכיך כמו חלאים מעשה ידי אמן "The curves of your thighs are like jewels, the work of an artist's hands") to support the contention that the Temple is a "work of Heaven" and more beautiful than anything made by an artist.

3. A tradition attributed to Rabbi Abba and Rabbi Ḥiyya in the name of Rabbi Yoḥanan in y. Meg. 1:13, 72b interprets the imperative phrases in Song 4:16 (עורי צפון ובואי תימן "Awake O North, and come O South") as a figuration of the eschatological rebuilding of the Temple and its sacrificial practice.

---

30 On the meaning אמנה in this section of the Mekilta of Rabbi Ishmael, see Cohen, "Analysis."

4. In a passage found in y. Sheqal. 6:1, 49d // y. Sotah 8:3, 22d, a phrase from Song 5:14 (ממלאים בתרשיש "inlaid with taršiš [beryl]") is employed as a figuration of the two tablets that contained the Ten Divine Utterances. In its context in the Song, the phrase appears as part of a longer description by the female protagonist of the male beloved's beauty. In the passages in the Palestinian Talmud, in the context of a longer discussion regarding how the two tablets were written, a certain Ḥananiah uses this phrase to support his assertion that the entire Torah was inlaid on the two tablets, a portion of the Torah written after every two commandments.

5. In a discussion between Rabbi and Rav Periri found in y. Pe'ah 7:4, 20b, Song 1:12 (עד שהמלך במסבו נרדי נתן ריחו) "When the king was on his couch, my nard gave its fragrance") is cited to demonstrate that the land of Israel manifested extraordinary fecundity only while the divine presence was resident in the Temple.

While the basic contours of these particular interpretations are deeply indebted to the earlier typological approach to the Song attested in the Tannaitic Midrashim, their attribution to later amoraic figures suggests that these passages appear in the Palestinian Talmud as novel interpretations. These new interpretations thus connect the Palestinian Talmud with other amoraic efforts, attested more fully in other works from Roman Palestine such as Song of Songs Rabbah and the Pesiqta of Rav Kahana, to develop and elaborate the rabbinic approach to interpreting the Song.[31]

A significant aspect of the interpretations of the Song found in the Palestinian Talmud is their emphasis on employing its verses as figurations of the experience of contemporary rabbinic culture rather than focusing on correlating them to an idyllic vision of Israel's scriptural history. In this case, these interpretations of the Song develop an interpretive approach found in just a few tannaitic works in which verses from the Song are employed to describe contemporary (and idealized) rabbinic culture and experience (e.g., m. Ta'an. 4:8; Mekilta of Rabbi Ishmael, Baḥodesh 1). The passages in the Palestinian Talmud include:

1. An aphoristic saying, which is attributed variously to Levi bar Nezira in y. Ber. 2:1, 4b, Shimon bar Nezira in y. Sheqal. 2:7, 47a, and bar Tira in y. Mo'ed Qat. 3:7, 83c, employs Song 7:10 (דובב שפתי ישנים "Dripping from the lips of sleeping ones")

---

[31] On the amoraic interpretation of Song of Songs Rabbah, see, for instance, Rapp-de Lange, "Rabbinische Liebe"; Kadari, "On the Redaction." On the interpretation of the Pesiqta of Rav Kahana, see, for instance, Anisfeld, *Sustain Me*.

to characterize the endurance of the teachings of sages after their death.³² The version of the saying from y. Ber. 2:1, 4b (MS Leiden, Scaliger 3) reads: כל האו' שמועה משם אומרה שפתותיו רוחשות עמו בקבר "If someone says a tradition in the name of its author, the author's lips move with him in the grave."

2. In y. Sanh. 4:2, 22a, in the context of a larger discussion about civil suits being decided on the basis of one witness, Rabbi Yannai engages in a discourse about the openness of the Torah to a plurality of interpretations rather than being constrained to one single interpretation. The Song is employed in two ways in this discourse. First, through the citation of the phrase ודגלו in Song 2:4, the passage proposes that there are 49 positive and 49 negative interpretations possible for every precept because the numerical values of the letters of this phrase added together equal 49 (6 + 4 + 3 + 30 + 6 = 49). Second, it takes the plural number of the word מישרים in Song 1:4 as an indication of the plurality of possible interpretations of the Torah.

3. In y. Ber. 2:7, 5b–c, Rabbi Shimon ben Laqish (known also as Resh Laqish) gives a eulogy for Rabbi Ḥiyyah bar Ada in which he employs Song 6:2 (דודי ירד לגנו לערוגות הבשם לרעות בגנים וללקט שושנים "My beloved has gone down to his garden to the beds of spice, to browse in the gardens and to pick lilies") as the main verse of the eulogy. Following the standard rabbinic approach to the Song, Resh Laqish interprets this verse as describing the journey of the blessed Holy One to the world ("the garden") in order to remove the righteous ("the lilies") among the nations of the worlds ("the gardens") and replant them in his personal garden of Israel. As Marie Roux and Yael Wilfand have recently argued, this eulogy echoes Roman political rhetoric, which similarly employs this floral metaphor. In this metaphor, "a higher being identifies the finest men from all the other nations and promotes them into a superior community," whether the Roman senatorial order in the case of the Roman exemplars or Israel in the case of this eulogy.³³

Together, these passages highlight the use of the Song in the Palestinian Talmud to valorize rabbinic society and interpretive culture and to claim the esteemed position of the Jewish people in the context of the Greco-Roman world. The focus of these passages on contemporary rabbinic society is a development from the earlier

---

32 Parallel passages in the Babylonian Talmud (b. Yevam. 97a; b. Sanh. 90b; b. Bekh. 31b) and Song of Songs Rabbah 7:10.1 that contain this saying attribute it to Rabbi Yoḥanan in the name of Rabbi Shimon (ben Yoḥai or ben Yehoṣadaq) or Rabbi Yoḥanan ben Tortah. Note that the printed edition of y. Mo'ed Qat. reads here בר טירא while a fragment of this passage from the Cairo Geniza (T-S F 17, 16) reads בר נזירא. Guggenheimer, *Jerusalem Talmud*, 611 n. 355, suggests that בר טירא in y. Mo'ed Qat. is likely a scribal error for בר נזירא.
33 Roux and Wilfand, "Homily," 315.

tannaitic exemplars, which primarily focused on interpreting verses from the Song as figurations of idealized personages, practices, and events in Israel's scriptural history. This shift in emphasis can be traced, in part, to the fact that these interpretations are found in a work that is organized as a commentary on the Mishnah and thus reflect concerns about contemporary rabbinic practice.[34]

The use of verses from the Song to support amoraic halachic decisions further highlights the contemporary interest of the interpretations of the Song found in the Palestinian Talmud. This usage is found in three passages in the Palestinian Talmud: y. Ber. 4:5, 8d; y. Shabb. 8:3, 11b; y. Avod. Zar. 2:8, 41c–d. The first two examples are brief while the third is more extended and developed. The first passage appears in a longer section of y. Ber. devoted to explicating the Amidah, the rabbinic prayer that is said in coordination with the daily Temple sacrifices. In this passage, Rabbi Abun interprets an enigmatic phrase in Song 4:4 (בנוי לתלפיות "built for talipiot") as indicated the three passages in the daily prayers when the Temple is mentioned: in the benediction said after eating a meal, in the fourteenth blessing of the Daily Amidah (in the enumeration and wording found in the Palestinian Talmud), and in the blessing said after the recitation of the paragraphs of the Shema (Deut 6:4–9; 11:13–21; Num 15:37–41). He interprets the lexeme תלפיות as meaning "a mound (תל) upon/towards which all mouths (פיות) may pray." Thus, he uses this phrase from the Song to characterize the site of the temple as a ruin to which people still orient their prayer after its destruction and pray for its restoration.

The second brief example appears in the context of a broader explanation of m. Shabb. 8:3. This mishnah discusses the quantity of a variety of objects (leather, parchment, ink, etc.) one may carry before violating the prohibition against carrying objects in a public domain on the Sabbath. Of particular interest in the discussion of this mishnah in y. Shabb. 8:3, 11b is why the Mishnah limits the measure of how much kohl one may carry to enough kohl "to apply to one eye" (כדי) לכחול על עין אחת). At this point the Palestinian Talmud presents a discussion between the Amoraim

---

34 In addition to these interpretations of the Song to valorize contemporary rabbinic culture, a verse from the Song is also employed in one instance in the Palestinian Talmud to clarify the meaning of an obscure word. In y. Shabb. 6, 8b, in the midst of long discussion of how to explain the difficult words in Isa 3:18–24, the anonymous interpreter employs Song 5:7 (נשאו את רדידי מעלי שמרי החמות "The watchmen of the walls took off my mantle from upon me") to justify the translation of the Hebrew word הרדידים from Isa 3:23 ("the mantles") with the word לסוטה, which also means something like "veil" or "mantle." This use of a verse from the Song mirrors examples found already in the Tannaitic Midrashim, wherein there are several instances in which the Song is employed to explain formal and linguistic features of other biblical texts. See the Mekilta of Rabbi Ishmael, Shirta 6 (Horovitz and Rabin, eds., *Mechilta*, 137–138); Beshallaḥ 5 (ibid., 101); Baḥodesh 8 (ibid., 234). A parallel version of the Beshallaḥ passage appears in the Mekilta of Rabbi Shimon bar Yoḥai, Beshallaḥ 24:2 (MS Firkovitch II A 268; Epstein and Melamed, *Mekhilta*, 87).

Rabbi Abun bar Ḥiyya and Rabbi Mana regarding whether a woman would paint only one eye with kohl and appear in public.³⁵ Rabbi Mana cites the Qere of Song 4:9 (לבבתיני באחת מעיניך) "You captured my heart with one of your eyes") to justify this practice. Rabbi Mana's interpretation is generated from the intertextual juxtaposition of m. Shabb. 8:3 and Song 4:9 on the basis of two words shared between the two: "one" אחת and "eye" עין. While this interpretation and the one from y. Ber. may seem unremarkable in and of themselves, it is important to note that the practice of employing the Song to justify the rabbinic halachic enterprise only occurs once in tannaitic literature (m. Avod. Zar. 2:5). The majority of tannaitic interpretations of the Song in relationship to the mitzvot focus instead on using verses from the work to give voice to the affective character of rabbinic piety.³⁶ In the case of these passages from y. Ber. and y. Shabb., the Song plays a markedly different role as the basis for justifying rabbinic legal judgment.

While verses from the Song play rather limited roles in y. Ber. 4:5, 8d and y. Shabb. 8:3, 11b, verses from the Song take center stage in the extended commentary on m. Avod. Zar. 2:5 found in y. Avod. Zar. 2:8, 41c–d, which develops substantially the interpretation of Song 1:2–3 found in this mishnah. The citation of Song 1:2–3 appears in the context of a conversation between Rabbi Ishmael and Rabbi Joshua that is recounted by Rabbi Judah regarding the justification for the designation of cheese made by non-Jews as forbidden for consumption by Jews. The substance of the dispute is whether the prohibition is rooted in biblical law or rabbinic restriction. In the course of their conversation, Rabbi Joshua shifts the discussion to inquire how Rabbi Ishmael pronounces the consonantal text of Song 1:2 and thus interprets the meaning of the verse. The relevant section of m. Avod. Zar. 2:5 reads:

הִשִּׂיאוֹ לְדָבָר אַחֵר, אָמַר לוֹ, יִשְׁמָעֵאל אָחִי, הֵיאַךְ אַתָּה קוֹרֵא כִּי טוֹבִים דֹּדֶיךָ מִיָּיִן, אוֹ כִּי טוֹבִים דֹּדַיִךְ. אָמַר לוֹ, כִּי טוֹבִים דֹּדַיִךְ. אָמַר לוֹ, אֵין הַדָּבָר כֵּן, שֶׁהֲרֵי חֲבֵרוֹ מְלַמֵּד עָלָיו, לְרֵיחַ שְׁמָנֶיךָ טוֹבִים:

A. He [Rabbi Joshua] shifted to another subject. He said to him, "Ishmael, my brother, how do you read [this verse]: "Your [masculine singular] love is better than wine" or "Your [feminine singular] love is better than wine?" [Song 1:2]."

B. He [Rabbi Ishmael] said to him [Rabbi Joshua], "Your [feminine singular] love is better than wine?"

---

35 For a broader discussion of stereotypes about women in the Palestinian Talmud, see Satlow, "Fictional Women."
36 On tannaitic interpretation of the Song in relationship to rabbinic piety, see Kaplan, *My Perfect One*, 95–133.

C. He [Rabbi Joshua] said to him [Rabbi Ishmael], "This reading [lit. 'matter', 'thing'] is not possible, because the next verse teaches regarding it, "the scent of your [masculine singular] oils are pleasant" [Song 1:3].

Rabbi Joshua's query of Rabbi Ishmael is based on legitimate uncertainty about who is uttering which words in the opening verses of the Song. The pronouns modifying various nouns in these verses can be read as either masculine or feminine depending on how you vocalize the consonantal text. The dominant interpretation of these verses, which is based both on the context of the verses and the pointing found in the Masoretic Text, understands the speaker of these verses as being the female protagonist of the Song. However, if one takes the second half of Song 1:2 in isolation, its consonantal text could be understood as the male lover of the Song extolling the love (or lovemaking) of the female protagonist. Rabbi Joshua presents this part of verse two to Rabbi Ishmael in isolation. In the context of rabbinic interpretation of the Song, the question is also about whether the speaker of this fragment is to be understood as God (identified with the male figure) or the people of Israel (correlated with the female protagonist). Rabbi Ishmael opts for the former and proposes a vocalization at odds with the consensus of interpretation. Rabbi Joshua points this disjunction out by appealing to the next verse (Song 1:3), wherein the pronoun can only be vocalized as referring to the male lover (and thus God) because of the context of the verse as a whole.

Though the discussion in this passage seems to be about the identity of speakers in these verses from the Song, its purpose must also be viewed in the broader context of this section of the Mishnah, which explores whether the prohibitions against gentile cheese are biblical or rabbinic in origin. Because Song 1:2–3 mention both wine and oil, they are relevant to this discussion because all three items of food are in some way prohibited to Jews under rabbinic law when they derive from or are handled by non-Jews. Rabbi Joshua's interpretation of these verses follows the standard rabbinic interpretation of the Song, which correlates God with the male lover and the Community of Israel with the female protagonist. His assertion that the speaker of these verses is the female protagonist characterizes the love of God, which she extolls in Song 1:2, as being greater than "wine" and by extension cheese and oil. In this interpretation, as Amit Gevaryahu, following Shlomo Naeh, notes, gentile cheese, wine, and oil are "forbidden by the Jews, or the rabbis, because Jews (or rabbis) love God more than wine or oil."[37] Thus, Song 1:2–3 become in this interpretation a way to articulate a theological rationale for rabbinic understandings of idealized Jewish practice.

---

37 Gevaryahu, "New Reading," 210, following Naeh, "Your Love," 428. See also Henshke, "For Your Love"; Freidenreich, *Foreigners*, 56; Rosenblum, *Food*, 87–88.

This use of Song 1:2–3 leads to a collection of texts in the amoraic discussion appended to it in the Palestinian Talmud that also offer interpretations of Song 1:2 as well as Song 7:10. The first of these appears at the beginning of y. Avod. Zar. 2:8, 41c (MS Leiden, Scaliger 3):

חברייה בשם רבי יוחנן דודים דברי סופרים לדברי תורה וחביבים יותר מדברי תורה וחכך
כיין הטוב שמעון בר בא בשם רבי יוחנן דודים דברי סופרים לדברי תורה וחביבים יותר
מדברי תורה כי טובים דודיך מיין.

- A. The colleagues in the name of Rabbi Yoḥanan: "The words of the Soferim are likened (*dodim*) to the words of Torah and are more pleasant than words of Torah. 'Your palate is like good wine' (Song 7:10)."
- B. Shimon bar Abba in the name of Rabbi Yoḥanan: "The words of the Soferim are likened (*dodim*) to the words of Torah and are more pleasant than words of Torah. 'For your friends (*dodeykha*) are better than wine' (Song 1:2)."[38]

In both traditions, which are linked to Rabbi Yoḥanan, the words of the Soferim, a group of scholars who preceded the Tannaim, are described as being comparable to and having greater value than the actual words of the Torah.[39] In the first tradition Song 7:10 is interpreted as a figuration of this assertion through the identification of the Soferim as the "palate" of the male figure in the Song. In the second tradition Song 1:2 provides the proof text for this assertion. This tradition utilizes a pun on the verbal form *dodim* ("to be likened") in order to connect this assertion to Song 1:2 through the appearance of the similar sounding plural noun form *dodeykha* in that verse. Rather than understanding *dodeykha* in this verse as "your love/lovemaking," as in the interpretation found in m. Avod. Zar. 2:5, Shimon bar Abba's interpretation of this word is better rendered as "companions" or "friends." Thus, the Soferim, who are understood to be the "companions" of God, are better than the words of Torah, which is correlated to "wine" in this verse.

The second example of an interpretation of Song 1:2 in y. Avod. Zar. 2:8, 41c appears in the context of a broader discussion about a statement attributed to the tannaitic figure Rabbi Ishmael in which he compares the relative severity of the words of Torah with the words of the Soferim. Later in the course of the discussion, Rabbi Ḥama bar Uqba raises a question regarding the mishnah cited at the beginning of this section. He asks, in effect, why Rabbi Joshua did not ask Rabbi Ishmael another question in order to distract him further from his line of argumentation.

---

38 Nearly identical versions of this tradition appear in y. Ber. 1:7, 3b and y. Sanh. 11:6, 30a.
39 For an introductory discussion of the Soferim, see Gilat, "Soferim."

Rabbi Ḥama bar Uqba suggests that he should have asked him about the five places in Torah whose syntax is difficult to parse with reference just to their consonantal text (Gen 4:7; 49:6–7; Exod 17:9; 25:34; Deut 31:16). Rabbi Tanḥuma proposes adding Gen 34:7 to this list. Before Rabbi Isaac adds Deut 4:14 to the list, the third generation Amora from Tiberias, Rabbi La (or Hela/Ela), recommends including the first part of Song 1:2 "may he kiss me with the kisses of his mouth" on this list.[40] The inclusion of Song 1:2 in this list makes sense given that the first part of the verse is clearly marked as having the male figure of the Song as its subject. As I noted earlier in my discussion of m. Avod. Zar. 2:5, the second half of this verse, however, could be understood as referring either to the male lover or the female protagonist depending on how you vocalize the second-person personal pronoun suffixed to "love making." How to vocalize and thus understand this pronoun is precisely the question posed earlier by Rabbi Joshua to Rabbi Ishmael in the mishnaic passage. The addition proposed to this list by the later amoraic figure, Rabbi La, might have not only distracted Rabbi Ishmael from the line of his argument, as Rabbi Ḥama bar Uqba suggested, but also subtly returned the conversation to Song 1:2, the verse that silenced Rabbi Ishmael in the first place in the framing discussion in the Mishnah.

The discussion in the Palestinian Talmud that comments on the end of m. Avod. Zar. 2:5 builds on and elaborates the interpretation of Song 1:2–3 found in the Mishnah and associated with Rabbi Joshua and Rabbi Ishmael in rather elaborate ways. First, this section of y. Avod. Zar. employs these verses in order to extoll the merits of the Soferim. Second, Rabbi La proposes including these verses among those whose syntax is difficult to parse without proper vocalization. His proposal serves to return the discussion back to the original discussion in the Mishnah. It also evinces the support of the editor of this tractate for Rabbi Joshua's position, as mediated through Song 1:2–3, regarding the forbidden status of gentile cheese, and by extension oil and wine, because this restriction serves as an expression of Israel's devotion to God.[41] Through this extended discussion, the later amoraic figures are then able to assert their own voice in the conversation on the meaning of these verses and by extension this practice. This extended discussion is the only example in the Palestinian Talmud in which the later Amoraim explicitly engage, develop, and respond to an interpretation of the Song found in tannaitic literature and in which they engage in sustained interpretation of verses from the Song. More importantly, this section of y. Avod. Zar. highlights the broadening of the use of the

---

40 On the various spellings of Rabbi La's name, see Strack and Stemberger, *Introduction*, 91.
41 On the irrational foundations of observing the commandments, see Heinemann, *Reasons*, esp. 24–25.

Song in amoraic literature from purely aggadic contexts to also being used to generate and to justify rabbinic legal decisions.

4 Conclusion

As I have shown in the preceding discussion, there is a remarkable degree of consistency in the hermeneutical approach to the Song found in both tannaitic literature and the Palestinian Talmud. The rabbinic sages, whose traditions are preserved in these various works, consistently correlate verses from the Song in a typological mode with idyllic and idealized understandings of scripture and of rabbinic society and practice. While the earlier tannaitic interpretations, particularly those found in the Tannaitic Midrashim, primarily correlated this work to an idealized vision of Israel's history and practice exemplified by the period of the exodus, Sinai Theophany, and wilderness wanderings, the amoraic interpretations found in the Palestinian Talmud exhibit a distinct emphasis in their interpretative approach to the Song. As I have argued in this essay, these passages present new interpretations of the Song through which these Amoraim valorize contemporary rabbinic society and halachah, claim to esteem the position of the Jewish people within the Greco-Roman world, and embed these rabbinic ideals in the Song alongside other scriptural works as the intended meaning of these texts. In part, this shift in emphasis may be the result of the fact that the earlier tannaitic interpretations of the Song appear in collections of midrashim arranged around Pentateuchal works. The focus of these works is on understanding the foundations of Israelite history and law found in the Torah. In contrast, the Palestinian Talmud is arranged as a commentary on the Mishnah, and its focus is more on shaping and chronicling contemporary rabbinic practice and society. In this regard, many of the verses drawn from the Song are often correlated in the Palestinian Talmud to the contemporary experience of the Amoraim who transmitted these interpretative traditions rather than intertextually to other verses in the Torah. In doing so, the Amoraim not only employ the Song to describe their contemporary experience but also develop the Song as a ready resource for providing scriptural support for their halachic positions. Thus, the Song in the Palestinian Talmud chronicles not just the past experience of ancient Israel but "drips" from the lips of the Amoraim as they describe their own idyllic and idealized rabbinic society and legislate ideal halachic practice for that society.

Bibliography

Anisfeld, Rachel A. *Sustain Me with Raisin-Cakes: Pesikta deRav Kahana and the Popularization of Rabbinic Judaism*. JSJ.S 133. Leiden: Brill, 2009.
Ben-Eliyahu, Eyal, Yehudah Cohn, and Fergus Millar. *Handbook of Jewish Literature from Late Antiquity, 135–700 CE*. Oxford: Oxford University Press, 2013.
Boyarin, Daniel. *Intertextuality and the Reading of Midrash*. Bloomington, IN: Indiana University Press, 1990.
Boyarin, Daniel. "'Language Inscribed by History on the Bodies of Living Beings': Midrash and Martyrdom." *Representations* 25 (1989): 139–151.
Boyarin, Daniel. *Tannaitic Midrash: Intertextuality and the Reading of Mekilta*, translated by David S. Luvish and Ruti Bar-Ilan. Jerusalem: Shalom Hartman Institute, 2011. (Hebrew)
Boyarin, Daniel. "Two Introductions to the Midrash on the Song of Songs." *Tarbiz* 56 (1986): 479–500. (Hebrew)
Cohen, Norman J. "Analysis of an Exegetic Tradition in the 'Mekhilta de-Rabbi Ishmael': The Meaning of 'Amanah in the Second and Third Centuries." *AJSR* 9 (1984): 1–25.
Elgvin, Torleif. *The Literary Growth of the Song of Songs during the Hasmonean and Early-Herodian Periods*. CBET 89. Leuven: Peeters, 2018.
Epstein, Jacob Nahum, and Ezra Zion Melamed, eds. *Mekhilta de-Rabbi Shimon ben Yoḥai*. Jerusalem: Meqitse Nirdamim, 1955.
Finkelstein, Louis, ed. *Siphre ad Deuteronomium*. New York: Jewish Theological Seminary of America, 1993.
Finkelstein, Louis. "The Sources of the Tannaitic Midrashim." *JQR* 31 (1941): 211–243.
Freidenreich, David M. *Foreigners and Their Food: Constructing Otherness in Jewish, Christian, and Islamic Law*. Berkeley, CA: University of California Press, 2011.
Gevaryahu, Amit. "A New Reading of the Three Dialogues in Mishnah Avodah Zarah." *JSQ* 19 (2012): 207–229.
Gilat, Yitzhak Dov. "Soferim." In vol. 18 of *Encyclopaedia Judaica*, edited by Michael Berenbaum and Fred Skolnik, 743–744. Detroit, MI: Macmillan Reference USA, 2007.
Goshen Gottstein, Alon. "Did the Tannaim Interpret the Song of Songs Systematically?" In *Vixens Disturbing Vineyards: Embarrassment and Embracement of Scriptures; Festschrift in Honor of Harry Fox (leBeit Yoreh)*, edited by Tzemah Yoreh, Aubrey Glazer, Justin Jaron Lewis, and Miryam Segal, 260–271. Boston: Academic Studies Press, 2010.
Guggenheimer, Heinrich W. *The Jerusalem Talmud: Second Order: Mo'ed, Tractates Ta'aniot, Megillah, Ḥagigah and Mo'ed Qaṭan (Mašqin)*. SJ 85. Berlin: de Gruyter, 2015.
Heinemann, Isaac. *The Reasons for the Commandments in Jewish Thought from the Bible to the Renaissance*, translated by Leonard Levin. Reference Library of Jewish Intellectual History. Boston: Academic Studies Press, 2008.
Henshke, David. "'For Your Love is More Delightful than Wine': Concerning Tannaitic Biblical Traditions." *JSIJ* 10 (2012): 1–24. (Hebrew)
Horovitz, H. Saul, ed. *Siphre ad Numeros adjecto Siphre zutta cum variis lectionibus et adnotanionibus*. Corpus Tannaiticum 2. Leipzig: G. Fock, 1917.
Horovitz, H. Saul, and Israel Abraham Rabin, eds. *Mechilta d'Rabbi Ismael cum variis lectionibus et adnotanionibus*. 2nd ed. Frankfurt: J. Kauffmann, 1931. Repr., Jerusalem: Shalem, 1997.
Kadari, Tamar. "On the Redaction of Midrash Shir HaShirim Rabbah." PhD diss., The Hebrew University of Jerusalem, 2004. (Hebrew)

Kalman, Jason. "Authorship, Attribution, and Authority: Jeremiah, Baruch, and the Rabbinic Interpretation of Lamentations." *HUCA* 90 (2019): 27–87.

Kaplan, Jonathan. "Martyrdom, Mysticism, and Disputation: Rabbi Akiva and the 'Beginning' of Rabbinic Interpretation of Song of Songs." In *The Song of Songs in its Context: Words for Love, Love for Words*, edited by Pierre Van Hecke, 287–310. BETL 310. Leuven: Peeters, 2020.

Kaplan, Jonathan. *My Perfect One: Typology and Early Rabbinic Interpretation of Song of Songs*. New York: Oxford University Press, 2015.

Kaplan, Jonathan. "The Song of Songs from the Bible to the Mishnah." *HUCA* 81 (2010/2013): 43–66.

Klein, Johannes. "Anregungen zur Interpretation der Samuelbücher aus dem Talmud." In *The Books of Samuel: Stories – History – Reception History*, edited by Walter Dietrich, 129–151. BETL 284. Leuven: Peeters, 2016.

Lieber, Laura S. *A Vocabulary of Desire: The Song of Songs in the Early Synagogue*. BRLA 40. Leiden: Brill, 2014.

Lieberman, Saul. "Mishnat shir ha-Shirim." In Gershom Scholem, *Jewish Gnosticism, Merkabah Mysticism, and Talmudic Tradition*, 118–126. 2nd ed. New York: Jewish Theological Seminary of America, 1965. (Hebrew)

Lieberman, Saul, ed. *The Tosefta*. 5 vols. New York: Jewish Theological Seminary of America, 1955–1988.

Meir, Ofra. "The Story as a Hermeneutic Device." *AJSR* 7/8 (1982/1983): 231–262.

Naeh, Shlomo. "'Your Love is Better than Wine': A New Look at Mishnah 'Abodah Zarah 2:5." In *Studies in the Talmud and Midrash: A Memorial Volume for Tirtsah Lifshitz*, edited by Moshe Bar-Asher, Joshua Levinson, and Berachyahu Lifshitz, 411–434. Jerusalem: Bialik, 2005.

Rapp-de Lange, Birke. "Rabbinische Liebe: Untersuchungen zur Deutung der Liebe des Hohenliedes auf das Studium der Tora in Midrasch Shir haShirim Rabba." PhD diss., Katholieke Theologische Universiteit in Utrecht, 2003.

Rosenblum, Jordan D. *Food and Identity in Early Rabbinic Judaism*. Cambridge: Cambridge University Press, 2010.

Roux, Marie, and Yael Wilfand. "'The Flower of the Whole World': A Homily on Converts from the Jerusalem Talmud Analyzed in Light of Greco-Roman Floral Motifs." *REJ* 179 (2020): 315–331.

Samely, Alexander. *Rabbinic Interpretation of Scripture in the Mishnah*. Oxford: Oxford University Press, 2002.

Satlow, Michael L. "Fictional Women: A Study in Stereotypes." In *The Talmud Yerushalmi and Graeco-Roman Culture III*, edited by Peter Schäfer, 225–243. TSAJ 93. Tübingen: Mohr Siebeck, 2002.

Stern, David. "Ancient Jewish Interpretation of the Song of Songs in a Comparative Context." In *Jewish Biblical Interpretation and Cultural Exchange: Comparative Exegesis in Context*, edited by Natalie B. Dohrmann and David Stern, 87–107, 263–272. Philadelphia, PA: University of Pennsylvania Press, 2008.

Strack, Hermann L., and Günter Stemberger. *Introduction to the Talmud and Midrash*, edited and translated by Markus Bockmuehl. 2nd ed. Edinburgh: T&T Clark, 1996.

Tomson, Peter J. "The Song of Songs in the Teachings of Jesus and the Development of the Exposition on the Song." *NTS* 61 (2015): 429–447.

Wyrick, Jed. *The Ascension of Authorship: Attribution and Canon Formation in Jewish, Hellenistic, and Christian Traditions*. Harvard Studies in Comparative Literature 49. Cambridge, MA: Harvard University Press, 2004.

Yadin-Israel, Azzan. *Scripture and Tradition: Rabbi Akiva and the Triumph of Midrash*. Divinations. Philadelphia, PA: University of Pennsylvania Press, 2015.

Yadin-Israel, Azzan. *Scripture as Logos: Rabbi Ishmael and the Origins of Midrash*. Divinations. Philadelphia, PA: University of Pennsylvania Press, 2004.

Tamar Kadari
The Exegesis of all Exegeses
The Uniqueness of Shir HaShirim Rabbah's Approach to the Song of Songs

Shir haShirim Rabbah[1] is an anthology of sayings attributed to sages who lived in the Land of Israel during the first centuries of the Common Era (0–500 CE). It was redacted at the end of the sixth century or the beginning of the seventh century in the Land of Israel,[2] though the identity of its redactor is unknown. Shir haShirim Rabbah is the earliest and lengthiest of the midrashic collections on the Song of Songs,[3] and belongs to the class of Amoraic aggadic midrashim.[4] The composition is primarily written in a combination of Hebrew and Galilean Aramaic, interwoven with Greek words.[5] The midrash has no clear internal division into sections. The division into eight chapters corresponding to the eight chapters of the Song of Songs, which appears in contemporary editions, was a much later development.

In this article we will examine the uniqueness of Shir haShirim Rabbah when considered as part of the history of the exegesis of the Song of Songs throughout the ages.

---

[1] Also known as *Song of Songs Rabbah* and *Canticles Rabbah*. The midrash opens with a verse from Proverbs (22:29): "Behold [*hazita*] a man skilled at his work," and so it came to be referred to also as *Midrash Hazita*.
[2] See Kadari, "New Textual Witnesses," 41–42. However, Lachs maintains that it was redacted later, between 650–750 CE. See Lachs, "Prolegomena to Canticles Rabba," 246–249.
[3] Another midrash on the Song of Songs was published concurrently under two different names: Buber, *Shir ha-Shirim Zuta*, and Schechter, *Agadath Shir ha-Shirim*. An additional midrash was published by Greenhut, *Midrash Shir ha-Shirim*. These collections are all smaller and probably later than Shir haShirim Rabbah.
[4] The creators of midrash were several thousand sages who lived in the first centuries CE, in the Land of Israel and Babylonia. They are generally divided into two groups—the Tannaim, who lived from about 0–200 CE and were active in the Land of Israel, and the Amoraim, who lived from about 200–500 CE and were active in the two geographic centers of Jewish life, the Land of Israel and Babylon. On halakhic and aggadic midrashim, see Lerner, "Works of the Aggadic Midrash," 138–145; Hirshman, "Aggadic Midrash."
[5] See GirÓn-Blanc, "Vocablos Griegos."

1 The Verses and their Interpretations as an Organizing Principle

One of the main characteristics of Shir haShirim Rabbah is the fact that the midrash is organized according to the order of the verses of the biblical book. Each verse is accompanied by a variety of interpretations attributed to different sages. Only five verses do not have commentary in Shir haShirim Rabbah, and four of them recur elsewhere in the scroll and are interpreted there.[6] This organizing style, proceeding verse by verse in a sustained manner, is known in scholarly literature as exegetical midrash.[7]

Despite the clear organization around biblical verses, the rabbis' central purpose was not to explicate difficult texts or passages. This can account for only a small part of the midrashim in Shir haShirim Rabbah. In essence, the meaning of the word "midrash," is literally searching out and exploring sacred scripture.[8] The sages studied the Bible deeply, intensely, and dealt with biblical verses in creative ways. In places where they reflect on what they were doing, their motives were matters of faith, and flowed from an educational philosophy that was about forging a strong, lively connection between the Torah and their lives, and making it meaningful and relevant to their contemporaries.

This is true of midrash more generally, and of Shir haShirim Rabbah in particular. The content of the different midrashic units that are linked to each verse of the Song of Songs is quite varied. A small fraction are concerned with interpreting rare words and phrases that appear nowhere else in the biblical text, but the vast majority involve long allegorical exegeses that encompass ideological and theological matters. We will analyze a few examples that reflect this diversity.

---

6 Song 3:5 השבעתי, Song 6:3 אני לדודי, Song 7:4 שני שדיך, Song 8:3 שמאלו, Song 8:4 השבעתי.
7 Exegetical midrash stands in contrast to homiletical midrash, in which the midrashic compositions are organized around a topic and do not interpret most of the verses of the biblical book. On exegetical and homiletical midrashim, see Stemberger, *Introduction*, 240.
8 In the Bible, the root D-R-SH originally meant to search for and explore after God (e.g., Deut 13:15; Gen 25:22). Over time, it underwent a dramatic shift to mean to search for and explore after the meaning of Scripture: "For Ezra devoted himself to search out—*li-drosh*—God's Torah." (Ezra 7:10).

2 A Wide Exegetical Range: From the Literal to the Allegorical

The Songs of Songs is written in elevated diction, as befits biblical poetry, and it contains unique words, unusual phrases, parallelism, and language rich with imagery and metaphor.[9] In a few places in Shir haShirim Rabbah, it seems as if the sages are attempting to clarify the textual meaning of various words and phrases that appear in the Song of Songs. But for the most part these attempts are actually a vehicle for delving into deeper layers of meaning, as seen in the following example.

The word *apiryon* (אַפִּרְיוֹן; usually translated as "palanquin") appears in a description of Solomon's wedding: "King Solomon made him a palanquin" (Song 3:9). This is a hapax legomenon and scholars disagree about the origin of this word.[10] Shir haShirim Rabbah 3:9.2 cites a midrash attributed to the tanna Rabbi Yehudah ben Rabbi Il'ai, who lived in the Land of Israel during the second century CE: "What is *apiryon*? A palanquin." Rabbi Yehudah proposes defining the word *apiryon* by reference to a familiar Greek word, φορεῖον, a kind of bed or chair with a canopy supported by poles used for transporting an individual outside.[11]

The literal meaning of the term *apiryon* is discussed in the context of a long allegorical midrashic unit, which identifies the palanquin with the Ark of the Covenant:

> *Shir haShirim Rabbah 3:9.2*
> Rabbi Yehudah ben Rabbi Il'ai interpreted the verses as referring to the ark. "A palanquin" [*apiryon*, Song 3:9] this refers to the ark.
> 1) What is *apiryon*? A palanquin.
> 2) It is as if a king had an only daughter, fair, lovely, and highly regarded, and he said to his servants, "My daughter is fair, lovely, and highly regarded; why do you not make her a palanquin? Make her a palanquin, for it is better that her beauty should be seen from out of the palanquin." So the Holy One, blessed be He, said: "My Torah is fair, lovely, and highly regarded.; why do you not make an ark for it? It is better that the beauty of My Torah should be discerned from out of the ark."
> 3) "King Solomon made him" [Song 3:9] the King unto Whom peace pertains.

---

[9] On the heightened features of different biblical genres and the problem of distinguishing between biblical poetry and prose, see Kugel, *Idea of Biblical Poetry*, 59–95.
[10] Scholars disagree about whether its origin is Indo-European (ancient Persian), Sanskrit, or Greek. See Koehler and Baumgartner, *Hebrew and Aramaic Lexicon*, 1:80.
[11] The Septuagint translated it as φορεῖον. See Aruk HaShalem, 1, 239b; Krauss, *Griechische und Lateinische Lehnwörter*, 434.

4) "Of wood from Lebanon" [Song 3:9] as it says, "And Bezalel made the ark of acacia-wood" [Exod 37:1]. "He made its posts of silver" [Song 3:10]—this refers to the two staves inside the ark which were of silver. "Its back of gold," [Song 3:10] as it says, "And he overlaid it with pure gold" [Exod 37:2]. "Its seat of purple wool" [Song 3:10]. Rabbi Tanhuma said: This refers to the veil which adjoined it. Rabbi Bibi said: This refers to the ark-cover, the gold of which resembled purple. "Within it was decked with love" [Song 3:10]—the tablets and the broken tablets were placed in the ark.[12]

We will first examine the third section of this midrashic unit, which offers an allegorical commentary on Song 3:9.

According to the allegorical approach, which is the prevailing exegetical method employed in Shir haShirim Rabbah, the Song of Songs alludes to an additional layer of spiritual meaning. The words "King Solomon made him a palanquin (*apiryon*)" are interpreted as referring to God, who is known as "the king to whom peace pertains" (section 3). The name *Shelomo* שלמה is interpreted as it sounds, but with a change of spelling: שלומו *shelomo*, as if it were a possessive noun: "his peace" or, as rendered here, "He to whom peace pertains." Peace belongs to the Almighty; He is referred to as "He who makes peace" (*sheha-shalom shelo*). This exegesis appears already in Tannaitic literature, and can also be found in ancient Christian commentary.[13]

In his allegorical exegesis on Song 3:9–10 (section 4), Rabbi Yehudah proposes reading the *apiryon* as a description of the Ark of the Covenant. He enumerates each of the components of the palanquin in turn—the posts, staves, and back—each of which is compared to one of the components of the ark. Like a palanquin, the ark was also made of wood, overlaid with gold, and covered with a purple curtain. The ark's purpose was to house the beloved Torah, that is, the Ten Commandments, just as the inside of the palanquin represented the love of the daughters of Jerusalem.

Rabbi Yehudah also incorporates a parable into his exegesis (section 2). The purpose of the parable is to further hone the connection between the palanquin and the ark, and to infuse the palanquin with religious significance. The parable features a king and his daughter who are bound to one another in love and concern. The king is aware of his daughter's many virtues, and he wishes for his subjects to

---

[12] English translation from *Song of Songs Rabbah* (Simon, trans.), 166–167, with some modifications. All quotes from Shir haShirim Rabbah are according to MS Vatican Ebr. 76. The last line, "within it was decked with love," is from the version preserved in two textual witnesses. For all textual variants of Shir haShirim Rabbah, see Kadari, *A Synoptic Edition*. For a description of MS Vatican 76 and its relationship to the other textual witnesses, see Steller, "Preliminary Remarks," 301–311.

[13] See *Mekhilta de-Rabbi Ishmael*, Masekhta de-Pisha, Bo 14 (Lauterbach ed., 1:75); and see Origen, *Song of Songs*, 51 (prologue 4): "It is, I think, unquestionable that Solomon is in many respects a type of Christ, first in that he is called the Peaceable."

admire and enjoy her beauty as he does. He asks his servants to make a palanquin for her so that others will be able to observe her publicly yet in a supervised, controlled setting that will befit her elevated status and keep her apart from the masses.

In this parable, the king's daughter represents the Torah, which is fair, lovely, and highly regarded. God commands the people of Israel to build an ark for the Torah so that they can admire and enjoy it. Like the palanquin, the ark was a square wooden structure decorated with expensive materials. Throughout their desert wanderings, the Israelites would cover it in fabric and transport it by means of poles. Even within the Tabernacle, it was impossible to see the ark because of the curtain that separated the sanctuary from the Holy of Holies.[14]

The analogy between the Torah and a king's daughter serves to anthropomorphize the Torah, or perhaps more accurately to feminize it.[15] The verses quoted from the Song of Songs underscore the special bond of love and esteem between God and His Torah. God wishes for the people of Israel, too, to admire and enjoy the Torah's beauty, and because of that, He employs the ark, which contains the tablets. This parable resolves the famous question about whether the Torah belongs to the creatures of the upper realm or the lower realm. According to the parable, the Torah is physically to be found within the camp of the Israelites, but the ark serves as a sort of royal home that attests to its elevated stature and uniqueness.

As we have seen, the literal interpretation of the word *apiryon* appears in Shir haShirim Rabbah in the context of a sophisticated allegorical exegesis which also contains a parable. This exegetical unit offers an excellent example of the interpretive richness found in Shir haShirim Rabbah, which deals with literal matters while also encompassing vivid images (a parable) and ideological concerns.

The vast majority of Shir haShirim Rabbah is comprised of allegorical exegesis of the Song of Songs.[16] Indeed, this long midrashic unit attributed to Rabbi Yehuda ben Rabbi Il'ai is just one of five allegorical midrashic units on these verses in Shir haShirim Rabbah. In the others, the sages propose that the *apiryon* is an allegory for the tabernacle, for Solomon's Temple, for the world, and for the throne of God's glory.[17] This brings us to the next characteristic of Shir haShirim Rabbah, namely its polysemic multiplicity.

---

14 See Tosefta Kippurim 2:15 (Leiberman, ed., 238).
15 On feminine imagery of the Torah, see Green, "Bride, Spouse, Daughter"; Wolfson, *Circle in the Square*, 1–28.
16 Some scholars argued that it was only on account of its allegorical exegesis that the Song of Songs was admitted into the biblical canon. See Cohen, "Song of Songs and the Jewish Religious Mentality"; Stern, "Ancient Jewish Interpretation," 89–92.
17 See Shir haShirim Rabbah 3:9.1–3:10.4.

3 A Polysemic Multiplicity of Views and Opinions

The richness of Shir haShirim Rabbah is reflected not just in the many types of interpretations and the various genres it contains, but also in the fact that each biblical verse is accompanied by a plethora of midrashim attributed to various sages holding different opinions.

Midrash Shir haShirim Rabbah is a collection of interpretations by different sages over the course of several centuries reflecting a range of opinions and ideas. Sometimes they are attributed to known sages, and sometimes they are anonymous. Each verse or sequence of verses in Shir haShirim Rabbah is accompanied by a plethora of allegorical exegesis covering a wide range of topics, without any clear unity or uniformity.[18]

This phenomenon is demonstrated by the following passage, in which various sages offer their understandings of the unique phrase *Shir haShirim* (שיר השירים; "song of songs"). The scroll opens with the heading, "The Song of Songs which is Solomon's." The phrase "song of songs" is an expression that occurs only once within the Bible. It is explained in Shir haShirim Rabbah 1:1.11: "Song of songs—the most praiseworthy of songs, the most exalted of songs, the finest of songs." The midrash explains the superlative phrase "Song of (all) Songs" by analogy to "the Sabbath of all Sabbaths" and "the Holy of Holies."[19] The Song of Songs is portrayed as a single song which is superior to all the other biblical songs.[20]

Later on, the midrash brings a dispute among four sages, two Amoraim and two Tannaim, each of whom proposes a different interpretation of the words Shir haShirim.

Shir haShirim Rabbah 1:2.1
1) "The Song of Songs, which is Solomon's" [. . .] Rabbi Yehudah ben Rabbi Simon said: It was said at Sinai. "The Song of Songs"—the song recited by the upright (*yesharim*) at Sinai, as it is said, "He is a shield to those who walk in uprightness" [Prov 2:7].
2) Rabbi Yitzhak said: The Song of Songs was recited at the Sea—that song which was said by the singing singers (*ha-sharim ha-shorerim*), of which it is said, "the singers in front, the minstrels last" [Ps 68:26].

---

18 According to Boyarin, the rabbis regarded the holy song as a hermeneutic key to the unlocking of the Torah. The reading method was not allegorical but rather intertextual. See Boyarin, *Intertextuality and the Reading of Midrash*, 105–107, 115.
19 A similar analogy appears in Origen, *Song of Songs*, 46 (prologue 4).
20 The Aramaic Targum on Song of Songs includes a list of all ten songs to which the Song of Songs is deemed superior. For the relationship between this list and the seven songs that appear in Origen, see Kugel, "Is There But One Song?"

3)   It was taught in the name of Rabbi Natan: The Holy One blessed be He in the glory of His greatness said it, as it is said, "The Song of Songs, which is Solomon's" [Song 1:1]—the king to whom peace pertains (*sheha-shalom shelo*).
4)   Rabban Gamliel said: The ministering angel said it. "The Song of Songs" [Song 1:1]—the song of the ministers (*shir hasarim*), the song that was said by the supernal ministers.[21]

Each of these four short interpretations of the words Shir haShirim ("Song of Songs") offers a different understanding of the name of the scroll. The sages are not interested in the literal meaning of these words. Their conviction is that the key to understanding the Song is to be found in the name of the book, which reflects its nature and contents. In order to reveal it, they use various plays on words. Here as elsewhere, the sages play creatively with biblical language, eliciting new ideas and original interpretations. The language of the Bible stimulated the rabbis' religious thinking and offered a way of wrestling with ideological and philosophical matters.

In the above dispute, the four sages attempt to answer the question of who sang or composed the Song of Songs. Although the Song is attributed to Solomon, each sage offers a different suggestion.

3.1 Rabbi Yehudah ben Rabbi Simon: The Song of the Israelites at Sinai

The first statement by Rabbi Yehudah ben Rabbi Simon uses a play on the word "songs" (*shirim*), switching the order of the letters so that *shirim* becomes *yesharim*. The word *yesharim* ("upright") describes the people of Israel at a particular historic moment, namely the revelation at Sinai. They merited the description "upright" on account of their willingness to receive the Torah.

This wordplay enables Rabbi Yehuda b. Rabbi Simon to give voice to his understanding of who composed the Song of Songs and when. According to Rabbi Yehudah ben Rabbi Simon's allegorical reading, the Song of Songs is the song that the children of Israel sang to God at Mount Sinai. At this unique moment of revelation they were able to see God face to face and to describe His physical appearance, like the descriptions of the beloved in the Song of Songs.

The ideological understanding behind this approach is that the Song of Songs gives voice to the deep love between the people of Israel and their God at the

---

[21] *Song of Songs Rabbah* (Simon, trans.), 20–21. These positions were brought as part of a larger dispute that contains two primary blocks of material: the dispute about "Where was it said?" (four positions) and the dispute about "Who said it?" (four positions).

moment when they wish to formalize their relationship. As such, the Song has elements that resemble the signing of a binding contract between lovers.

3.2 Rabbi Yitzhak: The Song of the Israelites at the Sea of Reeds

Rabbi Yitzhak proposes a different interpretation of the words *Shir haShirim*. He employs another wordplay that involves changing the vocalization so that the words are instead read as "singing singers" (*ha-sharim ha-shorerim*). The speakers in the Song are the Israelites singing the Song of the Sea at the splitting of the Sea of Reeds, on account of which they are referred to as "singers."

This wordplay captures Rabbi Yitzchak's allegorical interpretation, according to which the Song of Songs is a song that the people of Israel sang to God during the splitting of the Sea of Reeds. The impressive revelation that took place before all of Israel was accompanied by powerful singing, both of the Song of the Sea and of the Song of Songs. In this latter song the people of Israel express their praise and their gratitude to God for saving them from the Egyptians.

As opposed to the previous approach, according to Rabbi Yitzhak the song expresses the bond between lovers still in the early stages of their relationship. It is a love full of wonder and excitement, as befits the new religious experience that the Israelites underwent during the splitting of the sea.

The two first amoraic sayings depict the Song of Songs as recited by the people of Israel at a specific historical moment, at Sinai or at the Sea. This perception is consistent with the allegorical–historical approach.

The scholar Saul Lieberman contended that already during the tannaitic period (the years 0–200 in the Land of Israel) the rabbis had four different allegorical approaches, each of which comprised a consistent interpretation of the scroll as pertaining to a specific historical event or concept: The Sea of Reeds, Mount Sinai, the portable sanctuary, and Solomon's temple.[22] Each approach interpreted the entire scroll consistently, according to one specific historical event.

The various midrashim on the Song of Songs may contain some vestiges of these four distinct approaches, like the two first interpretations above, by Rabbi Yehuda ben Rabbi Simon and Rabbi Yitzhak. Yet Lieberman's theory still requires further examination. Shir haShirim Rabbah contains many different allegorical approaches and they are attributed to numerous rabbis. One approach can be connected to

---

22 See Lieberman, "Mishnat Shir haShirim"; cf. Gottlieb, "Jewish Allegory of Love."

several rabbis, and a single rabbi never interprets all of the verses systematically. Unfortunately, it is hard to identify any uniformity.[23]

3.3 Rabbi Natan: The Song of God

The third saying, by the tanna Rabbi Natan, focuses on the end of the verse, "the Song of Songs, which is Solomon's" [Song 1:1]. He interprets the name *Shelomo* as referring to God, "He to whom peace pertains (*sheha-shalom shelo*)."[24] This simple exegetical move enables Rabbi Natan to reconceive of the Song of Songs as a work written not by its declared author, King Solomon, but rather by God. The wordplay is a tool that enables Rabbi Natan to express his fundamental position with regard to his approach to the Song of Songs.

In contrast to the first two positions, which portrayed the Song of Songs as an earthly song sung by the people of Israel, Rabbi Natan suggests that it is a heavenly song spoken by God. According to this approach, the holiness of the Song of Songs arises from the fact that it is a divine song, and thus its place in the canon is indisputable.[25]

3.4 Rabban Gamliel: The Song of the Angels

The fourth and last saying by Rabban Gamliel uses a wordplay on "songs" (*shirim*), omitting the vocalization and switching the letter *shin* for *sin* so as to change the "singers" of the Song to the "ministers" (*sarim*), or to the "ministering angels" (*malachei hasharet*). Rabban Gamliel expresses his view of the Song as a heavenly song that the ministering angels sing before the Holy One blessed be He. Its content is similar to the *Qedushah* (doxology) recited in by the angels in heaven: "Holy, Holy, Holy."

The angels that envision the Almighty in His full beauty and splendor are able to give praise. Their praise includes the detailed physical descriptions of the beloved, which are part of the Song of Songs. Rabbi Akiva may have had this line of interpretation in mind when he stated that "The Song of Songs is the Holy of

---

23 See Goshen-Gottstein, "Did the Tannaim Interpret?"
24 As seen in the exegesis above.
25 The inclusion of the Song of Songs within the biblical canon was not a simple or self-evident process. The controversy regarding the sacred status of the scroll and its canonization emerges from a number of tannaitic sources, see *m. Yad.* 3.5; *b. Meg.* 7a; *Avot R. Nat.* I:1 (Schechter, ed., 2).

Holies"²⁶—and it was not for naught that he used a linguistic phrase reminiscent of the *Qedushah*.²⁷

By way of interim summary, we have seen four different positions with regard to the interpretation of the name of the Song. These various interpretations, which are based on play-on-words, strive to tackle difficult and significant questions pertaining to the way we are to understand the scroll as a whole, its authorship, and the context in which it was originally sung. As we saw, this dispute is a compilation of textual material from different historical periods—the first two opinions are attributed to Amoraim, who represent the approach that the Song of Songs is an earthly song; and the second two are attributed to Tannaim,²⁸ who understand the Song of Songs as a heavenly song sung by the Holy One Blessed Be He or by the angels. These sages express different and even conflicting interpretive perspectives. Nonetheless, the collection of statements was compiled by an editor who collected these materials and decided to present them in a certain order and manner.

4 Redaction: The Compositional Artistry of the Midrash

Shir haShirim Rabbah consists of lengthy commentaries on the biblical text, pedagogical sayings, ideological statements, stories, parables, and proverbs—and it contains almost no discussions of halakhic matters. Some of this material is comprised of earlier homilies on verses from the Song of Songs that appear in prior compositions.²⁹ This may testify to the existence of an ancient midrash on the Song of Songs that preceded Shir haShirim Rabbah, but is no longer extant. In spite of the composition's anthological character, the redactor's imprint and style are evident in the organization of the material, the formulation of the impressive opening and conclusion of the midrash, the ideological milieu and the preference for certain exegetical approaches.³⁰

---

26 See *m. Yad.* 3.5; *t. Sanh.* 12.10: "Rabbi Akiva said: One who raises his voice in the Song of Songs in the banquet house and makes it into a kind of [secular] song has no portion in the World to Come."
27 There are only a few extant traces of the approach that the Song of Songs is the song of the angels. See Kadari, "Friends Hearken to Your Voice," 194–195.
28 For a general division and dating of Tannaim and Amoraim, see n. 4.
29 On the phenomenon of parallels in Talmudic literature, see Lerner, "Works of the Aggadic Midrash," 148–149.
30 See Girón-Blanc, "Song of Songs in Song of Songs Rabbah," 857–870.

Midrash Shir haShirim Rabbah begins with an impressive opening designed by the editor, commenting on Song 1:1 and the beginning of Song 1:2. As we have seen above, the first words of the biblical scroll are regarded as the key to understanding fundamental issues regarding the book, such as: How should the Song of Songs be interpreted? What is the significance of the name of the biblical scroll, and what is its status vis-à-vis other biblical books? The opening also deals with the figure of King Solomon, to whom authorship of the scroll is attributed.

It is important to note that the five proems (*Petihtaot*) which appear at the beginning of the composition in contemporary editions are not part of the original midrash and were added at a later stage.[31]

5 Themes and Interreligious Polemic

One focus of the scholarly literature is the relationship between ancient Jewish and Christian exegesis on the Song of Songs.[32] According to some scholars the exegesis on the Song of Songs served as the main arena in which these interreligious clashes were played out. At the heart of the Jewish-Christian polemic lay the crucial question of the identity of the feminine beloved, God's true love—was it the people of Israel or the Church?[33]

The following passage deals with a question that preoccupied Jews and Christians during the early years of the common era, namely the identity of the chosen people.

> *Shir haShirim Rabbah 1:6.3*
> "Do not stare at me because I am black, because I am darkened by the sun" [Song 1:6]. Rabbi Isaac said: It happened once that a lady had an Ethiopian maidservant who went down with her companion to draw water from the spring. She said to her companion: Tomorrow my master is going to divorce his wife and marry me. She said to her: Why? [She answered:] Because he saw her hands stained. She said to her: Foolish one, listen to what you are saying. Here is his wife whom he loves exceedingly, and you say he is going to divorce her because he

---

31 See Kadari, "On the Origins of the Opening Proems."
32 The New Testament never directly quotes from the Song, yet there may be allusions to it in the Jesus traditions. See Tomson, "Song of Songs in the Teachings."
33 See de Lange, *Origen and the Jews*; Baer, "Israel, the Christian Church and the Roman Empire," 98–106; Urbach, "Homiletical Interpretations"; Clark, "Uses of the Song of Songs"; Kimelman, "Rabbi Yohanan and Origen"; Hirshman, *A Rivalry of Genius*, 83–94; Kadari, "Rabbinic and Christian Models of Interaction." Goshen-Gottstein argues that scholars read too much polemic into the exegesis of the Song of Songs and calls for a re-examination of the whole matter. See Goshen-Gottstein, "Polemomania."

once saw her hands stained. How then will he endure you who are stained all over and black from your mother's womb! So too do the other nations taunt Israel and say: This nation traded in its glory as it says, "They traded in their glory [for an ox that eats grass]" [Ps 106:20]. Israel says to them: If we who sinned only once are to be punished thus, how much more so you.[34]

The parable describes the situation of the nation of Israel, which sinned and seems to be spurned by God—like the beloved wife with the stained hands. The midrash gives voice to the claim made by the nations of the world, who assume that God banished Israel and will now choose a new wife. But the parable concludes by asserting that the gap between Israel and other nations is substantial and unbridgeable. The husband will not replace his beloved wife with a maidservant. Thus an identification of Jewish-Christian polemic can enrich our understanding of the messages and motives that lie at the heart of the ancient interpretations of the Song of Songs.

6 Summary

In this article we considered the place of Shir haShirim Rabbah in the history of the exegesis of the Song of Songs. We noted several of its primary characteristics. As we saw, the sages were aware of textual aspects such as hapax legomena, unique phrases, and syntactic features. Their midrashim involve creative interpretations and wordplays that give rise to new meanings. At times they offer literal interpretations, but their primary goal is to arrive at an understanding of the Song's deeper layers of significance.

We have seen that although the midrash adheres closely to the verses of the scroll, it offers a far-ranging diversity of interpretations. Each verse is accompanied by a plethora of varied exegeses, and thus the composition is quite long and complex. Most of these exegeses operate on the allegorical level and deal with the relationship between the people of Israel and God, which has been characterized by periods of closeness and distance over the course of Jewish history.

The Song describes various historical events which include moments of intimacy and love as well as moments of estrangement and frustration. At times the interpretations offered in Shir haShirim Rabbah offer more general keys to understanding the scroll, touching upon such questions as who wrote the scroll—was it a heavenly song composed by God or the angels, or perhaps an earthly song composed by the people of Israel? And if it was composed by the people of Israel, in what historical context was it first sung, and what sort of mood does it reflect?

---

34 *Song of Songs Rabbah* (Simon, trans.), 58.

In spite of these hermeneutical keys, Shir haShirim Rabbah contains no consistent or systematic approach to the entire scroll by any single sage. The midrash is rather an anthology that juxtaposes the statements of earlier and later sages, as well as parables, stories, and various interpretive approaches that were collected at a later time by an anonymous redactor. At the same time, it is clear that the midrash was shaped by a guiding hand, and the redactor may have had an agenda of his own. For instance, the redactor focused primarily on allegorical interpretations, which may suggest that the midrash was intended for a wide general audience. The allegorical interpretation may have also played a role in the interreligious polemic by demonstrating that the deep connection between God and the people of Israel endured throughout the generations.

Shir haShirim Rabbah constitutes a significant contribution to the rich and complex tradition of the interpretation of the Song of Songs throughout history.

Bibliography

Editions

Agadath Shir ha-Shirim, edited by Solomon Schechter. Cambridge: D. Bell, 1896.
Avot de-Rabbi Nathan, edited by Solomon Schechter. Prolegomenon by Menachem Kister. New York: JTS, 1997.
Mekhilta de-Rabbi Ishmael, edited by Jacob Z. Lauterbach. 2 vols. Philadelphia: JPS, 2004.
Nathan ben Yechiel. *Aruk HaShalem*, edited by Alexander Kohut. New York: Pardes, 1955.
Origen. *The Song of Songs: Commentary and Homilies*, translated by R. P. Lawson. ACW 26. Maryland: Mahwah Paulist, 1957.
Shir ha-Shirim Zuta, edited by Solomon Buber. Berlin: M'kize Nirdamim, 1894.
Song of Songs Rabbah: A Synoptic Edition, edited by Tamar Kadari. The Midrash Project, Schechter Institute of Jewish Studies Website: https://schechter.ac.il/midrash/shir-hashirim-raba/.
Song of Songs Rabbah, translated by Maurice Simon. In vol. 9 of *Midrash Rabbah*. London: Soncino, 1939.
Tosefta Kippurim, edited by Shaul Leiberman. New York: JTS, 1962.

Secondary Literature

Baer, Yitzhak Fritz. "Israel, the Christian Church and the Roman Empire: From the Days of Septimius Severus to the 'Edict of Toleration' of 313 C.E." *ScrHie* 7 (1971): 79–149.
Boyarin, Daniel. *Intertextuality and the Reading of Midrash*. Bloomington: Indiana University Press, 1990.

Clark, Elizabeth A. "The Uses of the Song of Songs: Origen and the Later Latin Fathers." In idem, *Ascetic Piety and Women's Faith: Essays on Late Ancient Christianity*, 386–427. SWR 20. Lewiston, NY: Edwin Mellen Press, 1986.

Cohen, Gerson D. "The Song of Songs and the Jewish Religious Mentality." In *The Samuel Friedland Lectures: Essays Brought Together in Honor of His 70th Birthday*, edited by Louis Finkelstein, Gerson D. Cohen, and Abraham J. Heschel, 1–21. New York: Jewish Theological Seminary, 1966.

Fishbane, Michael. *Song of Songs: The Traditional Hebrew Text with the New JPS Translation and Commentary by Michael Fishbane*. Philadelphia: JPS, 2015.

Girón-Blanc, Luis F. "Song of Songs in Song of Songs Rabbah." In vol. 2 of *Encyclopaedia of Midrash: Biblical Interpretation in Formative Judaism*, edited by Jacob Neusner and Alan J. Avery-Peck, 857–870. Leiden: Brill, 2005.

Girón-Blanc, Luis F. "Vocablos Griegos y latinos en Cantar de los Cantares Rabbâ." *Sef* 54 (1994): 271–306.

Goshen-Gottstein, Alon. "Did the Tannaim Interpret the Song of Songs Systematically? Lieberman Reconsidered." In *Vixens Disturbing Vineyards: Embarrassment and Embracement of Scripture; Festschrift in Honor of Harry Fox*, edited by Tzemah Yoreh, Aubrey Glazer, Justin J. Lewis, and Miryam Segal, 260–271. Boston: Academic Studies Press, 2010.

Goshen-Gottstein, Alon. "Polemomania: Methodological Reflection on the Study of the Judeo-Christian Controversy between the Talmudic Sages and Origin over the Interpretations of the Song of Songs." *JewSt* 42 (2003): 119–190. (Hebrew)

Gottlieb, Isaac B. "The Jewish Allegory of Love: Change and Constancy." *Journal of Jewish Thought & Philosophy* 2 (1993): 1–17.

Green, Arthur. "Bride, Spouse, Daughter: Images of the Feminine in Classical Jewish Sources." In *On Being a Jewish Feminist*, edited by Susannah Heschel, 248–260. New York: Schocken, 1995.

Hirshman, Marc. "Aggadic Midrash." In *Midrash and Targum, Liturgy, Poetry, Mysticism, Contracts, Inscriptions, Ancient Sience and the Languages of Rabbinic Literature*, edited by Shmuel Safrai, Zeev Safrai, Joshua J. Schwartz, and Peter Tomson, 107–131. Vol. 2 of *The Literature of the Sages*. CRINT 2/3b. Assen and Minneapolis: Brill 2006.

Hirshman, Marc. *A Rivalry of Genius: Jewish and Christian Biblical Interpretation in Late Antiquity*. Albany: State of New York Press, 1996.

Kadari, Tamar. "'Behold a Man Skilled in His Work' (Proverbs 22:29): On the Origins of the Opening Proems of Song of Songs Rabbah." *Tarbiz* 76 (2007): 155–174. (Hebrew)

Kadari, Tamar. "'Friends Hearken to Your Voice' (Song of Songs 8:13): Rabbinic Interpretations of the Song of Songs." In *Approaches to Literary Readings of Ancient Jewish Writings*, edited by Klaas Smelik and Karolien Vermeulen, 183–209. SSN 62. Antwerp: Brill & University of Antwerp, 2014.

Kadari, Tamar. "New Textual Witnesses to Midrash Song of Songs Rabbah." *Zutot: Perspectives on Jewish Culture* 13 (2016): 41–54.

Kadari, Tamar. "Rabbinic and Christian Models of Interaction on the Song of Songs." In *Interaction Between Judaism and Christianity in History, Religion, Art and Literature*, edited by Marcel Poorthuis, Joshua Schwartz, and Joseph Aaron Turner, 65–82. JCPS 17. Leiden: Brill, 2009.

Kimelman, Reuven. "Rabbi Yohanan and Origen on the Song of Songs: A Third-Century Jewish-Christian Disputation." *HTR* 73 (1980): 567–595.

Koehler, Ludwig, and Walter Baumgartner. *The Hebrew and Aramaic Lexicon of the Old Testament*. Vol. 1. Leiden: Brill, 1994.

Krauss, Samuel. *Griechische und Lateinische Lehnwörter im Talmud, Midrasch und Targum: Mit Bemerkungen von Immanuel Löw; Preisgekrönte Lösung der Lattes'schen Preisfrage*. Berlin: S. Calvary & Co., 1899.

Kugel, James L. "Is There But One Song?" *Bib* 63 (1982): 329–350.
Kugel, James L. *The Idea of Biblical Poetry: Parallelism and Its History*. New Haven: Yale University Press, 1981.
Lachs, Samuel T. "Prolegomena to Canticles Rabba." *JQR* 55 (1965): 235–255.
Lange, Nicholas R.M. de. *Origen and the Jews: Studies in Jewish-Christian Relations in Third-Century Palestine*. London: Cambridge University Press, 1976.
Lerner, Myron B. "The Works of the Aggadic Midrash and the Esther Midrashim." In *Midrash and Targum, Liturgy, Poetry, Mysticism, Contracts, Inscriptions, Ancient Science and the Languages of Rabbinic Literature*, edited by Shmuel Safrai, Zeev Safrai, Joshua Schwartz, and Peter J. Tomson, 133–229. Vol. 2 of *The Literature of the Sages*. CRINT 2/3a. Minneapolis: Fortress Press, 2006.
Lieberman, Saul. "Mishnat Shir ha-Shirim." In Gershom Scholem, *Jewish Gnosticism, Merkaba Mysticism, and Talmudic Tradition*, 118–126. 2nd edition. New York: Jewish Theological Seminary of America, 1965. (Hebrew)
Steller, H. E. "Preliminary Remarks to a New Edition of Shir Hashirim Rabbah." In *Rashi 1040–1990: Hommage q Ephra|m E. Urbach; IVe Congrčs européen des études juives, Paris-Troyes 6–13 Juillet 1990*, edited by Gabrielle Sed Rajna, 301–311. Paris: Éditions du Cerf, 1993.
Stemberger, Günter. *Introduction to the Talmud and Midrash*, edited and translated by Markus Bockmuehl. Edinburgh: T&T Clark, 1996.
Stern, David. "Ancient Jewish Interpretation of the Song of Songs in a Comparative Context." In *Biblical Interpretation and Cultural Exchange: Comparative Exegesis in Context*, edited by Natalie B. Dohrmann and David Stern, 87–107. Philadelphia: University of Pennsylvania Press, 2008.
Tomson, Peter J. "The Song of Songs in the Teachings of Jesus and the Development of the Exposition on the Song." *NTS* 61 (2015): 429–447.
Urbach, Ephraim E. "The Homiletical Interpretations of the Sages and the Exposition of Origen on Canticles and the Jewish-Christian Disputation." In *Studies in Aggadah and Folk-Literature*, edited by Joseph Heinemann and Dov Noy, 247–275. ScrHier 22. Jerusalem: Magnes Press, 1971.
Wolfson, Elliot R. *Circle in the Square: Studies in the Use of Gender in Kabbalistic Symbolism*. Albany: Suny Press, 1995.

Gerhard Langer
"I Slept but My Heart Was Awake"
Rabbinic Interpretations of Song of Songs 5:2

1 Introduction

Both Jewish and Christian tradition long explained the Song of Songs allegorically, but in the eighteenth century, following the work of Johann Gottfried Herder, Protestant exegetes finally began to interpret it as a collection of popular songs generated by a rural, "oriental" population and as the historical reminiscences of a love story from the circle of Solomon. Historical-critical interpreters in the twentieth century read the Song as a text about the love between a man and a woman, whether a collection of original, individual love songs or a literarily uniform composition. Many historical-critical exegetes still understand the Song in this way. More recently, however, the "old" traditions have been seen more positively as having an intrinsic value, and allegorical exegesis is no longer deemed far-fetched. Above all, scholars have contended more intensively with the unity of the book.[1]

Elisabeth Birnbaum, for example, has convincingly shown that the book should be read as a unity and, in the process, has also dealt critically with the historical figure of Solomon.[2] The Song of Songs criticizes a materially focused "love affair," turns refreshingly against hierarchies, and gives the woman an astonishingly significant and, above all, equal place. Solomon's kingdom, on the other hand, is material, enamored of status, and vain, a pale imitation of the conduct in life that is understood as good and right. Birnbaum even goes so far as to suspect a similar tendency in Christian and Jewish allegorical exegesis:

> The beloved, God or the Messiah, who is near to his beloved Israel just as he once was during the passage through the desert, who renounces pageantry and ostentation and loves his beloved passionately, would gain the advantage over a "Solomon-like" royal government. Solomon, in any case, would not be the one who "loves" "my soul," Israel. Everything in the Song of Songs that is so often praised—the personal, ardent and, to the greatest extent, equitable love of the two protagonists—could be made fruitful for the relationship between God and human beings.[3]

---
[1] For an overview of the history of interpretation of the Song, see Pardes, *Song*; Birnbaum, "Das Hohelied." On the question of the unity of Song of Songs, see Schoenfeld, "One Song or Many."
[2] See Birnbaum, "Just Call Me Salomo." On different interpretations of the Song of Songs, see the articles in Schwienhorst-Schönberger, ed., *Das Hohelied im Konflikt der Interpretationen*.
[3] Birnbaum, "Just Call Me Salomo," 262 (my translation from the German).

It is this relationship that is the focus of rabbinic exegesis. Rabbinically, the Song of Songs is considered to have been written by Solomon, for "the holy spirit rested on him and he composed these three books, Proverbs, Ecclesiastes, and the Song of Songs" (Song Rab. 1:1.7). It contains Solomon's wisdom: "He pondered the words of the Torah and investigated the words of the Torah. He made handles (ears) to the Torah" (Song Rab. 1:1.8).

The Song is considered to be an outstanding example of the fact that rabbinic literature also dealt extensively with an allegorical hermeneutical approach.[4] Thus, Jewish tradition interprets it for the most part (with the exception of medieval romantic lyric) as an allegorical/typological account of the love between God and his people Israel throughout history. In other interpretive variants, the messiah[5] or the Torah[6] become the beloved of Israel. Reference to the events around the exodus, to which elements such as the destruction of the temple and the exile are connected associatively, are seen as running consistently through the text.

As Daniel Boyarin has emphasized, the rabbis employed allegory not in order to import philosophical ideas into the Bible but rather to link texts with texts, that is, to argue intertextually.[7] Above all, the rabbis made full use of the potential of the Hebrew language for working out the many possible interpretations of Scripture.

In the following, I will use one example to show how the rabbis dealt with the Song of Songs. The example is intended to illustrate their hermeneutics and is in no way to be considered a comprehensive survey. I concentrate in the process on an exegesis of Song 5:2, in order to show, by comparison of two variant interpretations, that although the rabbis have a certain message, a close look also reveals small but significant differences in intention.

---

4 See Stemberger, *Einleitung*, 382; Girón Blanc, "Song of Songs," 857.
5 Thus, e.g., in a part of Pesiqta de Rab Kahana 5.7, the text I will analyze below.
6 Thus, e.g., in Leviticus Rabbah 19.1: "'His head is purest gold; [his hair is wavy and black as a raven]' (Song 5:11). 'His head'—this is the Torah, as it is written: 'The LORD brought me forth as the first of his ways' (Prov 8:22). [. . .] 'His hair is wavy' (NIV: 'his locks are curled')—these are the drawing lines. 'Black as a raven'—these are strokes of the letters, so R. Eliezer; and R. Yehoshua says the strokes (on the top of the letters in the Torah) contain piles (of ideas). By whom are they upheld? By he who studies morning and evening."
7 See Boyarin, *Intertextuality*, 108–110, etc.

Song 5 is a good example because here the desire of the woman for her beloved is especially clear. In 5:2 we read:

אֲנִי יְשֵׁנָה וְלִבִּי עֵר
קוֹל דּוֹדִי דוֹפֵק
פִּתְחִי־לִי
אֲחֹתִי רַעְיָתִי יוֹנָתִי תַמָּתִי
שֶׁרֹאשִׁי נִמְלָא־טָל, קְוֻצּוֹתַי רְסִיסֵי לָיְלָה

I slept but my heart was awake. / Listen! My beloved is knocking: / Open to me / my sister, my darling, my dove, my flawless one. / My head is drenched with dew, my hair with the dampness of the night.[8]

2 Song 5:2 in Pesiqta de Rab Kahana 5.6

Pesiqta de Rab Kahana is a midrash[9] on the readings on feasts and special Sabbaths as they were/are used in the synagogue. It originated in Palestine; though its content, structure, and language were shaped in the fifth century CE, it continued to develop for some time after that.[10] The name Pesiqta means "portion" or "chapter" in Aramaic (cf. Hebrew *pasuq*). The name acknowledges the fact that the midrash does not offer a continuous commentary but instead comments on sections of readings from the synagogue liturgy. Why the Pesiqta was attributed to Rab Kahana and which of the rabbis is designated by this name remains unclear. In addition, the number of chapters varies by edition. Mandelbaum's famous edition has twenty-eight chapters/*pisqaot* and nine appendices.

The passage from Pesiqta de Rab Kahana under study here[11] refers to the fourth of the four special Sabbaths,[12] two of which occur in the weeks leading up

---

[8] I use the NIV for English Bible translations but occasionally deviate from it when linguistically necessary.
[9] Midrash is a genre that is directly related to a religiously authoritative text (Bible), in which the latter is explicitly quoted or clearly alluded to and subsequently interpreted. Midrash is based on an understanding of the unity, clarity, and perfection of Scripture and applies hermeneutical methods (interpretation of intertextual references, rules of interpretation, etc.) to fill the gaps in the text and to connect the world of Scripture with the actual world of the reading/listening and interpreting people. For this definition, see Langer, *Midrasch*, 33.
[10] See Stemberger, *Einleitung*, 353–359.
[11] See similarly Pesiqta Rabbati 15 (which is dependent upon it). See also the short parallel in Exodus Rabbah 2:5.
[12] With four reading sections (*parashiyot*) in addition to the usual Torah readings: *Parashat Sheqalim* (on Exod 28:9–15), *Parashat Zakhor* (on Deut 25:17–19), *Parashat Parah* (on Num 19:1–22), and *Parashat ha-Hodesh* (on Exod 12:1–20).

to Purim and two of which take place in the weeks leading up to Passover. The fourth is *Shabbat ha-hodesh* ("the Sabbath of the month/new moon"), just before the beginning of the month of Nisan. The reading portion is Exod 12:1–20, which concentrates on the sanctification of the new moon and the commandments concerning Passover. Nisan was the first month of the year in the Torah's accounting.

The connection to the exodus tradition becomes clear through the context of the section.

2.1 Text of Pesiqta de Rab Kahana 5.6 (and parts of 5.7)

A—Israel reflects on its history with God

> "I slept but my heart was awake. Listen! My beloved is knocking: Open to me, etc."
> The congregation of Israel spoke before the Holy One, blessed be He:
> Lord of the Universe, "I slept"—concerning the temple; "but my heart was awake"—concerning the synagogues and houses of study.
> "I slept"—concerning the commandments; "but my heart was awake"—awake to do them.
> "I slept"—concerning the sacrificial offerings (הַקָּרְבָּנוֹת); "but my heart was awake"—concerning the commandments (הַמִּצְוֹת) and acts of charity (הַצְּדָקוֹת).
> "I slept"—concerning the end (of time)—"but my heart was awake"—concerning redemption.
> "I slept"—concerning redemption—but the heart of the Holy One, blessed be He, was awake to redeem us.
> R. Hiyya bar Abba said: From here we find that the Holy One is called "the heart of Israel," as it is written: "[My flesh and my heart may fail], but God is the strength of my heart and my portion forever" (Ps 73:26).

B—God redeems Israel in Egypt

> "Listen! My beloved is knocking"—this is Moses. "So Moses said: This is what the LORD says: About midnight I will go [throughout Egypt]" (Exod 11:4).

C—God urges Israel

> "Open me"—R. Yose said: The Holy One, blessed be He, said: open me (an opening the size of) a needle eye, and I open you an opening that camps and fortifications can enter.

D—God and Israel are bound together like siblings

"My sister" (אֲחֹתִי)—my sister (are the Israelites) in Egypt, because they were knitted closely (נִתְאָחוּ) to me by two commandments, the blood of the Passover (lamb) and the blood of circumcision.[13]

"My darling" (רַעְיָתִי)—my darling at the sea, because they demonstrated their love to me at the sea and said: "The LORD reigns for ever and ever" (Exod 15:18).

"My dove" (יוֹנָתִי)—my dove in Mara, because they excelled themselves before me by the commandments like a dove.

"My flawless one" (תַמָּתִי)—because they became flawless at Sinai, and said: "We will do and hear/obey" (Exod 24:7).

E—God suffers with Israel

R. Yannai says: "My twin sister."[14] I am not greater than she and she is not greater than I am.[15] R. Yehoshua from Sikhnin in the name of R. Levi: How is it with twins? If one has a pain in his head, the other feels it also. So the Holy One, blessed be He, says to His people: "I will be with him in trouble" (Ps 91:15).

F—God redeems Israel

"My head is drenched with dew"—"[When you, LORD, went out from Seir, when you marched from the land of Edom, the earth shook,] the heavens poured, [the clouds poured down water]" (Judg 5:4).

"My hair with the dampness of the night"—"The clouds poured down water" (Judg 5:4). When? In this month. "This month is to be for you the first month, the first month of your year" (Exod 12:2).[16]

Pesiqta de Rab Kahana 5.7 then continues with an exegesis of Song 2:8, which also speaks of the beloved who is coming,[17] and an excerpt of this passage demonstrates the close connection to the previous passage:

"Listen! My beloved! Look! Here he comes, leaping across the mountains, bounding over the hills." R. Yehuda and R. Nahman and the rabbis: R. Yehuda said: "Listen! My beloved! Look! Here he comes"—this is Moses, in the hour when he came to Israel and said: In this month you will

---

13 Slightly differently, see Braude and Kapstein, *Pesikta de-Rab Kahana*, 98: "God was saying: Israel, My own, My kin—you who bound yourselves irrevocably to Me in Egypt by two covenants of blood, the blood of Passover and the blood of circumcision."
14 One could read תומייתי (Oxford Ms) simply as Aramaic for תמתי, but it is clear from the following that it is connected to תאומים (twins).
15 Thoma and Lauer, *Die Gleichnisse der Rabbinen*, 139–140, suggest "older" instead of "greater," with reference to Genesis Rabbah 77.1.
16 According to the version of the Pesiqta de Rab Kahana reproduced on the Maagarim website, from the Mss. Oxford, Bodleian Library, 151. The passage there also appears with slight deviations in Parma, Biblioteca Palatina, 3122.
17 This passage is practically identical with Song Rabbah 2:8.1.

be redeemed. They said to him: Moses, our rabbi, how will we be redeemed? Did not the Holy One, blessed be He, say to our father Abraham: "[Know for certain that] for four hundred years [your descendants will be strangers in a country not their own and that they] will be enslaved and mistreated there" (Gen 15:13). And have we not reached only two hundred ten of them? He said to them: He can redeem you when he wishes and in your redemption he does not regard your calculations, rather he is "leaping across the mountains, bounding over the hills." (This means:) "Leaping over" calculations and "bounding over" reckonings and accountings. And in this month you will be redeemed. "This month is to be for you the first month" (Exod 12:2).

And R. Nehemia said: "Listen! My beloved! Look! Here he comes"—this is Moses in the hour when he came and said to Israel: In this month you will be redeemed. They said to him: Our rabbi Moses, how will we be redeemed, when Egypt was full of pollution from our idolatry? He said to them: He can redeem you when he wishes and in your redemption he does not look at your idolatry. [...] The rabbis said: "Listen! My beloved! Look! Here he comes"—this is Moses, in the hour when he came to Israel and said: In this month you will be redeemed. They said to him: Moses, our rabbi, how will we be redeemed, when no good deeds are in our hands? He said to them: "leaping across the mountains." (This means:) he does not regard your evil deeds. And whom does he regard? The righteous among you and their deeds, like Amram and his court of law.[18]

2.2 Hermeneutics and Explanation

The first verses of Song 5, as is usual in midrash, are "atomized," that is, broken up into small components. But a close look at these components has consequences for (a) the understanding of the text, (b) the understanding of history, and (c) the theology and worldview of the rabbis.

The *understanding of the text* is based on allegorical/typological exegesis. Most important, this exegesis moves exclusively within the framework of the textual world of the Hebrew Bible. Accordingly, the allegory does not refer to philosophical concepts, to abstract terms, or to persons outside the biblical context. The textual world of the Hebrew Bible fulfills all the "needs" of the rabbis. They find in it all the answers to their questions and all necessary proof texts. The Hebrew Bible is seen in its entirety as a unit. Each part can be related to the other parts. One can (with some caution) apply two terms to this: *canonical* and *intertextual. Canonical* refers to the entirety of the generally accepted texts of the Hebrew Bible, apart from a broad debate about the processes and duration of canonization. *Intertextuality* refers to various references to other texts within this canon. The intertextual reading practice of the rabbis builds on intrabiblical reading practice. The realm of interpretation is the biblical canon, in the light of which a single passage is interpreted. Therefore, midrash is, as Boyarin points out, basically a radical intertextual

---

[18] Later the "beloved" is identified with the messiah.

reading of this canon, in which the questions that arise in the reading, the so-called gaps, play a central role and are now filled. In principle, therefore, midrash can be understood as an intertextual—that is, textually dialogical—explanation of ambiguities and open questions—that is, of the gaps.[19]

It is this canonical-intertextual procedure that makes it possible for the rabbis to answer all the possible questions of their time and, at the same time, to demonstrate their world view. Applied to the Song of Songs and its exegesis, this means that it is not a woman and a man who encounter each other but rather (as a rule) Israel and its God or the messiah.[20]

The *understanding of history* is shaped by the conviction that the events central to Israel's history and essential to the formation of Israel's identity are to be found in the Bible. Of special significance are the exodus event and the circumstances surrounding the destruction of the temple, as well as the exile. Both are also treated in the exegesis of the Song of Songs, which undoubtedly emphasizes the events of the exodus. The understanding of history is not to be separated from the *world view* and theology of the rabbis, as a closer analysis of the text reveals.

The beginning of the text (A) explains the contrasts between "sleeping" and "waking."

A—Israel reflects on its history with God

> "I slept but my heart was awake. Listen! My beloved is knocking: Open to me etc."
> The congregation of Israel spoke before the Holy One, blessed be He:
> Lord of the Universe, "I slept"—concerning the temple; "but my heart was awake"—concerning the synagogues and houses of study.
> "I slept"—concerning the commandments; "but my heart was awake"—awake to do them.
> "I slept"—concerning the sacrificial offerings (הַקָּרְבָּנוֹת); "but my heart was awake"—concerning the commandments (הַמִּצְוֹת) and acts of charity (הַצְּדָקוֹת).
> "I slept"—concerning the end (of time)—"but my heart was awake"—concerning redemption.
> "I slept"—concerning redemption—but the heart of the Holy One, blessed be He, was awake to redeem us.
> R. Hiyya bar Abba said: From here we find that the Holy One is called "the heart of Israel," as it is written: "[My flesh and my heart may fail], but God is the strength of my heart and my portion forever" (Ps 73:26).

Modern exegetes of Song 5:2 often think of dream situations,[21] and my own inclination is to read the beloved's sleeping as perhaps meaning that she does not yet have

---

19 See Boyarin, *Intertextuality*. Cf. Langer, *Midrasch*, 16–17, etc.
20 The messianic interpretation is strengthened in the Middle Ages; see Kozodoy, "Messianic Interpretation."
21 See, e.g., Zakovitch, *Hohelied*, 212–214; Spencer, *Song of Songs*, 115; Pardes, *Song*, 9.

any sexual experience with her beloved and her waking heart as expressing her willingness to engage with him. The rabbis, though, interpret sleeping in this case as the negatively connoted laxity of the congregation of Israel.

In several parts of section A, the contrast between sleeping and waking is interpreted in terms of the history of Israel and its God. Thereby, the rabbis associate sleeping with sloth and negligence, but there is no indication at all of any reference to sin or malice. Whoever neglects the commandments is, to be sure, not to be praised but clearly rises above the one who consciously does not keep them or even intentionally transgresses them. The prophetic criticism of Israel is not taken up here. Rather, it appears to be the case that Israel may have slipped into catastrophe because of its negligence.

The text masterfully illustrates the alternatives of sleeping and waking with examples that indicate a temporal sequence in history. After the temple, there follows the synagogue and the *bet midrash* (house of study); after the offerings, there follow the *mitzvot* (commandments) and good deeds. Thus, two periods are made accessible in principle: the time before the destruction of the temple and the time afterward or, more exactly, the current time in which the rabbis find themselves. One has the impression that Israel is awakened in the rabbinic era. But there is a puzzling differentiation between sloth in regard to the commandments and the fact that they are nevertheless fulfilled with an attentive eye. This is evocative of Exod 24:7, which is named explicitly later in the text: "Then he took the book of the covenant and read it to the people. They responded, 'Everything the LORD has said we will do and hear/obey.'" In Hebrew, the people's answer sounds shorter: נַעֲשֶׂה וְנִשְׁמָע. The doing of the commandments comes before the hearing/obeying of them. What does it mean, then, that one has slept in regard to the *mitzvot*? Were they not understood completely; was one not aware of their function, their significance, their impact?

The last part of the enumeration is striking: the people slept in regard to the end of days. This seems to mean that the people did nothing to make possible or to accelerate the arrival of the messiah or of the messianic time. Thereby, the rabbis not only fire a broadside against every sort of messianic interpretation of the wars against Rome, but they emphasize the inability and impossibility of any individual being able to bring about salvation and redemption. Here the passage reaches it high point. The speech is no longer about Israel's heart but about God. God is the one who guarantees salvation. The concern, therefore, is primarily to place trust in God, who, for his part, does not sleep. Thus the beginning of the longer section places the focus on trust in God, on his devotion to and love for Israel. This is emphasized especially by the citation from Ps 73: God is Israel's assurance. The text impresses this fact upon the reader.

After the explanation of the opposition "sleeping" and "being awake," there follows the second, shorter section (B) on the beloved's knocking.

B—God redeems Israel in Egypt

> "Listen! My beloved is knocking"—this is Moses. "So Moses said: This is what the LORD says: About midnight I will go [throughout Egypt]" (Exod 11:4).

Once again, the text contains a historical reference to a concrete situation within the framework of the exodus events, namely, to the warning about the midnight passage of the angel of death and the killing of all the firstborn among the Egyptians. Moses proclaims the message of the beloved, the words of God making himself known powerfully to Pharaoh. These words are the beginning of liberation from the yoke of Egypt.

The third section (C) shows beautifully how both the literal and the allegorical meaning of the text can be perceptible at the same time.

C—God urges Israel

> "Open me"—R. Yose said: The Holy One, blessed be He, said: open me (an opening the size of) a needle eye, and I open you an opening that camps and fortifications can enter.

The beloved awaits nothing more eagerly than that the female beloved open the door to him—or, better, that she open *herself* to him. The text is conspicuously silent about repentance or atonement. One may of course read such things into the text when the speech is about openness to God, but the text can be interpreted just as well as an expression of trust in God, who will act on his own initiative. Israel must open itself to its own deliverer.

Section D explains the various designations for the female beloved once again, as in section A, in a historicizing sense.

D—God and Israel are bound together like siblings

> "My sister" (אֲחֹתִי)—my sister (are the Israelites) in Egypt, because they were knitted closely (נִתְאֲחוּ) to me by two commandments, the blood of the Passover (lamb) and the blood of circumcision.
> "My darling" (רַעְיָתִי)—my darling at the sea, because they demonstrated their love to me at the sea and said: "The LORD reigns for ever and ever" (Exod 15:18).
> "My dove" (יוֹנָתִי)—my dove in Mara, because they excelled themselves before me by the commandments like a dove.
> "My flawless one" (תַמָּתִי)—because they became flawless at Sinai, and said: "We will do and hear/obey" (Exod 24:7).

Above all, this section employs linguistic interpretation. Whereas section A focuses on the contrast between "earlier/lazy" and "later/awake," here the focus is on deriving meaning from the particular root used in each case. What follows is a historicizing explanation in which it is always God who speaks.

"My sister" (אֲחֹתִי) leads to the derivation of a sibling relationship between God and Israel. "Sister" can undoubtedly carry a figurative sense, that is, it can also mean the female beloved. In any case, the term connotes an extremely close relationship. The basic reference text for this is Ezek 16, which deals with the relationship between God and Israel/Jerusalem.[22] It is a strained love relationship because Israel, in Ezekiel's view, does not sufficiently appreciate God's love and worships foreign gods. For this it is punished, though God finally returns to Israel, and there is a lasting reconciliation. The rabbis focus on Ezek 16:1–14, where God turns to the helpless baby Israel and raises her until she is grown and ready for marriage. Among other things, he sees the infant lying in her blood and grants her life. Since the word for blood appears in a grammatically dual form in the text (בְּדָמַיִךְ חֲיִי, "in your blood live"), the rabbis interpret the text to mean that there are two forms of blood involved. In our text, one "blood" refers to the brushing of the doorposts with the blood of the Passover lamb, and the second "blood" refers to circumcision.

The two "bloods" are already combined in the Mekilta,[23] Pisḥa 5, as a rationale for why Israel was released from Egypt. Later texts interpret the connection even more broadly. In an exegesis in Exodus Rabbah[24] (19.5), for example, the Passover blood is mixed together with the blood of circumcision as the Israelites, one after the other, let themselves be circumcised in order to be permitted to eat from the flesh of the lamb at Passover, from which, according to Exod 12, no uncircumcised person is permitted to eat. Then God kisses the circumcised Israelites. Thus the love poetry of the Song of Songs is, quite appropriately, applied to Israel.

The terms of endearment increase in intensity as the text continues. "My darling" (רַעְיָתִי), in the rabbis' view, refers to another segment of the love story, closely connected with the exodus. At the crossing of the Sea of Reeds in Exod 15:18, it is said, Israel proved its love for God. The subject is a confession of God's permanent power and his ability to defeat the enemies of Israel.

The next stage is Mara, on the Sinai Peninsula. Here, the Israelites once again demonstrate their ardent love for God. In Mara, according to the Babylonian Talmud (b. Sanh. 56b), the Israelites receive ten directives, whereby a further three fundamental commandments—namely, to establish courts of justice, to keep the Sabbath,

---

22 See Langer, *Drama*.
23 The Mekilta de Rabbi Ishmael is an early midrash on Exodus, perhaps from the third century CE. See Stemberger, *Einleitung*, 301–308.
24 Exodus Rabbah is a midrash on Exodus consisting of two parts. Part 1 (chapters 1–14) is on Exod 1–10, and part 2 (chapters 15–52) is on the rest of Exodus. Part 2 seems to be older than part 1, which may have been written around the tenth century. See Stemberger, *Einleitung*, 374–375.

and to honor parents—were added to the seven Noahide laws.[25] Through these commandments, Israel excelled itself before all the peoples and distinguished itself from them. This "excelled" has also intruded itself—via Sipre Deuteronomy[26] 301 on Deut 26—into the Passover haggadah, where Israel in Egypt was excelled/distinguished when it became a great people. A commentary in the London Haggadah, from the Rhenish rabbinical school, relates it, for example, to the Hebrew language and to the *tzitzit* on clothing, thereby emphasizing the focus on "distinction."[27]

The dove is a recognized symbol of love, for which Othmar Keel, among others, has provided numerous examples.[28] Likewise, the dove is often equated with Israel.[29] In Song Rabbah 1:15.2, 4; 4:1.2, for example, Israel is compared to the dove in so far as the latter is considered to be a model of decency. Israel distinguishes itself from all other peoples in this way. In another passage, the dove is a symbol of Israel concealing itself from its enemies (for example, in the Mekilta de Rabbi Shimon bar Yohai on Exod 19:17, with reference to Song 2:14). The connection between dove and Mara is only one possibility. As Ilana Pardes recently pointed out, Rabbi Akiva "read the Song's dove against the backdrop of Mount Sinai, [and] there are others who set it in the context of another pivotal moment in Exodus: the crossing of the Red Sea."[30]

"My flawless one" makes reference to Sinai, where the commandments were given. It is here where Israel speaks the portentous words of Exod 24:7: "Everything the LORD has said, we will do and obey." Through their commitment to observing the *mitzvot*, Israel has become flawless.

E—God suffers with Israel

> R. Yannai says "My twin sister" (תומייתי, read תְּאוֹמָתִי). I am not greater than she and she is not greater than I am.
> R. Yehoshua from Sikhnin in the name of R. Levi: How is it with twins? If one has a pain in his head, the other feels it also. So the Holy One, blessed be He, says to His people: "I will be with him in trouble" (Ps 91:15).

---

[25] The seven Noahide laws are a set of commandments for all human beings (see Gen 9). They appear in b. Sanhedrin 56ab and were repeated by Maimonides in his *Mishneh Torah Shoftim*, "Laws of Kings and Their Wars" 8.11–13.
[26] Sipre Deuteronomy is a relatively early midrash on Deuteronomy, perhaps from the third century CE. See Stemberger, *Einleitung*, 326–330.
[27] See the London Haggadah, f. 12v. For a German edition and translation, see Goldstein, ed., *Die Londoner Haggada*, 23.
[28] See Keel, *Deine Blicke sind Tauben*, 53–62; idem, *Das Recht der Bilder*, 143–168.
[29] See, e.g., S. Stern, *Jewish Identity*, 82–84.
[30] Pardes, *Song*, 34.

This exegesis, attributed to R. Yannai, is astonishing, breaking with the style of the preceding lines. The text could also be read in an exhortative sense, that is, that Israel ought to make the effort to become flawless again like it once was on Sinai. This idea, of course, is not wrong, but R. Yannai's reading now places the focus on another point and therewith turns the reader's attention back to God. He reads not "my flawless one" (תַמָּתִי) but rather "my twin sister" (תְּאוֹמָתִי), once again taking up the beginning of the enumeration, at the point where the sibling nature of the two beloveds is mentioned. If God has connected himself to Israel as a sibling, there are important consequences. This is illustrated by a *mashal*, a parable,[31] with an especially poignant effect: God and Israel are like twins, and when Israel suffers, God also feels it. God's compassion is addressed here in a more than explicit manner.[32] God's commitment to his people, accordingly, is based primarily not on Israel keeping the covenant with God but rather on the close love relationship, which is interpreted as the closest of kinship. The whole segment thus reads like an evocation of a close relationship that binds God just as it does Israel.

The last part (F) concentrates on Judg 5:4, a section from the Song of Deborah.[33]

F—God redeems Israel

> "My head is drenched with dew"—"[When you, Lord, went out from Seir, when you marched from the land of Edom, the earth shook,] the heavens poured, [the clouds poured down water]" (Judg 5:4).
> "My hair with the dampness of the night"—"The clouds poured down water" (Judg 5:4).
> When? In this month. "This month is to be for you the first month, the first month of your year" (Exod 12:2).

This is a song in praise of God, who saves. The subject is the omnipotence of this God and his commitment to Israel, the partisan support of Israel for all time. We have thus arrived once again at the beginning, just as section A ends with God's salvation being near. And when is this salvation celebrated and ritually reenacted? At the feast of Passover. The passage thus confirms the rabbinic tendency to ascribe redemption to God's initiative and to believe it will take place in spite of Israel's misconduct.

---

31 See, e.g., D. Stern, "Parables."
32 See Thoma and Lauer, *Die Gleichnisse der Rabbinen*, 139–140. An important indication of the Godlikeness of the human being and of the human being's dignity undoubtedly lies behind the statement.
33 For a brief overview of the rabbinic interpretation on Deborah, see Kadari, "Deborah 2."

2.3 Conclusion

What is the message of the rabbis in Pesiqta de Rab Kahana 5.6? I think it is the following: Whoever celebrates Passover should move purposefully through the past. The experience of the destruction of the temple and of the end of the sacrificial worship service stands painfully before the mind's eye. These imaginative acts allow one to critically call to mind one's own negligence. At the same time, it is important to commemorate the experience of deliverance from Egypt, which will become the fundamental paradigm for the coming redemption. Just as God did not act according to calculation at that time and did not place the correct conduct of the people on the scales of judgment, so will Israel's conduct in the future also not be the decisive criterion for the redemption. Israel should trust in God. The covenantal commitment, which has deep symbolism in circumcision and achieved its highest point with the acceptance of the *mitzvot* on Sinai, is Israel's abiding duty and objective; but it is not the only criterion for the coming redemption.

3 Song 5:2 in Song of Songs Rabbah 5:2.2

3.1 Text of Song of Songs Rabbah 5:2.2

A—Israel reflects on its history with God

> "I slept"—The congregation of Israel spoke before the Holy One, blessed be He: Lord of the Universe, "I slept"—concerning the *mitzvot*; "but my heart was awake"—concerning the good deeds (גְּמִילוּת חֲסָדִים).
> "I slept"—concerning the good deeds/acts of charity (הַצְּדָקוֹת); "but my heart was awake"—to do them.
> "I slept"—concerning the sacrificial offerings (הַקָּרְבָּנוֹת)—"but my heart was awake"—to recite the Shema and the prayer (תְּפִלָּה).
> "I slept"—concerning the temple—"but my heart was awake"—concerning the synagogues and the houses of study.
> "I slept"—concerning the end (of time)—"but my heart was awake"—concerning redemption.
> "I slept"—concerning redemption—but the heart of the Holy One, blessed be He, was awake to redeem me.
>
> R. Hiyya bar Abba said: From here we find that the Holy One is called "the heart of Israel," as it is written: "[My flesh and my heart may fail,] but God is the strength of my heart and my portion forever" (Ps 73:26).

B—God redeems Israel in Egypt

"Listen! My beloved is knocking"—through Moses in the hour, when he said: "So Moses said, This is what the LORD says: About midnight I will go throughout Egypt" (Exod 11:4).

C—Repentance

"Open me"—R. Yasa said: The Holy One, blessed be He, said to Israel: My children, open me an opening of repentance (תְּשׁוּבָה) (the size of) a needle eye, and I open you an opening that wagons and carriages can pass through.

R. Tanhuma and R. Hunia, and R. Abbahu in the name of Resh Lakish (said): It is written, "Let be, and know that I am God, etc." (Ps 46:11). The Holy One, blessed be He, said to Israel: Let be your evil deeds and know that I am God. R. Levi said: When Israel would practice repentance even for one day, they would be redeemed immediately, and immediately the son of David would come. What is the (biblical) reason? "For he is our God, and we are the people of His pasture, the flock under His care. Today, if only you would hear His voice" (Ps 95:7).

R. Yudan and R. Levi said: The Holy One, blessed be He, said to Israel: Let go your evil ways and practice repentance even for a wink of the eye and know that I am God.

D—God and Israel are like siblings

"My sister" (אֲחֹתִי)—my sister (are the Israelites) in Egypt, because they were knitted closely (נִתְאָחוּ) to me by two commandments, the blood of the Passover (lamb) and the blood of circumcision, as it says: "Then I passed by and saw you kicking about in your blood, and as you lay therein I said to you, In your blood live!" (Ezek 16:6)—(the first in your blood) this is the blood of the Passover, "and I said to you, In your blood live!"—this is the blood of circumcision. "My darling" (רַעְיָתִי)—because they demonstrated their love to me at the sea and said: "He is my God and I will praise him" (Exod 15:2) (and) "The LORD reigns for ever and ever" (Exod 15:18).

"My dove" (יוֹנָתִי)—in Mara, because from there on they received commandments and excelled themselves before me with all manner of commandments and acts of charity and good deeds like a dove which is excelled above all other birds, as it is written, "There the LORD issued a ruling and instruction for them" (Exod 15:25).

"My flawless one" (תַמָּתִי)—because they became flawless with me at Sinai, and said: "Everything the LORD has said, we will do and hear/obey" (Exod 24:7).

E—God suffers with Israel

R. Yannai says: "My twin sister" (יְתמוֹאתִי): I am not greater than she and she is not greater than I am.

R. Yehoshua from Sikhnin in the name of R. Levi: my twin sister—how is it with twins? If one has a pain in his head, the other feels it also. So, if one dares to say, the Holy One, blessed be He, says to His people: "I will be with him in trouble" (Ps 91:15).

F—God redeems Israel

"My head is drenched with dew"—with reference to: "The earth shook, the heavens poured down rain" (Ps 68:8; cf. Judg 5:4).

"My hair with the dampness of the night"—with reference to: "The clouds poured down water" (Judg 5:4).[34]

3.2 Explanation

At first glance, the interpretation of Song 5:2 in Song Rabbah[35] just takes up the interpretation of Pesiqta de Rab Kahana. But a closer look shows that Song Rabbah elaborates on this template and explains it further.

In a comparison of the A elements in the two variants, the following differences stand out:

Pesiqta de Rab Kahana	Song of Songs Rabbah
Temple neglected—substituted with synagogues and houses of study	—
Mitzvot neglected	*Mitzvot* neglected
Mitzvot done	Acts of charity done
Offerings neglected—*mitzvot* and acts of charity done	Offerings neglected—substituted with *prayers*
—	Temple neglected—substituted with synagogues and houses of study

The differences should not be overstated, but they are still worth mentioning. Very briefly, we can say that *mitzvot* (complemented by acts of charity) stand at the center of this part in the Pesiqta, whereas acts of charity are at the center in Song Rabbah. And only in Song Rabbah do the prayers (the Shema and the Amidah = the *shmoneh esreh*) occur explicitly as a substitution for the temple service.

The Song Rabbah version evokes biblical texts like Prov 21:21:

רֹדֵף צְדָקָה וָחָסֶד יִמְצָא חַיִּים צְדָקָה וְכָבוֹד

"Whoever pursues righteousness and love finds life, prosperity, and honor."

The Talmud (b. Bava Batra 9b) comments, "Rabbi Yehoshua ben Levi says: Anyone who is accustomed to performing acts of charity deserves to have sons who are masters of wisdom, masters of wealth, and masters of aggadah." Although this text may not have

---

34 Following Ms. Vatican, Biblioteca Apostolica ebr., 76.
35 On Song Rabbah and the Song of Songs, see Siquans, "Das Hohelied"; and the contribution of Tamar Kadari in this volume.

been known to the authors of Song Rabbah, it nevertheless sums up their attitude well. Perhaps it is only a small shift of emphasis from *mitzvot* to the practice/acts of charity, but it is precisely the nuances in what they choose to emphasize that make these two texts, Pesiqta de Rab Kahana 5.6 and Song Rabbah 5:2.2, so fascinating.

The differences become even clearer in element C. Song Rabbah heavily encourages the people to change their thinking and emphasizes penance and repentance. This section thus distinguishes itself most clearly from Pesiqta de Rab Kahana. It is followed by the passage through the exodus events, with stops in Egypt (night of Passover), the sea, Mara, Sinai, the wanderings through the desert, and the story up to the time of Deborah. As in other parts of Song Rabbah, dew becomes an expression for God's intervention (see Song Rab. 1:14.3; 2:2.6; 8:6.3, in each case with reference to Hos 14:6).

4 Conclusion and an Outlook for the Targum

In contrast to Pesiqta de Rab Kahana, the midrash in Song Rabbah aims more intensely at the appeal to repentance. The differences thus lie above all in the evaluation of Israel's own contribution to its salvation/redemption. In Song Rabbah 5:2.2, the willingness to repent is stressed; in Pesiqta de Rab Kahana, it is trust in the saving God.

The targum of the Song of Songs (which perhaps dates to the ninth century)[36] follows the tendency of Song Rabbah. Though space does not permit a thorough analysis, the outline of the targum to Song 5:2 is as follows:

> [5:2] After all these matters, the people, the house of Israel, sinned.
> The LORD handed them over to King Nebuchadnezzar of Babylon, and he carried them into exile.
> While in their exile, they were like a sleeping man who is not able to rouse himself from his slumber.
> And the voice of the Holy Spirit was admonishing them by means of the prophets, rousing them from their heart's slumber.
> The LORD of all worlds answered and said,
> "Turn in repentance! Open your mouth, rejoice, and praise me,
>   O my sister,
>   my beloved,
>   congregation of Israel,
>   who is likened to a dove in your perfect deeds.

---

[36] See the contribution of Günter Stemberger in this volume.

For the hair of my head is filled with your tears, like a man whose hair is drenched with the dew of heaven. And my locks are like a man whose locks are filled with raindrops that descend at night."[37]

According to the targum, Israel was—so to speak—in a state of shock during the Babylonian exile, from which the Holy Spirit, with the help of the prophets, awakened it. Israel's conscience is being addressed, and Israel is once again heard by God, whose hair drips with the tears of Israel's mourning. The targum emphasizes the elements of repentance and praise of God, but indirectly it also appeals to God's intervention because of Israel's tears, which are not only an expression of lament but also an appeal to God to redeem Israel.

To conclude, the view of the Song of Songs as a collection of ardent love songs is in principle not lost in the process of rabbinic interpretation in the midrash (and the targum). The examples discussed here demonstrate boldly and clearly that the love between God and Israel possesses a depth and intensity that can hardly be better expressed than through a love song like the Song of Songs. In addition, these texts demonstrate that when it comes to the ostensible difference between literal and allegorical interpretation, that the rabbis have no problem with the text being both at once.

Bibliography

Birnbaum, Elisabeth. "Das Hohelied: Unerschöpflich, unabschließbar, uninterpretierbar?" *BiKi* 3 (2018): 126–134.

Birnbaum, Elisabeth. "'Just Call Me Salomo?' Hld 3,6–11 und 8,11–12 als Fallbeispiele der Hoheliedinterpretation." In *Das Hohelied im Konflikt der Interpretationen*, edited by Ludger Schwienhorst-Schönberger, 233–264. Frankfurt am Main: Peter Lang, 2017.

Boyarin, Daniel. *Intertextuality and the Reading of Midrash*. ISBL. Bloomington: Indiana University Press, 1990.

Braude, William G., and Israel J. Kapstein. *Pesikta de-Rab Kahana: R. Kahana's Compilation of Discourses for Sabbaths and Festal Days*. London: Jewish Publication Society, 1975.

Girón Blanc, Luis-Fernando. "Song of Songs in Song of Songs Rabbah." In vol. 2 of *Encyclopaedia of Midrash*, edited by Jacob Neusner and Alan Avery-Peck, 857–870. Leiden: Brill, 2005.

Goldstein, David, ed. *Die Londoner Haggada aus der British Library: Ein hebräisches Manuskript aus der Mitte des 15. Jahrhunderts . . .*, translated by Felicitas Heimann. Freiburg: Herder, 1985.

Jastrow, Marcus. Dictionary of the Targumim, the Talmud Babli and Yerushalmi, and the Midrashic Literature: English and Hebrew Edition. Accessed March 18, 2021. http://www.tyndalearchive.com/TABS/Jastrow/index.htm.

---

[37] Text according to Paris Heb. 110, in Litke, *Targum Song of Songs*, 259.

Kadari, Tamar. "Deborah 2: Midrash and Aggadah." *Jewish Women: A Comprehensive Historical Encyclopedia*. December 31, 1999. Jewish Women's Archive. https://jwa.org/encyclopedia/article/deborah-2-midrash-and-aggadah.

Keel, Othmar. *Das Hohelied*. ZBKAT 18. Zürich: Theologischer Verlag, 1986.

Keel, Othmar. *Das Recht der Bilder gesehen zu werden: Drei Fallstudien zur Methode der Interpretation altorientalischer Bilder*. OBO 122. Göttingen: Vandenhoeck & Ruprecht, 1992.

Keel, Othmar. *Deine Blicke sind Tauben: Zur Metaphorik des Hohen Liedes*. SBS 114/115. Stuttgart: Katholisches Bibelwerk, 1984.

Keel, Othmar. *Vögel als Boten: Studien zu Ps 68,12–14, Gen 8,6–12, Pred 10,20 und dem Aussenden von Botenvögeln in Ägypten; mit einem Beitrag von Urs Winter zu Ps 56,1 und zur Ikonographie der Göttin mit der Taube*. OBO 14. Göttingen: Vandenhoeck & Ruprecht, 1977.

Kozodoy, Maud. "Messianic Interpretation of the Song of Songs in Late-Medieval Iberia." In *The Hebrew Bible in Fifteenth-Century Spain: Exegesis, Literature, Philosophy, and the Arts*, edited by Jonathan Decter and Arturo Prats, 117–147. Leiden: Brill, 2012.

Langer, Gerhard. *Das Drama des Bundes: Ezechiel 16 in rabbinischer Perspektive*. HBS 11. Freiburg: Herder, 1997.

Langer, Gerhard. *Midrasch*. UTB 4675. Tübingen: Mohr Siebeck, 2016.

Litke, Andrew W. *Targum Song of Songs and Late Jewish Literary Aramaic: Language, Lexicon, Text, and Translation*. STAS 15. Leiden: Brill, 2019.

Maagarim. The Historical Dictionary Project of the Academy of the Hebrew Language. Accessed August 27, 2021. https://maagarim.hebrew-academy.org.il/Pages/PMain.aspx.

Mandelbaum, Bernard. *Pesiqta de Rav Kahana: According to an Oxford Manuscript with Variants . . . with Commentary and Introduction*. 2nd ed. 2 vols. New York: Jewish Theological Press, 1987.

Mann, Jacob. *The Bible as Read and Preached in the Old Synagogue: A Study in the Cycles of the Readings from Torah and Prophets, as well as from Psalms, and in the Structure of the Midrashic Homilies I; The Palestinian Triennial Cycle; Genesis and Exodus; With a Hebrew Section Containing Manuscript Material of Midrashim to These Books; Prolegomenon by Ben Zion Wacholder*. New York: Ktav, 1971.

Pardes, Ilana. *The Song of Songs: A Biography*. Lives of Great Religious Books. Princeton: Princeton University Press, 2019.

Schoenfeld, Devorah. "One Song or Many: The Unity of the Song of Songs in Jewish and Christian Exegesis." *HS* 61 (2020): 123–142.

Schwienhorst-Schönberger, Ludger. "Das Hohelied als Allegorie." In *Das Hohelied im Konflikt der Interpretationen*, edited by Ludger Schwienhorst-Schönberger, 11–56. Frankfurt am Main: Peter Lang, 2017.

Schwienhorst-Schönberger, Ludger, ed. *Das Hohelied im Konflikt der Interpretationen*. Frankfurt am Main: Peter Lang, 2017.

Siquans, Agnethe. "Das Hohelied als Deuteschlüssel für das Buch Exodus in Schir ha-Schirim Rabba." In *Das Hohelied im Konflikt der Interpretationen*, edited by Ludger Schwienhorst-Schönberger, 287–322. Frankfurt am Main: Peter Lang, 2017.

Stemberger, Günter. *Einleitung in Talmud und Midrasch*. 9th ed. Munich: Beck, 2011.

Stern, David. *Parables in Midrash: Narrative and Exegesis in Rabbinic Literature*. Cambridge: Harvard University Press, 1991.

Stern, Sacha. *Jewish Identity in Early Rabbinic Writings*. Leiden: Brill, 1994.

Spencer, F. Scott. *Song of Songs*. Wisdom Commentary 25. Collegeville: Liturgical Press, 2016.

Thoma, Clemens, and Simon Lauer. *Die Gleichnisse der Rabbinen: Erster Teil; Pesiqtà de Rav Kahanà (PesK); Einleitung, Übersetzung, Parallelen, Kommentar, Texte*. JudChr 10. Bern: Peter Lang, 1986.

Zakovitch, Yair. *Das Hohelied*. HTKAT. Freiburg im Breisgau: Herder, 2004.

Erik Wade
Reading the Old English *Life of Saint Mary of Egypt* with Abbot Hadrian of Africa
The Influence of Byzantine Readings of the Song of Songs on Early Medieval England

> *Nigra sum sed formosa*
> I am black but beautiful
> —Vulgate Song of Songs 1:4 (Hebr. 1:5)
>
> Western beauty culture has helped destroy
> black communities and black women in particular.
> —Kim Hall[1]

In 670, two monks arrived in England from Rome: Abbot Hadrian, born in Africa, and Archbishop Theodore, born in Tarsus (in what is now Turkey). Sent by the pope to reform the English church, Hadrian and Theodore brought Greek and Roman theology, legends, and literary works with them, as well as teaching Biblical exegesis, Greek, and Latin. Scholars tend to diminish Hadrian and Theodore's non-European origins, dismissing the idea that their backgrounds could have affected their teaching or changed England. Mary Rambaran-Olm argues that Hadrian's presence has gone so unexamined because it would upend white supremacist ideas of English history: "The fact that Hadrian, 'the man by nation of Africa,' may have been Black further disrupts the established account of British history that early English studies maintains."[2]

Hadrian and Theodore introduced the English to the Byzantine legend of St. Mary of Egypt—a black-skinned saint modeled on both the Bride and Groom of the Song of Songs—who spent the end of her life in a desert, repenting for her sexual sins, her clothes falling to pieces, and her only food desert plants. Likewise, when Hadrian and Theodore taught the Song of Songs, they chose not to justify or explain the Bride's blackness, unlike every other major commentator on the Song. Their

---
[1] Hall, *Things of Darkness*, 264.
[2] Rambaran-Olm, "A Wrinkle in Medieval Time," 397.

Note: My thanks to Bettina Bildhauer, Jessica Hines, Rebekka Rüger, and Annette Schellenberg for their thoughtful comments on this article. My gratitude to Mary Rambaran-Olm for sharing her knowledge of Hadrian. Additional thanks to Danielle Allor and Stacy Klein for working through the Latin with me and offering insightful suggestions and readings. All errors that remain are my own.

teachings are preserved in a series of Biblical glosses, based on notes taken down by their students.³

Both of these texts—the *Life of Saint Mary of Egypt* and the glosses—suggest that Hadrian and Theodore defied the usual Roman and Greek exegesis that claimed that the Bride's blackness was metaphorical or that blackness is not beautiful. The Vulgate version of the Song stated that the Bride is "black but beautiful," influencing centuries of English attitudes towards Black women. Kim Hall argues that the Bride represented "the central paradox of black beauty" in the minds of centuries of white English writers who could not imagine that blackness *could* be beautiful.⁴ But, in seventh-century England, Hadrian and Theodore read the Bride inaugurated a forgotten English tradition of reading Black women as beautiful.

Modern scholars have overlooked this tradition due to their own belief that blackness is not beautiful and their unwillingness to credit Hadrian in particular with innovation in English theology. Rambaran-Olm argues that contemporary scholars have sidelined Hadrian's role in shaping the English church, likely due to Hadrian's African origins.⁵ (Rambaran-Olm notes that scholars also emphasize Hadrian as "North" African, without evidence, as a way to imply he was white).⁶ Similarly, scholars discussing the Old English version of the *Life of Saint Mary of Egypt* assume that Mary is ugly and masculine due to her blackness. Yet, the *Life* only describes Mary as *sweart* ("black"), not ugly. The most recent editor of the Old English *Life* states that Mary's nudity and blackness "contradicts all conventional images of femininity."⁷ Scholars describe Mary as having a "*sweart* female body that is both repulsive and titillating," as an "exotic woman," and as a contradiction whose "body is repulsive yet (who) is the bride of Christ."⁸ These attitudes suggest why scholars have given little attention to how Hadrian and Theodore fostered a tradition of recognizing black beauty through their exegesis on the Song and their teaching of texts like the *Life of Saint Mary of Egypt*. In what follows, I analyze first Hadrian and Theodore's commentary on the Song, then the *Life*, in order to argue that they read blackness as beautiful in the Song and in Song-inspired texts. Finally,

---

3 I have reproduced and translated the glosses in Appendix 1 of this article.
4 See Hall, *Things of Darkness*, 107–116, quote at 110.
5 See Rambaran-Olm, "A Wrinkle in Medieval Time." Hall has similarly criticized "the curious absence of discussions of English interaction with Africa in new historicist work" on the early modern period (*Things of Darkness*, 260). The scholarly refusal to consider premodern English interactions with African societies is long-standing and pervasive.
6 Rambaran-Olm, "A Wrinkle in Medieval Time," 405–406 n. 82.
7 Magennis, ed., *Old English Life*, 5.
8 Quotes respectively are Rulon-Miller, "Sexual Humor," 104; Scheil, "Bodies and Boundaries," 137; Coon, *Sacred fictions*, xiii.

in an appendix, I provide the text—along with my translation—of their commentary on the Song, in hopes of bringing this unique work to a larger audience.

1 Comments on the Song of Songs—The Canterbury Glosses

Despite evidence that Hadrian and Theodore's backgrounds influenced their theology, scholars have downplayed their non-European origins.[9] Hadrian and Theodore likely introduced knowledge of a Persian saint to England, Theodore may have designed a floorplan for the St. Gall's monastery in Switzerland (whose layout resembles Syrian monasteries), and Hadrian introduced an African riddling tradition.[10]

The records of their classroom teaching include glosses on the Song of Songs that name Hadrian as the source of several opinions.[11] Bernard Bischoff and Michael Lapidge draw attention to one gloss on the Song that twice cites Hadrian as the authority:

> Stipate. stringite Adrianus dicit .i. remissionem peccatorum per baptismum. Domum uini ecclesiam dicit.
>
> Compass. "Hold in check," said Hadrian, that is, the remission of sins through baptism. He also says that the house of wine (II.4: *cellam uinariam*) represents the Church.[12]

Bischoff and Lapidge argue that Hadrian's reading of the *cellam uinariam* ("house of wine") shows that Hadrian read the Song as a theological metaphor: "Hadrian's comments represent an early attempt to interpret the (unambiguous) sexual language of the Song of Songs in terms of the soul and the Church."[13] Yet, a careful study of the glosses suggests that Hadrian and Theodore emphasized a literal reading of the Song.

---

9 See Rambaran-Olm, "A Wrinkle in Medieval Time"; Wade, "*Pater* Don't Preach."

10 Rambaran-Olm, "A Wrinkle in Medieval Time," summarizes these influences and the scholarly reluctance to name them.

11 See Bischoff and Lapidge, eds., *Biblical Commentaries*; Lapidge, "School of Theodore and Hadrian"; Pheifer, "Canterbury Bible Glosses."

12 Latin and translation quoted from Bischoff and Lapidge, eds., *Biblical Commentaries*, 177. The glossed line from the Song here is "compass (*stipate*) me about with apples (*malis*) because I languish with love." Bischoff and Lapidge note that Hadrian seems to have mistaken the Latin *malis* for "evils," rather than "apples," and thus understood *stipate* ("compass") as meaning "protect me against" (*Biblical Commentaries*, 177). The glosses naming Hadrian appear in two continental manuscripts (see Bischoff and Lapidge, eds., *Biblical Commentaries*, 177, 542).

13 Bischoff and Lapidge, eds., *Biblical Commentaries*, 144.

In what follows, I refer to the author of the unnamed glosses as "Hadrian," for ease and due to Hadrian's clear authorship of the two named glosses, but these glosses likely reflect the teaching of both Hadrian and Theodore. However, we only know for sure that Hadrian taught the Song, as the glosses on it never mention Theodore. Following Rambaran-Olm's argument that scholarship has sidelined Hadrian in favor of Theodore, I emphasize Hadrian as a theologian and innovator.[14] Rambaran-Olm argues that Hadrian's early role in influencing the treatment of the Song should technically make him a Church Father.[15] Hadrian was the pope's first choice for Archbishop, but Hadrian declined and suggested Theodore as a suitable candidate. Theodore had asked Hadrian to accompany him to ensure Theodore—trained in the Greek eastern Church—kept his theology sufficiently Roman.[16] Both the pope and Theodore saw Hadrian as a theologian and monastic of rare gifts, yet scholars rarely credit Hadrian with any innovations in England, preferring to attribute them to Theodore. I seek to push back on this scholarly narrative by emphasizing Hadrian as a theologian.

In this study, I focus on the Leiden Glossary, as it is the most comprehensive version of the Biblical glosses. A Scottish or German monk likely produced the Leiden Glossary in the eighth century in the same Swiss monastery whose floor-plan has been attributed to Theodore.[17] Though written in Latin letters, the glossary contains many Greek words and Greek characteristics, including *xp* in the name of Christ (*xpistus*), for instance.[18] This Greek style reflects Hadrian and Theodore's Greek influence. Bischoff and Lapidge argue that "the 'Leiden Family' glossaries represent the teaching of Theodore and Hadrian" almost certainly.[19] As such, the Leiden glosses on the Song show us their early, influential teaching of the Song in England.

The Leiden glosses reveal that Hadrian and Theodore's analysis of the Song is more original than some of their other Biblical commentaries. Hadrian and Theodore's other Biblical commentaries exhibit clear influence by Origen and likely influence by Theodoret of Cyrhus, for instance, but scholars have noted no apparent debts to Apponius.[20] However, even though these authorities all wrote famous commentaries on the Song, they do not seem to have influenced Hadrian's interpretation.

---

14 See Rambaran-Olm, "Wrinkle in Medieval Time."
15 Personal communication, Jan 27th, 2021.
16 This story is recounted in Bede's *Ecclesiastical History*, Book IV, Ch. 1. See The Venerable Bede, *Bede's Ecclesiastical History of the English People*, edited and translated by Bertram Colgrave and Roger A. B. Mynors.
17 See Hessels, *An Eighth-century Latin-Anglo-Saxon Glossary*, xi–xiii.
18 See Hessels, *An Eighth-century Latin-Anglo-Saxon Glossary*, xxix–xxx.
19 See Bischoff and Lapidge, eds., *Biblical Commentaries*, 178.
20 See Bischoff and Lapidge, eds., *Biblical Commentaries*, 219–220, 223–224.

In the appendix, I describe the slight parallels to Hadrian's readings in the work of other commentators, which lead me to two hypotheses:[21] First, Hadrian's reading is original, as far as I can determine. Hadrian likely knew Apponius' commentary but did not rely on it. If there is a debt to fellow African theologian Origen, it is extremely slight. Hadrian's analysis resembles Theodoret in its literalism, but there seems little indication of any direct influence. Second, the Venerable Bede, the most well-known early English exegete of the Song, likely did not know Hadrian's commentary, as there is little clear influence on his own commentary. Given the plethora of continental copies of these glosses, scholars should seek instead for Hadrian and Theodore's influence on later continental writers' analysis of the Song.

Hadrian reads the Song's eroticism literally, as a holy eroticism, an approach unlike other commentators. Hadrian thinks that the first line of the Song describes a literal kiss from Christ:

> Osculetur me; ista oscula que execlesie porrexit xpistus quam baptismi nitore mundatam et ornatam per spiritum sanctum.

> Kiss me: those kisses which Christ extended to the Church, that have been cleaned and dressed with the splendor of baptism by means of the Holy Spirit.[22]

Hadrian uniquely reads the kiss as Christ's kiss to the Church after the Church's baptism.

Most exegetes read the Song's eroticism entirely as a metaphor, yet—from the opening lines—Hadrian shows a marked unwillingness to do so. In the Song's first few lines (Song 1:1–4), the Bride calls the Bridegroom's breasts better than wine and says young maidens love him because his name is like oil poured out. She says they run eagerly after the smell of his ointments. Most exegetes maintain these lines cannot be read literally. Bede insisted that these lines could not be taken literally.[23] Yet Hadrian does not gloss away the kisses, the ointments, the maidens running, or many other controversial parts of the Song's human world.

Hadrian glosses many of these lines in order to stress that these loving and sexual metaphors reflect the love of a person entering the Christian faith through baptism. The line "Draw me: we will run after thee to the odour of thy ointments" is glossed to suggest that ointments signify baptism: *Odor ungentorum, donum quod in baptismate accipimus* ("The smell of ointments, which we receive as a gift of

---

21 I have compared the glosses to the commentaries on the Song by Apponius, Gregory, Origen, and Theodoret, as well as to Bede's later commentary, in case Hadrian's commentary influenced Bede.
22 Latin from Hessels, *An Eighth-century Latin-Anglo-Saxon Glossary*, 11–12, hereafter cited in-text by gloss number as *"LG."* This is gloss 1. All translations are my own. Notes on my translations and occasional changes to the Latin appear in the appendix.
23 See Wade, "Birds and the Bedes."

baptism") (*LG*, 3). Likewise, Hadrian glosses the oil poured out as *chrisme* ("anointment oil/chrism") (*LG*, 6). When the Song states that the beams of the house are cedar, Hadrian notes that this *significat apostolos* ("signifies the apostles") (*LG*, 11). The Song becomes, in Hadrian's reading, a direct account of love between Christian and Christ.

Hadrian glosses some phrases as metaphorical, glossing *ubera* ("breasts") as *apostoli* ("apostles") (*LG*, 2). Hadrian glosses *Nomen tuum* ("your name") as *xpistianiam a xpisto et chrismam* ("Christian, from 'Christ' and 'chrism'") (*LG*, 5). Similarly, the young maidens who love the Groom are glossed as *ecclesie . uel anime de numero gentium* ("Church. Or the spirit of the number of people") (*LG*, 7). Hadrian glosses wine as the prophets (*LG*, 4). These readings sometimes stray into metaphor, but more commonly, they retain their erotic meanings alongside spiritual ones.

Hadrian's reading does not erase eroticism and thus bucks the trend among Christian exegetes to emphasize the divide between the literal and spiritual meaning of the Song in order to explain away the Song's erotic overtones. When Hadrian's students gathered around him in Canterbury, they apparently heard him talk primarily about the literal level of the Song: explicating various references in the text that English readers might not have understood, including spikenard, golden collars, cypress trees, figs, litters, and aloe (*LG*, 8; 9; 10; 12; 13; 18). Hadrian's interpretations of the Song rarely suggest allegory or metaphor. He reads three lines allegorically: the cedar beams and the Bridegroom's breasts representing apostles, and the wine cellar representing the Church. Instead, Hadrian reads the literal level as having a spiritual meaning: the ointment and oil poured out are ointments and oils of baptism. The kiss is Christ's kiss. The odor is the odor of the ointments of baptism. The Bridegroom's name is the name "Christian," while the young women running after him are the members of the Church or their spirits. Hadrian, then, does not avoid the Song's literal level (as Bede does) or see it as a play of symbols (as Origen does). Hadrian thinks the Song can be understood more literally. Hadrian innovatively saw the Song's *literal* level as about the Bride of Christ, rather than seeing the Song as being a metaphor for the Bride of Christ.

The commentary on the cedar beams shows how Hadrian saw the human and spiritual levels interplaying:

> *Tigna tecta cedri natura arborum cedri inputribili uigore consistunt quarum sucus uermibus est obuius; significat apostolos.*
>
> Ceiling beams of cedar, born of cedar trees standing with incorruptible vigor whose sap is hostile to worms; signifies the apostles. (*LG*, 11)

Hadrian implies that cedar trees' "incorruptible vigor" and hostility to worms help us see *how* this wood signifies the incorruptible and vigorous apostles, whose very nature is hostile to corrupting influences. For Hadrian, we better understand the Song's spiritual message through a careful examination of its literal level.

Hadrian and Theodore's other Biblical commentaries also tend towards literal exegesis, which was a likely result of Hadrian and Theodore's influence by the Antioch school of exegesis.[24] The Antioch school was a group of Syrian monastics who sought to burnish their credentials as exegetes by claims to deeper learning and to avoiding speculation through focus on the literal Biblical text. While they didn't entirely abstain from allegorical interpretation, they did so far more than the opposing Alexandrian school.[25] One might assume that Syrian-born Theodore would be the source of an Antiochian influence, while African-born Hadrian would be more likely to have trained in the Alexandrian school. However, Hadrian had ample opportunity to have contact with Syrian theology due to his political involvements with the Byzantine government. Hadrian worked on behalf of the Byzantine Emperor Constens II (possibly as an interpreter and emissary) prior to traveling to England.[26] Hadrian's contacts brought him to a trusted position in Rome and in the Byzantine Court, making him the person whom the pope turned to when picking the new English archbishop. That work also could have easily brought him into contact with the Antioch school.

The other most unique part of Hadrian's commentary is his apparent disinterest in explicating the Bride's blackness. The glossary has no gloss on *Nigra sum* ("I am black"), the only early commentary on the Song that I know of that ignores this line. Medieval exegetes produced enormous commentary on this line, trying to adjust the lines to suggest blackness wasn't beautiful or desirable.[27] Origen's commentary on that single line amounts, in a recent translation, to some *twenty-two pages* wrestling with the Bride's blackness.[28] Alone among early commentators, Hadrian did *not* address the Bride's blackness. For him, apparently, the idea of a black Bride required no explanation.

Hadrian's reading would be unusual even in the Byzantine context, but in western Europe, where Jerome's Vulgate translation represented blackness as ugly, this reading was radical. While the Greek text of the Song reads Μέλαινά εἰμι καὶ καλή ("I am black and beautiful"), Jerome translated the line as *Nigra sum sed*

---

[24] See Bischoff and Lapidge, eds., *Biblical Commentaries*, 243–249; Pfiefer, "Canterbury Bible Glosses," 293.
[25] On the debate over the nature of the Antioch school, see Schor, "Theodoret."
[26] See Bischoff and Lapidge, eds., *Biblical Commentaries*, 123–132.
[27] See De Weever, *Sheba's Daughters*, xii–xvi, 79–84, 177–178; Hall, *Things of Darkness*, 107–116; Holsinger, "Color of Salvation"; Wade, "Birds and the Bedes."
[28] See Origen, *Commentarius in Canticum* (*Comm. Cant.*) II 1,1–57 (Fürst and Strutwolf, eds., 176–199; Lawson, trans., 91–113).

formosa ("I am black but beautiful").[29] While the Vulgate version emphasizes the Bride's blackness and beauty as contradictory, Byzantine commentators relying on the Greek version *also* found the Bride's blackness troubling.[30] Jerome's translation solidified anti-Black views among early medieval English commentators, including Bede. Haruko Momma delineates how Old English texts often associated blackness with sin and demons.[31] Eleventh-century English monastic Goscelin of Saint-Bertin stated that Jesus loved Black women too, no matter how black, ugly, or foul they were:

> No woman of Ethiopia is so black, none so ugly, so foul, if she love[s] (Christ) purely, that she does not draw grace and splendour from his beauty [...] he had as a type of Christ and the church an Ethiopian as his wife (Exod 2:15–21; Num 12:1), a queen of Ethiopia, which is to say black, but when Christ makes her fair, beautiful.[32]

Goscelin implies that blackness is negative, and he associates Black women with ugliness and foulness. Jacqueline de Weever has traced negative medieval European depictions of Black women from this period onward, which were often tied to ideas about the Bride.[33] Yet, if Goscelin and Bede represent the dominant reading of the Bride's blackness, Hadrian represents another, less remembered, approach, one in which the Bride's blackness and beauty required neither qualification or explanation.

Hadrian and Theodore's other commentaries also do not depict blackness negatively. In their commentaries on the book of Numbers, they explain that people were concerned about Moses' Ethiopian wife because Moses had her in wedlock, not because of her race:

> *Propter uxorem eius Æthiopissam [XII. 1]. Tractatores dicunt ut ipsi suspicionem haberent contra eum quod ipsam in coniugio haberet, quia in uno tabernaculo erant; quod non erat credendum nisi tantum secum habens et circumducens, ut sanctus Petrus postea suam uxorem.*

> Because of his wife the Ethiopian [XII. 1]. Commentators say that Mary and Aaron held a suspicion against Moses because he had her in wedlock, since they were in the one tabernacle; a situation which was not to be countenanced unless he kept her with him and led her around, as St. Peter was later to lead around his wife.[34]

---

[29] See Betancourt, *Byzantine Intersectionality*, 182. Lapidge and Bischoff argue that Hadrian and Theodore worked from a Vulgate Bible but that they referenced a Greek version (*Biblical Commentaries*, 190–198). For instance, the commentaries on the Song have *Redimicula* ("necklaces") where the Vulgate has *Murenulas* ("necklaces") (*LG*, 8).
[30] See Betancourt, *Byzantine Intersectionality*, 182–185, 201.
[31] Momma, "The Theater of Race," 420–422.
[32] Barnes and Hayward, trans., "Goscelin's *Liber Confortatorius*," 194–195.
[33] De Weever, *Sheba's Daughters*.
[34] Bischoff and Lapidge, eds., *Biblical Commentaries*, 376–377.

Hadrian and Theodore did not represent Ethiopians or blackness as the subject of deserved prejudice. This contrasts sharply to their treatment of Muslims, for instance, who received harsh scorn from them.[35] These issues of blackness were not merely theoretical in England; as Paul Edward Montgomery Ramírez has shown, archeological evidence shows that people of African descent—including people we would now call "Black"—were living in England throughout the first millennium.[36] Both Hadrian and Theodore's unprejudiced take on the Bride's blackness and their literal reading of the Song's sexuality may provide insight on how they read another Song-inspired text they likely brought to England: the tale of Saint Mary of Egypt.

2 The Old English *Life of Saint Mary of Egypt* and Its Echoes of the Song

Since Hadrian and Theodore likely conveyed the legend of Mary of Egypt to England, their commentary on the Song can help us understand how they might have understood the legend.[37] Scholars suggest that Mary's feast-day was celebrated in England as early as the late seventh-century, right when Hadrian and Theodore were teaching.[38] Twelve pre-Conquest English calendars include the feast of St. Mary of Egypt, and all but two date it to April 9th (the Greek date, not the Roman date), suggesting the influence of a Greek tradition (and thus likely Theodore and Hadrian).[39]

There were three different versions of Mary's story, but Hadrian and Theodore probably brought the version of the legend written by Sophronius.[40] The two earliest versions of Mary's tale, one attributed to John Moschus and one to Cyril of Scythopolis, described her as a nun or cantor who fled men who desired her.[41] Sophronius, John Moschus' student, is the probable author of a third Greek version in the 600s, which became wildly popular.[42] A ninth-century translator, likely Paul

---

35 See Bischoff and Lapidge, eds., *Biblical Commentaries*, 324–325, 455–456.
36 Montgomery Ramírez, "Colonial representations of race." Montgomery Ramírez details the racist frameworks that museums and scholars have used for considering these medieval remains (ibid).
37 See Magennis, ed., *Old English Life*, 12.
38 See Ó Riain, *Anglo-Saxon Ireland*, 19.
39 See Magennis, ed., *Old English Life*, 12.
40 See Magennis, ed., *Old English Life*, 3–10.
41 See Kouli, "Life of St. Mary of Egypt"; Walsh, "Ascetic Mother," 61.
42 See Walsh, "Ascetic Mother," 62. Maria Kouli has translated Sophronius' Greek text ("Life of St. Mary of Egypt"). While some scholars question Sophronius's attribution, it is the most accepted theory. For discussion of the debate, see ibid., 65–66; Shoemaker, *Life of the Virgin*, 11–12.

of Naples, translated the Sophronius version into Latin; the Latin version spread around western Europe, where it reached England and was translated into Old English.[43]

Theodore and Hadrian presumably introduced the Sophronius version of Mary's legend to England, in which Mary is not merely a woman fleeing the possibility of sexual sin but was herself a former sexual sinner. Hadrian and Theodore seem less likely to have known the two earlier versions of the legend of Mary of Egypt by John Moschus and Cyril of Scythopolis. There is almost no evidence that Hadrian or Theodore knew Cyril's writings.[44] They possibly had read John Moschus' work, but, given that they probably knew Moschus' work through his student Sophronius, if they were familiar with Moschus' version of the legend, they probably also knew Sophronius' longer version.[45] Theodore and Hadrian seem to have read some of Sophronius' other works.[46] Moreover, Theodore and Sophronius both likely lived in Constantinople around the same time in the 630s and may have been acquainted.[47] Even if Theodore and Sophronius hadn't met, Theodore may have participated in a council condemning the doctrine of monotheletism in Rome, a council where he would have gotten to know Sophronius's student, Maximus the Confessor.[48] Theodore knew Maximus' work, and Maximus could have provided Theodore with Sophronius's writings.[49] If Theodore and Hadrian brought the legend of Mary of Egypt to England, they doubtless brought the Sophronius version.

The Sophronius version begins with a Palestinian monk named Zosimus, who sees a dark naked figure running through the desert and pursues it. The figure is a naked, black-skinned woman with short white hair, to whom Zosimus lends his cloak. She is Mary of Egypt, though she isn't named until the end of the narrative. Convinced of her holiness, Zosimus begs for her story.

---

[43] See Magennis, ed., *Old English Life*, 3, 10–14. Hugh Magennis provides editions and translations of both the Latin and the Old English text (ibid., 55–209).
[44] See Bischoff and Lapidge, eds., *Biblical Commentaries*, 463.
[45] See Bischoff and Lapidge, eds., *Biblical Commentaries*, 225–226, 523.
[46] See Bischoff and Lapidge, eds., *Biblical Commentaries*, 226, 254, 509, 524.
[47] See Bischoff and Lapidge, eds., 60, 63–64; Guglielmo Cavallo argues that Theodore could have known Sophronius or Maximus the Confessor from other meetings as well ("Theodore of Tarsus," 66). The Biblical commentaries from Hadrian and Theodore include one opinion attributed to Sophronius that does not appear in Sophronius' extant writing, suggesting they may have known of his opinions from other sources or firsthand (see Bischoff and Lapidge, eds., *Biblical Commentaries*, 219, 310–311, 442, 502). Theodore was familiar with the Greek verse-form anacreontics, which Sophronius famously practiced (see Lapidge, "Career," 24).
[48] See Lapidge, "Career," 24.
[49] See Bischoff and Lapidge, eds., *Biblical Commentaries*, 219.

Mary tells him that she grew up in Alexandria, where she turned to a life of sexual pleasure, before travelling to Jerusalem. In Jerusalem, she tried to enter a temple but an invisible force barred her way. She prayed to an image of the Virgin Mary, asking the Virgin to intercede with God for her. The unseen barrier vanished, and Mary entered the church. Later, the Virgin's voice told her that she must repent her life of sin. Mary fled into the desert and remained there for forty-seven years.

Zosimus begs for more information but Mary defers his request and asks him to return the following year with the sacrament for her. The following year, Zosimus witnesses her walking across the River Jordan to meet him. She takes the sacrament and accepts his blessings, then asks him to return in another year. The next year, Zosimus returns to find Mary lying dead, and he buries her. Zosimus then returns to his monastery and spreads Mary's story.

In what follows, I focus on the Old English translation of this *Life of Saint Mary of Egypt*, even though it was translated well after Hadrian was buried. An Anglian author likely translated the Old English *Life* in the tenth century.[50] The Old English *Life* appears in three partial manuscript witnesses, most completely in an early eleventh-century text that also preserves Ælfric's *Lives of Saints*.[51] The Old English *Life* serves as a record of the English reception of the legend that Hadrian and Theodore introduced.

2.1 Skin Color and Mary of Egypt

Scholarship on the Old English *Life* often assumes that Mary's blackness makes her ugly or masculine, even though the *Life* just describes her as *sweart* ("black"), never as ugly. Contemporary medievalists argue that Mary's blackness makes her masculine; one scholar claims that Mary's "short, white hair, her 'sweartes' body, and her emaciated frame all lend her the literal, material aspect of a man or of a manly woman."[52] Other scholars argue that Mary represents the medieval concept of the "loathly lady," since she appears "naked, starving, white-haired and blackened by the sun."[53] Scholars argue, without textual evidence, that Mary was beautiful and white before entering the desert, where the sun turned her black and unattractive: "her once gorgeous body is now extremely unattractive, and the Old English text describes how the desert sun has rendered her complexion dry and swarthy."[54]

---

50 See Magennis, ed., *Old English Life*, 23.
51 See Magennis, ed., *Old English Life*, 14–30.
52 Heron, "Lioness in the Text," 29.
53 Watt and Lees, "Age and Desire," 60.
54 Heron, "Lioness in the Text," 28.

Andy Orchard likewise states that Mary's "physical appearance, naked, with blackened skin and sun-bleached (and short) hair is a precise negative of the sumptuous garments, bright white flesh, and dark flowing hair that were the badge of her former trade," a claim made more extraordinary by the fact that the *Life* never describes Mary's appearance before she entered the desert.[55] One scholarly article describes Mary as a "wench," a derogative term that Carissa Harris argues white people have long applied to Black women to paint them as overly sexual.[56] Byzantinist scholars, by contrast, rarely (if ever) conflate Mary's blackness with ugliness, a lack of femininity, or exoticism. Old English scholars—like most medieval Song of Song exegetes—conflate blackness with ugliness over and over again.

The *Life*, however, describes Mary as desirable, rather than as ugly. Zosimus's first proper look at Mary is the only physical description of her:

> þær soðlice man geseah westweardes on þæt westen efstan, and witodlice þaet wæs wifman þæt þær gesewen wæs. Swiðe sweartes lichaman heo wæs for þære sunnan hæto, and þa loccas hire heafdes wæron swa hwite swa wull and þa na siddren þonne oþ þone swuran.

> Ða wisan Zosimus georne behealdende wæs and for þære gewilnedan swetnysse þære wuldorfæstan gesihðe he fægen gefremed ofstlice arn.

> there he truly saw a person hastening westward in the wasteland, and truly that was a woman who he saw there. Very black of body she was because of the sun's heat, the locks of her head were as white as wool and reached no further than to her neck.

> Then Zosimus was eagerly beholding this matter and because of the desired sweetness of this glorious sight, he quickly went with joy. (213–222)[57]

Mary is black and has white hair down to her neck. Such represents the entirety of Mary's physical description. The text characterizes Mary as desirable and beautiful. Zosimus pursues the *gewilnedan swetnysse þære wuldorfæsten gesihðe* ("desired sweetness of this glorious sight"). Later, Zosimus thinks of Mary's *gewilnodan andwlitan* ("desired countenance") (762); he describes her as *swa rihtwislicre gesihðe* ("so righteous a sight") (798); and he recounts her *deorwurðan andwlitan* ("dear-worthy face") (841–842). On his last journey into the desert to meet her, Zosimus looks for *þære gewilnedan gesihðe and wilnunge þære stowe* ("the desired sight and the place of his desire") (870–871). Nothing in these descriptions suggests Mary's blackness is ugly or masculine. Instead, Mary appears beautiful and desirable, with the text specifying the *swetnysse* ("sweetness") of her appearance. She is thus both *sweart* ("black") and *swet* ("sweet"), the words' alliteration and aural similarity suggesting

---

55 See Orchard, "Hot Lust in a Cold Climate," 203.
56 See Maslanka, "From Wench to Wonder Woman"; Harris, "A History of the Wench."
57 Quotes from the Old English *Life* are from Magennis, ed., *Old English Life*, 58–121, cited by line numbers in text. All translations are my own.

the translator means us to read them together. The English translator thus emphasizes the connection between blackness and beauty more than the Latin or Greek originals.

All three versions of the *Life*—Latin, Greek, and Old English—strongly imply Mary was born black. Hadrian knew the story through the Greek *Life*, which suggests that Mary was born black, not that she was sunburnt. The Greek original says Mary's "body was black, *as if* tanned by the scorching of the sun."[58] By contrast, the Latin and the Old English versions state that she *was* burned by the sun, but that was just the standard explanation for black skin. The well-known classical theory of environmental determinism argued that the local environment caused skin color and other characteristics.[59] The word "Ethiopian," often synonymous in European texts with Black people, itself meant "sun-burnt" in Greek, while the Old English word for "Ethiopian," *Sigelhearwan*, likely also referred to being sunburnt.[60] Isidore of Seville saw Ethiopians' sun-caused blackness as their essential trait: "Ethiopia is so called after the color of its inhabitants, who are scorched by the proximity of the sun."[61] Writing in England around the same time the *Life* was translated into Old English, Goscelin used environmental determination as a metaphor for spiritual failure, asking God to "Protect me [. . .] from the face of the Ethiopian sun blackening souls."[62] Furthermore, the translator compares Mary's *loccas* "locks" to *wull* "wool," another frequent feature of classical and medieval descriptions of Black people.[63] The *Life* itself never states that Mary became black in the desert, an assumption made by modern scholars but unlikely to have been made by medieval readers.

Like other African readers of the legend of Mary, Hadrian probably did not regard Mary's blackness as significant or even racial. Judging from the Biblical commentaries, Hadrian saw nothing remarkable about blackness. Scholars like Geraldine Heng and Sierra Lomuto argue that skin color was not the only marker of race in the Middle Ages.[64] Hadrian may not have seen blackness as racial or may have regarded it as natural human variation, not in need of explanation. We might see a partial parallel in the nameless fourteenth-century Ethiopian translator of the *Life* into Ge'ez.

---

58 "μέλαν τω σώματι, ως εξ ηλιακης φλογός." Greek from Migne, ed., *Patrologia Grecae* 87/3, 3705. The translation is from Kouli, "Life of St. Mary of Egypt," 76 (emphasis mine).
59 See Betancourt, *Byzantine Intersectionality*, 186, 194; Snowden, *Blacks in Antiquity*, 25, 172–177.
60 See Betancourt, *Byzantine Intersectionality*, 177; Tolkien, "Sigelwara Land," 95–111. On environmental determinism's ongoing legacy in the Middle Ages, see Weeda, *Ethnicity in Medieval Europe*.
61 Barney et al., trans., *Etymologies*, 293.
62 Barnes and Hayward, trans., "Goscelin's *Liber Confortatorius*," 114.
63 Snowden, *Blacks in Antiquity*, 6–8, 102, 173–174.
64 See Heng, *Invention of Race*, 15–54, 181–256; Lomuto, "Mongol Princess."

This translator cut down the *Life* from its Greek version, and eliminated any explanation for Mary's blackness: "[Zosimus] saw [the figure] again, and perceived that it was going naked; the color of its body was black, and the hair of its head was white as wool and went down to its shoulders."[65] The Ge'ez translation excised the explanation for Mary's blackness ("tanned by the scorching of the sun") that appears in the Greek and Latin versions of the *Life*.[66] The Ethiopian translator required no explanation for Mary's blackness. Similarly, Hadrian saw no reason to gloss the Bride's blackness and likely would have seen no reason to decipher Mary's blackness.

For Hadrian, Mary's sun-burned blackness would resonate with the Bride from the Song, who says "the sun hath altered my colour" (Song 1:5). Scholars describe Mary's appearance as a clear reference to the Bride.[67] The *Life* never quotes the Song, but the *Life* has relatively few Biblical quotations compared to other works from its period.[68]

2.2 Echoes of the Song of Songs in the *Life of Saint Mary of Egypt*

The *Life* nonetheless mirrors the Song heavily, something scholars have yet to fully examine. Clare Lees and Gillian Overing note that few scholars have written figural analysis of the *Life*, including of its relationship to the Song.[69] When Zosimus first encounters Mary, she flees from him and then tells him to avert his eyes because of her nudity, echoing Song 6:4 ("Turn away thy eyes from me, for they have made me flee away"). Likewise, Mary's emergence from the desert parallels Song 8:5 ("Who is this that cometh up from the desert, flowing with delights, leaning upon her beloved?") and Song 3:6 ("Who is she that goeth up by the desert"). Zosimus first perceives Mary's dead body as *swa swa scinende sunne* ("something just like a shining sun") (883–884), echoing Song 6:9 ("Who is she that cometh forth as the morning rising, fair as the moon, bright as the sun").

The references to the Song appear in Mary's later, holy life, not in her earlier sexual life, emphasizing that Mary's eroticism was rechanneled into her spirituality. Irina Dumitrescu argues that the *Life*'s scene of pursuit—alone with its entangled ideas

---

65 Gunderson and Huehnergard, "An Ethiopic Version," 160.
66 See Kouli, "Life of St. Mary of Egypt," 76.
67 See Schiel, "Bodies and Boundaries," 154; Lees and Overing, *Double Agents*, 158; Lees and Watt, "Age and Desire," 58–59; Dumitrescu, *Experience of Education*, 143–144; Burrus, S*ex Lives of Saints*, 148–149; Coon, *Sacred Fictions*, xiii.
68 See Magennis, ed., *Old English Life*, 122–129; Krueger, "Scripture and Liturgy."
69 See Lees and Overing, *Double Agents*, 174.

about desire—alludes to the Song: "The Song, with its depiction of a bride and bridegroom approaching each other yet kept apart, represents a similar understanding of the way desire is evoked, frustrated, and increased."[70] Chapter 3 of the Song serves as a basis for the *Life*, as it describes seeking the beloved in the city, then discovering them in the desert. Mary first appears to Zosimus like some sort of *wildeora* (wild animal) (226), echoing Song 8:14 ("Flee away, O my beloved, and be like to the roe, and to the young hart"). Later, Zosimus waits for Mary to return like *se gleawesta hunta, gif he þær mihte þæt sweteste wildeor gegripan* ("the cleverest hunter, if he might capture there the sweetest wild animal") (873–875). Zosimus brings Mary the fruits of the palm-tree, a reference to Song 7:7–8 ("I will go up into the palm tree, and will take hold of the fruit thereof"). The *Life* echoes the Song's eroticism in Mary's scenes with Zosimus and thus suggests that Mary becomes the Bride *after* her repentance.

2.3 Eroticism and Queerness in the *Life of Saint Mary of Egypt*

The Song parallels in Mary's saintly life show that Mary's eroticism continues to cling to her even after she repents and that she represents a complexly erotic saintly figure.[71] For Dumitrescu, Zosimus pursuing Mary across the desert suggests how the *Life* uses imagery from the Song to remind us of the role of desire in the *Life*.[72] Diane Watt and Clare Lees argue that scholars into the 1990s tended to focus on Mary's sexuality before the desert, reducing her to her sexual past and not considering her ongoing sexuality.[73] Virginia Burrus argues that many sexual-sinners-turned-saints "have consistently been read as repenting of their transgressive sexuality, [but . . .] their sanctity inheres in their unrepentant—if nonetheless transfigured—seductiveness."[74]

Since Hadrian didn't regard the Song's eroticism as dangerous, he may have considered these echoes of the Song in Mary's behavior as a holy woman to be appropriate. Hadrian saw the Song as a spiritual text, but he did not understand that spirituality to be separated from the sexual. The kiss, the sweet odor, the lover pursued, the ointments poured out—all of these could be spiritual in themselves. For Hadrian, the Song's kiss, odor, and ointments all mark baptism and the entrance into Christianity. Likewise, the *Life* emphasizes Mary's need for the sacraments of baptism, brought to her through her Song-inspired relationship with Zosimus.

---

70 Dumitrescu, *Experience of Education*, 143–144.
71 See, for instance, Scheil, "Bodies and Boundaries."
72 See Dumitrescu, *Experience of Education*, 143–144.
73 See Watt and Lees, "Age and Desire," 65–66.
74 Burrus, *Sex Lives of Saints*, 13.

Christ-like Mary is both the Bride and the Bridegroom of the Song, while Zosimus can only ever be the Bride running after Mary. As Lynda Coon notes, "The wizened desert hermit is both the eschatological Messiah and Christ's bride."[75] Mary's role as Bride and Bridegroom makes her relationship to Zosimus queer. Watt and Lees suggest that both Zosimus and Mary achieve desires in the desert that are remarkably queer: Zosimus seeks masculine love and instruction, while Mary turns towards the love of the Virgin Mary.[76] The parallels between Mary and Christ further this queerness, as Zosimus pursues Mary across the desert. Scholars have noted the numerous parallels between Mary and Christ in the text. Mary walks on water and levitates.[77] Mary's solitude in the desert parallels Christ's solitary temptations in the desert.[78] Zosimus plays Doubting Thomas to Mary's Christ, asking astonished questions about her ability to survive in the desert.[79] After Mary's death, Zosimus cleans her feet with his tears like Mary Magdalene did to Christ.[80] Mary's Christ-like nature requires us to see her as the Bridegroom, while Zosimus must be the Bride striving to better herself so that she may be worthy of Christ.

2.4 The *Life* as a Model for Christian Emulation of the Song of Songs

The *Life* thus suggests that the Song's literal, human level provides a model for a Christian life, a model emphasizing the need for human connection. Zosimus and Mary embody this approach to spirituality, whose successes the *Life* contrasts to the failed spiritual practices of Zosimus' monastery. The *Life* shares with Hadrian's reading of the Song a fundamental belief that the spiritual life cannot be a life severed from the human world.

The *Life* shows the Christian need for connection with the world by contrasting the asceticism of Zosimus' problem-ridden Palestinian monastery with Mary's desire for worldly connection even after entering the desert. Zosimus' monastery exemplifies the ascetic, solitary life, as it is unknown to the outside world and unaware of the outside world's practices. The monastery is in a desolate, uninhabited locale and is thus *eac swilce uncuð þam landleodum him sylfum* ("even unknown to the people of that land themselves") (131–132). Within the monastery, a similar

---

75 Coon, *Sacred Fictions*, 93.
76 See Watt and Lees, "Age and Desire," 63–65.
77 See Coon, *Sacred Fictions*, 10; Heron, "Lioness in the Text," 28.
78 See Coon, *Sacred Fictions*, 84–85.
79 See Coon, *Sacred Fictions*, 88.
80 See Coon, *Sacred Fictions*, 88.

kind of forgetting characterizes their monastic practice. The isolated monks themselves do not know of the outside world, to such an extent that they do not know of sinful, worldly topics:

> þær næfre unnytte spræce næron ne geþanc goldes and seolfres oþþe oþra gestreona, ne furðon se nama mid him næs oncnawen, ac þæt an wæs swiðost fram heom eallum geefst, þæt heora ælc wære on lichaman dead and on gaste libbende. Mid þam soðlice hi hæfdon ungeteorodne mete, þæt wæron þa godcundan gespræcu.
>
> there was never unnecessary speech nor any thought of gold and silver or other treasures, not even the names of which were known among them, but they all hastened towards that one thing, that each of them was dead in body and living in spirit. At the same time, they truly had the untiring food: that is, the divine words. (108–114)

The monks do not even know the names of silver and gold. The Old English translator added this detail, which does not appear in the Latin version. Abandoning the world, the monks hasten towards the goal of living as spiritual, rather than physical, beings.

The monks not knowing the words for silver and gold would have struck Hadrian as troubling, since these terms appear frequently in the Bible. The monks thus either did not read the Bible or they did not fully understand it. Such an idea would be antithetical to Hadrian's Antioch-school-trained mind, which stressed the importance of understanding every Biblical term in its literal sense.

The text also describes the monastery itself as being corrupted with unnoticed spiritual failures that Mary must correct, from her superior position balanced between the worldly and the spiritual. When Mary first meets Zosimus, she tells him the monastery has unspecified failures, but she forbids him to speak of them until the appropriate time. At the end of the *Life*, Zosimus discloses these failures to the abbot, who *soðlice ongeat sume þa mynsterwisan to gerihtanne, swa swa seo halige ær foresæde, ac he þa sona Gode fultumigendum gerihte* ("truly understood that some monastic practices must be set right, just as the holy one foretold earlier, but he then soon righted them with God's help") (954–956). This passage differs from the Latin version, in which the abbot corrects specific individuals within the monastery. Instead, the Old English author has Mary correct the entire monastery's practices, critiquing their vision of ascetic perfection.

The Old English *Life* thus contrasts the isolated monastery's failures with the holiness of Mary, who still desires connection with the world. While scholars often describe the *Life* as strictly ascetic and about solitary holiness, the *Life* itself is not so clear-cut.[81] Mary asks Zosimus about the world in their first meeting:

---

81 See Magennis, "St Mary of Egypt and Ælfric," 99–112.

> *sege me hu nu todæge on middanearde Cristes folc sy gereht and hu ða caseres, oððe hu is nu gelæswod seo heord Cristes rihtgeleaffullan gesamnunga.*
>
> say to me now how today Christ's folk are ruled in the world and how are the emperors, or how the herd of Christ's right-believing congregation are pastured. (308–311)

Mary asks Zosimus for news of the outside world, an act that would be in defiance of Zosimus' monastery's rules. Mary shows that an interest in the physical world does not contradict with holiness or spiritual pursuits. Given Hadrian's own involvement with the Byzantine emperor, it seems clear that he would not see an involvement in politics as contrary to monastic ideals.

Zosimus' own choice to pursue Mary, like the Bride seeking the Bridegroom, defies his monastery's rules, but it leads to spiritual betterment for himself and the monastery. The monks went out into the wilderness once a year for solitary contemplation, and they avoided each other in the desert. When Zosimus goes into the desert, however, he seeks not solitude but he strives to

> *sumne fæder on þam westene funde, þe hine on sumum þingum getimbrede þæs þe he sylf ær ne cuðe.*
>
> find some father in the desert, so that he (the father) might instruct him (Zosimus) in some things that he had not earlier known. (193–195)

What Zosimus finds is not a desert father but a desert mother, who rewards his decision to defy his monastery's usual solitary practice. The monks have gone into Mary's desert for forty-seven years, yet Zosimus is the first one to meet her, because he was the first to follow a figure he encountered, rather than fleeing from them. Their ascetic practice kept them from her, while Zosimus' choice to chase connection improves both himself and the monastery.

The *Life* uses the Song as a model for proper living—not just in terms of the relationship of the church to God, but in terms of the relationship of Christians to each other. Like the Song, the *Life* suggests Christian perfection should be sought in the connections between Christians. The human, literal level of understanding can lead to deeper spiritual understanding. Zosimus asks when he meets Mary,

> *Eala, ðu gastlice modor, geswutela nu hwæt þu sie of þære gesihþe, forþam þu eart soðlice Godes þinen.*
>
> Oh, you spiritual mother, reveal now what you are in your appearance, because you are truly God's thane. (289–291)

Zosimus asks her what she is in her appearance. He understands that she is holy and a servant of God. What he asks is not her generality—that which she shares with all saints and holy people—but her specific individuality, as embodied in her black, beautiful, mortal body. Everything that follows—all of Mary's story and the assistance she provides the monastery and Zosimus—comes about as a result of Zosimus seeking, rather than refusing, connection.

3 Conclusion

While the glosses on the Song may suggest why Hadrian and Theodore brought the legend of Mary of Egypt to England, we can only ever speculate whether their reading of the legend influenced the early reception of Mary of Egypt.

Two moments in the Old English *Life* could hint that English writers passed down Hadrian's approach. The Old English writer twice glosses unfamiliar foods with their English equivalents, a practice from Hadrian and Theodore's teachings. First, the translator glosses *palmtreowa wæstmum* ("palm-tree fruits") as *þe we hatað fingeræppla* ("what we call finger-fruits [dates]") (780–781). A short while later, the translator glosses lentils: *lenticula, þæt syndon pysan* ("lentils, which are peas") (849). In both instances, the translator saw necessary to ensure that English readers understood the literal level of the *Life*. Could these glosses within the *Life* suggest that a reading practice based in careful, literal interpretation survived in England from Hadrian and Theodore's Canterbury school? We may never know.

If Hadrian and Theodore brought the *Life* to England, then their vision of a hagiographical tradition differed from that of the Benedictine Reform and Ælfric, just as their reading of the Song of Songs differed from Bede's reading. Rambaran-Olm has diagnosed how the scholarly sidelining of Hadrian in particular causes scholars to overlook the radical contributions that Hadrian, along with Theodore, made to early English culture. Their interpretation of the Song shows that they did not see its human level as antithetical to its spiritual message, suggesting how they could find the humanity of the legend of St. Mary of Egypt acceptable. Kim Hall has shown that, by the early modern period, most English writers discussing the Song's Bride saw blackness and beauty as polar opposites.[82] However, the Leiden Glosses and the *Life* hint that—while lecturing about the meaning of cedars, figs, and oil poured out—Hadrian quietly introduced an alternate tradition in the first millennium in England, one that understood women could be both beautiful and Black.

---

82 See Hall, *Things of Darkness*, 107–116.

Appendix: Hadrian on The Song of Songs

Unpublished glosses from the Milan and Berlin manuscripts

> *Stipate. stringite Adrianus dicit .i. remissionem peccatorum per baptismum. Domum uini ecclesiam dicit.*[83]

> Compass. "Hold in check," said Hadrian, that is, the remission of sins through baptism. He also says that the house of wine (II.4: cellam uinariam) represents the Church.[84]

The Leiden Glosses

1. *Osculetur me; ista oscula que execlesie*[85] *porrexit xpistus quam baptismi nitore mundatam et ornatam per spiritum sanctum odoris sui ; Gratia inuitat ut sponsam;*[86]
   Kiss me: those kisses which Christ extended to the Church, that has been cleaned and dressed with the splendor of baptism by means of the Holy Spirit; the grace of his odor attracts the Bride;[87]
2. *Ubera ; apostoli;*
   Breasts; apostles;[88]
3. *Odor ungentorum, donum quod in baptismate accipimus .*
   The odor of ointment, a gift we receive in baptism.
4. *Uina; prophete;*[89]
   Wines; prophets;[90]

---

83 The manuscripts are Milan, Biblioteca Ambrosiana, M. 79 sup.; & Berlin, Staatsbibliothek Der Stiftung Preussischer Kulturbesitz, Grimm 132,2.
84 Bede treats the "house of wine" similarly to Hadrian. See Bede, *In Cantica Canticorum* (*In Cant.*) I 7 (Hurst, ed., 200–201; Holder, trans., 67).
85 I take *execlesie* as *execlesiae* here.
86 The manuscript is Leiden University Library, Voss. Lat. Q. 69. Punctuation copied from Hessel's edition, based on the manuscript (Hessel xxx). I have occasionally altered the punctuation in my translations for readability.
87 It is possible that the scribe has written *odoris sui* for *oris sui*, and thus everything from *odoris* onward is meant to be a separate gloss reading *oris sui; Gratia inuitat ut sponsam* ("his mouth; grace invites the bride").
88 This reading corresponds to Apponius' commentaries. See Apponius, *In Cantica Canticorum* (*In Cant.*) I 20–21 (Vregille and Neyrand, eds., 168–172).
89 Assuming that both nouns should be in the same case, I take *prophete* as *prophetae* here.
90 This reading resembles Apponius, who states that "Wine was the word of the messages carried by angels who spoke to the prophets or in the prophets—such as the Prophet Zachaxias" (*Vinum enim erat uerbum nuntiorum delatum per angelos | qui ad prophetas uel in prophetis loquebantur— sicut ait Zachaxias propheta)*; Apponius, *In Cant.* I 19 (Vregille and Neyrand, eds., 168; translation my own). Hadrian's reading here thus approximates Apponius' reading, but Hadrian takes wine as the prophets, not the prophecy related to them.

5. *Nomen tuum : xpistianiam a xpisto et chrismam*
   Your name: Christian, from Christ and chrism.[91]
6. *Unguentum; exinanitum. Chrisme uocabulum dedictum est quod non ante dicitur chrisma quam super hominem fuerit fusum;*
   Oil; being poured out. The term "chrism" is contradicted because it is not said before unction which is poured out over a man;[92]
7. *Aduliscentule; ecclesie . uel anime de numero gentium*[93]
   Young women; Churches or the spirits of the multitude of the people.[94]
8. *Redimicula; sunt ornamenta ceruicis;*
   Necklaces: these are ornaments of the neck;
9. *Nardum spica unde faciunt unguenta;*
   Spike-nard, from which ointment is made
10. *Cyprus : arbor est similis salice habens flores miri odoris et butros*[95] *. sicut erba pratearum.*
    Cypress: a tree that is similar to the willow, having flowers of wonderful scent and buds, like meadow plants.
11. *Tigna tecta cedri natura arborum cedri inputribili uigore consistunt quarum sucus uermibus est obuius; significat apostolos*;
    Ceiling beams of cedar, by the nature of cedar trees standing with incorruptible[96] vigor whose sap is hostile to worms; signifies the apostles ;[97]
12. *Ficus protulit grossos suos flore ipsius . antequam aperiantur sic dicuntur*
    The fig tree puts forth its young figs by flower of itself; before it is opened, as it is said[98]
13. *Ferculum lectum est quod portari potest;*
    A litter is a bed which it is possible to carry;
14. *Amana: et libanus . sanir et hermon montes sunt*
    Amana and Lebanon (Amana is in Lebanon?). Sanir and Hermon are mountains[99]

---

91 Bede likewise makes the connection to chrism, Gregory connects the name to Christ, and Apponius relates the name to Christ and to chrism. See Apponius, *In Cant.* I 22–23 (Vregille and Neyrand, eds.,173–177); Bede, *In Cant.* I 1 (Hurst, ed., 190–192; Holder, trans., 40–41).
92 This gloss seems to be distinguishing when to call this oil *unguentum* and when to call it *chrism*.
93 I take *aduliscentule, ecclesie,* and *anime* as *aduliscentulae, ecclesiae,* and *animae* respectively.
94 This reading resembles Origen in some aspects, though its fragmentary nature makes identification difficult; other commentaries have no equivalent reading. See Origen, *Comm. Cant.* I 4,1–30 (Fürst and Strutwolf, eds., 150–165; Lawson, trans., 74–77).
95 Taken as *botros*.
96 Theodoret's commentary also emphasizes the "incorruptibility" of the cedar, though his commentary otherwise differs from Hadrian's (Theodoret, *Commentary*, 53).
97 Bede suggests the beams are "holy preachers," while Origen argues they are priests; see Bede, *In Cant.* I 5 (Hurst, ed., 196–199; Holder, trans., 62); Origen, *Comm. Cant.* III 3,1–6 (Fürst and Strutwolf, eds., 302–303; Lawson, trans., 174–176). Apponius likewise suggests they are holy men of the church, but he suggests they are those who succeeded the apostles; see Apponius, *In Cant.* I 23–24 (Vregille and Neyrand, eds., 319–323).
98 This seems to reference the fact that fig trees do not flower conventionally but put forth flowers within their figs. My thanks to Danielle Allor for this point.
99 This is slightly garbled, as Amana, Sanir, and Hermon are all mountains in Lebanon. It seems likely the meaning has been altered in transmission.

15. *Emissiones tue : munera delectabilia;*
    Your emissions/plants: delectable gifts
16. *Crocus herbe flos est modice mire odoris.*
    Saffron is the flower of a plant of uncommonly mild scent.
17. *Fistola : arbor est boni odoris non boni saporis;*
    Sweet cane: a tree which (has) a good scent (but) not a good taste;
18. *Murra et aloe . herbe sunt;*
    Myrrh and aloe are herbs;
19. *Gutta . de arbore currit; idest balsamum;*
    The drop, which runs from the tree; that is, the balsam;
20. *Cassia . erba est similis coste;*
    Cassia, an herb which is similar to costus;[100]
21. *Elate palmarum; folia palmarum que eleuentur sursum quia non pendent deorsum sicut aliarum arborum;*
    Raised palms; palm leaves that are raised up because they do not hang down like the other trees;
22. *Areola dicitur ubi aqua diriuatur in ortum et stat in modico stagnello ipse dicitur ereola propter inrigationem ubi crescunt aromata;*[101]
    A small garden bed that is said to be where water is directed into the garden and remains in a small pool; it is said to be the garden bed near the irrigation where the spices grow;
23. *Aminab : proprium nomen uiri:*
    Aminab: proper name of the man.
24. *Salamitis concubina dauid que ministrabat ei in senectute,*
    Salamitis: David's concubine who attended him in his old age.
25. *Uinum candidum ; piperatum . uel mellatum;*
    White wine ; spiced or honey;
26. *Mustum facitur de malis granatis. id est malis punicis;*
    Made fresh from pomegranates, that is Punic apples;

Bibliography

Apponius. *Commentaire sur le Cantique des Cantiques*. Vol. 1 of *Livres I–III*, translated and edited by Bernard de Vregille and Louis Neyrand. Paris: Les Éditions Du Cerf, 1997.

Barnes, William R., and Rebecca Hayward, trans. "Goscelin's *Liber Confortatorius*." In *Writing the Wilton Women: Goscelin's Legend of Edith and Liber Confortatorius*, edited by Stephanie Hollis, 99–207. Turnhout: Brepols Publishers, 2004.

Barney, Stephen A., Wendy J. Lewis, Jennifer A. Beach, Oliver Berghof, with the collaboration of Muriel Hall, eds. and trans. *The Etymologies of Isidore of Seville*. New York: Cambridge University Press, 2006.

---

[100] Taking *coste* here as *costum/costus*. This likely refers to chrysanthemum balsamita ("costmary").

[101] I take *ortum* as *hortum* here.

Bede, The Venerable. *Bede's Ecclesiastical History of the English People*, edited and translated by Bertram Colgrave and R. A. B. Mynors. Oxford: Oxford at the Clarendon Press, 1969.

Bede, The Venerable. "In Cantica Canticorum Libri VI." In *Bedae Venerabilis Opera, Pars II: Opera Exegetica 2B*, edited by David Hurst, 164–375. CCSL 119B. Turnhout: Brepols, 1983.

Bede, The Venerable. *On the Song of Songs and Selected Writings*, translated by Arthur Holder. Mahwah, NJ: Paulist Press, 2011.

Betancourt, Roland. *Byzantine Intersectionality: Sexuality, Gender & Race in the Middle Ages*. Princeton: Princeton University Press, 2020.

Bischoff, Bernhard, and Michael Lapidge, eds. *Biblical Commentaries from the Canterbury School of Theodore and Hadrian*. Cambridge: Cambridge University Press, 1994.

Burrus, Virginia. *The Sex Lives of Saints: An Erotics of Ancient Hagiography*. Divinations: Rereading Late Ancient Religion. Philadelphia: University of Pennsylvania Press, 2007.

Cavallo, Guglielmo. "Theodore of Tarsus and the Greek Culture of His Time." In *Archbishop Theodore: Commemorative Studies on His Life and Influence*, edited by Michael Lapidge, 54–67. Cambridge: Cambridge University Press, 1995.

Coon, Lynda L. *Sacred Fictions: Holy Women and Hagiography in Late Antiquity*. Philadelphia: University of Pennsylvania Press, 1997.

De Weever, Jacqueline. *Sheba's Daughters: Whitening and Demonizing the Saracen Woman in Medieval French Epic*. New York: Routledge, 2015.

Dumitrescu, Irina. *The Experience of Education in Anglo-Saxon Literature*. Cambridge: Cambridge University Press, 2018.

Gunderson, Jaime, and John Huehnergard. "An Ethiopic Version of the Life of Mary of Egypt." *Vostok (Oriens)* 3 (2019): 151–169.

Hall, Kim F. *Things of Darkness: Economies of Race and Gender in Early Modern England*. Ithaca, NY: Cornell University Press, 1995.

Harris, Carissa. "A History of the Wench," Electric Literature, 03.06.2019, https://electricliterature.com/a-history-of-the-wench/.

Heng, Geraldine. *The Invention of Race in the European Middle Ages*. Cambridge: Cambridge University Press, 2018.

Heron, Onnaca. "The Lioness in the Text: Mary of Egypt as Immasculated Female Saint." *Quidditas: Journal of the Rocky Mountain Medieval and Renaissance Association* 21 (2000): 23–44.

Hessels, John Henry, ed. *An Eighth-century Latin-Anglo-Saxon Glossary: Preserved in the Library of Corpus Christi College, Cambridge (ms. No. 144)*. Cambridge: Cambridge University Press, 1890.

Holsinger, Bruce. "The Color of Salvation: Desire, Death, and the Second Crusade in Bernard of Clairvaux's *Sermons on the Song of Songs*." In *The Tongue of the Fathers: Gender and Ideology in Twelfth-Century Latin*, edited by David Townsend and John Andrew Taylor, 156–186. Philadelphia: University of Pennsylvania Press, 1998.

Kouli, Maria. "Life of St. Mary of Egypt." In *Holy Women in Byzantium: Ten Saints Lives in English Translation*, edited by Alice-Mary Talbot. Washington, DC: Dumbarton Oaks, 1996.

Krueger, Derek. "Scripture and Liturgy in the Life of Mary of Egypt." In *Education and Religion in Late Antique Christianity: Reflections, Social Contexts and Genres*, edited by Peter Gemeinhardt, Lieve Van Hoof, and Peter Van Nuffelen, 131–141. London: Routledge, 2016.

Lapidge, Michael. "The Career of Archbishop Theodore." In *Archbishop Theodore: Commemorative Studies on His Life and Influence*, edited by Michael Lapidge, 1–29. CSASE 11. Cambridge: Cambridge University Press, 1995.

Lapidge, Michael. "The School of Theodore and Hadrian." *Anglo-Saxon England* 15 (1986): 45–72.

Lees, Clare, and Gillian R. Overing. *Double Agents: Women and Clerical Culture in Anglo-Saxon England*. Religion and Culture in the Middle Ages. Cardiff: University of Wales Press, 2009.

Lomuto, Sierra. "The Mongol Princess of Tars: Global Relations and Racial Formation in *The King of Tars* (c. 1330)." *Exemplaria* 31 (2019): 171–192.

Magennis, Hugh, ed. *The Old English Life of St. Mary of Egypt: An Edition of the Old English Text with Modern English Parallel-Text Translation*. Exeter: University of Exeter Press, 2002.

Magennis, Hugh. "St Mary of Egypt and Ælfric: Unlikely Bedfellows in Cotton Julius E. vii?" In *The Legend of Mary of Egypt in Medieval Insular Hagiography*, edited by Erich Poppe and Bianca Ross, 99–112. Dublin: Four Courts Press, 1996.

Maslanka, Christopher. "From Wench to Wonder Woman: Lenten Discipline and Miraculous Powers in the *South English Legendary*'s Life of Saint Mary of Egypt." *Essays in Medieval Studies* 29 (2013): 27–41.

Migne, Jacques-Paul, ed., *Patrologia Graeca* 87/3. Paris, 1865.

Momma, Haruko. "The Theater of Race and Its Supporting Actors: A Tale of Two Islands." *New Literary History* 52 (2021): 407–429.

Montgomery Ramírez, Paul Edward. "Colonial Representations of Race in Alternative Museums: The 'African' of St Benet's, the 'Arab' of Jorvik, and the 'Black Viking.'" *International Journal of Heritage Studies* 27, (2021): 1–16.

Orchard, Andy. "Hot Lust in a Cold Climate: Comparison and Contrast in the Old Norse Versions of the Life of Mary of Egypt." In *The Legend of Mary of Egypt in Medieval Insular Hagiography*, edited by Erich Poppe and Bianca Ross, 175–204. Dublin: Four Courts Press, 1996.

Ó Riain, Pádraig. *Anglo-Saxon Ireland: The Evidence of the Martyrology of Tallaght*. H. M. Chadwick Memorial Lectures 3. Cambridge: Department of Anglo-Saxon, Norse, and Celtic, University of Cambridge, 1993.

Origen. *Der Kommentar zum Hohelied*, translated and edited by Alfons Fürst and Holger Strutwolf. Orig. WD 9,1. Berlin: de Gruyter, 2016.

Origen. *The Song of Songs: Commentary and Homilies*, edited and translated by Richard P. Lawson. Westminster, MD: The Newman Press, 1957.

Pheifer, Joseph D. "The Canterbury Bible Glosses: Facts and Problems." In *Archbishop Theodore: Commemorative Studies on His Life and Influence*, edited by Michael Lapidge, 281–333. Cambridge: Cambridge University Press, 1995.

Rambaran-Olm, Mary. "A Wrinkle in Medieval Time: Ironing Out Issues Regarding Race, Temporality, and the Early English." *New Literary History* 52 (2021): 385–406.

Rulon-Miller, Nina. "Sexual Humor and Fettered Desire in Exeter Book Riddle 12." In *Humour in Anglo-Saxon Literature*, edited by Jonathan Wilcox, 99–126. Cambridge: Boydell & Brewer, 2000.

Scheil, Andrew P. "Bodies and Boundaries in the Old English Life of St. Mary of Egypt." *NP* 84 (2000): 137–156.

Schor, Adam M. "Theodoret on the 'School of Antioch': A Network Approach." *JECS* 15 (2007): 517–562.

Shoemaker, Stephen J. *The Life of the Virgin: Maximus the Confessor*. New Haven, CT: Yale University Press, 2012.

Snowden, Frank M. *Blacks in Antiquity: Ethiopians in the Greco-Roman Experience*. Cambridge, MA: Harvard University Press, 1970.

Theodoret of Cyrus. *Commentary on the Song of Songs*, translated by Robert C. Hill. Brisbane: Centre for Early Christian Studies, 2001.

Tolkien, John R. R. "Sigelwara Land." *Medium Ævum* 3 (1934): 95–111.

Wade, Erik. "*Pater* Don't Preach: Byzantine Theology, Female Sexuality, and Histories of Global Encounter in the 'English' *Paenitentiale Theodori*." *The Medieval Globe* 4.2 (2018): 1–29.

Wade, Erik. "The Birds and the Bedes: Race, Gender, and Sexuality in Bede's *In Cantica Canticorum*." *postmedieval: a journal of medieval cultural studies* 11 (2020): 425–433.

Walsh, Efthalia Makris. "The Ascetic Mother Mary of Egypt." *GOTR* 34 (1989): 59–69.

Watt, Diane, and Clare A. Lees. "Age and Desire in the Old English *Life of St. Mary of Egypt*: A Queerer Time and Place?" In *Middle-Aged Women in the Middle Ages*, edited by Sue Niebrzydowski, 53–68. Cambridge: D. S. Brewer, 2011.

Weeda, Claire. *Ethnicity in Medieval Europe, 950–1250: Medicine, Power and Religion*. Suffolk: York Medieval Press, 2021.

Günter Stemberger
Targum Song of Songs, the History of Israel, and the Study of Torah

Aramaic translations of the Bible, *targumim* (singular, *targum*), have a very long history. The earliest examples are those found at Qumran (fragments of Leviticus and Job), but the liturgical use of such translations is not attested before the early rabbinic period. Mishnah Megillah 4:4 rules that when reading the Torah, the text is to be translated after every single verse, whereas for the prophets one may read up to three verses before they are translated into Aramaic. The reason for this practice of translation is that in the talmudic period (first millennium CE) most people no longer understood the Hebrew of the biblical text. In order to clearly distinguish the targum as Oral Torah from the biblical text, it could not be delivered from a written copy.[1] But texts that were not part of the liturgical reading, mainly the Writings, among them the Five Scrolls with the Song of Songs, did not receive an early targum.

1 Targum Song of Songs: Its Language, Date, and Country of Origin

All the targumim of the Five Scrolls are rather late (sixth–ninth century) and are not free translations of the biblical text but rather a mixture of targum and midrash.[2] This is also true of Targum Song, which does not simply follow the biblical text but has its own agenda. In its plain sense, the Song of Songs is a collection of profane love songs that never even mention God. To justify its inclusion within the collection of biblical books, the Song had to be interpreted in an allegorical way and infused with religious meaning. According to R. Akiva, "the whole world is not as worthy as the day on which the Song of Songs was given to Israel; for all the writings are holy but the Song of Songs is the holy of holies" (m. Yad. 3:5). Even the earliest rabbinic interpretations of the Song of Songs say it refers to the relationship between God and Israel, starting with the covenant at Mount Sinai and the building

---

1 For details, see Flesher and Chilton, *Targums*.
2 Sperber, *Hagiographa*, adds the subtitle: "Transition from Translation to Midrash" and the note, "These texts are not Targum-texts but Midrash-texts in the disguise of Targum" (viii). But see also Alexander, "Translation."

of the temple (thus m. Ta'an. 4:8, based on Song 3:11; King Solomon, mentioned in this verse, is understood to be a reference to God). The text is therefore always connected with the biblical readings at Pesach. The targum takes up this tradition but expands it considerably and applies it systematically.

Unlike nearly all other targumim or earlier midrashim, Targum Song does not compile different traditions and sources in a more or less redacted form but impresses its fully coherent agenda on its historical interpretation of Song of Songs. It seems to be not the collective work of many rabbis over a long period of time but rather the work of an individual author, something new in rabbinic literature and a late phenomenon, most comparable to the equally late (eighth–ninth century) Seder Eliyahu Rabbah.[3]

The assignment of the targumists to the rabbinic movement is problematic in spite of many parallels between targumim and midrashim. But in the case of the author of Targum Songs, there is no doubt that he was highly familiar with rabbinic traditions; Philip Alexander even speaks of "such a learned Rabbinic work as Tg. Cant."[4] This does not necessarily mean that the author was formally a member of a rabbinic school, but he certainly was fairly close to such schools. Most of the ideas expressed in the targum have close parallels in rabbinic texts. They are frequently seen as dependent on rabbinic traditions, but the relationship is not so clear-cut. As Alexander insists, this approach views rabbinic tradition "essentially as a collection of finished literary works. This is problematic. Rabbinic tradition seems to have been in a very fluid state in late antiquity [. . . and] to a greater or lesser degree textually unstable."[5] This objection is certainly correct but should not be exaggerated.

---

[3] As Alexander, "Tradition," 336, states, "The exegetical schema is so clever and so consistently applied that it is reasonable to postulate behind it a single, creative mind. Here is, possibly, one early rabbinic text to which we can assign an author in the modern sense of the term." The designation of the targum as an "early rabbinic text" is problematic, but the claim of an individual author is certainly justified.

[4] Alexander, Targum, 9.

[5] Alexander, Targum, 39. See also 44–45, and idem, "Tradition," 321–330. Junkermann, "Relationship" (a doctoral thesis written under the guidance of Philip Alexander), offers a most detailed analysis of the parallels between Song of Songs Rabbah and Targum Song. As a result of her case studies, she insists time and again that "although most of the elements of the Targum can be found individually in the Midrash, some are absent, and the Targum's interpretation cannot be found anywhere as a unified exegetical package in the Midrash. It really strains credulity to suppose that so creative a homilist as the Targumist could only have created his Targum by cherry-picking among the options of the Midrash and so creating his strong, coherent reading of the biblical text" (159; cf. 166, 175, 221, 225–227). As she concludes a first summary, "The resemblances between the Targum and the Midrash are more readily explained by supposing that both belonged to the same broad Palestinian tradition of Bible interpretation in late antiquity, and are drawing on that, rather than directly on each other" (186). And again: "that relationship is misconceived if it is understood in

At the time of the creation of this targum, many rabbinic works already existed in a rather, though never fully, stable form.⁶ But even when authors had access to a written copy of a text, they used its ideas and standard phrases with considerable freedom. The extent of the library accessible to the author of the targum cannot be ascertained; he clearly did not produce a mere pastiche of rabbinic traditions but rather used them with great freedom.

Regarding the date of the targum, nearly all scholars agree on its redaction in the early Islamic period in Palestine. Some insist that it had many much earlier sources, going back at least to the early third century CE.⁷ That the author of the midrash used earlier texts and traditions is clear. But this does not really influence the question of dating. The proposed date is based mainly on its relationship to rabbinic traditions, hints of the situation at the time of its composition, and, above all, its language. Alexander, who proposes a date "around the eighth–ninth centuries C.E.,"⁸ regards the Aramaic of this targum as "a purely literary dialect [. . .] created by someone who knew Jewish literature in both eastern and western dialects as well as in the Targumic Aramaic of Onq[elos] and Jon[athan], and [who] was quite happy to combine for literary purposes elements drawn from all three of these dialectal groups."⁹ The main argument for a date of composition in the Islamic period is the collection of loanwords from Arabic, "a strong indication that our Targumist's vernacular was Arabic, as was that of his intended readership."¹⁰ The same time frame is supported by the very positive description of the Hasmoneans, who in classical rabbinic literature are ignored or, if mentioned, viewed rather critically (more on this later).

But these arguments, though widely accepted, have recently been contested, with good reason, by Andrew Litke. The targum's language is Jewish Literary Aramaic (mainly that of Onkelos and Pseudo-Jonathan), not Palestinian Aramaic. Since Onkelos was also studied in the western diaspora, this language was more universal and "opens up the distinct possibility that the Targum was composed

---

terms of literary dependency or literary borrowing by the Targum from the Midrash. Both are different crystallisations of exegesis on Song of Songs drawn from the vast reservoir of oral midrash on that biblical book which had collected in the Rabbinic schools in late antiquity" (231).

6 In favor of written midrashim at an early point (with the special example of Lam. Rab.), see Mandel, "Between Byzantium," 93; this applies especially in Palestine, whereas in Babylonia the same text might be transmitted orally and thus lead to a separate recension.

7 Thus, e.g., Loewe, "Apologetic Motifs," 167–168. Menn, "Thwarted Metaphors," 238, sees the targum as "composed in Palestine between the fifth to eighth centuries CE."

8 Alexander, *Targum*, 12, and in other publications.

9 Alexander, *Targum*, 10.

10 Alexander, *Targum*, 12.

outside of Palestine."[11] The uncontested Arabisms in the targum all occur in a list of gemstones in 5:14 in the western recension, which is most likely a later addition. The lack of more Arabisms is striking, especially if one assumes that Arabic was the native language of the targumist. The eschatology of the targum resembles formulations found in Saʿadia and might be drawn from this tenth-century thinker. The use of the late Latin word *olibanum* (with the Greek ending, *olibanon*) for "frankincense" in 4:11, "first attested in tenth- and eleventh-century manuscripts in Italy,"[12] might also hint at this time. The targum (and its popularity) may be connected with the incorporation of Song of Songs into the liturgy, which is not attested before chapters 10–21 of Massekhet Soferim, possibly composed in Byzantium or southern Italy.[13] These and other considerations lead Litke to consider the possibility that the author of Targum Song spoke Greek and lived in a diaspora community (perhaps Byzantium or southern Italy) in the tenth or eleventh century.[14] This alternative date and setting of Targum Song is worthy of serious consideration.

2 Targum Song of Songs and the History of Israel

Early rabbinic traditions saw the Song of Songs as alluding to an increasing number of events in biblical history.[15] Especially noteworthy is the Mekilta, with its many quotations of the Song, which it takes as references not only to Israel's redemption from Egypt in all its details and to the revelation at Sinai but also to the author's contemporary situation, as when, because of the description of the beloved in 5:10–16, the nations want to join Israel (6:1: "Which way has your beloved turned, that we may seek him with you?," a possible allusion to increased proselytism in the time of the Mekilta), an offer that Israel does not accept (6:3: "I am my beloved's and my beloved is mine"; Mek. Shirata 3). The primordial experience of redemption in the exodus also strengthens Israel's hope in the final redemption, the ingathering of the exiled Israelites from Lebanon and the Amana (4:8: "Come with me from Lebanon, my bride; come with me from Lebanon. Depart from the peak of Amana"), connecting the name Amana with faith (אֱמוּנָה, *'emunah*) in Moses, as stated in Exod 14:31: "Israel saw the great work that the Lord did against the Egyptians. So the people feared the Lord and believed (ויאמינו, *va-yaʾaminu*) in the Lord and in his servant

---

11 Litke, "Following the Frankincense," 292.
12 Litke, "Following the Frankincense," 306.
13 See Blank, "It's Time," 4–5.
14 See Litke, "Following the Frankincense," 307.
15 See Stemberger, "Midraschim zum Hohenlied."

Moses" (Mek. Beshallaḥ 7). Thus the events of the exodus are consistently read in connection to the Song of Songs.

The historical interpretation of the Song of Songs is greatly expanded in the classical midrashim. In Lev. Rab., the garden is understood as the garden of Eden and recalls the creation; many great persons in the biblical history—Abraham, Jacob, Elijah, David, Daniel—are discovered in the Song (Lev. Rab. 31.4 on Song 7:6). The Pesiqta de Rab Kahana goes even further: Pesiq. Rab Kah. 5 (parallel Pesiq. Rab. 15, and to a large extent also Song Rab. on Song 2:8–13) is a homily on Exod 12 for the Shabbat before or on the first day of Nisan. Song 2:10, "Arise, my love, my fair one, and come away," is taken in Pesiq. Rab Kah. 5.9 to refer to the "daughter of Abraham who made me beloved in the world, who made me fair, you daughter of Isaac who made My name fair throughout My world when his father bound him on the altar, and go away, you daughter of Jacob, he who hearkened to his father and his mother."[16] This connection to the history of the patriarchs, especially the reference to the Akedah—a topic traditionally connected with Pesach—became traditional. The interpretation of Song 2:10–13 begins with the redemption from Egypt, the forty years in the desert up to the settlement in the promised land, and the destruction of the Canaanites and leads up to the offering of the firstfruits in the temple. In a second round, these verses are connected to Daniel and Ezra and the end of the seventy years of the Babylonian exile. "The voice of the turtledove is heard in our land" (Song 2:12) becomes a reference to Cyrus, whom God has charged "to build him a house at Jerusalem in Judah" (Ezra 1:2)—a topic that also becomes traditional in later interpretations of the Song. A third round of interpretation connects these verses to Elijah, the messiah, and the final redemption.

This interpretation in the Pesiqta sees in the Song the whole of history, from the creation of the world up to the final redemption. Later interpretations, for example Song Rabbah, follow this general line and fill it in with many details, including postbiblical developments. Thus, Song Rabbah sees "the foxes, the little foxes, that ruin the vineyards" (2:15) as Esau, that is, Rome and its generals; "the cleft mountains" (הרי בתר, *harei bater*; 2:17) are understood as a reference to the battle for Betar during the Bar Kokhba revolt; Usha, the site of the new beginning of the rabbinic movement in the Galilee after the revolt in the 140s, is discovered in 2:5, "sustain me with raisins" (באשישות, *ba-'ashishot*).

Targum Songs takes up this line of interpretation. But unlike the authors of the earlier rabbinic literature, with which he was fully familiar, the targum's author does not limit this historical approach to the interpretation of a few verses within the Song of Songs but applies it to the whole text from beginning to end. This inten-

---

16 Translation from Braude and Kapstein, *Pĕsiḳta dĕ-Raḇ Kahăna*, 105, slightly adapted.

tion is already noticeable in the first lines of the targum, which begins with an enumeration of ten songs that were uttered in the world:[17] Adam uttered the first song when the Sabbath day came and protected him (Ps 92:1); second is the song sung by Moses and the Israelites at the Red Sea (Exod 15:1); third is the song of the Israelites when the well of water was given to them (Num 21:17); the fourth song is the song of Moses before his death (Deut 32:1); and the fifth song is that of Joshua during his war with Gibeon (Josh 10:12). These songs are followed by the song of Barak and Deborah after the victory over Sisera (Judg 5:1), the song of Hannah (1Sam 2:1), and those of David (2Sam 22:1) and Solomon (Song of Songs). The final song is that of the exiles when they return from their places of exile, as depicted by Isaiah (Isa 30:19). All these songs are biblical and thus limited to biblical history up to David, preceded by Adam and the creation; but they are opened up to later history in the targum's interpretation of the Song and to final redemption in the quotation from Isaiah.

This enumeration of biblical songs at the beginning of the targum introduces one of its basic ideas: Israel's history is the key to understanding the Song of Songs. But the beginning, with Adam, is not taken up again in the targum, and, above all, this list does not give the slightest idea how the targumist will draw out Israel's history in his interpretation, most of all its postbiblical developments. As Philip Alexander understands the text,

> The Targumist offers a strikingly coherent reading of Canticles. [...] His distinctive contribution was to read the Song *systematically* as a cryptic *history* of that relationship [an allegory of God's relationship with Israel], starting with the Exodus from Egypt and concluding with the Messianic Age. [...] He divides the long history of Israel into three great periods, each of which begins with an exile, leads to an exodus, and culminates in an occupation of the Land, the building of the Temple, the establishment of the monarchy, and the abiding of the Shekhinah in the midst of the people. [...] Thus the history of Israel is seen as following the pattern of estrangement from God, reconciliation, and communion—three exiles (Egypt, Babylon, and Edom), three exodusses (under Moses, Cyrus, and the Messiah), culminating in three Jewish States (under Solomon, the Hasmoneans, and the Messiah).[18]

The approach of Targum Song is exceptional not only in its coherent and continuous reading of Israel's history in the Song of Songs but also in its integration of the history of the Hasmoneans, which most earlier rabbinic literature had passed

---

17 The midrash on the ten songs has a long prehistory, starting with Mek. Shirata 1. See Brady, "Use of Eschatological Lists," 497–504; Alexander, *Targum*, 206–209. As Brady, "Use of Eschatological Lists," 496, remarks, comparable lists occur in Tg. Ruth and Tg. Esth. II: "Each of these three lists is characterized by the fact that (1) they include ten items; (2) each end[s] with an eschatological figure/event; and (3) each list serves as a prologue to the Targum in question."
18 Alexander, *Targum*, 13.

over in silence. Rabbinic texts dealing with John Hyrcanus, Alexander Jannaeus, Hyrcanus II, and Aristobulus II or Mariamne are more frequent; but references to Hashmonay (as proper name of an individual) or the collective Hasmoneans (בני/בית חשמוני, *bnei/beit hashmoni*) are extremely rare in early texts (only once in the Mishnah, never in the Tosefta or in the halakhic midrashim); only in the Babylonian Talmud and in Megillat Antiokhos are they mentioned frequently. This late additional information may have come from increased contact with Arabs and Christians in Babylonia in the late Sasanian and early Islamic periods, when many originally Jewish traditions came home again, and even more so in the eighth and ninth centuries, when Baghdad's climate was one of discussion and exchange among the different religious communities. This late historical context may explain the sudden importance of the Hasmoneans in Targum Song.[19] Even more astonishing, when compared to earlier rabbinic texts, is the absolutely positive picture of the Hasmoneans:

> As for the royal house of the Hasmoneans, all of them are full of commandments like a pomegranate, let alone Matitiah the High Priest and his sons, who are righteous and maintain the commandments and words of the Torah with yearning.
>
> Then the Greeks arose and gathered sixty kings from the sons of Esau. Clad in chainmail, they rode on horses as horsemen, in addition to eighty rulers from the sons of Ishmael who ride on elephants, let alone the rest of the countless peoples, nations, and tongues. They appointed the wicked Alexander over them as leader, and he came to wage war with Jerusalem.
>
> At that time, the congregation of Israel (who is compared to a perfect dove) was wholeheartedly worshipping her Lord, seizing the Torah, and wholeheartedly studying the words of the Torah. Her merits were as pure as the day she went out from Egypt. It was then that the Hasmoneans, Matitiah, and all the people of Israel went out and waged war against them. And the Lord delivered them into their hands. (Targum Song 6:7–9)[20]

The Hasmoneans are idealized as being "full of commandments like a pomegranate, let alone Matitiah the High Priest and his sons, who are righteous and maintain the commandments and words of the Torah with yearning" (6:7), a description that hardly fits the image of the Hasmoneans in the books of Maccabees, Josephus, or earlier rabbinic texts.[21] Their complete adherence to the words of the Torah will be a subject of the next section.

---

19 See Stemberger, "Maccabees." Alexander, "From Poetry," 112–121, offers a detailed evaluation of the Maccabees in Targum Song. The appendix (126–128) lists the major references to the Hasmoneans in Talmud and midrash, including references to individual members of the dynasty.
20 Translation from Litke, *Targum Song*, 265, 267.
21 For Alexander, "From Poetry," 115, "The positive evaluation of the Hasmoneans may in part be dictated by the Targumist's scheme of history. He needed a climax to his second exodus, the exodus

3 The Study of Torah

It is generally recognized that besides the history of Israel, the dominant theme within Targum Song of Songs is the study of the Torah, including all its institutions. This topic is introduced at the very beginning of the targum:

> Solomon the prophet said: "Blessed be the name of the Lord who gave us the Torah at the hands of Moses, the Great Scribe, [both the Torah] written on the two tablets of stone, and the Six Orders of the Mishnah and Talmud by oral tradition, and [who] spoke with us face to face as a man kisses his friend, out of the abundance of the love wherewith He loved us more than the seventy nations." (Targum Song 1:2)[22]

Thus, God has given Israel both the written Torah on the two tablets and the Oral Torah in the form of the six orders of the Mishnah and its elaboration in the Talmud at the hands of Moses; both have coexisted since Sinai and are equally God's word, transmitted by the kisses of his mouth (Song 1:2). Mishnah and Talmud are not later traditions that should be done away with in order to return to the pure message of the biblical text, as claimed by critics of the rabbinic movement since at least the eighth century, a group that later emerged as the schismatic Karaites. Rather, these traditions are as old and as valid as the written Torah and distinguish Israel from the nations of the world, Christians as well as Muslims. These claims are at the core of the rabbinic movement. To proclaim them right after the enumeration of the ten songs that form the proem of the targum is a programmatic statement: the Song of Songs expresses rabbinic teachings and values. Both expressions of the Torah, written and oral, are not only given by God to Israel; God himself still studies them day and night in the presence of ten thousand angels:

> Then Israel began to speak in praise of the Sovereign of the World, and thus she said: "My pleasure is to worship that God who, wrapped by day in a robe as white as snow, engages in [the study of] the Twenty Four Books [comprising] the Torah, the words of the Prophets, and the Writings, and [who] by night engages in [the study of] the Six Orders of the Mishnah, and the radiance of the glory of whose face shines like fire on account of the greatness of the wisdom and reasoning with which He discloses new meanings all day long; and He will publish these to His people on the great day." And His banner [waves] over ten thousand times ten thousand angels who serve before Him. (Targum Song 5:10)

This is found in Song 5:10: "My beloved is all radiant and ruddy, distinguished among ten thousand." *Radiant* is connected to the white robe in which God is clad

---

from Babylon, which completely reversed the conditions of exile and led to the re-establishment of statehood and Temple. This could only have come with the Hasmoneans."

22 Translation here and in the following taken from Alexander, *Targum*.

when studying by day, comparable to the robe of the rabbinic scholar; *ruddy* is the glowing fire at night. God thus gives an example to the rabbinic scholar who is also supposed to study the Torah day and night, based on Josh 1:8: "This book of the law shall not depart out of your mouth; you shall meditate on it day and night." In the same way as the rabbis, God discloses new meanings in the Torah; the rabbis in their activity are the perfect counterpart of God and his company in heaven; there is no need for more justification.[23]

Tha targum understands Song 1:7, "Tell me, you whom my soul loves, where you pasture your flock," as Moses's question to God at the point of his death, asking how Israel will be sustained in spite of her sins. The answer is found in Song 1:8, "Pasture your kids beside the shepherds' tents":

> Let her walk in the ways of the righteous, let her order her prayer on the instructions of the leaders and guides of her generation, and let her teach her sons, who are likened to the kids of goats, to go to the synagogue and house of study and in virtue of this they will be provided for in exile, until I send them the King Messiah. (Targum Song 1:8)

In the time of exile, before the coming of the messiah, Israel will survive by virtue of the synagogue and the house of study, under the guidance of the leaders of the generation, clearly understood as the heads of the rabbinic movement. Israel thus continues its way of life under Moses, as Song 3:4 is understood: "Scarcely had I passed them, when I found him whom my soul loves. I held him, and would not let him go until I brought him into my mother's house, and into the chamber of her that conceived me." The targum reads:

> Scarcely a moment passed before the Lord turned from His fierce anger and commanded Moses the prophet to make the Tent of Meeting and the Ark, and He caused His Shekhinah to dwell therein. And the people of Israel were bringing their offerings and engaging in the study of the words of the Torah in the chamber of the house of study of Moses their teacher and in the room of Joshua son of Nun, his minister. (Targum Song 3:4)

"My mother's house" is the tent of meeting, where the Israelites bring their offerings, but its equivalent is also "the house of study of Moses their teacher" and that of Joshua, his successor. In the targum Moses is mainly Moshe Rabbenu (thus again

---

[23] Parts and variants of this presentation may be found in rabbinic texts. The closest parallel is the equally late Midr. Ps. 19:7: "And from where [do we know] that the Holy One, Blessed be He, is occupied with Scripture by day and with Mishnah by night? For it is written: 'My beloved is all radiant and ruddy.' When he occupies himself with Scripture by day, his face is bright as snow. And 'my beloved' (דודי [*dodi*]) means nothing but the 24 books [of Scripture], since in gematria דודי is 24. And when he occupies himself with Mishnah by night, his face is red." For more rabbinic parallels, see Alexander, *Targum*, 155–156.

in 3:7), who teaches Torah in his *beit midrash* (house of study) and is succeeded by Joshua, starting the chain of tradition leading up to the rabbis in the time of the targum. The first passage through history concludes with the dedication of Solomon's Temple, which the targum sees in Song 4:1, "How beautiful you are, my love, how very beautiful!" But this beauty is eclipsed by that of the sages of the Sanhedrin who teach Israel, whom the targum finds in the same verse, "Your eyes are doves behind your veil":

> On the day that King Solomon offered up a thousand burnt offerings on the altar [...], a *bat qol* [divine voice] went forth from the heavens and thus said: "How beautiful are you, Assembly of Israel, and how beautiful are the leaders of the assembly and the Sages sitting in the Sanhedrin, who enlighten the people of the House of Israel, and [who are] like fledglings, the young of the dove." (Targum Song 4:1)

Priests and Levites are praised, especially the high priest with his prayer (not sacrifices!) on the Day of Atonement (Targum Song 4:2–3); but these again are outshone by the (rabbinic) academy. "Your neck is like the tower of David, built in courses; on it hang a thousand bucklers, all of them shields of warriors" (4:4) is thus understood:

> The Head of the College, who is your teacher, is as strong in meritorious acts and as great in good deeds as was David, King of Israel. Upon the utterance of his mouth the world was built, and on the teaching of the Torah, in which he was engaged, the people of the House of Israel were depending, and [through it] they were victorious in battle as if they were holding in their hands all kinds of weapons of the warriors. (Targum Song 4:4)

The head of the college (ריש מתיבתא, *resh metivta*) appears in the Babylonian Talmud, but there it is a function—the rabbi who presides at a meeting of study (e.g., b. Nid. 14b); only in the Islamic period does it become a title, conferred upon the leading teacher in the geonic academy for life, unless he is promoted to the highest rank of gaon. This is clearly the understanding of the targum, which thus compares the head of the college of its time with David; the people of Israel depend on his teaching—no small praise for the leading teaching institution of his time.

Song 5:2 ("I slept") introduces the targum's second pass through history, when Nebuchadnezzar led Israel into exile. "While in exile, they were like a sleeping man." But: "Listen! my beloved is knocking" (Song 5:2)—the prophets and God himself successfully tried to awaken Israel and "went down to Babylon, to the Sanhedrin of the Sages" (Targum Song 5:2). Israel again engages in the study of Bible and Mishnah (Targum Song 5:12), God frees them from their exile under the direction of Cyrus (Targum Song 6:2), and the temple is rebuilt. And again not only is the temple praised (Targum Song 6:4), but even more so is the study of the Torah:

> Cause your teachers, the Sages of the Great Assembly, to sit round in a circle before Me, for they acknowledged My kingship, in exile, and instituted the school for the teaching of My

Torah. And the rest of your students and the people of the land proclaimed Me as just through the word of their mouth, like the sons of Jacob, who gathered stones and raised a monument on Mount Gilead. (Targum Song 6:5)

The men of the Great Assembly (or Great Synagogue), in rabbinic thought, are the bridge from the biblical to the proto-rabbinic period of Simeon the Righteous and the Five Pairs; last among them are Ezra and Nehemiah, the founders of the new community in Jerusalem. Israel shows itself worthy of its regained freedom: "At that time the Assembly of Israel, which is likened to the perfect dove, was worshipping the Sovereign of the World with one heart, and was devoted to the Torah and engaging in the study of the words of the Torah with a perfect heart" (Targum Song 6:9). And because God saw "that they were righteous and were engaging in [the study of] the Torah, the Lord said through His Word: 'I will not again crush them'" (Targum Song 6:12).

The author of the targum finds the situation of his own time (or what he wishes it were) in Song 7:2: "Your navel is a rounded bowl that never lacks mixed wine. Your belly is a heap of wheat, encircled with lilies." It symbolizes "the Head of your College through whose merit all the world is sustained, just as the fetus is sustained through its navel in the belly of its mother." He knows how "to pronounce pure or impure, innocent or guilty, and the words of the Torah never fail [to flow] from his mouth. [. . .] Seventy Sages surround him, like a round threshing-floor" (Targum Song 7:2). The head of the college, surrounded by the Sanhedrin, sees his treasuries

> full of the holy tithes, votive and freewill offerings, which Ezra the priest, Zerubbabel, Jeshua, Nehemiah, and Mordechai Bilshan, the Men of the Great Assembly, who are compared to roses, ordained for their benefit, so that they might be enabled to engage in the study of the Torah day and night. (Targum Song 7:3)

Early in rabbinic history, the rabbis already regarded their studies as the replacement of the temple sacrifices that were no longer possible. They therefore claimed the priestly gifts, tithes, and freewill offerings as their own. This was, to a great extent, wishful thinking. In the Islamic period this claim was renewed, with greater success, although the geonic schools to a great extent still depended on the contributions of the diaspora. To underline this claim, the author of the targum states that Ezra and Nehemiah, in the time of the Second Temple, had already transferred these gifts to the rabbinic schools.

The study of the Torah will also be central in messianic times. "Let us go out early to the vineyards, and see whether the vines have budded" (Song 7:13), in the understanding of the targum, means that Israel rises early to search the Torah to see whether the time for the redemption has come. "The mandrakes give forth fragrance, and over our doors are all choice fruits, new as well as old, which I have laid up for you" (Song 7:14) the targum reads as God's words to the King Messiah:

> The term of the exile is already completed, and the merit of the righteous has become as fragrant before Me as the scent of balsam. The Sages of the generation are fixed at the doors of the schools, diligently studying the words of the Scribes and the words of the Torah. Arise now, and receive the kingdom that I have stored up for you. (Targum Song 7:14)

The targum interprets Song 8:1—"O that you were like a brother to me, who nursed at my mother's breast! If I met you outside, I would kiss you, and no one would despise me"—as addressed to the King Messiah as well:

> Come, be a brother to us, and let us go up to Jerusalem and suck out with you the reasons for the Torah, just as an infant sucks at the breast of its mother. For all the time that I was wandering outside my land, when I was mindful of the Name of the Great God and gave up my life for His divinity, even the nations of the earth did not despise me. (Targum Song 8:1)

Even in the diaspora ("outside"), Israel openly confessed her faith in God, and the nations did not despise her. But now the messiah should join Israel in Jerusalem in the study of the reasons of the Torah; this study has not ended with redemption. "O you who dwell in the gardens, my companions are listening for your voice; let me hear it" (Song 8:13) is understood to be God's words to Israel at the end of days:

> You, Assembly of Israel, who are likened to a little garden among the nations, and [who] sit in the House of Study with the members of the Sanhedrin, and with the rest of the people, who listen to the voice of the Head of the College, and learn from his mouth the teachings of the Torah, cause Me to hear the sound of your words, when you sit to acquit and to condemn, and I will approve all that you do. (Targum Song 8:13)

Even now, at the end of days, Israel is still sitting in the house of study, led by the Sanhedrin and the head of the college. The rabbinic institutions endure; their legal decisions are still valid, now openly approved by God, who listens to their voice.

Let us conclude: whoever reads the Song of Songs without preconceived ideas will never arrive at an understanding of the text at all comparable to that of the targum. But the rabbis and the authors of the targumim did not read the Song of Songs in the plain sense. Being part of the Bible, it must have religious meaning. For Jews, it is the relationship between God and Israel in the course of history; rabbinic Jews also discover in it their highest religious values, high up among them the study of Torah. This was also the approach of the targum. What distinguishes its author from all earlier rabbinic readings of the text is the fully consistent reading of it—understanding the Song of Songs, from beginning to end, as the presentation of Israel's history from creation to final redemption, dominated by the ideal of the study of Torah under its rabbinic institutions, the head of the college, the Sanhedrin, and the house of study. Once the premises of this reading are accepted, one cannot but admire the targum as fully successful in its enterprise.

Bibliography

Alexander, Philip S. "From Poetry to Historiography: The Image of the Hasmoneans in Targum Canticles and the Question of the Targum's Provenance and Date." *JSP* 19 (1999): 103–128.

Alexander, Philip S. *The Targum of Canticles: Translated, with a Critical Introduction, Apparatus, and Notes.* ArBib 17A. Collegeville, MN: Liturgical Press, 2003.

Alexander, Philip S. "Tradition and Originality in the Targum of the Song of Songs." In *The Aramaic Bible: Targums in their Historical Contexts*, edited by Derek R. G. Beatty and Martin McNamara, 318–339. JSOTSup 166. Sheffield: JSOT Press, 1994.

Alexander, Philip S. "'Translation and Midrash Completely Fused Together'? The Form of the Targums to Canticles, Lamentations and Qohelet." *AS* 9 (2011): 83–99.

Blank, Debra Reed. "It's Time to Take Another Look at 'Our Little Sister' Soferim: A Bibliographical Essay." *JQR* 90 (1999–2000): 1–26.

Brady, Christian M. M. "The Use of Eschatological Lists within the Targumim of the Megilloth." *JSJ* 40 (2009): 493–509.

Braude, William G., and Israel G. Kapstein. *Pĕsikṭa dĕ-Raḇ Kahăna: R. Kahana's Compilation of Discourses for Sabbaths and Festal Days.* Philadelphia: Jewish Publication Society of America, 1975.

Flesher, Paul, Virgil McCracken, and Bruce Chilton. *The Targums: A Critical Introduction.* Leiden: Brill, 2011.

Junkermann, Penelope Robin. "The Relationship between Targum Song of Songs and Midrash Rabbah Song of Songs." PhD diss., Manchester, 2010.

Litke, Andrew W. "Following the Frankincense: Reassessing the Sitz im Leben of Targum Song of Songs." *JSP* 27 (2018): 289–313.

Litke, Andrew W. *Targum Song of Songs and Late Jewish Literary Aramaic: Language, Lexicon, Text, and Translation.* Supplements to Aramaic Studies 15. Leiden: Brill, 2019.

Loewe, Raphael. "Apologetic Motifs in the Targum to the Song of Songs." In *Biblical Motifs: Origins and Transformations*, edited by Alexander Altmann, 159–196. STLI 3. Cambridge, MA: Harvard University Press, 1966.

Mandel, Paul D. "Between Byzantium and Islam: The Transmission of a Jewish Book in the Byzantine and Early Islamic Periods." In *Transmitting Jewish Traditions: Orality, Textuality and Cultural Diffusion*, edited by Yaakov Elman and Israel Gershoni, 74–106. New Haven: Yale University Press, 2000.

Menn, Esther M. "Thwarted Metaphors: Complicating the Language of Desire in the Targum of the Song of Songs." *JSJ* 34 (2003): 237–273.

Sperber, Alexander. *The Hagiographa: Transition from Translation to Midrash.* Vol. 4A of *The Bible in Aramaic*. Leiden: Brill, 1968.

Stemberger, Günter. "Midraschim zum Hohenlied und Geschichte Israels." In idem, *Judaica Minora, I: Biblische Traditionen im rabbinischen Judentum*, 248–255. TSAJ 133. Tübingen: Mohr Siebeck, 2010.

Stemberger, Günter. "The Maccabees in Rabbinic Tradition." In idem, *Judaica Minora, I: Biblische Traditionen im rabbinischen Judentum*, 256–265. TSAJ 133. Tübingen: Mohr Siebeck, 2010.

Elliot R. Wolfson
Do Not Wake or Arouse Love
Erotics of Time and the Dream of Messianic Waiting

> Oh, sister, when I come to knock on your door
> Don't turn away, you'll create sorrow
> Time is an ocean but it ends at the shore
> You may not see me tomorrow
>   Bob Dylan, "Oh, Sister"

According to a passage attributed to Saadiah Gaon, "Know, my brother, that you will find great differences in interpretation of the Song of Songs. In truth they differ because the Song of Songs resembles locks to which the keys have been lost."[1] The simplicity of comparing a text to a series of locks for which the keys have been misplaced might prevent one from pondering the depth of insight expressed by this image. Multivocality is understood as a consequence of the fact that the meaning of the text is no longer retrievable and not because there is no such meaning. The hermeneutical ambiguity is bolstered by the historical record of Jews and Christians through the centuries cultivating an abiding exegetical interest in the Song. Prima facie, this claim seems trivial as it could be made for other books in the scriptural canon. And yet, ironically enough, the one book that, at least when read according to its contextual sense, is lacking any allusion to the *Heilsgeschichte* of the people of Israel has been allocated an inordinate religious significance.

It would not be an exaggeration to say that the reading of the Song served as one of the most important channels in which the virulent exchanges between the two faiths were enacted. Inasmuch as clerical authorities and lay practitioners in both liturgical communities steadfastly maintained the covenantal privilege of being the special recipient of divine love, it was only natural that commentaries and sermons on the Song would act as a prism to refract theological controversies, debates, and disagreements. As one might expect, however, the polemical element was apt to enhance the intrigue of the other and thereby increase the possibility of mutual influence.

In this article, I will focus on the erotics of time and the deferment of the messianic redemption, as signposts that simultaneously mark the point of divergence within the convergence of the divergent and the point of convergence within the divergence of the convergent. The specific topics explored in this article lend cre-

---

[1] Cited in Pope, *Song of Songs*, 89.

dence to the larger claim that the condemnation of the other bespeaks contiguity with the other, and this is so even when the other has preached intolerance or perpetrated violence in the socio-political arena.[2]

1 Iconographic Text, Envisioning the Invisible, and Allegorizing the Erotic

There are a variety of literary settings in which the ideal of spiritual eroticism has found expression, but one medium that has been especially significant in the history of Judaism and Christianity is the commentarial tradition on the Song of Songs, the biblical book that most overtly employs tropes of conjugal love and carnal sexuality.[3] As Bernard McGinn astutely articulated the matter,

> Among the many intimate bonds between Jewish and Christian mystical traditions none is more important than the fact that both found in the Song the mystical text par excellence. For Jews and Christians, the Song was not some excuse for the surreptitious use of forbidden motifs, but was the authorized model that guided their personal appropriation of the divine-human encounter.[4]

From the formative period when rabbinic Judaism and Christianity evolved as distinct faith communities, the Song presented a unique hermeneutical problem: how does one interpret the exclusively sensual language of a book canonized as part of sacred Scripture?

Early rabbinic interpreters, as their Christian counterparts, adopted exegetical strategies to deal with the challenge of infusing a work that on the surface is not about God, Israel, or the covenantal bond between them, with hallowed meaning. One strategy formulated in the rabbinic academies was the allegorical approach, to interpret the erotic imagery of the earthly lover and beloved as a reference to the relationship between God and Israel. This is the orientation that is most frequently mentioned in conjunction with the rabbis, but it must be noted that the exegetical comments on the Song scattered in literature of both the tannaitic and the

---

[2] See the section "Setting of Boundary and the Proximity of the Other," in Wolfson, "Textual Flesh," 190–194.
[3] For a more extensive discussion, see Wolfson, *Language, Eros, Being*, 334–345. I have taken the liberty to repeat some of my analysis here. The sacred nature of the literal sense of the erotic language in the Song of Songs has been pursued by a number of other scholars. For instance, see Walsh, *Exquisite Desire*; Carr, *Erotic Word*, 109–151.
[4] McGinn, "Language of Love," 217. See, more recently, Stern, "Ancient Jewish Interpretation"; Pardes, *Song of Songs*, 22–58.

amoraic periods indicates that the rabbinic reading was not uniform or monolithic. On the contrary, even the main metaphorical explanation adopted by the rabbis splintered into smaller symbolic applications that do not add up to one coherent picture, although each is centered on locating the utterance of the poem at a particular moment in Israel's sacred history. The correlation of the Song and the historical narrative, beginning with creation and ending with messianic redemption, is implicit in some of the rabbinic pericopae[5] but fully developed in the Aramaic Targum.[6] We can thus distinguish two main types of allegorical approach, one that relates more generally to the relationship of God and Israel and the other that relates more specifically to the historical highlights of the Jewish people from creation to redemption.

In both cases, for the rabbinic exegetes, in contrast to their Patristic counterparts, the internal meaning of the Song is not predicated on undermining the external form of the scriptural metaphor.[7] On the contrary, the allegoresis intended by the midrashic reading is an intensification of the literal carnality and the consequent application of erotic imagery to the divine.[8] To underline the point, let me note the observation of André LaCoque,

> a thoroughgoing allegorization of the text obliterates eros in favor of an altogether disincarnate agape. From the second century CE, the book has traditionally been read [. . .] as an allegory of the mutual quest for God and humanity. By this means, the female author is dispossessed of her property, which becomes the possession of scribes, sages, and church fathers.[9]

I am uncertain about the contention that the alleged female author of the Song divested herself of her femininity, but of greater concern is the claim regarding the

---

[5] See Kaplan, *My Perfect One*, 47–93.
[6] See Alexander, *Targum of Canticles*, 1–71, esp. 13–26. See also the detailed literary-textual analysis in Junkermann, "Relationship." For a more nuanced analysis of the role of gender roles in the Targumic interpretation, see Menn, "Thwarted Metaphors."
[7] My approach can be compared profitably to the hypothesis of Landy, *Paradoxes of Paradise*. For discussion of the metaphorical import of the literal sense of the biblical text, see Hendel, "Life of Metaphor." On metaphor and intertextuality, see LaCoque, *Romance*, 24–33.
[8] See Kaplan, "Song of Songs from the Bible"; idem, *My Perfect One*, 15–45.
[9] LaCoque, "I Am Black and Beautiful," 163. On the gender identification of the author of the Song of Songs as female, see LaCoque, *Romance*, 16–23, 39–53, and especially the interpretation of the repeated oath not to rouse love on 64: "The composer of the Canticle did not make it her business to praise the chaste love between Israel and her God or between Israel and Wisdom personified. [. . .] What the poet is doing here is shedding her societal chains; she is shouting her freedom from gender stereotypes. She is daringly mocking consecrated definitions and formulas." See also the collection of studies in Brenner and Fontaine, eds., *Song of Songs*.

disincarnate agape as it applies to the rabbinic sages.[10] On the contrary, the allegorization of the text embraced by the rabbis amplified the tangibility of the eroticism based on their perception that the allegorical nature of eros is specularized through the erotic nature of allegory.[11] Such a thematic reciprocity reinforces one of the more striking and influential ideas promulgated by the metaphorical reading of the Song, to wit, the assumption that this collection of poems is equivalent to the Torah in its entirety.[12] It appears that some rabbinic sages reacted to Origen's claim that Christians had been granted direct revelation in contrast to Jews who must rely on mediators. Consider the following passage from Song of Songs Rabbah:

> R. Azariah and R. Judah bar R. Simon said in the name of R. Joshua ben Levi [...] It is written, "Moses commanded us the Torah" [Deut 33:4]. In the entire Torah there are 613 commandments. The numerical value of the letters [in the word] Torah is 611. These are the commandments that Moses spoke to us. However, "I am [the Lord your God]" and "You will not have [other gods besides me]" [Exod 20:1–2] we have not heard from the mouth of Moses but from the mouth of the holy One, blessed be he. That is [the meaning of the verse] "O that you would kiss me with the kisses of your mouth" [Song 1:2].[13]

The kiss of the Song alludes to the direct revelation of God to Israel, but this is not a onetime event in the rabbinic mentality. Every time the text is studied and interpreted, it is as if it were revealed anew. The rabbinic understanding of an ongoing revelation, which unfolds through an unbroken chain of interpretation, is not based on a static conception of the eternity of Torah set in opposition to time and therefore resistant to the fluctuation of historical contingency. Rather, it is grounded in a conception of temporality that calls into question the linear model of aligning events chronoscopically in a sequence stretched invariably between before and after. The rabbinic hermeneutic champions a notion of time that is circular in its linearity and linear in its circularity.[14] The study of Torah, accordingly, demands that one be able to imagine each day, indeed each moment of each day, as an occasion for the novel recurrence of the Sinaitic theophany.

---

[10] A formulation that is closer to my own position is offered by the apposition of the naturalist and the mystical interpretations of the Song in LaCoque, *Romance*, 6–15.

[11] On the role of metaphor and rethinking the allegorical-literal nexus, see Pardes, *Song*, 3–21.

[12] This idea was exploited by the medieval kabbalists for whom the equation of Torah and the Song is related to their reading the latter as the drama of the *hieros gamos* in the divine realm. See Green, "Shekhinah"; idem, "Song of Songs in Early Jewish Mysticism"; idem, "Intradivine Romance"; Wolfson, *Language*, 351–371; Devine, "Active/Passive." This is not the place to respond to Devine's claim that the zoharic authors echoed the depatriarchalizing themes of the biblical text, but suffice it to say that it is based on very questionable interpretations of the zoharic material.

[13] Song Rabbah 1:13 (Dunasky, ed., 13).

[14] See Wolfson, *Alef, Mem, Tau*, 55–117, esp. 58–59, 63–65; revised version in Wolfson, *Suffering Time*, 72–253, esp. 87–89, 117–119.

I surmise that the nexus between the Sinaitic revelation and the Song is the underlying meaning of the oft-cited remark attributed to Aqiva *kol ha-ketuvim qodesh we-shir ha-shirim qodesh qodashim*, "all of the writings are holy, but the Song of Songs is the holy of holies" (m. Yad. 3:5). That is, just as the sanctity of the holy of holies outweighs the sanctity of all other holy places, so the Song is the most sacrosanct book of holy writ, for it encapsulates the holiness of the entire canon. The Song is thus the inner sanctum wherein lay the measure of holiness that delineates the parameters of sanctified space. Here it is worth noting the Islamic tradition, "The entire Koran is a symbolic, allusive (*ramz*) story, between the Lover and the Beloved, and no one except the two of them understands the truth or reality of its intention," and the interpretation offered by Henry Corbin: "Clearly the entire 'science of the heart' and all the creativity of the heart are needed to set in motion the *ta'wîl*, the mystic interpretation which makes it possible to read and to practice the Koran as though it were a variant of the Song of Songs."[15] As it happens, from the scholar of Islamic esotericism we can deduce a fundamental tenet of the rabbinic approach to the Song of Songs: the erotic drama divulges the paradoxical juxtaposition that characterizes the mystery of revelation, the unconcealing of the concealment that is the concealing of the unconcealment, the breach in time, the historical irruption, that tears away the cloak of the unhidden conserved in its hiddenness. The point is made poignantly in another comment attributed to Aqiva in the midrashic anthology Shir ha-Shirim Zuta, which is linked exegetically to the opening verse, "The Song of Songs by Solomon" (Song 1:1): "This is to teach you that all the wisdom of Solomon was equal to the Torah. R. Aqiva said, Had the Torah not been given, the Song of Songs would have been sufficient to guide the world."[16] The notion that this biblical book is commensurate to the entire Torah no doubt underlies as well the opinion of the rabbis who located the utterance of the Song at Sinai.[17] Recitation of the poem, which expresses figuratively the love between God and Israel, occurred when the divine glory was revealed in the giving of the Torah.

---

15 Corbin, *Creative Imagination*, 251.
16 Schechter, ed., *Agadath Shir Hashirim*, 5. The original Hebrew of this passage is somewhat enigmatic, *illu lo nitnah ba-torah shir ha-shirim keda'y hayyetah linhog et ha-olam*. My rendering presumes that the word *ba-torah* is a corruption of *ha-torah*, a reading that is confirmed by the passage cited by the thirteenth-century kabbalist, Isaac Ibn Sahula, in his commentary on the Song, which is mentioned by Schechter, ed., *Agadath Shir Hashirim*, 49. See also Lieberman, *Midreshei Teiman*, 14 n. 1. Lieberman suggests that the correct reading is *illu lo nitnah ba-torah ela shir ha-shirim*, which should be translated as "Had nothing been given in the Torah except for the Song of Songs."
17 For the various spatial and temporal locations for the utterance of the Song, see Song Rabbah 1:12 (Dunasky, ed., 12). See Lieberman, "Mishnath Shir ha-Shirim," 118–121. The influence of this rabbinic tradition is reflected, for instance, in the liturgical poem for Pentecost composed by Eleazar bi-R. Qillir, which is organized around verses from the Song. See Elizur, "New Findings."

To locate the narration of the Song at the Sinaitic epiphany underscores the fact that the moment that the Torah was revealed to Israel is itself erotically charged. This can be explained in terms of the prevalent depiction of the epiphany at Sinai in matrimonial language,[18] but it also embraces the more esoteric claim that the Torah as revealed word entails the structure of the parable from which we can infer the paradox of metaphorical representation basic to the dynamic of eros with its disclosure of reality through the appearance of image, the uncovering of truth through the covering of untruth.

Treating the Song as inherently parabolic, and comparing it to all of Torah, opens up the possibility that one can meaningfully posit that speech—the linguistic gesture that may be expressed as verbal gesticulation, graphic inscription, or mental avowal of word-signs—has a threshold, but semiosis—the interpretation of those signs—is infinite. The text of the Song, as the Torah more generally, conceals what it reveals in the revelation of what it conceals; that is, if the truth is invisible, it can be disclosed only to the extent that it is occluded in its unveiling. Insofar as the Torah, the primordial parable or the parable of the primordial, is the image of that which has no image, it points to the convergence of the literal and the figurative: what is literally true is the figuration of that which has no figure, the icon of the invisible, and thus human beings do not have the ability to grasp the actual divested of the metaphorical veneer. Following the suggestion of Ellen F. Davis, I would say that the Song can be read iconographically.[19] Just as the icon, especially as it has functioned in Eastern Orthodox Christianity, is the sensible portal through which the worshipper gains entry to the transcendent realm, the biblical book is the holy of holies in and through which one envisions the invisible in its invisibility.[20]

The iconographic text imparts that the impossibility of presence, the rallying call of postmodern hermeneutics, is inseparable from the impossibility of absence inasmuch as there cannot not be presence but in the presence of absence in the manner that there cannot not be absence but in the absence of presence. Rather than viewing the spatio-temporal world as illusionary, it should be seen as allusive: the corporeal points to the spiritual in a way that is analogous to the claim that the esoteric meaning of the scriptural text is accessible only through the guise

---

18 See Wolfson, *Circle in the Square*, 4–7.
19 See Davis, "Reading the Song Iconographically."
20 According to Davis, implicit in the description of the Song of Songs as the inner sanctuary of the Temple is the correlation of the latter and the Garden of Eden. See Davis, "Reading the Song Iconographically," 178–179. The pioneering essay that emphasized the connection of the Song of Songs and the narrative about Eden in the third chapter of Genesis is Trible, "Depatriarchalizing." See also Landy, "Song of Songs and the Garden of Eden"; idem, *Paradoxes of Paradise*; Davidson, "Theology of Sexuality"; Walsh, *Exquisite Desire*, 148–154.

of the exoteric meaning. The internal light is seen through the external garment and not by discarding it.[21] Needless to say, appreciating this point has an impact on how we assess the relationship of the literal to the figurative. The notion of the symbolic nature of language, and the further assumption regarding the linguistic nature of reality, raise the possibility of a hermeneutic buttressed by an alternative conception of temporality, one that would not necessarily privilege a linear conception of time that imposes upon the researcher the historicist presumption that a cultural phenomenon is best apprehended by understanding historical context synchronically.

2 *Dugma* of the *Dugma*: Convergence of the Literal and the Figurative

The equation of Torah and the Song of Songs opens a path that uncovers the ground of rabbinic poetics: just as in the particular case of the Song the contextual meaning is figurative, so the hermeneutical pattern of Scripture in general is related to the poetic configuration of metaphor, the *mashal* in Hebrew, which presumes an interplay of inner and outer signification, the duplicity of meaning, the secret exposed through the shrouding of the secret. In the midrashic anthology, Shir ha-Shirim Rabbah, the nature of the Song is elucidated by a discussion of the parables (*meshalim*) that Solomon composed in order to clarify the meaning of Scripture,[22] an activity that is epitomized in the statement, "Until Solomon arose there was no similitude (*dugma*)."[23] Interpreting the description of Solomon in Eccl 12:9 as one who "weighed, pondered, and composed many parables," *izzen we-ḥiqqer tiqqen meshalim harbeh*, the anonymous midrashist remarks, "He made handles for the Torah." The parables composed by Solomon are depicted idiomatically as handles (*oznayim*), for just as one can carry a basket more effectively if it has a handle, so the parables make the meaning of Torah comprehensible to one who possesses a discerning ear (*ozen*). The Song may be considered the *dugma* of the *dugma*, that is, the paradigm of paradigms, the metaphorical figuration that renders dissimilar things similar through the prism of the symbolic imagination. Alternatively expressed, the Song is the poem *par excellence*, for the contextual sense overlaps

---

21 See Wolfson, *Language*, 222–224.
22 See Stern, *Parables in Midrash*, 63–67.
23 Song Rabbah 1:8 (Dunasky, ed., 5). Many of the pericopae included in this anthology are predicated on the implicit identification of the Song and the Torah. Only such an assumption can account for the specific application of verses from the Song to the Torah.

with the figurative. The convergence of *peshaṭ* and *mashal* is indicative of the larger hermeneutical claim regarding the poetic nature of Torah, which in turn expresses and is expressed by the desire that resonates in the language of the Song. The symbolic reading of this book proffered by rabbinic interpreters revolves around the recognition of the essentially metaphorical nature of eros and the concurrent affirmation of the essentially erotic nature of metaphor. The mutuality of metaphor and eros is such that both materialize in the space between absence and presence. Here it is apposite to recall that Derrida spoke of metaphor as the withdrawal of truth as nontruth.[24] What does this mean? How can truth withdraw as nontruth? How can the truth withdrawn as nontruth remain the truth that is withdrawn? We can make sense of this only if we appreciate that truth and nontruth are not polar opposites, as common wisdom might dictate, but rather there is no reality of truth but what appears through the screen of nontruth, no face that is not itself a mask betraying the pretense of being a face beneath the mask.

Support for the assumption regarding the parabolic nature of the literal meaning may be gleaned from the approach to the Song offered by Solomon ben Isaac, better known by the acronym Rashi. According to Rashi's school of exegesis, the main interest is the plain sense (*peshaṭ*) to be determined by focusing on the grammar and the philology of the text. Rabbinic comments are to be considered only to the extent that they can help in the exposition of the historical-contextual sense. In theory, this is a major revision from the midrashic sensibility, since rabbinic tradition becomes a handmaiden to Scripture and is verified by independent criteria. Rashi applies this principle to the Song as well. However, in the introduction to his commentary to this book, he notes that there were various interpretations that deviated from the plain sense of the text and that his ambition is to understand the literal sense of the text even as he allows for the use of rabbinic interpretations. A verse may have multiple meanings but none of them can go against the primary contextual sense—*ein miqra yoṣe midei peshuṭo*.[25] In the final analysis, the literal for him is figurative because the plain sense of the text is about Israel's exilic condition, which reflects the exile of the divine presence.[26] The book was composed by Solomon as a parable—the technical terms Rashi used are *mashal*, *dugma*, and *dimyon*—to express the displaced state of the Jewish people, their longing for redemption, and their appeal to God's good graces based on Israel's glorious past and the divine promises.[27] The woman desiring her beloved is a

---

[24] See Derrida, "Retrait of Metaphor," 128. I have discussed this Derridean text previously in Wolfson, "Suffering Eros," 343; idem, *A Dream*, 202.
[25] See Kamin, *Rashi's Exegetical Categorization*, 77–87.
[26] See Kamin, *Rashi's Exegetical Categorization*, 251–256.
[27] See Kamin, "'Dugma' in Rashi's Commentary."

metaphorical depiction of Israel's being abandoned by and separated from God. The beloved remembers her acts of loyalty from her youth and thus recalls that they were bound together in an eternal bond, and assures her that the separation is not a divorce. In spite of the lover's misdeeds, if love is genuine, the beloved forgives her. Rashi's goal is to give some comfort to Israel by reminding them that they will always belong to God as the beloved to the lover.

The reconstructed plot of the Song, its presumed plain sense, is an allegorical narration of Israel's sacred history. The *peshaṭ* cannot be fully severed from what Rashi calls *dugma*; that is, the literal sense is a figure for the different events of Israel's history in relation to God. The assumption is that the Song in its plain sense conveys this figurative meaning. Consider Rashi's commentary on the first verse:

> *Let him kiss me with the kisses of his mouth.* This is a song in her [the maiden's] mouth, in her exile and widowhood. [And it means:] Would that I be kissed by King Solomon with the kisses of his mouth, as of yore; for though there are places that [have the custom to] kiss on the hand or shoulder, I desire and yearn that he treats me as before, like a groom with a bride [who kiss one another] mouth to mouth. *For your love is* to me *better than* any *wine* banquet. Now all this is an explication of the [plain] sense (*bei'ur mashma'o*). It is formulated in figurative terms (*dugma*) because God gave [the people] Israel His Torah and spoke with them face to face; and this love remains sweeter than any other enjoyment. They are [also] assured by Him that He will return and explicate its secret meanings and some of its deepest mysteries; and they supplicate Him to fulfill His promise. This is [the deeper meaning of the phrase]: *May He kiss me with the kisses of His mouth.*[28]

Rashi preserves both the literal and the allegorical meanings. The text is, in the first instance, about the desire of one of Solomon's wives for his passionate love, to be kissed again as when she was a young bride, but it is also about Israel's desire to be restored to God and to be kissed by him as it was at Sinai when the Torah was given.[29] The language of the text is read concomitantly on the horizontal and the vertical planes. Rashi's mentioning the secrets to be explicated when the divine returns is an allusion to the messianic age when the deeper mysteries will be disclosed with the same intimacy that was experienced at the Sinaitic revelation.[30] The dialectical nature of the Song, with the strong expression of desire followed by the suspension of that desire, well suited the Jewish belief in the messiah whose coming is always a matter of not coming.

---

28 I have utilized the translation of Rashi's passage in Fishbane, *Song of Songs*, 247.
29 On Rashi's constructing a counter-narrative to Christian triumphalism, including in his commentary on the Song, see Signer, "God's Love for Israel."
30 On the trope of the messiah in Rashi's commentary on the Song, see Kozodoy, "Messianic Interpretation," 123–126.

3 Waiting to Wait: Dream and the Deferment of Consummation

The Song of Songs is a compendium of love poems that has no plot but it does have a framework, as indicated by the interconnection between the beginning and the end, a framework shaped by the celebration of passion marked by the tension between separation and unification, infatuation and fulfillment. A number of scholars have noted the central role played by the imagination in the Song and have likened it to a dream in which the sequence of events does not necessarily follow a logical transition.[31] One of the most lucid accounts of this perspective was given by Solomon Freehof:

> Many of the images and incidents in the book are clearly such as have to do with dreams and sleeping. How frequently does the book speak of lying in bed at night or the bed of Solomon? How often does it refer to the events that will last until the day dawn and the shadows flee? And over all the mysterious improbable landscape is heard the plea: "I beg you, O daughters of Jerusalem, do not awaken love until it desireth." In other words, "Do not awaken me. Let me continue to dream." Once the book is read thus, its very disorder makes sense. The book is not the story of two lovers seeking each other in actual places, but in imaginary. "On my bed at night I sought my beloved" (III, 1). In other words, the book is a sequence of dreams. [...] While we may have here a series of dreams from several dreamers, the magic succession of scenes, the endless moving about in enchanted motion, and the overvividness of the descriptions, all suggest strongly that the entire book is chiefly a record of the contents of dreams.[32]

Freehof, correctly in my opinion, pinpointed the key rhetorical element that makes sense of the literary anomalies of this book, if indeed it should even be referred to by this taxonomy. The dearth of logical or chronological order can be explained if one postulates an oneiric framing of the compilation of poetic fragments. The erotic yearning expressed herein should be decoded in relation to lovers playing out their fantasy in an imaginary domain of the dream. Moreover, reading the book as a sequence of dreams casts light on the motive of the rabbis to endow the book with a symbolic interpretation to the extent that the textual topography mimics the dreamscape in blurring the distinction between the literal and the figurative:

> We may well assume that they who studied the book so carefully in order to bring it into the canon,—and especially Rabbi Akiba who seemed particularly devoted to the book,—sensed that such was its real nature. Then precisely for that reason it had a special appeal to them. They did not take dreams lightly. The dream was the vehicle of communication between God

---

31 See Pope, *Song of Songs*, 132–141; Fisch, *Poetry with a Purpose*, 80–103; Landy, "Song of Songs and the Garden," 514–515, 521, 526 n. 45; idem, "Song of Songs," 316; Tanner, "Message," 146–147; LaCoque, *Romance*, 8.
32 Freehof, "Song of Songs," 401.

and man. God spoke to the prophets in dreams. God gave to wise men their understanding of the depths of life in dreams (Job IV, 13). God foretold man his destiny through dreams. Dreams were therefore sacred communications between the Divine and man. Therefore, to interpret the dream was not just therapeutics as it is with us, but a religious duty. This they did, and in the only way in which a dream can be properly interpreted, namely, symbolically. The symbol seemed clear to them. The very love-language of the dream enabled them to interpret it all as a description of the eternal love between Israel and God. [. . .] As in a dream the beloved are parted, lost to each other, seeking each other; so God seeks Israel, but Israel seems lost from His presence. Then Israel, in repentance, seeks God and God seems far away. Finally they find each other for "Many waters cannot quench out love nor the floods overwhelm it." Israel is forever united with God. "I am my beloved's and He is mine." No wonder this interpretation of a dream, God's communication to man, was described by Akiba as Holy of Holies.[33]

Freehof's explication is susceptible of too easily narrowing the gap separating the biblical author and the rabbinic interpreters. However, his accentuating the dreamlike nature of the text is instructive in illumining its intrinsically symbolic character. As readers we are never certain if we are in a dream or if we are to imagine that what is described poetically is really taking place. The confusion, I submit, is intentional insofar as it communicates that this want of clarity may itself be symptomatic of the reality of love and the texture of erotic desire.

In piercing through the prism of the dream, we discern the invariable and unsettling truth that the image is true to the degree that it is false and false to the degree that it is true. The veracity of this truth breaks with the law of the excluded middle (P or ¬P) and the corollary principle of noncontradiction (a thing cannot be both P and ¬P in the same respect and at the same time) to which we steadfastly adhere as the logical foundations of our sensory and cognitive experience in the world, much as the conventional distinction between good and evil serves as the axiological foundation for humanity's political experience and the social-communal behavior necessary for its promotion.[34] To treat truth and deception as indistinguishable is a sign of foolishness and weak-mindedness. The exception, however, is the dream about which it can be said that it embodies the paradoxical collapse of the difference between real and unreal. As I have written elsewhere, dream-images, like images in a mirror, are veritable because they are imagined, but they are imagined as false; that is to say, they are not what they appear to be and thus appear not to be what they are. It is logically impossible to rule out the possibility that what we estimate to be wakefulness is a dream, perhaps a dream that one is waking from a dream.[35] Just as in a dream there is no basis to distinguish fact and

---

33 Freehof, "Song of Songs," 401–402.
34 See Wolfson, *A Dream*, 16, 46–47, 62–63, 110, 153, 188–189, 210.
35 See Wolfson, *A Dream*, 62.

fiction, so with respect to the Song of Songs, we do not have a solid epistemological criterion by which to discriminate what is real from what is being imagined to be real. The surplus of metaphoricity displayed by the book gives rise determinatively to a semantic indeterminacy. The intense yearning for sexual union is tempered by the need to defer gratification whence we discern that desire is centered on lack; indeed, it is the prolificacy of lack that illumines the profusion of desire. But here it is necessary to exercise caution as the trajectory of desire does not move unilaterally from lack to fullness or from fullness to lack. It swings rather like a pendulum from one pole to its opposite, constantly seeking the other manifest in its nonmanifestation and nonmanifest in its manifestation. To suffer eros one must succumb to the disquiet of craving, to walk the path of want that can want no path to walk, to confront the presence absently present in the absence presently absent.

Fluctuating between consummating and postponing desire is rendered most forcefully in the refrain that is couched as an oath taken by the maiden in the name of her female companions, the daughters of Jerusalem, "Do not wake or arouse love until it desire" (Song 2:7; 3:5; 5:8; 8:4). The exhortation that love should not be stimulated until the pertinent time attests not only to the fact that there is no desire without lack, but that, more profoundly, the lack itself constitutes the temporal reflexivity of the desire to desire. Sensuous lust is tethered to time since the craving satiated in one moment invariably gives way to another craving that must be satiated in the next moment; the relentless pursuit of pleasure resembles the continuous ebb and flow of chronological succession marked by the intransient transience and the permanent impermanence. Satisfaction of our physical cravings—always in and of the moment—is never anything but temporary, and hence timebound. Time is overcome in the momentariness of time implemented in the present recovering the future and anticipating the past. The warning not to enflame love before its time imparts to us this rudimentary truth about the nature of time as the liminal space between sleep and wakefulness. In this respect, the temporal comportment of the erotic transmitted by the Song bears the character of a dream. Moreover, the pledge not to hasten love provided the rationale to read this text messianically.[36] To wait for the messiah—whether understood in the traditional sense of a messianic figure or in a more contemporary sense as the messianicity of a future that is impending without presuming the advent of a redeemer—is a waiting for the sake of waiting, and hence it requires the patience of deferral that is the metrics of the diachronic synchronicity of the length of time. Precisely because the end is imminent at all times, the pursuit of pressing the end, *deḥiqat ha-qeṣ*, is discouraged. The mutual

---

[36] The thematic link between the Song and the messianic redemption is the basis for the custom to read this biblical work at the Passover seder as well as on the intermediate Sabbath of that holiday.

yearning of beloved and lover in the Song, the solicitation to effectuate the cohabitation that is realized only through its denial, provides a narratological construction within which to substantiate the temporal tensiveness essential to the messianic delay of the future concretized in the kenotic abundance of the present, the today adjourned until tomorrow because tomorrow continually transpires today.

Both Christian and Jewish interpreters discerned that the oscillation between absence and presence in the Song, and the repeated admonition not to provoke love before the appropriate time, are fitting characterizations of the messianic kerygma. Although the two religious communities are often distinguished based on the presumption that, for Jews, the messianic promise is expressive of an event yet to take place in historical time, whereas Christian eschatology is anchored in the notion of kairetic time informed by the expectation of a second coming of the messiah, that is, the belief that the completion of time is achieved not as the climax of a linear process but in the potentiality of Christ's return in each moment disrupting the temporal sequence, the fact is that one can discover in Jewish sources as well the chiastic paradox that undergirds the diremptive temporality of the Christian parousia: *the future is already present as the present that is always future*.[37] This form of hope is not expressed by waiting for someone to arrive or for something to take place in the ordinary procession of time but as an expectation of the unexpected, the unforeseeable intrusion that engenders the renewal of what has previously transpired as what is yet to transpire, the disjuncture within time through which we grasp the flow of time. The messianic dogma of Judaism, in a manner congruent to but not identical with Christian soteriology, betokens a tension between the absent presence of the past and the present absence of the future. Redemption, consequently, is always of the future that retrieves the past and ruptures the present.

The Song of Songs, on this score, is the instantiation of the messianic template as a complex wavering between prescience and reminiscence, between the presence of absence and the absence of presence, between the nongivenness of the given and the givenness of the nongiven, between the disappearance that has appeared and the appearance that will disappear.[38] One would think that the bond of matrimonial devotion is eternal and thus, as it is famously proclaimed, "For love is as strong as death" (Song 8:6).[39] Notwithstanding the imperishability of eros presumed

---

[37] See Wolfson, *Suffering Time*, 598, and references to other works of my own cited there in n. 81.
[38] I have reworked the comment from Wolfson, *Suffering Time*, 603.
[39] On death and desire in the Song, see Walsh, *Exquisite Desire*, 159–184, esp. 160–161: "When the woman finally asserts that 'love is as strong as death,' her sentiment is no cliché or glib assurance about the worthiness of desire as death's only real contender. Instead, given the considered skill of the figurative expression throughout the Song, we know that she means for this simile to be freighted with multivalent meanings. Love and death are, for the desiring woman of the Song, *equal* forces

by its being equated with thanatos, the measure of lovesickness is in the ephemeral seeking and not in the irrevocable possessing the subject of affection; the durability of the quest thus depends on being faithful to the vow not to wake or to incite love until the endtime. Love overpowers death to the extent that love, like death, exemplifies the possibility of the impossibility of bending the timeline such that not yet is no more insofar as no more is not yet. The endtime is not the end of time but the time of the end that cannot end and remain the time of the end. From this time that is not in time, the terminus that is not capable of terminating, we fathom the fecundity of eros in the perpetual depletion of waiting to wait for love to desire its own arousal.

Bibliography

Alexander, Philip S., ed. *The Targum of Canticles: Translated, with a Critical Introduction, Apparatus, and Notes*. ArBib 17A. Collegeville: Liturgical Press, 2003.

Brenner, Athalya, and Fontaine, Carole R., eds. *The Song of Songs: A Feminist Companion to the Bible*. Sheffield: Sheffield Academic Press, 2000.

Carr, David M. *The Erotic Word: Sexuality, Spirituality, and the Bible*. Oxford: Oxford University Press, 2003.

Corbin, Henry. *Creative Imagination in the Ṣūfism of Ibn ʿArabī*, translated by Ralph Manheim. Princeton: Princeton University Press, 1969.

Davidson, Richard M. "Theology of Sexuality in the Song of Songs: Return to Eden." *AUSS* 27 (1989): 1–19.

Davis, Ellen F. "Reading the Song Iconographically." In *Scrolls of Love: Reading Ruth and the Song of Songs*, edited by Peter S. Hawkins and Lesleigh Cushing Stahlberg, 172–184. New York: Fordham University Press, 2006.

Derrida, Jacques. "The Retrait of Metaphor." In *The Derrida Reader: Writing Performances*, edited by Julian Wolfreys, 102–129. Lincoln: University of Nebraska Press, 1998.

Devine, Luke. "Active/Passive, 'Diminished'/'Beautiful,' 'Light' from Above and Below: Rereading Shekhinah's Sexual Desire in Zohar al Shir ha-Shirim (Song of Songs)." *FemTh* 28 (2020): 297–315.

Dunasky, Shimshon, ed. *Shir ha-Shirim Rabbah*. Jerusalem: Dvir, 1980.

Elizur, Shulamit. "On the Role of the Yozer in the Legacy of Eleazar bi-Rabbi Qillir: New Findings." *Tarbiz* 66 (1997): 351–394. (Hebrew)

Fisch, Harold. *Poetry with a Purpose: Biblical Poetics and Interpretation*. Bloomington: Indiana University Press, 1988.

Fishbane, Michael. *The JPS Bible Commentary: Song of Songs*. Philadelphia: Jewish Publication Society, 2015.

Freehof, Solomon B. "The Song of Songs: A General Suggestion." *JQR* 39 (1949): 397–402.

---

of life. The subtextual contest between love and death in the Song, in our psyches, has been a draw, not a victory. The poet, to be sure, is aware of desire's potency and costs, along with its rewarding pleasures. The Song affirms the paradox that human desire is the life force and is associated with death itself" (emphasis in original).

Green, Arthur. "Intradivine Romance: The Song of Songs in the Zohar." In *Scrolls of Love: Reading Ruth and the Song of Songs*, edited by Peter S. Hawkins and Lesleigh Cushing Stahlberg, 214–227. New York: Fordham University Press, 2006.
Green, Arthur. "Shekhinah, the Virgin Mary, and the Song of Songs: Reflections on a Kabbalistic Symbol on a Kabbalistic Symbol in Its Historical Context." *AJSR* 26 (2002): 1–52.
Green, Arthur. "The Song of Songs in Early Jewish Mysticism." In *The Heart of the Matter: Studies in Jewish Mysticism and Theology*, edited by Arthur Green, 101–116. Philadelphia: Jewish Publication Society of America, 2015.
Hendel, Ronald. "The Life of Metaphor in Song of Songs: Poetics, Canon, and the Cultural Bible." *Bib* 100 (2019): 60–83.
Junkermann, Penelope Robin. "The Relationship between Targum Song of Songs and Midrash Rabbah Song of Songs." PhD diss., University of Manchester, 2010.
Kamin, Sarah. "'Dugma' in Rashi's Commentary on Song of Songs." *Tarbiz* 52 (1982–1983): 41–58. Repr., in *Jews and Christians Interpret the Bible*, 13–30. Jerusalem: Magnes, 1991. (Hebrew)
Kamin, Sarah. *Rashi's Exegetical Categorization in Respect to the Distinction between Peshat and Derash*. Jerusalem: Magness Press, 1986. (Hebrew)
Kaplan, Jonathan. *My Perfect One: Typology and Early Rabbinic Interpretation of Song of Songs*. Oxford: Oxford University Press, 2015.
Kaplan, Jonathan. "The Song of Songs from the Bible to the Mishnah." *HUCA* 81 (2010): 43–66.
Kozodoy, Maud. "Messianic Interpretation on the Song of Songs in Late-Medieval Iberia." In *The Hebrew Bible in Fifteenth-Century Spain: Exegesis, Literature, Philosophy, and the Arts*, edited by Jonathan Decter and Arturo Prats, 117–150. Leiden: Brill, 2012.
LaCoque, André. "I Am Black and Beautiful." In *Scrolls of Love: Reading Ruth and the Song of Songs*, edited by Peter S. Hawkins and Lesleigh Cushing Stahlberg, 162–171. New York: Fordham University Press, 2006.
LaCoque, André. *Romance, She Wrote: A Hermeneutical Essay on Song of Songs*. Eugene: Wipf & Stock, 2006.
Landy, Francis. *Paradoxes of Paradise: Identity and Difference in the Song of Songs*. Sheffield: Almond Press, 1983.
Landy, Francis. "The Song of Songs." In *The Literary Guide to the Bible*, edited by Robert Alter and Frank Kermode, 305–319. Cambridge, MA: Harvard University Press, 1987.
Landy, Francis. "The Song of Songs and the Garden of Eden." *JBL* 98 (1979): 513–528.
Lieberman, Saul. *Midreshei Teiman*. Jerusalem: Wahrmann Books, 1970.
Lieberman, Saul. "Mishnath Shir ha-Shirim." In *Jewish Gnosticism, Merkabah Mysticism, and Talmudic Tradition*, edited by Gershom Scholem, 118–126. New York: Jewish Theological Seminary of America, 1965.
McGinn, Bernard. "The Language of Love in Christian and Jewish Mysticism." In *Mysticism and Language*, edited by Steven T. Katz, 202–235. Oxford: Oxford University Press, 1992.
Menn, Esther M. "Thwarted Metaphors: Complicating the Language of Desire in the Targum of the Song of Songs." *JSJ* 34 (2003): 237–273.
Pardes, Ilana. *The Song of Songs: A Biography*. Princeton: Princeton University Press, 2019.
Pope, Marvin H. *Song of Songs: A New Translation with Introduction and Commentary*. AB 7C. New York: Doubleday, 1977.
Schechter, Solomon, ed. *Agadath Shir Hashirim*. Cambridge: Deighton Bell, 1896.
Signer, Michael A. "God's Love for Israel: Apologetic and Hermeneutical Strategies in Twelfth-Century Biblical Exegesis." In *Jews and Christians in Twelfth-Century Europe*, edited by Michael A. Signer and John Van Engen, 123–149. Notre Dame: University of Notre Dame Press, 2001.

Stern, David. "Ancient Jewish Interpretation of the Song of Songs in Comparative Context." In *Jewish Biblical Interpretation and Cultural Exchange: Comparative Exegesis in Context*, edited by Natalie B. Dohrmann and David Stern, 86–107. Philadelphia: University of Pennsylvania Press, 2008.

Stern, David. *Parables in Midrash: Narrative and Exegesis in Rabbinic Literature*. Cambridge, MA: Harvard University Press, 1991.

Tanner, J. Paul. "The Message of the Song of Songs." *BSac* 154 (1993): 142–161.

Trible, Phyllis. "Depatriarchalizing in Biblical Interpretation." *JAAR* 41 (1973): 30–48.

Walsh, Carey Ellen. *Exquisite Desire: Religion, the Erotic, and the Song of Songs*. Minneapolis: Fortress Press, 2000.

Wolfson, Elliot R. *A Dream Interpreted within a Dream: Oneiropoiesis and the Prism of Imagination*. New York: Zone Books, 2011.

Wolfson, Elliot R. *Alef, Mem, Tau: Kabbalistic Musings on Time, Truth and Death*. Berkeley: University of California Press, 2006.

Wolfson, Elliot R. *Circle in the Square: Studies in the Use of Gender in Kabbalistic Symbolism*. Albany: State University of New York Press, 1995.

Wolfson, Elliot R. *Language, Eros, Being: Kabbalistic Hermeneutics and Poetic Imagination*. New York: Fordham University Press, 2005.

Wolfson, Elliot R. "Suffering Eros and Textual Incarnation: A Kristevan Reading of Kabbalistic Poetics." In *Toward a Theology of Eros: Transfiguring Passion at the Limits of Discipline*, edited by Virginia Burrus and Catherine Keller, 341–365. New York: Fordham University Press, 2006.

Wolfson, Elliot R. "Textual Flesh, Incarnation, and the Imaginal Body: Abraham Abulafia's Polemic With Christianity." In *Studies in Medieval Jewish Intellectual and Social History: Festschrift in Honor of Robert Chazan*, edited by David Engel, Lawrence H. Schiffman, and Elliot R. Wolfson, 189–226. Leiden: Brill, 2012.

Wolfson, Elliot R. *Suffering Time: Philosophical, Kabbalistic, and Ḥasidic Reflections on Temporality*. Leiden: Brill, 2021.

Ariel Zinder
Of Songs and Sequels
The Song of Songs in the Hebrew Liturgical Poetry of al-Andalus

"My sun, how much longer will you set and not rise
    My root, how much longer shall it wither and not bloom?
I call on you, my lovers, and adjure you
    Please speak to my beloved who has fled.
Why does my companion who espoused me now revile me?
    Since He has left me I scream both night and day
Thus do I cry out and stand trembling before Him,
    Perhaps my beloved will smell my plea like myrrh
The all-merciful one shall command His lovingkindness
    And if I have no merit—let Him remember the covenant of Abraham"
"Remember, my awesome one, remember my salvation
    Lean against me, you shall not be a burden to bear.
Arise and shine, for your light that was extinguished comes
    And the glory of God has shone upon you."[1]

This poem was written in al-Andalus by renowned poet and philosopher Solomon Ibn Gabirol (ca. 1021–1058). There are two dramatic speakers in this lyric vignette. The first is a female speaker bemoaning her current plight as an abandoned wife and expressing some hopes for the future. In the last two verses, the husband speaks out, and his words convey intimacy and consolation, as well as a promise of assistance. The two lovers express these sentiments through the overt use of the Song of Songs. The wife adjures her companions following Song 5:8, and she later addresses the fleeing of her lover following Song 8:14. Her lover calls her "my awesome one" (*'ayyumati*), following Song 6:4 and 6:10. These echoes of the Song reinforce the tension inherent in the dialogue and infuse the poem with a sense of urgency and intimacy. And yet, this poem was not intended to explore romantic or erotic frustration and hope. Instead, it establishes this scene as an allegorical representation of human-divine relations. The poem itself makes this clear as soon as it mentions Abraham and God in vv. 5 and 7, pointing to its allegorical meaning: the separated lovers represent Israel (as the abandoned wife) and God (as the con-

---

[1] Ibn Gabirol, *Shirei ha-kodesh*, 2:466. I thank Tzvi Novick for his wonderful contribution to the translation.

Note: My thanks go to Ilana Pardes and Tamar Kadari for their generous and thoughtful suggestions.

soling lover or husband). In fact, the regular audience of this poem would surely know this even before v. 5, because the poem was specifically written for liturgical performance in the synagogue. In such a context, a medieval Jewish poet could rely on his listeners to decipher his use of the Song of Songs as a way of addressing the pressing questions of exile and covenant.

Ibn Gabirol's poem is but one example of a larger phenomenon. Several Jewish poets from medieval al-Andalus wrote similar poems or dedicated parts of larger compositions to allegorical dialogues between, or descriptions of, these two lovers. Several scholars have discussed this body of poems, its historical and cultural origins, and its conventions, in some cases offering detailed readings of specific poems.[2] And yet, these poems have rarely been discussed as a unique chapter in the long and winding story of the Song's reception. Ilana Pardes took a significant step forward in this direction, as she included Andalusian liturgical poetry in her account of pivotal moments in the reception and interpretation of the Song.[3] Following Pardes, I wish to delve deeper into the specific case of Andalusian *piyyut* (liturgical poetry). In the following pages, I will first situate this poetic phenomenon in its historical context and briefly describe its central textual and performative characteristics. I will then refer to one crucial aspect of reception. Ultimately, I will argue that the central gesture of reception in these poems was one of fictional expansion and disjunction. The liturgical poets of al-Andalus inherited a rich understanding of the Song, paid close attention to its clues and opportunities, and proposed multiple variations of and sequels to the original tale, ultimately turning the Song of Songs into a literary universe that one can traverse and understand anew.

1 The Allegory of Love in the Liturgical Poetry of al-Andalus

The poems we shall discuss here all belong to the long tradition of Hebrew liturgical poetry, known as *piyyut* (pl., *piyyutim*). Beginning in the fourth or fifth century CE, Jewish liturgy featured not only fixed prayers but also poetic supplements and insertions into those prayers. The earliest forms of piyyut were crafted in late antique Palestine, and the genre spread in later centuries to several communi-

---

2 See Scheindlin, *Gazelle*; Levin, "Bikashti"; Huss, "Peshat 'o 'alegoriyah."
3 See Pardes, *Song*, 59–97.

ties in the Middle East, North Africa, and western Europe.⁴ The earliest authors of piyyut in al-Andalus who are known to us appear only in the tenth century. At first, these poets followed the poetic conventions of eastern, mostly Baghdadi, liturgical poetry. But early on, and especially following Ibn Gabirol, Andalusian piyyut claimed a style of its own and prided itself on its departures from eastern influence and poetics. As we shall soon see, the emergence of this new style had much to do with the fact that the poets who cultivated it were also great masters of nonliturgical poetry, discussing themes such as mundane love, wine banquets, and more.⁵

The new style of these Jewish Andalusian poets was the result of multiple shifts and innovations of the time. One such shift, which was of the utmost importance, took place in linguistics and biblical exegesis. This was the renewed appreciation of biblical language, which began in al-Andalus in the late tenth century. For exegetes and linguists this renewed interest in literal language led to a new form of commentary, known as *peshat*, aimed at listening to Scripture as a "language of men."⁶ In poetry, this new attitude also led to a new poetic style, as poets prided themselves on the emulation of biblical diction and rhetoric, which they performed in their liturgical and nonliturgical poetry alike.⁷

These changes pertained to the Bible as a whole, and yet their impact on the reception of the Song was profound. Biblical commentators in al-Andalus now examined the Song not only for its allegorical meanings but also for its literal plotline and character formation as well. Some commentators even wrote two parallel commentaries on the Song, one regarding the literal tale of love and the other regarding its hidden allegorical meanings.⁸ Similarly, the poets of al-Andalus could listen to the Song afresh, and borrow its language with great delight, for the sake of their poems of human or divine love. It is *this* Song, newly appreciated and heard afresh, that lies at the heart of the liturgical poems we are discussing here. And indeed, during the eleventh and twelfth centuries, the Jewish liturgical poets of al-Andalus modeled dozens of liturgical poems on the Song. As Pardes notes, these poems display "a greater insistence on the literal even within the allegorical level."⁹ Even when the poem is meant to represent God and Israel, it does so through rhe-

---

4 For an overview of piyyut, see Lieber, "Piyyut."
5 See Scheindlin, *Gazelle*, 6–25; Fleischer, *Shirat ha-kodesh*, 331–412. For an introduction to the Hebrew poetry of al-Andalus and a translation of selected poems, see Cole, *Dream of the Poem*.
6 See M. Cohen, *Rule of Peshat*, 68–84. As Cohen shows, this new approach to Scripture also led to an appreciation of it on literary grounds. See also M. Cohen, "Best of Poetry," 15–57.
7 For a detailed discussion of the place of the Bible in the Hebrew poetry of al-Andalus, see Brann, *Compunctious Poet*, 23–58.
8 See Reif, "Abraham Ibn Ezra."
9 Pardes, *Song*, 78.

torical exchanges, flowery metaphors, and epithets, all coming from the literal tale of the two lovers.

While this new approach to Scripture and to the Song was a crucial element in the creation of piyyut, one cannot understand the allegories of love in Andalusian piyyut solely on the basis of this linguistic shift. Woven into these allegorical poems, alongside their allusions and quotes from the Song, were strands of other textual and interpretive traditions. In fact, the story of the reception of the Song in these poems is precisely the story of the fusion of the literal and vibrant language of the Song with these other traditions. As several scholars have noted, the language of the Song was translated into such allegorical love lyrics through its fusion with four other distinct poetic and textual traditions: (1) biblical tradition at large, including multiple cases of the allegorization of Israel as a desolate wife; (2) rabbinic homiletical literature, otherwise known as midrash; (3) pre-Andalusian piyyut; and (4) contemporary nonliturgical poetry, especially erotic poetry.[10]

The allegorical lyrics of the Andalusian poets owe their unique and powerful diction to the creative fusion of these four traditions. Their impact is evident in Ibn Gabirol's poem cited above. The poem incorporates imagery and rhetoric from the Song as well as echoes of Isa 54:5–6, in which the prophet tells Israel, "For God hath called thee as a wife forsaken and grieved in spirit."[11] The impact of midrash is similarly felt, especially through the overall allegorical key of the poem. It was the sages of late antique Palestine who first suggested that one should read *dodi* ("my beloved") as a reference to God and *'ayyumati* ("my awesome one") as a reference to Israel, and it was this prevalent understanding of the Song that allowed Ibn Gabirol to use those epithets so freely.[12] From early piyyut Ibn Gabirol inherited not only the poetic use of the Song but also the daring and taunting rhetoric, aimed at awakening God by asking, "Why does my companion who espoused me now revile me?"[13] Finally, Ibn Gabirol's poem relates to nonliturgical poetry, especially erotic poetry, in Arabic and in Hebrew, as it was practiced and widely accepted in Jewish circles in al-Andalus. The Jewish cultural elite of al-Andalus was well versed in such poetry, and there can be little doubt that the audience of the synagogue heard

---

10 See Scheindlin, *Gazelle*, 18–25; Pardes, *Song*, 71–81.
11 All translations from here on are from the King James Version or the Jewish Publication Society Bible (1917), with slight emendations by the present author.
12 See Pardes, *Song*, 22–43; Boyarin, *Intertextuality*, 105–116; Kadari, "Friends." In this context I should add that the Andalusian poets indeed relied primarily on the overall allegorical key. Only rarely did they allude to a highly specific midrashic homily. The importance of this aspect will be developed later.
13 For the early roots of such daring references to God in piyyut, see Lieber, "There Is None Like You."

echoes of such mundane poetry in the lofty descriptions of Israel's lovesickness. In fact, one central feature of medieval Arabic erotic poetry is the adoption of the frustrated or abandoned lover's point of view. Most erotic poems in al-Andalus were crafted as painful monologues of such frustrated lovers. It is no wonder that such motifs could be easily embedded in the allegorical representations of the frustrated Israel.[14]

I have pointed out the presence and impact of these four strands of poetic discourse in Ibn Gabirol's poem. One could easily cite many other examples of this poetic, cultural, and theological *tour de force*. Practically all major Hebrew poets of al-Andalus wrote such poems, using various techniques and poetic forms, many of which have been described and discussed in previous scholarship.[15] Indeed, one can see these four strata as complementary aspects of the same phenomenon: lyrical and allegorical poems, written in a biblical idiom yet presented as contemporary and urgent interventions in the exilic state, gaining their powerful effect especially from the idiom of erotic frustration and longing.

2 The Creative Reception of the Song

We shall now turn to the more specific question of how such poems played a part in the reception of the Song of Songs in their time. The poems' debt to the Song is obvious, and it is apparent in several linguistic, stylistic, and rhetorical aspects. And yet, the *literary form* that this debt takes remains to be explained. One could simply argue that the later poem echoes the Song. Yet, from a strictly literary point of view, such a description is insufficient. *Echoing* is a vague term that suggests an elusive form of contact between the biblical text and the later poem. Alternatively, one may suggest that this is a simple case of intertextual allusion. Yet, using these terms would suggest that the Andalusian piyyutim stand as autonomous texts, with their own premise and substance, into which the poets wove the Song's verses as foreign,

---

14 See Levin, "Bikashti." In some cases, piyyutim of this sort displayed well-known motifs from Arabic love poetry, almost to the point of blurring the line between human erotic discourse and words of prayer. Such cases are by no means the majority of allegorical piyyutim in al-Andalus. Furthermore, they do not play a substantial role in the drama of the reception of the Song since they do not incorporate clear quotes or elaborate allusions to the biblical text.

15 It should be noted that scholars sometimes highlight the crucial role that mundane erotic poetry played in crafting such liturgical poetry while paying less attention to the two other strands that make up these unique poems. Yet, as surprising as this sacred-secular dialogue may be, it is the present author's position that the allegorical liturgical poems of love were equally influenced by the poetics of the biblical sources and by the various traditions and conventions of piyyut.

biblical intertexts. This might be true of many modern poetic dialogues with the Song, but in the case of Andalusian piyyut, there is no such clear division between text and intertext. The biblical text gives the later piyyut its entire premise, its dramatic structure, and its distribution of characters. The later poem does not allude *to* the Song of Songs. In some way it inheres *in* the Song.

Given the poem's close proximity to the biblical Song, might we see it as an adaptation or a rewriting of the biblical Song? This would seem appropriate if we had heard the dramatic personae of the poem reenacting the biblical scenes. But the woeful scene of a desolate wife does not appear anywhere in the Song, and the poem can therefore not be seen as a reenactment of one of its scenes. Undoubtedly, there are dark moments in the biblical Song that explore the constant threat of parting or disappearing. Yet in none of them does the text suggest either long-term separation or the anguish such separation might bring. Thus, as the biblical protagonists of the Song indeed seem to be those speaking in such poems, they are enacting an entirely unfamiliar scene. The tone of their dialogue, the scope of their story, indeed the *mise en scène* are altered. As a result of these alterations, one cannot see the poems either as intertextual allusions or as adaptations. They belong to the biblical tale, and yet they are foreigners in it. As such, the question arises, How do these late pieces achieve the puzzling feat in which they both receive and preserve the biblical text while altering its literary makeup?

In order to answer this question one does indeed need to hold fast to a *literary* reading of the Song and its belated poetic supplement. By this I mean to suggest that the best way of addressing the Song's reception in Andalusian piyyut is to place its allegorical meanings in brackets and direct the interpretive gaze at the *literal* level of the lovers' tale. Such bracketing might sound absurd given that the poems' primary message was the same historical-allegorical meaning as that which is bracketed. The answer, I would suggest, is found in Ibn Gabirol's poem and others like it. As we saw, the dramatic personae in the poem gave only slight hints as to the decoding of their utterances. Such decoding is easily performed, of course, but the text itself barely gestures in that direction and leaves it to take place in the minds of its readers or listeners. The poem's main *textual* thrust is the exquisite fictional drama of the two speakers.[16] In fact, such an emphasis on the lovers' tale might be expected of poets who lived in an era of literal exegesis and were themselves masters of lyrical utterances of love and frustration. Simply put, Ibn Gabirol and his fellow poets meant to convey allegorical meanings yet did so by exploring the literal language of the Song. It is only fitting, then, that we should follow suit.

---

[16] The poem's dramatic structure brings to mind the ancient understanding of the Song as a drama, as described by Origen. See Kadari, "Rabbinic and Christian Models," esp. 69–71.

The bracketing of the encoded message allows us to go beyond vague descriptions of echoing and delve further into a more nuanced description of the relations between the various texts. Only after such a description is achieved can one return to the overladen questions of the religious, theological, and ideological meanings of these late texts. Therefore, for the moment, I ask you to think of the Song as a literary representation of a lovers' tale, as we examine the way in which that same tale is recounted in later, and highly creative, pieces of poetry.

When the liturgical poems of al-Andalus are approached through these questions, they turn out to embody a strange and fascinating scene of reception. For as the rhetoric, imagery, and narrative of the Song settle into the medieval poems, they do so through two interconnected techniques of disjunction and displacement. One occurs on the level of the narrative. It is true that the biblical Song's plot is tumultuous and quite elusive, but one can easily point to its outermost limits. In the biblical lovers' tale, we do not hear how the lovers met, nor do we hear of the later years of their lives, after the courtship was over. And yet, as we saw, in Ibn Gabirol's poem their dramatic dialogue takes place precisely at such a later stage, after the lovers' marriage and separation, a stage clearly absent from the biblical Song. In these poems, the two protagonists of the lovers' tale have outlived the biblical account, and thanks to the poem they are now living in the biblical Song's sequel, so to speak. Thus one aspect of the poem's gesture of reception is this act of *surpassing* the biblical Song's plot.

The other aspect occurs on the linguistic and grammatical level. For not only do the poets of al-Andalus extend the Song's plot, they tend to depict its *later* phase while using and altering various phrases from the *earlier* phase. The protagonists describe their life as separated lovers yet do so with the words they used before the separation. Sometimes this is done via a change of tense, at other times through grammatical changes or some shift in the identity of the speaking persona or its addressees.[17] In Ibn Gabirol's poem cited above, for instance, the female lover adjures not her female friends (the "daughters" from Song 5:8) but rather a group of *male* friends or lovers; she also changes the imperative "flee, my lover" (Song 8:14) to a description in the past tense: "my lover *has* fled." Such changes are, of course, related to the narrative shifts, yet they also contribute to the unique nature of this gesture of reception. While the first aspect is based on an extension of the Song, which explores the uncharted lands of its aftermath, the second aspect is based on a notion of constant reuse. Even in altered circumstances, the words of the initial love story can be used. Even if the narrative must be stretched, it must also, somehow, cling to the words of the preliminary narrative.

---

[17] For a brief account of such shifts and reversals, see Pardes, *Song*, 76–81.

3 The Poetics of Transduction

I would like to address these two gestures of reception one by one, beginning with the gesture of narrative extension. To that end, let us examine another textual example from al-Andalus. The following is one strophe from a longer liturgical poem, most probably penned by another eleventh century poet, the eminent rabbi from Lucena, Isaac Ibn Ghiyyat (1038–1064):

> Let Him restore my serenity and fraternity, / my beloved who did attack me
> Despite those loving passions / with kisses of his mouth he did kiss me
> Since I despised and did not love him / at the time when he loved me
> And he fled like a dove and turned away, / and like a widow deserted me,
> And in pain as she who delivers a firstborn / I called him, and he did not answer me.
> In my torments I sought him every night, / until the city watchers caught me.
> Where can I seek you, my beloved?/ Where will I find you? Turn to me
> I have returned to you, Here I am! / Now, let me kiss your hand.[18]

The female speaker represents the contemporary exiled Israel, and her words clearly echo the Song of Songs. Yet, from a purely narrative perspective, the poem stands in stark contrast to the Song itself, for it follows a story line that does not exist in the biblical tale. Nowhere does the Song suggest an actual marriage between the lovers, and it certainly does not suggest widowhood. Of course, one can cite various verses in which the female lover is lonely or in jeopardy, but nowhere can one find any reference to her legal marital status. Thus, even as the poem goes on to describe the familiar scene of a nightly sojourn (based on Song 3:1–4), we are forced to imagine a yet-unheard-of scene: gone is the playful and vibrant lovesick girl, as we now envision the frantic and hopeless wandering of an abandoned wife who thinks of herself as a widow.[19]

Simply put, Ibn Ghiyyat's poem introduces us to the biblical Song's sequel. No matter how confusing the Song of Songs may be, it is safely framed within a time and space of amatory courtship. The time and space of widowhood and estranged husbands must surely reside beyond that tale. Of course, such a gesture of narra-

---

18 Ibn Ghiyyat, *Shirei Isaac Ibn Giyyat*, 250 (translated by Tzvi Novick). The text in this edition is flawed. I have amended it according to one of its versions found in a Genizah document, Cambridge University Library, Ms. T-S NS 134.137. On the poet and his literary and philosophical oeuvre, see Sáenz-Badillos, "Ibn Ghayyat."
19 The image of Israel as a widow bears a great resemblance to one of the most famous medieval interpretations of the Song. In the commentary by Rashi (R. Shlomo Itzhaki, France, 1040–1105), the female protagonist of the Song is described as a "woman stuck in widowhood." See M. Cohen, *Rule of Peshat*, 100–105. As far as I know, there is no direct link between Rashi's image of the widow and its appearance in Andalusian piyyut, but the matter needs further research.

tive expansion is familiar enough to us moderns, especially in our days of abundant prequels and sequels in the cinema. Yet in premodern Jewish literature it is quite rare. As we will soon see, such an extension of the Song's plot has certain roots in midrash and pre-Andalusian piyyut, but it rarely attains or rises to the level of such a large-scale dramatization. Needless to say, extensions of other biblical narratives are hard to find. One can find midrashic accounts of Abraham's childhood years or Balaam's aftermath, but these are almost always elaborate techniques for filling the gaps within the biblical narrative itself. The Andalusian poem, on the other hand, does not address a gap in the plot but rather *creates* such a gap by prolonging the life of the narrative's heroes.

However rare such a phenomenon was in the premedieval era, in the allegorical poetry of al-Andalus it became the norm. All major liturgical poets from al-Andalus wrote poems similar to the verses of Ibn Gabirol and Ibn Ghiyyat. Given the shifts and conjunctions found in them, one cannot regard such poems as mere echoes of the biblical Song or as poems vaguely following it. Rather, this group of poems takes part in a gesture of reception that Lubomir Dolezel has called *transduction*. The term is derived from the obsolete verb *traduce*, which the Oxford English Dictionary defines as follows: "To put (a text, etc.) into another form or mode of expression, especially into another language; to translate, render; to alter, modify, reduce." In Dolezel's work the term specifically designates the gesture of taking one text's fictional world, which he calls the *protoworld*, and putting it into another form. This can be done by keeping certain elements of the original's plot, characters, and events and rewriting them within a new narrative framework. Such rewriting, he suggests, "tak[es] the literary work beyond the communicative act into an open, unlimited chain of transmission."[20] Transduction occurs when one literary text does more than simply allude to another text. It occurs when one text embraces another text's fictional world and goes on to tell the story differently, in another language or setting, or in a more expansive or contracted time frame. Dolezel himself demonstrates such transductions in postmodernist rewrites of classic literary works, such as J. M. Coetzee's novel *Foe* (1986), which is woven around Daniel Defoe's *Robinson Crusoe*. While addressing such rewrites, he mentions three distinct types of transduction in these works: transposition, expansion, and displacement. Of these three types, expansion is the one that best describes the gesture of reception we have found in the piyyut of al-Andalus. The strategy of expansion, writes Dolezel,

---

20 Dolezel, *Heterocosmica*, 205.

extends the scope of the protoworld, by filling its gaps, constructing a prehistory or posthistory, and so on. The protoworld and the successor world are *complementary*. The protoworld is put into a new co-text, and the established structure is thus shifted.[21]

When the world of the Song of Songs enters the liturgical poetry of al-Andalus, an expansion occurs. The medieval poems relate to the biblical tale by expanding the fictional world of the Song. As Dolezel says of postmodern fiction, such expansions simultaneously rejuvenate the protoworld and challenge it. For indeed, the Andalusian poets' motivation for adopting and perfecting this strategy was surely not merely artistic. That was their way of adapting the biblical narrative to the contemporary situation of the poem's audience. Nevertheless, such motivation should not prevent us from seeing the specific literary strategy that was at work here.

It should be noted that within Andalusian piyyut, this extension never turns into a fully developed narrative sequel to the biblical tale. Given their lyrical nature, these poems are primarily concerned with highly charged moments or dramatic exchanges that occur within this belated chapter of the love story. In many poems we hear the protagonists speak for themselves, sometimes in monologue form and sometimes in dialogue. At other times a third dramatic persona, figured as a precentor or a representative of the community, speaks of the abandoned wife and of her husband, sometimes identifying with the former's pain or promising the imminent return of the latter. Furthermore, it should be noted that within these sequels, it is unclear where these belated events take place. Only rarely is the deserted wife placed in Spain or some other specific country. Often she is simply displaced and outside of her beloved Jerusalem. She is in exile, of course, yet the poets saw no need to mention her specific location.

4 The Poetics of Transduction in al-Andalus and Its Precedents

As we confront this fascinating poetics of expansion, two major questions arise. One is the historical question, namely, what conditions allowed this poetics to evolve and take such deep root in al-Andalus. The second question is one of poetics: How do the disjunctions work? I will address the former question briefly, as it has been discussed

---

21 Dolezel, *Heterocosmica*, 207. A similar phenomenon is addressed by Gerard Genette under the heading "continuation." See Genette, *Palimpsests*, 161–162.

in scholarship, and will then focus on the second, which has yet to be described in contemporary literary terms.

The poets of al-Andalus were not the first to toy with the question of the Song's sequel, just as they were not the first to wed the Song's imagery to the prophetic figuration of Israel as an abandoned wife. However, I would suggest that they were among the first to give this notion such a widespread grasp and such a detailed literary representation. Though I do not wish to discuss the multiple early hints at the expansion of the Song's plot, I will point out a few influential precedents, thereby clarifying both the traditionalism and the novelty of the Andalusian school. Gerson Cohen has described "the direct and continuing chain of the imagery of Israel as the wife and God the husband" and suggested that this chain allowed for the Song's canonicity.[22] Yair Zakovitch has further suggested that there was an innerbiblical continuum between the Song of Songs and the prophetic representations of husband and wife.[23] Yet, the Bible lays no claim to a continuous narrative that begins with the Song and continues with Isaiah, and therefore it falls short of an actual precedent for the poetics of transduction in al-Andalus. Such linkage does appear, though, in early midrash and piyyut. In one midrashic homily from Song of Songs Rabbah, for example, one sage discusses the verse "We shall rejoice in you" (Song 1:4) and explicates it through a parable of an older, abandoned woman who rejoices upon hearing of her lover's return. The parable includes references to Isa 60:4, where God addresses Israel and says, "Lift up thine eyes round about and see [. . .] thy sons come from far."[24] The juxtaposition of the Song's female lover and the old mother in Isaiah suggests that the two women figures of these separate biblical works may be seen as a single protagonist who moves from youthful love to desolation and then to renewed joy in the time of redemption.[25]

The possibility of seeing Israel's exile as a prolonged narrative of love and separation can be glimpsed in early piyyut as well. One famous example is a piyyut by Elazar Birabi Qalir, who lived in Palestine during the latter half of the sixth century. The poem figures female and male protagonists. First we hear the female figure

---

22 G. Cohen, "Song," 11.
23 See Zakovitch, *Song*, 111–113.
24 Song of Songs Rabbah 1:4. For an English translation, see Simon, *Midrash Rabbah*, 49–50.
25 Another well-known example of linking the Song to exile and suffering appears in the midrashic compilation called Sifre. In it there is a parable of Rabbi Yohanan, who meets an impoverished mother "gleaning barley-corn from under the hooves of the beasts" after the destruction of Jerusalem and says that her situation reveals the tragic meaning of the words "o thy way forth by the footsteps of the flock" (Song 1:8); *Sifrei*, 365. These homilies were probably part of a minor midrashic tradition that interpreted the Song as an allegorical representation of exile among the nations. For a detailed account of this tradition, see Kadari, "Nismeḥu."

(representing Israel) exclaiming, "My husband has thrown me away and deserted me / He does not remember the devotion of my youth." To this the male figure replies in the next poem, "My black one, I shall never forsake you / I will return a second time and gather you in, / your words of dispute are over / my undefiled, I shall never desert or forget you."[26]

While the female speaker makes no use of the Song of Songs, she is the one who sets the scene. She was married and later deserted; they experienced nuptial joy, and then she was forgotten. And yet, she does not use the language of the Song. It is only through the husband's reply that we are shocked into the realization that the desolate and forgotten wife is the same woman who was called "black and beautiful" and "undefiled" in Song 1:4; 5:2. In other words, we realize that this dialogue takes places in a fictional expansion of the biblical tale. In this belated episode, the husband calls her "my black one" simply to remind her who she once was and what she meant to him.

These precedents suggest that the imaginative leap beyond the Song's narrative frame, and the creative linkage of the comely shepherdess with the deserted Mother Zion, were already close at hand in late antique Palestine. However, examples of transduction in pre-Andalusian midrash or piyyut are rare, as they are in targum, another important late-antique genre consisting of creative translations of the Bible into Aramaic.[27] In all three genres, the central gesture of reception of the Song is a gesture of unraveling and decoding the Song, which stands as a veiled depiction of Israel's *past*. Such creative work was usually achieved by referring to small units of the Song and relating these to the exodus, the building of the temple, and more.[28] The dominance of the backward glance in these genres naturally precludes any dominant use of expansion and transduction. These were fabulous acts of interpretation, as well as complex ideological statements about the importance of the covenant, but they only indirectly addressed their own times and the distant future.[29]

---

26 The poem is included in Elizur, *Kedushah*, 32–33.
27 See Alexander, "Tradition and Originality."
28 For this phenomenon in midrash, see Boyarin, *Intertextuality*, 105–116. See also Urbach, "Homiletical Interpretations;" Lieberman, "Mishnat." For piyyut, see Lieber, *Vocabulary*, esp. 26–44.
29 This does not mean, of course, that the authors of midrash, piyyut, and targum were preoccupied with nostalgia or with mere stories of the past. Their narratives of the past were surely a part of their response to their historical situation of exile and uncertainty. The difference between them and the Andalusian poets was not necessarily one of national ideology but rather one of literary and interpretive technique. For an elucidation of the non-nostalgic mode of early piyyut, see Lieber, *Vocabulary*, 80–90.

The shift we can detect in the Song's reception in Andalusian culture has to do with the release of its poets and exegetes from this interpretive paradigm. Once it was removed, the Song could be fully examined as a trove of discourse of love and frustration, which the gifted poets of al-Andalus could turn into spirited dialogues not so much about the past but rather about the present. In such a context the literal meanings of various verses could be heard anew, their erotic overtones could be retrieved, and there was no need to refer solely (or even primarily) to the events of the past.[30]

Before returning to the literary evaluation of these poems, I would add one last comment as to the emergence of the poetics of transduction in al-Andalus. There was one more cultural shift that served as a catalyst for this new poetics. This was what might be termed the lyricization of piyyut. In earlier generations, authors of piyyut took great care to place each individual poem in a highly specific structure. Many piyyutim referred to the specific holiday for which they were written or to the Torah portion about that event; other piyyutim were modeled on elaborate linguistic schemes, as each verse began or ended with a series of biblical words; lastly, many piyyutim were written as parts of large-scale compositions and could not be easily understood outside those compositions. In al-Andalus this all changed substantially, especially in the work of Ibn Gabirol and later poets. Instead of linking each and every piyyut to certain words, portions of the Torah, or unique ritual contexts, the Andalusians wrote many poems that addressed larger themes such as exile, redemption, or praise of God.[31] This double release, both from elaborate linguistic formulas and from specific calendrical events, enabled poets to craft short, lyrical explorations of universal themes. This high degree of poetic freedom must have played an important role in the popularity of a more flexible use of the Song's materials and, eventually, in the expansion of its narrative. Instead of the sophisticated and rather quizzical poetry of earlier generations, Ibn Gabirol and later poets displayed a greater degree of poetic license and produced lyrical adaptations of the Song of Songs, which were meant primarily to address the congregation's yearning and suffering in their own historical reality.

---

30 One might wonder whether some historical events made the poets of al-Andalus more attentive to the symbolic potential of the Song to represent the historical present rather than the past. I believe that there is no sufficient evidence for such a suggestion. The themes of exilic desolation and hopes for redemption were by no means new in the synagogue poetry of Jewish communities. It is just that these were rarely expressed through the use of the Song. For this to occur there was need not for some historical shift but rather for a cultural one.
31 See Fleischer, *Shirat ha-kodesh*, 385–395.

5 Transduction and Interpretation: The Song's Apparatus in a New Context

Thus far I have described the phenomenon of transduction in these poems and addressed its unique historical terms of possibility. However, a descriptive poetics of this phenomenon cannot suffice, and we must seek to understand how this technique reflects a reevaluation of the Song's meaning. Therefore the next step is an assessment of the ideological and moral relations between the Song and its Andalusian extensions. What do the later poems reveal about the biblical Song? What form of evaluation can be found within them—one of positive glorification or perhaps critical suspicion? Do the protagonists maintain their integrity and energy, or are they diminished in some way?

Naturally, the poems themselves do not offer any explicit argument regarding their own position vis-à-vis the biblical tale, and such arguments can only be sought through our own active interpretation of the poems. Therefore, the following suggestions should not be seen as an attempt at divining the understanding of the historical, eleventh-century audience of these poems. Rather, I wish to point to certain insights and evaluations that these poems evoke, whether the historical audience was aware of them or not.

As a first step, we should address the full scope of transduction in these poems. For as noted earlier, the poets of al-Andalus did not achieve this only by extending the narrative of the biblical tale. The power of their poetic reception of the Song is also due to their use of specific verses and phrases from the Song. In this sense, the poems both extend the biblical tale and enact its repetition through difference. The time frame of the poems is a later era of separation, but the words exchanged are the ones of old. Thus God as the male speaker consoles his abandoned spouse with the same words he used to court her, and his wife describes her woes and hopes through the images and phrases of her younger, amatory self. Now one might dismiss this simply as a literary convention or as an innocent textual effect. The lovers speak the language of the Song, one might suggest, simply because the choice of characters entails a certain diction that was available in that specific biblical episode. To this I would reply that the motivation behind the poets' use of the Song's language does not, and cannot, fully account for the *results* of their poetic choices. Be their motivation as it may, the results of this poetic choice are startling and fascinating. For while the words of adoration and courtship now resound in a context of separation and sorrow, those same words are submitted to renewed scrutiny. One might say that the biblical words are now reinterpreted, and even the seemingly innocent compliment of a courting shepherd is now on display as the damning evidence of that shepherd's later betrayal.

As this displacement of verses occurs within the aforementioned narrative expansion of the Song, one can truly encounter the profound impact of these acts of transduction. Indeed, such poems do not simply echo the Song. They traverse the Song as if it were a vast symbolic universe that can be expanded and contracted and in which phrases and scenes disappear and resurface, acquiring new meanings each time. Thus the poets of al-Andalus address the lovers' tale only to produce a body of poetic interventions in that same narrative. Not only do these poems ask what happened later, but they also provoke a new assessment of events which took place at the time of the tale itself.

The outcome of this change is the submission of the Song of Songs to various interpretations and reevaluations. Key events and phrases of the Song are tested and twisted so that their resonance becomes wider and more complex. Suddenly, phrases that appeared to be innocent or entirely positive in the Song's original context acquire a somber or even ominous tone. Conversely, narrative moments in the biblical tale that depict mishaps or misunderstandings turn out to be beneficial precedents for the lovers' ability to overcome adversity.

An example of these insertions of the Song's language into the expanded narrative can be found in the following poem, written by poet and exegete Abraham Ibn Ezra († 1187):

My awesome one, you were barren thus long
Arise and swell, for you have been pitied
How beautiful and pleasant you are.

My companion, there is life in your face and dew among your teeth
Beauty and grace surround you, your earrings adorn you
And you have painted your eyes.

My beloved among gazelles, arise and swell in the night
Then shall you rejoice in dance and your breasts shall be like clusters of the vine
If you have sinned—it was for conjuring spirits!

How have you been raged at, most beautiful of women,
Shining forth like the dawn. You have been disgraced
If you have fallen—you shall arise.

Why should you complain? Arise, my daughter and come with me
I shall bring you to the house of my splendor, I am your husband and you are my wife
Adorn yourself, and be consoled.[32]

---

32 Ibn Ezra, *Shirei ha-kodesh*, 1:200–201.

The speaker in this poem is the male protagonist, allegorically representing God. The whole poem is addressed to his beloved, and it is composed of a mixture of consolation, chastisement, and provocation to action. The poem includes clear references to the lovers' mutual past, to their (and especially her) current condition, and to the prospect of their joint future. As in previous examples, this poem is based on the premise of the two lovers of the Song while actively displacing it. This is already evident in the first three verses. The male speaker calls his beloved "my terrible one" (cf. Song 6:4, 10) and adds a consoling message: you will be barren no more, you can rise for you have obtained compassion. He then ends with a direct quote from Song 7:7: "How fair and how pleasant art thou." We are clearly in a belated episode, after a time of harsh separation and barrenness.

A detailed analysis of the vast intertextual apparatus of this poem is beyond the scope of the current essay, so instead I will point to two key moments in the poem's reception of the Song, in which the poetics of transduction indeed provoke a renewed interpretation and evaluation of the original biblical text. The first moment is the instructive use of the epithet *'ayyumati* ("my terrible one") in v. 1. The term itself is puzzling in the biblical context, and it has been variously explained by multiple commentators over the years, including Ibn Ezra himself. Since it is part of a verse of praise ("You are beautiful as Tirzah"), it is usually explained as a positive term, designating the lover's (and Israel's) daunting beauty or righteousness. It is tempting to suggest that this term in itself acquires a new meaning here and exposes Israel's own fears in the face of daunting forces, but it should be mentioned that the epithet is quite common in piyyut and it does not necessarily carry such interpretive weight. However, what should be stressed is the small grammatical difference between the biblical phrase and Ibn Ezra's wording. In Song 6:4, the lover tells his beloved that she is "awesome as an army with banners." In the poem the beloved is referred to as "*my* awesome one." Her position in the poem, from this very first word, is mediated by the male speaker's presence. She is *his* beloved, and he is the one who compliments her features, directs her actions, and even points to her faults (v. 8). In other words, this poem places the words of the biblical Song in the framework of a single mindset. Gone is the wonderfully dialogic nature of the Song, which allows the two lovers to exchange words and caresses as if they were equals, and instead we follow the male speaker as he coaches his addressee in her distress. By this I am referring not only to the fact that he is the only speaker but also to the way he encapsulates his lover in his own evaluations and perceptions. This is clearly felt in the final words of the first strophe as well. The speaker quotes Song 7:7 and says, "How beautiful and pleasant you are." In their original context, these words convey the male lover's appreciation of his beloved's actual physical beauty, which he wishes to possess. In the context of Ibn Ezra's poem, these biblical words are no longer an appreciation but rather an estimation, a promise of hidden beauty, a way of strengthening the male protagonist's position as the sole redeemer of the barren wife.

Another striking reevaluation of the biblical words in the poem occurs in the fourth strophe. Here the speaker of the poem uses two well-known phrases from the Song to describe his beloved. She is the "most beautiful of women" (Song 1:8) and the one who is "Shining forth like the dawn" (6:10). Yet both positive phrases are placed within a distich that suggests ominous counterparts to these compliments: the most beautiful of women has now been the object of anger, and the one who looks like the dawn is now disgraced. Furthermore, these verses all rhyme, with the negative words in the first and last hemistiches, thus encapsulating the positive words. The result is a terrifying musical feat in which the woman's beauty rhymes with the fury she absorbs, and her ability to shine forth rhymes with her own disgrace.

In both cases, the same words of the biblical tale are placed in a new rhetorical and musical context and resonate differently. Naturally, they also raise our awareness of certain aspects of the biblical text itself. For indeed, once the male protagonist's text is freshly examined, his commanding and objectifying tendencies reveal themselves. Similarly, the Song's multiple ideal depictions of that most "beautiful of women" acquire an ominous tone once they are read in light of this poem. After all, the Song itself details the female lover's endangered position, as she is susceptible to the beating of the city's guards or to the various cries of the unruly male crowd. In a way, then, the Song prepares us for an understanding of the ways beauty and disgrace can rhyme. It is simply the poem's elucidation that makes this so manifestly clear.

6 Conclusion, or: The Song of Songs as a Promise and an Indictment

Once we realize the full scope of the relations between the biblical Song and its Andalusian adaptations, the complicated question of allegory and ideology can be allowed back into our discussion. We have learned that a large portion of such Andalusian piyyut addresses the Song through disjunction and thus exposes it to renewed scrutiny. Now we must adapt our reading to the historical audience and equate the lovers' tale with the glorious past of Israel and its God. Given such a deciphering of the allegory, where does the renewed scrutiny inherent in the poems lead us? What do these poems have to say on a historical and ideological level? My suggestion is that this scrutiny leads to two primary conclusions. One is that in these poems, the love story between God and Israel is very much alive, despite the prolonged exile. The other is that the glorious days of intimacy between God and Israel are a distant memory; that Israel's disappointment and desolation turn even the most delicate of images or promises into a cause for bitter complaint. These two perceptions of the glorious past are not necessarily contradictory. They speak to the ambivalence of medieval Jewish communities toward their self image as both a chosen *and* an exiled people. Such ambivalence is well documented and needs no elaboration here. Rather, once again, I wish to focus on the question of the text itself. This double perspective makes the Song of Songs into a marvelously dual phenomenon. It is both a reminder of the divine promise of assistance and redemption and an indictment of a God who has been distant for too long. This double perspective is achieved primarily through the literary techniques detailed in this article. The biblical Song is shown to be flexible and susceptible to temporal stretching, and yet at the same time it is this elasticity that causes the original particles to sound anew and generate the pain of yearning for a renewed embrace. It is only in this unique setting that the biblical lover's words "flee [*beraḥ*], my love" can turn into a bitter-yet-hopeful address in Ibn Gabirol's poem: "Please speak to my beloved who has fled [*baraḥ*]." The change of tense reveals the force of this transduction: the same characters speak of the same love with the same words and similes, but oh, so much has changed.

Bibliography

Alexander, Philip S. "Tradition and Originality in the Targum of the Song of Songs." In *The Aramaic Bible*, edited by Derek R. G. Beattie and Martin J. McNamara, 318–339. JSOTSup 166. London: Bloomsbury, 1994.
Boyarin, Daniel. *Intertextuality and the Reading of Midrash*. Bloomington: Indiana University Press, 1990.
Brann, Ross. *The Compunctious Poet*. Baltimore: Johns Hopkins University Press, 1991.
Cohen, Gerson D. "The Song of Songs and the Jewish Religious Mentality." In *The S. Friedland Lectures: Essays Brought together in Honor of His 70th Birthday*, 1–21. New York: Jewish Theological Seminary, 1966.
Cohen, Mordechai Z. "'The Best of Poetry . . .': Literary Approaches to the Bible in the Spanish Peshat Tradition." *The Torah U-Madda Journal* 6 (1995): 15–57.
Cohen, Mordechai Z. *The Rule of Peshat*. Philadelphia: University of Pennsylvania Press, 2020.
Cole, Peter, ed. and trans. *The Dream of the Poem: Hebrew Poetry from Muslim and Christian Spain, 950–1492*. Princeton: Princeton University Press, 2007.
Dolezel, Lubomir. *Heterocosmica: Fiction and Possible Worlds*. Baltimore: Johns Hopkins University Press, 1998.
Elizur, Shulamit, ed. *Kedushah ve-shir*. Jerusalem: self-published, 1988. (Hebrew)
Fleischer, Ezra. *Shirat ha-kodesh ha-'ivrit bimey habbeinayim*. Jerusalem: Keter, 1975. (Hebrew)
Genette, Gerard. *Palimpsests: Literature in the Second Degree*, translated by Channa Newman and Claude Doubinsky. Lincoln: University of Nebraska Press, 1976.

Huss, Matti. "Peshat 'o 'alegoriyah: Shirat ha-ḥeshek shel Shmu'el Hanagid." *Meḥkarei Yerushalayim be-sifrut 'ivrit* 15 (1995): 35–73. (Hebrew)
Ibn Ezra, Abraham. *Shirei ha-kodesh shel Abraham Ibn Ezra*, edited by Israel Levin. 2 vols. Jeruslaem: The Israeli National Academy of Science, 1976. (Hebrew)
Ibn Gabirol, Solomon. *Shirei ha-kodesh le-rabbi Shlomo Ibn Gabirol*, edited by Dov Yarden. 2 vols. Jerusalem: American Academy for Jewish Research, 1972. (Hebrew)
Ibn Ghiyyat, Isaac. *Shirei Isaac Ibn Giyyat*, edited by Yonah David. Tel Aviv: Aḥshav, 1987. (Hebrew)
Kadari, Tamar. "'Friends Hearken to Your Voice': Rabbinic Interpretations of the Song of Songs." In *Approaches to Literary Readings of Ancient Jewish Writings*, edited by K. A. D. Smelik and Karolien Vermeulen, 181–209. SSN 62. Leiden: Brill, 2014.
Kadari, Tamar. "Nismeḥu li leylot le-leylot." *Mada'ei ha-yahadut* 53 (2018): 45–168. (Hebrew)
Kadari, Tamar. "Rabbinic and Christian Models of Interaction on the Song of Songs." In *Interaction between Judaism and Christianity in History, Religion, Art and Literature*, edited by Marcel Poorthuis, Joshua J. Schwartz, and Joseph Turner, 65–82. JCPS 17. Leiden: Brill, 2009.
Levin, Israel. "Bikashti 'et she-'ahavah nafshi." *Hasifrut* 3 (1971–1972): 116–149. (Hebrew)
Lieber, Laura. "Piyyut." *Encyclopaedia of Judaism*. 2006. Accessed June 23, 2021. http://dx.doi.org/10.1163/1872-9029_EJ_COM_0143.
Lieber, Laura. "'There Is None Like You among the Mute': The Theology of *Ein Kamokha Ba-Illemim* in Context, with a New Edition and Translation." *Crusades* 6 (2007): 15–35.
Lieber, Laura. *A Vocabulary of Desire: The Song of Songs in the Early Synagogue*. BRLA 40. Leiden: Brill, 2014.
Lieberman, Saul. "Mishnat Shir ha-Shirim." In *Jewish Gnosticism, Merkaba Mysticism and Talmudic Tradition*, by Gerschom Scholem, 118–126. 2nd ed. New York: Jewish Theological Seminary, 1965. (Hebrew)
Pardes, Ilana. *The Song of Songs: A Biography*. Princeton: Princeton University Press, 2019.
Reif, Stefan C. "Abraham Ibn Ezra on Canticles." In *Abraham Ibn Ezra y Su Tiempo*, edited by Fernando Díaz Esteban, 241–249. Madrid: Asociación Española de Orientalistas, 1990.
Sáenz-Badillos, Angel. "Ibn Ghayyat." *EJ* 9:676–677.
Scheindlin, Raymond. *The Gazelle*. New York: Oxford University Press, 1999.
Sifrei. Translated by Shraga Silverstein. Sefaria. Accessed June 12, 2021. https://www.sefaria.org/Sifrei_Devarim?p2=Sifrei_Devarim.305.1&lang=en.
Simon, Maurice, trans. *Midrash Rabbah: Song of Songs*. London: Soncino Press, 1939.
Urbach, Ephraim E. "The Homiletical Interpretations of the Sages and the Expositions of Origen on Canticles, and the Jewish-Christian Disputation." *ScrHie* 22 (1971): 247–275.
Zakovitch, Yair. *Song of Songs: Riddle of Riddles*. LHBOTS 673. London: T&T Clark, 2019.

Jonathan Vardi
A Vocabulary of Love
The Song of Songs in the Secular Hebrew Love Poetry from Muslim Spain

1 The Gift of Vocabulary

The Golden Age of Hebrew poetry in Muslim Spain (al-Andalus) was the first major school of secular Hebrew literature to emerge after the canonization of the Bible. For over a thousand years, poetry in Hebrew was written mainly for liturgical purposes. Beginning in tenth century Cordoba, a massive corpus of poetry was written not merely for functional purposes, but also "for the sake of art." This new school of poetry emulated the masterpieces of Arabic poetry and expressed the emotional, poetic, and aesthetic values of the new Jewish elite who became integrated into the upper echelons of Muslim administration and had adopted many features of the lifestyle of Muslim high society, first in Cordoba, the capitol of the Omayyad caliphate, and later on in the many small states (*ṭā'ifa*; pl. *ṭawā'if*) that split off from it in the eleventh century. Thus, while the language of this innovative style was strictly purist biblical Hebrew, its form, meter, rhyme, genres, and motifs were all drawn from Arabic. However, the Hebrew poets of al-Andalus did not cease writing liturgical poetry (*piyyut*; pl. *piyyutim*); on the contrary, they embraced it. Gradually, the revolutionary style of their secular poetry penetrated the liturgical mode.

Unlike the language of the classical *piyyut* that emerged in Byzantine Palestine, which consisted of a mixture of biblical, rabbinic, and specific liturgical vocabulary, the Hebrew poets of al-Andalus exalted the Bible and considered it not only as the holy scripture but also a codex of literary masterpieces and the pinnacle of Hebrew style. Thus, they restricted themselves almost entirely to biblical Hebrew. When they attempted to revive the genre of love poetry in Hebrew—maybe for the first time since the Song of Songs—they were inevitably influenced by this ancient text.

In liturgical poetry, the allegoric mode flourished. Poets borrowed numerous motifs and tropes from secular love poetry and applied them to the traditional allegory of love between God as a husband and the feminine personification of Israel as his wife. Thus, even though the poetic form and style of some *piyyutim* may have resembled certain aspects of Arabic love poetry, their themes were still extensions (may we say fanfic?) of the allegoric interpretation of the Song of Songs: they dwelled on the same love story and the same characters but adopted it to fit a situation in which the lovers are apart (since Israel is in exile and the Temple of Jerusalem has been destroyed).[1]

This was not the case for secular love poetry. While the Song of Songs tells the story of mutual love in which both the man and woman celebrate each other's physical presence, and while some allegoric Andalusi *piyyutim* took up the voice of the female Israel by expressing her longing and faithfulness to her God-lover, the basic story of most secular poems was different. These poems were always presented from the perspective of a male speaker, who voiced his unrequited love for a beautiful yet cruel beloved, either female or male. Clearly, this narrative framework differed considerably from the Song of Songs, regardless of whether it is interpreted literally or allegorically. However, the Song of Songs gave this newly born Hebrew genre an invaluable birth present: the gift of vocabulary. Since Hebrew was not a spoken language, none of the secular genres could use a "living" speech; yet the Song of Songs offered—particularly for the genre of love—a lively, affecting, convincing, and ready-made *discours amoureux*.

2 Wine and Love

During the first two generations of Hebrew Andalusi poetry, poets were still seeking out ways to adapt Hebrew poems to Arabic conventions. The poet who managed to design a Hebrew pattern to most literary genres belonged to the third poetic generation; it was the great statesman, military commander, rabbi, philologist, and poet Samuel Ha-Nagid (Ismāʿīl ibn Naghrila; 993–1056). His contemporaries acknowledged him as the first major poet of the school; in the twelfth century, the historian Abraham ibn Daud wrote that while the first generation of Hebrew poets "began to chirp," by contrast "in the days of Samuel Ha-Nagid they sang aloud."[2] This metaphor of poets as songbirds refers to a famous wine poem by the great eighth century Abbasid poet Abū Nuwās. In a wine poem celebrating the spring equinox (the Persian *Nowruz*), the poet declares that "the birds sang after previously stammering."[3] By shifting this metaphor to literary history, Ibn Daud implied that with Samuel Ha-Nagid a poetic spring has arrived.

The contribution of the Song of Songs to secular poetry may be demonstrated by comparing the language of Ha-Nagid in the two "Arabic" genres of wine (*kham-*

---

[1] For the distinction between secular love poems and religious allegoric ones, see Huss, "Secular Poetry."
[2] Ibn Daud, *Sefer ha-Qabbalah*, 102; Hebrew text: ibid., 73.
[3] Wagner, ed., *Der Dīwān*, 243.

riyyāt) and love (ghazaliyyāt). To capture the subtle details of an aristocratic wine banquet, Ha-Nagid sometimes had to "chase his words to the edges of Hebrew" (as the modern poet Nathan Alterman has written in a different context).[4] The relatively common biblical word כּוֹס (kos, cup), being the etymological equivalent of the Arabic ka's, was clearly appropriate in Hebrew wine poems, but was not always sufficiently exquisite. To depict an extravagant cup, Ha-Nagid sometimes used it within constructs such as כּוֹס אֶקְדָּח. The hapax legomenon אֶקְדָּח (eqdaḥ; Isa 54:12) refers originally to a kind of precious stone and derives from the root ק-ד-ח which is connected to piercing or kindling (not to be confused, as Israeli students often do, with a gun, the meaning of the same word in modern Hebrew). The expression kos eqdaḥ thus means a cup that radiates like a gem, as a result of the artisan's high craftsmanship but also because of the shimmering wine that fills it. However, the readers or listeners of Ha-Nagid could not miss the similarity to the parallel Arabic word qadaḥ, which means a large drinking cup. In another poem, Ha-Nagid omitted the word kos and used the rare word alone (perhaps, after already introducing the construct form, he could rely on his audience to understand a shorter version), but shifted it to the feminine form of אֶקְדָּחָה (eqdaḥa). Since in Arabic both cup and wine are feminine, the whole genre ascribes feminine qualities to this beverage. Another surprising feminine lexical option is the rare word אֲשִׁישָׁה (ashisha); the original meaning of the word is uncertain, but it clearly belongs to the semantic field of food or drink. It is mentioned in Song 2:5 as a parallel to apples, and in 2Sam 6:19 it is used in a description that includes a loaf of bread. The Hebrew philologists of al-Andalus tended to interpret this word as a wine cup (cf. Hos 3:1);[5] Ha-Nagid utilized it in several wine poems to depict a precious goblet.

These kind of lexical problems and brilliant solutions were unnecessary in the genre of love. The basic vocabulary was available, as is, in the Song of Songs. The ordinary metaphorical terms for the beloved woman or man עָפְרָה, עֹפֶר, צְבִיָּה, צְבִי (gazelle, doe, fawn) reflected Arabic terms such as ghazāl (the etymological origin of gazelle); among other reasons, such as the similarity between צְבִי (ṣebi; gazelle) and the Arabic ṣabī (boy), they were probably chosen over other biblical terms for antelopes also because these appear in the Song of Songs.[6] However, the Song did not only give this new genre a vocabulary of names and epithets but also a rich symbolic language of figures and tropes. When Ha-Nagid wants to depict a young "fawn" who engages in a brilliant poetic flirt, he writes that when the youth saw him drinking his wine, he offered him something even more attractive:

---

[4] Alterman, 'ir Hayona, 292.
[5] See Menaḥem ben Saruq, Maḥberet, 34–35.
[6] The main exception, יעלה, usually appears as part of the idiom יעלת חן (Prov 5:19).

אֲשֶׁר רָאָה בְיָדִי כוֹס וְאָמַר / 'שְׁתֵה מִבֵּין שְׂפָתַי דַּם עֲנָבִים'.

> [the fawn] who saw a cup in my hand and said:
> Drink your grape-blood (wine; cf. Deut 32:14) from between my lips.[7]

The hidden metaphor, comparison, and erotic invitation—kiss me, for my kiss is better than wine—was clear to the listeners and readers since it alludes to the opening of the Song (1:2): "Oh give me the kisses of his mouth: for your love is more delightful than wine." Similarly, in another poem, the act of kissing is described as drinking not only wine but also milk from each other's lips, as in Song 4:11 ("honey and milk are under your tongue"):

שְׁתֵה יַיִן וְחָלָב מִשְּׂפָתַי / וְתֵן תַּגְמוּל לְיֵינִי וַחֲלָבִי.

> drink wine and milk of my lips;
> reward me for my own wine and milk (i.e., answer my kisses with yours).[8]

Elsewhere, Ha-Nagid incorporates the Song's description of the woman's belly, "hedged about with lilies" (7:3), probably to describe the belly (perfumed with lilies?) of his own (male) flirting-partner.[9] Even when the poet gives credence to the superstition that the lover's gaze may cast an evil eye on the beloved, he has no better words to warn him than the ones from the Song ("Set out, my beloved, swift as a gazelle"; 2:17; cf. 8:14):

סוֹב דְּמֵה לַצְּבִי וְהִרְחַק לָךְ, פֶּן / אֶחֱמוֹד יָפְיְךָ וְתֻלְקֶה בְעֵינִי.

> Set out and be as swift as a gazelle, distance yourself lest
> I yearn for your beauty and my eye will hurt you.[10]

Anyhow, the Song of Songs was also a resource for wine poems. Most works in this genre were not devoted to wine drinking alone, but rather to the enchanting setting of the banquet which was usually held in a lush garden in springtime, to the sound of birds, rivulets, and music. The Song of Songs was certainly a major biblical resource for descriptions of spring.[11] The beautiful (male or female) servants who poured the wine were also an attraction of these banquets; often their physical

---

7 Ha-Nagid, *Dīwān*, 305 no. 183. Translations of Medieval poetry are all mine; biblical translation usually follow the new-JPS translation.
8 Ha-Nagid, *Dīwān*, 299 no. 166.
9 See Ha-Nagid, *Dīwān*, 296 no. 160.
10 Ha-Nagid, *Dīwān*, 297 no. 163.
11 See, e.g., Ha-Nagid, *Dīwān*, 285 no. 135, נִרְאוּ בְנֵי הַתּוֹר בְּאַרְצֵנוּ ("turtledoves are seen in our land"), following Song 2:12.

descriptions were based on passages from the Song in which the lovers metaphorically describe each other's body in detail.[12]

Finally, in Arabic wine poetry it is not unusual for the poet to mention the geographical origin of his wine, in order to praise its quality. Hebrew wine poetry did not maintain this tradition since the purist restriction to biblical language prevented the poets from using the actual names of places. Two poems by Ha-Nagid are probably exceptions, in which he recites the verse אַשְׁקְךָ מִיַּיִן הָרֶקַח מֵעֲסִיס רִמֹּנִי ("I would let you drink of the spiced wine, of my pomegranate juice"; Song 8:2).[13] In these poems, it is quite possible that the poet was not referring to actual fruit juice, but rather to the wine whose origin is Ha-Nagid's hometown, Granada (i.e., a pomegranate, and often in Hebrew poetry: רימון).

3 Arabic Motifs

In the courtly Arabic love poetry written in al-Andalus, poets often mentioned names of places in the Arabian Peninsula. These places were previously described in eastern Arabic classical love poetry, either in the *nasīb*-section (amatory prelude) of the celebrated pre-Islamic *qaṣāʾid* (s. *qaṣīda*, polythematic long poem) or in the sentimental heart-breaking *ʿudhrī* poems about mad, eternal love. Michael Sells noted that "features of ancient Bedouin lovers had become through centuries of symbolic condensation the perfect vehicle for the Andalusian longing for the homeland."[14] Ha-Nagid, who aspired to achieve this kind of effect in his own love poetry, utilized the symbolic *topoi* from the Song of Songs:

> אָשׁוּט כְּהֹלֵךְ עֲלֵי גִבְעַת לְבוֹנָה וְאֶד- / בִּיק אֶת לְחָיַי אֱלֵי מִדְרַךְ הֲלִיכְיְכִי.
>
> I wander like a nomad upon the hill of frankincense,
> and lay my cheek where your feet have trod.[15]

The *topos* of this poem is the landscape of the biblical pastorale. The "hill of frankincense" has a double meaning: literally, it may be the actual hill where the perfumed beloved walked, leaving behind her a wonderful scent. At the same time, it is part of a biblical arcadia, the scenery of the Song of Songs (4:6; גִּבְעַת הַלְּבוֹנָה) and the most appropriate location for Hebrew love poetry.

---

12 See e.g., the descriptions of the female servant's lips and the male servant's arms (Ha-Nagid, *Dīwān*, 288 no. 140, 290; no. 145), in which the description follows Song 4:3; 5:14.
13 Ha-Nagid, *Dīwān*, 286 no. 137, 288; no. 140.
14 Sells, "Love," 146.
15 Ha-Nagid, *Dīwān*, 299 no. 167.

Solomon ibn Gabirol (ca. 1021–1058), Ha-Nagid's young contemporary, also adapted from the Song of Songs in order to play with Arabic motifs. One of his most brilliant references to the Song is connected to the Hebrew adaptation of the dominant Arabic poetic form, the *qaṣīda*.[16] Although the Hebrew *qaṣīda* dates back to the tenth century with Dunash b. Labrat's panegyrics to his patron Ḥasday ibn Shaprut, the Hebrew poets seemed to hesitate about using the amatory prelude (*nasīb*). The Hebrew poets did start their *qaṣā'id* with an introductory section before reaching the "aim" (*qaṣd*) of the poem (i.e., the praise of its recipient); however, in the first generations of the poetic school, the opening section was still not dedicated to the theme of love. For example, Dunash's poem דְּעֵה לִבִּי חָכְמָה ("know, my heart, wisdom"), that is traditionally considered the first Hebrew *qaṣīda*, begins with a long didactic section (adhering to the Arabic genre of ascetic poetry, *zuhd*) before praising Ḥasday.[17] Samuel Ha-Nagid refrained from amatory themes in most of his *qaṣā'id* as well; nevertheless, he was still at the focus of the erotic *nasīb*'s entrance into Hebrew literature. He was involved with four of the earliest Hebrew amatory preludes: two were written by Ha-Nagid and the other two opened *qaṣā'id* that were written in his honor: the panegyric of Joseph ibn Ḥasday to Samuel Ha-Nagid;[18] the latter's response-poem to the former;[19] Ha-Nagid's poem צְבִי נָעִים,[20] in which he curiously declares that the whole amatory prelude is merely an allegory, just like the Song of Songs(!);[21] and Ibn Gabirol's *qaṣīda* מִי זֹאת כְּמוֹ שַׁחַר,[22] whose reference to the Song of Songs is most fascinating.

The most common motif in the ancient Arabic *nasīb* was the *aṭlāl*—the traces of an abandoned camp: the poet goes to the places where his beloved's tribe used to dwell, sees the ruins, remembers the delightful nights he spent with her, and cries over her loss in the infinite desert. This section often starts with a question of *anagnorisis*, recognition: "lo, whose traces do I see?" etc. Another ancient theme describes a desert encounter with a travelling lady: the beloved and her tribe are about to break camp; the poet sees her at the moment of departure, bids her farewell, asks whether she will remain faithful to him, etc.[23]

Ibn Gabirol's *nasīb* manages to intertwine these two motifs: upon his encounter with the woman-nomad, the speaker begins with a question of *anagnorisis*: "lo,

---

16 For this poetic form in Arabic see, for example, Jacobi, "Qaṣīda."
17 See Schirmann, *Hebrew Poetry*, 35–40.
18 See Schirmann, *Hebrew Poetry*, 172–175.
19 See Ha-Nagid, *Dīwān*, 164–169.
20 See Ha-Nagid, *Dīwān*, 221–222. Traditional "Arabian" motifs occur also in ha-Nagid's introduction to the poem היום מחר, without an explicit erotic discourse. See ibid., 200.
21 Regarding this declaration, see Huss, "Secular Poetry."
22 See Ibn Gabirol, *Secular Poems*, 98 no. 159.
23 See Jacobi, "Nasīb," 978–983.

who is this beauty." Surprisingly, this scene, which, when located at the beginning of a *qaṣīda* seems so "Arabic," is in fact a quotation from Song 6:10 ("Who is she who shines through like the dawn, Beautiful as the moon, radiant as the sun"), with minimal adaptation to the poem's meter and rhyme:

מִי זֹאת כְּמוֹ שַׁחַר עוֹלָה וְנִשְׁקְפָה, / תָּאִיר כְּאוֹר חַמָּה, בָּרָה מְאֹד יָפָה?

Who is she that like the dawn does shine / glowing like sunlight, radiant, very beautiful?[24]

The desert is not mentioned directly in this poem; but it enters the reader's mind both because of the Arabic connotations of a desert scene and the parallel question in Song 3:6 ("Who is she who comes up from the desert"). Thus, Ibn Gabirol not only facilitates the incorporation of Arabic motifs into Hebrew poetry by mediating them through famous biblical verses but also reveals the literary imagination of his cultural milieu, by reading the Song of Songs and seeing a *nasīb*-like scene.

Ibn Gabirol makes another significant reference to the Songs of Songs in one of his miniature poems. Remarkably, this time the poet actually mocks the Song. After comparing the beautiful ephebe's teeth to icicles and pearls, he adds that he "wonders about the wise Solomon, who compared pearls to flocks."[25] Obviously, Ibn Gabirol is referring to the Song's verse about the beloved woman's teeth ("your teeth are like a flock of ewes climbing up from the washing pool"; 6:6). As Uriah Kfir has recently shown, Ibn Gabirol deliberately uses the Song of Songs as a poetic cliché.[26] Criticizing the pastoral imagery of the Song, Gabirol manages to imitate the boasting denunciation of the modern (*muḥdath*), urban Arabic poets of their pre-Islamic predecessors of the Arabic peninsula. The "modern" poets bragged that they had a superior lifestyle, preferring the garden to the desert and plenty of wine to goat milk; at the same time, they manifested their discontent with the celebrated "Arabic" motifs such as describing the abandoned abodes and camel journeys, or when in particular they expressed their contempt for the usage of beasts as symbols of beauty. While Ibn Gabirol seems to criticize King Solomon for his pastoral simile, he actually constructed the Song of Songs as the biblical analogy of pre-Islamic poetry by casting it as an obsolete yet admired corpus that only a saucy young poet could courageously dismiss. Thus, he actually offered Hebrew poetry its own glorious past. This miniature poem shows that the Hebrew love poetry did not blindly embrace the entire imagery of the Song of Songs as a whole; however, by refuting an "inappropriate" simile from the Song and revealing it as an "archaicism," Ibn Gabirol successfully revives even the most "futile" image.

---

24 Ibn Gabirol, *Secular Poems*, 98 no. 159.
25 Ibn Gabirol, *Secular Poems*, 132 no. 205.
26 See Kfir, "Solomon vs. Solomon."

4 Interpretation

The creative process of transmuting the Song of Songs into "modern," Arabic-style love poetry was not unidirectional. The Jewish intellectuals of al-Andalus did not only interweave images from the Song into their own poems; inevitably, their own aesthetic and poetic ideal of love poetry influenced the way they read the Song itself. We have seen how Ibn Gabirol considered the poetic questions of the Song, "who is she who shines through like the dawn" and "who is she that comes up from the desert," as resembling an Arabic *nasīb*. This case is not exceptional. A fascinating interpretation of the Song, influenced by the conventions of Arabic love poetry can be found in *Kitāb al-Uṣūl* ("The Book of Roots"), the famous dictionary of the eleventh century grammarian Abu-l-walīd Marwān Yona (Jonah) ibn Jannāḥ, who was a bitter rival of Samuel Ha-Nagid, and probably an occasional patron of Ibn Gabirol.²⁷

The biblical verb לִבַּבְתִּנִי (Song 4:9), deriving from the root which denotes "heart" (לבב), is usually interpreted as "you have captured my heart" (new JPS translation) or "ravished my heart" (KJV translation). That is, it is clear that the beloved woman does *something*, although it is not quite clear what, to her lover's heart. Ibn Jannāḥ's brilliant solution to this question is affected by the Arabic twice: first by a philological inquiry of a parallel root, and second by the conventions of Arabic love poetry. To determine the meaning of this verb, he compares it to the equivalent Arabic denominative verb *qalaba*, which derives from the parallel noun *qalb* ("heart"). Although the basic meaning of the verb is to turn something upside down, one of its connotations is to strike someone's heart. This meaning actually fits a very common convention in Arabic (and later Hebrew) love poetry: the beloved's glance is compared to a deadly arrow because it makes the lover die of love. This is exactly how Ibn Jannāḥ reads Song 4:9 (לִבַּבְתִּנִי אֲחֹתִי כַלָּה לִבַּבְתִּנִי בְּאַחַת מֵעֵינַיִךְ בְּאַחַד עֲנָק מִצַּוְּרֹנָיִךְ; "you have captured my heart, my sister, my bride, you have captured my heart with one [glance] of your eyes, with one coil of your necklace"). According to his dictionary, the glance of the beloved does not only capture her lover's heart, but rather, poetically, slays it: "לבבתני; the translation is *qalabtinī* ('you have struck my heart'), or *aṣabti qalbī* ('you have hit my heart') with the arrow of your eyes'."²⁸

---

27 To the rivalry between the two grammarians, see Wilhelm Bacher's introduction to: Ibn Jannāḥ, *Sefer Haschoraschim*, XV–XX; Schirmann, *History*, 205–206. To the panegyrics of Ibn Gabirol in honor of Ibn Jannāḥ, see Ibn Gabirol, *Secular Poems*, 63 no. 114, and probably also ibid., 79 no. 132, that praises a grammarian without mentioning his name, and ibid., 34 no. 61, whose recipient's first name is Jonah. See Vardi, "Between Shemuel Ha-Nagid," 458, 443 n. 26.
28 Ibn Jannāḥ, *Book of Hebrew Roots (Kitāb al-Uṣūl)*, 343.

This figure of speech repeats itself in a love poem by Ibn Jannāḥ's great rival, Samuel Ha-Nagid, in which the quotation from the Song of Songs functions not only poetically but also exegetically.

רַעְיָה, צְבִי מִבּוֹר-שְׁבִי – הֲתִפְתְּחִי? / רֵיחַ בְּגָדַיִךְ לְבַשְׂרוֹ שִׁלְחִי!
הֲבְמֵי אֲדָמִים תִּמְשְׁחִי שִׂפְתָיַיִךְ, / אוֹ דַם עֳפָרִים תִּמְרְחִי עַל הַלְּחִי?
דּוֹדִים לְדוֹד תַּגְמוּל אֲהָבָיו תִּתְּנִי, / רוּחִי וְנִשְׁמָתִי מְקוֹם מָהֳרֵךְ קְחִי.
לֵב בִּשְׁתֵּי עֵינַיִךְ אִם תִּפְלְחִי – / בְּאַחַד עֲנָק מִצַּוְּארוֹנַיִךְ יְחִי!

> O beloved, shall you release a gazelle from its prison? /
> Do send him the scent of your garments to herald him!
> Is it rubies-water you anoint your lips with, /
> Or rather the blood of fawns upon your cheek?
> Give love to your lover as a reward for his love, /
> Take my soul and my spirit instead of your bride price.
> If you slay a heart with both of your eyes—/
> It will come back to life with one coil of your necklace.[29]

In the beginning of the poem, the speaker unusually refers to himself as a "gazelle," which is primarily reserved for the beloved; thus, the poem presents the speaker's desire to become a "gazelle" in the eye of his beloved. He addresses her and begs her to free him from the "prison" of desire; in order to do so, this gallant lover needs no more than the heady fragrance of her garments.

The second verse, however, reveals the "cruel-hearted" side of the beloved, who does not tend to return her suitors' love: the red of her lips and cheeks may come either from a miraculous lipstick of melted rubies or from the blood of "fawns," that is, the dead young men who fell fatally for her. The speaker seems to waver between the hope of earning the woman's love and deadly despair facing her refusals. The next verse expresses hope once again: he offers her a fair trade of her love for his love, but also an eternal devotion with his soul as the bride's price.

The final verse seems to strike a balance between the beauty and fatality of this woman. It does so by using an extended version of Song 4:9. The entire line is based upon this biblical verse, but the verb לבבתני is missing. The verb תפלחי ("you slay") replaces it: instead of the rare and difficult verb, Ha-Nagid uses a verb whose meaning is unequivocal. This is a poetic choice of a poet who was also a philologist and bible commentator; he loads the poetic line with enough biblical references to evoke recollections of the verse from the Song and then implies that the meaning of the missing and obscure word is the one in the poem instead. In this case (and actually in many others; Ibn Jannāḥ's dictionary is very helpful when reading

---

29 Ha-Nagid, *Dīwān*, 297 no. 161.

Ha-Nagid's poetry) it turns out that Ha-Nagid agreed with his opponent-linguist as regards to the meaning of this word.

The final line thus poetically "emends" Song 4:9. The beloved's glance, according to literary conventions, is deadly. That is why the biblical poet writes that his beloved "slayed him with [the arrow-glance of] one of her eyes." This appears to make the second component of this verse redundant: did she kill him again with "one coil of her necklace" (Song 4:9)? Ha-Nagid endows the second part with a special verb of its own, thus constructing a binary opposition that could actually fit a biblical parallelism: if you slay my heart with [*one*, nay, even if you kill me with] *both* of your eyes, this death will not be absolute. All I need is one coil of your necklace to revive. This extreme sensibility of a courtly lover envelopes the poem and closes it beautifully: he who needs only the fragrance of his beloved's garments to alleviate his desire, is the one who only needs a coil of her necklace to rise from passionate death.

5 Conclusion

The Song of Songs played a major part in the creation of Hebrew love poetry in al-Andalus: it provided poets with the proper vocabulary and imagery to write love poetry in Hebrew once again after more than a thousand years. Their usage of the Song, however, was not naïve at all. The convention of Arabic *ghazal* and standards of courtly love could not authorize straightforward borrowing from the Song. The ways of utilizing the biblical material in Hebrew-Andalusi poetry constantly shifted between recitation, adaptation, emendation, exegesis, and even parody. Rethinking the Song of Songs in terms of Arabic love poetry did not only help shape a parallel Hebrew genre but also altered the way in which the Song of Songs was read by Jews in al-Andalus, at least with regard to its literal meaning, before considering it allegorically.

Bibliography

Alterman, Nathan. *'ir Hayona*. Tel-Aviv: Hakibutz Hameuḥad, 1958.
Ha-Nagid, Samuel. *Dīwān*, edited by Dov Jarden (*Divan Shmuel Hanagid: Ben Tehillim*). Jerusalem: Hebrew Union College, 1967.
Huss, Matti. "Secular Poetry or Religious Allegory: The Love Poems of Samuel Ha-Nagid." *Jerusalem Studies in Hebrew Literature* 15 (1995): 35–73. (Hebrew)
Ibn Daud, Abraham. *Sefer ha-Qabbalah: The Book of Tradition*, edited and translated by Gershon D. Cohen. Philadelphia: The Jewish Publication Society of America, 1967.

Ibn Gabirol, Solomon. *Secular Poems*, edited by Haim Brody and Jefim Schirmann. Jerusalem: Schocken, 1974.
Ibn Jannāḥ, Abu-l-walīd Marwān Yona. *Sefer Haschoraschim*, edited by Wilhelm Bacher, translated by Jehuda Ibn Tibbon. Berlin: M'kize Nirdamim, 1896.
Ibn Jannāḥ, Abu-l-walīd Marwān Yona. *The Book of Hebrew Roots (Kitāb al-Uṣūl)*, edited by Adolf Neubauer. Oxford: Clarendon Press, 1875.
Jacobi, Renate. "Nasīb." In vol. 7 of *Encyclopaedia of Islam: Second Edition*, edited by Peri Bearman, Thierry Bianquis, Clifford Edmund Bosworth, Emeri Johannes van Donzel, and Wolfhart P. Heinrichs, 978–983. Leiden: Brill, 1993.
Jacobi, Renate. "Qaṣīda." In vol. 2 of *Encyclopedia of Arabic Literature*, edited by Julie Scott Meisami and Paul Starkey, 630–633. London: Routledge, 1998.
Kfir, Uriah. "Solomon vs. Solomon: The Fabrication of a Hebrew-shuʿūbite Polemic." In *'His Pen and Ink Are a Powerful Mirror': Andalusi, Judaeo-Arabic, and Other Near Eastern Studies in Honor of Ross Brann*, edited by Adam Bursi, Sarah Jean Pearce, and Hamza M. Zafer, 118–139. Christians and Jews in Muslim Societies 4. Leiden: Brill, 2020.
Menaḥem ben Saruq. *Maḥberet*, edited by Herschell Filipowski. London: The Hebrew Antiquarian Society, 1854.
Schirmann, Jefim, ed. *Hebrew Poetry in Spain and Provence*. Jerusalem: Bialik Institute, 1956.
Schirmann, Jefim. *The History of Hebrew Poetry in Muslim Spain*, edited by Ezra Fleischer. Jerusalem: Magnes Press & Ben-Zvi Institute, 1995. (Hebrew)
Sells, Michael. "Love." In *The Literature of Al-Andalus*, edited by María Rosa Menocal, Raymond P. Scheindlin, and Michael Sells, 126–158. Cambridge: Cambridge University Press, 2000.
Vardi, Jonathan. "Between Shemuel Ha-Nagid and the Poets of Zaragoza." *Tarbiz* 84 (2016): 437–467.
Wagner, Ewald, ed. *Der Dīwān des Abū Nuwās*. Vol. 3. Wiesbaden: Steiner, 1988.

Ludger Schwienhorst-Schönberger
Bernard of Clairvaux
The Song of Songs as an Instruction on the Spiritual Life

1 Introduction

The 86 *Sermones super Cantica Canticorum* (abbreviation: SC)[1] are not only the most extensive, but also the most significant work by Bernard of Clairvaux (1090–1153). They are based upon sermons that the famous Cistercian had held over a longer period from 1135 to 1153 in front of his community of monks in the abbey that he had founded in *Clara Vallis* (Clairvaux) in the Northeast of France in 1115. In these sermons, the abbot presents a continuous interpretation of the Song of Songs 1:1–3:1. This interpretation is not a Bible commentary (*expositio*) in its strict sense but a series of homilies or sermons. A sermon (*sermo*) presents a theme according to principles provided by a biblical text. This text is not commented upon verse-by-verse, as would be the case in a commentary, but it forms the point of departure for the discussion of themes that were considered important for the life of a monk. There is no doubt that Bernard indeed did deliver sermons on the Song of Songs. Their precise wording has not been preserved, however. The *Sermones super Cantica Canticorum*, which have been handed down in different versions, are no exact transcripts, but renderings of the original sermons that have been meticulously and skillfully revised and reconstructed according to the highest literary standards—one of the most aesthetic medieval works of literary art known to us today.[2] Because of its religious and literary quality, this work has surpassed all other writings of Bernard by far in its influence.[3]

In his method of scriptural interpretation, Bernard depends on the legacy of the Church Fathers, as does medieval theology in general. Patristic exegesis, as it was handed down to the Middle Ages in the works of Origen, Ambrose, Augustine, Jerome, and Gregory the Great, represents the uncritical methodical and hermeneutical framework within which Bernard reads and interprets Holy Scripture.

---

[1] The English translations of Bernhard's sermons are own translations, based on the following translations and editions: Bernard, *On the Song of Songs I* (Walsh, trans.); Bernard, *On the Song of Songs II* (Walsh, trans.); Bernhard, *Sämtliche Werke* (Winkler, ed.); Bernard, *Super Cantica 1–35* (Leclercq et al., eds.); Bernard, *Super Cantica 36–83* (Leclercq et al., eds.).
[2] See Köpf, "Einleitung," 30.
[3] See Dinzelbacher, *Bernhard*, 177.

Note: I thank Dr. Hanneke Friedl for translating my text from German to English.

Despite lively developments in philosophy, theology, and exegesis, conscious continuity with its patristic legacy remains one of the most important characteristics of the medieval period, albeit with methodical adaptations. Early scriptural interpretations thus became a model, referential text, and irrevocable part of every new exegetical initiative.[4] Several important recent contributions have led to the rediscovery and reappraisal of the exegesis of the Church Fathers.[5] An animated discussion now attempts to determine whether the scriptural interpretation of the Early Church and Middle Ages can contribute towards mitigating or even partially solving the aporia and the one-sidedness of modern historical-critical exegesis.[6] Without discussing this aspect in detail, we may simply briefly remind ourselves of the principles of patristic scriptural interpretation.[7] These include: (1) the polysemy and ambiguity of biblical texts (the "multiple senses of Scripture"), (2) the doctrine of the unity of Scripture (*unitas scripturae*), (3) the importance of the biblical canon as the interpretational context and determiner of meaning for biblical texts, (4) the importance of intertextuality, (5) the distinction between the intention of an author and the meaning of a text, (6) the influence of the community of reception on the exposition and determination of the meaning of polysemic texts.

Bernard's position must be determined somewhat more accurately within this greater flow of thought. Our famous Cistercian was one of the main exponents of so-called *monastic theology*, which had experienced its culmination in the twelfth century. The distinction between monastic and scholastic theology can be attributed to the medievalist Jean Leclercq, who essentially distinguishes between two types of Christian scholarly discipline. Whereas scholastic theology was taught—as is evidenced by the name—in urban clerical schools situated adjacent to the cathedrals and was conceived as a preparation for the *vita activa*, the monasteries gave birth to an educational form that was detached from any particular objective, showing contemplative tendencies, indeed a theology of the monasteries, the monastic theology. In his classical work, *The Love of Learning and the Desire for God: A Study of Monastic Culture*, Leclercq describes monastic theology and its addressees as follows:

> they are spiritual men who must have the *doctrina spiritus*. They are the 'perfect' to whom, according to St. Paul, words of wisdom must be spoken: *sapientiam loquimur.* They are men who constantly, 'for a long time, have been concerned with celestial realities' [...] in a word,

---

4 See Prügl, "Mittelalter," 127.
5 See Reiser, *Bibelkritik*; idem, *Autorität der Schrift*.
6 See Schwienhorst-Schönberger, "Wiederentdeckung," 402–425.
7 See Fiedrowicz, *Prinzipien*; idem, *Theologie der Kirchenväter*, 97–187; Schwienhorst-Schönberger, "Der vierfache Schriftsinn," 275–202; Pollmann, "Alte Kirche," 9–11; Prügl, "Mittelalter," 125–133; Drecoll, "Kirchengeschichte Patristik und Mittelalter," 105–140.

they are contemplatives. [...] This theology assumes on the part of the teacher and on the part of his audience, a special way of life, a rigorous asceticism, or as they say today a 'commitment.' Rather than speculative insights, it gives them a certain appreciation, of savoring and clinging to the truth and, what is everything, to the love of God.[8]

Whereas scholastic theology strives towards examining, asking critical questions (*quaerere*), and attaining knowledge (*scire*), monastic theology deals with longing (*desiderare*) and experience (*experiri*). Leclercq considers Bernard's homilies on the Song of Songs an exemplary piece of monastic theology. They are a contemplative speech, a *theoreticus sermo*,

not oriented toward learning but toward spirituality. He insists that one must go beyond the rational methods which may be properly applied to matters of faith. He is therefore assuming that the teacher and his pupils have received a God-given gift and personal grace. It is God really who does the teaching; consequently it is to Him that we must pray. In this light, just as there is no theology without moral life and asceticism, so there is no theology without prayer. Its effect will be the establishment of a certain contact with God.[9]

With Ambrogio Piazzoni, one can take a further step and distinguish an earlier and a later school of thought within monastic theology. Piazzoni mentions Rupert of Deutz, Lawrence of Durham, Bruno, abbot of Segni, Honorius Augustodunensis, Richard, abbot of Préaux, and Arnold of Bonneval as exponents of the earlier school of thought, whereas Bernard of Clairvaux and his pupils would represent the later school. Their primary concern was not secular knowledge, but spiritual experience.[10]

In his basic understanding of the Song of Songs, Bernard likewise shares in the tradition of early Christian thought, which in turn depends on Jewish tradition. This understanding differs sharply from modern views on the book, although one should add that the discussion of earlier viewpoints has been taken up anew recently.[11] However, this discussion can and should not be explained here. Jewish and Christian traditions both understand the Song of Songs figuratively. The love between the man and the woman that is extolled in the Song is understood as an image of the love between God and His people. The man symbolizes God and, in the Christian tradition, Christ, the Bridegroom (see Matt 9:15 par.; John 3:29); the woman represents the people of Israel and, in the Christian tradition, the Church.

---

8 Leclercq, *Love of Learning*, 6.
9 Leclercq, *Love of Learning*, 6–7.
10 See Piazzoni, "Exégèse vétéro-monastique et néo-monastique," 143–156.
11 Zur jüngeren Diskussion, see Schellenberg and Schwienhorst-Schönberger, *Interpreting*; Schwienhorst-Schönberger, *Konflikt der Interpretationen*; idem, *Das Hohelied der Liebe*; idem, "Der theologische Charakter des Hoheliedes," 269–286; Heereman, *Behold King Solomon*.

Within the Christian tradition, this basic understanding has developed in three directions, according to an ecclesiological, a mystical, and a Mariological understanding. In the ecclesiological interpretation, the woman represents the Church. According to the mystical understanding she represents the soul of the individual believer, and in the Mariological reading she represents the Virgin Mary. Bernard's homilies accentuate the mystical understanding of the Song of Songs. One might understand these sermons as a *vademecum* of the spiritual life. Before exploring this according to a few exemplary interpretations, let us consider, together with the Protestant Bernard-expert, Ulrich Köpf:

> Influenced by Bernard, the Cistercians largely eschewed the Mariological interpretation in favor of the mystical. Greek theology constituted an important reference: Gregory of Nyssa, portions from Pseudo-Dionysius the Areopagite, and particularly Origen were being read anew. The twelfth century was the scene of a veritable Origen Renaissance. The works of the Alexandrian were largely available in Clairvaux, and his influence on Bernard and his contemporaries cannot be denied. William of Saint-Thierry had already written a commentary wholly concentrated on the mystical interpretation in 1135/1138. Bernard has directly treated this commentary, which had doubtlessly influenced his thought. The work of the abbot of Clairvaux constitutes the unquestionable zenith in the history of mystical interpretations of the Song of Songs. Bernard however does not merely pass over the literal meaning (*sensus literalis*) of the book. He occasionally considers all three levels of meaning consecutively, albeit with a definite preference for the deeper meaning, that of the "spiritual sense" (*sensus spiritualis*), which refers to the Church, and the "moral sense" (*sensus moralis*), which has the individual in its view and culminates in a mystical interpretation.[12]

In his sermons, Bernard presents the Song of Songs "as a handbook for the practical religiosity of his monks. Through his homilies, he turned the explication of the Bible, which had until then belonged to theoretical theology, into a means of spiritual guidance of the soul."[13]

Before turning to some of these sermons, we provide an overview over the contents of the complete work. We should remember, however, that Bernard was often led by associations. Therefore, it hardly is possible to recognize any strictly thematical structure in the text. A simplified structure would consist of two main parts, each containing five sections:[14]

I. SC 1–38: Dogmatic themes
    (1) SC 1–9: Incarnation, trinity, creation
    (2) SC 10–16: Confession and penance

---

[12] Köpf, "Einleitung," 36 (own translation from the German).
[13] Dinzelbacher, *Bernhard*, 177 (own translation from the German).
[14] In accordance with Winkler, "Einleitung," 37–41.

    (3) SC 17–24: Grace
    (4) SC 25–34: Eschatology
    (5) SC 35–38: Knowledge of self, Knowledge of God, Knowledge of the world
II. SC 39–86: Themes from moral theology and ecclesiology
    (1) SC 39–48: The doctrine of virtue
    (2) SC 49–62: Love as the primary fruit of salvation
    (3) SC 63–69: The danger to the church through hypocrisy and heresy
    (4) SC 70–75: God-given love as a gift of the spirit
    (5) SC 76–86: The doctrine of the mystery of the church (ending Song 3:3)

2 A Holy Contemplative Discourse (SC 1)

The first sermon provides a suitable entry into an understanding of the whole collection of sermons. Using the Song of Songs as a starting point, the abbot of Clairvaux introduces the monks entrusted to his care to the higher echelons of spiritual life. He assumes that the first two phases of human maturation, as they have been described in Christian tradition since Origen, have largely been completed. Bernard's sermons on the Song therefore are not addressed to novices on the pathway of spiritual growth:

> The novices, the immature, those but recently converted from a worldly life, do not normally sing this song or hear it sung. Only the mind disciplined by persevering study, only the man whose efforts have borne fruit under God's inspiration, the man whose years, as it were, make him ripe for marriage years measured out not in time but in merits—only he is truly prepared for nuptial union with the divine partner. (SC 1,12)

To make the "teaching of Christ" accessible within a philosophically oriented concept of reality, Origen had ordered the three Greek philosophical disciplines, namely ethics (*disciplina moralis*), physics (*disciplina naturalis*), and theology (*disciplina inspectiva*) according to the three Solomonic books of Proverbs, Ecclesiastes, and the Song of Songs. According to Origen, these three books at the same time represent three stages of human maturation: The book of Proverbs addresses novices (*incipientes*) in the spiritual life, the book of Ecclesiastes addresses those who have advanced (*proficientes*) in spirituality and the Song those who have reached perfection (*perfecti*). In the book of Proverbs, a youthful person is introduced to the virtues. He is taught "the avoidance of evil and the doing of good" (SC 1,2). The book of Ecclesiastes calls upon the young man who has reached adulthood with the maxim *Vanitas, vanitatum, vanitas vanitatum, omnia vanitas* to let go of the transient world and direct his senses towards that which is intransient. The person who had advanced in spiritual life and has completed this process of detachment can set out to meet the divine Bridegroom and become unified with Him in the heavenly bridal chamber. The Song directs the human soul on this pathway that is to be taken on the last stage of spiritual life, which leads to perfection.

It is about this last stage, the mystical way in its true sense, that Bernard wishes to speak in his sermons on the Song of Songs. It is noteworthy, however, that he changes the first two phases around, which might have something to do with his primary addressees. The first and fundamental decision at the onset of monastic life is the "denial of the world" (*contemptus mundi*), which is associated with entry into the monastery. Bernard reminds his monks: "Now, unless I am mistaken, by the grace of God you have understood quite well from the book of Ecclesiastes how to recognize and have done with the false promise of this world (*mundi huius cognoscere et contemnere vanitatem*)" (SC 1,2). Subsequently, the monk is to cleanse his life of all error within this new form of life, that is, to live morally well. That is the theme of the book of Proverbs. After having overcome the love of the world (*amor mundi*) according to the teachings of the book of Ecclesiastes, and the love of self (*amor sui*) with the aid of the book of Proverbs, they now enter the third and decisive phase of their spiritual life: "Having previously tasted and received these two books [. . .] approach this third [i.e., the Song of Songs] that, if possible, you may recognize its greater force" (SC 1,2). The bride and groom conduct a "holy and contemplative discourse which [. . .] may be delivered only to well-prepared ears and minds" (SC 1,3).

Bernard now wishes to guide his monks on this third stage of their spiritual pathway, using the Song of Songs as directive. This section of the road is not without its dangers, either. One can stumble on this road and go astray. The Song of Songs is a willing spiritual guide on this dangerous pathway, and the abbot of Clairvaux wishes to explain the Song to his monks as such. His sermons represent a form of spiritual guidance that addresses the whole community. His explications however also have paradigmatic significance. Although Bernard directly addresses his confrères, the weight of his words transcends the monastic world to a certain extent. Directly addressing the increasing number of laypersons living in cities who grew interested in spirituality, however, would become the privilege of the exponents of the spiritual movement of the thirteenth and fourteenth centuries, especially those representing Rhenish mysticism (Meister Eckhart, Johannes Tauler, Henry Suso). The true Master of spiritual guidance, however, is not Bernard, but Christ. In relation to Him, the interpreter of Scripture is nothing but a recipient. Bernard therefore prays: "For I myself am one of the seekers, one who begs [. . .] for the food of my soul, the nourishment of my spirit [. . .] O God most kind, break your bread [. . .] through my hands indeed [. . .] but with an efficacy that is all your own" (SC 1,4).

These introductory remarks leading to the first sermon are of fundamental importance for the discussion of the relation between present-day exegesis and the history of interpretation if one wished to avoid talking past each other. Whoever lacks understanding of the ideas of spiritual guidance or spiritual experience will find it difficult to access Bernard's sermons on the Song of Songs. Modern exegesis alone does not provide access to the spiritual life. This is not meant as criticism, but only as a sober statement. Modernity has brought a new orientation in the field of Biblical Studies. The self-restraint exercised in modern exegesis has led to great accomplishments, which still continue today. Considered against the backdrop of the history of interpretation, one must, however, acknowledge that this self-restraint comes at a price. It is only the very particular form of Biblical Studies that displays openness for the experiences and insights of the spiritual pathway that will be able to engage in constructive dialogue with Bernard. Devoid of spiritual experience, this will be impossible. Ulrich Köpf, confirms: "Own experience is the prerequisite of an understanding of texts in which others have captured their experiences."[15] Experience, according to Köpf, is one of the central concepts of the *Sermones super Cantica Canticorum*.[16] Bernard expresses this as follows in his image-rich language: "Unction alone teaches such a song, and experience (*experientia*) alone can comprehend it. Let the adept (*experti*) have insight; let all others (*inexperti*) ardently desire, not as much to understand as to experience" (SC 1,11). Bernard essentially follows a reception-aesthetical approach: The understanding of a text depends on the constitution of the awareness of its recipient. This is true especially for higher forms of understanding. Recipients' comprehension may however be refined through spiritual exercises. Bernard presupposes, as has been noted, familiarity with this discipline in his monks. Whoever is not familiar with it, will not be able to comprehend the Song of Songs: "Just as a light is poured out in vain on sightless or closed eyes, so 'a worldly person cannot accept anything of the Spirit of God' [1Cor 2:14]" (SC 1,3).

The prerequisites for any constructive exchange between modern exegesis and spiritual Scriptural interpretation in some of its forms have improved in the last years, especially because modern and post-modern society is rediscovering mysticism and experience-based forms of spirituality.[17] Whereas academic theology has long been suspicious of this trend, the tables seem to be turning here,[18] including in Protestant theology. With the latter, the opinion used to be that mysticism was a

---

15 Köpf, "Einleitung," 37 (own translation from the German).
16 See Köpf, *Religiöse Erfahrung*.
17 See McGinn, *Foundations of Mysticism*, XI: "The global ecumenical situation in which we now find ourselves has facilitated a new level of awareness and discussion of the richness of humanity's spiritual heritage. From both the specifically Christian and the ecumenical point of view, mysticism is a topic of central concern today." For two practical examples among many others, see Jalics, *Kontemplative Exerzitien*; Keating, *Centering Prayer*.
18 See Kieslinger, *Keatings 'Centering Prayer.'*

Catholic and Orthodox matter which had nothing to do with the Gospel of Christ.[19] This is no longer the case. Martin Luther's mystical roots are increasingly being discovered.[20] In the period subsequent to Luther, mystical movements have likewise distinctly shaped Protestant theology and piety.[21]

3 The Kiss of his Mouth as Mediator between God and Mankind (SC 2)

The prophets of the Old Testament, thus Bernard, longed for a direct encounter with God. They knew about the beauty of the Divine Anointed and about the grace that is poured out over his lips (Ps 45), but that God would unite Himself with mankind, they could only yearn for. This desire for a direct encounter with God is expressed in the opening verse of the Song of Songs, "Let him kiss me with the kiss of his mouth":

> This was the kiss for which just men yearned under the old dispensation, foreseeing as they did that in him they would "find happiness and a crown of rejoicing," [Sir 15:6] because in him were hidden "all the jewels of wisdom and knowledge" [Col 2:3]. Hence their longing to taste that fullness of his. (SC 2,3)

This kiss announces "the mystery of the incarnate Word" (SC 2,7). It was "bestowed on the world for two reasons"—the strengthening of "those who wavered" and the

---

[19] See Leppin, *Mystik*, 116–118: "Für den Protestantismus hatte mystische Frömmigkeit ihren spezifischen Ort verloren, der immer ihr Zentrum gewesen war: das Kloster. Dennoch wurden gerade durch Luther mystische Wege in gebrochener Weise fortgeführt, und evangelische Theologen bedienten sich immer wieder mystischer Sprache und des mystischen Erbes um auszudrücken, was mit der für das reformatorische Denken zentralen Lehre von der Rechtfertigung, von der Gerechtsprechung des Sünders ohne eigenes Verdienst, gemeint war. [. . .] Doch in der Folgezeit traten im Protestantismus viel stärker die gleichfalls bei Luther angelegten kritischen Wendungen gegen die Mystik in den Vordergrund [. . .] In Verbindung mit der Rationalität der Aufklärung im 19. Jahrhundert, aber auch teils sehr scharfen Reaktionen darauf im 20. Jahrhundert wurde sich die protestantische Theologie vor allem des deutschen Sprachraums weitgehend einig, dass Protestantismus und Mystik unvereinbar seien."
[20] See Leppin, *Fremde Reformation*; Nicol, *Meditation*.
[21] See Zimmerling, *Mystik*, 10–11: "Die Beschäftigung mit evangelischer Mystik schließt eine Wiederentdeckung verschütteter Frömmigkeitstraditionen ein. Darin scheint mir die Voraussetzung für eine echte Bereicherung evangelischer Theologie und Spiritualität durch die Mystik zu liegen. [. . .] Dadurch ergibt sich ein neues Bild der Theologie- und Spiritualitätsgeschichte. Es wird erkennbar: Evangelisches Christentum und evangelischer Glaube sind ohne Mystik gar nicht denkbar." See Leppin, *Ruhen in Gott*; McGinn, *Mysticism in the Reformation*.

appeasing of "the desires of the fervent" (SC 2,9). The kiss is "no other than the Mediator between God and man, himself a man, Christ Jesus" (SC 2,9).

4 The Kiss of the Lord's Feet, Hands, and Mouth (SC 3)

Bernard considers the question why the opening sentence of the Song of Songs does not simply state "let him kiss me." Why is "with his mouth" added? Apparently, there must be other kinds of kisses too (SC 4,1). Bernard distinguishes between three types of kisses and recognizes the three stages on the spiritual path which he has identified in the first sermon. There is the kiss of his feet for the novices, the kiss of his hands for the intermediaries, and the kiss of his mouth for those who have reached perfection.

At the onset of his third sermon, Bernard reminds his monks of the goal of spiritual life, which is why he first refers to the kiss of the mouth. It is an expression of a profound experience of God. It is hard to explain the exact meaning of this image. Only the person who has experienced as much will truly be able to grasp it. Therefore, Bernard opens his third sermon with the words "Today we read in the book of experience (*Hodie legimus in libro experientiae*)" (SC 3,1). He wishes to fathom whether anyone can repeat the words "Let him kiss me with the kiss of his mouth" from own experience. Soberly he states that this might not be the case for all: "Not every man can speak thus with affection, but whoever has received such a spiritual kiss from the mouth of Christ even once, is surely shaken to the core by this particular experience, so that he freely wishes for its repetition" (SC 3,1). Bernard here addresses a familiar phenomenon associated with spiritual experience, of which we must consider four aspects. This kind of experience shakes a person to the core of his existence. It secondly is only brief, at least when it occurs for the first time. Whoever experiences it, begins to long for its reoccurrence. Thirdly, only those who have had such an experience can really understand it. It is an *immediate* experience, that is, one that cannot be mediated through words. According to Bernard, the plea "let him kiss me with the kiss of his mouth" expresses the longing for such an experience. It is a spiritual experience, which is why Bernard speaks of a "spiritual kiss" (*spirituale osculum*). He describes it as follows:

> I think that nobody can grasp what it is, except the one who receives it. For it is "a hidden manna" and only he who eats it still hungers for more. It is "a sealed fountain" to which no stranger has access; only he who drinks still thirsts for more. (SC 3,1)

The mystical traditions of many religions describe this experience according to different anthropological and theological concepts. This will not be further treated here. Bernard however explains the experience Christologically.

There is a risk that those who are instructed about this kind of experience could try to actively pursue it. That would lead them astray. Their aim should much rather be to gain a realistic self-estimation. Each should acknowledge his own position on the spiritual pathway and find the correct step that he should personally take. It would be presumptuous if a soul that is still "burdened with sins, still subject to carnal passions, devoid of any knowledge of spiritual delights (*suavitatem spiritus*)" made such a request, "unacquainted as it is with the joys of supernatural life" (SC 3,1). Thus it is logically consistent that Bernard initially speaks about the first two kisses. He begins with the *kiss of his feet*. For an inexperienced soul it is inappropriate to "rashly aspire to the lips of a most benign Bridegroom" (SC 3,2). It would be presumptuous. Such a soul should rather prostrate itself at the feet of the Lord and, like the biblical publican, turn its eyes to the earth rather than to heaven. Then its "eyes, accustomed only to the darkness" will not be "confused by the brightness of the heavens, overpowered by its glory, and vanquished by its reverberating brilliance, only to be covered in the blindness of a gloom even more impenetrable than before" (SC 3,2). An important insight into the art of spiritual direction becomes apparent here: it is usually counterproductive to "push" someone towards an experience of enlightenment. What is necessary, rather, is the patient and sustainable transformation of the empirical ego, if the penetrating divine Light truly is to be welcomed and if it is to permanently transform, illuminate and endear a person from within. If the person who is to receive these gifts is unprepared or insufficiently prepared, and if he presumptuously reaches for "things too sublime" (see Ps 131), it might result in bedazzlement or even delusion, as Bernard explains. Therefore the woman rightly speaks in the Song of Songs: "I am black, yet beautiful, daughters of Jerusalem" (Song 1:5). She acknowledges her own sinfulness with these words—thus Bernard, in an interpretation that also does justice to the original meaning of the text, in my opinion.[22] The confession of own sins has nothing to do with a false form of humility, but is a realistic self-observation which, in its concentration on God, opens a pathway towards healing. As did the sinful woman in the Gospel, the person who has reached insight in his own sinfulness should prostrate himself before the Lord, however not in order to remain there, but to experience forgiveness, healing, and "upliftment": "Humble yourself as this happy penitent did so that you may be rid of your wretchedness. Prostrate yourself on the ground, take hold of his feet, soothe them with kisses, sprinkle them with your

---

22 See Schwienhorst-Schönberger, *Hohelied*, 41–46.

tears" (SC 3,2). The person who then remains within the dynamics of self-observation and does not fixate himself onto the initial sudden recognition but chooses to be someone who truly hears, will hear the sentence: "'Your sins are forgiven' [Luke 7:48], to be followed by the summons, 'Awake, awake, captive daughter of Zion, awake, shake off the dust' [Isa 52:1–2]" (SC 3,2).

The kiss of his hands symbolizes the subsequent second phase, in which the upright posture is stabilized. This means that the consistent practice of doing good should be internalized and become his habitus. This is the most certain safeguard against falling back into the old way of life, which would be a fall down the abyss. This, too, is a gracious gift of God: "He who gave the grace to repent, must also bestow the power to persevere, that I do not anew commit regrettable deeds, worse than my previous ones" (SC 3,3). Bernard's sobering and realistic assessment teaches us that progress on the road of maturation, if it is to be sustainable, should take place gradually: "I do not wish to suddenly be the highest, my desire is to advance by degrees (*paulatim proficere volo*)" (SC 3,4). At this stage, it is too early yet for the kiss of the mouth. The person making progress should still learn to discern his own limitations:

> You will please him [scil. God] more readily if you live within the limits proper to you, and do not set your sights at things beyond you. It is a long and formidable leap from the foot to the mouth, a manner of approach that is not commendable. Consider for a moment: still tarnished as you are with the dust of sin, would you dare touch those sacred lips? Yesterday you were lifted from the mire, today you wish to encounter the glory of his face? No, his hand must be your guide to that end. (SC 3,4)

Only when this person has stabilized himself at the level of the kiss of the hand, then he may glance ahead to that which is higher, to the "kiss of highest dignity and wonderful sweetness" (SC 3,5). At the end of his third sermon, Bernard recapitulates the order of the three kisses:

> This is the way, the order of procedure: first, we cast ourselves at his feet, we weep before the Lord who made us, deploring that which we have done. Then we reach out for the hand that will lift us up, that will steady our trembling knees. And finally, when we shall have obtained this through many petitions and tears, we humbly dare to raise our eyes to his mouth, not merely to gaze upon it, but to receive its kiss. (SC 3,5)

It is this intimacy, too, that is the deepest desire of the Psalmist: "My face looks to you, Lord, I do seek your face! [Ps 27:8]" (SC 3,6).

The path that has been described is the way of ascent. In the Christian tradition, particularly in Augustine, the Platonic idea of ascent is associated with the Songs of Ascent (Pss 120–134), Psalms that were prayed during the pilgrimage to Jerusalem. They ultimately deal, thus Augustine, with an *ascensus in corde*, an "ascent in the heart."²³ Bernard, too, is familiar with this tradition (SC 1,10). The three kisses refer to the threefold ascent of the soul to God (SC 4,1).

5 God—the Being of all Things (SC 4)

At the beginning of the fourth sermon, Bernard again summarizes the thoughts of his previous sermon, a method that he often uses, and which demonstrates that his sermons are thematically interrelated. He places the theme of the Song of Songs in the overall structure of an ordered spiritual path:

> The first kiss is dedicated to the beginnings of our conversion, the second is granted to those who are proficient, the third however will only be experienced in those rare cases of perfection. From it alone, this rare kiss that is placed in the last position, does our portion of Scripture that we have started to expound, commence (SC 4,1).

In pointing out that an immediate experience of God, which is expressed in the kiss of the mouth, is a rare occurrence, Bernard again proves himself an experienced spiritual director. He dedicates the rest of his fourth sermon to the development of a doctrine of God as the "Being of all things" (SC 4,4), which will not be further explored here.

We will now look at sermons 35 to 38. These stand at the end of the first sub-collection of sermons, and in their thematic development they elaborate the connection between knowledge of self, knowledge of God, and knowledge of the world. This connection has played an important part in the history of Christian mysticism.

6 Relapse (SC 35,1)

Bernard opens sermon SC 34 with the words from the second half of Song 1:7: "If you do not know yourself, go forth!" (*Si te ignoras, egredere*!). The explication of the verse, however, he at first delays. In an excursus, he initially explains different forms of humility. This is a method that recurs in his sermons. He only returns to Song 1:7 in sermon SC 35. In this verse Bernard explains, the Bridegroom speaks to his beloved. He speaks very harshly to her, as would an irate master to his slave or an indignant mistress to her slave-girl: "Away from here! Away from me! Get yourself out of my sight and out of my house!" (SC 35,1). The Bridegroom however

---

23 See Schwienhorst-Schönberger, "Lieder des Aufstiegs."

stipulates: *Si te ignoras*—"If you do not know yourself." This is what matters to Bernard: in as far as the bride is ignorant about herself, she should depart from her Bridegroom.

Bernard reconstructs a scene that could serve as a backdrop to this phrase from the Song of Songs. He designs, so to speak, the scenery on a stage and attempts to reconstruct the larger communicative context from which an understanding of this quotation may emerge. He assumes the bridegroom to be the speaker of the sentence. This is possible, but not undisputed. Modern-day commentaries provide two possible stances in this regard. Othmar Keel is of the opinion that the statement could be best understood when attributed to the female companions of the bride. According to Keel, it is not the groom, but the companions who express this summons.[24] Hans-Peter Müller, on the other hand, understands the sentence as does Bernard: as the words of the male speaker.[25] This is, moreover, a fine example of the ambiguity of the text. The text itself does not identify the speaker of the words "If you do not know yourself, go forth!" The reader can only guess.

Bernard now asks: Where is the bride to go from, and where should she go to? His answer: Apparently, the bride has previously been close to her Beloved, but is now summoned to leave him. Bernard expresses this in the idiom of his time. He states that nothing is more terrifying for the soul that once had tasted the presence of God than being driven from that very presence:

> Would that soul regard a temporary experience of hell as more horrible, more punitive, than having once tasted the sweetness of this spiritual desire, to have to go out again to the allurements or rather the irksome demands of the flesh [1John 2:15–16], and be involved as before in the insatiable prurience of the body's senses? Ecclesiastes says: "The eye is not satisfied with seeing, nor the ear filled with hearing" [Eccl 1:8]. […] To attempt to turn this holy soul away from that good, would cause him to feel as if driven out of Paradise, from the very gateway to glory. Therefore I say to you: There is nothing more terrifying for someone who has once received this bounty than, abandoned by grace, to have to go out again to the fleshly consolations, which are really desolations, and to endure once more the tumult of physical desire. (SC 35,1)

The experience described here by Bernard is not seldom encountered on the spiritual pathway. It may occur that a person is confronted with an existential experience but is unprepared for it. Whoever has had no contact whatsoever with religious tradition, might not know how to deal with such an encounter. The experience would usually then disappear again, leaving the person confused and despondent. Such a person might be overjoyed about that which he had encountered and simultaneously saddened and confused by its sudden and complete disappearance. Everything

---

24 See Keel, *Hohelied*, 58.
25 See Müller, *Hohelied*, 17.

now seems worse than before. Having once seen the Light, this person is now all the more aware of the misery in which he still finds himself. Bernard seems to assume a situation such as this. He speaks about the tremendous heartache caused by the disappearance of the divine presence, once tasted: "I say to you: There is nothing more terrifying for someone who has once received this bounty" (SC 35,1).

Bernard now attempts to understand this experience in the light of Scripture. Why is the soul being sent away from God, having once tasted Him? Why does He say: "Away from here"? Bernard's answer: because this soul is still ignorant of itself. It has not yet truly observed itself and therefore does not truly know itself. Therefore, the summons, "Away from here!" applies under the condition which is indicated in Scripture itself: "if you do not know yourself." Knowledge of self thus is the prerequisite for the continuation of a life in communion with the Bridegroom. Without knowledge of self, thus Bernard, there can be no knowledge of God.

7 Chastened Sensuality (SC 35,2–9)

Bernard continues by asking: Where should the soul go, and what should it do on being sent away? He finds the answer in the continuation of the sentence quoted previously. The summons "go forth!" is continued with the words "and pasture your kids (*et pasce haedos tuos*)." Bernard comments:

> Know yourself unworthy of that familiar and sweet contemplation of things heavenly, things of the spirit, divine things. Therefore go forth from that heart of yours which has been my sanctuary (*egredere de sanctuario meo, corde tuo*), where it was your custom to drink sweet draughts from the secret, holy teachings of truth and wisdom. Much rather, like a worldly person, let yourself be entangled in feeding and enjoying the senses of your flesh. Since through them sin enters the soul like death through the windows [Jer 9:21], he calls the restless, wanton senses of the body kids, which signifies sin. (SC 35,2)

These and similar words, which we often find in Bernard, might provoke objection in a modern reader. Is this not proof of a type of contempt for the body that is typical of an unhealthy, "platonically" inspired Christianity, which severs people from the energies that vitalize them? None less than Friedrich Nietzsche famously accused Christianity of exactly this. In *Jenseits von Gut und Böse* we read: "Das Christentum gab dem Eros Gift zu trinken—er starb zwar nicht daran, aber entartete, zum Laster."[26] In his encyclical *Deus caritas est*, even Pope Benedict XVI acknowledges

---

26 Quoted according to Nietzsche, *Werke in drei Bänden*, 2:639 (no. 168).

"Nowadays Christianity of the past is often criticized as having been opposed to the body; and it is quite true that tendencies of this sort have always existed" (5).

Hearing Bernard against this background, we notice that he very well knows how to distinguish within the sphere of sensuality. Every person that has cultivated a degree of self-observation arguably knows that there are forms of sensuality that leave a stale aftertaste. There are ways of enjoying food that might seem pleasurable in the moment, but soon afterwards reveal unpleasant mental and physical consequences. Unbridled sensuality might provide temporary gratification, yet it does not satiate the deeper longing of the soul. A person is aware that something is deficient, but seeks his fulfilment on a false, that is superficial, level, which leads to the danger of addiction. Superficially, he consumes much, but internally he remains hungry. He is missing something. That which he is missing, however, cannot be found in superficial sensory perception. Bernard distinguishes between misdirected and appropriate sensuality. People often have a deficient perception of the inner quality of a matter. Bernard seems to have in mind a form of sensuality that races along the surface of things, failing to perceive and taste inner, divine qualities, when he speaks of "the restless, wanton senses of the body." The goat-kids, he says, are "the restless, wanton senses of the body (*vagos ac petulantes corporis sensus*)," not meaning all senses of the body as such. Elsewhere he states that this form of sensuality arouses rather than satiates desires. The restless and wanton senses are unable to perceive that which is celestial among that which is earthly (SC 35,2). This is what it is all about: finding God in everything. Bernard does not aim at dissociation from sensuality as such; he strives for dissociation from a superficial form of sensuality. The soul of the person who succumbs to superficial sensuality remains uncomforted; he remains the eternal beggar. He subjects himself, says Bernard, "to the shameful task of serving the body, of obeying the flesh, of satisfying stomach and palate, and begging throughout the world, this world whose form is passing away, for a means to gratify, to some degree, a perpetually ravenous curiosity" (SC 35,3). This is the end of a soul that leaves the divine abode: it reaches a place of unsatiated longing. This is the end of a soul that does not know itself.

8 Knowledge of Self (SC 36,1–5)

What does it mean, though, to have self-knowledge? Bernard investigates this in the subsequent sermon, SC 36. He distinguishes three types of ignorance. The first has to do with external matters. In this area, it is impossible to know everything, and it is not necessary, either. There are many sciences and professions of which we know little to nothing. This has no effect on our salvation—to the contrary. The person who pursues knowledge of the external beyond measure and for the wrong reasons, is at risk of becoming haughty. Bernard quotes Paul: "Do not strive towards more knowledge than is necessary but strive towards knowledge to think with sober judgement [Rom 12,3]" (SC 36,2). However, there are two types of dangerous ignorance: ignorance relating to self and ignorance relating to God. Bernard writes:

> I wish therefore that before everything else a man should know himself, because not only usefulness but right order demand this. Right order, since what we are is our first concern; and usefulness, because this knowledge gives humility rather than self-importance, it provides a basis on which to build. For unless there is a durable foundation of humility, the spiritual edifice has no hope of standing. (SC 36,5)

Bernard distances himself from a false understanding of humility. Appropriate humility signifies an attitude that establishes itself, as it were, of its own accord when a person enters onto the pathway of self-knowledge. Bernard, again, states:

> There is nothing more effective, more adapted to the acquiring of humility, than to find out the truth about oneself. There must be no dissimulation, no attempt at self-deception, only a facing up to one's real self (*statuat se ante faciem suam*) without flinching and turning aside. (SC 36,5)

Bernard brings a beautiful description of the pathway of self-knowledge. We readily flinch and turn aside from our true self. We easily deceive ourselves. Doing so, we live in falsehood. Our perception is blurred, so that we can hardly recognize the people and things around us, let alone God. Bernard's remedy is the pathway of self-knowledge. Practically of its own accord, it leads the person to true humility:

> How can he [scil. the soul] escape being genuinely humbled on acquiring this true self-knowledge, on seeing the burden of sin that he carries, the oppressive weight of his mortal body, the complexities of earthly cares, the corrupting influence of sensual desires; on seeing his blindness, his worldliness, his weakness, his embroilment in repeated errors; on seeing himself exposed to a thousand dangers, trembling amid a thousand fears, confused by a thousand difficulties, defenseless before a thousand suspicions, worried by a thousand needs; one to whom vice is welcome, virtue repugnant? Can this man afford the haughty eyes, the proud lift of the head? With the thorns of his misery pricking him, will he not rather be changed for the better? Let him be changed and weep, changed to mourning and sighing, changed to acceptance of the Lord, to whom in his lowliness he will say: "Heal me because I have sinned against you." [Ps 41:5]. (SC 36,5)

The concepts and images applied by Bernard are not all equally accessible to us today. I do believe, however, that we are well familiar with many of the experiences that he describes. The knowledge of self leads us into a form of humility that freely introduces itself to us: it is neither feigned nor artificial, nor is it accepted grudgingly. It results from personal insight and experience; it is a humility that corresponds to the truth of our lives.

This insight into our own self can wrestle us down. The illusions and pretty self-images we used to cultivate and still do, are shattered. We hit the ground of reality. We see who we truly are: a being, forfeited to death.

9 Knowledge of God (SC 36,6–7)

Bernard now takes a next step. The person who halts at knowledge of self, will despair. Seeing ourselves in our misery, need, and relinquishment unto death, truly grasping this awareness and not allowing anything that transcends it to enter our minds, will lead to desperation. Beside self-knowledge, another form of insight now comes into view: knowledge of God (*notitia Dei*). Bernard instructs us:

> As long as I look at myself, my eye is filled with bitterness. But if I look up and fix my eyes on the aid of the divine mercy, this happy vision of God soon tempers the bitter vision of myself, and I say to him: "I am disturbed within so I will call you to mind from the land of the Jordan" [Ps 42:7]. (SC 36,6)

This most probably is the point at which the path of contemplation distinguishes itself from the path of Zen. The latter, as is well known, does not include the word "God." In Zen, the knowledge of self is perpetuated until the ego is recognized as the last great illusion. The ego, thought-through and experienced substantially, reveals itself as one great delusion. When this delusion is shattered, the person finds liberating redemption. I am unsure whether there is a real distinction from Christian tradition here. Scholars and scholarly literature hold differing opinions on this question.[27] Bernard uses expressions that can be found similarly in Zen, for instance when he says that a person without self-knowledge could not be saved (SC 37,1). We could find similar statements in Zen. There, however, the pathway of desperation is followed consistently until the desperate person is "not there" anymore. He finds himself again at a place which one can at best describe as "placelessness." Christian tradition is not unfamiliar with these experiences either. Christianity however has a different set of concepts to verbalize that which can really only be expressed with great difficulty. The other reality (which principally is nothing other than this reality) to which the person advances on the pathway of self-knowledge, is designated the divine reality. And Christianity speaks of God as the Redeemer and Savior. "God, the Redeemer and Savior" does not imply that He is a magician.

---

27 See Enomiya-Lassale, *Zen*.

Unfortunately, this is a widespread misunderstanding. Christian understanding recognizes regularities of divine action that must be understood, from a human point of view, as an anthropological-soteriological constant. Bernard describes it as the order of divine action:

> By this kind of experience, and in this way, God makes himself known to us for our good. When a man first discovers that he is in difficulties, he will cry out to the Lord who will hear him and say: "I will deliver you and you shall glorify me" [Ps 50:15]. In this way your self-knowledge will be a step to the knowledge of God; he will become visible to you accordingly, as his image is being renewed within you. And you, "gazing confidently on the glory of the Lord with unveiled face, will be transformed into that same image with ever increasing brightness, by the work of the Spirit of the Lord" [2Cor 3:18]. (SC 36,6)

The interrelation of self-knowledge and knowledge of God becomes apparent here. Bernard's description is founded on biblical creation theology. According to Gen 1:26, man is made as the image ("statue") of God. Through the Fall, this image was disfigured—thus the Christian interpretation. To remain in the imagery: The statue fell down, into the dust. This is the sense in which Christian tradition speaks of the Fall of Mankind. Man has fallen to the ground as did the person (*anthropos*) who had fallen prey to the robbers in the parable of the Good Samaritan (Luke 10:25–37).[28] The self-knowledge that Bernard wishes us to gain, commences at this point: A person recognizes what has become of him. He sees himself in his misery and removal from God. From his distress, he calls to God for salvation. In Christ, God, who is gracious and full of lovingkindness, turns to this person who has "fallen prey to the robbers"—as did the Good Samaritan—and helps him up. Thus, by degrees, the person is restored to being the image of God. In this way, knowledge of self smoothly transforms into knowledge of God. To recognize God, man does not have to look to the outside, but must rather continue on the path of self-knowledge to the very end. In the restored image of God, he will then recognize God Himself. This is what Bernard means when he says: "and in his image, which is restored in you, he [scil. God] will be seen" (SC 36,6)." Bernard takes one further step and, with the apostle Paul, he states: "Gazing confidently on the glory of the Lord with unveiled face, you will be transformed into that same image [2Cor 3:18]" (SC 36,6).

---

28 See Heither and Reemts, *Adam*, 21.

10 Knowledge of Self, Knowledge of God, Knowledge of the World (SC 37)

Whoever has completed this process may now, thus Bernard, obtain further knowledge, including that of the world. This leads him back to his point of departure: Having achieved knowledge of self and of God, additional knowledge of the world can no longer lead to haughtiness.

In Bernard's own words, we may summarize the results of the two forms of insight:

> It was but right that he who wept when faced with the truth about himself, should rejoice on seeing the Lord [. . .]. It bears out the truth in the Prophet's words: "Those who sow in tears shall reap in jubilation." We find the two kinds of knowledge within these words: that of ourselves in the sowing in tears; and that of God, in the reaping in joy. (SC 37,4)

I consider the sequence of events important. Insight into the condition of the self has priority. It is the prerequisite for knowledge of God. These two sets of insight serve as a correction of a false attitude. A person can over- or under-estimate himself. Both attitudes are malignant. Both lead to misguidance and both are an impediment to maturation:

> And as the fear of God (*timor Dei*) springs up within you from knowledge of self (*notitia tui*), and love of God (*Dei amor*) from the knowledge of God (*ex Dei notitia*), so on the contrary, pride (*superbia*) comes from want of self-knowledge (*de ignorantia tui*) and despair (*desperatio*) from want of knowledge of God (*de Dei ignorantia*). (SC 37,6)

One might object: There is no eschatological precondition included here! Ultimately, in life hereafter, we will behold God. Here, on earth, we have no alternative but to believe in Him. Bernard contradicts: The blissful condition that God has in mind for every person can already be experienced here on earth, should man be willing to commit himself into the healing Hands of God. "What else is there to hold you back from the way of salvation? This is what I say: you know nothing about God, yet you will not believe what we have heard. I should like you to at least believe those whom experience has taught" (SC 38,2). The way in which Bernard distinguishes between faith in and knowledge of God is demonstrated here: "You know nothing about God, yet you will not believe what we have heard. I should like you to at least believe those whom experience has taught (*Deum ignoratis, sed non creditis auditui nostro. Vellem vos vel expertis credere*)" (SC 38,2). Faith here serves as a substitute for an experience that has not come into fruition. The particular profile of monastic theology, oriented towards contemplation, becomes clear here once more. Monastic theology is interested in the *cognitio Dei experimentalis*, the knowledge of God based on experience. Only when this is not attainable, or when people are unwilling to walk this troublesome pathway, only then does Bernard say that they should at least believe those who have had the experience. With Volker Leppin one could describe the text of the Song of Songs in Bernard's sermons as the mediator of personal spiritual experience: Bernard's

> mystagogic sermons need the biblical text as mediator to de-individualize personal experience, to set it within the biblical text and thus make it conveyable. By these means, the abbot is able to lead his brothers into mystical experience, which is meant to be edifying in the truest sense of the word: constructive of their spiritual experience.[29]

Bibliography

Bernard of Clairvaux. *On the Song of Songs I: Sermons 1–20*, translated by Kilian Walsh, introduced by M. Corneille Halflants. CiFS 4. Kalamazoo, MI: Cistercian Publications, 1981.

Bernard of Clairvaux. *On the Song of Songs II: Sermons 21–46*, translated by Kilian Walsh, introduced by Jean Leclercq. CiFS 7. Kalamazoo, MI: Cistercian Publications, 1983.

Bernhard von Clairvaux. *Sämtliche Werke*, edited by Gerhard B. Winkler. Vols. 5–6. Innsbruck: Tyrolia-Verlag, 1994–1995.

Bernard of Clairvaux. *Super Cantica 1–3*, edited by Jean Leclercq, Charles H. Talbot, and Henri M. Rochais. SBO I. Rome: Editiones Cistercienses, 1957.

Bernard of Clairvaux. *Super Cantica 36–83*, edited by Jean Leclercq, Charles H. Talbot, and Henri M. Rochais. SBO II. Rome: Editiones Cistercienses, 1958.

Dinzelbacher, Peter. *Bernhard von Clairvaux: Leben und Werk des berühmten Zisterziensers*. Darmstadt: Wiss. Buchgesellschaft, 1998.

Drecoll, Volker. "Kirchengeschichte Patristik und Mittelalter." In *Schriftauslegung*, edited by Friederike Nüssel, 105–140. ThTh 8. Tübingen: Mohr Siebeck, 2014.

Enomiya-Lassalle, Hugo M. *Zen und christliche Mystik*. Freiburg i. Br.: Aurum, 1986.

Fiedrowicz, Michael. *Prinzipien der Schriftauslegung in der Alten Kirche*. TC 10. Bern: Peter Lang, 1998.

Fiedrowicz, Michael. *Theologie der Kirchenväter: Grundlagen frühchristlicher Glaubensreflexion*. Freiburg i. Br.: Herder, 2007.

Heereman, Nina S. *"Behold King Solomon on the Day of his Wedding": A Symbolic-Diachronic Reading of Song 3,6–11 and 4,12–5,1*. BETL 320. Leuven: Peeters, 2021.

Heither, Theresia, and Christina Reemts. *Biblische Gestalten bei den Kirchenvätern: Adam*. Münster: Aschendorff, 2007.

Jalics, Franz. *Kontemplative Exerzitien: Eine Einführung in die kontemplative Lebenshaltung und in das Jesusgebet*. Würzburg: Echter, 1994, 2020.

Keating, Thomas. *Intimacy with God: An Introduction to Centering Prayer*. New York, 2014.

Keel, Othmar. *Das Hohelied*. ZBK.AT 18. Zürich: TVZ, 1986, 1992.

Kieslinger, Kristina. *Ethik, Kontemplation und Spiritualität: Thomas Keatings 'Centering Prayer' und dessen Bedeutung für die Theologische Ethik*. SThE 155, Basel: Schwabe / Würzburg: Echter, 2020.

---

29 Leppin, *Mystik*, 59.

Köpf, Ulrich. "Einleitung." In vol. 5 of Bernhard von Clairvaux. *Sämtliche Werke*, edited by Gerhard B. Winkler, 27–47. Innsbruck: Tyrolia-Verlag, 1994.

Köpf, Ulrich. *Religiöse Erfahrung in der Theologie Bernhards von Clairvaux*. BHTh 61. Tübingen: Mohr-Siebeck, 1980.

Leclercq, Jean OSB. *The Love of Learning and the Desire for God: A Study of Monastic Culture*, translated by Catharine Misrahi. New York: Fordham University Press, 1977 (Translated from *L'amour des lettres et le désir de Dieu*. Paris: Les Éditions du Cerf, 1957).

Leppin, Volker. *Die christliche Mystik*. München: C. H. Beck, 2007.

Leppin, Volker. *Die fremde Reformation: Luthers mystische Wurzeln*. München: C. H. Beck, 2016.

Leppin, Volker. *Ruhen in Gott: Geschichte der christlichen Mystik*. München: C. H. Beck, 2021.

McGinn, Bernard. *Mysticism in the Reformation (1500–1650): Part 1*. Vol. 6 of *The Presence of God: A History of Western Christian Mysticism*. London: Herder & Herder, 2019.

McGinn, Bernard. *The Foundations of Mysticism: Origins to the Fifth Century*. Vol 1, *The Presence of God: A History of Western Christian Mysticism*. New York: Herder & Herder, 1991.

Müller, Hans-Peter. *Das Hohelied*. ATD 16/2. Göttingen: Vandenhoeck & Ruprecht, 1992.

Nicol, Martin. *Meditation bei Luther*. Göttingen: Vandenhoeck & Ruprecht, 1991.

Nietzsche, Friedrich. *Werke in drei Bänden*. Vol. 2. München: Hanser, 1977.

Piazzoni, Ambrogio. "Exégèse vétéro-monastique et néo-monastique." In *L'exégèse monastique au Moyen Âge (XIe – XIVe siècle)*, edited by Gilbert Duhan and Annie Noblesse-Rocher, 143–156. EAMA 5. Paris, 2014.

Pollmann, Karla. "Alte Kirche: Einführung." In *Handbuch der Bibelhermeneutiken: Von Origenes bis zur Gegenwart*, edited by Oda Wischmeyer, 9–11. Berlin: de Gruyter, 2016.

Prügl, Thomas. "Mittelalter: Einführung." In *Handbuch der Bibelhermeneutiken: Von Origenes bis zur Gegenwart*, edited by Oda Wischmeyer, 125–133. Berlin: de Gruyter, 2016.

Reiser, Marius. *Bibelkritik und Auslegung der Heiligen Schrift: Beiträge zur Geschichte der biblischen Exegese und Hermeneutik*. WUNT 217. Tübingen: Mohr Siebeck, 2007.

Reiser, Marius. *Die Autorität der Schrift im Wandel der Zeiten: Studien zur Geschichte der biblischen Exegese und Hermeneutik*. Fohren-Linden: Carthusianus, 2016.

Schellenberg, Annette, and Ludger Schwienhorst-Schönberger, eds. *Interpreting the Song of Songs— Literal or Allegorical?* BToSt 26. Leuven: Peeters, 2016.

Schwienhorst-Schönberger, Ludger. *Das Hohelied der Liebe*. Freiburg: Herder, 2015.

Schwienhorst-Schönberger, Ludger, ed. *Das Hohelied im Konflikt der Interpretationen*. ÖBS 47. Frankfurt: Peter Lang, 2017.

Schwienhorst-Schönberger, Ludger. "Der theologische Charakter des Hoheliedes: Evidenzen und Konsequenzen." In *The Song of Songs in its Context: Words for Love, Love for Words*, edited by Pierre Van Hecke, 269–286. BETL 310. Leuven: Peeters, 2020.

Schwienhorst-Schönberger, Ludger. "Der vierfache Schriftsinn—ein Einblick und ein Ausblick." *JBTh* 31 (2016): 275–202.

Schwienhorst-Schönberger, Ludger. "Lieder des Aufstiegs: Die alttestamentlichen Wallfahrtspsalmen und der platonische Gedanke des Aufstiegs." In *Lasst euch versöhnen mit Gott: Der Heilige Rock als Zeichen der ungeteilten Christenheit*, edited by Philipp Thull and Hermann-Josef Scheidgen, 23–36. Nordhausen: Traugott Bautz, 2012.

Schwienhorst-Schönberger, Ludger. "Wiederentdeckung des geistigen Schriftverständnisses: Zur Bedeutung der Kirchenväterhermeneutik." *ThGl* 101 (2011): 402–425.

Winkler, "Einleitung." In Bernhard von Clairvaux. *Sämtliche Werke*, edited by Gerhard B. Winkler, 31–43. Vol 6. Innsbruck: Tyrolia-Verlag, 1995.
Wischmeyer, Oda, ed. *Handbuch der Bibelhermeneutiken: Von Origenes bis zur Gegenwart*. Berlin: de Gruyter, 2016.
Zimmerling, Peter. *Evangelische Mystik*. Göttingen: Vandenhoeck & Ruprecht, 2015.

Hannah W. Matis
Preaching the Song of Songs at Admont
A Minority Report from the Twelfth Century

In the history of spirituality, medieval exegesis of the Song of Songs is indissolubly associated with the sermon cycle of Bernard of Clairvaux. In the popularization of Jean Leclercq, a distinctive "monastic spirituality" as practiced by the Cistercians evolved in contrast with, and in reaction to, the scholastic method, a spirituality characterized by ruminative *lectio divina* and a yearning, affective approach which resurrected the Song as a mystical text for the rest of the Middle Ages.[1] Brian Stock underscored the centrality of the Song text in Cistercian spirituality as a case study for his influential model of the "textual community," in particular noting the layers of oral superstructure accumulating around, but still oriented toward, the written text of scripture.[2] The association between the Cistercian choir monk and the text of the Song of Songs is therefore fairly firm, and as a consequence, the monastic spirituality of the Song of Songs in the twelfth century has tended to gender as male. The monk's conception of his female soul notwithstanding, when one envisions a monastic audience for sermons on the Song of Songs in the twelfth century, it is invariably male bodies and male psycho-sexual development that have attracted the most critical attention.[3]

1 Exegesis and Reform at the Monastery of Admont

While Bernard of Clairvaux may be the most famous exegete of the Song of Songs in the twelfth century, he was hardly the only one, however; nor were all of the Song's readers male. The double monastery of Admont, now in Austria, represents a very different sort of twelfth-century textual community from that of Bernard's Cistercians. Part of the Hirsau Reform, and contemporary with the huge upsurge in women converts who joined the Premonstratensian canons, Admont and the other houses in its orbit stressed the presence and inclusion of women alongside men

---

[1] See LeClercq, *Love of Learning*, 191–235.
[2] See Stock, *Implications of Literacy*, 403–454.
[3] See LeClercq, *Monks and Love*; Newman, *Boundaries of Charity*; Turner, *Eros and Allegory*; Casey, *Athirst for God*.

in monastic life.⁴ The *Speculum virginum*, the highly influential dialogue between a young virgin, Theodora, and her spiritual advisor, Peregrinus, on the nature of her vocation, may have been modeled on the same Peregrinus who was a monk at Hirsau and a religious woman at a mixed community like the nearby Zwiefalten.⁵ Women arrived at Admont around 1120, and in numbers in the 1130s and 1140s. They were generally wealthy and aristocratic, perhaps more so than the men of the community, something that certainly occurred in the few early official Cistercian women's foundations.⁶ As a consequence, the community was sufficiently financially secure that the Admont women could devote themselves entirely to reading and study. Contemporaries of Herrad of Hohenbourg and Hildegard of Bingen, like them the women of Admont were literate and even learned, amassing a magnificent collection of texts in the community library, possibly including the manuscript that contained the *St. Trudperter Hohelied*.⁷ Tellingly, the female head of house in a Hirsau community was known not as an abbess or prioress but as the *magistra*. Admont was particularly known for its biblical exegesis, most notably producing the Old Testament scholar Irimbert (d. 1176), abbot of the community in the last four years of his life, who composed a commentary on the Song of Songs, as well as on the books of Joshua, Judges, Kings, and Ruth.⁸

While this may seem an unusual field of specialization, it was very much in the tradition of Hrabanus Maurus and Carolingian allegorical "encyclopedic" exegesis on the Old Testament. Irimbert chose to begin his exegetical career with a commentary on the Song of Songs, an indication, perhaps, both of his personal confidence as an exegete and the confidence of Admont itself in the 1140s.⁹ What is most unusual, however, is that Irimbert's Song commentary was almost certainly copied by women. Precisely because of Admont's insistence on the complete enclosure of the women and the utter segregation of the genders, to be breached only in direst emergency, Admont was required to have two separate scriptoria. The paleographical study of Alison Beach has uncovered the hands of multiple women scribes at work on the manuscript containing Irimbert's Song commentary, as well the names of two women thanked by him, Regilind and Irmingart, who transcribed Irimbert's

---

4 See McNamara, *Sisters in Arms*, 233–288; Hotchin, "Female Religious Life"; Griffiths, *Nuns' Priests' Tales*, 27. A parallel study of the Lippoldsberg community, also affiliated with the Hirsau Reform, is Hotchin, "Women's Reading."
5 The critical edition is provided by Seyfarth, ed., CCCM 5; see Mews, "Virginity, Theology, and Pedagogy."
6 See Berman, *White Nuns*, 20.
7 See Ohly, *Hohelied-Studien*, 269–271.
8 A table and rough chronology of Irimbert's exegetical works can be found in Turner, "Irimbert," 31–32.
9 See Alberi, "'Better Paths,'" 898–900.

works and may also have overseen their copying in the women's scriptorium.[10] This suggests a certain amount of ongoing contact between the men and women of Admont, probably via the communicating window in the door to the women's house that Irimbert describes. Irimbert described preaching to the women in this way himself, only to discover that the women were taking down his words secretly by dictation.[11] Humility topos, certainly, but it underscores the degree to which Irimbert's careful distance from a group of educated women created moments for their own initiative and self-direction.

In her study of the manuscripts produced by the Admont scriptoria, Beach has drawn critical attention to the large collection of sermons, exegesis, and other anonymous material collected by Bernard Pez and published indiscriminately in the *Patrologia Latina* under the name of Godfrey of Admont, abbot from 1137/38 to 1165.[12] There is no evidence that Godfrey, while an estimable abbot, was responsible for any or all of this, and a strong likelihood that the women of Admont may be not only the copyists of the corpus, but also the authors of at least some of it. Beach has noted the difficulty of identifying any one author at work in what seems to have been, overall, a genuinely collaborative exegetical enterprise, and it is entirely possible that, as Stephen Borgehammer suggests, even when they took down Irimbert's preaching the nuns may still have exercised a good deal of creative editorial initiative.[13] It was the nuns' community which kept the series of manuscripts containing the sermons for Sundays and feast days printed by Pez and then Migne. Irimbert acknowledged that the nuns preached on certain feast days, and two striking small illuminations on the title pages of two of the manuscripts containing homilies for feast days depict veiled religious women holding books and gesturing with one hand, pointing to the probability of women preaching and teaching within their own circle.[14] Conversely, if the homilies were written by Irimbert or someone from the men's community, it was also entirely possible for a woman preacher to expound in real time upon the written sermon from which she preached.

In sum, it is not possible to know with any degree of certainty who wrote, preached, illuminated, or copied the sermons found now in the *Patrologia Latina*

---

10 See Beach, *Women as Scribes*, 84–103.
11 *Nulla ad fenestram accedit loquendi gratia nisi a magistra accepta licentia, nisi abbatem adesse videant, cui soli ut filiae patri loqui audeant.* Irimbert of Admont, *Ven. Irimberti abbatis Admontensis*, Report XVI (Pez, ed. *Bibliotheca ascetica antiquo-nova* 8), quoted in the edition by Lutter, "Christ's Educated Brides," 199 n. 27.
12 See *Homiliae Dominicales*, cols. 21–120 (Migne, ed., PL 174).
13 See Borgehammer, "Who Wrote."
14 See Beach, "Listening for the Voices," 190. The illuminations of nuns preaching are Admont, Stiftsbibliothek MS 58, fol. 1v and Admont, Stiftsbibliothek MS 62, fol. 2r; they are reproduced in the article by Beach as figures 1 and 2.

or even who heard them preached, except that, in all likelihood, Abbot Godfrey was only indirectly involved. But there is a greater than usual probability, with evidence of female scribes and aristocratic, literate women in positions of authority within a fairly autonomous women's community, that these sermons were written, preached, heard, illuminated, or copied by women, or some permutation and combination of all of the above. Moreover, Admont was a self-consciously reformed community whose particular identity centered around biblical exegesis and the rejection of outside influence and interference, which meant that Admont did not, like many women's houses in German-speaking lands at the time, unofficially adopt some aspects of Cistercian observance. Its reform was, in its way, more old-fashioned. Like Hildegard, who linked her visionary vocation to her special understanding of scripture, even the Admont women's license to preach amongst themselves may well have been located in highly traditional Carolingian discourses around the need to reform the church through correct biblical interpretation, and precisely because of the women's very desire to keep themselves above suspicion by preserving their own strict enclosure.[15]

When Admont took up the Song of Songs in sermons, therefore, the community did not immediately adopt the style of exegesis of Bernard of Clairvaux, or indeed, take up the Song of Songs as a love song between Christ and the individual soul in its Latin exegesis.[16] Instead, the Admont sermons reveal an exegetical approach to the Song of Songs that was predominantly Marian, building on the Song commentary of Rupert of Deutz, developing liturgical traditions around the Marian feasts of the church, and traditions of writing for religious women that encouraged them to take the Blessed Virgin as a model for their own piety. Ironically, there is a late-twelfth century copy of Bernard's "Morimund" or "M" recension of the *Sermons on the Song of Songs* preserved at Admont, suggesting the community was well aware of Bernard's work.[17] The sermons kept in the women's community, however, preserve a twelfth-century Latin reading of the Song that was perhaps later eclipsed by the popularity of Bernard's sermon cycle, or by home-grown vernacular texts

---

15 *Et repente intellectum expositionis librorum, uidelicet psalterii, euangelii et aliorum catholicorum tam ueteris quam noui testamenti uoluminum sapiebam, non autem interpretationem uerborum textus eorum nec diuisionem syllabarum nec cognitionem casuum aut temporum habebam.* Hildegard of Bingen, "Protestificatio," in idem, *Scivias*, lines 30–34 (Führkötter, ed., CCCM 43). A nuanced account of enclosure in early medieval women's communities in Lotharingia, and the pressure brought to bear in the eleventh century to follow Benedictine observance, is Vanderputten, *Dark Age Nunneries*, 135–154.
16 Bernard himself, for all of his importance in the subsequent history of Marian devotion, does not seem to have gravitated toward a Marian reading of the Song of Songs. See Fulton, *From Judgment to Passion*, 303–304.
17 See Davis, "Bernard of Clairvaux's *Sermones*."

like the *St. Trudperter Hohelied*: an interpretation of the Song of Songs in which the women of Admont accessed the biblical text, even to understand their own bridal vocation, primarily through the radiant figure of Mary.

2 Early Medieval Exegesis of the Song of Songs

A complex ecosystem of exegesis had grown up around the Song of Songs in the early Middle Ages, nurtured by the flexibility of allegorical interpretation and the encyclopedic range of ambitious Carolingian scholars like Hrabanus Maurus and Paschasius Radbertus. Carolingian biblical scholarship on the Song of Songs had built on the intersecting legacies of Gregory the Great and the Venerable Bede, who had invited early medieval exegetes to interpret the Song of Songs almost exclusively as a love song between Christ and his church.[18] To Alcuin, the beautiful body of the Bridegroom, compared in the Song of Songs to ivory and gold, underscored the regal Christology of the period, while the Song's descriptions of the Bride's luscious lips and breasts were transmuted into urgent calls for preaching, baptism, and nurturing pastoral care.[19] The teachers of the Carolingian reform saw themselves as integral parts of the body of the Bride; in this reading of the Song of Songs, eroticism was, if anything, deployed rhetorically to articulate longing, urgency, and the imminence of spiritual reality.[20] As a result of the early medieval commentary tradition, the Song of Songs became a very natural text to use in connection with ecclesiology and church reform. This continued in the eleventh century, albeit in a slightly different form, with the exegetes associated with the Gregorian Reform emphasizing, not their shared, corporate clerical identity, but the Bride's solitude, signifying her freedom from secular ties, her watchfulness, and her purity.[21]

---

18 See the Venerable Bede, *In Cantica Canticorum Libri VI* (Hurst, ed., CCSL 119B, 165–375). Bede compiled a small florilegium of extracts from the works of Gregory the Great guided his own interpretation of the Song of Songs and which make up Book VI of the Bedan commentary.
19 The most recent critical edition is Alcuin, *Commento al Cantico dei Cantici* (Guglielmetti, ed.).
20 It is most likely this "anagogical" dimension of Song exegesis, as well as certain obvious points of contact such as John's vision of Christ or the New Jerusalem as a Bride, which encouraged nearly all exegetes from the ninth century onwards to write commentaries both on the Song of Songs and the Apocalypse. See Matter, "Apocalypse"; idem, "Exegesis."
21 An example is the commentary of Robert of Tombelaine, part of which is attributed to Gregory the Great (Migne, ed., PL 79; 150). Another is the commentary by the layman John of Mantua, *Tractatus Iohanni Mantuani in Cantica Canticorum ad semper felicem Matildam* (Bischoff and Taeger, eds., *Spicilegium Friburgense* 19, 25–155), which is dedicated to Matilda of Tuscany.

While the commentary tradition on the Song of Songs was overwhelmingly institutional and ecclesiological in the early Middle Ages, the reading of the Song of Songs as an allegory between Christ and the individual soul survived, particularly in the context of treatises and letters written to women in the monastic life, often as descriptions of, or as advocates for women's enclosure. Inevitably, these were modeled on the monastic rhetoric of Jerome, particularly his "Letter to Eustochium," and however ambivalent Jerome's attitude to his female correspondents may seem to the modern reader, the figure of Jerome was a potent patristic license for those priests and monks who developed their own spirituality through pastoral relationships with religious women.[22] Alcuin, Paschasius Radbertus, and Peter Damian all address aristocratic women in terms of the language of the Song of Songs, exhorting them to seek their heavenly Bridegroom and to find peace in their confinement through the consolation of their bridal status.[23] At the same time, Paschasius Radbertus returns to Mary as the preeminent model for the enclosed woman, the Virgin Mother to both virgins and widows.[24] Paschasius, writing in his authorial persona as Jerome, addressed his Song-strewn letter known as *Cogitis me*, which would be incorporated into the office of matins for the feast of the Assumption, specifically to the women's community at Soissons, which was dedicated to the Virgin.[25]

3 Rupert of Deutz and the Marian Interpretation of the Song of Songs at Admont

The prominence of Marian feasts for the Admont community, as well as the use of the Song of Songs to narrate Mary's experience, is plainly apparent in the sermon collection. At one point, the Song is referred to simply and unilaterally as "that book of our Lady Mary."[26] Admont's volume of festival sermons contains five sermons devoted to the Annunciation, a sermon for the vigil of the Assumption, no less than

---

22 See Griffiths, *Nuns' Priests' Tales*, 77–110.
23 Peter Damian wrote only a few letters to women, all from the 1060s: Letters 66 and 123, and the three letters to the Empress Agnes, 104, 124, and 149, published in the series *The Letters of Peter Damian, The Fathers of the Church: Medieval Continuation* (Blum and Resnick, trans.).
24 This is most clearly expressed in Paschasius Radbertus, *Expositio in Ps 44* (Paulus, ed., CCCM 94).
25 See Paschasius Radbertus, *De assumptione sanctae Mariae uirginis* (Ripberger, ed., CCCM 56C, 109–162) and Fulton, *From Judgment to Passion*, 248. It would be Carolingian liturgists who made the intuitive leap to use selections from the Song of Songs within the office of the Assumption in the first place; see Fulton, "'Quae est ista,'" 101–116.
26 *Homiliae Dominicales*, Homily 4, col. 37A.

eight sermons for the feast of the Assumption, and five for the feast of the nativity of the Virgin. While not all of these sermons refer explicitly to the Song of Songs, many do, even when the guiding scriptural pericope does not. Conversely, most, if not all, references to the Song of Songs in the entire sermon corpus occur in connection with the Virgin, with a few acknowledging the older exegetical tradition of seeing the Bride of the Song of Songs as a figure for the church, and very occasionally, in isolated moments, as the individual soul. One Admont sermon for Palm Sunday, taking as its text "Ascendam in palmam" (Song 7:8), describes Christ ascending to Jerusalem to take hold of its fruit, the human race. The preacher describes how those in the Palm Sunday procession wear only albs, to signify redeemed souls who have left the body behind in the dust of the earth, while the cantors, who signify the angels, wear both albs and copes (*cappis*). On Easter Day, however, everyone will be clad in both, as on the day of resurrection.[27] One homily on the Last Supper compares Christ's declaration that his disciples will see him in a little while to the mysteriously departing Bridegroom of the Song (Song 8:14).[28] Another homily on the pools of Beth-zatha (John 5:1–9) compares the spiritual life to the invalids waiting for the angel to stir the waters; we languish with love (Song 5:8) while we complain to the daughters of Jerusalem, symbolizing those just souls whom we will join when we leave this wretched life.[29]

More frequently, however, the sermons track alongside and take exegetical cues from the Song commentary of Rupert of Deutz. Unlike many of the twelfth-century commentators, Rupert of Deutz, like Irimbert, did not immediately adopt the language of the schools but deliberately turned instead toward biblical interpretation as a tool for reform—a stance that would influence Hildegard, not least.[30] Bishop Cuno of Regensberg, Rupert's particular friend and patron, seems to have enthusiastically circulated copies of Rupert's Marian commentary throughout Bavaria in the years of his bishopric, between 1126 and 1132, which may well have been when Admont first received the work, since a twelfth-century copy from Admont survives.[31] If so, the arrival of Rupert's commentary virtually coincided with the implementation of reform and the admittance of women to Admont, and over time the community seems to have made a point of collecting Rupert's broader exegetical oeuvre.[32] The Admont sermons are not slavish adaptations of Rupert's work,

---

27 See *Homiliae Dominicales*, Homily 44, cols. 293A–294B.
28 See *Homiliae Dominicales*, Homily 50, col. 333C–D.
29 See *Homiliae Dominicales*, Homily 27, cols. 183D–184B.
30 See Griffiths, *Garden of Delights*, 75.
31 See Van Engen, *Rupert of Deutz*, 5. An Admont manuscript of Rupert's commentary is the "I" text in Rupert of Deutz, *Commentaria* (Haacke, ed., CCCM 26).
32 See Beach, *Women as Scribes*, 132.

however, departing from the narrative provided by his commentary at several points, and they certainly do not invoke him explicitly as an authority, as one might expect.

For example, in the Admont collection of Dominical sermons, the fourth sermon embarks on a careful reading of the fifth chapter of the Song of Songs, "Aperi mihi, soror mea," as a retelling of the Annunciation. Interestingly, Rupert interprets this particular passage, probably taking his cue from the Song reference to the bride's tunic, as an allegory of the crucifixion; for Rupert, "anima mea liquefacta est" (Song 5:6) is a reference to the soul-piercing sword of Mary's sorrow at Christ on the cross.[33] For the writer of the Admont sermon, however, the voice calling for the bride to open her door is that of Gabriel to Mary, "my sister, my bride, my dove": sister as a daughter of Abraham, dove-like in her simplicity. The tunic the Bride has taken off corresponds to the skin garments of Genesis, and to carnal desire more generally; myrrh (Song 5:5), to the mortification of the flesh.[34] The Bridegroom reaching in to touch the Bride through the keyhole (*foramen*) is the Holy Spirit's entrance to the Virgin's womb; in this reading, "my belly trembled at his touch" (Song 5:4) has a particularly vivid resonance.[35] The festival sermons on the Annunciation return to the Song of Songs, and to Song 5:6 in particular; the writer acknowledges that while the Bride in this passage can be understood as the church, it is even more particularly appropriate to Mary. The Bride's search for her beloved through the city in the rest of the Song chapter corresponds to Mary's search for her beloved amidst a fallen world, the Bride's encounter with the guards of the city to her protection by the Holy Spirit and by the angels, who take away the cloak of original sin from her.[36]

The other Song narrative adapted for the Annunciation, "the feast above all other feasts," is the invitation to the daughters of Jerusalem to go see King Solomon, crowned by his mother on his wedding-day (Song 3:11). The Annunciation is the moment, the author repeats twice, that Christ becomes the Bridegroom for the first time and Mary the Bride, in the "wedding-chamber" of Mary's womb

---

[33] *Ibi ignis, ibi gladius, ignis amoris, gladius doloris, et anima mea uictima erat holocausti.* Rupert of Deutz, *Commentaria*, lines 292–328, quotation at lines 318–319 (Haacke, ed., CCCM 26, 112–113).
[34] [. . .] *continua abstinentia multisque laboribus virgineum corpus suum castigaret, ne quando carnalis concupiscentiae vitium sibi appropinquaret.* *Homiliae Dominicales*, Homily 4, cols. 40B; 42A.
[35] See *Homiliae Dominicales*, Homily 4, col. 41C.
[36] [. . .] *ut nata est, Spiritus sanctus in sui eam custodiam suscepit, ut, protectionis ejus munimine obumbrata, florens inter spinas rosa absque spinarum injuria in altum cresceret, ex qua dulcissimus totius suavitatis, totius munditiae et castitatis flosculus suo in tempore potenter emergeret* [. . .] *angelicos convenienter spiritus accipere possumus, quorum specialem custodiae et protectionis diligentiam haec Virgo gloriosa tanto majorem circa se promuerit, quanto in carne praeter carnem vivens per singularis vitae innocentium prima omnium angelicae vitae imitata est excellentiam.* *Homiliae Festivales*, Homily 31, col. 769D; cols. 770D–771A.

with the kiss with which the Song begins.³⁷ Christ is crowned by his mother and by the Synagogue with the double crown of the Incarnation and the Passion; in his reading of the passage, Rupert explicitly invokes the crown of thorns.³⁸ With the rather abrupt re-emergence of *Synagoga* from the early medieval commentary tradition, in which she was regularly paired with and pitted against *Ecclesia*, it is a reminder that the anti-Jewish aspects of early medieval exegesis hardly disappeared with the Marian interpretation of the Song. Other Old Testament figures could be coopted into this narrative as well. The kiss of the Song's opening verses makes another cameo appearance in an allegorical homily on Samson and Delilah, which the preacher interprets as Christ's love for fallen humanity: it was no other, neither angel nor man, but from Christ himself that Mary asked and received his kiss, along with a burning love of God and neighbor beyond all earthly things.³⁹

In the Admont sermon corpus, the "spotlessness" of the Bride is not something Mary is born with, but rather is something granted to her by God—the removal of original sin—after much spiritual searching and asceticism. Signified in the Bride's encounter with the night watchmen and their theft of her cloak or veil (Song 5:7), this moment in the Song narrative is projected backwards such that it becomes a kind of prerequisite to the Annunciation: earlier in the same chapter, the Bride rises to open the door to her beloved, naked and already free from original sin.⁴⁰ In this way, the discontinuous poetry of the Song of Songs allowed for a certain amount of theological ambiguity and development precisely because it did not bind a particular theological teaching concerning Mary to a linear, prosaic narrative. Another Admont Annunciation sermon suggests that, already extraordinary to begin with,

---

37 [. . .] *quia in thalamo illo, beatissimae Virginis utero, idem Filius Dei sponsus factus est et sponsa; sponsus secundum divinitatem, sponsa secundum humanitatem.* [. . .] *Hodie dulcissimum illud osculum Patris et Spiritus sancti, quod erat Filius Dei, ad quod suspirabant antiqui Patres ab initio saeculi, dicente in persona ipsorum Salomone Osculetur. Homiliae Festivales*, Homily 20, col. 760B; 762B. Cf. Rupert of Deutz, *Commentaria*, lines 1–42 (Haacke, ed., CCCM 26, 10–11).
38 See Rupert of Deutz, *Commentaria*, lines 296–333 (Haacke, ed., CCCM 26, 68–69).
39 *Non alium, inquit, non angelum, non hominem expecto sed ipse me osculetur osculo oris sui. Dudum mihi per ora prophetarum suorum locutus est Dominus, veniat et ipse, humiliet et exinaniat se, et osculetur me osculo oris sui. Nonne ex Dalilis istis una, beata Dei genetrix Maria erat, quam credimus supra omnes homines [tanto] majori instantia hujusmodi dilectionis oscula postulasse, quanto majori dilectionis Dei et proximi desiderio prae cunctis mortalibus flagrabat? Homiliae Dominicales*, Homily 42, col. 280C.
40 *Surrexi, inquam, corpore et anima ab omni originali siue actuali peccato libera. Nec propter me hoc factum est, quasi ego virtutum meritis alios praecellens tali munere sublimare digna sim, sed ut aperirem dilecto meo, hoc est, ut porta illi fierem per quam cum carne ex me sumpta transiret ad hominem. Homiliae Dominicales*, Homily 4, col. 41D.

Mary's original sin was removed and her growth in virtue accelerated as she was literally conformed to the virtues of the Christ child growing within her.[41]

4 The Admont Sermons on the Assumption of the Virgin

The nine sermons on the Assumption reiterate and further develop many of these themes, which are then in turn further reinforced by another sequence on her nativity. As the first homily on the vigil for the Assumption says, rather coyly, "we should say something in her praise, as best we can."[42] As a group, the Assumption sermons splice together a collection of scriptural texts which loosely follow, if occasionally tangentially and out of order, the collects for the Assumption as recorded in the Antiphoner of Compiègne; interestingly, they do not incorporate such readings for the feast as would become traditional, such as the woman clothed with the sun (Rev 12).[43] The scriptural texts employed by the Admont sermons include the seven-columned hall built by Wisdom (Prov 9), Mary and Martha (Luke 10), "Arise, my love" (Song 2:10–11), "You are altogether beautiful, my love (Song 4:7), Ps 71, "Quae est ista" (Song 3:6), and Wisdom's hymn in Ecclesiasticus (Sir 24:1–22). Wisdom personified bookends the series, therefore, and interestingly, both the text from Proverbs and the hymn from Ecclesiasticus refer to nard, "a humble but sweet-smelling herb," which the sermon writer wastes no time in comparing to Mary and linking back to the Song of Songs (Song 1:11). Likewise, in the nativity series, one homily would return to Mary as Wisdom from Prov 8.[44] The two Assumption homilies on Mary and Martha are an interesting effort at reading, not just the New Testament, but a gospel text allegorically, with the two sisters corresponding, respectively, to

---

41 *Hoc sane pallio, quia haec Virgo beata, utpote in peccatis concepta et nata, nequaquam caruit, audita quidem credidit, sed quomodo fieri possent, penitus ignoravit [. . .] totius concupiscentiae macula, originali crimine indita, funditus deperiit, quia licet ab ipso nativitatis suae ortu cunctis virginibus incomparabilis esset, ab ipso tamen novae et inauditae salutationis angelicae obsequio meritis sanctior, virtutibus celsior per omnia ei, quem conceperat, conformatur, quemadmodum ex sequentibus ejus dictis manifeste declaratur.* Homiliae Festivales, Homily 31, col. 772B–D.
42 *Quia gloriosa beatissimae Virginis Mariae assumptionem celebraturi sumus dignum est, ut de laude ejus, prout poterimus, aliquid loqui curemus.* Homiliae Festivales, Homily 63, col. 957A. The homilies on the Assumption are Homilies 63–71, those on the Virgin's nativity are Homilies 74–78.
43 A table of the collects for the Assumption from the Antiphoner of Compiègne can be found in Fulton, "'Quae est ista,'" 105–108.
44 [. . .] *humilis herba, sed suaveolens.* Homiliae Festivales, Homily 63, col. 958AB; Homily 71, col. 988B; Homily 77, col. 1014D.

Mary's soul and her life of bodily asceticism.⁴⁵ The short third homily emphasizes Mary's role as intercessor and argues that the multiplicity of names in the Song arises from her many virtues.⁴⁶ The next homily begins by operatically praising "Blessed Mary, mistress of the world, queen of heaven, empress of the angels, unique matter [*materia singularis*] of all the sacraments," then praises her bodily integrity, before returning again to the removal of her original sin through Christ.⁴⁷ Both the seventh Assumption homily, "Quae est ista," and the nativity homily which also returns to that particular verse follow the interpretation popularized by the *Transitus Mariae*, which envisions the speaker as the Holy Spirit and the angels.⁴⁸ The Bride of the Song, beautiful as the dawn, coming up from the desert like a column of incense (Song 3:6; 6:10), is Mary at her Assumption, surrounded by angels, having passed through the bitter incense of the Passion.⁴⁹

Two illuminations in the Admont manuscript containing these sermons correspond, respectively, to the feast of her nativity, depicting the Virgin as a child with Anne and Joachim, and to her Dormition. In the illumination of the Dormition, the soul of Mary is depicted in a triumphant embrace with Christ. Stefanie Seeburg has argued that both images were intended to depict the Virgin as a model for the nuns' own vocations.⁵⁰ For the nuns of Admont, speculation and devotion around the life of Mary was hardly a matter of purely academic interest: Mary was the preeminent personification for their own piety, virgin and mother, representing in her own body the two populations of a women's religious community, virgins and widows. Sermons celebrating the Marian feasts were occasions, not least, to bring the community together, and perhaps the women's community with the men's as well. In this endeavor, Admont, which had built its identity around supporting and

---

45 *Quia Martha* irritans, *vel* provocans, *vel etiam Syro sermone* dominans *interpretatur, recte hujus nominis etymologia beatissimae Virginis corpus figuratur, quod jejuniorum, vigiliarum et totius continentiae nimietate hostem antiquum irritat.* Homiliae Festivales, Homily 65, col. 966D.
46 *Quando quidem multis ac diversis adornata erat virtutibus, multis etiam ac diversis eam Spiritus sanctus honorare voluit nominibus.* Homily 66, *Homiliae Festivales*, col. 972B.
47 *beata Maria, mundi domina, coelorum regina, angelorum imperatrix, sacramentorum omnium materia singularis.* [. . .] *Habuit ergo mater innocentiae maculam, nullam videlicet aliam nisi originalis peccati culpam, qua in ortu suo non caruit, quia ut caeteri Adae filii sine crimine in mundum prodire non potuit. In deliciis enim concepta et nata usu naturae hoc cum aliis peccatoribus habuit commune, ut originale peccato tandiu subjaceret, donec ipse ejus Unigenitus per semetipsum a Matre et per Matrem ejusdem originalis peccati maculam ab omnibus tolleret atque deleret. Homiliae Festivales*, Homily 67, cols. 974B–975AB.
48 Rupert of Deutz hesitates at making this passage explicitly about the Assumption, see Rupert of Deutz, *Commentaria*, lines 8–58 (Haacke, ed., CCCM 26, 60–61).
49 *Homiliae Festivales*, Homily 70, col. 985BC; Homily 77, cols. 1017D–1019C.
50 See Seeberg, "Illustrations," 112–117, illuminations reproduced as figures 14 and 16.

lauding women's religious vocation as brides of Christ, thus drew upon already existing discourses within the early medieval church, one strong element of which since Jerome was the use of Song exegesis. At the same time, a reformer in the twelfth century trying to convey the spiritual reality of the church in the most vivid and urgent way possible must have felt that *Ecclesia* could have used an exegetical makeover from the purely institutional allegory of Bede and Gregory. The Marian interpretation of the Song of Songs represented a particularly potent answer to both halves of this conundrum, born of the religious needs of the twelfth century. While all exegetes, not least Rupert of Deutz and certainly Bernard of Clairvaux, recognized the interpretation rested on a hermeneutical leap of faith, Mary understood as the Bride of the Song could hold the space for both ecclesiological and individual women's readings of the Song to coexist together. The Admont sermons sometimes admit that the Marian interpretation of the Song is not the only one available, but then insist that the scriptural text is especially and particularly appropriate for the Virgin.[51] In this way, it was in the context of the Marian narrative that the nuns of Admont were allowed to read the Song as applicable to the individual soul in the early days of reform. Mary, therefore, acted as a kind of exegetical guardrail for how bridal mysticism would look in practice.

Bibliography

Primary Sources

Alcuin. *Commento al Cantico dei Cantici: Con i commenti anonimi Vox ecclesie Vox antique ecclesie*, edited by Rossana E. Guglielmetti. Florence: SISMEL, 2004.
Bede, The Venerable. "In Cantica Canticorum Libri VI." In *Bedae Venerabilis Opera, Pars II: Opera Exegetica 2B*, edited by David Hurst, 164–375. CCSL 119B. Turnhout: Brepols, 1983.
Hildegard of Bingen. *Scivias*, edited by Adelgundis Führkötter. CCCM 43. Turnhout: Brepols, 1978.
Homiliae Dominicales et Festivales, edited by Jacques-Paul Migne. PL 174. Paris, 1854.
Irimbert of Admont. *Ven. Irimberti abbatis Admontensis de incendio monasterii sui, ac de vita et moribus virginum sanctimonialium parthenonis Admuntensis Order. S. Ben. Narratio*, edited by Bernhard Pez. Bibliotheca ascetica antiquo-nova 8. Regensburg, 1725.

---

51 For example, *Haec utique licet ex persona Ecclesiae dixerit, speciali tamen et nobilissimae illius, qui feminam nescit, sponsae, dominae nostrae scilicet perpetuae Virgini Mariae, specialius ascribuntur. Homiliae Festivales*, Homily 31, col. 768A; *In cujus lectionis area, licet multorum et magnorum expositorum, tam modernorum quam antiquorum, subtilia et sublimia desudaverint ingenia, odorifera tamen et sub palea litterae recondita tam gloriosae Matris virginis quam praecelsi Filii regis, adhuc innumera redolent mysteria. Homiliae Festivales*, Homily 65, col. 964C; Homily 66, col. 972A.

John of Mantua. *Tractatus Iohanni Mantuani in Cantica Canticorum ad semper felicem Matildam*, edited by Bernhard Bischoff and Burkhard Taeger. Spicilegium Friburgense 19. Fribourg: Universitätsverlag, 1973.
Paschasius Radbertus. *De assumptione sanctae Mariae uirginis*, edited by Albert Ripberger. CCCM 56C. Turnhout: Brepols, 1985.
Paschasius Radbertus. *Expositio in Ps 44*, edited by Beda Paulus. CCCM 94. Turnhout: Brepols, 1991.
Peter Damian. *The Letters of Peter Damian; The Fathers of the Church: Medieval Continuation*, translated by Owen Blum and Irven Resnick. Washington D.C.: Catholic University Press, 1989–2013.
Rupert of Deutz. *Commentaria in Canticum Canticorum*, edited by Hrabanus Haacke. CCCM 26. Turnhout: Brepols, 1974.
Speculum virginum, edited by Jutta Seyfarth. CCCM 5. Turnhout: Brepols, 1990.

Secondary Sources

Alberi, Mary. "'The Better Paths of Wisdom': Alcuin's Monastic 'True Philosophy' and the Worldly Court." *Speculum* 76 (2001): 896–910.
Beach, Alison I. "Listening for the Voices of Admont's Twelfth-Century Nuns." In *Voices in Dialogue: Reading Women in the Middle Ages*, edited by Linda Olson and Kathryn Kerby-Fulton, 187–198. Notre Dame: University of Notre Dame Press, 2005.
Beach, Alison I. *Women as Scribes: Book-Production and Monastic Reform in Twelfth-Century Bavaria*. Cambridge: Cambridge University Press, 2004.
Berman, Constance. *The White Nuns: Cistercian Abbeys for Women in Medieval France*. Philadelphia: University of Pennsylvania Press, 2018.
Borgehammer, Stephen. "Who Wrote the Admont Sermon Corpus? Gottfried the Abbot, His Brother Irimbert, or the Nuns?" In *De l'homilie au sermon: Histoire de la prédication médiévale*, edited by Jacqueline Hamesse and Xavier Hermand, 47–51. Louvain-la-Neuve: Brepols, 1993.
Casey, Michael. *Athirst for God: Spiritual Desire in Bernard of Clairvaux's Sermons on the Song of Songs*. Kalamazoo: Cistercian Publications, 1988.
Davis, Lisa Fagin. "Bernard of Clairvaux's *Sermones super Cantica Canticorum* in Twelfth-Century Austria." In *Manuscripts and Monastic Culture: Reform and Renewal in Twelfth-Century Germany*, edited by Alison I. Beach, 285–310. Medieval Church Studies 13. Turnhout: Brepols, 2007.
Fulton Brown, Rachel. *From Judgment to Passion: Devotion to Christ and the Virgin Mary, 800–1200*. New York: Columbia University Press, 2002.
Fulton Brown, Rachel. "'Quae est ista quae ascendit sicut aurora consurgens?' The Song of Songs as the *Historia* for the Office of the Assumption." *MST 60* (1998): 55–122.
Griffiths, Fiona J. *The Garden of Delights: Reform and Renaissance for Women in the Twelfth Century*. Philadelphia: University of Pennsylvania Press, 2007.
Griffiths, Fiona J. *Nuns' Priests' Tales: Men and Salvation in Medieval Women's Monastic Life*. Philadelphia: University of Pennsylvania Press, 2018.
Hotchin, Julie. "Female Religious Life and the *cura monialium* in Hirsau Monasticism, 1080–1150." In *Listen, Daughter: The Speculum Virginum and the Formation of Religious Women in the Middle Ages*, edited by Constant J. Mews, 59–83. London: Palgrave, 2001.
Hotchin, Julie. "Women's Reading and Monastic Reform in Twelfth-Century Germany: The Library of the Nuns of Lippoldsberg." In *Manuscripts and Monastic Culture: Reform and Renewal in Twelfth-*

Century Germany, edited by Alison I. Beach, 139–189. Medieval Church Studies 13. Turnhout: Brepols, 2007.

LeClercq, Jean. *The Love of Learning and the Desire for God: A Study of Monastic Culture*. New York: Fordham University Press, 2000.

LeClercq, Jean. *Monks and Love: Psycho-historical Essays*. Oxford: Clarendon Press, 1979.

Lutter, Christina. "Christ's Educated Brides: Literacy, Spirituality, and Gender in Twelfth-Century Admont." In *Manuscripts and Monastic Culture: Reform and Renewal in Twelfth-Century Germany*, edited by Alison I. Beach, 191–213. Medieval Church Studies 13. Turnhout: Brepols, 2007.

Matter, E. Ann. "The Apocalypse in Early Medieval Exegesis." In *The Apocalypse in the Middle Ages*, edited by Richard K. Emmerson and Bernard McGinn, 38–50. Ithaca: Cornell University Press, 1992.

Matter, E. Ann. "Exegesis of the Apocalypse in the Early Middle Ages." In *The Year 1000: Religious and Social Response to the Turning of the First Millenium*, edited by Michael Frassetto, 29–40. London: Palgrave, 2002.

McNamara, Jo Ann Kay. *Sisters in Arms: Catholic Nuns through Two Millennia*. Cambridge, MA: Harvard University Press, 1996.

Mews, Constant. "Virginity, Theology, and Pedagogy in the *Speculum Virginum*." In *Listen, Daughter: The Speculum Virginum and the Formation of Religious Women in the Middle Ages*, edited by Constant J. Mews, 15–40. London: Palgrave, 2001.

Newman, Martha G. *The Boundaries of Charity: Cistercian Culture and Ecclesiastical Reform, 1098–1180*. Stanford: Stanford University Press, 1996.

Ohly, Friedrich. *Hohelied-Studien: Grundzüge einer Geschichte der Hohelied-Auslegung des Abendlandes bis um 1200*. Wiesbaden, Franz Steiner Verlag, 1958.

Seeberg, Stefanie. "Illustrations in the Manuscripts of the Admont Nuns from the Second Half of the Twelfth Century: Reflections on Their Function." In *Manuscripts and Monastic Culture: Reform and Renewal in Twelfth-Century Germany*, edited by Alison I. Beach, 99–121. Medieval Church Studies 13. Turnhout: Brepols, 2007.

Stock, Brian. *The Implications of Literacy: Written Language and Models of Interpretation in the Eleventh and Twelfth Centuries*. Princeton: Princeton University Press, 1983.

Turner, Denys. *Eros and Allegory: Medieval Exegesis of the Song of Songs*. Kalamazoo: Cistercian Publications, 1995.

Turner, Shannon Marie. "Irimbert of Admont and His Scriptural Commentaries: Exegeting Salvation History in the Twelfth Century." PhD diss., Ohio State University, 2017.

Vanderputten, Steven. *Dark Age Nunneries: The Ambiguous Identity of Female Monasticism, 800–1050*. Ithaca: Cornell University Press, 2018.

Van Engen, John. *Rupert of Deutz*. Berkeley: University of California Press, 1983.

Rabea Kohnen
Voices Shifting and Voices Layered
The Song of Songs in Medieval German Commentaries

1 Introduction

> *Ecce pulchra es amica mea ecce tu pulchra oculi tui columbarum*
> *Ecce tu pulcher es et dilecte mi decorus, lectulus noster floridus*
>
> Behold thou art fair, O my love, behold thou art fair, thy eyes are as those of doves.
> Behold thou art fair, my beloved and comely. Our bed is flourishing.[1]

The Song of Songs mainly consists of two voices talking to each other and about one another. They praise their beloved, talk about their emotions, describe imagined or remembered tender encounters, or express their longing to meet again. The text does not convey much biographical information about those lovers, though, which opens up an imaginative space for every recipient to identify with one of them (or both).[2] This is a common feature of lyrical speech and supports the assumption that the Song of Songs is a collection of previously independent love songs.[3] The different voices of the separate songs would only become the voices of the same two lovers in the act of reception, when readers identified with the textual voices by projecting their own internal voices onto them.[4] In such an understanding, bride and groom are viewed as functional entities, but only in a very restricted sense as literary characters.[5]

Christian reception of the Song of Songs from antiquity until at least the end of the Middle Ages operated from quite different base assumptions. Authorship by King

---

1 Song 1:15–16 (Vulg. 1:14–15). English translation from the *Douay-Rheims* edition.
2 See Exum, *Song of Songs*, 8.
3 For an introduction to the ongoing discussion of the Song of Songs' genre, see Zakovitch, *Das Hohelied*, 30–40; Exum, *Song of Songs*, 28–46.
4 For the underlying methodological framework of this assumption, see Zymner, "'Stimme(n)' als Text."
5 In contrast, one could argue that a literary character is already completely present in the recipients imagination as soon as it is mentioned and is only modified after that. See Grabes, "Wie aus Sätzen Personen werden." For an in-depth discussion of the production of characters in the act of reception, see Jannidis, *Figur und Person*. For a reflection on the voices of the Song of Songs, see Fischer, *Das Hohelied Salomos*, 136–172.

Solomon, which seems rather doubtful to modern scholars,[6] guaranteed the artistic and even biographical unity of the Song of Songs, as it was often seen as a bridal song written for the pharaoh's daughter.[7] Moreover, the first Christian exegetes adopted the allegorical reading of the Song of Songs from the Jewish tradition, understanding the groom and bride not, or at least not only, as human lovers but also and more prominently as representations of God and his believers. In this way *sponsus* and *sponsa*, the terms for groom and bride in the Latin tradition, were seen as characters, but in a fluid sense of the concept. The *sponsus* was King Solomon and God at the same time, the *sponsa* an actual bride of Solomon but also a personification of the church, an image of the human soul, or in later times Mary as the perfect representative of both.[8] These different layers of historical and allegorical understanding also led to different concepts of *sponsus* and *sponsa*—ranging from voices with minimal physicality to fully formed characters with their own biographies—which I want to explore in this paper.

In my explorations of these designs, I will focus on three commentaries on the Song of Songs in the German vernacular, one each from the eleventh, twelfth, and thirteenth centuries. Even though these three texts differ enormously in many regards, they share some common features. As literary rewritings, they are as much adaptations of the Song of Songs as they are exegetical works aimed at a better understanding of this inspiring yet provocative biblical book. In addition to their ways to design *sponsus* and *sponsa* as voices and/or as characters, all three add another entity, who moderates, relates to, and comments on these voices. In a narrative text, we would refer to such an entity as *narrator*, and in a nonliterary text we might even call it the *author*.[9] To abstain from judgment regarding the genre and fictionality of the works discussed here and to make a clear distinction between the historical author and the center of utterances as part of the text, I will refer to this entity as the *primary voice*.[10] The validity of the

---

6 See Murphy, *Song of Songs*, 3.
7 Theodore of Mopsuestia argued vehemently for such an understanding and refuted all allegorical interpretation of the Song of Songs. See Ohly, *Hohelied-Studien*, 55–56.
8 For an overview of the tradition, see Ohly, *Hohelied-Studien*; Matter, *Voice of My Beloved*; Turner, *Eros and Allegory*; Scheper, "Spiritual Marriage"; Astell, *Song of Songs in the Middle Ages*.
9 The relationship between historical authors and narrators as a feature of a text is a topic of ongoing debate in literary studies. The distinction is even more challenging for medieval literature and therefore even more controversial. As an introduction, see Jannidis, "Zwischen Autor und Erzähler"; Unzeitig, "Von der Schwierigkeit"; Reuvekamp-Felber, "Autorschaft als Textfunktion."
10 Wolf Schmid (with reference to Bertil Romberg) advocated for the terms *primary narrator* and *secondary narrator* as replacements for the sometimes misleading terms *extradiegetic narrator* and *intradiegetic narrator* proposed by Gérard Genette (see Schmid, *Elemente der Narratologie*, 80). As the texts analyzed here are only partly narrations, I have opted for an even more general term.

term *voice* as a narratological concept has been the subject of discussion for some time, mostly because of its metaphorical nature and its hermeneutic ambiguity.[11] I would argue, though, that these are precisely the features of the concept that make it stimulating and useful with regard to medieval reception of the Song of Songs.[12]

The three commentaries I will explore—*Expositio in Cantica Canticorum* by Williram of Ebersberg, the anonymously authored *Lehre der liebenden Gotteserkenntnis*, and *Hohelied* by Brun of Schönebeck—inherit the dialogic nature of the Song of Songs as their basic compositional principle, but they construct very different dialogues between the voices of *sponsus* and *sponsa*, the primary voice and the (implied) recipients, the voice of text and the voices of textual tradition. This is partly due to the different times, contexts, and audiences they were created for, but I would also argue that it was an effect of the literary power of the Song of Songs, which had an enormous impact on medieval theology and art alike.

2 Dialogue as Soliloquy: Williram of Ebersberg and His *Expositio in Cantica Canticorum*

2.1 Author, Work, and Context

Williram of Ebersberg (1010–1085) wrote his *Expositio in Cantica Canticorum*[13] while he was the abbot of a small Benedictine monastery in Ebersberg, where he does not seem to have been very happy.[14] In the dedication of this book to King Henry IV, Williram expresses a great desire to return to "his monastery" *(monasterium meum)* from his exile. He also mentions greater aspirations he once harbored and how those where shattered by the death of Henry III.[15] We do not know if the king received a copy of the book or if he deigned to answer the unhappy abbot, but we know that Williram died in 1085 in Ebersberg, never having returned from what felt like exile to him. The preface of the *Expositio* gives options for what he

---

[11] For an outline of research history and an overview of current topics and positions in the discussion, see Blödorn, Langer, and Scheffel, eds., *Stimme(n) im Text*.
[12] In so doing, I was inspired in particular by Aczel, "Hearing Voices in Narrative Texts," and Jannidis, "Wer sagt das?"
[13] The relevant critical edition is Williram, *Expositio* (Lähnemann and Rupp, eds.; references hereafter are to this edition); for a translation into English, see Williram, *Expositio* (Meyer, ed.).
[14] For a discussion of this point, see Schupp, *Studien*, 174–201.
[15] See Williram, *Expositio*, 2–3, 5–14.

might have meant by "his monastery," as its title reads *Incipit Praefatio Willirami Babinbergensis Scolastici Fuldensis monachi in Cantica Canticorum* ("here starts the preface of the [commentary] on the Song of Songs by Williram, master of the school from Bamberg and monk from Fulda").[16] Even if the monastery at Fulda did not shine as brightly in Williram's lifetime as it had when Hrabanus Maurus taught there in the ninth century, it was still an important political, spiritual, and intellectual center with an impressive library.[17] The monastery of Michaelsberg in Bamberg, where Williram was *scholasticus*, was not as grand, but it easily outshone the provincial Ebersberg.[18] We know that Williram was of noble descent, and his literary works reflect an extensive education, so his political aspirations as a young man might have been well justified.[19] The contribution he made with his commentary on the Song of Songs, though, lets his exile in Ebersberg appear to be a lucky turn of events—if not for Williram himself then surely for the history of German literature.

The importance of the *Expositio* for the history of German literature is grounded in its chronological position, complex composition, and broad reception alike. The century before Williram saw a curious gap in the tradition of writing in the German vernacular, and the next big increase did not happen for another hundred years. As a result, the *Expositio* is an important reference point from both a linguistic and an artistic perspective.[20] The broad reception of this work is documented in the large number of codices and even early prints but also shows itself in later literary works that refer to Williram.[21] Even though the *Expositio* has been criticized by modern scholars for being exegetically conservative, its mastery of verse and prose and of Latin and German, and the ingenuity with which these elements are combined, has always guaranteed the work a well-deserved space in the history of German literature.[22]

Williram's understanding of the Song of Songs is deeply rooted in Carolingian theology, and the *Expositio* has been shown to be directly based on a commentary written by Haimo of Auxerre, which is itself a reworking of the widely known work of the Venerable Bede on the subject.[23] This tradition that Williram drew

---

16 Williram, *Expositio*, 4–5.
17 See Patzold, "Schrifttum und Kultur im Kloster Fulda."
18 See Jung, Kempkens, and Gehringer, eds., *Tausend Jahre Kloster Michaelsberg Bamberg (1015–2015)*.
19 See Gärtner, "Williram von Ebersberg OSB."
20 See Kartschoke, *Geschichte der deutschen Literatur*, 174–179.
21 See Gärtner, "Zu den Handschriften."
22 See Zerfaß, *Die Allegorese*, 15.
23 See Schupp, *Studien*, 21–59. Thus the many ideas presented in the *Expositio* are at least four hundred years old. If we take into regard how much Bede took from Gregor the Great, we could

upon understood the Song of Songs as a dialogue between Christ as the *sponsus* and the church in her different historical manifestations as the *sponsa*.²⁴ This ecclesiastical reading is the oldest version of an allegorical understanding of the Song of Songs and might even have been influential for its canonization in the Jewish Tanakh.²⁵ What makes Williram's version so fascinating—and even daring in a way—is the literary form and use of layout he chose. The *Expositio* is not a single text to be read from beginning to end but a composition of five strands of text existing in dynamic relation to each other.

Regarding the category of voice, I would argue that in the interaction between Williram's exegetical understanding and the particular form of his text, the dialogue of the Song of Songs between *sponsus* and *sponsa* is shifted to a soliloquy of the *sponsa*. The isolation and multiplication of each single verse invites such an impression; splitting the *sponsa* into more than one allegorical persona pushes it even further. I will illustrate this rather abstract idea using Williram's discussion of the flowery bed as an example.²⁶

2.2 Únser bétte ist wóla geblûomet

	Vox Ecclesiae	
Stramen habet nostrum redimicula plurima florum.	Lectus noster floridus.	Únser bétte ist wóla geblûomet.
Si requiem praebes vernant virtute fideles. Floret honestatis plus copia tempore pacis.		So íh dechêina wîla gerûowet bín a persecutione, so wíl íh des de mêr bíderbe scêinan durh dînen wíllon in contemplatione, vigiliis, ieiuniis, elemosynis et caeteris bonis operibus.²⁷

---

add another two hundred years to that count. For a discussion of the Carolingian interpretation of the Song of Songs, see Matis, *Song of Songs*.
24 See Matter, *Voice of My Beloved*, 86–122.
25 See Stern, "Ancient Jewish Interpretation," 89–92.
26 For a broader discussion of the exegetical and literary reception of the flowery bed in the Middle Ages, see Lerchner, *Lectulus Floridus*, 45–59, 301–306, 427–446.
27 Williram, *Expositio*, 32.

	The voice of the church	
Our litter has many ribbons of flowers.	Our bed flourishing.	Our bed is adorned beautifully with flowers.
If you grant rest, the faithful flourish with virtue. Honor blossoms more abundantly in time of peace.		As soon as I have rested from persecution for a short time, I shall appear all the more diligent in meditation, vigilance, fasting, almsgiving and other good works for your sake.[28]

In the original manuscript layout, the verses of the biblical Song of Songs are placed in the middle of the page and written in a larger script then the rest of the text. This center is framed by Latin verses on the left and German prose on the right. Those columns consist of two parts each, the first being a transformation of the biblical verse and the second a commentary on it.[29] In the *praefatio*, Williram describes this layout as a girding of the biblical verse that should open up its understanding.[30] Thus the biblical verses are central in more than one way: they are at the heart of the *Expositio* both with regard to their position on each single page and in the overall endeavor to understand them better by paraphrasing them in different ways. But even though the biblical verses are highly visible, they only appear in a transformed way. The *tituli* do not mark the speakers as *sponsus* and *sponsa* in a literal sense as two human lovers but rather offer an allegorical reading as the basis for understanding.[31] In this example, the speaker is marked as the *vox ecclesiae*, the "voice of the church." The way Williram labels the voices goes back to Bede but creates new forms of meaning in the textual ensemble of the *Expositio*.[32] Curiously, the speaking entity is presented not as the church itself but as the voice of the church. In this way, even though *sponsus* and *sponsa* talk about their bodies, their corporality

---

[28] All translations into English are my own but are often greatly indebted to the cited editions, their translations, and commentary.
[29] The edition by Lähnemann and Rupp maintains this layout of the oldest manuscripts. It is lost in most medieval copies, though, and a significant number of them only transmit certain parts. See Lähnemann and Rupp, "Von der Leiblichkeit."
[30] See Williram, *Expositio*, 4–5, sentence 7.
[31] For the *tituli*, see Schupp, *Studien*, 201–204; Hartmann, "*Odor Spiritualium Virtutum*," 136–139. For a discussion of traces a primary voice leaves in a dramatic text, see Jahn, "Narrative Voice."
[32] In Bede's work a table of contents summarizing the allegorical narrative (181–184) is followed by the Latin text of the Song of Songs with corresponding indications of speakers (185–189), as preliminaries before the actual commentary begins (see Beda Venerabilis, "In Cantica Canticorum Libri VI").

is reduced, the imagination of readers guided to a sublime understanding of their bodily love. Nevertheless, the importance of the category of voice is stressed as the only remaining physical quality of the protagonists.

This, in turn, raises the recipient's attention to the quality of each voice, its style and tone,[33] making the multiplication of each utterance in different linguistic registers all the more intriguing. The voice of the church speaks not only the words of Scripture but also their transformation into Latin poetry and German prose. The small changes in each expression, combined with the differences in language, tone, and style, indicate some kind of shift in the center of utterance, in how the speaking entity is not quite identical with itself. This impression holds even more true for the exegetical part, as the voice of the church is not interpreted by the primary voice of a commentator but continues to speak for itself. Friedrich Ohly calls attention to this "Form der dramatischen Selbstauslegung des Wortes" ("form of dramatic self-explanation of the word") as a means by which Williram transfers the dialogic nature of the Song of Songs to its exegesis.[34] Williram himself explained this form in his *praefatio* as a means to lend greater authority to his interpretation and to achieve a greater emotional impact in his readers.[35] This is interesting because he used a literary strategy—building characters and letting them talk within a text— as a way to generate theological authority.

Each column has unique features, even though the content-related differences between both are small.[36] But where the Latin verses aspire to beauty of expression by following the models and rules of antique poetry, the German prose is much more direct and offers a catechetical orientation to the Christian system of belief by using technical terms in Latin.[37] While the Latin verses describe a universal truth in a form close to a proverb ("Honor blossoms more abundantly in time of peace"), the German prose follows the ecclesiological focus of Haimo much more closely, even incorporating central terms from his commentary. Allowing *sponsus* and *sponsa* to explain themselves also leads to a certain blending of voices, as the explanations they utter have been formed in a long exegetical tradition. Haimo's

---

[33] Following Richard Aczel ("Hearing Voices in Narrative Texts"), these are the main features that make a literary voice recognizable, and therefore the term *voice* is meaningful.
[34] Ohly, *Hohelied-Studien*, 102. See also Zerfaß, *Die Allegorese*, 103.
[35] See Williram, *Expositio*, 4–5.
[36] Regarding the dialogic character of both the Song of Songs and its explanation in the *Expositio*, the example of the flowery bed is interesting in so far as the Latin verses address Christ ("If you grant rest") while in the German prose the bride talks about and probably even to herself ("As soon as I have rested").
[37] For this relationship between the Latin and German parts of the text, see Lähnemann, "Reimprosa," esp. 210.

commentary in particular can be "heard" not only in what *sponsus* and *sponsa* say but also in how they phrase their words.[38]

Just as the voice of the biblical *sponsa* remains audible in the transformation to Latin poetry and German prose, the voice or voices of exegetical tradition remain audible in the explanatory words of the *sponsa* for everyone familiar with that tradition. It is therefore not surprising that there is a difference in the tone and stylistic profile not only between the Latin verse and the German prose but also between the transformation of the biblical verse and its explanation. Thus the reader is offered not exegetical alternatives so much as different forms of expression with their own perspectives and centers of gravity. The main aim of the twofold commentary is not to explore different meanings but to unfold the same meaning in different forms, to offer more than one cognitive and linguistic channel of understanding. Regarding the category of voice, the different modes of voice lead to the impression that multiple voices of the church are in constant dialogue with one another.

This impression of soliloquy as dialogue or dialogue as soliloquy evoked in each verse also holds true for the shaping of the Song of Songs as some kind of salvation history in the underlying plot of Williram's commentary. This history is told by multiplying the voice of the *sponsa*: she appears not only as the voice of the church (*vox ecclesiae*) but also as the voice of the synagogue (*vox synagogae*) and even once as the church of the heathens (*vox ecclesiae electae de gentibus*). Like his predecessors Bede and Haimo, Williram presents the Song of Songs as a tale about the union between Christ and the church, but the dialogic nature of Williram's explanation strengthens the impression of an interpersonal drama mainly evolving between the synagogue and the church. Thus the central dialogue in the *Expositio* is not so much between *sponsus* and *sponsa* but between different versions of the *sponsa*, telling

---

[38] See Williram, *Expositio*, 32–33: *Lectulus Ecclesiae est qualiscunque tranquillitas, vel requies praesentis vitae. Nam quasi in bello est Ecclesia, dum pro Christo diversa tolerat certamina, quasi vero in lectulo requiescit, cum aliquantula pace sibi concessa fruitur. Sed hic lectulus floridus est, hoc est, varietate virtutum quasi vernantibus floribus distincta est requies Ecclesiae. Tunc enim liberius contemplationi divinae insistit, tunc ieiunia, vigilias et caetera bonorum operum liberius exsequitur* ("The bed of the church is any rest or respite from the present life. For the church is at war, when she fights various battles for Christ; but she rests in the bed, when it enjoys that she has been granted a little time of peace. But the bed is adorned with flowers, which means the respite of the church is adorned by a multitude of virtues as if they were spring flowers. For she gives herself freely to divine contemplations at some times and at other times, she devotes herself to fasting, vigilance, and other good works"). It is one of the great merits of the edition by Lähnemann and Rupp that it makes such comparisons available at a glance.

herself about her struggles, her rest, and her love for Christ.[39] The dialogic nature of the Song of Songs is therefore multiplied in Williram's *Expositio*, but the dialogue between *sponsus* and *sponsa* becomes less audible.

3 Polyphonic Harmonies: *Lehre der liebenden Gotteserkenntnis*

3.1 Work and Context

In the twelfth century, interest in the Song of Song increased enormously. More than thirty works commenting on it are preserved in Latin from that time, as many as from all preceding centuries combined.[40] The reasons for this intensified discussion are linked to the monastic reforms of this time: the Song of Songs seems to have been ideal material to articulate a more intimate relationship between believers and God, which had great appeal for the growing number of laypeople drawn to the spiritual life.[41] The most famous representative of this movement was Bernard of Clairvaux, who also shaped medieval reception of the Song of Songs for centuries to come.[42] His powerful and elegant prose, as well as his interpretation of the *sponsa* as the human soul in search of God within the framework of a monastic community, was a great inspiration for the German poet who wrote *Lehre der liebenden Gotteserkenntnis* (*How to Know God Lovingly*), better known as *Das St. Trudperter Hohelied* in German studies.[43] The *Lehre* is the first medieval commentary on the Song of Songs completely written in a vernacular, and it does not refer back to a single Latin source. In addition to Bernard's tropological reading of the Song of

---

39 See, for example, versicles 76 (Williram, *Expositio*, 138–139) and 86 (ibid., 156–157). The voice of Christ also treats the three voices of the *sponsa* as different entities talking to one of them about the other; see, e.g., versicle 131 (ibid., 268–271).
40 See the list in Matter, *Voice of My Beloved*, 203–210.
41 See Leclercq, "New Recruitment."
42 See Bernard of Clairvaux, *Sermones Super Cantica Canticorum*. Bernard's understanding of the *sponsa* as the human soul is not entirely new, of course, but goes back to a long yet at times sparse tradition with the commentary and homilies of Origen (see Origenes, *Der Kommentar zum Hohelied*) as a clear reference point. The intensity with which Bernard focuses on this perspective and gives it new actuality is quite remarkable, however.
43 See the critical edition by Ohly, ed., *Das St. Trudperter Hohelied* (references hereafter are to this edition under the label *Lehre*). The name *St. Trudperter Hohelied* is misleading as only one manuscript was found at St. Trudpert and the author names his work quite clearly in the epilogue (Ohly, "Kommentar," 306).

Songs, the Marian interpretation established in the works of Rupert of Deutz had significant influence on its author as well.[44]

We do not know who composed the *Lehre*, nor are we sure where or when exactly it was written. The content and history of transmission both point to a reformed female monastery, though.[45] Different monasteries have been discussed as potential origins, but there seems to be a strong recent tendency to place the *Lehre* in the Benedictine monastery of Admont in Styria and to date it around 1160.[46] Regarding the actual author, Friedrich Ohly favors a male spiritual advisor to the nuns, and one could easily suggest Irimbert of Admont, who not only held this office in Admont around 1160 but who also wrote a Latin commentary on the Song of Songs.[47] As the nuns of this monastery where highly educated themselves and are known to have been active not only as scribes but also as authors, we also have good reason to suspect that one of them composed the *Lehre*.[48] But whoever the author may have been, he or she crafted a work that is as unique in its theological independence (from any single author, school, or even way of understanding the Song of Songs) as in its fluid literary form, which combines features of different genres into artful prose.[49]

The exegesis of the Song of Songs is framed by two opening sections and one closing section, each with an agenda and center of gravity of its own. While the first opening establishes a communicative situation and emphasizes virtues and vices,[50] the second praises the Song of Songs and shapes an ideal reception community;

---

[44] See Rupert of Deutz, *Commentaria in Canticum Canticorum*. Before Rupert and parallel to him, the mariological reading of the Song of Songs was developed in the liturgical context of the Marian feast; see Huber, "Unfolding Song." For further sources of the *Lehre* and its allegorical dimensions, see Ohly, "Kommentar," 332–334.
[45] See Küsters, *Der verschlossene Garten*, 64–177.
[46] See Ohly, "Kommentar," 328; Stridde, "St. Trudperter Hohelied," 425; Spitz, "Zur Lokalisierung"; Küsters, *Der verschlossene Garten*, 88–99.
[47] Ohly, "Kommentar," 328. On Irimbert of Admont, see Li, "Irimbert of Admont"; Braun, "Irimbert von Admont."
[48] Josef Haupt was the first to suggest female authorship of the *Lehre*, in 1864 (see Haupt, "Einleitung," xxii–xxiv), even though his attribution to two specific abbesses has been criticized, with good reason (see Ohly, *Hohelied-Studien*, 8). Johann Wilhelm Braun pointed in this direction again in 1973 (see Braun, "Irimbert von Admont," 289–291), and the extensive work done on the female monastery in Admont during the twelfth century in recent years seems to make such an assumption all the more probable (see Borgehammar, "Who Wrote the Admont Sermon Corpus"; Lutter, *Geschlecht und Wissen*, 52–125; Beach, *Women as Scribes*, 65–103; Seeberg, *Die Illustrationen*). These questions are also discussed by Hannah W. Matis in this volume (see her contribution on pp. 199–212).
[49] See Spitz, "*Ez ist sanc aller sange*."
[50] See Ohly, "Der Prolog"; Keller, "Verborgene Küsse"; Wisniewski, "Der Aufbau."

the closing is more didactic in nature.[51] In between them, the commentary proper follows the order of the biblical text but deals with each verse differently in terms of length, style, and exegetical focus. There has been an intense debate over the question whether the *Lehre* is a mystical text or even the first work of mysticism in the German vernacular. But even though there are mystic elements in the emotional depth of the soul's quest for God, the strong emphasis on the monastic community sets the character of the *Lehre* apart from later forms of mysticism.[52] Regarding the use and treatment of polyphony,[53] strategic ambiguity and the presence of a strong primary voice seem to be the main features of the *Lehre*.

3.2 Want ich bin selp der bluome

> *Unser bette daz ist geblüemet. [. . .] [D]az quît: die bluomen nehabent niht vil nutzes an in newane den gedingen, des nâch gênten wuochers. von diu sô sprich ich, daz unser bette wole geblüemet sî, want ich bin selp der bluome, dâ dîne inneren sinne ane gewunnesament werdent. Dir smecket wole der liliebluome mîner natiurlichen kiusche, dir lîchet ouch der rôsenbluome mîner getriuwelichen martere. [. . .] [V]one diu smeckent ouch mir dîne bluomen, diu lilie dîner kiusche, diu rôse dîner kestigunge. [. . .] [M]it disen bluomen sol umbestecket sîn daz bette, daz quît der muot dâ got ane ruowet. [. . .] [W]ant aber unser samet wesen niht nemac sîn, sô heizzet ez mêre ein bluome danne ein wuocher.*[54]

> Our bed is full of flowers. [. . .] This means: The flowers themselves have no use except the expectation of the fruit that will come from them. Therefore, I say, our bed is beautiful with flowers, for I myself am the flower in which your inner senses shall delight. The lily blossom of my natural chastity is fragrant to you. You also like the rose blossom of my devoted passion. [. . .] Therefore, your flowers are also perfume to me: the lily of your chastity, the rose of your asceticism. [. . .] With these flowers, the bed is said to be surrounded, that is, the mind in which God rests. [. . .] But because we cannot be together permanently, the community is called flower rather than fruit.

I have left out some parts of the passage not only because of its overall length but also because the *Lehre* deals with Song 1:16 and 1:17 at the same time, integrating an explanation of the cedars and cypresses. Even the trimmed text, though, offers a glimpse of the beauty and clarity of the prose, as well as the ingenuity of the exege-

---

51 See Suerbaum, "Die Paradoxie," 36.
52 This argument is made most strongly by Christine Stridde, who also offers insights on the previous discussion (see Stridde, *Verbalpräsenz und göttlicher Sprechakt*; idem, "Die performative Zumutung").
53 Friedrich Ohly describes the *Lehre* as "vielgliedrig polyphon" ("diversely polyphonic") with regard to the leading of the voice and the theological content alike (Ohly, "Kommentar," 330).
54 *Lehre*, 74–76.

sis and the enriching use of ambiguity and fluid transfers between the voices. For example, it may take the recipient some time to figure out who is actually speaking, as this verse is traditionally attributed to the *sponsa*. It comes as a surprise to slowly discover that Christ is the speaker of the first part. The first hint is that he calls himself "the flower in which your inner senses shall delight," but only when he mentions his passion does this shift in speaker become clear. The idea of the flower being a promise of future fruit has roots in the exegetical tradition, but the way it is presented here as a speech of Christ and the following alignment with the virtues of *sponsus* and *sponsa* seem to be new contributions made by the *Lehre*.[55]

After identifying the speaker, though, the recipient is still left wondering whom he is talking to. In his commentary on the passage, Friedrich Ohly sees Mary as the addressee, which would be consistent with a Marian interpretation in which the *sponsus* is God in one of the Trinitarian forms and the *sponsa* is Mary. This also fits well with the verse before, where Mary speaks and interprets the beauty of the *sponsus* in terms of the birth she gave him as a virgin.[56] However, Christ could also be addressing the implicit recipient herself, in her monastic life, with the description of the virtues he enjoys in his beloved one ("chastity," "asceticism," "repentance," "renunciation of the world"). This reading offers a smooth transition to the primary voice interpreting Christ's interpretation of himself with less-poetic words, defining the bed as the *muot*[57] in which God rests, addressing the recipients. In the commentary on the next verse (Song 2:2), Christ talks about *mine erwelten sêle* ("my chosen souls"),[58] as the lilies among thorns, which would also align with a tropologic understanding of the bride addressed here being the human soul. Such an understanding would closely echo the interpretation of Bernard of Clairvaux, who saw the *lectulus floridus* as a communal place of rest for Christ and the monks he addressed with his sermons individually but even more in monastic community.[59]

The very last sentence of the passage sustains this tendency toward ambiguity, as it could be spoken either by Mary or by the primary voice. If we assign it to Mary, *unser samet wesen*, the being-together of *sponsus* and *sponsa*, would refer to the time Mary and Christ spent together, that is, the time between the incarnation and

---

55 Ohly, "Kommentar", 667–675.
56 *[D]în geburt, diu was magetliche von mir*, "your birth was virgin through me"; *Lehre*, 74.
57 The semantics of this Middle High German term are broader than its modern equivalent *Mut* and the English term *mood*. It addresses the human interior across a wide range, from mind, sense, and courage to soul and heart; see Ehrismann and Classen, *Ehre und Mut, Âventiure und Minne*, 148–151.
58 *Lehre*, 76.
59 See Lerchner, *Lectulus Floridus*, 53–54. Bernard refers to the *lectulus floridus* as the monastery addressing the collective but also asking the individual to act according to monastic virtues (see Bernard of Clairvaux, *Sermones super Cantica Canticorum*, 56–58).

birth of Christ and his passion and the resulting salvation of mankind, echoing the understanding of Rupert of Deutz.[60] If we assign this sentence to the primary voice instead, the *unser* would imply a community, the joining of every soul with Christ. The flowery promise would then turn into a fruit in the afterlife in the final connection between God and the human soul, which reflects the abovementioned interpretation of Bernard of Clairvaux. Thus the ambiguity of the *sponsa* as Mary, the individual soul, or even the monastic community of souls allows different voices in the exegetical tradition to be heard at the same time, adding to the exegetical richness of the interpretation. The ambiguity of the voices taking part in this passage is a characteristic feature of the *Lehre*. It should not be understood, though, as assigning the decision about who is speaking to the recipient; rather, a plurality of voices are singing together, merging perspectives.[61]

What this passage fails to convey is the ubiquitous presence of a primary voice, in contact with and coordinating all other voices. Friedrich Ohly describes the richness of this primary voice and its communicative modes:

> He counts himself to the congregation as a nameless bearer of his office, he turns to the congregation as a "you" facing him with admonition and encouragement turned toward it, he emerges in the authorial prayer for inspiration as an I, in the prayer to Mary and to God, in the humble formula and in narrative-technical remarks.[62]

If we take this one step further and ask how the primary voice engages in dialogues, the answer is equally complex and can only be hinted at here. Nevertheless, two main communicative axes are obvious: the dialogue between the primary voice and the individual and collective recipients on the one hand and the dialogue between the primary voice and Mary and Christ on the other.[63] In both cases, the primary voice alternates between the first-person singular, which creates an impression of individuality,[64] and the first-person plural, which encourages the recipient to

---

60 See Lerchner, *Lectulus Floridus*, 56; Rupert lets Mary speak here, and she interprets the *lectulus* as her uterus, where Jesus rested for nine months (see Rupert of Deutz, *Commentaria in Canticum Canticorum*, 1:35).
61 I agree here with Suerbaum, "Die Paradoxie," 36–39.
62 Ohly, "Kommentar," 328: "Als namenloser Träger seines Amts im *wir* sich zur Gemeinde zählend, im Predigtton der Duform mit Abmahnung und Ermunterung ihr zugewandt, tritt er als Ich im Autorgebet um Inspiration, im Gebet zu Maria und zu Gott, in der Demutsformel und in erzähltechnischen Bemerkungen hervor."
63 The dialogue between the primary voice and the collective of recipients is already modeled in the prologue (*Lehre*, 10–27); the dialogue between the primary voice leads to complex constellations in the transition to the commentary proper (ibid., 34–38).
64 This becomes most prominent in passages like the prayer for inspiration in the second introductory passage (*Lehre*, 30).

identify with the primary voice in a collective of believers. Indeed, the text gives frequent encouragements to hear not only a single primary voice but a collective one. For example, the lines "now sing, beloved ones, since you never became hoarse from worldly singing. This voice shall not sound for the ears of men, it reaches out to the realm of the Most High"[65] indicate that the following text should be sung by many instead of being spoken by one. Furthermore, they reverse the order of speakers (Christ and Mary) and recipients in an invitation for every reader or listener to join the song.

This diversity within the primary voice (individual teacher, member of a group, or even a whole group speaking) on the one hand and the multiplication of the dialogues (between Mary and Christ, between one of them and the primary voice, or between the primary voice and its addressees) on the other leads to a complex communicative setting. This setting gains an additional dynamic from the shifts and ambiguities regarding both the voice we hear at any given moment as the speaker of an utterance and the echoes of the exegetical tradition audible within them.

4 Dialogues and Dialogism: Brun of Schönebeck and His *Hohelied*

4.1 Author, Work, and Context

Brun of Schönebeck was a warrior, a poet, and a successful event manager—or at least this is how the *Schöppenchronik* portrays him.[66] He lived as a member of the upper class in the second half of the thirteenth century in the prosperous Hanseatic city of Magdeburg. Only parts of his literary work have survived to today, but he seems to have been well respected in his time and in the following centuries.[67] Nevertheless, his impressive commentary on the Song of Songs (*Hohelied*)[68] is far less well-known than Williram's *Expositio in cantica canticorum* or the *Lehre der*

---

[65] *Lehre*, 40: *nû singet ir liebesten, wan ir ne heiser enwurdet von weltlicheme sange. Disiu stimme enlûtet niht ze den ôren der menschen, si recket sich in daz rîche des aller hoehesten.*
[66] See Janicke, *Magdeburger Schöppenchronik*, 168–169. For an introduction to the *Schöppenchronik*, see Keil, "Magdeburger Schöppenchronik." On the grail festival that Brun organized according to the *Schöppenchronik*, see Wolff, "Das Magdeburger Gralsfest Bruns von Schönebeck."
[67] Wolfgang Spangenberg lists him among the *Meistersinger*, even though no lyrical texts by Brun are conserved (see Spangenberg, *Von der Musica*, 125). For an overview on Brun's oeuvre, see Riedmann, "Brun von Schönebeck."
[68] The text edition is Brun of Schönebeck, *Werke*.

liebenden Gotteserkenntnis. There are many reasons for this, among them the great increase in German literary production in the late thirteenth century in general and in religious literature in particular, which has left many works of the time largely undiscovered by modern scholars. Arwed Fischer, who edited the first and so far only edition of Brun's works, must take some of the blame for this neglect as well, though, as he clearly detested the texts and influenced many later readers with his impression of an author without talent and with only a superficial education.[69] However, the lack of research is also due to the often befuddling nature of Brun's *Hohelied* itself, which is a child both of scholastic theology in full bloom and of courtly literary traditions, in a unique and often troubling mix.

In his *Hohelied*, Brun cites and uses many sources, from antique literature to church fathers to contemporary theologians, but the *Expositio in Cantica Canticorum*, written by Honorius Augustodunensis in the twelfth century, certainly had the greatest influence on the overall architecture of his commentary.[70] Honorius's life and work would merit a discussion of their own,[71] but to understand Brun's adaptation better, two features of the *Expositio* are paramount: the highly differentiated scholastic exegetic method and the creative construction of a new plot. Honorius was one of the few medieval authors who really sought the fourfold sense of writing in the smallest details,[72] which made his commentary a great source of knowledge but also sometimes quite tiresome and confusing for a modern reader not trained in scholastic methods. However, Honorius gave his *Expositio* a new and captivating structure by embedding the dialogue of the Song of Songs in a bridal-quest narrative of his own design. In addition to taking these two features over from Honorius—detail-oriented yet wide-ranging scholastic method and freedom in storytelling—Brun was highly influenced by German courtly literature, most sig-

---

69 In his introduction, he states: "Daß Brun alles in allem ein recht dürftiger geist gewesen ist, davon wird sich jeder leser seines reimwerkes bald überzeugen. Zum 'dichter' vollends fehlt ihm ungemein viel" ("Every reader of his rhyming work will soon be convinced that Brun was, all in all, a rather poor mind. In any regard he lacks a great deal to be a 'poet'"); Brun of Schönebeck, *Werke*, 19. This judgment is even upheld by authors who clearly see the scope of Brun's knowledge and education; see, e.g., Hagenlocher, "Littera meretrix," esp. 136–137.
70 See Hübner, "Das Hohe Lied des Bruns von Schönebeck und seine Quellen."
71 See Matter, *Voice of My Beloved*, 49–85, and Cohen, "Synagoga conversa." For the *Expositio* and for the life and other works of Honorius, see Rappl, "Meinen Namen will ich deshalb in Schweigen hüllen"; Flint, *Ideas in the Medieval West*.
72 In addition to looking for the literal meaning of biblical texts, medieval exegesis also explored different variants of allegorical readings. For a short introduction to the terms and systems used, see van Liere, "Medieval Bible," 210–240. With regard to Honorius, see Matter, "Voice of My Beloved," 52–76.

nificantly by Wolfram of Eschenbach, who is well-known for his bold moves, love of mysteries, and high-profile narrator figures.[73]

Brun's *Hohelied* consists of 12,719 verses divided into four parts of widely differing length. In the first, Brun constructs a new *sensus litteralis* by writing his own Song of Songs, using the verses of the biblical text as a quarry.[74] The three following parts each use a selection of those verses and offer three different allegorical readings. The first part, which takes up nearly half of the total verses, is a mariological interpretation. Nearly a third of the text is then used for a tropological interpretation in the third part, before the last and significantly shorter part offers an ecclesiastical reading. Even though these three ways of interpreting the bride of the Song of Songs as Mary, the human soul, and the church had already been combined in earlier commentaries,[75] Brun seems to have been the first to arrange them so decisively as parallel options within one work. This structure, combined with other inspirations from Honorius and Wolfram, gave Brun's work a specific profile and led to the intensification of two trends that could already be observed in the *Lehre*: first, the voices of the biblical Song of Songs are increasingly treated as literary characters within a narration, and second, the primary voice is developed as a center of gravity, engaging in dialogues of its own. This primary voice claims the name *brun schonebeke* for itself, and therefore I will call this center of utterance Brun in the following.[76]

4.2 Ich buwe uf mime zwickel

do di brut mit lobes zil	When the bride had praised
den brutegam gelobete vil,	the bridegroom much to glorify him,
do begunden si ein hus schouwen,	they saw a house
daz was gemachet durch rouwen	made for resting,

---

[73] See Volfing, "Song of Songs as Fiction."
[74] He took the idea for this plot from Honorius but developed it further into a consistent narrative: Solomon sends his messenger Fortitudo to the pharaoh's daughter with a love letter, and she agrees to marry him. When she arrives at his court, she is welcomed warmly and engages in dialogue with different groups of people, talking about her beloved. At the marriage feast, Mandragora, the girl without a head, is introduced and crowned with a golden head by Solomon (Brun, *Werke*, 3–28 [vv. 62–913]).
[75] All three perspectives are taken, for example, in the *Lehre*, but one could argue that they were already available as options for Ambrose; see Ohly, *Hohelied-Studien*, 32–46.
[76] Brun, *Werke*, 2 (v. 31).

schone und richeit si im jach,	she said it was beautiful and splendid,
do von si dese wort sprach:	so she said these words:
lectus noster floridus	*Our bed is flourishing*
min lip der ist schon gar,	My beloved one is very beautiful
unse bette ist blumenvar	and our bed made of flowers.[77]

The flowery bed becomes part of a small narrative in Brun's own version of the Song of Songs, as the two lovers happen across it. The *sponsa* then describes the bed, and after the passage cited above she is led into it by the *sponsus*. Brun's new ordering of the biblical verses, with Song 5:12 followed by Song 2:6 and 1:12, creates a new context and emphasizes the *sponsa*'s praise of the *sponsus* rather than the exchange between them. This focus on the acts of speaking, especially by the *sponsa*, is also evident in the frequency with which speech words like *gelobete* (vowed), *jach* (said), and *sprach* (said) appear. The inclusion of the biblical text leads to some repetitions, as the quality of the house is first described, then addressed in Latin, and then followed by a translation into German. This form of citation also lets the reader keep in mind that Brun's rewriting of the Song of Songs aims not to replace the biblical text but to explore it, with certain literary liberties, in a playful way.

Having thus been marked as literature in the second degree,[78] the primary voice can distance itself from the strange and "rough" (*rou*, v. 814) biblical text and designate itself as the expert who can make it understandable for knights and laborers alike, with the help of Christ (vv. 815–817). By setting the primary voice in opposition to its biblical object of reference, the text transforms this voice into a narrator or exegete as a character with self-consciousness and a personal profile. This "Brun" then gives the impression that his narration and explanation of the Song of Songs is an action that is happening right now, and he includes his recipients in this daring process. An even clearer instance of this dynamic appears in the commentary on the flowery bed in the third part of *Hohelied*, where Brun interprets the *sponsa* in terms of the human soul. Thus the interpretation of the flowery bed comes quite late in Brun's text and is wedged in between interpretations of Song 5:8 and 4:17, with no explicit connection to either verse. These two verses are also spoken by the bride, which further decreases the dialogue between *sponsus* and *sponsa* in the explanation. The passage begins with the citation of the Latin verses of Song 1:16–17, followed by a translation into German as direct speech by the *sponsa* but introduced as something the *sponsa* spoke loud and joyfully (*mit*

---

[77] Brun, *Werke*, 26 (vv. 818–826).
[78] See Genette, *Palimpseste*. What Genette describes here as "littérature au second degré" is a broad range of transformations from one text to another (like parody, translation, or continuation), which he sees in an even wider field of relationships between texts.

vrouden obirlut, v. 8390). The explanation first focuses on the wooden parts of the house:

daz ist also man uns seit	That is, as we are told,
uf ein ture vulmunt geleit.	placed on a splendid foundation.
durch waz sal manz lenger sparn:	For what should it be longer saved up?
ich will durch den vulmunt varn	I am going to break up the foundation
und will das nedirteil ufkeren.	and turn the lowest to the top.
sol ich dese rede untweren,	If I am to untangle this talk,
ich buwe uf mime zwickel	I trust my wedge
so der zimmerman uf den bickel	like the carpenter his pick
und vare biz an den vollemunt.	and go right through to the foundation.[79]

This is quite obviously not a commentary on the biblical verse but Brun reflecting on his own exegetical practice in a metaphorical way. His presentation of his approach to the text seems quite daring indeed. To understand the meaning of the flowery house, it must be demolished completely, its foundations turned upside down. This is in fact how Brun as author deals with the Song of Songs from the beginning: his rewriting and exegesis are both based on the principle of not leaving a single stone unturned. Nevertheless, Brun's method shows a shocking lack of respect for the biblical text and its sanctity. And just as Brun blurs the line between remaking and explaining throughout *Hohelied*, he does so on a smaller scale here, as he first has to invent the splendid foundation of the flowery house, which is nowhere mentioned in the Song of Songs, before he can break it apart. As for the category of voice, passages like this—and there are many more[80]—make the primary voice the main protagonist of this text and Brun's literary and exegetical praxis the main events of the text.

This primary voice does not engage in dialogues with *sponsus* or *sponsa* but is in constant contact first with the implied recipients, for whom it undertakes the strenuous endeavor of squeezing meaning out of the Song of Songs, and second with the literary and exegetical tradition, which the voice incorporates frequently, often with a special twist. Both can be seen in the treatment of Song 1:16–17 as well. After Brun has demolished the flowery house, he turns to explaining *pulcher es dilecte mi et decorus*, addressing his audience with the words, "Gentlemen you shall know without mockery; the beloved of the bride is God himself" (*wizzet ir hirren sundir spot, / der brut libe ist selber got*).[81] The flippant way in which the primary voice addresses his audience is typical, even though the groups of people addressed change and mostly include women as well. They always remain lay people, though,

---

79 Brun, *Werke*, 251–252 (vv. 8398–8406).
80 A long, complex, and striking passage of this kind connects the rewriting of the Song of Song in the first part to the commentary proper (Brun, *Werke*, 28–35 [vv. 913–1153]).
81 Brun, *Werke*, 251 (vv. 8410–8411).

who are not as well versed in the fine points of theology and exegesis as Brun himself. The way the narrator/exegete shows off his knowledge on the one hand and calls himself a dumb Saxon on the other leads to a creative tension that is released through jokes and personal piety alike.[82]

In the second dialogue with tradition, Brun cites many authorities by name and even more indirectly. A direct quotation does not mean that he adopted the author's exact wording, though. For example, to describe the beauty of God as the *sponsus*, Brun picks up Augustine's argument that the beauty of creation is a testimony to the even greater beauty of its creator:

daz got an im selber schone si,	You can see that God himself is beautiful
daz seht an den creaturen da bi.	in the being he created.
di mogen sprechen so man gicht:	They can say, as one does:
her geschuf uns wir selben nicht.	"He created us, we did not do it ourselves."
gotes schonde urkundet sus	In that way Saint Augustine
der heilige Augustinus:	testified to the beauty of God.
	He who created is better than what is good,
qui creavit bona melior est. qui creavit	he who created is more beautiful than what
pulchra pulchrior est. qui creavit dulcia	is beautiful, he who created is sweeter than
dulcior est. qui creavit magna maior est.	what is sweet, he who created is bigger than what is big.[83]

This idea appears both in a sermon by Augustine and in his *Confessions*.[84] Brun's phrasing, however, is much closer to the third sermon on the Last Supper by Bernard of Clairvaux, which addresses the twofold nature of Christ, for whom it was necessary to accept human form but who is still God as the highest being and creator of everything: "there is no one greater, better, more beautiful, sweeter or dearer than him" (*ipse est quo nullus maior, nullus melior, quo nullus pulchrior, nullus dulcior,*

---

[82] References to Brun being a *tumber Sachse* can be found in v. 8557 and v. 8580 (Brun, *Werke*, 256). Comic relief is used when Brun admits, after long and complex reflections on the power of God and his wish to speak the truth, that he is now sweating with fear regarding his task (v. 1133). Nevertheless, Brun often shows deep veneration and personal piety, especially with regard to Mary. See, for example, vv. 12480–12519.

[83] Brun, *Werke*, 251–252 (vv. 8412–8420).

[84] See most extensively chapter 2 of Augustinus, "Sermo 241" (MPL 38, 1133–1138) and, closer to Brun's version, in *Confessions*: *tu ergo, domine, fecisti ea, qui pulcher es (pulchra suntenim), qui bonus es (bona sunt enim), qui es (sunt enim). nec ita pulchra sunt nec ita bona sunt nec ita sunt, sicut tu conditor eorum, quo comparato nec pulchra sunt nec bona sunt nec sunt* ("So, Lord, you have made them; and you are beautiful [so they are beautiful], and you are good [so they are good], and you exist [so they exist]. They are neither beautiful nor good nor existent in the same way as you, who are their creator; compared to you they are not beautiful or good or existent"); Augustinus, *Confessions*, 198–201 (11.4).

nullos charior).[85] It is noteworthy that neither of the works cited by Augustine or by Bernard deal with the Song of Songs themselves, which may offer a glimpse of the scope of foreign texts and ideas that Brun incorporated into his treatment of this biblical book. The voices of tradition are even more perceptible here than in the *Lehre*, as Brun references Augustine by name and cites Bernard (nearly) verbatim. Even though this is no dialogue in a strict sense, it is nevertheless a strong form of dialogicity, a concept outlined by Mikhail Bakhtin and elaborated by Julia Kristeva under the label *intertextuality*.[86]

In rewriting the Song of Songs and the threefold commentary on it alike, Brun decreases the intensity of the dialogue between *sponsus* and *sponsa*, treating them instead as literary characters under the total control of the narrator/exegete.[87] This primary voice engages with its implied audience frequently, but the real dialogue established in Brun's *Hohelied* is between the text and the textual tradition before it, combining exegetical knowledge and literary techniques in surprising ways.

5 Conclusion

It may have been pure coincidence that three commentaries on the Song of Songs were preserved in the German vernacular, one each from the eleventh, twelfth, and thirteenth centuries, but the opportunity to compare these three as windows onto their own times, their exegetical, cultural, and literary contexts, is nevertheless precious. All three not only adapt and transform the dialogue between *sponsus* and *sponsa* as it is offered in the Song of Songs but incorporate its central principle of dialogicity in individual ways.

(1) Voice and Dialogue: The dialogue between *sponsus* and *sponsa* loses power and consistency in all three commentaries examined here. This is not surprising, given that medieval exegesis has a tendency to focus on single verses or even single words of the biblical text. Exploring their depth often means isolating them from their original contexts. Furthermore, the dissipation of the dialogue between

---

85 Bernard of Clairvaux, "De verbis Domini in coena" (MPL 184, 890). Meister Eckhart's rephrasing of Augustine, which is nearly identical to Brun's text, could be an interesting path to shed some new light on Brun's educational career and intellectual networks (edited and commented on in Meister Eckhart, *Traktate, Lateinische Werke*, 560, 889).
86 See Bakhtin, "Das Wort im Roman"; Kristeva, "Dialog und Roman." For an overview, see Allen, *Intertextuality*.
87 See the weaving of Mary done by the primary voice in vv. 2730–2745 (Brun, *Werke*, 83) as a striking example of this.

sponsus and *sponsa* in the medieval commentaries is not so surprising if we regard the many passages in which the Song of Songs does not take the form of a dialogue itself but only alludes to such a communicative situation by alternating the voices of *sponsus* and *sponsa*, without them really engaging with one another. Nevertheless, all three commentaries emphasize the category of voice and the stylistic or personal profile of each voice, as an audible quality. Williram explores the stylistic scope of the single voice by employing different languages and styles, the *Lehre* pays great attention to the actual act of singing in fluid harmonies, and even Brun gives an impression of how certain verses are spoken, even though the voice of the narrator/exegete receives his greatest attention.

(2) Voices and/as Characters: Reading for the plot is essential in all three commentaries, even though each constructs quiet a different plot. Williram's *Expositio* tells the tale of the church and her journey to God, with all its hardships and triumphs. This turns the voices of the Song of Songs into characters with specific personal histories but also creates tension between the corporality of narrated events and the abstractness of the church or the synagogue, which are personifications instead of persons. The role of Christ and his biography as a part of this salvation history, though, reveals a great interest in the capacity of the Song of Songs to adapt to different plots. With the rise of mariological interpretation in the twelfth century, the Song of Songs was used frequently to recount the life of Mary as well as the life of Christ, often with a focus on incarnation and passion. This is also true for the *Lehre*, which does not construct a cohesive biographical plot but includes such elements frequently. Thereby, *sponsus* and *sponsa* are given a new corporality as Christ and Mary, and the other allegorical dimensions of the *sponsa* are blended into Mary as a representative of both the church and the human soul. The life of Mary is an important model for Brun, as well, in the second part of his *Hohelied*. The construction of a new plot between Solomon and his Egyptian bride is even more striking, as it so clearly shows the freedom of storytelling encountered with some frequency in medieval exegesis of the Song of Songs.

(3) A New Voice: All three commentaries feature a primary voice that cannot be understood only as a rhetorical function but that is instead endowed with an individual quality of speech and biographical fragments that let us imagine a fully shaped character. In Williram's *Expositio*, the primary voice can only be heard explicitly in the *tituli* and in a few remarks within the *Selbstauslegungen*, but "Williram" nevertheless is given a personal profile and a biographic identity in the introductory texts, in which he also takes responsibility for the form and content of the work. In contrast, the primary voice of the *Lehre* is not even named, and the only biographical information given is its role as a teacher and member of a (female) monastic community. The shifts between these roles and between the individual *I*

and collective *we* are one essential part of the works' fluidity. In Brun's *Hohelied*, the primary voice is probably even more essential, as it is the center of gravity that pulls the diverse units, ideas, and sources of this work together, that holds the attention of the reader and makes the acts of narration and explanation the real events of the text, like demolishing a house or weaving Mary as a piece of art. Biographical information is given in bits and pieces, but even more impactful is the power and even audacity of the voice itself.

(4) Intertextual Voices: The voices of exegetical, theological, and literary traditions can be heard in all three commentaries, even if they draw attention to those voices differently. This cannot be surprising in a genre that is as bound to the authority of previous writings as medieval biblical commentary was. Regardless of whether we call this heteroglossia, dialogicity, or intertextuality, the presence of foreign speech in our own is an integral part of every text, probably of every human utterance. It is already apparent in the Song of Song itself, which also incorporates genres, literary roles, modes of speech, and metaphors predating its creation. If the allegorical potential of the love songs played any part in their compilation, revision, and integration into the biblical canon, then the crossing of literary and exegetical interest goes very far back indeed. It is not only the multiplication of dialogues between *sponsus* and *sponsa* (and quiet often *sponsae*), primary voice, and audience but also the complex communicative relationships between the Song of Songs, the exegetical tradition as an ever-growing resource, and the individual commentary that interrelate to one another, creating complex communicative settings and fascinating works of art and exegesis alike.

Bibliography

Primary Sources

Augustinus, Aurelius. *Confessions*, edited by Carolyn J. B. Hammond. LCL 27. Cambridge: Harvard University Press, 2016.

Augustinus, Aurelius. "Sermo 241: In Diebus Paschalibus 12, de Resurrectione Corporum, Contra Gentiles." In vol. 35 of *Opera omnia*, edited by Jacques-Paul Migne, 1133–1138. MPL 38. Paris, 1863.

Beda Venerabilis. "In Cantica Canticorum Libri VI." In *Opera, Pars II: Opera Exegetica 2B*, edited by David Hurst, 164–375. CCSL 119B. Turnhout: Brepols, 1983.

Bernard of Clairvaux. "De Verbis Domini in Coena: Sermo III." In vol. 3 of *Opera omnia*, edited by D. Jean Mabillon, 889–895. MPL 184. Paris: 1862.

Bernard of Clairvaux. *Sermones Super Cantica Canticorum: Sermones 1–35*, edited by Jean Leclercq, Charles H. Talbot, and Henri M. Rochais. Vol. 1 of *Sancti Bernardi Opera*. Rome: Editiones Cistercienses, 1957.
Bernard of Clairvaux. *Sermones Super Cantica Canticorum: Sermones 39–86*, edited by Gerhard B. Winkler. Vol. 6 of *Sämtliche Werke*. Innsbruck, 1995.
Brun of Schönebeck. *Werke*, edited by Arwed Fischer. Tübingen: Litterarischer Verein Stuttgart, 1893.
Hieronymus, Sophronius E. *Biblia sacra vulgata: Lateinisch/Deutsch*, edited by Michael Fieger, Widu-Wolfgang Ehlers, and Andreas Beriger. Sammlung Tusculum. 6 vols. Berlin: de Gruyter, 2018.
Janicke, Karl, ed. *Magdeburger Schöppenchronik*. Vol. 1 of *Die Chroniken der deutschen Städte: Vom 14. bis in's 16. Jahrhundert*. Leipzig, 1869.
Meister Eckhart. *Traktate, Lateinische Werke*, edited by Niklaus Largier and Ernst Benz. Vol. 2 of *Werke*. Frankfurt am Main: Deutscher Klassiker-Verlag, 2008.
Ohly, Friedrich, ed. and trans. *Das St. Trudperter Hohelied: Eine Lehre der liebenden Gotteserkenntnis*. Bibliothek des Mittelalters 2. Frankfurt am Main: Dt. Klassiker-Verl., 1998.
Origenes. *Der Kommentar zum Hohelied*, edited by Alfons Fürst and Holger Strutwolf. Orig.WD 9/1. Berlin: de Gruyter, 2016.
Rupert of Deutz. *Commentaria in Canticum Canticorum—Kommentar zum Hohenlied: Lateinisch/Deutsch*. 2 vols. FC 70. Turnhout: Brepols, 2005.
The Holy Bible (Douay-Rheims): Translated from the Latin Vulgate. 1609. Repr., Baltimore, MD, 1914.
Williram of Ebersberg. *Expositio in Cantica Canticorum: An Edition and Translation with Forward and Backward Concordances to the German Text*, edited by Christopher J. Meyer. Ann Arbor: University Microfilms International, 1988.
Williram of Ebersberg. *Expositio in Cantica Canticorum: Und das Commentarium in Cantica Canticorum Haimos von Auxerre*, edited by Henrike Lähnemann and Michael Rupp. Berlin: de Gruyter, 2004.

Secondary Sources

Aczel, Richard. "Hearing Voices in Narrative Texts." *New Literary History* 29 (1998): 467–500.
Allen, Graham. *Intertextuality*. The New Critical Idiom. London: Routledge, 2010.
Astell, Ann W. *The Song of Songs in the Middle Ages*. Ithaca, NY: Cornell University Press, 1990.
Bakhtin, Mikhail. "Das Wort im Roman." In *Die Ästhetik des Wortes*, edited by Mikhail Bakhtin, 154–300. Edition Suhrkamp 967. Frankfurt a. M.: Suhrkamp, 2005.
Beach, Alison I. *Women as Scribes: Book Production and Monastic Reform in Twelfth-Century Bavaria*. Cambridge Studies in Palaeography and Codicology 10. Cambridge: Cambridge University Press, 2004.
Blödorn, Andreas, Daniela Langer, and Michael Scheffel, eds. *Stimme(n) im Text: Narratologische Positionsbestimmungen*. Narratologia 10. Berlin: de Gruyter, 2008.
Borgehammar, Stephan. "Who Wrote the Admont Sermon Corpus: Gottfried the Abbot, His Brother Irimbert, or the Nuns?" In *De l'homélie au sermon: Histoire de la prédication médiévale*, edited by Jacqueline Hamesse and Xavier Hermand, 47–51. Louvain-la-Neuve: Institut d'études médiévales de l'université catholique de Louvain, 1993.
Braun, Johann W. "Irimbert von Admont." *FMSt* 7 (1973): 266–323.
Cohen, Jeremy. "Synagoga conversa: Honorius Augustodunensis, the Song of Songs, and Christianity's 'Eschatological Jew.'" *Spec* 79 (2004): 309–340.

Ehrismann, Otfrid, and Albrecht Classen. *Ehre und Mut, Âventiure und Minne: Höfische Wortgeschichten aus dem Mittelalter*. München: Beck, 1995.

Exum, J. Cheryl. *Song of Songs: A Commentary*. OTL. Louisville: Westminster John Knox Press, 2005.

Fischer, Stefan. *Das Hohelied Salomos zwischen Poesie und Erzählung: Erzähltextanalyse eines Poetischen Textes*. FAT 72. Tübingen: Mohr Siebeck, 2010.

Flint, Valerie I. *Ideas in the Medieval West: Texts and Their Contexts*. VCS 268. London: Variorum Reprints, 1988.

Gärtner, Kurt. "Williram von Ebersberg OSB." In vol. 10 of *Die Deutsche Literatur des Mittelalters: Verfasserlexikon*, edited by Kurt Ruh, Burghart Wachinger, and Franz J. Worstbrock, 1156–1170. Berlin: de Gruyter, 2010.

Gärtner, Kurt. "Zu den Handschriften mit dem deutschen Kommentarteil des Hoheliedkommentars Willirams von Ebersberg." In *Deutsche Handschriften 1100–1400: Oxforder Kolloquium 1985*, edited by Volker Honemann and Nigel F. Palmer, 1–34. Tübingen: Max Niemeyer Verlag, 1988.

Genette, Gérard. *Palimpseste: Die Literatur auf Zweiter Stufe*, translated by Wolfram Bayer and Dieter Hornig. Aesthetica 168. Frankfurt am Main: Suhrkamp, 2015.

Grabes, Herbert. "Wie aus Sätzen Personen werden: Über die Erforschung literarischer Figuren." *Poet.* 10 (1978): 405–428.

Hagenlocher, Albrecht. "Littera meretrix: Brun von Schönebeck und die Autorität der Schrift im Mittelalter." *ZfdA* 118 (1989): 131–163.

Hartmann, Heiko. "*Odor spiritualium virtutum*: Die Allegorese der Düfte im *Hohelied*-Kommentar Willirams von Ebersberg." In *Begegnung mit Literaturen: Festschrift für Carola L. Gottzmann zum 65. Geburtstag*, edited by Petra Hörner and Roswitha Wisniewski, 133–150. Berlin: Weidler-Buchverlag, 2008.

Haupt, Joseph. "Einleitung." In *Das Hohe Lied: Übersetzt von Willeram, erklärt von Rilindis und Herrat, Äbtissinen zu Hohenburg im Elsasz (1147–1196)*, edited by Joseph Haupt, 1–34. Vienna, 1864.

Huber, Jane E. "Unfolding Song: The Matins Celebration for the Marian Feast of the Assumption; Early Origins to Medieval Example." PhD diss., Union Theological Seminary, 2013.

Hübner, Annemarie. "Das Hohe Lied des Bruns von Schönbeck und seine Quellen." In *Festgabe für Ulrich Pretzel: Zum 65. Geburtstag dargebracht von Freunden und Schülern*, edited by Werner Simon, Wolfgang Bachofer, and Wolfgang Dittmann, 43–54. Berlin: E. Schmidt, 1963.

Jahn, Manfred. "Narrative Voice and Agency in Drama: Aspects of a Narratology of Drama." *New Literary History* 32 (2001): 659–679.

Jannidis, Fotis. *Figur und Person: Beitrag zu einer historischen Narratologie*. Narratologia 3. Berlin: de Gruyter, 2008.

Jannidis, Fotis. "Wer sagt das? Erzählen mit Stimmverlust." In *Stimme(n) im Text: Narratologische Positionsbestimmungen*, edited by Andreas Blödorn, Daniela Langer, and Michael Scheffel, 151–164. Narratologia 10. Berlin: de Gruyter, 2008.

Jannidis, Fotis. "Zwischen Autor und Erzähler." In *Autorschaft: Positionen und Revisionen*, edited by Heinrich Detering, 540–556. DFG-Symposion 2001. Stuttgart: Metzler, 2002.

Jung, Norbert, Holger Kempkens, and Horst Gehringer, eds. *Tausend Jahre Kloster Michaelsberg Bamberg (1015–2015)*. Vol. 7 of *Veröffentlichungen des Diözesanmuseums Bamberg*. Petersberg: Imhof. Begleitpublikation zur Sonderausstellung *Im Schutz des Engels* vom 26. Juni bis 4. Oktober 2015, 2015.

Kartschoke, Dieter. *Geschichte der deutschen Literatur im frühen Mittelalter*. München: Deutscher Taschenbuch Verlag, 2000.

Keil, Gundolf. "Magdeburger Schöppenchronik." In vol. 5 of *Die Deutsche Literatur des Mittelalters: Verfasserlexikon*, edited by Kurt Ruh, Burghart Wachinger, and Franz J. Worstbrock, 1132–1142. Berlin: 1985.

Keller, Johannes. "Verborgene Küsse—gefesselte Füße." In *Verstellung und Betrug im Mittelalter und in der mittelalterlichen Literatur*, edited by Matthias Meyer, 75–87. Aventiuren 7. Göttingen: V&R Unipress, 2015.

Kristeva, Julia. "Dialog und Roman bei Bachtin (1967)." In vol. 3 of *Literaturwissenschaft und Linguistik: Ergebnisse und Perspektiven; Zur linguistischen Basis der Literaturwissenschaft, II*, edited by Jens Ihwe, 345–375. Frankfurt a. M.: Athenäum Fischer Taschenbuch Verlag, 1972.

Küsters, Urban. *Der verschlossene Garten: Volkssprachliche Hohelied-Auslegung und monastische Lebensform im 12. Jahrhundert*. StH 2. Düsseldorf: Droste, 1985.

Lähnemann, Henrike. "Reimprosa und Mischsprache bei Williram von Ebersberg: Mit einer kommentierten Ausgabe und Übersetzung seiner *Aurelius-Vita*." In *Deutsche Texte der Salierzeit: Neuanfänge und Kontinuitäten im 11. Jahrhundert*, edited by Stephan Müller and Jens Schneider, 205–237. Mittelalterstudien 20. München: Wilhelm Fink, 2010.

Lähnemann, Henrike, and Michael Rupp. "Von der Leiblichkeit eines 'gegürteten Textkörpers': Die *Expositio in Cantica Canticorum* Willirams von Ebersberg in ihrer Überlieferung." In *Text und Text in lateinischer und volkssprachiger Überlieferung des Mittelalters: Freiburger Kolloquium 2004*, edited by Eckart C. Lutz, 95–116. Wolfram-Studien 19. Berlin: Schmidt, 2006.

Leclercq, Jean. "New Recruitment—New Psychology." In *Monks and Love in Twelfth-Century France: Psycho-Historical Essays*, edited by Jean Leclercq, 8–26. Oxford: Clarendon Press, 1979.

Lerchner, Karin. *Lectulus Floridus: Zur Bedeutung des Bettes in Literatur und Handschriftenillustration des Mittelalters*. Pictura et Poesis 6. Köln: Böhlau, 1993.

Li, Shannon M. "Irimbert of Admont and His Scriptural Commentaries: Exegeting Salvation History in the Twelfth Century." PhD diss., Ohio State University, 2017.

Liere, Frans van. *An Introduction to the Medieval Bible*. Introduction to Religion. Cambridge: Cambridge University Press, 2014.

Lutter, Christina. *Geschlecht und Wissen, Norm und Praxis, Lesen und Schreiben: Monastische Reformgemeinschaften im 12. Jahrhundert*. VIÖG 43. Wien: Böhlau-Verlag, 2005.

Matis, Hannah W. *The Song of Songs in the Early Middle Ages*. SHCT 191. Boston: Brill, 2019.

Matter, E. Ann. *The Voice of My Beloved: The Song of Songs in Western Medieval Christianity*. Philadelphia: University of Pennsylvania Press, 1992.

Murphy, Roland E. *The Song of Songs: A Commentary on the Book of Canticles or the Song of Songs*. Hermeneia 22. Minneapolis: Fortress Press, 1990.

Ohly, Friedrich. "Der Prolog des *St. Trudperter Hoheliedes*." *ZfdA* 84 (1953): 198–232.

Ohly, Friedrich. *Hohelied-Studien: Grundzüge einer Geschichte der Hoheliedauslegung des Abendlandes bis um 1200*. Wiesbaden: Franz Steiner, 1958.

Ohly, Friedrich. "Kommentar." In *Das St. Trudperter Hohelied: Eine Lehre der liebenden Gotteserkenntnis*, edited and translated by Friedrich Ohly, 317–1267. Frankfurt am Main: Dt. Klassiker-Verl., 1999.

Patzold, Steffen. "Schrifttum und Kultur im Kloster Fulda im späten 9. und frühen 10. Jahrhundert." In *Konrad I: Auf dem Weg zum "Deutschen Reich"?*, edited by Hans-Werner Goetz, Simon Elling, and Gerd Althoff, 229–244. Bochum: Winkler, 2006.

Rappl, Stephanie. "Meinen Namen will ich deshalb in Schweigen hüllen: Honorius Augustodunensis als Regensburger Gelehrter." In *Kleine Regensburger Literaturgeschichte*, edited by Rainer Barbey and Erwin Petzi, 21–25. Regensburg: Verlag Friedrich Pustet, 2014.

Reuvekamp-Felber, Timo. "Autorschaft als Textfunktion: Zur Interdependenz von Erzählerstilisierung, Stoff und Gattung in der Epik des 12. und 13. Jahrhunderts." *ZfdPh* 120 (2001): 1–23.

Riedmann, Josef. "Brun von Schönebeck." In vol. 1 of *Die Deutsche Literatur des Mittelalters: Verfasserlexikon*, edited by Kurt Ruh, Burghart Wachinger, and Franz J. Worstbrock, 1056–1062. Berlin: de Gruyter, 1978.

Scheper, George L. "The Spiritual Marriage: The Exegetic and Literary Impact of the Song of Songs in the Middle Ages." PhD diss., Princeton University, 1971.
Schmid, Wolf. *Elemente der Narratologie*. Berlin: de Gruyter, 2014.
Schupp, Volker. *Studien zu Williram von Ebersberg*. Bibliotheca Germanica 21. Bern: Francke, 1978.
Seeberg, Stefanie. *Die Illustrationen im Admonter Nonnenbrevier von 1180: Marienkrönung und Nonnenfrömmigkeit—die Rolle der Brevierillustration in der Entwicklung von Bildthemen im 12. Jahrhundert*. Imagines Medii Aevi 8. Wiesbaden: Reichert, 2002.
Spangenberg, Wolfhart. *Von der Musica: Singschul*, edited by András Vizkelety and translated by Andor Tarnai. Vol. 1 of *Sämtliche Werke*. Ausgaben deutscher Literatur des 15. bis 18. Jahrhunderts 29. Berlin: de Gruyter, 1971.
Spitz, Hans-Jörg. *"Ez ist sanc aller sange*: Das *St. Trudperter Hohelied* zwischen Kommentar und Dichtung." In *Germanistische Mediävistik*, edited by Volker Honemann, 61–88. Germanistik 4. Münster: LIT-Verlag, 2000.
Spitz, Hans-Jörg. "Zur Lokalisierung des *St. Trudperter Hohenliedes* im Frauenkloster Admont." *ZfdA* 121 (1992): 174–177.
Stern, David. "Ancient Jewish Interpretation of the Song of Songs in a Comparative Context." In *Jewish Biblical Interpretation and Cultural Exchange: Comparative Exegesis in Context*, edited by Natalie B. Dohrmann and David Stern, 87–108. Philadelphia: University of Pennsylvania Press, 2008.
Stridde, Christine. "Die performative Zumutung: Sprechakt, Deixis und Imagination im *St. Trudperter Hohelied*." In *Imagination und Deixis: Studien zur Wahrnehmung im Mittelalter*, edited by Kathryn Starkey, 85–103. Germanistik. Stuttgart: Hirzel, 2007.
Stridde, Christine. *Verbalpräsenz und göttlicher Sprechakt: Zur Pragmatik spiritueller Kommunikation zwischen St. Trudperter Hohelied und Mechthilds von Magdeburg Das fließende Licht der Gottheit*. Germanistik. Stuttgart: Hirzel, 2009.
Stridde, Christine. "St. Trudperter Hohelied." In *Das geistliche Schrifttum*, edited by Wolfgang Achnitz, 425–429. Vol. 2 of *Deutsches Literatur-Lexikon*. Berlin: de Gruyter, 2011.
Suerbaum, Almut. "Die Paradoxie mystischer Lehre im *St. Trudperter Hohenlied* und im *Fließenden Licht der Gottheit*." In *Dichtung und Didaxe: Lehrhaftes Sprechen in der deutschen Literatur des Mittelalters*, edited by Henrike Lähnemann, 27–40. Berlin: de Gruyter, 2009.
Turner, Denys, *Eros and Allegory: Medieval Exegesis of the Song of the Songs*. CistSS 156. Kalamazoo: Cistercian Publications, 1995.
Unzeitig, Monika. "Von der Schwierigkeit zwischen Autor und Erzähler zu unterscheiden: Eine historisch vergleichende Analyse zu Chrétien und Hartmann." In *Erzähltechnik und Erzählstrategien in der deutschen Literatur des Mittelalters: Saarbrücker Kolloquium 2002*, edited by Wolfgang Haubrichs, Eckart C. Lutz, and Klaus Ridder, 59–81. Veröffentlichungen der Wolfram-von-Eschenbach-Gesellschaft 18. Berlin: Schmidt, 2004.
Volfing, Annette. "The Song of Songs as Fiction: Brun von Schönbecks *Das Hohe Lied*." In *"Vir ingenio mirandus,"* edited by William Jones, William Kelly, and Frank Shaw, 137–154. Göppinger Arbeiten zur Germanistik 710. Göppingen: Kümmerle, 2003.
Wisniewski, Roswitha. "Der Aufbau des Prologs zum *St. Trudperter Hohen Lied*." In *Festschrift für Herbert Kolb zu seinem 65. Geburtstag*, edited by Barbara Haupt and Klaus Matzel, 775–780. Bern: Lang, 1989.
Wolff, Ludwig. "Das Magdeburger Gralsfest Bruns von Schönebeck." *Niederdeutsche Zeitschrift für Volkskunde* 5 (1927): 202–216. Repr., Wolff, Ludwig. *Kleinere Schriften zur altdeutschen Philologie*, edited by Werner Schröder, 401–417. Berlin: de Gruyter, 1967.

Zakovitch, Yair. *Das Hohelied*. HThKAT. Freiburg im Breisgau: Herder, 2004.
Zerfaß, Christiane. *Die Allegorese zwischen Latinität und Volkssprache: Willirams von Ebersberg Expositio in Cantica Canticorum*. Göppinger Arbeiten zur Germanistik 614. Göppingen: Kümmerle, 1995.
Zymner, Rüdiger. "'Stimme(n)' als Text und Stimme(n) als Ereignis." In *Stimme(n) im Text: Narratologische Positionsbestimmungen*, edited by Andreas Blödorn, Daniela Langer, and Michael Scheffel, 321–348. Narratologia 10. Berlin: de Gruyter, 2008.

Christopher Ocker
An Ecology of Desire
Pierre d'Ailly's First Theological Work, a Latin Commentary on the Song of Songs

In 1401, Christine de Pizan (ca. 1365–1430) was a writer seeking a voice in the entourage of the Queen of France, Isabeau de Bavière. Soon she would become the public defender of the moral power of women in government, implicitly criticizing that queen for insufficiently asserting herself at court.[1] But now, still establishing a career after her husband's death, Christine set her target on a man, Jean de Montreuil, provost of the cathedral of Lille, and the approving essay he just wrote on the *Roman de la Rose*.[2]

Christine criticized the *Roman* as a morally degrading, woman-hating book. Controversy followed. The importance of the ensuing *querelle des femmes* was assured not only by the cameo of the *Roman*, France's most celebrated medieval romance novel, and not only by Christine's wisdom, wit, and critical insight, but also by the growing political instability of King Charles VI's court, during a particularly volatile phase of the French-English struggles of attrition and intrigue known as the "Hundred Years War."[3] As is well known to historians of women, France, and medieval literature, for Christine de Pizan, an allegory of love and the manner of its engendering had assumed political importance.

---

1 In general, see Hult, "*Roman de la Rose*." For Christine's writing and Isabelle, see Green, "Isabeau de Bavière"; Hult's "Introduction" in Christine de Pizan, *Debate of the Romance*, 32–57. For Christine's use of allegory, see Akbari, "Movement from Verse to Prose." Badel, "Pierre d'Ailly," established d'Ailly's participation in the debate, on the evidence of this work in comparison with a Pentecost sermon by d'Ailly.
2 Begun by Guillaume de Lorris in the second quarter of the thirteenth century and completed by Jean de Meun a half century later, the *Roman* is the most famous poem written in Old French. It presents a dream-vision that tells an allegorical story of a young man's frustrated romantic conquests. While Guillaume de Lorris's section of the poem leaves the lover's "rose" protected and inaccessible, and him inconsolably sad, Jean de Meun's completion of the story increases the lover's aggression, portrays women's resistance to male desire negatively, and concludes with the male's sexual conquest.
3 See Kennedy, "Christine de Pizan."

Note: I am grateful to Christopher Schabel for advice and to Varda Koch Ocker for criticism and help with Hebrew. Unless noted, all translations are my own.

https://doi.org/10.1515/9783110750799-014

Hidden in the background of the *querelle des femmes* were a primary text of idealized medieval love, the biblical Song of Songs, and a theologian. Pierre d'Ailly (1350/1–1420) contributed to Christine's side of the debate over the *Roman de la Rose*. So too, more famously, did d'Ailly's former student and friend, Jean Gerson (1363–1429), the current chancellor of the University of Paris. D'Ailly had preceded Gerson as chancellor of the university, while also serving as confessor to the French king. In 1401, he was the bishop of Cambrai and well connected to the royal court. D'Ailly's contribution to the *querelle des femmes* took the form of an essay called *Le Jardin amoureux de l'âme devote*, a prose text culminating in a poem of seventy-seven verses. The entire text was based on the allegorical tradition of Song of Songs commentary. It was structured like the *Roman de la Rose*, producing an evocative exchange between biblical and romance genres. D'Ailly replaced the lovers' garden of the *Roman* with "the Amorous Garden where the real God of love lives [. . .] where sweet Jesus lives and to which he calls his beloved [. . .] 'Come into my garden, my sister, my bride' (Cant. 5:1)."[4] The little book was an impassioned, intimate narrative of love for and from Christ. D'Ailly's *Le Jardin* became one of the most popular of several vernacular parabiblical poems and paraphrases circulating in fifteenth- and sixteenth-century France.[5] But this well studied text was not where d'Ailly's interest in the Song of Songs began. His starting point is my subject.

Not many Latin commentaries on the Song of Songs were written in the late Middle Ages. D'Ailly wrote one as a young man, a fact hardly known today beyond a small circle of d'Ailly specialists.[6] The Latin commentary was his earliest strictly theological work, produced in 1374 as the Old Testament lectures required by a *cursor biblicus* at the University of Paris.[7] The *cursor biblicus* was the "Bachelor of the Bible" at a first turning point in his progress toward completion of the Bachelor of Theology degree. After four years of hearing lectures, the student was required to lecture on a book of the Old Testament and a book of the New Testament, and then to do the same with Peter Lombard's *Four Books of Sentences*: hear, prepare, and deliver lectures. D'Ailly gave his Old Testament lectures four years after he was made Master of Arts and while he was still performing *magister artis* functions.[8] The vast majority of bible commentaries written in Europe from the early

---

[4] Hult's translation in Christine de Pizan, *Debate of the Romance of the Rose*, 71–83. The French original may be found misattributed to Gerson, *Oeuvres complètes*, 7/1:144–154.
[5] See Hoogvliet, "'Car Dieu veult'"; idem, "Encouraging Lay People." It is available in a fine English translation. See Hult in the previous note.
[6] See Stegmüller and Reinhardt, *Repertorium Biblicum*, 4:228 n. 6410.
[7] The year is given in the explicit of his inaugural lecture. See Paris, BNF, Arsenal Ms-520, fol. 187v.
[8] "Secular" students were required to complete a Master of Arts before beginning theology degrees. "Regular" students, that is, members of religious orders, who were often members of the

thirteenth century to the early sixteenth were texts composed for this curriculum. It was common among "secular" theology students in the later fourteenth century to lecture in the Arts faculty while working up through theological degrees. D'Ailly, Master of Arts and *cursor biblicus*, had already produced a number of significant philosophical works, including at least the beginning, and perhaps also the completion, of a treatise on Boethius' *Consolatio philosophiae*, which he probably, at least initially, composed as lectures for Arts students.[9]

Typically, each set of a theology Bachelor's lectures—Old Testament, New Testament, and *Sentences*—would begin with a *principium*, an inaugural lecture. After the *principium* would come a running commentary on the biblical book, beginning with its preface. Prefaces to sections and books of the bible were found in most medieval Vulgate manuscripts and in the "standard" commentary on the bible, the Ordinary Gloss, a complex text of interlinear and marginal comments that was assembled and evolved into its standard shape during the formative years of the European university, in the twelfth and early thirteenth centuries.[10] After treating the preface, a *cursor biblicus* would then proceed through the source text by chapter and line (verse divisions only came in the sixteenth century), sometimes selectively. In d'Ailly's case here, the Song of Songs, he covered the entire book.

D'Ailly's inaugural lecture and running commentary have survived in a single author-approved manuscript from d'Ailly's Collège de Navarre and in an incunabulum edition.[11] As far as I know, the text has not been studied before. I offer the

---

mendicant orders, entered the course in theology on the strength of their prior studies in the religious order's schools.

9 That the *Expositio* represents d'Ailly's Old Testament lectures as *cursor biblicus* in Paris has been long known, as well as the fact that a *principium in cursu bibliae* included in the seventeenth-century edition of Jean Gerson represents d'Ailly's inaugural lecture for his New Testament Bachelor of Theology requirement, which consisted of commentary on the Gospel of Mark. See Salembier, *Petrus de Alliaco*, 13, 197–199; the edition by Du Pin in Pierre d'Ailly, "Principium in cursu bibliae," 610–617. The *Recommendatio sacrae scripturae* initiated his master's lectures in the theology faculty. Salembier put the *Recommendatio* at 1380 (see Salembier, *Petrus*, 235 n. 1). The year was corrected by Courtenay and Schabel to 1381 (see Schabel, "Redating," 69; Glorieux, "Les années d'études de Pierre d'Ailly," 132). Chappuis (*Le Traité de Pierre d'Ailly*, 1:ix) also has 1374 for the beginning of Gerson's *cursor biblicus* lectures, but uses later dates and date ranges for key philosophical and theological works (*Conceptus* >1368<1375, *Insolubilia* >1372<1375, Peter Lombard's *Sentences* 1376–1377, *De Anima* >1377<1381, *Consolatio philosophiae* >1377<1381, ca. 1380). Schabel ("Redating," 70–71) suggests that the philosophical works and the *Consolatio* preceded the *cursor biblicus* lectures.

10 See Ocker and Madigan, "After Beryl Smalley," 91–94 and the literature noted there.

11 Glorieux ("Les années d'études," 130–132) noted the *Principium* for the Song of Songs is the *Descriptio imaginaria visionis de horto S. Scripturae*, which carries an *explicit* of 1374. It is found in BNF, Arsenal Ms-520, fols. 177–188. I will be using this manuscript for d'Ailly's *Principium* or first

observations below to introduce the commentary and call attention to its interpretive practice on the example of the inaugural lecture and a single chapter: Song of Songs 4.[12] D'Ailly, I believe, manifests an unappreciated feature of the practical poetics of the medieval bible, namely, the way commentaries facilitated a fluid movement between text, historical imaginary, figurative expression, and emotion. This quaternary movement, it seems to me, can be said to form a late medieval "ecology" of biblical literature, a framework suggested by both the text of the Song of Songs and its interpretation.

---

inaugural lecture as *cursor biblicus*. The commentary proper follows in BNF, Arsenal Ms-520, fols. 188–205. The commentary proper was published as Petrus de Alliaco, *Expositio super Cantica*, fols. 30r–56v. I will be using this incunabulum for the commentary proper. A second manuscript of only the running commentary, without the inaugural lecture, can be found in Vienna ÖNB Codex 11585, fols. 37–93. This manuscript both is late and appears to be a copy of the printed edition. The Codex in which it is found bears a 1538 date at several places: fol. 37r, *Anno 1538*; fol. 110r, *Anno 1538 ipso die Egidij quae erat die dominica factus est a me iste sermo in monasterio monialium S. Mariae magdalenae in assumptione cuiusdam virginis nouiciae* (fols. 93v–170v = Johannes Cochlaeius, *Sermone novem*); fol. 209v, 1538 *In vigilia Assumptionis deiparae virginis Mariae* (fols. 200r–217v = Johannes Cochlaeus, *Sermones quinque*); fol. 209v, *In festo Assumptionis Mariae* 1538. It already belonged to the Vienna Hofbibliothek in 1576. After lecturing on the Song of Songs, d'Ailly as *cursor biblicus* treated the Gospel of Mark to fulfill the university's New Testament requirement. These lectures have been edited, along with another hermeneutical work that he produced later as Master of Theology, a *Recommendatio* treating Matt 16:16–18. They were published in the eighteenth century in *Ioannis Gersonii opera omnia*, 1:603–610 (*Recommendatio*), 610–617 (*Principium*). Glorieux ("Deux éloges de la sainte") offers a French translation of both. Dahan ("Histoire de l'exégèse chrétienne," 309–317, here 315) and Glorieux in an earlier essay ("Deux éloges de la sainte écriture," 114) refer only to the *Principium* for Mark's Gospel.

12 Few commentaries on the Song of Songs were produced in the fourteenth and fifteenth centuries, and only two have been studied closely, the *Postilla* by Nicholas of Lyra and a commentary by Denys the Carthusian. Lyra is famous for working out a "historical" interpretation of the text. Denys the Carthusian has usually been taken to exemplify an older tradition of ecclesiastical and mystical allegory. Since Henri de Lubac, the contrast of these two commentators has illustrated an alleged competition between literal-historical and mystical interpretation before Renaissance and Reformation. I've argued elsewhere on the basis of commentary practices that this contrast didn't really exist in the way de Lubac imagined: there was no competition between literal-historical and allegorical ways of knowing. If anything, there was a growing tendency to fuse the two. In Ocker, *Biblical Poetics*, 75–78, 112–183, and passim, I saw this as a breakdown of a Victorine view of biblical signification. I now think that alternative mystical and rhetorical approaches can be seen in different medieval biblical interpreters since Carolingian times. Consider Ocker, "Hebrew Idiom."

1 The Inaugural Lecture

Addressing an audience of "the most reverend fathers, masters, and lords," d'Ailly begins his Old Testament inaugural lecture on the bible with the description of an alluring dream.[13] "'Come into my garden': the words are recited from Solomon Canticles 5," he says, opening the discourse, in effect reminding his audience that this text, a familiar line of an antiphon from the Feast of the Nativity of Mary, comes from the Song of Songs.[14] He describes a lush garden in the paroxysms of May. A maiden sits in the garden, so beautiful he cannot find words to describe her, "and this maiden, with a coy and jaunty expression on her face, looking at me with friendly eye, was saying in the clearest voice a foretasted word," a *verbum praelibatum*, perhaps a whisper: "come into my garden."[15] The assembled masters and lords would have noticed the young Bachelor's evident relish in accenting this sensuality. One might have recalled a wandering mind while chanting. D'Ailly, in his dream, then notices King Solomon, an aged and grave man, wearing his crown, holding his scepter and a book. Solomon explains how this garden is a likeness of sacred scripture, where a person contemplates divine wisdom in a garden of spiritual delights. The maiden is the divine wisdom that presides above, condescended to human beings in the humble speech of sacred writing. Solomon gave d'Ailly the theme for his lecture.

What follows is a clearly scholastic exercise. It occasionally flashes a broader erudition with citations of classical authors and the much-appreciated, but superficially used, *Anticlaudianus* and *De planctu naturae* by the twelfth-century encyclopedist Alan of Lille, all of this self-consciously structured by divisions of his subject matter, which he illustrates in line graphs built around the syntactical elements of simple and compound sentences.[16] And his ruling metaphor is promiscuously indulged. Scripture is a most pleasant garden, by virtue of the strength of its enclosure, its bright and agreeable ornamentation, and its fertility (Figure 1). These will constitute the three parts of the lecture.

---

[13] See Pierre d'Ailly, *Descriptio imaginaria visionis*, BNF, Arsenal Ms-520, fol. 177r.

[14] Song 5:1, and the *incipit* of the inaugural lecture: Ueni in [h]ortum meum, verba sunt diuine sapientie a sapiente Salomone Cant. 5 capitulo recitata. See the Antiphon for *Nativitas Mariae*: https://gregorien.info/chant/id/8430/0/de and http://cantusindex.org/id/005325.

[15] Pierre d'Ailly, *Descriptio imaginaria*, BNF, Arsenal Ms-520, fol. 177r: [. . .] hec autem uirgo me humili et hylari vultu ac oculo beniuolo respiciens uoce serenissima uerbum dicebat prelibatum, ueni in ortum meum.

[16] There are twenty-four of these in the *Descriptio imaginaria*, some of which couple phrases around a conjunction or verb, others of which offer brief lists of subthemes. There is much about this text of obvious interest to the intellectual historian, such as this one, that must be left for another time.

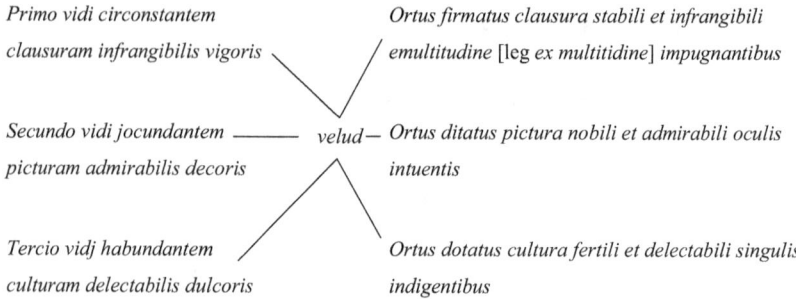

Figure 1: Basic division of the concept of garden. BNF, Arsenal Ms-520, fol. 178r.

He breaks it down a bit further, linking each characteristic (strength, prettiness, fertility) to effects (Figure 2). The garden's stable enclosure "has" a strength that rejects the envious (part one of the lecture). "Was having," to be exact: the entire lecture unfolds in the imperfect tense, as a retelling of his dream. The garden's excellent visual form has a beauty that attracts the eyes (second part). Its fertility has a renewing calmness (third part).

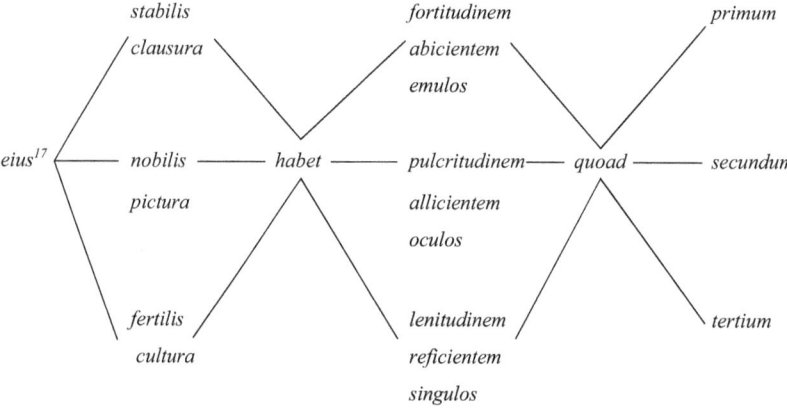

Figure 2: Basic division of part 1 of the inaugural lecture. BNF, Arsenal Ms-520, fol. 178r.

---

17 *ms* iiii eius. This is written at the left margin, with the beginning of the first term (iiii) possibly cut off. It is impossible to tell if iiii is intended as a number (in which case it should be read as iii) or an abbreviated word. The meaning seems clear without it.

Verses from the Song of Songs that mention these three basic attributes are noted, along with other biblical intertexts, in the manner of Christian typology, documenting a link between the Song of Songs and Christ.[18]

Each part of d'Ailly's discourse, yet again, breaks down one of these three features of the garden. In part one, he describes four defensive gates to the enclosure, which, against the degraders of holy scripture, are defended by flawless truth, proven fidelity, God-given humility, and the bible's soaring charity.[19] The degraders are identified (poets, idolaters, heretics, and sinners), and so are the defenders, maidens who stand guard repelling them. All these characters are eruditely described by turns.

In part two, which treats the garden of scripture's visual beauty, d'Ailly argues that beauty is both internal and external, applying the distinction between internal and external seals on the book beside the enthroned God in Rev 5:1.[20] Inside, there is the erudition of totalities, and outside the stimuli of particulars; inside, complete understanding, and outside, sensual delight; inside the secrets of divine wisdom, and outside human philosophy in the literature of the nations. This brings d'Ailly, the Arts Master, to describe the beauty of the external images as the Liberal Arts, which can be illustrated by ancient histories. He emphasizes their complementary, preparatory relationship to theology.[21] The superiority of biblical knowledge to the knowledge otherwise scattered about the nations (i.e., the relationship of theology to the Liberal Arts) comes from its universality (it begins at creation, then extends through Israel to all nations) and its interiority, or as he says,

> So I saw in the aforementioned internal image of sacred scripture four parts distinguished from one another, of which the first contained the law of Moses, which drives away evil; true history, which neglects nothing; concealed prophecy, which exceeds understanding; and gospel teaching, which exceeds everything.[22]

---

18 E.g., for the first point, the strength of the enclosure, he cites Song 4:12; Ps 86:1; Eph 2:20; 1Cor 10:4. I find it unhelpful to make a sharp distinction between allegory and typology. Consider Luxon, *Literal Figures*, 53–54 and passim. Also Ocker, "Typology"; idem, "Fourfold Sense." I am also discarding Paul Ricoeur's distinction between allegory (an image that discards the literal meaning and functions independently of it) and symbol (the literal meaning remains and embellishes the figurative meaning), in favour of a view that metaphor and metonymy interact with one another and allow "allegorical insight to re-illuminate the literal meaning." (Wilson, "Metaphoric and Metonymic," 225).
19 See Pierre d'Ailly, *Descriptio imaginaria*, BNF, Arsenal Ms-520, fols. 178r–181r.
20 See Pierre d'Ailly, *Descriptio imaginaria*, BNF, Arsenal Ms-520, fol. 181v.
21 See Pierre d'Ailly, *Descriptio imaginaria*, BNF, Arsenal Ms-520, fols. 181v–184r.
22 Pierre d'Ailly, *Descriptio imaginaria*, BNF, Arsenal Ms-520, fol. 182v: *Vidi itaque in predicta sacre scripture interiori pictura partes quatuor abinvicem condistinctas. Quarum prima continebat Sac-*

Solomon singing his wedding song belongs to the third category here, "concealed prophecy, which exceeds understanding."[23] It all falls under a familiar Christian umbrella of promise and fulfillment.[24] A brief survey of biblical literature follows.

Part three of the inaugural lecture divides and subdivides the metaphor of the scripture-garden's fertility into four quantities and dimensions of things: the great plenitude of plants growing from the earth, the great diversity of living creatures, the breadth of its rivers and fountains, and the height of its wooded mountains (Figure 3).[25]

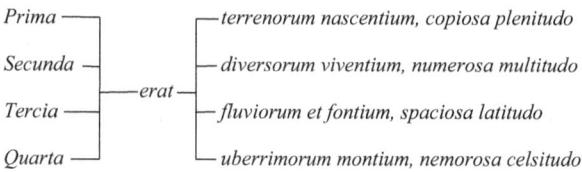

Figure 3: Basic division of part 3 of the inaugural lecture. BNF, Arsenal Ms-520, fol. 184v.

Each of these is then divided again. The plants are divided into powerful herbs, fragrant flowers, leafy trees, and pleasing fruits, and he surveys these types of plants in the bible (Figure 4).[26]

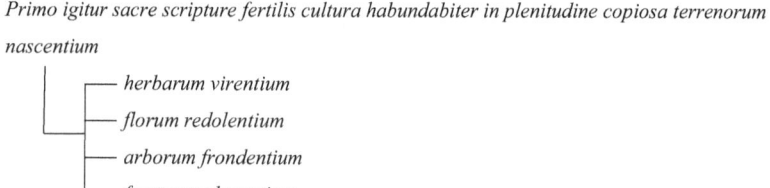

Figure 4: The abundance of living things born of the earth. BNF, Arsenal Ms-520, fol. 184v.

---

ram legem mosaycam, que malum repellit veritatem hystoricam, que nullum fefellit latenciam propheticam, que sensum excellit doctrinam euangelicam, que totum precellit.
23 Pierre d'Ailly, *Descriptio imaginaria*, BNF, Arsenal Ms-520, fol. 183r: *Illic Salomon rex pacificus et amabilis domino, prius mores corrigit, vitam dirigit, virtutes erigit, et tandem prophetiam aggreditur, dum ecclesiam suit et christum sanctarumque nuptiarum dulce canit epythalamium.*
24 For this in late medieval commentaries, see Ocker, *Biblical Poetics*, 8–30 and passim.
25 See Pierre d'Ailly, *Descriptio imaginaria*, BNF, Arsenal Ms-520, fols. 184r–187v.
26 See Pierre d'Ailly, *Descriptio imaginaria*, BNF, Arsenal Ms-520, fols. 184v–185v.

He notes the medicinal effects of herbs, the variety and physical associations of plant odors, the variety, natural purposes, and benefits of branching trees for themselves and other creatures (attributing the natural cause of intellect to the tree of life in Paradise), and the variety of fruits represented in the bible.

Living creatures are divided into those moving on earth, living in water, flying through air, and finally the humans (Figure 5), who play in a garden, "for people of every race (*gens*), of every populace (*plebs*), of every tribe, of every sex, of every nation, of every condition are met, of whom some undertake distinct duties, some carry out diverse jobs, others go on their way in delightful diversions."[27]

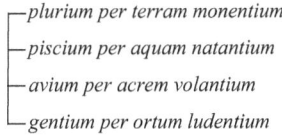

—plurium per terram monentium
—piscium per aquam natantium
—avium per acrem volantium
—gentium per ortum ludentium

Figure 5: Division of living creatures. BNF, Arsenal Ms-520, fol. 185v.

Again, each is described in turn, with liberal citation of biblical texts. The same is true for the last two sections of the inaugural lecture's part three, spacious rivers and fountains[28] and high, forested mountains.[29] In the former, scattered biblical references are used to emphasize rivers and fluids as elements of natural fertility. The latter insinuates allegory more strongly than most of the inaugural lecture, by carrying the reader from mountain to bridal allegory (again, the past imperfect serves the inaugural lecture's framing fiction of a rehearsed dream):

> The fourth fertile agriculture of holy scripture was abounding in the sheer height of the trees on its most copious mountains. For the mountains found in the garden of holy scripture are of such remarkable height and abundance, in which the variety of woods, the loftiness of groves, the density of trees, the viridity of plants and softness of flowers, the sweet sound of birds, make that garden lovely and cheerful, that Christ, the bridegroom longing to live there indulgently with his bride "comes leaping in the mountains and bounding across the hills," Canticle 2.[30]

---

27 See Pierre d'Ailly, *Descriptio imaginaria*, BNF, Arsenal Ms-520, fols. 185v–186v; quotation ibid., fol. 186r: *Illic enim de omni gente, de omni plebe, de omni tribu, de omnj sexu, de omni natione et de omni conditione reperiuntur homines, quorum alij distinctis occupantur officijs, alij varijs exercentur laboribus, Alij ludis delectabilibus spaciantur.*
28 See Pierre d'Ailly, *Descriptio imaginaria*, BNF, Arsenal Ms-520, fol. 187r.
29 See Pierre d'Ailly, *Descriptio imaginaria*, BNF, Arsenal Ms-520, fols. 187r–187v.
30 Pierre d'Ailly, *Descriptio imaginaria*, BNF, Arsenal Ms-520, fol. 187v: *Quarto igitur sacre scripture fertilis cultura habundabat in celsitudine nemorosa uberrimorum montium. In ortu namque scripture sacre reperiuntur montes celsitudinis mirabilis et inestimabilis ubertatis in quibus nemo-*

Some hasty references to biblical mountains (Zion, the Mount of Olives, Mount Carmel, etc.) conclude this fourth subpoint. Another brief graph and a few sentences recapitulate the entire lecture (Figure 6).

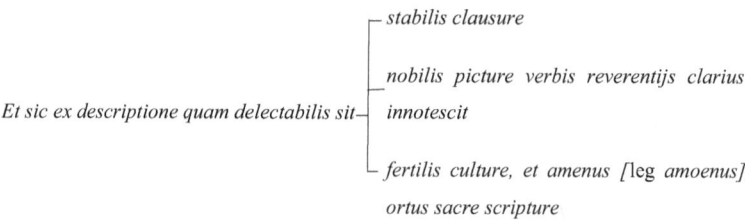

Figure 6: Recapitulation. BNF, Arsenal Ms-520, fol. 187v.

D'Ailly finishes with an admonition, "He who is its cultivator and equally preserver allows us to enter this garden, that we may be able to make passage to the kingdom in which he lives and reigns for ever and ever. Amen."[31] The manuscript then adds a two-page condensed version of the lecture (reproducing the main graphs),[32] before turning to the preface and the proper text of the Song of Songs.

This first bible lecture made only the most restrained attempt to link biblical interpretation to the philosophy d'Ailly was teaching as a master in the Arts faculty. In part, this reflects a late scholastic desire to see the work of Arts and Theology faculties as separate but complementary domains. It also reflects the immaturity of this first exercise, in which the scholar laid a groundwork upon which he would expand through each step of his education.[33] In the Arts faculty, he had already proved his command of terminist logic.[34] An *Insolubilia* treatise and a commentary on Aristotle's *De anima*, along with his *De consolatio* treatise, had put this mastery

---

rosa pluralitas Arboris proceritas silvarum condempsitas [leg *condensitas*], *herbarum viriditas florumque suavitas, et Avium dulcis sonoritas, ortum ipsum amenum efficiunt et jocundum propter quod Christus sponsus cum sponsa sua ibi delectabiliter habitare cupiens "venit saliens in montibus et transiliens colles," Can. secundo.*

31 Pierre d'Ailly, *Descriptio imaginaria*, BNF, Arsenal Ms-520, fol. 187v: *Propter quod divina sapientia ibi residens et habitans perpetua mansione vestrum quemlibet ad hunc ortum accedere, et secum manere, suauiter exhortatur, dicens verbum prius protheumate vestris reverentijs propositum veni in ortum meum. Ad quem ortum nos pervenire concedat ille, qui eius cultor est pariter atque custos, ut inde ad regnum transire valeamus. In quo ipse idem vivit et regnat in secula seculorum Amen.*

32 See Pierre d'Ailly, *Descriptio imaginaria*, BNF, Arsenal Ms-520, fols. 188r–188v.

33 Illustrative of this process in the previous generation was Johannes Klenkok, who left a particularly good trail of manuscript revisions; see Ocker, *Johannes Klenkok*, 16–41.

34 It is better to describe his method as "terminist" rather than "nominalist," as I explain in *The Hybrid Reformation*, 100-155.

on display. In his first *cursor biblicus* lecture, the task was to outline a complementary but hierarchical relationship between natural knowledge and theology.

The inaugural lecture on the Old Testament constituted a first pass. He took a second pass in his New Testament inaugural lecture, which preceded his exposition of the Gospel of Mark. The New Testament inaugural lecture was based on Mark 1:27, where a crowd, witnessing Jesus command an unclean spirit in a boy to keep silent, remarks, in Jerome's Latin, *quaenam doctrina haec nova* ("what is this new doctrine?"). D'Ailly used the contrast between old and new to describe features that distinguished the work of each of four "schools" or spheres of knowledge: the school of *sermocinales scientiae* (grammar and logic, rhetoric, poetics), the school of mathematics (arithmetic, music, geometry, astrology), the school of jurisprudence (*in qua contentiose disceptantur quaestiones civiles et politicae*), and the school of theology.[35] In this, he recognizes the difference between the language-oriented trivium and the quantitative-oriented quadrivium in the faculty of Liberal Arts (his first two schools), and ranks them beside fields that obviously represent the faculties of law and theology. He took a final pass at the same four-fold division of learning in the inaugural lecture that began his commentary on Peter Lombard's *Sentences*, required of a Bachelor of the Sentences before attaining the Master of Theology degree.[36] His overarching conceptualization of fields was conventional, and he kept it through his entire educational career.

What appears in the first inaugural lecture is a framework intellectually more raw than what d'Ailly produced at later stages of his education. For the biblical interpreter it is also more interesting, because it depended less on the application of this grand-scale organization of knowledge than on the image of the garden and its narrative and intertextual dimensions. The *cursor biblicus'* first theological lecture emphasizes a sensuality that is not merely erotic but fundamentally naturalistic. The garden becomes something more concrete than an allegorical figure. Its physical attributes determine its pleasantness: its material design, the life growing there, and the productivity of that life. These attributes exercise agency: the enclosure's protection of a biosphere, the visual attraction of its beauty, and its self-replicating productivity. Breaking these things down further allows d'Ailly to describe a more intricate architecture that joins the natural world to human experiences and actions, and which forms an important realm of human knowledge, but which he also documents with scattered biblical passages. D'Ailly never denies an allegorical reading of the text, and he indulges a comprehensively naturalistic view of the bible as the basis of Christian reading.

---

35 See Pierre d'Ailly, "Principium in cursum bibliae," 610–617.
36 See Chappuis, *Le Traité de Pierre d'Ailly*, 2:13–16.

The Ordinary Gloss, as the name implies, the "standard" medieval reference commentary, offers an instructive comparison to d'Ailly's inaugural lecture. It includes a "Prothemata" and, in one of its versions, a Prologue.[37] The Prothemata discusses Solomon's authorship and the text's principal character as a wedding song mystically describing the marriage of Christ and the church, in an allegory that moves the reader to consider heavenly and divine things. The Gloss documents this movement by interpreting Solomon's name and the title Song of Songs, adding a brief description of the book's "matter" ("husband and wife, that is, head and church"), "mode" (the desire that binds head and members), and "end" (the love of God). It offers a description of the four people believed to appear in the poem, allegorical observations on where the characters are located (house, garden), and the Song's effect — to move the soul toward the good.[38] These hasty allegorical associations are repeated and elaborated in the Prologue, which was written by Raoul of Laon and Anselm of Laon. They describe the Song of Songs as the culmination of a Solomonic trilogy. While the Book of Proverbs addresses beginners, like parent to child, teaching honest and decent behaviour, the Book of Ecclesiastes admonishes a person to abandon the world for contemplation. The Song uses terrestrial likenesses to show how we come to eternal glory. Solomon's trilogy propels the reader from moral infancy to spiritual self-realization, the goal of reading. In this manner, allegorical interpretation is aligned with a grandiose redemptive purpose.

Just how pervasive this conviction of allegory's redemptive purpose became is suggested by the most famous literal interpreter of the Middle Ages, Nicholas of Lyra (ca. 1270–1249). Lyra's preface to the Song of Songs also emphasized the allegorical value of the book, saying it cannot be taken as erotic prose.[39]

D'Ailly paraphrased and adapted observations from the Gloss's Prothemata after his inaugural lecture, when, in place of a commentary on the standard prologue, he offered mostly his own brief reworking of the Prothemata.[40] The Song of Song is a wedding song by Solomon, he says. Its purpose is to document the

---

37 All references to the Ordinary Gloss are from the text edited by Martin Morard (2017) in *Glossae Scripturae Sacrae-Electronicae*, 30 (Cantica), which collates the base text of the *Biblia latina cum Glossa ordinaria* (Strasbourg 1480) with the critical apparatus of *Glossae ordinariae*. See https://gloss-e.irht.cnrs.fr/php/editions.php?livre=../sources/editions/GLOSS-liber30.xml, accessed 17 May 2021. For the two versions, see ibid., 30.2 n. a.

38 *Glossae Scripturae Sacrae-Electronicae*, Prothemata, 30.1.

39 Lyra says the text cannot be about the love of husband and wife, because that would be carnal. See Nicholas of Lyra, *Postilla*, 30: *propter quod descriptio talis amoris non videtur ad libros Sacrae Scripturae canonicos pertinere, maxime quia huiusmodi libri Spiritu Sancto dictante sunt scripti*.

40 References to the commentary itself are to the incunabulum edition, here, Petrus de Alliaco, *Expositio*, fol. 30r. Where the manuscript contains significant variants, these are noted in parentheses with a reference to the folio in BNF, Arsenal Ms-520.

spiritual love of husband and wife, that is, Christ and the church, and he adds, "see the Gloss." The Song advocates a triple purpose, departure from vice, progress into virtue, and the consummation of good works, he explains, adapting the Gloss's view of the book's purpose. D'Ailly adds an observation about his task in expounding a small book, of only eight chapters, "short in words but long in meanings." It is not "to focus on curious expressions and narrative flow between chapters and parts," but to identify the four voices (groom, bride, friends, young women) as they appear.[41] His stated purpose, then, is to document the structure of the narrative's dialogue.

2 The Commentary

The commentary proves to be a bit more than that. To document the structure of dialogue, d'Ailly divides each of the Song's eight chapters into parts. Chapters one, two, four, and eight have eight parts. Chapters three and seven have five parts. Chapter five has nine parts. At the beginning of each part, d'Ailly identifies a narrative voice: "the groom speaks," the bride, the friends, or the young women speak. Line diagrams scattered throughout the commentary reinforce his sense of how narrative structures can be organized and layered in the text and visually represented.

The tone of d'Ailly's exegesis is set in his exposition of Song 1 (and the chapter's first of eight parts), which shows how seriously he takes the allegorical significations justified by his Prologue commentary. Using the first words of the Song of Songs, "He kisses me with the kiss of his mouth" (Song 1:2), he signals a strictly allegorical reading: "these are the words of the church in the character of the ancient people who desired the coming of Christ in the flesh."[42] The point is reinforced by alternative readings of the phrase. God the Father kisses God the Son "'with a kiss of

---

41 Petrus de Alliaco, *Expositio*, fol. 30r: *In processu expositionis huius libri non intendo insistere curiosis dictionibus seu continuationibus capitulorum uel partium adinuicem. Sed quia liber iste dialogus est in quo sunt quattuor personatus, sponsi uidelicet et sponse, sodalium et adolescentularum, sicut ex dictis patet: ideo solum intendo uti quadam distinctione clausularum, ut appareat quando sponsus loquitur uel sponsa, uel sodales sponsi, uel adolescentule sponse.*

42 For this and the following, Petrus de Alliaco, *Expositio*, fol. 30r: *Et sunt uerba ecclesie in persona antiquorum Christi aduentum in carem desiderantium. Prima pars dicit ergo* Osculetur me *scilicet Deus Pater* osculo oris sui id est unione filii dei. *Uel* Osculetur me osculo oris sui *id est non loquatur michi Moyses uel Ysaias uel alius prophetarum: sed ore suo Filius Dei me erudiat. Uel* Osculetur me osculo oris *sui id est blandum et hylarem se michi exhibeat, non asperum uel terribilem sicut in ueteri testamento.*

his mouth,' that is, by the union of the Son of God." Or, "with the kiss of his mouth" means that "Moses, Isaiah, or another prophet does not speak to me but the Son of God teaches me." Or it means God "displays Godself to me openly and happily, not cruelly and fearfully as in the Old Testament." These typically supersessionist interpretations are underscored by d'Ailly's close reading of the phrase's grammar and imagery. The text says "the kiss of his mouth": "not with his mouth," he explains, to distinguish between the kissing of the Father and the Son (the Word), illustrating the Trinity's distinction of persons in the one divine substance, while the lips of those kissing signify the natural conjunction of humanity and the Word of God. The bodily internal panting of those kissing signifies the union of divine and human spirit, and the approaching movement of two bodies signifies the co-participation of the passions of Christ and Christians. In addition, the kiss is triple, to the feet (for remission of sins), hands (for the action of grace), and the mouth (for mutual pleasure).[43] In this manner, words connected to each other in a certain way—the text's grammar and diction—reach beyond Solomon's bridal poem to a love more supreme and divine.

We easily see the same interest documented in his treatment of Songs 4, which I have chosen for closer scrutiny.[44] The groom speaks in each of the chapter's eight parts, but d'Ailly parses his lavish blandishments to the bride into elements of Christian religious convention. The chapter begins boldly with entreating blandishment (4:1). This is the Vulgate text, which I compare to the Hebrew:

הִנָּךְ יָפָה רַעְיָתִי הִנָּךְ יָפָה עֵינַיִךְ יוֹנִים מִבַּעַד לְצַמָּתֵךְ שַׂעְרֵךְ כְּעֵדֶר הָעִזִּים שֶׁגָּלְשׁוּ מֵהַר גִּלְעָד:	*Quam pulchra es, amica mea! quam pulchra es! Oculi tui columbarum, absque eo quod intrinsecus latet. Capilli tui sicut greges caprarum quae ascenderunt de monte Galaad.*
You are gorgeous, my dear one, you are gorgeous, your eyes like doves behind your braid,[45] your hair like a flock of goats come down from Mt. Gilead	How beautiful you are, my dear! How beautiful you are! Your eyes of doves, apart from what is concealed within. Your hair like flocks of goats rising from Mt. Gilead.

The Vulgate struggles with the vocabulary of "braid" or, as often rendered, "veil" (לְצַמָּתֵךְ מִבַּעַד, *quod intrinsecus latet*), but otherwise conveys the original's direct, uncompromising flattery, which is relentlessly sustained throughout the chapter. Part one of this chapter, d'Ailly explains, is in

> the voice of the groom who commends the church of the gentiles in many ways and shows her admirable beauty, and he says *O my love, how beautiful you are* [Song 4:1], in working, *how*

---

[43] See Petrus de Alliaco, *Expositio*, fols. 30v–31r.
[44] See Petrus de Alliaco, *Expositio*, fols. 42r–46r; BNF, Arsenal Ms-520, fols. 196r–199v.
[45] Rashi on Song 4:1 describes the term צמה as a braid or device for restraining hair; see *Shir Ha-Shirim im Perush Rashi*, 18.

beautiful in preaching. *your doves' eyes*, that is, they are teachers and simple prelates, who are spiritual and pursuing the flowings of scripture. *apart from what is concealed within*, that is, apart from the heart's intention, which is known to God alone, or apart from the beauty of interior virtues, which is hidden to people, or apart from the clarity of eternal retribution, which is now neither seen nor appears. *your hair*, that is humbly faithful and simple, delicately gentle, holding fast to Christ in faith, hope, and love. *like flocks of goats*, in rapidity of work, in ascending contemplation, in descending compassion and for the choice of better fodder. *which arose from Mt. Gilead*, that is from the mountain of holy scripture, where there is a pile of testimonies to the promise of rewards for good deeds and the threat of suffering for evil deeds. Or *Mt. Gilead* is Christ, to whom the multitude of martyrs attest. For martyr and witness are the same and from this mountain, that is from her faith and virtue, all the penitent arise from the depth of vices to the height of virtues.[46]

Is the emotional force of the original text carried into d'Ailly's technical, allegorical exposition? I think a fair answer must be no; Christian allegory does not sustain the emotional intensity of the Hebrew or Jerome's translation.

Yet to transpose such feeling seems to be d'Ailly's exact intention, as he continues through the chapter (and the entire book) part-by-part, connecting words in the text with features of the church. Part one (Song 4:1–6) compliments the bride. He associates most of the imagery of part one to preachers and connects the similes that describe the bride's beauty with their moral, attitudinal, and emotional attributes. A very brief part two (Song 4:6), "I will go to the mountain of myrrh, and to the hill of frankincense," is associated with the mortification of the flesh and the grace conferred by devotion. An equally brief part three (Song 4:7), "My love is total beauty and flawless," summarizes the beauty the groom earlier described in parts, which he associates with Christ's atoning death on the cross. The association of imagery with points of Christian doctrine continues in part four.

---

46 I quote the incunabulum edition and note significant variants from the manuscript. Petrus de Alliaco, *Expositio*, fol. 42v; BNF, Arsenal Ms-520, fol. 196r–v: [. . .] *vox sponsi, ecclesiam de gentibus multipliciter commendantis et eius pulchritudinem I* [fol. 42v] *admirabilem ostendentis, et dicit,* O *amica mea quam pulchra es operatione quam pulchra predicatione oculi tui columbarum id est doctores et prelati simplices sunt et spirituales et fluentis* [ms *fluentes*] *scripturarum insistentes absque eo quod intrinsecus latet, id est absque intentione cordis: que soli deo patet, uel absque virtutum interiorum pulchritudine que homines latet, uel absque eterne retributionis claritate: que modo non uidetur nec apparet,* capilli tui, *id est fideles et graciles humilitate, molles mansuetudine: Christo capite adherentes fide, spe, et caritate sicut greges caprarum, in uelocitate operis, ascensu contemplationis* [ms add. in marg. *Christo* [. . .] *contemplationis*]*, descensu compassionis, et electione pastus melioris,* que ascenderunt de monte Galaad, *id est de monte scripture sacre, ubi est aceruus testimoniorum de promissione premiorum bonis, et de comminatione suppliciorum maliis. Uel mons Galaad est Christus, cui attestatur multitudo martyrum. Martyr enim et testis idem sunt et de hoc monte, id est de fide et uirtute eius, ascenderunt omnes penitentes ab imo uiciorum ad alta uirtutum.*

In part four (Song 4:8), "Come from Lebanon, my bride, come from Lebanon. Come, you will be crowned," the groom, who earlier said (Song 4:6) he will go to the bride, now bids her to move, saying "come" three times. This either points to faith in the Trinity; or to heart, hearing, and work; or to faith, hope, and love. The term Lebanon means splendour, a definition taken from the Ordinary Gloss, and thus indicates primarily splendour of conscience and intention and secondarily purity of life and deed.[47] The verse's additional references to the peaks of Mounts Amana, Sanir, and Hermon are translated as classes of sins (disquiet, pride, luxury, avarice), and so to summon the bride while mentioning these mountains is to summon her to leave sin. Or alternatively, "you will be crowned from the top of Amana" may refer to the converts of preachers, or one of several other possible significations that d'Ailly explores.

Part five (Song 4:9) is dominated by the Vulgate's repeated phrase, "you wound my heart, my sister." The reader of Hebrew may feel that Jerome botched his translation of idioms in this passage,[48] but d'Ailly is drawn to the text's idiomatic eccentricity (Jerome's choice of the verb *vulnerare* for לִבַּבְתִּנִי, the expressions "one of your eyes, one of your necklaces"). These words encourage the interpreter to link the text to the passion of Christ, whose wound was two-fold, one of suffering and compassion, while the phrase "in one of your eyes" refers to the unity of preaching, that is the teaching that is preached, the coitus that occurs during contemplation, a coitus of practical and temporal things, or the coitus of those who hear with one heart and mind. References to the bride's anatomy in the Vulgate's rendition of the sixth part (Song 4:10–11), breasts, her "udders," her "wine," the smell of her unguents, her lips a dripping honeycomb, milk and honey under her tongue, and the smell of her clothes are translated in an even more brutal manner. The breasts are teachers of children who give the milk of simple doctrine, and the wine of her breast is the simple doctrine itself. Appealing to the Ordinary Gloss, the odor of her unguents is the reputation of the faith which is produced by charity. Her honeycomb lips are holy eloquence, milk and honey under the tongue, like divine speech, sweeter than honey. Her scented garment is the reputation of good works.

In the seventh part (Song 4:12–15), the groom recites a litany of sexualized garden metaphors applied indulgently to the bride in both the Hebrew original and Jerome's translation. D'Ailly recognizes its sexuality, but diverts the reader to other things. D'Ailly says, "the voice is the groom describing the beauty of the bride

---

47 See *Glossa ordinaria*, 30.4, Song 4:8.
48 לִבַּבְתִּנִי אֲחֹתִי כַלָּה לִבַּבְתִּנִי בְּאַחַת (בְּאַחַד כתיב) מֵעֵינַיִךְ בְּאַחַד עֲנָק מִצַּוְּרֹנָיִךְ; *Vulnerasti cor meum, soror mea, sponsa; vulnerasti cor meum in uno oculorum tuorum, et in uno crine colli tui.*

differently than before. He treated her as a beautiful woman. Now he treats her as a garden and a field."[49] As in the previous parts, the poem's intense display of erotic metaphor seems to be stripped away by doctrine. For the garden carries d'Ailly to Eden, whose diverse trees are the saints, where the tree of life is Christ, and where the tree of the knowledge of good and evil are teachers "who have knowledge of good and evil" (*sed lignum scientie uite boni et mali sunt doctores qui habent scientiam boni et mali*) and the variety of plants and the animals they support indicate mercies, virtues, and many other things.[50]

The eighth part (Song 4:16), "Arise, north wind, come south wind, blow through my garden, let its perfumes flow," d'Ailly again attributes to the voice of the groom, now encouraging the bride to be patient, after describing her beauty as woman and garden. The winds signify the persecuting devil and a love-kindling Holy Spirit. And with this, his exposition of Song 4 ends.

3 An Ecology of Desire

How should one read a medieval commentary? Any commentary minces its text into bits, and then inelegantly chews them with clinically precise expositions. In addition, a first course of lectures by a Bachelor of the Bible is a work produced in a student laboratory, in which all the technicians were male. It reflects the tastes, norms, and practices of a faculty and a school. An evaluation of d'Ailly as biblical interpreter will have to wait for a comprehensive study of his biblical interpretation, in the context of his complete education and ecclesiastical career. But what we are given here, in a work of his intellectual youth, has great value as a reflection of a biblical interpreter's starting point, an engagement with a text that relies on inherited assumptions and reference works, like the Ordinary Gloss, which could very well have been open on his lectern as he worked through the exposition. As an element of a curriculum, the commentary must be read with its required inaugural lecture. As a commentary, it must be read with the presumption that its base text, as a complete poetic narrative, had already triggered the scholar's pleasure and wonder. D'Ailly's attempt to underscore the poem's organizational structure

---

49 Pierre d'Ailly, *Expositio*, fol. 45v; BNF, Arsenal Ms-520, fol. 198r: *Septima pars.* Ortus conclusus soror mea sponsa, ortus conclusus *Vox est sponsi: sponse pulchritudinem aliter quam prius describentis. Comparauerat enim eam mulieri formose: nunc orto seu culture fructuose, et causam vide in glossa.*
50 Pierre d'Ailly, *Expositio*, 45v; BNF, Arsenal Ms-520, fol. 198r.

made explicit a deliberate arrangement of voices in the eight chapters of Solomon's poetic prose.

The inaugural lecture suggests a naturalistic superstructure for biblical reading. D'Ailly's audience could take for granted the Songs's natural erotism, which d'Ailly insightfully understands not merely as an individual or a couple's sexuality but as a biosphere. The university's curriculum studies its natural, civic, and theological dimensions. The narrative produces certain associations that we might not expect in a hermeneutical work, for example, its insight that sexual desire, interestingly, is something communicated between lovers but also among friends: it is not merely emotional but also social.

The commentary proper tries to document word by word, phrase by phrase, not merely the historical voices it cursorily identifies, and even less the grammar and rhetoric of an author, but the concepts that define the church as a spiritual world. The commentary is pedantic. Its purpose is not to replace the original writing but to expand the natural associations of the Song's language and narrative, to integrate a spiritual world into its setting, into its garden. A school's curriculum exercises such transposition. It can allow the text to remain an erotic poem, but it encourages the scholar to read the poem also as something else, which the theologian says is better. The indulgent admiration and longing of lovers becomes something more inclusive and widely shared. The text's sexuality is expanded into a love with dimensions far greater than a lover's conquest of another. Its sexuality is expanded, not denied or replaced.

In contrast with modern critical commentaries (and perhaps also some Renaissance-Reformation ones), d'Ailly's commentary does not merely "observe" the text, its grammar, or very much of its biblical author's environment. Nor is it a direct, fluent expression of mystical prose. The commentary is an instrument, a tool, perhaps even a machine. It expands the dialogue of lovers in the Song of Songs and the setting in which it occurs to a dialogue of writing and readers. If one thinks of the commentary as a tool operating within a certain "ecology," and that ecology as co-agent in the operation of the tool, one could say, the commentary as book, the lecture as discourse, the university as curriculum all constitute each other. The commentary enables an aspiration for an entire life-world, one in which a young man or a woman hearing the Song of Songs can imagine oneself as intimately pursued by a beautiful and solicitous God-man within and beyond the garden of this world. To appreciate the "ecology" to which the commentary belongs is to learn something about not only the commentary as mechanism used to make meaning, but also about the "affordances" of an environment acting on the tool—the form and content of an environment affecting the tool's shape and uses, including, in this instance, the possibilities of gender and affection in that environment. The commentary-instrument becomes a participatory element of a shared habitation, a place of open communication between text, its imaginary, and readers. To the critical historian, this goes beyond a fusion of perceptual horizons in the old-fashioned, Gadamerian sense. The commentary is cohabitant, by means of interwoven ideas and by means of the physicality of commented texts and readers. Fundamental to the "ecology" of these things are not only the figures interpreted by the commentary, but the proper setting to which the Song of Songs is assigned; not merely a reader's self-insertion into an ancient erotic dialogue or its current, reconstituted presence, but a transcending desire, documented by words and phrases in a book (or a chant, a sermon, a painting), which couples biblical figures to readers, readers to biblical figures.

There was, by implication, something enduring here in this first theological work, which a Protestant reformer might have ridiculed as reckless allegorizing. It was something an older Pierre d'Ailly would remember and apply a quarter century later during the controversy over the *Roman de la Rose*.

4 A Vernacular Afterlife

Twenty-five years later, when d'Ailly composed a third-person description of experiences in the garden of God in the prose and verse of *Le jardin amoureux de l'âme devote*, he replicated the Song of Songs. Near the culmination of *Le jardin*, we hear the sound of devout souls chanting spiritual songs like birds, singing in "total agreement between the heart and the mouth and a perfect concord between voice and thought." This triggers a kind of spiritual orgy:[51]

> At the sound of this melody, the beloved women and the men, lovers, come to disport themselves joyously, manifesting a spiritual joy, without unseemly merriment. There the lovers assemble their amorous company and lead a joyous life thinking and speaking of love; there they get down on their knees to pay homage to the God of love, giving themselves over obediently to his amorous service; there they come to his school to hear the amorous law, where the art of loving is completely enclosed. It is the school of Jesus Christ where he teaches the divine law [. . .] It is the art of loving well, which no human creature can know through native reasoning unless it has been disciplined and taught by the word of divine Scripture. This art was never known by Virgil or Ovid or the others who taught how to love foolishly and deceptively and to foolishly honor Cupid, the false god of love, and his wanton mother, Venus.

Seeing all this going on, the sacred soul, "very pleased and delighted," joins in, and hoping to draw others into the menagerie, "makes an effort to praise her beloved and deliver her sweet praises to him," and she sings,[52]

---

51 Translated by Hunt, Pierre d'Ailly, "Le jardin," 80–81.
52 Translated by Hunt. Pierre d'Ailly, "Le jardin," 82–83.

> [. . .] Love made him create the beautiful world
> and adorn the firmament with stars;
> he made the elements harmonize
> as he appeased their contrariety;
> In plants he rejuvenated the greenery,
> he made beasts see to procreation;
> by him force was given to things,
> by him worth was bequeathed to them
> > in equitable measure.

She continues, marveling at the creation of human beings, the incarnation, crucifixion and atonement, the law of grace, and the reward of eternity. It is, in essence, a paraphrase of the Creed, from creation to beatitude. The song ends with two stanzas to love,[53]

> It is a sweet thing to love loyally
> since love is the foundation of all good things.
> There is in good love sweetness without gall
> for those who know how to maintain it gently;
> for sweet pleasure greatly assures its gift
> and sweet hope feeds its desire:
> If such sweetness is fully tasted,
> true lovers can find in it
> > sweet nourishment.
> Let us now have the warmth of this love.
> Let us love him who is beautiful without foulness;
> let us love the beautiful one who is loved by him,
> let us love for his sake all created beauty
> > lacking vulgar filth.

D'Ailly had managed to express in French verse what he once pursued in a Latin commentary, a love constant, pure, and complete, like a Platonic love, yet loving within the created world.

Bibliography

Akbari, Suzanne Conklin. "The Movement from Verse to Prose in the Allegories of Christine de Pizan." In *Poetry, Knowledge and Community in Late Medieval France*, edited by Adrian Armstrong, Sylvia Huot, and Sarah Kay, 136–148. London: Boydell and Brewer, 2008.

Badel, Pierre-Yves. "Pierre d'Ailly, auteur du *Jardin amoureux*." *Rom.* 97 (1976): 369–381.

---

[53] Translated by Hunt. Pierre d'Ailly, "Le jardin," 82–83.

Chappuis, Marguerite. *Le Traité de Pierre d'Ailly sur la Consolation de Boèce: Qu. 1*. 2 vols. Amsterdam: B. R. Grüner, 1993.
Christine de Pizan. *Debate of the Romance of the Rose*, edited and translated by David Hult. Chicago: University of Chicago, 2010.
Dahan, Gilbert. "Histoire de l'exégèse chrétienne au Moyen Âge (Conference)." *Annuaires de l'École pratique des hautes études* 112 (2003): 309–331.
Gerson, Jean. *Oeuvres complètes*, edited by Palémon Glorieux. 10 vols. Paris: Desclée, 1960–1973.
Glorieux, Palémon. "Deux éloges de la sainte écriture par Pierre d'Ailly." *MScRel* 29 (1972): 113–129.
Glorieux, Palémon. "Les années d'études de Pierre d'Ailly." *RTAM* 44 (1977): 127–149.
Glossae ordinariae. Pars 22: *In Canticum Canticorum*, edited by Mary Dove. CCCM 170.22. Brepols: Turnhout, 1997.
Glossae Scripturae Sacrae-Electronicae 30 (Cantica), edited by Martin Morard. 2017. https://gloss-e.irht.cnrs.fr/php/editions.php?livre=../sources/editions/GLOSS-liber30.xml, accessed 17 May 2021.
Green, Karen. "Isabeau de Bavière and the Political Philosophy of Christine de Pizan." *Historical Reflections/Réflexions Historiques* 32 (2006): 247–272.
Hoogvliet, Margriet. "'Car Dieu veult estre serui de tous estaz': Encouraging and Instructing Lay People in French from the Late Middle Ages to the Early Sixteenth Century." In *Discovering the Riches of the Word: Religious Reading in Late Medieval and Early Modern Europe*, edited by Sabrina Corbellini, Margriet Hoogvliet, and Bart Ramakers, 111–140. Leiden: Brill, 2015.
Hoogvliet, Margriet. "Encouraging Lay People to Read the Bible in the French Vernaculars: New Groups of Readers and Textual Communities." *CHRC* 93 (2013): 239–274.
Hult, David F. "The *Roman de la Rose*, Christine de Pizan, and the *querelle des femmes*." In *The Cambridge Companion to Medieval Women's Writing*, edited by Carolyn Dinshaw and David Wallace, 184–194. New York: Cambridge University Press, 2003.
Kennedy, Angus. "Christine de Pizan, Orléans, and Burgundy." *MAe* 88 (2019): 134–139.
Luxon, Thomas H. *Literal Figures: Puritan Allegory and the Reformation Crisis of Representation*. Chicago: University of Chicago Press, 1995.
Nicholas of Lyra. *Postilla of Nicholas of Lyra on the Song of Songs*, edited and translated by James G. Kiecker. Milwaukie: Marquette University Press, 1998.
Ocker, Christopher. *Biblical Poetics Before Humanism and Reformation*. Cambridge: Cambridge University Press, 2002.
Ocker, Christopher. "Hebrew Idiom and Figurative Reading between Theodolf of Orléans and the Victorines: An Unstable Textuality." In *From Theodulf to Rashi: Texts, Techniques, and Transfer in Western European Exegesis (650–1100)*, edited by Johannes Heil, Hanna Liss, and Sumi Shimahara, 297–349. Leiden: Brill, 2021.
Ocker, Christopher. *Hybrid Reformations*. Cambridge: Cambridge University Press, forthcoming.
Ocker, Christopher. *Johannes Klenkok: A Friar's Life*. Philadelphia: American Philosophical Society, 1992.
Ocker, Christopher. "The Fourfold Sense." In vol. 9 of *Encyclopedia of the Bible and Its Reception*, edited by Dale Allison, Jr., Volker Leppin, Choon-Leong Seow, Hermann Spieckermann, Barry Dov Walfish, and Eric Ziolkowski, 551–556. Berlin: de Gruyter, 2014.
Ocker, Christopher. "Typology." In *Oxford Guide to the Historical Reception of Augustine*, edited by Willemien Otten and Karla Pollmann, 1342–1348. Oxford: Oxford University Press, 2013.
Ocker, Christopher, and Kevin Madigan. "After Beryl Smalley: Thirty Years of Medieval Exegesis." *JBRec* 2 (2015): 87–130.
Pierre d'Ailly. *Descriptio imaginaria visionis de [h]orto S. Scripturae*. Paris: BNF, Arsenal Ms-520, fols. 177–188.

Pierre d'Ailly. *Expositio super Cantica*, fols. 30r–56v. Paris: Antoine Caillaut, 16 September 1483 (GW M31951).

Pierre d'Ailly. *Expositio super Cantica canticorum*. Paris: BNF, Arsenal Ms-520, fols. 188–205.

Pierre d'Ailly. "Le jardin amoureux de l'âme devote" (1402). In Christine de Pizan, *Debate of the Romance of the Rose*, edited and translated by David Hult, 71–83. Chicago: University of Chicago 2010.

Pierre d'Ailly. "Principium in cursu bibliae." In vol. 1 of *Ioannis Gersonii opera omnia*, edited by Louis Ellies Du Pin, 610–617. The Hague: Pierre du Hont, 1728.

Pierre d'Ailly. "Recommendatio sacrae scripturae." In vol. 1 of *Ioannis Gersonii opera omnia*, edited by Louis Ellies Du Pin, 603–610. The Hague: Pierre du Hont, 1728.

Salembier, Louis Joseph. *Petrus de Alliaco*. Lille: J. Lefort, 1886.

Schabel, Chris. "Redating Pierre d'Ailly's Early Writings and Revisiting His Position on the Necessity of the Past and the Future." In *Pierre d'Ailly: Un esprit universel à l'aube du XVe siècle*, edited by Jean-Patrice Boudet, Monica Brînzei, Fabrice Delivré, Hélène Millet, Jacques Verges, and Michel Zink, 61–82. Paris: Académie des Inscriptions et Belles-Lettres 2019.

Shir Ha-Shirim im Perush Rashi, edited by Meir Leibush Malbim. Vilna: Widow and Brothers Romm, 1891.

Stegmüller, Friedrich, and Klaus Reindhardt. *Repertorium Biblicum Medii Aevi*. 11 vols. Madrid: Consejo Superior de Investigaciones Cientificas, 1950–1980.

Wilson, Raymond J., III. "Metaphoric and Metonymic Allegory: Ricoeur, Jakobson, and the Poetry of W.B. Yeats." *AHus* 42 (1994): 219–227.

Lieke Smits
Lovers, Gardens, and Wounds
An Exploration of the Medieval Iconographies of the Song of Songs

The vivid, sensory imagery of the Song of Songs, with its descriptions of the beauty of nature and the appearances of a bride and bridegroom, constitutes a rich sourcebook for artists. In the late medieval Christian West, further inspiration was provided by mystical writing describing a personal love relationship between de human soul and Christ, making ample use of the Song's vocabulary. The richness of the material opens up fruitful avenues for research into the medieval art of bridal mysticism. Yet, in 2003 Bernard McGinn noted that only specialized studies on the topic have been published, while a general overview is lacking.[1] McGinn contrasts this lack with research on the art of late medieval Passion piety, which has resulted in publications providing a general overview such as James H. Marrow's 1979 *Passion Iconography in Northern European Art of the Late Middle Ages and Early Renaissance*.

Almost two decades later, the gap identified by McGinn has unfortunately not been filled. Although the field has progressed with innovative specialized studies, a general overview on medieval iconographic traditions based on the Song is still lacking. It should, however, be noted that images of bridal mysticism are regularly discussed in studies of medieval women's visual culture. The art of German nuns, for example, including many motives related to the Song of Songs, has been studied extensively by Jeffrey F. Hamburger and is central to the exhibition catalogue *Krone und Schleier*.[2] For the Low Countries, Paul Vandenbroeck's *Hooglied* first gave an overview of the art of religious women, placed in their historical context.[3] Moreover, Barbara Baert has regularly discussed the iconology of the Song of Songs from an interdisciplinary approach informed by the visual and anthropological turns.[4] These studies have all contributed to our understanding of the importance of the

---

[1] See McGinn, "On Mysticism & Art."
[2] See Frings and Gerchow, *Krone und Schleier*.
[3] See Vandenbroeck et al., *Hooglied*. Despite its title, *Hooglied* does not specifically focus on the iconography of the Song of Songs.
[4] See Baert, "Je hebt mijn hart verwond"; idem, "Gaze"; idem, *Interruptions and Transitions*.

Note: Parts of this chapter are based on my doctoral dissertation ("Performing Desire") and a short article in Dutch ("Door de ogen").

Song of Songs to late medieval art, and the creativity with which the textual material was visualized and materialized.

The lack of a general overview of the iconography of bridal mysticism, or more broadly of the medieval iconographical traditions based on the Song of Songs, might be explained by its variety and complexity, resulting in difficulties in clearly demarcating the subject matter. The iconography of Passion mysticism, in contract, is easier to identify. It follows the narrative sequence of the Gospel, and the additional, apocryphal narratives gathered in medieval Passion books. Non-narrative meditation images such as Christ as Man of Sorrows, sometimes called *Andachtsbilder*, are clearly recognizable as part of Passion iconography through their subject matter: the suffering body of Christ. The art of bridal mysticism, however, is not so easily defined. Illustrations of the Song of Songs usually do not depict the literal level of the text, and the love dialogue lacks a clear narrative, making narrative image cycles rare. Book illustrations pose little problems when it comes to identification, as they are found next to the text in Bibles and biblical commentaries. However, motifs like floral imagery taken from the Song and found in media like panel paintings do often not straightforwardly refer to, but merely allude to the Canticle. The various exegetical levels on which the Song was explained, such as the literal, mystical, allegorical and Mariological, have moreover resulted in a wide variety of illustrations. This heterogeneity of the images and the ways they relate to the text of the Song makes it difficult to compile and summarize the subject matter.

In this article I will provide a more elaborate overview of the above-sketched visual material, providing a beginning of a systematic inventory of the reception of the Song of Songs in medieval visual culture. Because an exhaustive overview of artworks is not possible within the scope of this article, I will discuss different ways in which medieval images relate to the Song of Songs, beginning with images that have a strong connection to the text, which I call visual exegesis, and ending with artwork that are hardly recognizable as bridal iconography, but can be interpreted within this context. The scope will be limited to Christianity in Western Europe, with a focus on the late medieval period.[5]

---

[5] It should be noted that we also find Jewish artistic interpretations of the Song in this time and region, which will not be discussed here, because they relate to a different exegetical tradition. On the different approaches of Jewish and Christian artists, see Bartal, "Medieval Images."

1 Visual Exegesis

In order to understand the different exegetical levels of the Song that artists have illustrated, it is necessary to start with a brief oversight the medieval commentary tradition.[6] Building on the interpretations of the Song by Origen of Alexandria (ca. 185–252), most medieval commentators operated on two levels of exegesis. Foremost, the Song of Songs could be read allegorically, as the love relationship between God or Christ and the Church. In the second, tropological or moral interpretation, the bride personified the human soul, making it a text about mystical desire for union with the divine.[7] The Cistercian abbot and mystic Bernard of Clairvaux (ca. 1090–1153) elaborated on the tropological meaning in his eighty-six *Sermons on the Song of Songs*. These are seen as a foundation of bridal mysticism, a tradition that had appeal beyond the male monastic context, and reached religious women and laypeople.[8] In Bernard's and other medieval commentaries, for example by the Benedictine Rupert of Deutz (ca. 1075–1130), the bride not only personified the human soul and the Church, but also Mary, emphasizing her role in the Incarnation.[9] These identifications were not mutually exclusive, but could overlap.

Images visualizing the allegorical interpretation can be found in Bibles and commentaries, where the Song of Songs is usually not accompanied by elaborate image cycles. Illustrations are most often found in the opening initial of the Song's first verse[10]: the "O" of *Osculetur me osculo oris sui* ("Let him kiss me with the kiss of his mouth").[11] While the mystical interpretation of the Song gained popularity in the twelfth century, in the initials the identification of bridegroom and bride with Christ and Ecclesia remained prevalent. We can see them exchanging affective gestures like a kiss, embrace, or chin chuck (Figure 1), or seated next to each other on heavenly thrones.[12] Ecclesia can be recognized by her attributes, such as an aureole, banner, chalice, church building, or an architectural crown. Sometimes

---

[6] On the medieval exegetical tradition, see Ohly, *Hohelied-Studien*; Riedlinger, *Makellosigkeit*; Herde, *Hohelied*; Matter, *Voice*; Astell, *Song*; Turner, *Eros and Allegory*.
[7] The literal and anagogical meanings of the text received little attention. On the apocalyptic interpretation of the Song of Songs, see Matter, "Love Song." On a fifteenth-century Italian manuscript with rare literal illustrations including gazelles and stags on a mountain (Song 2:9: "My beloved is like a gazelle or a young stag"), see Hamburger, "Cantique."
[8] See Gregory, *Marrying Jesus*.
[9] On Mary and the Song of Songs, see Fulton, *From Judgment*.
[10] In the Hebrew text and English translations this is Song 1:2; the Vulgate leaves out the superscription and thus counts differently.
[11] Wechsler, "Change"; Malaise, "L'iconographie biblique." English Bible quotations in this chapter are from the Douay-Rheims edition.
[12] The chin chuck is described in Steinberg, "Metaphors," 281.

she is depicted alone, without her bridegroom, or both Christ and the Synagogue are present. As identified by Judith Glatzer Wechsler, the mid-twelfth century saw the rise of a new iconographical type: an initial "O" with Mary and the Christ Child on her lap, sometimes exchanging affective gestures.[13] This can be understood within the context of Mariological commentaries. In addition to the initials, we can also find miniatures illustrating the Song of Songs. In these cases we also find depictions of the literal level of the Song: King Solomon, who was thought to be the writer of the love dialogue, with his bride, the Shulamite or Queen of Sheba. In some of these miniatures she is a black woman, in accordance with Song 1:5 (Vulg. 1:4): "I am black but beautiful, O ye daughters of Jerusalem, as the tents of Cedar, as the curtains of Solomon."[14]

Figure 1: Initial "O" with bride and bridegroom as Christ and Ecclesia in a Bible from the second half of the twelfth century. Paris, BnF, MS Lat. 16745, fol. 112v (detail).

---

13 See Wechsler, "Change."
14 See Bindman and Gates, *Image*, 66, 159.

Image cycles with visual exegesis can be found in biblical picture books.[15] An example is the so-called *Bible moralisée*, a type of book originally developed for the early thirteenth-century French court.[16] Each page contains short text passages: biblical verses followed by a short moralizing commentary. The majority of the page is reserved for eight medallions containing illuminations, giving visual interpretations of the text. Each time, the biblical text and its accompanying illustration is followed by a moralizing interpretation in both text and image. In *Bibles moralisées* the Song of Songs takes up no less than 26 folios. In one manuscript, for example, we see a roundel with the youthful bride and bridegroom accompanied by two female companions, next to the text "Draw me: we will run after thee to the odor of thy ointments" (Song 1:3 [Engl. 1:4]; Figure 2). In the roundel below their places have been taken, typologically, by Ecclesia, with aureole, crown, and chalice, and Christ, bearded and with cruciform nimbus. In the accompanying text, Ecclesia asks Christ to help her in her ascent to heaven. It has been argued that the books were intended to prompt private discussion about meanings and connections between their reader-viewers, putting their exegetical knowledge into practice.[17] Thus, the images would not only offer visual exegesis, but can be seen as visual aids in the active performance of exegesis by the readers-viewers themselves.

A similar system of visual exegesis can be found in the *Biblia pauperum*. This type of biblical picture book has its origin in the thirteenth-century monastic milieu, in Bavaria or Austria. The Gospel is central, and Old Testament scenes are only depicted as typological precedents of events from Jesus' life. In the characteristic tripartite lay-out that became standard in the fourteenth and fifteenth centuries, the main event is pictured in the middle, with two supporting scenes at the sides.[18] The various text blocks identify the scenes and explain the typological connections. In a blockbook version of the *Biblia pauperum*, a scene from the Song of Songs is found on a page with Three Women at the Tomb as central image (Figure 3). To the left we see Ruben at the well and to the right the bride seeking her beloved, with a banderol citing Song 3:1: "I sought him, and found him not." Just as with the *Bible moralisée*, the reader-viewer is expected to reflect on the connections between the images. Rather than giving an allegorical interpretation, the Song of Songs is presented as foreshadowing of the events of the Passion.

---

15 On methods of visual exegesis in the Middle Ages, see Esmeijer, *Divina Quaternitas*.
16 On the *Bible moralisée*, see Lowden, *Making*; Haussherr, *Bible moralisée*.
17 See Lowden, "Reading," 515–516.
18 See Henry, "Iconography."

Figure 2: Two roundels with bride and bridegroom and Ecclesia and Christ in a *Bible moralisée*, ca. 1230–1250. Paris, BnF, MS Lat. 11560, fol. 67v (detail).

A picture book completely devoted to the Song of Songs is the so-called blockbook *Canticum Canticorum*.[19] Is was produced in the Southern Low Countries around 1465, possibly for a readership of religious women.[20] Each of the sixteen

---

19 See Meertens and Delen, *Canticum* (including a facsimile); Petev, "Typology and Format"; Aronberg Lavin, "New Allegory."
20 See Engammare, "Blockbuch," 320–323.

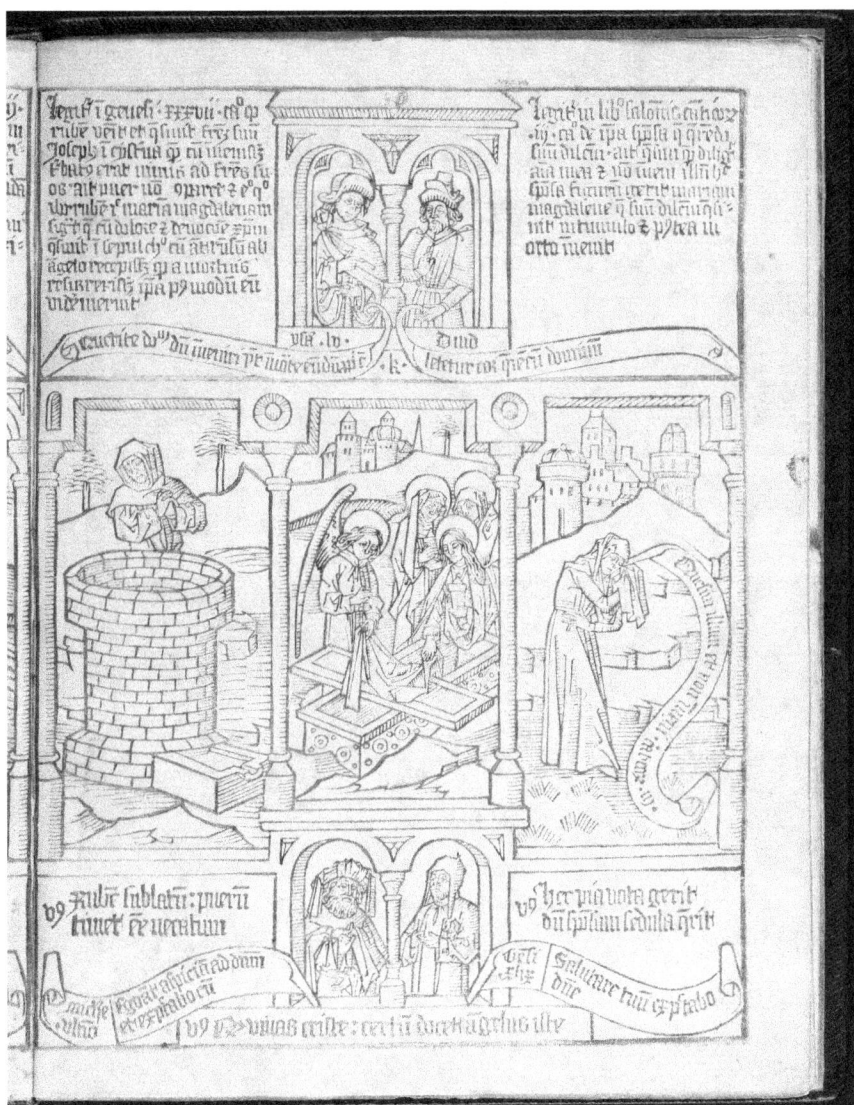

Figure 3: Ruben at the well/the three women at the tomb/the bride seeks the beloved in a blockbook *Biblia pauperum*, ca. 1470. Library of Congress, Rare Book and Special Collections Division, Incun. X .B562.

pages shows two illustrations, containing banderols with quotations and paraphrases from the Song in Latin, which do not follow the sequence of the biblical text (Figure 4). Two editions of the blockbook are known, the second one providing a Middle Dutch title: *Dit is die voorsienicheit van marien der mod' godes En is geheten in latyn cantic* ("This is the providence of Mary, the Mother of God, which

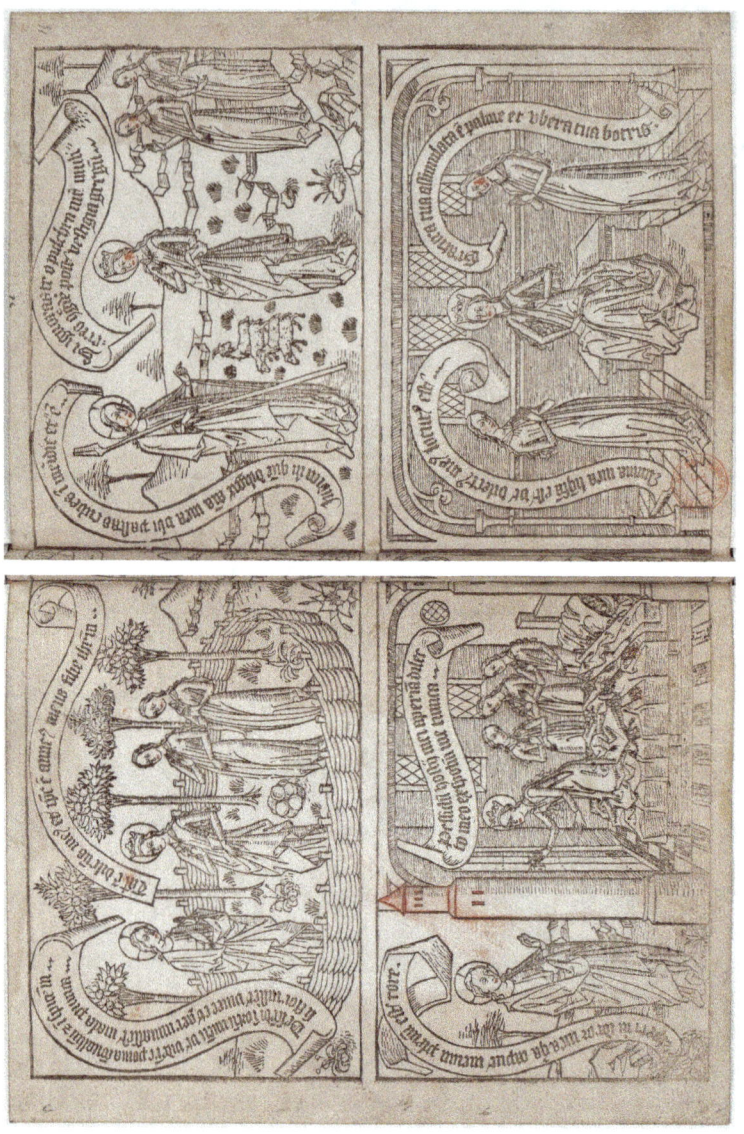

Figure 4: Opening from a blockbook *Canticum Canticorum*, Southern Netherlands, ca. 1465. Paris, BnF, Rés. XYLO-27, fols. 7v–8r.

is called in Latin the *Canticum*").[21] As this title indicates, the bride in the blockbook represents Mary, but it should be kept in mind that this does not exclude the possibility of her personifying the Church and human soul at the same time. The Sponsa is consistently depicted with aureole and crown, while the bridegroom has the cruciform halo of Christ. Other than the *Bible moralisée* and *Biblia pauperum*, the blockbook provides no written commentary; the exegesis is purely a visual one. It is more complex and less prescriptive than the two other books, as Todor Petev notes, which makes it an "extremely dense and resonant meditational device which could be used time and again in the course of one's spiritual ascension."[22] The woodcuts in the blockbook show striking similarities with mid-fourteenth-century murals in the Cistercian convent at Chełmno in Poland.[23] A likely explanation is that both compositions are based on a now-lost common source.

2 Horticultural Allusions

Another category of image related to the Song of Songs involve more subtle allusions to the biblical love dialogue in the form of horticultural motives. The Song speaks of fruit and palm trees, vineyards, sweet fruits, lilies, and other fragrant flowers, and an enclosed garden (*hortus conclusus*):

> My sister, my spouse, is a garden enclosed, a garden enclosed, a fountain sealed up. Thy plants are a paradise of pomegranates with the fruits of the orchard. Cypress with spikenard. Spikenard and saffron, sweet cane and cinnamon, with all the trees of Libanus, myrrh and aloes with all the chief perfumes. The fountain of gardens: the well of living waters, which run with a strong stream from Libanus. (Song 4:12–15)

This horticultural imagery was often connected to the virginity of Mary. She was depicted in an enclosed garden with lilies and other flowers, for example at the moment of the Annunciation, but also in depictions of Mary as queen of heaven or blessed mother with the Christ Child, sometimes accompanied by saints or companions (Figure 5).

Horticultural imagery has been interpreted in the context of bridal mysticism by Reindert Falkenburg. In *The Fruit of Devotion*, he studies the presence of fruits and flowers in late medieval paintings of Mary and Child from Flanders. These can, he argues, be connected to the popular "spiritual garden treatises" that made use of

---

21 See Petev, "Typology and Format," 331.
22 Petev, "Typology and Format," 356.
23 See Bartal, "Your Beloved."

Figure 5: *The Little Garden of Paradise*, Upper Rhenish Master, ca. 1410–1420. Städel Museum, Frankfurt am Main, CC BY–SA 4.0 license.

the Song of Songs in order to incite mystical desire. Examples include the late fourteenth-century *Dets dbuec van den palmboeme* ("This is the Book of the Palm Tree"), *Thoofkijn van devotien* ("Garden of Devotion") printed by Gerard Leeu in 1487, and *Die geestlicke boomgaert der vruchten* ("The Spiritual Orchard of Fruits"), printed seven times between 1500 and 1546. The texts focus either on God's pleasure in the virtues of the soul, represented by fruits and flowers, or on cultivating compassion for Christ's suffering.[24] Parallel with these texts, Falkenburg interprets the fruits and flowers as consumptive metaphors that, by bringing to mind the relationship between the soul and God, were meant to incite emotions and prepare the viewer for mystical union.

A similar interpretation can be given of the so-called "enclosed gardens," produced in the early sixteenth century in the Southern Low Countries and Germany.[25] These cabinets are mixed-media objects, containing compositions made up of silk flowers, small statues, seals, pilgrim badges, glass pearls, semi-precious stones, and

---

24 See Falkenburg, *Fruit*, 20–55.
25 See Baert, *Late Mediaval 'Enclosed Gardens'*; Baert et al., "Late Medieval Enclosed Gardens."

Figure 6: *Enclosed Garden with Calvary and Hunt on the Unicorn*, Mechelen, 1510–1520. Museum Hof van Busleyden, Mechelen – foto: Hervé Pigeolet, KIK-IRPA.

relics, among other things (Figure 6). Most of these artifacts would have been made by professional craftsmen, but in some cases they were compiled by monastics who would use them in their devotion.[26] They can be interpreted as paradisical gardens, but also the enclosed garden from the Song of Songs, where the meeting between bride and bridegroom takes place. As Baert argues, these objects invite sensory engagement, but also direct their audience towards interiorization.[27] A different perspective on garden imagery in general and enclosed gardens specifically is offered by Andrea Pearson, who argues that this iconography was highly intertwined with the moralization of human bodies, as it relates to sex, gender, and disability.[28]

These images and objects with horticultural elements cannot unequivocally be interpreted as illustrations of the Song. They also contain references to Paradise, or, for example, to the virtues that were associated with flowers. For those familiar with spiritual garden treatises and other texts of bridal mysticism, they would have

---

26 Some were owned by lay people; see Pearson, "Sensory Piety."
27 See Baert, "Art and Mysticism"; see also Pearson, "Sensory Piety."
28 See Pearson, *Gardens*.

a relation to the Song. As such, they are potent examples of the major but complex influence of the Song of Songs on medieval imagery.

3 Dramatization of the Narrative

Illustrations related to the Song of Songs can also be found in late medieval texts related to bridal mysticism, that develop a dramatized narrative out of the love dialogue. In many of these, the search of the soul for her beloved heavenly bridegroom is central. An example is the literary tradition of the so-called Daughter Zion Allegory, studied extensively by Annette Volfing.[29] The narrative originated in various Latin prose versions, and exists in different German and Middle Dutch versions.[30] In these texts, the soul is personified by the lovesick Daughter Zion, in many ways comparable to the bride of the Canticle, who is assisted by personifications of virtues that mediate between her and the divine bridegroom. Caritas shoots an arrow in Christ's heart, making him fall in love with the soul. An incunable printed by Gheraert Leeu contains seven woodcut illustrations, culminating in Caritas firing her arrow while Oratio collects the blood from his wound (Figure 7). In the closing paragraph the narrator urges the Daughter to carry on Caritas' wounding. The soul wounding her bridegroom refers to Song 4:9: "Thou hast wounded my heart, my sister, my spouse, thou hast wounded my heart with one of thy eyes, and with one hair of thy neck." Thus, the reader is invited to participated in the dramatic narrative by taking on the role of bride.

A striking example that is related to the Daughter Zion Allegory from the German-speaking area is the mystical love dialogue *Christus und die minnende Seele* ("Christ and the Loving Soul"). It is usually accompanied by 20–24 images, either in manuscript or print, and probably originated as an illustrated broadsheet made for Dominican nuns.[31] Each image shows Christ and the loving soul in the guise of a nun or bride. In the first part of the narrative, Christ attempts to free the soul from all worldly manners by mistreating her. Then he starts wooing her, leading to their eventual union. Some of the scenes contain elements that we can recognize from the Song of Songs, such as the bride wounding her beloved with an arrow, and lying

---

[29] See Volfing, "Middle High German Appropriations"; idem, *Daughter*.
[30] Examples include the mid-fifteenth-century verse text *Tochter Sion* by the Franciscan Lambrecht of Regensburg, the Middle Dutch *Vander dochtere van Syon een devoet exercitie*, called the *Devotio Moderna Daughter Zion* by Volfing, printed by Gheraert Leeu, and the so-called *East Middle Dutch Daughter Zion*.
[31] See Gebauer, *Christus*; Volfing, *Daughter*, 171–182; Williams-Krapp, "Bilderbogen-Mystik"; Hamburger, "Visual," 172.

Figure 7: Caritas shoots an arrow at Christ in *Vander dochtere van Syon een devoet exercitie*, Antwerp: Gheraert Leeu, 1492. The Hague, Koninklijke Bibliotheek, 150 B 66, fol. b 4r.

in bed. Other scenes are new. Some seem to relate to contemporary romance, such as Christ wooing the soul by playing the violin (Figure 8). The soul sitting next to a distaff, which Christ forbids her to use because she should devote her time only to him, refers to the life of religious women.[32] Such admonishments are clearly meant as instructions to reader-viewers, and encourage them to imagine themselves in the scenes.

Figure 8: Christ playing the violin for the loving soul, fragment of the broadsheet *Christus und die minnende Seele*, fifteenth century. Bayerische Staatsbibliothek München, Einbl. III,52 f (detail).

The wounding of Christ by the bride or Caritas is a recurring theme in late medieval iconography. It combined bridal mysticism with the popular imagery of Christ's wounds. In a iconographic type called the "Crucifixion by the Virtues," the personification of Caritas or the Sponsa pierces Christ's side.[33] A unique image of the soul wounding Christ is found in a manuscript made around 1300 for a Flemish nun,

---

[32] See Diskant Muir, "Love and Courtship"; Hamburger, *Nuns*, 183.
[33] See Kraft, "Bildallegorie"; Hamburger, "Visual," 170–171. An example of the bride piercing Christ's side can be found in the Regensburg Lectionary from the second half of the thirteenth century (Oxford, Keble College Library, MS 49, fol. 7r).

known as the Rothschild Canticles.[34] The book is a Latin florilegium with biblical, theological, and liturgical excerpts. It contains an elaborate and unique illustration program, with many illuminations that are mystical in nature. In his foundational study of the manuscript and its images, Hamburger points out their mystagogical function: serving as "vehicles of mystical devotion; they 'transport' the reader, structuring experience rather than instructing through the provision of an exemplary model."[35] The wounding of Christ is depicted on fols. 18v and 19r (Figure 9). On fol. 18r the top image represents bride and bridegroom meeting and embracing in the garden. Below, the bride-soul is seated. She is holding a spear and keeps back her veil, as if to free her eyes. The spear transgresses the miniature's frame, and when we look at the opposite page, we can see it is directed at the side wound of the naked Christ, who is depicted as Man of Sorrows with the instruments of his Passion. What we see here is a visualization of Song 4:9. The soul has wounded Christ with her gaze, and has thus gained access to his heart, where mystical union takes place.[36] This can be seen as an invitation to the reader-viewer, to likewise contemplatively look at the image in order to reach mystical depths. The example from the Rothschild Canticles suggests that the Song of Songs did not only influence medieval iconography, but that bridal mysticism also shaped the way of looking at the image of Christ.

4 Desire as Key

The influence of bridal mysticism on the perception of the image of Christ cannot only be deduced from visual, but also from textual evidence. A popular topos in late medieval devotions was that Christ's posture on the cross, with his nodded head and outstretched arms, were an expression of his desire for a kiss and embrace.[37] The

---

34 According to Hamburger, *Rothschild Canticles*, the manuscript was made for a woman, probably a nun or canoness (3), with Flanders and the Rhineland as possible regions of origin (8). Wybren Scheepsma has identified a Dionysian quotation in the manuscript as Middle Dutch, making it plausible that the book was produced, or at least read, in the Low Countries (see Scheepsma, "Filling in," *passim*). On the basis of a prayer that has its origins in a hagiographical text that was unknown outside the abbey of Bergues-Saint-Winnoc in current French Flanders, Barbara Newman argues that the compiler was a monk of this abbey, who may have produced it for a canoness at the local abbey of Saint-Victor (see Newman, "Contemplating the Trinity").
35 Hamburger, *Rothschild Canticles*, 1–2.
36 For interpretations of this image, see Hamburger, *Rothschild Canticles*, 72; Biernoff, *Sight and Embodiment*, 160; Camille, *Medieval Art*, 37–39; Smits, "Wounding," 6–7. On the heart as *locus* of mystical union, see Hamburger, *Nuns*, 101–128. On queer interpretations of the side wound, see Lochrie, "Mystical Acts"; Sauer, "Queer Time."
37 See Lipton, "Sweet Lean"; idem, "Images."

Figure 9: The bride and bridegroom embracing and the bride wounding the bridegroom in the Rothschild Canticles, Flanders, ca. 1300. New Haven, Beinecke Rare Book and Manuscript Library, Yale University, MS 404, fols. 18v–19r.

origins of this idea can be found in visionary literature, where saints and mystics are embraced by the crucified Christ. The earliest known example is a vision by the Benedictine Rupert of Deutz (d. 1129), which he recorded in two commentaries, one of which was on the Song of Songs. He describes how the crucified Christ on the altar in church allowed him to reach him for a kiss and embrace, with mutual desire.[38] A more influential vision was ascribed to Bernard of Clairvaux, although it was only recorded after his death. A witness described how he encountered Bernard praying and lying prostrate in church before the altar, when "a cross with the Crucified on it appeared on the floor in front of him. The most blessed man adored and kissed it with deepest devotion. Then it seemed as if that Majesty, detaching his arms from each side of the cross, embrace the servant of God and drew him to himself."[39] This vision was not only transmitted textually; the *amplexus Bernardi* became a popular type of image.[40] The depictions do not follow the literal text of the vision. Rather than portraying Bernard prostrate and the crucifix lying on the floor, the crucifix is depicted upright, with Bernard kneeling in front of it. This way, the connection with material culture is strengthened, as the impression is created that, as in Rupert's vision, and actual image of the crucifix comes to life.

Probably influenced by such visions, we also find meditations on the Passion that encourage the reader to see in Christ's posture his desire for a kiss and embrace. An elaborate example making use of quotations from the Song is from a twelfth-century text known as the *Meditatio de passione Christi*, likely written by a Cistercian and surviving in a manuscript that belonged to the Carthusians in Diest.[41] The text describes the beauty of the Crucified Christ, from his head to his arms, side, and feet. There is a focus on his wounds, but rather than gruesome evidence of his suffering, they are presented as openings that allow for a dialogue between devotee and crucified, to whom the words of the Song are assigned:

> [Jesus is] sweet in the inclination of the head: for, inclining his head on the cross, [Jesus] seems as if to say to his beloved: "O my beloved! You who so often have desired to enjoy the kiss of my mouth, announcing to me through my companions: Let him kiss me with the kiss of his

---

38 See Meier-Staubach, "Ruperts von Deutz."
39 *Notus est mihi monachus, qui beatum Bernardum abbatem aliquando reperit in ecclesia solum orantem. Qui cum prostratus esset ante altare, apparebat ei quaedam crux cum suo crucifixo super pavimentum, posita coram illo, quam idem vir beatissimus devotissime adorabat, ac deosculabatur. Porro ipsa majestas, separatis brachiis a cornibus crucis, videbatur eumdem Dei famulum amplecti, atque astringere sibi.* Conrad of Eberbach, *Exordium magnum Cisterciense* (Griesser, ed., 102–103; Ward and Savage, trans., 137).
40 See Posset, *"Amplexus Bernardi"* (including a catalogue); France, *Medieval Images*; Diskant Muir, *Saintly Brides*, 91–115.
41 See Brussels, Bibliothèque Royale, MS 5246–5252, fol. 18vb, late twelfth/early thirteenth century.

mouth [Song 1:1; Engl. 1:2], I am ready, I incline my head, I offer my mouth, kiss me however many times it pleases." [. . .] Sweet in the extension of his arms: for, extending his arms to us, he shows that he himself desires our embraces.[42]

For devotees familiar with this text, images of the crucified Christ bearing no visual traces of the Song of Songs could be perceived as representations of the heavenly bridegroom. A similar, more widely read meditation describing Christ from head to feet is Arnulf of Louvain's hymn *Oratio Rhythmica*. Some Middle Dutch versions of the text start with a rubric referencing Bernard's vision, and seem to promise the reader a similar experience:

> Here begins a devout prayer that Saint Bernard made, to mourn the passion of our Lord; and one reads how Saint Bernard once read this prayer out in front of the cross of our Lord. And it was seen that the image detached itself from the cross, and came down and embraced Saint Bernard. And it has been endowed by the Papal Throne with a splendid indulgence.[43]

Two manuscripts from the Low Countries illustrate this text; one with an image of Bernard embracing the feet of the crucifix (Figure 10), and one with an image of a female Augustinian embracing Christ.

In these examples, the reader is instructed to look at images of the crucified Christ, bearing no trace of the imagery of the Song of Songs, through the eyes of the bride. Bridal desire functions as a key to unlock a potential in the images for interaction and animation.

---

[42] *Dulcis in inclinatione capitis: inclinans enim caput in cruce quasi dilecte sue dicere videtur:* "O *dilecta mea, quae tociens desiderasti frui osculo oris mei, nuncians mihi per sodales meos, osculetur me osculo oris sui. Ego paratus sum, caput inclino, os porrigo, osculare quantumlibet vel placet* [. . .]." *Dulcis in extensione brachiorum: extendens enim brachia nobis, insinuat quod amplexus nostros ipse desideret. Meditatio de passione Christi*, edited by Lipton, "Sweet Lean," 1206; translation adapted from ibid., 1182.

[43] "Hier beghint een ynnich gebet dat Sinte Bernaert gemaect heft, mede te bescreyen ons heren passie; ende men leest hoe, in eenre tijt, Sinte Bernaert dit ghebet las voerden cruce ons heren. Ende het waert ghesien, dattet beelde hem vanden cruce loesde, ende gaf hem neder, ende omhelsde Sinte Bernaert. Ende het is vanden Stoele van Roomen met schoenen aflaet beghaeft." Stracke, "Arnulf van Leuven," 410, from Antwerp, Bibliotheek van het Ruusbroecgenootschap, MS 17.

Figure 10: Bernard of Clairvaux embraces the foot of the cross in a Manuscript fragment, Zwolle, ca. 1480. Museum Catharijneconvent, Utrecht, ABM h111 / photo Ruben de Heer.

5 Conclusion

In this article I have presented different ways in which the Song of Songs influenced medieval visual culture. Apart from direct illustrations of the text, we find complex puzzles of visual exegesis, ambiguous allusions to the Song's spiritual garden, illustrations of dramatized narratives influenced by bridal mysticism, and images in which references to the Song are absent, but the perception of which was influenced by bridal desire. This variety and complexity make the influence of the Song of Songs on medieval art a rich subject, but also one that is difficult to define and demarcate. It should also be noted that the types of iconography described here lived on after the Middle Ages. In the devotional art of early modern religious women, many of the medieval themes are creatively expanded and developed.[44] Iconography related to the Song is also found in the art of well-known painters such as Michelangelo and Rembrandt.[45]

In this limited exploration, several recurring themes have come forward. Images related to the Song of Songs could express theological truths, offer tools for exegesis and meditation, and transport the viewer to a mystical space. They could also cross over with images of worldly love, and convey ideas about the human body. Often an active role is preserved for the viewer: as exegete connecting texts and images, or as subject of desire, taking on the role of bride. The love dialogue provided characters, settings, props, and a script with which interactions with Christ could be played out in creative ways.

Bibliography

Aronberg Lavin, Marilyn. "A New Allegory of Divine Love: The Netherlandish Blockbook 'Canticum Canticorum.'" In *Manuscripta Illuminata: Approaches to Understanding Medieval and Renaissance Manuscripts*, edited by Colum Hourihane, 259–274. Princeton: Index of Christian Art, 2014.

Astell, Ann W. *The Song of Songs in the Middle Ages*. Ithaca: Cornell University Press, 1990.

Baert, Barbara. "Art and Mysticism as Horticulture: Late Medieval Enclosed Gardens of the Low Countries in an Interdisciplinary Perspective." In *Art and Mysticism: Interfaces in the Medieval and Modern Periods*, edited by Louise Nelstrop and Helen Appleton, 104–127. London: Routledge, 2018.

Baert, Barbara. "The Gaze in the Garden: Mary Magdalene in *Noli me tangere*." In *Mary Magdalene: Iconographic Studies from the Middle Ages to the Baroque*, edited by Michelle Erhardt and Amy Morris, 189–221. Leiden: Brill, 2012.

---

[44] See Verheggen, *Beelden*; Kilroy-Ewbank, "Love Hurts"; Melion, "Eyes."
[45] See Lavin and Aronberg Lavin, *Liturgy*.

Baert, Barbara. *Interruptions and Transitions: Essays on the Senses in Medieval and Early Modern Visual Culture*. Leiden: Brill, 2019.

Baert, Barbara. "'Je hebt mijn hart verwond': Hooglied in beeld." In *Hooglied: Bijbelse liefde in beeld, woord en klank*, edited by Hans Ausloos and Ignace Bossuyt, 59–105. Leuven: Acco, 2008.

Baert, Barbara. *Late Medieval 'Enclosed Gardens' of the Low Countries: Contributions to Gender and Artistic Expression*. Louvain: Peeters, 2016.

Baert, Barbara, Hannah Iterbeke, and Lieve Watteeuw. "Late Medieval Enclosed Gardens of the Low Countries: Mixed Media, Remnant Art, Récyclage and Gender in the Low Countries (Sixteenth Century Onwards)." In *The Agency of Things in Medieval and Early Modern Art: Materials, Power and Manipulation*, edited by Grażyna Jurkowlaniec, Ika Matyjaszkiewicz, and Zuzanna Sarnecka, 33–47. New York: Routledge, 2017.

Bartal, Ruth. "Medieval Images of 'Sacred Love': Jewish and Christian Perceptions." *Assaph: Studies in Art History* 2 (1996): 93–110.

Bartal, Ruth. "'Where Has Your Beloved Gone?': The Staging of the *Quaerere Deum* on the Murals of the Cistercian Convent at Chełmno." *Word & Image* 16 (2000): 270–289.

Biernoff, Suzannah. *Sight and Embodiment in the Middle Ages*. Basingstoke: Palgrave Macmillan, 2002.

Bindman, David, and Henry Louis Gates, Jr., eds. *The Image of the Black in Western Art the Early Christian Era to the "Age of Discovery": Africans in the Christian Ordinance of the World*. Cambridge, MA: Harvard University Press, 2010.

Camille, Michael. *The Medieval Art of Love: Objects and Subjects of Desire*. London: Laurence King, 1998.

Diskant Muir, Carolyn. "Love and Courtship in the Convent: St. Agnes and the Adult Christ in Two Upper Rhine Manuscripts." *Gesta* 47 (2008): 123–145.

Diskant Muir, Carolyn. *Saintly Brides and Bridegrooms: The Mystic Marriage in Northern Renaissance Art*. Turnhout: Brepols, 2012.

Eberbach, Conrad of. *Exordium magnum Cisterciense, sive: Narratio de initio Cisterciensis Ordinis*, edited by Bruno Griesser. Rome: Editiones Cistercienses, 1961. (Translated by Benedicta Ward and Paul Savage as *The Great Beginning of Cîteaux: A Narrative of the Beginning of the Cistercian Order; The Exordium Magnum of Conrad of Eberbach*, edited by E. Rozanne Elder. Cistercian Fathers Series 72. Collegeville: Cistercian Publication, 2012.)

Engammare, Max. "Das Blockbuch 'Canticum Canticorum': Die erste Serie von Abbildungen des Hohenliedes." In *Blockbücher des Mittelalters: Bilderfolgen als Lektüre*, edited by Gutenberg-Gesellschaft, 319–237. Mainz: Phillip von Zabern, 1991.

Esmeijer, Anna C. *Divina Quaternitas: A Preliminary Study in the Method and Application of Visual Exegesis*. Assen: Van Gorcum, 1978.

Falkenburg, Reindert. *The Fruit of Devotion: Mysticism and the Imagery of Love in Flemish Paintings of the Virgin and Child, 1450–1550*. Amsterdam: Benjamins, 1994.

France, James. *Medieval Images of Saint Bernard of Clairvaux*. Kalamazoo: Cistercian Publications, 2007.

Frings, Jutta, and Jan Gerchow, eds. *Krone und Schleier: Kunst aus mittelalterlichen Frauenklöstern*. Exhibition catalogue. Kunst- und Ausstellungshalle der Bundesrepublik Deutschland, Bonn and Ruhrlandmuseum, Essen. München: Hirmer, 2005.

Fulton, Rachel. *From Judgment to Passion: Devotion to Christ and the Virgin Mary, 800–1200*. New York: Columbia University Press, 2002.

Gebauer, Amy. *"Christus und die minnende Seele": An Analysis of Circulation, Text and Iconography*. Wiesbaden: Reichert Verlag, 2010.

Gregory, Rabia. *Marrying Jesus in Medieval and Early Modern Northern Europe*. Farnham: Ashgate, 2016.

Hamburger, Jeffrey F. "Le Cantique des cantiques: Un rare commentaire illustré dans l'Italie du Quattrocento." *Art de l'enluminure* 59 (2016): 2–59.

Hamburger, Jeffrey F. *Nuns as Artists: The Visual Culture of a Medieval Convent.* Berkeley: University of California Press, 1997.

Hamburger, Jeffrey F. *The Rothschild Canticles: Art and Mysticism in Flanders and the Rhineland circa 1300.* New Haven: Yale University Press, 1990.

Hamburger, Jeffrey F. "The Visual and the Visionary: The Image in Late Medieval Monastic Devotions." *Viator* 20 (1989): 161–182.

Haussherr, Reiner. *Bible moralisée: Prachthandschriften des hohen Mittelalters; Gesammelte Schriften.* Petersberg: Michael Imhof, 2009.

Henry, Avril. "The Iconography of the Forty-Page Blockbook Biblia Pauperum: Form and Meaning." In *Blockbücher des Mittelalters: Bilderfolgen als Lektüre*, edited by Gutenberg-Gesellschaft, 263–288. Mainz: Philip von Zabern, 1991.

Herde, Rosemarie. *Das Hohelied in der lateinischen Literatur des Mittelalters bis zum 12. Jahrhundert.* MBM 3. Centro Italiano di Studi sull'Alto Medioevo: Spoleto, 1968.

Kilroy-Ewbank, Lauren G. "Love Hurts: Mystical Marriage in the Art of New Spain." In *Visualizing Sensuous Suffering and Affective Pain in Early Modern Europe and the Americas*, edited by Heather Graham and Lauren G. Kilroy-Ewbank, 313–357. Leiden: Brill, 2018.

Kraft, Heike. "Die Bildallegorie der Kreuzigung Christi durch die Tugenden." PhD diss., Freie Universität Berlin, 1976.

Lavin, Irving, and Marilyn Aronberg Lavin. *The Liturgy of Love: Images from the Song of Songs in the Art of Cimabue, Michelangelo, and Rembrandt.* Franklin D. Murphy Lectures 14. Lawrence, KS: Spencer Museum of Art, University of Kansas, 2001.

Lipton, Sara. "Images in the World: Reading the Crucifixion." In *Medieval Christianity in Practice*, edited by Miri Rubin, 173–185. Princeton: Princeton University Press, 2009.

Lipton, Sara. "'The Sweet Lean of His Head': Writing about Looking at the Crucifix in the High Middle Ages." *Spec.* 80 (2005): 1172–1207.

Lochrie, Karma. "Mystical Acts, Queer Tendencies." In *Constructing Medieval Sexuality*, edited by Karma Lochrie, Peggy McCracken, and James A. Schultz, 180–200. Minneapolis: University of Minnesota Press, 1997.

Lowden, John. *The Making of the Bibles Moralisées.* 2 vols. University Park: Pennsylvania State University Press, 2000.

Lowden, John. "'Reading' Images and Texts in the *Bibles moralisées*: Images as Exegesis and the Exegesis of Images." In *Reading Images and Texts: Medieval Images and Texts as Forms of Communication; Papers from the Third Utrecht Symposium on Medieval Literacy, Utrecht, 7–9 December 2000*, edited by Mariëlle Hageman and Marco Mostert, 495–525. Turnhout: Brepols, 2005.

Malaise, Isabelle. "L'iconographie biblique du Cantique des cantiques au XIIe siècle." *Scr.* 46 (1992): 67–73.

Marrow, James H. *Passion Iconography in Northern European Art of the Late Middle Ages and Early Renaissance: A Study of the Transformation of Sacred Metaphor into Descriptive Narrative.* Kortrijk: Van Ghemmert, 1979.

Matter, Edith Ann. "The Love Song of the Millennium: Medieval Christian Apocalyptic and the Song of Songs." In *Scrolls of Love: Ruth and the Song of Songs*, edited by Peter S. Hawkins and Lesleigh Cushing Stahlberg, 228–243. New York: Fordham University Press, 2006.

Matter, Edith Ann. *The Voice of My Beloved: The Song of Songs in Western Medieval Christianity.* Philadelphia: University of Pennsylvania Press, 1990.

McGinn, Bernard. "On Mysticism & Art." *Dædalus* 132.2 (2003): 131–134.

Meertens, Maria, and Adrien Jean Joseph Delen. *Canticum Canticorum: Het blokbloek Canticum Canticorum als godsdienstig kunstwerk/Het blokboek Canticum Canticorum als graphisch kunstwerk*. 3 vols. Antwerp: Standaardboekhandel, 1949.

Meier-Staubach, Christel. "Ruperts von Deutz literarische Sendung." In *Aspekte des 12. Jahrhunderts: Freisinger Kolloquium 1998*, edited by Wolfram Haubrichs, Eckart Conrad Lutz, and Gisela Vollmann-Profe, 29–52. Wolfram-Studien 16. Berlin: Schmidt, 2000.

Melion, Walter S. "'Eyes Enlivened and Heart Softened': The Visual Rhetoric of Suffering in Gebedenboek Ruusbroecgenootschap HS 452." In *Visualizing Sensuous Suffering and Affective Pain in Early Modern Europe and the Americas*, edited by Heather Graham and Lauren G. Kilroy-Ewbank, 269–312. Leiden: Brill, 2018.

Newman, Barbara. "Contemplating the Trinity: Text, Image, and the Origins of the Rothschild Canticles." *Gesta* 52 (2013): 133–159.

Ohly, Friedrich. *Hohelied-Studien: Grundzüge einer Geschichte der Hoheliedauslegung des Abendlandes bis um 1200*. Wiesbaden: Steiner, 1958.

Pearson, Andrea. *Gardens of Love and the Limits of Morality in Early Netherlandish Art*. Leiden: Brill, 2019.

Pearson, Andrea. "Sensory Piety as Social Intervention in a Mechelen Besloten Hofje." *Journal of Historians of Netherlandish Art* 9.2 (2017). DOI: 10.5092/jhna.2017.9.2.1.

Petev, Todor. "Typology and Format in the Netherlandish Blockbook *Canticum Canticorum*, ca. 1465." *Visual Resources* 13.3–4 (1998): 331–361.

Posset, Franz. "*Amplexus Bernardi*: The Dissemination of a Cistercian Motif in the Later Middle Ages." *Citeaux* 54 (2003): 251–400.

Riedlinger, Helmut. *Die Makellosigkeit der Kirche in den lateinischen Hoheliedkommentaren des Mittelalters*. BGPhMA 38.3. Münster: Aschendorff, 1958.

Sauer, Michelle M. "Queer Time and Lesbian Temporality in Medieval Women's Encounters with the Side Wound." In *Medieval Futurity: Essays for the Future of a Queer Medieval Studies*, edited by Will Rogers and Christopher Michael Roman, 199–220. Berlin: de Gruyter, 2021.

Scheepsma, Wybren. "Filling in the Blanks: A Middle Dutch Dionysius Quotation and the Origins of the Rothschild Canticles." *MAe* 70 (2001): 278–303.

Smits, Lieke Andrea. "Door de ogen van de bruid: Hooglied en middeleeuwse beeldcultuur." *Transparant* 31.3 (2020): 17–21.

Smits, Lieke Andrea. "Performing Desire: Bridal Mysticism and Medieval Imagery (c. 1100–1500)." PhD diss., Leiden University, 2019.

Smits, Lieke Andrea. "Wounding, Sealing, and Kissing: Bridal Imagery and the Image of Christ." *MAe* 88 (2019): 1–22.

Steinberg, Leo. "Metaphors of Love and Birth in Michelangelo's Pietàs." In *Studies in Erotic Art*, edited by Theodore Bowie and Cornelia V. Christenson, 231–335. New York: Basic Books, 1970.

Stracke, Desideer Adolf. "Arnulf van Leuven O.Cist. versus Gelukz. Hermann Jozef O.Praem." *Ons Geestelijk Erf* 24 (1950): 27–50.

Turner, Denys. *Eros and Allegory: Medieval Exegesis of the Song of Songs*. Kalamazoo: Cistercian Publications, 1995.

Vandenbroeck, Paul, et al. *Hooglied: De beeldwereld van religieuze vrouwen in de Zuidelijke Nederlanden vanaf de 13e eeuw*. Creatrices 1. Brussels: Vereniging voor Tentoonstellingen van het Paleis voor Schone Kunsten, 1994.

Verheggen, Evelyne. *Beelden voor passie en hartstocht: Bid- en devotieprenten in de Noordelijke Nederlanden, 17de en 18de eeuw*. Zutphen: Walburg Pers, 2006.

Volfing, Annette. "Middle High German Appropriations of the Song of Songs: Allegorical Interpretation and Narrative Extrapolation." In *Perspectives on the Song of Songs/Perspektiven der Hoheliedauslegung*, edited by Anselm C. Hagedorn, 294–316. BZAW 346. Berlin: de Gruyter, 2005.

Volfing, Annette. *The Daughter Zion Allegory in Medieval German Religious Writing*. London: Routledge, 2017.

Wechsler, Judith Glatzer. "A Change in the Iconography of the Song of Songs in 12th and 13th Century Latin Bible." In *Texts and Responses: Studies Presented to Nahum N. Glatzer on the Occasion of his Seventieth Birthday by his Students*, edited by Michael A. Fishbane and Paul R. Flohr, 73–93. Leiden: Brill, 1975.

Williams-Krapp, Werner. "Bilderbogen-Mystik: Zu 'Christus und die minnende Seele': Mit Edition der Mainzer Überlieferung." In *Überlieferungsgeschichtliche Editionen und Studien zur deutschen Literatur des Mittelalters: Kurt Ruh zum 75. Geburtstag*, edited by Konrad Kunze, Johannes Gottfried Mayer, and Bernhard Schnell, 350–364. Tübingen: de Gruyter, 1989.

Stefan Gasch
Singing the Song of Songs in the Late Middle Ages and the Renaissance
The Evidence of the Alamire Manuscripts

The Song of Songs is without any doubt one of the most fascinating and maybe most enigmatic books of the Bible. With its figurative language that often appeals to all of the five senses, it is certainly the most poetic. From the very first words (*Osculetur me osculo oris sui*; 1:2 = Vulg. = 1:1[1]) to the last sentence (*fuge dilecte mi et adsimilare capreae hinuloque cervorum super montes aromatum*; 8:14) the reader joins in with the chorus of the daughters of Jerusalem to participate in an intimate dialogue of two lovers praising each other's bodily qualities, thereby creating an erotically charged atmosphere of harmony and yearning.

Although the entry of the text into the history of Christian theology seems to have taken place already in the third century CE, it took centuries before it was established in Christian liturgy. It is noteworthy that the text was not a part of the *proprium missae* where the texts of the Psalms, Gospels or prophetic writings played a more important role, but in the daily Liturgy of the Hours, where the poem was particularly linked with the Feast of the Assumption. Contrary to the tradition of Origen, Alcuin, or Beda Venerabilis, however, in this liturgical setting the text was interpreted in Marian terms, a reading that seems to have solidified by the time of Rupert of Deutz, Honorius of Autun, and Bernard of Clairvaux, after which the indispensable link between the *sponsa* (the bride of the Song) and the Virgin Mary was established.[2]

The increasing emphasis placed on Marian devotion intensified the use of the Song as the basis of a multitude of motets or motet cycles during the fourteenth, fifteenth, and sixteenth centuries. As these texts gained currency in courtly or secular environments and through emerging liturgical customs, this book became one of the most important lyrical sources for composers, whose voluminous output from the fourteenth through the seventeenth centuries does not facilitate an examination of the repertoire, but demands a differentiated consideration of the subject.

Considering the richness of musical settings, it becomes understandable why scholarship has often limited itself to certain subsets of this repertoires, sources, or

---

[1] For the Latin text of the Vulgate, see Beriger et al., *Biblia Sacra Vulgata*, 3:928–947. The Vulgate does not have Song 1:1 (the superscription) and thus counts differently in the first chapter.
[2] See Stenzl, *Der Klang*, 1:22–23.

compositional techniques. Shai Burstyn was one of the first scholars to explore an entire century of polyphonic settings of the *Canticum Canticorum*,[3] while scholars such as Jane Elizabeth Dahlenburg or Remi Chiu concentrated on textual observations, a certain period of time or a particular repertoire.[4] In many cases, however, discussions of polyphonic settings were either embedded in larger contexts, whether the discussion of the genre of the motet as a whole[5] or of the œuvre of an individual composer.[6] Only Jürg Stenzl has taken on the challenge of sketching a detailed picture of the development of the Song of Songs in liturgy (function) and music (meaning) from the ninth through the fifteenth centuries, discussing the complex transmission of the text and its allegorical readings while covering a broad scope of compositions.[7] Stenzl, however, closes his observations with Josquin Desprez' *Ecce tu pulchra es*, the final piece in Petrucci's first print of masses by Josquin,[8] leaving out the expansive polyphonic tradition the *Canticum* was still to enjoy as the sixteenth century unfolded, culminating in such important works as Giovanni Pierluigi da Palestrina's *Canticum* settings.[9]

This is where the following contribution intends to pick up the thread. As it seems unreasonable to attempt to sketch an overview of the development of such settings during the sixteenth century in such a limited space, the following observations concentrate on the group of manuscripts from the scribal workshop of Petrus Imhoff, or Alamire[10] (ca. 1470–1536), a native of Nuremberg in Bavaria, who moved to the Low Countries around 1500 and worked for the Habsburg-Burgundian Court under Philip the Fair, Archduke Charles (later Emperor Charles V), and Margaret of Austria.

Such a choice offers several advantages: due to their date of origin most of the compositions and none of the sources were considered by Stenzl. As the compositions examined cover a spectrum of about sixty years of musical development, they thus offer an expanded perspective on the polyphonic tradition of the *Canticum Canticorum*. Also, the compiling of the musical material (which was usually done in consideration of the recipient) and the inclusion of certain compositions in par-

---

[3] See Burstyn, "Fifteenth-century Polyphonic Settings"; idem, "Power's *Anima mea*"; idem, "Early 15th-Century Polyphonic Settings."
[4] See Dahlenburg, "Motet c. 1580–1630"; Chiu, "Motet Settings"; Thomas, "Devotional Love."
[5] See Cumming, *Motet in the Age of Du Fay*.
[6] See Higgins, "Love and Death."
[7] See Stenzl, *Der Klang*.
[8] Josquin Desprez, *Liber primus Missarum Josquin* (Venice: Ottaviano Petrucci, 1502).
[9] Giovanni Pierluigi da Palestrina, *Motettorum quinque vocibus liber quartus* (Rome: Alessandro Gardano, 1583/1584).
[10] The name A-La-Mi-Re is a pseudonym. It refers to the usual name for the tone A, which, in the three hexachords on C, F, and G had the solmization syllables for this tone: "la," "mi," and "re."

ticular manuscripts should allow statements with regard to the intended meaning and function of the musical pieces. This is especially significant because a change in the perception and function of these texts can be observed during this period. This, to my opinion, becomes particularly evident in the transformation of these texts to polyphonic music: until far into the fifteenth century settings of the Song of Songs had been motivated primarily by a practical use in the liturgy. From the last quarter of the fifteenth century onwards, however, polyphonic works on this textual basis were granted more and more space also in private devotion. Due to the ever-flourishing devotion to the Virgin Mary, the once liturgical texts and melodies were freed bit by bit from the constraints of the church. The broad community of believers adopted them and developed them into new forms that were suitable for lay veneration.

The group of Alamire manuscripts thereby is a selection of sources, which was only available to a wealthy upper class and thus also reflects the (religious) practices of this class. Due to their specificity in terms of repertoire, geography, and audience these sources also contributed to the formation of the musical canon of the time and, not least, show certain coherence due to the continuity of the scribal workshop. The compositions within this group can thus be considered as *pars pro toto*: they exemplify a new understanding of the text, which emerges around 1500 and they document the different types of text setting available (as motet, as motet-chanson, as devotional prayer, as liturgical music in the broadest sense).

1 The Song of Songs in the Alamire Manuscripts

The complete group of surviving calligraphic music manuscripts, most of which were prepared under the supervision of Petrus Alamire (ca. 1470–1543), encompasses more than 60 beautifully illuminated music manuscripts.[11] Those manuscripts—47 choirbooks and sets of partbooks, as well as 14 sets of detached leaves and fragments—were prepared for a small group of European rulers such as Charles V, Margaret of Austria, Emperor Maximilian I, Frederick the Wise of Saxony, Pope Leo X, or Henry VIII, but also on commission from brotherhoods, churches, or such wealthy patrons as the Fugger family of Augsburg. With over 600 polyphonic masses, motets, and secular works from between 1480 and 1535 these sources provide a substantial part of the contemporary repertoire of Franco-Flemish polyphony.

---

11 For digital high-resolution reproductions for most of the manuscripts, see the *Integrated Database for Early Music* of the Alamire Foundation: https://idemdatabase.org.

Not all of the more than 50 manuscripts of the scribal workshop contain works on texts of the Song of Songs (see the Appendix on pp. 306–308): the large group of choirbooks (nos. 3–8, 10, 12–15) stands out in particular. Most of them, however, will be left aside as they do not transmit motets, but—with regard to Song of Songs settings—either Pierre de la Rue's five-voice mass on the monophonic antiphon *Ista est speciosa*,[12] or so-called parody masses, i.e., masses that are based on existing polyphonic compositions, by Lupus Hellinck or Noel Bauldeweyn. As unexplored as the topic of (parody) masses on texts from the Song of Songs is, it is a subject of research in its own right and therefore shall not be considered in the following.[13]

To concentrate on polyphonic settings of the Song of Songs thus means to focus on the compositions transmitted in the two choirbooks Brussels, MS 9126 and London, MS Royal 8.G.vii; the two chansonniers Florence, MS Basevi 2439 and Brussels, MS 228; as well as in the two sets of partbooks Vienna, Mus.Hs. 15941 and Vatican, MS Pal. lat. 1976–1979. Notwithstanding the small number of only six manuscripts, the 13 compositions under discussion offer a broad spectrum of musical practices of the time, may it be liturgy, piety, or private devotion.

2 A Repertoire for Representation: Settings of *Anima mea liquefacta est* (Song 5:6–8) and *Osculetur me* (Song 1:2 = Vulg. 1:1)

A first look at the Song of Song compositions in the Habsburg-Burgundian court complex reveals that Pierre de la Rue—"court composer" to Margaret of Austria, long-time singer in her court chapel, and by far the most well-represented composer in all the manuscripts of this scriptorium—is only represented by his *Missa Ista est speciosa*. This mass would have been suitable for many of the numerous

---

[12] La Rue's mass is included in the seven Alamire manuscripts shown in Table 1, but is missing in any sources outside the Habsburg-Burgundian circle.
[13] This gap in research has yet to be addressed. Among the masses to be researched belong (apart from the already mentioned masses) works by composers such as Arnold de Lantins (*Missa O pulcherrima*), Pierre de Manchicourt (*Missa Ego flos campi*; *Missa Quo abiit dilectus tuus*), Dominique Phinot (*Missa Quam pulchra es*), Giovanni Pierluigi da Palestrina (*Missa Nigra sum*; *Missa Sicut lilium inter spinas*), Clemens non Papa (*Missa Nigra sum*), Cristóbal de Morales (*Missa Vulnerasti cor meum*), Matthieu Gascongne (*Missa Nigra sum*) as well as anonymously transmitted compositions in Dresden, MS Grimma 56 (*Missa Ego flos campi*), Munich, Mus.ms. 65 (*Missa Vulnerasti cor meum*), or Prague, MS 59 R 5117 (*Missa Vulnerasti cor meum*).

devotional services of the Virgin Mary and is his only polyphonic work, which is based on a monophonic antiphon.

In contrast, the following distribution of passages from the Song of Song emerges (Table 1):

Table 1: Motets based on the Song of Songs in the Habsburg-Burgundian Court Manuscripts.

Text incipit	Number of works (composer)
Anima mea liquefacta est (Song 5:6–8)	4 (Isaac, Ghiselin, Weerbeke, Compère)
Tota pulchra es (Song 4:7)	3 (2 anon., Agricola)
Descendi in hortum (Song 6:11)	2 (Josquin?, de Orto) + 1 (anon.) as 2.p. of *O pulcherrima mulierum* (Févin?)
Osculetur me (Song 1:2)	2 (Barbireau, Gascongne)
O pulcherrima mulierum (Song 5:9 / 5:17)	1 (Févin?) + 1 (anon.) as 2.p. of *Tota pulchra es* (anon.)
Quam pulchra es (Song 7:7)	1 (Bauldeweyn)
Veni dilecte mi (Song 7:12)	1 (Bauldeweyn) as 2.p. of *Quam pulchra es*

That *Anima mea liquefacta est* is represented by such a high number of settings should come as no surprise.[14] The antiphon was an integral part of the Liturgy of the Hours for Marian and virgin feasts and initially served as an antiphon for Benedictus (Lauds) and Magnificat (Vespers) before becoming an independent Marian votive antiphon. The extensive distribution and popularity of this relatively long antiphon (at 39 words), which had been integrated into Office cycles for the Feast of the Nativity of Mary since the eleventh century,[15] is probably due to the dramatic nature of the text (Song 5:6–8), which thematises the plight of a woman separated from her lover. Finding herself alone in the middle of the night, she begins to search for her beloved in the city, but she is only found by the guards who beat her, wound her, and take away her cloak. In a final outcry she beseeches the daughters of Jerusalem to tell the lover that she is languishing with love.

---

14 See the detailed analysis in Stenzl, *Der Klang*, 1:49–52.
15 Stenzl, *Der Klang*, 1:45–48.

The dramatic content[16] is vividly staged in the melodic style of the monophonic antiphon, which is characterised by the choice of mode of the plainchant (authentic on *g*) and its structural components such as the wide ambitus, intervallic leaps of a fourth, a fifth or even a seventh (at "filiae Jerusalem"), and rich melismas.[17]

The passionate text as well as the musical qualities of this antiphon could explain the fascination that it held for composers and the inclusion of their settings in the manuscripts under discussion. In our context, two of the sources are worthy of attention in several respects. Although the two manuscripts differ in format and were produced at different times, both were designed as chansonniers and both were intended for women: Florence, MS Basevi 2439 for an unknown member of the Agostini Ciardi family of Siena, and Brussels, MS 228 for Margaret of Austria, Governor of the Habsburg Netherlands and daughter of Emperor Maximilian I.[18]

Both sources are also among the most extensive chansonniers of the early sixteenth century and represent important documents for music at the beginning of this century. While the Basevi manuscript was produced in an Italian oblong format, reflecting the first polyphonic prints of Ottaviano Petrucci,[19] Margaret's chansonnier, prepared about ten years later and sumptuously decorated, reflects her musical taste at the court in Mechelen and compiles settings connected to Margaret's family.[20]

In both manuscripts the works are divided into three-part and four-part compositions and both manuscripts share a similar orientation with regard to the Song of Songs repertoire: they both include Loyset Compère's (ca. 1445–1516) *Plaine d'ennuy / Anima mea*; and a (different) motet on *Anima mea liquefacta est*: in Flor-

---

16 Compared to the Vulgate version, the text of the antiphon exhibits minimal changes in 5:6 and 5:7, whereas the acclamation *adiuro vos* in 5:8 was left out.

17 See Stenzl, *Der Klang*, 2:14.

18 The earlier of the two manuscripts, Florence, MS Basevi 2439, with a date of origin between 1505 and 1508, is one of the earliest manuscripts of the Habsburg-Burgundian workshop. The manuscript was produced by scribe B, at a time when Petrus Alamire had not yet taken over the workshop. All manuscripts prepared by or under the direction of "scribe B" were copied before 1510: Brussels, MS 9126; Jena, MS 22; Oxford, MS Ashmole 831; Verona, MS 756; Vatican, Biblioteca Apostolica Vaticana, MS Chigi C.VIII.234 (Chigi Codex); and Vienna, Cod. 1783. For the development of the scribal workshop and the individual manuscripts, see Kellman, *Treasury*.

19 See Kellman, *Treasury*, 78–79.

20 As the manuscript is not mentioned in an inventory of Margaret's library from 1516, but is listed in a later inventory from 1523, the chansonnier was probably completed at some time before 1523. The inclusion of the mourning motet *Proch dolor* for Margaret's father, who had died in 1519, could point to a date of origin around 1520. See Kellman, *Treasury*, 69.

ence, MS Basevi 2439 a setting by Johannes Ghiselin (Verbonnet) (ca. 1460–after 1507) and in Brussels, MS 228 a setting by Gaspar van Weerbeke (ca. 1445–after 1516). As an additional piece, the Florentine manuscript transmits Alexander Agricola's (ca. 1445/1446–1506) *Belles sur toutes / Tota pulchra es.*

The works of Compère and Agricola belong to the group of so-called motet-chansons, a subgenre of chanson whose popularity peaked during the last quarter of the fifteenth century. Such works, usually for three voices, perform a secular French text in the two upper voices and are built on a Latin monophonic melody (in these cases of liturgical antiphons), which is presented in the lower voice.

While the French text of the upper voices in Agricola's *Belles sur toutes / Tota pulchra es* reflects on Song 4:7 (*Tota pulchra es amica mea, et macula non est in te*),[21] the relationship between the two texts in Compères *Plaine d'ennuy de longue main / Anima mea liquefacta est* is more complex and less apparent.[22]

Text in discantus and tenor	Text in bassus
Plaine d'ennuy de longue main actainte de desplaisir en vie langoureuse, Dis a par moy que seroy bien heureuse Se par la mort estoit ma vie estainte.	*Anima mea liquefacta est. Filiae Jerusalem, nuntiate dilecto meo quia amore langueo.*
Ne pensez pas que le dye par fainte Car sans cela me tiendray maleureuse Plaine dennuy de longue main actainte Se desplaisir en vie langoureuse.	
Sans dieu ne puis venir a mon attainte Auquel je fais pryere douloureuse De non me voir en forme rigoureuse Se je demeure a tousjours de noir tainte.	

Compère uses an abbreviated version of Song 5:6–8 by employing the first four words of v. 6 and v. 8 in its entirety. The misfortune of the beloved is set against the grieving text of the *rondeau quatrain* of the two upper voices (a topos in chanson poetry of the time). Unusually, the singer of this text is not an unhappy courtier, who searches in vain for his absent lady, but the grieving lady herself. This becomes clear in the second stanza where she prays painfully ("pryere douloureuse") to God (thereby ren-

---

21 See Agricola, *Opera omnia*, 4:52–53.
22 See Finscher, *Loyset Compère*. Compère's setting is also included in Margaret's other chansonnier, Brussels, MS 11239, fols. 27v–29r. A modern edition of the motet can be found in Compère, *Opera omnia*, 5:6.

dering the motet-chanson a devotional composition) and states that she will "remain as the black coloured woman" ("Se je demeure tousjours de noir tainte").[23]

Compère's setting seems to be connected with another work found in the same manuscript: Gaspar van Weerbeke's *Anima mea liquefacta est*.[24] As Ludwig Finscher and Martin Picker have argued, Compère employs in his tenor the opening and closing sections of essentially the same melody (transposed down a fourth) that Weerbeke uses in the tenor of his motet.[25] It cannot be ruled out that Compère borrowed his material directly from Weerbeke, but since both composers were fellow singers at the Sforza court in Milan in the 1470s, it is also possible that they both relied on "a common chant source which is no longer extant."[26] Although both compositions were included in Brussels, MS 228, they were notated in different sections of the manuscript and the compiler of Margaret's music book might not have been aware of the relationship between the two compositions.

Weerbeke's *Anima mea liquefacta est* as well as Johannes Ghiselin's three-voice setting of the same text in Florence, MS Basevi 2439[27] again provide evidence for the broad popularity of this text. Both composers set an abbreviated version of the text to music, leaving out the last verse; both pieces are typical for the Latin compositions of "song-motets," which were often included in chansonniers; neither work is polytextual (which underlines their devotional character); and neither one is based on a monophonic cantus firmus, which normally assigns them a function outside the liturgy. The two compositions can thus be seen as exemplary for this genre:[28] unlike chansons they are fully texted with one Latin text, they are imitative but with sections of homophonic and syllabic text treatment in addition to fermatas that structure the text (Weerbeke more rigorously structures the text by means of caesuras, cadences, and general rests, but both Ghiselin and Weerbeke make a homophonic halt at *vocavi* to illustrate the unanswered call for the beloved); both also feature a climactic change to triple meter at the end of the composition.[29]

---

23 Stenzl assumes that this text section refers to Song 1:5 (Vulg. 1:4; *Nigra sum*). See Stenzl, *Der Klang*, 1:221.

24 For a modern edition of this motet, see Weerbeke, *Collected Works*, 3:7–9.

25 Compère's contra corresponds at measures 5–11 to measures 6–13 of Weerbeke's tenor, and at measures 15–38 with Weerbeke's measures 56–72. See Finscher, *Loyset Compère*, 215–217; Picker, *Chanson Albums*, 84.

26 Maniates, "Combinative Techniques," 164.

27 For a modern edition of Ghiselin's *Anima mea liquefacta*, see Ghiselin-Verbonnet, *Collected Works*, 1:6–8.

28 This term, used by modern scholarship, is problematic since it is applied to a wide range of music from the fifteenth and sixteenth centuries, usually describing compositions for three voices often included in secular sources.

29 See Meconi, "Sacred Tricinia," 165–166.

Song-motets, many of which address the Virgin Mary, thus demonstrate their multifaceted function between official liturgy and private devotion and offer insights into the devotional culture that continuously flourished in the last quarter of the fifteenth century.[30]

When turning from the intimate atmosphere of private devotion in a chansonnier owned by a noblewoman to the formal gift exchange of music books, we find another setting of *Anima mea*: a four-voice motet by Heinrich Isaac (ca. 1450–1517). This work by the court composer of Emperor Maximilian I is transmitted in one of the choirbooks: London, MS Royal 8.G.vii, a manuscript that underwent a shifting process of development. Originally planned for Anne of Brittany and Louis XII, King of France, it was later presented to Henry VIII, King of England, and Katherine of Aragon.[31]

Isaac's composition belongs to the group of pieces included at the very end of the choirbook, which "was clearly compiled according to a plan."[32] Unlike the aforementioned settings, Isaac does not compile different sections from the Song of Songs or alter the text in any other manner. Instead, he sets the entirety of Song 5:6–8 to music and devises a polyphonic setting from the Latin monophonic chant, divided into three sections: *Anima mea—Invenerunt me—Filiae Hierusalem*.[33] Isaac thus chose to emphasise the dramatic situation: in the *prima pars* the beloved describes her nightly routine (her arousal from sleep, her search, her calling out), while the contemptuous treatment of the wandering lover by the guards is set to music in the *secunda pars*, and in the last verse (*tertia pars*) the daughters of Jerusalem are implored from the first-person to report to her beloved that she is lovesick.

Isaac, however, does not employ the typical layout of a tenor motet in which the plainchant is treated in long note values in the tenor. Instead, Isaac treats the monophonic cantus firmus more flexibly and fashions a texture characterised

---

[30] Weerbeke's motet, however, did have a liturgical function as the piece was composed as part of the composer's motet-cycle *Ave, mundi Domina*, which was sung during mass in place of the Offertorium (*loco offertorii*). These cycles, commonly known as *motetti missales* reflect a special liturgical tradition at the Sforza court and were conceived as alternatives to the Mass Ordinary. See Filippi and Pavanello, *Motet Cycles*, as well as the websites http://motetcycles.ch and https://www.gaffurius-codices.ch.
[31] The names of Anne and Louis were entered in red ink in Antoine de Févin's motet *Adiutorium nostrum* (fols. 4v–6r), but erased and replaced by "Katherina" and "Henricus Rex." The manuscript is also illuminated with miniatures and borders in the Ghent-Bruges style, as well as the heraldic emblems of the new recipients (the coats of arms, the Tudor rose, the pomegranate). See Kellman, *Treasury*, 110–111. Honey Meconi reasonably assumes the preparation of the manuscript around 1513. See Meconi, "Another Look," 24.
[32] Kellman, *Treasury*, 110.
[33] For a detailed analysis of the motet, see Kempson, "Motets of Henricus Isaac," 1:156–158. A modern edition can be found in Isaac, *Opera omnia*, 10:32–38.

by syllabic text treatment, imitative counterpoint, and—to emphasise particular passages—repetitions of text and music. Isaac's motet thus clearly makes use of the modern technique of imitation, which is the reason why Emma Kempson has argued that *Anima mea liquefacta est*—along with some other Marian motets (among them Isaac's *Tota pulchra es*, which is not transmitted in manuscripts from the Habsburg-Burgundian workshop)—belongs to the "most elaborate and sophisticated of all of Isaac's chant settings."[34]

The fact that the choirbook was planned to honour and celebrate the English royal couple may explain why Isaac's motet was included in the London choirbook,[35] and why it is accompanied by two other motets on texts from the Song of Songs: after the first gathering, which features motets praying for offspring, comes the first Song of Song motet at the start of the second gathering, *Descendi in ortum meum*. The composer of this piece chooses to use the word *meum* instead of *nucum* (Song 6:10) and to omit the name *Sulamit* (Song 6:12), allowing for a more personal yet neutral perspective.[36] In the second motet, *Tota pulchra es amica mea / Salve—O pulcherrima mulierum / Salve*, the admiration of the lover for the beloved is expressed over an ostinato based on the opening motif from the *Salve, Regina* antiphon, which situates the composition in a pseudo-liturgical context, oscillating between devotion for the heavenly and the earthly queen.[37] Isaac's *Anima mea liquefacta est* finally thematises the desire of a beloved for her lover and thus becomes part of a larger plan to present three Song of Songs motets to the royal couple, each from a different perspective.

The second choirbook from the complex of manuscripts of interest to this investigation is Brussels, MS 9126. Like the Basevi Codex, the choirbook was also prepared by scribe B and was completed between November 1504 and January 1506 for the only son of Emperor Maximilian I, Philip the Fair, and his wife Juana of Castile.[38] Again, the manuscript was precisely tailored to the royal couple. This is evident not only in the book's rich decoration, which includes donor portraits,

---

34 Kempson, "Motets of Henricus Isaac," 148.
35 It is in fact one of the very few motets by the composer to be found in manuscripts from the Alamire scriptorium. The other compositions by Isaac in the Habsburg-Burgundian manuscript complex are *Alma Redemptoris Mater* (Vatican, Cod. Pal. lat. 1976–1979), *Angeli, archangeli throni* (Vatican, MS Chigi C.VIII.234), and *La mi la sol* (Florence, MS Basevi 2439).
36 The composition is attributed to Josquin Desprez only in Vienna, Mus.Hs. 15941, which will be discussed below (see pp. 299–304). Although the manuscript is in generally reliable in terms of attributions, the counterpoint is untypical for Josquin (see Patrick Macey, Jeremy Noble, Jeffrey Dean, and Gustave Reese, art. "Josquin (Lebloitte dit) des Prez").
37 The motet is not available in a modern edition.
38 See Kellman, *Treasury*, 73.

initials, the princely mottos, and Philip's status as Duke of Burgundy and archduke of Austria, but also in the musical repertoire, which—with the exception of works by Josquin—contains compositions by the singer-composers of Philip's chapel designed to fulfil liturgical needs: eight works by Pierre de la Rue (two of which are unica), five works by Alexander Agricola (one unicum), and one motet each by Marbrianus de Orto (ca. 1460–1529) and Jacobus Barbireau (1455–1491).[39] It is not clear, however, how or why Barbireau's *Osculetur me* was included in this manuscript, which was compiled more than ten years after this composer's death.[40] Barbireau was also not a member of Philip's chapel. Nevertheless, he seemed to have had close connections with the Habsburg family: he was sent on a diplomatic mission to Buda in late 1479 and 1480 by Maximilian; in 1488 the Emperor "ordered payment of 70 pounds to Barbireau for the musical education during two years of the son of one of his equerries;" and in January 1490 Queen Beatrix of Hungary and Bohemia called Barbireau a "musicus praestantissimus" and "familiaris" of Maximilian.[41]

Text in discantus, contratenor, and bassus	Song	Text in tenor
1.p.		1.p.
Osculetur me osculo oris sui; quia meliora sunt ubera tua vino.	1:2–3	–
Fragrantia unguentis optimis, oleum effusum nomen tuum;		
ideo adolescentulae dilexerunt te.		
Ego flos campi et lilium convallium.	2:1–2	–
Sicut lilium inter spinas sic amica mea inter filias.	2:6	
Laeva eius sub capite meo, et dextera illius amplexabitur me.		
2.p.		2.p.
Adiuro vos filiae Jerusalem per capreas cervosque camporum,	2:7–9	*Surge*
ne suscitetis neque evigilare faciatis dilectam, quoadusque ipsa velit.		
Vox dilecti mei ecce iste venit saliens in montibus transiliens colles.		
Similis est dilectus meus capreæ, hinnuloque cervorum,		
en ipse stat post parietem nostrum, despiciens per fenestras, prospiciens per cancellos.		
Amen.		

---

39 On the structure of the musical content, see Gasch, "Pierre de la Rues Sieben Freuden," 39–41. Although Josquin was not a member of the chapel, he most likely met La Rue und Agricola in 1501 during the visit of Philip at the French court and in 1503 during the meeting of the rulers in Lyons. See Kellman, *Treasury*, 73.
40 All of Barbireau's other sacred compositions (*Kyrie Pascale, Missa Faulx perversa, Missa Virgo parens Christi*) are also found in the Habsburg-Burgundian manuscript complex. An edition of them can be found in Barbireau, *Opera omnia*, 2:1–7.
41 Kooiman et al., "Biography of Jacob Barbireau," 38, 51.

Unlike Isaac's composition, the text of Barbireau's only known four-part motet is a not a continuous passage from the Song of Songs (for the text, see p. 297), but a compilation from the first two chapters with a closing "Amen" at the end. As with all compiled text settings, this piece too has no original cantus firmus, which is why a new monophonic chant (in the fourth mode) is introduced in the tenor. Brussels, MS 9126 is the only surviving source for the motet, but unfortunately does not provide a text for this tenor melody beyond the single word "Surge" at the beginning of the *secunda pars*, suggesting that the motet was bitextual. The composition itself is composed mainly in free polyphony but with passages of imitation derived from the plainchant melody. Other features, such as motifs based on the rhythmic scansion of words or the rhythmic densification at the end of phrases or sections, heighten the emotional poetry.

The other Song of Songs motet in Brussels, MS 9126 with the text incipit *Osculetur me* is a four-part setting by Matthieu Gascongne, who can be documented around 1517/1518 as a singer and composer at the French royal chapel.[42] The motet is composed in two *partes* and compiles various passages from the first chapter of the Song, the *prima pars* drawing on Song 1:2–4 (Vulg. 1:1–3) and the *secunda pars* using sections from Song 1:5–7 (Vulg. 1:4–6).[43] Differences in the text, however, shows that this antiphon was not as strongly anchored in liturgical tradition as, for example, *Anima mea liquefacta est* and therefore was subject to change or at least to a more flexible textual treatment. The motet—which praises the intimate action of kissing, alluding to the bodily beauty of the lover through the senses of touching, smelling and tasting—was included in the so-called Palatini partbooks (Vatican, MS Pal. lat. 1976–1979), which at first glance seems surprising given the enmity between the House of Habsburg and the French monarch François I. These works, however, "supplemented the exclusively Netherlandish works" and helped to establish a musical canon that would "transform the landscape of the literate musical culture of Renaissance Europe"[44] through the production of lavishly decorated manuscripts.

---

42 An edition of the motet can be found in Willaert, *Opera omnia*, 9:219–225.
43 *Osculetur me osculo oris sui; quia meliora sunt ubera tua vino. Fragrantia unguentis optimis, oleum effusum nomen tuum; ideo adolescentulae dilexerunt te. Trahe me post te curremus in odorem unguentorum tuorum—Nigra sum sed formosa filia Jerusalem quia decoloravit me sol posuerunt me custodem in vineis indica mihi quem diligit animam meam ubi pascas ubi cubes ne vagari incipiam per greges sodalium tuorum.*
44 Anderson, "Palatini Partbooks Revisited," 96.

3 Music for Private Devotion: The Partbook Sets Vienna, Mus.Hs. 15941 and Vatican, MS Pal. lat. 1976–1979

Both Gascongne's motet as well as the aforementioned *Descendi in ortum meum* in the London manuscript finally brings us to the two partbook sets Vienna, Mus.Hs. 15941 and Vatican, MS Pal. lat. 1976–1979. Together with Vienna, Mus.Hs. 18825 (another partbook set which is not relevant to this investigation), these four sources are the only manuscripts in the entire Habsburg-Burgundian complex to compile motets exclusively.

Vienna 15941 and Vatican 1976–1979 are closely related as twelve of the 32 motets contained in Vienna are concordant with the 38 motets in the Vatican partbooks, which were prepared between 1528 and 1534 for Queen Anne, daughter of Louis I of Bohemia and Hungary, and her husband Ferdinand, King of the Romans and brother of Emperor Charles V.[45] Its creation for these recipients is made clear by its musical program organized into four sections,[46] the last of which includes concordances for *Descendi in hortum meum* and Bauldeweyn's *Quam pulchra es*.

Of all the manuscripts in the Habsburg-Burgundian court complex, however, Vienna, Mus.Hs. 15941 transmits the broadest range of works on texts from the Song of Songs, both quantitatively and in terms of text selection (see Table 2). I have shown elsewhere that this manuscript was prepared for Raymund Fugger the Elder for devotional reasons,[47] but only the first 13 of its 32 motets were compiled for Raymund[48] and directly refer to local conditions in Raymund's hometown of Augsburg.

---

[45] See Kellman, *Treasury*, 130–132, 159; Anderson, "Palatini Partbooks Revisited," 94–95. While Kellman proposes Mary of Hungary as the commissioner of the partbooks, Anderson argues that Margaret of Austria would have been a more reasonable candidate.
[46] Nos. 2–7 make reference to the recipients (emphasising Anne); nos. 8–13 honour the Virgin Mary and close with a motet for Christ; nos. 14–23 praise Christ and the Crucifixion and close with a motet for Mary; and nos. 24–37 mix works for Mary and Christ.
[47] See Gasch, "Pierre de la Rue's *Ave, Regina caelorum*." The manuscript is incomplete: only the contratenor, tenor, and bassus partbooks are extant; the discantus part is missing.
[48] I henceforth use the sigla Vienna, Mus.Hs. 15941^{I} and Vienna, Mus.Hs. 15941^{II} to indicate the two sections. That both sections were once independent is evident through the coat of arms of the Fugger family, which is painted in all extant partbooks on fol. 11v (leaving fol. 11r blank in all partbooks), and individualised by the initials "RF" on the red background of the coat of arms. On the *verso* pages of Vienna, Mus.Hs. 15941^{II} (fol. 52v and fol. 50v) on the other hand, blank space has been left in all partbooks for a coat of arms that was never executed. Both sections were indexed separately, with the pieces listed in order of appearance. Moreover, the beginning of the second section starts on a *folium versum* after a *folium rectum* that exhibits signs of frequent use. This may indicate that the *recto* pages (fol. 52r in contratenor and tenor partbooks, fol. 50r in the bassus

Table 2: Contents of Vienna, Mus.Hs. 15941[I+II].

Section	No.	Incipit	Composer
I	1	*In principio erat verbum*	Josquin Desprez
	2	*In exitu Israel*	Josquin Desprez
	3	*Qui habitat in adiutorium*	Josquin Desprez
	4	*Salve, Regina*	Josquin Desprez
	5	*Descendi in ortum meum*	Josquin Desprez?
	6	*Quam pulchra es*	Noel Bauldeweyn
	7	*Celeste beneficium*	Jean Mouton
	8	*Ave, Regina caelorum*	Pierre de La Rue
	9	*Ave, Roche sanctissime*	anon.
	10	*Miseremini mei*	Jean Richafort?
	11	*Tota pulchra es*	anon.
	12	*O florens rosa*	Laurentius de Vourda
II	13	*Ave fuit prima salus*	Jean Mouton
	14	*Gratia plena ipsa*	Ninot le Petit (Jean Mouton?)
	15	*Salve, Mater Salvatoris*	Pierre de La Rue
	16	*Factum est silentium in caelo*	Jean Mouton
	17	*Amicus Dei Nicolaus*	Jean Mouton
	18	*Ave, mundi spes Maria*	Josquin Desprez
	19	*Alma chorus Domini*	Mathurin Forestier
	20	*Laudate Deum in sanctis eius*	Jean Mouton
	21	*Homo quidam fecit cenam*	Antoine de Févin
	22	*Puer natus est nobis*	Jean Mouton
	23	*Deus in adiutorium*	Nicolas Champion
	24	*Gaude Maria virgo*	Pierrequin de Thérache
	25	*Illuminare Jerusalem*	Jean Mouton
	26	*Egregie Christi martyr*	Jean Mouton?
	27	*Descendi in ortum meum*	Marbrianus de Orto
	28	*Nesciens Mater Virgo*	Antoine de Févin
	29	*O pulcherrimum mulierum*	Antoine de Févin?
	30	*Ave caro Christi cara*	Noel Bauldeweyn
	31	*In illo tempore assesserunt*	Jean Mouton
	32	*De profundis clamavi*	Nicolas Champion

The three motets based on the Song of Songs in the manuscript Vienna, Mus.Hs. 15941[I] (nos. 5, 6, and 11) belong to a group of six polyphonic antiphon settings for the veneration of the Virgin Mary. Nearly all of this Marian repertoire corresponds

---

partbook) had been used as covers for the fascicle. In any case, it seems that Vienna, Mus.Hs. 15941[II] was put aside after the music had been copied. The two originally independent sections, however, were bound together before they were sent to Raymund Fugger.

with either the liturgy of the Diocese of Augsburg, or the liturgy at the Augsburg Carmelite monastery of St Anne, to which the Fugger family had made enormous endowments.[49] All of these compositions could thus have been used liturgically in Augsburg. Raymund Fugger, however, possibly perceived the music of his book in a rather different way: the psalm settings could serve as prayers for salvation from diseases and evil, while the texts for St Anne (the patron saint of the monastery where the Fugger family had erected their memorial chapel) and the Virgin had a dual function that could be read not only as prayers of devotion but also as prayers against the plague or the French pox. Facing the possibility of an all-to-early death which such diseases could bring, Raymund Fugger apparently tried to collect musical texts in preparation for his last hour.[50] Vienna, Mus.Hs. 15941^1 thus can be seen as an aural, visual, and haptic book of polyphonic prayers, assembled to fit the personal demands of the commissioner.[51]

All three polyphonic settings (*Descendi in hortum meum*[52] and *Quam pulchra es* by Noel Bauldeweyn, as well as the anonymous *Tota pulchra es*) are suitable for the Feast of the Assumption of Mary and could indeed be performed with organ music during second Vespers.[53] While the first two motets set familiar texts—both were widely used in liturgy for Marian and virgin feasts, *Descendi in hortum* (like *Anima mea liquefacta est*) being an antiphon with a coherent text excerpt, *Quam pulchra es* being a compiled antiphon text established in the twelfth and thirteenth centuries—*Tota pulchra es* is not a motet based on Song 4:7 as it would seem to be. The motet reveals that changes to the repertoire of Vienna, Mus.Hs. 15941^1 were probably made up to the very last stage of compilation: the index of this first section does not mention the motet, and it seems therefore likely that this composition was included

---

49 See Scheller, *Memoria an der Zeitenwende*; Bushart, *Die Fuggerkapelle*.
50 Vienna, Mus.Hs. 15941^1 forms the companion volume to Vienna, Mus.Hs. 18825, which (most likely) was also commissioned by Raymund Fugger and contains music for the Easter season until the Sunday of Ascension.
51 It is not known whether the partbooks were ever used, since there is no documentary evidence that the Fuggers employed a vocal ensemble to perform the music. Nevertheless, all partbooks of Vienna, Mus.Hs. 15941 bear signs of use, such as yellowing and fingerprints at the side and page margins. Besides, at ca. 19 × 27,5 cm the size of the partbooks is quite large and big enough to accommodate a small ensemble singing from it. It is in fact the largest of the manuscripts in comparison to the Basevi codex (16,8 × 24 cm) or the Palatini partbooks (15,8 × 21 cm) discussed above.
52 Vienna, Mus.Hs. 15941 is the only source that attributes the work to Josquin. The *New Josquin Edition* counts the motet as an *opus dubium* among Josquin's works on stylistic grounds. See Josquin Desprez, *New Edition of the Collected Works*, 14:27.
53 Evidence for this can be found in Munich, University Library, MS 4° Cod. ms. 170, one of several organ books of the family's organist Bernhard Rem. *Quam pulchra es* and *Descendi in hortum meum* can be found on fol. 88r–v; the antiphon *Tota pulchra es*, which was also used during first Vespers, is on fols. 85r and 87r. None of the motets, however, is available in modern edition.

after the index had been completed (together with the motet *Ave, Roche sanctissime*, which is likewise missing from the index). The inclusion at a late stage in the production process (possibly on the request of Raymund Fugger) can be understood when examining the text, which reveals itself to be a devotional motet in the proper sense:

> Tota pulchra es amica mea
> et macula non est in te.
> O Maria sis pro nobis advocata in hora mortis
> et a peccatis nos protegat
> ut iubilemus perhenniter in celis.

The motet thus further emphasises the musical program of Vienna, Mus.Hs. 15941^{I} with its strong focus on Marian motets. This program expresses the faith of the commissioner, who views the Virgin Mary as the most important intercessor before God, through a free textual expansion of the biblical poem set to music.

In this context, it becomes clear once again how often the vocabulary of these texts, used in the context of Marian worship, gave expression to the fervent nature of devotion to the Virgin Mary as intercessor, Mother of God, and beloved. Adoration of the earthly beloved, whose roots lie in the biblical tradition, thus becomes a transcendental devotion to the heavenly Mother. This has all the more significance for the Fugger family, since family members prayed in their eponymous chapel while standing under their donated organ with two massive organ shutters depicting the risen Christ on one, but the *Assumptio Mariae* on the other.[54] In contrast to most other medieval altarpieces, the patrons were thus not painted in close proximity to biblical scenes, but became even a living part of it.

Vienna, Mus.Hs. 15941^{II} too, greatly favours motets for the Virgin Mary, but with reversed signs: while Vienna, Mus.Hs. 15941^{I} demonstrates a clear preference for works by Josquin[55] with only one motet by Mouton, Vienna, Mus.Hs. 15941^{II} in turn highlights motets by Mouton and includes just one composition by Josquin. Even more interesting is the overall program of this section, which combines works by other French composers (such as Pierrequin de Thérache, Antoine de Févin, or Mathurin Forestier) with pieces by composers who had a close relationship to Margaret of Austria and her court in Mechelen (Pierre de la Rue, Nicolas Champion, Marbrianus de Orto, Noel Bauldeweyn).

---

[54] See Bushart, *Die Fuggerkapelle*, Tafel X–XII.
[55] The Fugger family had a special interest in works by Josquin, which can also be seen in the choirbooks Vienna, Cod. 4809 and Vienna, Mus.Hs. 11778. These manuscripts, which were also prepared in the Habsburg-Burgundian scribal workshop, solely contain masses by Josquin and could have been commissioned by Jakob Fugger ("the rich") for the prestigious and newly endowed family chapel.

De Orto's *Descendi in ortum meum* is a polyphonic setting of Song 6:10 (*prima pars*) and Song 6:12 (*secunda pars*).[56] The text for the short *O pulcherrima mulierum* (45 measures),[57] however, is a free compilation of various textual extracts (*O pulcherrima mulierum | vulnerasti cor meum | soror mea, columba mea*), which are set in imitative counterpoint and delineated from one another by means of cadences and fermatas. This composition thus continues the group of the devotional motets *Tota pulchra es* contained in Vienna, Mus.Hs. 15941^I, and the above-mentioned *Tota pulchra es amica mea | Salve—O pulcherrima mulierum | Salve* in the London manuscript (MS Royal 8.G.vii).

Song	1.p. (Text in discantus and contratenor)	1.p. (Text in tenor and bassus)
4:7	Salve	Tota pulchra es amica mea et macula non est in te.
7:2		Quam pulchri sunt gressus tui,
1:14 / 4:1		oculi tui columbarum
7:6		et comae capitis tui sicut purpura regis.
7:5		Collum tuum sicut turris eburnea.
7:7		Quam pulchra es et quam decora carissima.
4:8		Veni de Libano, veni coronaberis.
Song	2.p. (Text in discantus and contratenor)	2.p. (Text in tenor and bassus)
5:9 / 5:17	O pulcherrima mulierum,	Salve
2:10	surge propera amica mea,	
2:10	columba mea, formosa mea et veni,	
2:14	ostende mihi faciem tuam,	
	sonet vox tua in auribus meis,	
	vox enim tua dulcis est et facies tua decora.	

The text of this motet thus combines two Marian antiphons, and (similar to the anonymous motet for Raymund Fugger in Vienna, Mus.Hs. 15941^I) the *Tota pulchra es* of the lower voices is only a quotation that serves as a reminder of the actual antiphon. This idea of musical remembering is continued in the two upper/lower voices: by singing the characteristic opening motif of the *Salve, Regina* in form of a canonic ostinato, which is used as a substitute for the missing cantus firmus, they immediately evoke the perhaps best-known Marian antiphon.[58] The texts sung by

---

56 De Orto's motet is not available in a modern edition.
57 The motet has been ascribed to various composers. A transcription of the motet is provided in Shine, "Motets of Jean Mouton," 2:644–646.
58 Since the thirteenth century, the four non-biblical antiphons *Alma Redemptoris Mater*, *Ave, Regina caelorum*, *Regina caeli*, and *Salve, Regina* conclude the Liturgy of the Hours. These are the

the non-ostinato voices, however, are no longer based on centuries-old liturgical antiphons from the Song of Songs.[59]

Such free textual compilations are almost without exception typical of the continental approach to this text repertoire.[60] At the beginning of the sixteenth century this repertoire is increasingly adapted to an individual's needs and serves as vivid testimony to the continued ascendancy of Marian devotion that produced countless works of art at this time.

4 Conclusion

Six centuries of theological appropriation, whose central content was to exclude any literal reading and to allegorically identify the Virgin Mary as the *sponsa*, finally led to the inclusion of the erotic texts of the Song of Songs into the Liturgy of the Hours during the ninth century. Because of this Marian reading of the poem, the ever-changing interpretation of the text during the following centuries was always connected with the veneration of Mary and is mirrored in polyphonic settings of the Song of Songs in the Early Modern Period. The contexts—in the present case it is the richly illuminated manuscripts that function as carriers of musical texts—can thereby contribute to an understanding of this changing approach to the biblical text and its use in daily practices.

The repertoire of Song of Song motets in the Alamire manuscripts thus vividly illustrates the coexistence of liturgy and Marian devotion and uncovers the role of the music as the intermediary element between the sacred and the secular: while the Marian antiphons were still used in liturgy at the end of the fifteenth century, in private Marian devotion the selection of texts from the Song of Songs no longer follows liturgical practice but increasingly detaches itself from the liturgy as polyphonic cantica antiphons. This is exactly, why the manifold polyphonic appearances of the Song of Songs contained in the Alamire manuscripts—as (para-)liturgical music, as votive antiphons used for private devotion, as private chamber music of mourning, as items which could replace elements of the mass ordinary—are

---

most important Marian antiphons, which were set to music in countless motets (mostly on the basis of their monophonic cantus firmi). In the course of the fifteenth century, a special singing tradition developed for the *Salve*. During these *Salve* services, which formed part of daily devotion from the early fifteenth century onwards, the *Salve, Regina* was sung together with many other devotions in honour the Virgin Mary.

59 There is evidence of a tradition for the antiphon text of the *secunda pars*, which has been known since the second third of the fifteenth century. See Strohm, *Bruges*, 133.
60 See Stenzl, *Der Klang*, 1:187.

not mere polyphonic settings of Marian antiphons but are individually designed musical texts and prayers which ought to fulfil particular needs.

To discover these needs, the religious backgrounds as well as the sociocultural context behind those compositions is a fascinating task. It means to reveal the contemporary history of the text,[61] which is crucial for the musical history and may help to bring us closer to the answer to the question of whether music can capture the inherent meaning of a text at all.

List of Library Sigla

Brussels, MS 228 = Brussels, Koninklijke Bibliotheek / Bibliothèque royale, MS 228
Brussels, MS 6428 = Brussels, Koninklijke Bibliotheek / Bibliothèque royale, MS 6428
Brussels, MS 9126 = Brussels, Koninklijke Bibliotheek / Bibliothèque royale, MS 9126
Brussels, MS 11239 = Brussels, Koninklijke Bibliotheek / Bibliothèque royale, MS 11239
Brussels, MS 15075 = Brussels, Koninklijke Bibliotheek / Bibliothèque royale, MS 15075
Dresden, MS Grimma 56 = Dresden, Sächsische Landesbibliothek – Staats- und Universitätsbibliothek Dresden, MS Grimma 56
Florence, MS Basevi 2439 = Florence, Conservatorio di Musica Luigi Cherubini, MS Basevi 2439
's-Hertogenbosch, MS 72B = 's-Hertogenbosch, Archief van de Illustre Lieve Vrouwe Broederschap, MS 72B
Jena, MS 2 = Jena, Universitätsbibliothek, MS 2
Jena, MS 4 = Jena, Universitätsbibliothek, MS 4
Jena, MS 22 = Jena, Universitätsbibliothek, MS 22
London, MS Royal 8.G.vii = London, British Library, MS Royal 8.G.vii
Munich, Mus.ms. 6 = Munich, Bayerische Staatsbibliothek, Mus.ms. 6
Munich, Mus.ms. 65 = Munich, Bayerische Staatsbibliothek, Mus.ms. 65
Oxford, Bodleian Library, MS Ashmole 831
Prague, MS 59 R 5117 = Prague, Národní knihovna České republiky, MS 59 R 5117
Vatican, MS Capp. Sist. 34 = Vatican, Biblioteca Apostolica Vaticana, MS Capp. Sist. 34
Vatican, MS Pal. lat. 1976–79 = Vatican, Biblioteca Apostolica Vaticana, MS Pal. lat. 1976–1979
Verona, Biblioteca Capitolare, MS 756
Vienna, Cod. 1783 = Vienna, Österreichische Nationalbibliothek, Handschriftensammlung, Cod. 1783
Vienna, Cod. 4809 = Vienna, Österreichische Nationalbibliothek, Handschriftensammlung, Cod. 4809
Vienna, Cod. 11883 = Vienna, Österreichische Nationalbibliothek, Handschriftensammlung, Cod. 11883
Vienna, Mus.Hs. 11778 = Vienna, Österreichische Nationalbibliothek, Musiksammlung, Mus.Hs. 11778
Vienna, Mus.Hs. 15497 = Vienna, Österreichische Nationalbibliothek, Musiksammlung, Mus.Hs. 15497
Vienna, Mus.Hs. 15941 = Vienna, Österreichische Nationalbibliothek, Musiksammlung, Mus.Hs. 15941
Vienna, Mus.Hs. 18825 = Vienna, Österreichische Nationalbibliothek, Musiksammlung, Mus.Hs. 18825
Vienna, Mus.Hs. 18832 = Vienna, Österreichische Nationalbibliothek, Musiksammlung, Mus.Hs. 18832

---

61 See Stenzl, *Der Klang*, 1:19.

Appendix

Compositions based on the Song of Songs in the Scribal Workshop of the Habsburg-Burgundian Court

No.	Shelfmark	Time of Origin[62]	Composer	Title	Remarks
1	Brussels, MS 9126	ca. 1505	Jacobus Barbireau	Osculetur me	fols. 174v–177r
2	Florence, MS Basevi 2439	ca. 1505–1508	Loyset Compère	Plaine d'ennuy / Anima mea	fols. 50v–51r
			Alexander Agricola	Belles sur toutes / Tota pulchra es	fols. 63v–64r
			Johannes Ghiselin (Verbonnet)	Anima mea liquefacta est	fols. 92v–94r
3	Brussels, MS 6428	ca. 1512	[Pierre de la Rue]	Missa Ista est speciosa	
4	Jena, MS 2	1512–1525	Pierre de la Rue	Missa Ista est speciosa	
5	Vienna, Mus.Hs. 15497	ca. 1514–1516	[Pierre de la Rue]	Missa Ista est speciosa	
6	Vatican, Capp. Sist. 34	ca. 1515–1516	[Pierre de la Rue]	Missa Ista est speciosa	
7	Jena, MS 4	ca. 1516–1518	Pierre de la Rue	Missa Ista est speciosa	
8	London, MS Royal 8.G.vii	ca. 1516–1522	[Josquin Desprez?]	Descendi in ortum meum	fols. 10v–12r = Vienna, Mus. Hs. 15941 = Vatican, MS Pal. lat. 1976–9
			anon.	Tota pulchra es amica mea / Salve 2.p. O pulcherrima mulierum / Salve	fols. 26v–28r ≠ Vienna, Mus. Hs. 15941
			[Heinrich Isaac]	Anima mea liquefacta est 2.p. Invenerunt me custodes 3.p. Filiae Jerusalem nuntiate dilecto	fols. 59v–62r

---

62 Datings are given according to Kellman, *Treasury*. A name in square brackets indicates, that the name of the composer has been identified via concordant sources.

(continued)

No.	Shelfmark	Time of Origin[62]	Composer	Title	Remarks
9	Brussels, MS 228	ca. 1516–1523	[Gaspar van Weerbeke]	Anima mea liquefacta est	fols. 47v–48r
			[Loyset Compère]	Plaine d'ennuy de longue main / Anima mea	fols. 55v–56r
10	Vienna, Cod. 11883	ca. 1475–1540	[Lupus Hellinck]	Missa Quam pulchra es	
11	Vienna, Mus.Hs. 15941	ca. 1519–1525	[Josquin Desprez?]	Descendi in ortum meum	fols. 29v–31r = London, MS Royal 8.G.vii = Vatican, MS Pal. lat. 1976–1979
			Noel Bauldeweyn	Quam pulchra es et quam decora 2.p. Veni dilecte mi egrediamus	fols. 31r–32r = Vatican, MS Pal. lat. 1976–1979
			anon.	Tota pulchra es amica mea	fols. 37r–38r ≠ London, MS Royal 8.G.vii
			Marbrianus de Orto	Descendi in ortum meum 2.p. Revertere Sulamitis	fols. 80v–81r
			Antoine de Févin?/ [Noel Bauldeweyn]/ [Costanzo Festa]/ [Jean Mouton]	O pulcherrima mulierum 2.p. Descendi in ortum meum	fols. 82v–83r
12	Vienna, Mus.Hs. 18832	ca. 1521–1525	Pierre de la Rue	Missa Ista est speciosa ("Pleni" only)	fol. 13r
13	Brussels, MS 15075	after 1524, before 1534	Pierre de la Rue	Missa Ista est speciosa	
14	Munich, Mus. ms. 6	ca. 1508–1530	[Noel Bauldeweyn]	Missa Quam pulchra es	
15	's-Hertogenbosch, MS 72B	ca. 1530–1631	[Noel Bauldeweyn]	Missa Quam pulchra es	

(continued)

No.	Shelfmark	Time of Origin[62]	Composer	Title	Remarks
16	Vatican, MS Pal. lat. 1976–1979	ca. 1531–1532	[Josquin Desprez?]	*Descendi in ortum meum*	fols. 85r–86v = London, MS Royal 8.G.vii = Vienna, Mus. Hs. 15941
			[Noel Bauldeweyn]	*Quam pulchra es et quam decora* 2.p. *Veni dilecte mi egrediamus*	fols. 89r–90r = Vienna, Mus. Hs. 15941
			[Matthieu Gascongne]	*Osculetur me*	fols. 102r–105r

Bibliography

Agricola, Alexander. *Opera omnia*. Vol. 4: *Motetta, Contrafacta*, edited by Edward R. Lerner. Corpus Mensurabilis Musicae 22. American Institute of Musicology, 1966.

Anderson, Michael Alan. "The Palatini Partbooks Revisited." *Journal of the Alamire Foundation* 11 (2019): 85–96.

Barbireau, Jacob. *Opera omnia*. Vol. 2: *Motet and Chansons*, edited by Bernhard Meier. Corpus Mensurabilis Musicae 7. American Institute of Musicology, 1957.

Beriger, Andreas, Widu-Wolfgang Ehlers, and Michael Fieger, eds. *Biblia Sacra Vulgata: Lateinisch-Deutsch*. Vol. 3: *Psalmi—Proverbia—Ecclesiastes—Canticum Canticorum—Sapientia—Iesus Sirach*. Boston: de Gruyter, 2018.

Burstyn, Shai. "Early 15th-Century Polyphonic Settings of Song of Songs Antiphons." *AMl* 49 (1977): 200–227.

Burstyn, Shai. "Fifteenth-century Polyphonic Settings of Verses from the Song of Songs." PhD diss., Columbia University, 1975.

Burstyn, Shai. "Power's *Anima mea* and Binchois' *De plus en plus*: A Study in Musical Relationships." *MusDisc* 30 (1976): 55–62.

Bushart, Bruno. *Die Fuggerkapelle bei St. Anna in Augsburg*. München: Deutscher Kunstverlag, 1994.

Chiu, Remi. "Motet Settings of the Song of Songs ca. 1500–1520." Master's Thesis, Schulich School of Music, McGill University, Montreal, 2006.

Compère, Loyset. *Opera omnia*. Vol. 5 [Motet-chansons, Chansons, Frottole, Opera dubia], edited by Ludwig Finscher. Corpus Mensurabilis Musicae 15. American Institute of Musicology, 1972.

Cumming, Julie E. *The Motet in the Age of Du Fay*. Cambridge: Cambridge University Press, 1999.

Dahlenburg, Jane Elizabeth. "The Motet c. 1580–1630: Sacred Music Based on the Song of Songs." PhD diss., University of North Carolina at Chapel Hill, 2000.

Desprez, Josquin. *New Edition of the Collected Works: Critical Commentary*. Vol. 14: *Motets on Texts from the Old Testament*, edited by Richard Sherr. Utrecht: Koninklijke Vereniging voor Nederlandse Muziekgeschiedenis, 2002.

Filippi, Daniele V., and Agnese Pavanello, eds. *Motet Cycles between Devotion and Liturgy*. Schola Cantorum Basiliensis Scripta 7. Basel: Schwabe, 2019.

Finscher, Ludwig. *Loyset Compère (c. 1450–1518): Life and Works*. Musicological Studies and Documents 12. Rome: American Institute of Musicology, 1964.

Gasch, Stefan. "Pierre de la Rue's *Ave, Regina caelorum* and Praying against the Plague in Augsburg." In *Pierre de la Rue and Music at the Habsburg-Burgundian Court*, edited by David J. Burn, Honey Meconi, and Christiane Wiesenfeldt. Turnhout: Brepols, forthcoming.

Gasch, Stefan. "Pierre de la Rues Sieben Freuden: Einige Bemerkungen zur Motette *Gaude virgo mater Christi*." *Die Tonkunst* 5 (2011): 34–43.

Ghiselin-Verbonnet, Johannes. *Opera omnia*. Vol. 1: *Motets*, edited by Clytus Gottwald. Corpus Mensurabilis Musicae 23. American Institute of Musicology, 1961.

Higgins, Paula. "Love and Death in the Fifteenth-Century Motet: A Reading of Busnoy's *Anima mea liquefacta est / Stirps Jesse*." In *Hearing the Motet: Essays on the Motet of the Middle Ages and Renaissance*, edited by Dolores Pesce, 142–168. Oxford: Oxford University Press, 1997.

Isaac, Heinrich. *Opera omnia*. Vol. 10: *Motets: Part I*, edited by Edward R. Lerner. Corpus Mensurabilis Musicae 65. American Institute of Musicology, 2011.

Kellman, Herbert. *The Treasury of Petrus Alamire: Music and Art in Flemish Court Manuscripts, 1500–1535*. Ghent: Ludion, 1999.

Kempson, Emma. "The Motets of Henricus Isaac (c.1450–1517): Transmission, Structure and Function." 2 vols. PhD diss., King's College London, University of London, 1998.

Kooiman, Elly, Dale C. Carr, and Anne-Marie Palmer. "The Biography of Jacob Barbireau (1455–1491) Reviewed." *Tijdschrift van de Vereniging voor Nederlandse Muziekgeschiedenis* 38 (1988): 36–58.

Macey, Patrick, Jeremy Noble, Jeffrey Dean, and Gustave Reese. "Josquin (Lebloitte dit) des Prez." Updated and revised version 23 February 2011, *Grove Music Online*, Oxford University Press.

Maniates, Maria Rika. "Combinative Techniques in Franco-Flemish Polyphony: A Study of Mannerism in Music from 1450–1530." PhD diss., Department of Music, Columbia University, New York, 1965.

Meconi, Honey. "Another Look at Absalon." *Tijdschrift van de Koninklijke Vereniging voor Nederlandse Muziekgeschiedenis* 49 (1998): 3–29.

Meconi, Honey. "Sacred Tricinia and Basevi 2439." *I Tatti Studies in the Italian Renaissance* 4 (1991): 151–199.

Picker, Martin. *The Chanson Albums of Marguerite of Austria: Manuscripts 228 and 11239 of the Bibliothèque Royale de Belgique, Bruxelles*. Los Angeles: University of California Press, 1985.

Scheller, Benjamin. *Memoria an der Zeitenwende: Die Stiftungen Jakob Fuggers des Reichen vor und während der Reformation (ca. 1505–1555)*. Veröffentlichungen der Schwäbischen Forschungsgemeinschaft 4/28. Studien zur Fuggergeschichte 37. Berlin: de Gruyter, 2004.

Shine, Josephine M. "The Motets of Jean Mouton." 3 vols. PhD diss., University of New York, 1953.

Stenzl, Jürg. *Der Klang des Hohen Liedes: Vertonungen des Canticum Canticorum vom 9. bis zum Ende des 15. Jahrhunderts*. 2 vols. Salzburger Stier. Würzburg: Königshausen & Neumann, 2008.

Strohm, Reinhard. *Musik in Late Medieval Bruges*. Oxford: Clarendon Press, 2003.

Thomas, Wimberly Grace. "Devotional Love in the Late Spiritual Madrigal Cycles of Orlando di Lasso and Giovanni Pierluigi da Palestrina." PhD diss., University of Bangor, 2009.

Weerbeke, Gaspar van. *Collected Works*. Vol. 3: *The Motet Cycles*, edited by Andrea Lindmayr-Brandl. Corpus Mensurabilis Musicae 106. Neuhausen: American Institute of Musicology, 1998.

Willaert, Adrian. *Opera omnia*. Vol. 9: *Liber quinque missarum IV vocum 1536*, edited by Helga Meier. Corpus Mensurabilis Musicae 3. Neuhausen: American Institute of Musicology, 1987.

Bernard McGinn
Early Modern Women Comment on the Song of Songs

The Song of Songs has been both a stumbling block and an opportunity in the history of the reception of the Bible—a stumbling block for those who wonder how this collection of erotic poems made it into the canon of sacred scripture, and an opportunity for exegetes, both Jewish and Christian, to show how the language of human love is an apt resource for expressing the love between God and the community of believers, as well as God and the individual. The defense of the Song goes back at least as far as the second-third centuries CE, when Rabbi Akivah ben Joseph vindicated the sacred character of the Song against its unnamed opponents by claiming, "The whole world is not worthy of the day the Song of Songs was given to Israel," and when Origen of Alexandria (185–253/4) said, "This Song is to be preferred to all [biblical] songs."[1] The Song of Songs can be described as the "Magna Carta" of Jewish and Christian mysticism.

The story of the readings, especially the mystical readings, of the Song in Judaism and Christianity is immense. Not surprisingly, given the patriarchal cast of these traditions, the great majority of its interpreters have been male, despite the strong feminine voice in the Song's love poems. Nonetheless, if the voice of the Bride is conceived of as representing the community of the faithful, both men and women can claim equal membership in the congregation. In the Christian Bible, the Bride is also identified with the individual soul (*psyche* in Greek, *anima* in Latin), but these feminine nouns apply to both men and women. The fact that so many male mystics identified with the Bride of the Song contributed much to the tradition of gender malleability in Christian mysticism. But the gender-crossing of male to female is not the whole story. Women also pondered the words of the Song of Songs and even wrote down their thoughts about the Bible's book of love.

The voices of women, while not totally absent, were generally muted in the first millennium of Christian history. The thoughts of individual women occasionally break through—Perpetua in the second century; Macrina and Monica in the fourth; Dhuoda in the ninth century; Hrotswitha in the tenth. It was only in the twelfth century, however, with figures like Heloise of the Paraclete and Hildegard of Bingen, that we really begin to hear what women were thinking in some detail, not

---

[1] For these passages and general remarks on the use of the Song in mysticism, see McGinn, "Language of Love," 207.

only about their relation to God, but also about how they understood the Bible.[2] It is no accident that Hildegard is the first woman who leaves us substantial materials on the meaning of the Song of Songs. The formidable abbess (1098–1179)—visionary, poet, musician, dramatist, theologian, and more, was also an original exegete.[3] Her major trilogy of works, as well as her many letters, cite half of the verses of the Song of Songs (58 of 116), sometimes just as proof texts, but also with some extended interpretations.[4] From the late twelfth century, we also have the Middle High German paraphrase and interpretation of the Song of Songs usually known as the *Sankt Trudperter Hohelied*, composed for the nuns at Admont about 1160. This was probably written by the nuns' chaplain, but could have been composed by a member of the community.

The thirteenth century began the period of the great outpouring of mystical literature by women, much of it in the vernacular. A number of these mystical writers, such as Beatrice of Nazareth (1200–1268), Angela of Foligno (1248–1309), and the beguine Marguerite Porete (1250–1310), do not use the Song. At least five major figures do. Clare of Assisi (1194–1253) used the erotic tropes of the twelfth-century male commentators on the Song, especially the Cistercians, to present her teaching about the love between Jesus and the "Poor Clare" nuns. Two great beguine mystics made even more extensive employment of the Song of Songs. The Flemish Hadewijch of Antwerp (ca. 1240) used the Song some thirty times in her *Visions, Letters*, and *Songs (Poems in Stanzas)*.[5] She was especially drawn to two verses: the opening (Song 1:1), "Let him kiss me with the kiss of the mouth," and Song 2:16, "My Beloved to me and I to him who feeds among the lilies." The German beguine Mechthild of Magdeburg (1207–1282) cites the Song some twenty times in her multi-genre collection, *Das fliessende licht der gotheit*, at times re-imagining the verses in her own poems and mini-dramas. The most extensive use of the Song of Songs is found in the Latin works of the Cistercian nuns of Helfta in Saxony at the end of the century. The *Liber specialis gratiae* ascribed to Mechthild of Hackeborn (1241/2–1298), and the *Legatus divinae pietatis* of her disciple Gertrude the Great (1256–1301) and other members of the community contain about one hundred and twenty references to the Song of Songs.[6]

---

2 I have set out some of the history of women's views of the Song of Songs in two previous essays: primarily for the early period in McGinn, "Women Reading the Song of Songs"; and a more general treatment in idem, "Women Interpreting the Song of Songs."
3 See McGinn, "Hildegard of Bingen."
4 For Hildegard on the Song, see McGinn, "Women Reading the Song of Songs," 284–290.
5 See Hart, *Hadewijch: The Complete Works*.
6 On the thirteenth-century women, see McGinn, "Women Interpreting the Song of Songs," 254–261.

The women mystics of the fourteenth and fifteenth centuries, alas, did not make much use of the Song. Important mystics like Catherine of Siena (1347–1381) and Julian of Norwich (1342–1416) very rarely cite the book. The Franciscan Catherine of Bologna (1413–1463) did not quote it in her major work, the *Sette armi spirituali*, although some of the mystical works produced under her inspiration in the Franciscan convents of Ferrara and Bologna do, especially the treatise called *I dodici Giardini*, which sketches the soul's journey to "unitive love" with the Beloved through twelve gardens of virtues. The most important woman mystic of the late fifteenth century, Catherine of Genoa (1447–1510), rarely cites scripture at all, let alone the Song of Songs. We are left, then, with a rather anomalous picture of women using the Song of Songs in the medieval period—fairly extensive use in the twelfth and thirteenth centuries, but rather restricted employment among fourteenth- and fifteenth-century women.

The paucity of use in the period 1300–1500 does not prepare us for the explosion of interest in the Song of Songs among Early Modern mystical women of the sixteenth and seventeenth centuries. I have not tried to trace the many citations of the Song among the scores of women mystical writers of this period, nor in the numerous *vitae* about them penned by their confessors and spiritual directors. What I want to present as evidence of this remarkable flowering is how female mystical exegetes began the practice of writing commentaries on the Song, as well as including commentarial sections on the book in their treatises. I have thus far identified nine such "commentaries," and there may be more to be discovered as the texts of relatively unknown women are edited and made public.[7] What is more, these commentaries are spread across the spectrum of female religiosity

---

7 I list the nine commentaries in chronological order: (1) Teresa of Avila (1515–1572), Carmelite, *Meditaciones sobre los Cantares*, first written about 1566 and revised 1572–1575; (2) Battistina Vernazza (1497–1587), Augustinian, with two treatises: *Trattato sopra "Osculetur me osculo"* of 1575–1576, and *Trattato sopra "Quis mihi det,"* written before 1585; (3) Jeanne de Cambry (1581–1639), Augustinian, wrote her *Traicté de la ruine de l'amour propre et bastiment de l'amour divin*, about 1604 to 1616; it was first published in 1623; (4) Mariana de San José (1568–1638), Augustinian, has a *Commentario al "Cantar de los Cantares"* of ca. 1622–1627; (5) Marguerite d'Arbouze (1580–1626), Benedictine; some passages from her verbal comments on the Song were cited in the *Vie admirable...* by her confessor Jacques Ferraige in 1628; (6) Cecilia del Nacimiento (1570–1646), Carmelite, has two *Glossae*, the first on Song 2:16 (*Dilectus meus mihi et ego illi*) of 1634, the second on the sleep of the Bride (Song 3:5 and 5:2) of 1637; (7) Marie de l'Incarnation (1599–1672), Ursuline, gave an *Entretien spiritual sur l'Épouse des Cantiques*, to her nuns about 1634, but the work was not published until 1682; she also made extensive use of the Song in her *Relation de 1654*; (8) Marguerite Romanet of Savoy (d. 1663), lay woman, whose *Commentary* appears to be lost, but some passages are cited by her Carmelite confessor, Paul de Saint-Sacrament; and (9) Jeanne Guyon (1648–1713), lay woman, with her *Commentaire au Cantique des cantiques de Salomon* of 1684.

with two Carmelite authors, three Augustinians, an Ursuline, a Benedictine, and two laywomen.

What precipitated this new stage in the relation between women mystics and the Song of Songs? Women, as noted, had turned to the Song of Songs since at least the twelfth century to help express their longing for union with their divine Lover. Why was there a renewed interest in the Song among women beginning in the second half of the sixteenth century, and why does it so often take the turn to commentary? It is not easy to say. I have previously suggested that the role of some of these women (e.g., Teresa of Avila, Marie de l'Incarnation) as leaders of communities of religious women with an obligation to instruct their charges may have been a factor,[8] but this is certainly not true of all the women. Some of them (e.g., Teresa of Avila, Cecilia del Nacimiento) say that they wrote under obedience to their confessors and spiritual directors, but they all appear to have been personally emboldened to write primarily from their own inner experience. Teresa of Avila's example and fame as a mystic may have provided a cover for some of these women, but her *Meditaciones* did not appear in the first editions of her works and were scarcely well-known. There seem to be few, if any, common denominators among these nine writers, but there is no question that they represent a new chapter in the reception of the Bible's book of love. In a short article, it is not possible to provide a detailed study of all nine of these authors, especially because some of their texts are difficult to access today. In this context I will briefly investigate five of the comments that are readily available as a contribution to the ongoing recovery of the story of women and the Song of Songs.

1 Teresa of Avila

The obvious place to begin is Teresa of Avila (1515–1582), who is both the first and the most important woman to take up the task of commenting on the Song.[9] Of course, Teresa, powerful figure as she was, did not claim to be a "real" biblical commentator, because in her historical situation that was a position that could be

---

8 See McGinn, "Women Interpreting the Song of Songs," 264–265.
9 Teresa's *Meditaciones* can be found in Steggink and de la Madre de Dios, eds., *Santa Teresa de Jesús*, 423–468. I will use the translation of Kavanaugh and Rodriguez, trans., *Collected Works*, 215–260, which uses a slightly different enumeration of sections within chapters from the BAC edition. I will make use of some insights from my article, McGinn, "'One Word Will Contain,'" 21–40. There is a considerable literature on Teresa on the Song of Songs that is surveyed in this article.

held only by learned male clerics (*letrados*).¹⁰ The Carmelite foundress paid real, if somewhat ironic, deference to these "learned clerics" in the text that she said was no more than her partial "meditations" on *some* verses from the Song of Songs. Nonetheless, both the "prologue" and chapter 1.1–9 of the *Meditaciones* can be described as an exercise in the subversion of hermeneutical patriarchy by defending the right of women to comment on the Bible.

The mother of the Carmelite reform's intention in the prologue and chapter 1 was not negative or hostile; rather, she was positive and pastoral, designing her work to help her nuns drink spiritual wisdom from the inexhaustible riches of the Song of Song. In order to effect this, however, Teresa had to defend the right of women to be biblical exegetes—the first such defense in the history of Christianity. According to the prologue, for a number of years God had given Teresa "great delight" in hearing or reading some of the words of the Song of Songs, even when she did not completely understand the Latin. So, following the opinion of "some people she was obliged to obey," she says, "I shall write something about the understanding the Lord gives me of what is contained in the words that bring delight to my soul about this path of prayer" (prol. 3).¹¹ Since Scripture deals with divine mysteries, we should expect that many things in it will be beyond our understanding, something that pertains both to women and to men (ch. 1.1). It is God who infuses understanding in us without our effort, although learned exegetes still must work at interpreting the text. Not only is God's gift of understanding essential, but we must also recognize the inexhaustibility of the richness of the word of God: "For one word of his will contain within itself a thousand mysteries, and thus our understanding is only very elementary" (ch. 1.2)—an ancient theme.¹² God chose the unusual style of the Song to communicate the same message of love found in the life of the Savior, and Teresa says that the words of the book proved a guide to her, so that through them "she understood that it was possible for a soul in love with its Spouse to experience all these favors, swoons, deaths, afflictions, delights, and joys in relation to him" (ch. 1.6).¹³ Here the Carmelite introduces a key theme

---

10 Although the work was approved by Teresa's confessor, Domingo Bañez in 1577, in 1580 a later confessor, Diego de Yanguas, when he discovered that she had written a commentary on the Song, commanded her to destroy it. This she dutifully did, but only with the knowledge that copies had already been disseminated to other houses of the Reform. See McGinn, "'One Word Will Contain,'" 25.
11 Steggink and de la Madre de Dios, eds., *Santa Teresa de Jesús*, 423; Kavanaugh and Rodriguez, trans., *Collected Works*, 215.
12 Steggink and de la Madre de Dios, eds., *Santa Teresa de Jesús*, 424; Kavanaugh and Rodriguez, trans., *Collected Works*, 217.
13 Steggink and de la Madre de Dios, eds., *Santa Teresa de Jesús*, 425; Kavanaugh and Rodriguez, trans., *Collected Works*, 218.

of her exegesis, one she shares with Bernard of Clairvaux and many male exegetes, that is, the reciprocity between the book of the Song and the "book of experience."[14]

Chapter 1.8 reaches the heart of Teresa's defense of women as exegetes.[15] The words of the Song of Songs are so rich and enigmatic, she says, "that when I asked learned men to explain what the Holy Spirit meant by them and what the true meaning was they answered that the doctors wrote many commentaries and yet never explained them fully." Hence, there is no reason why she cannot proceed with her reading, but under two conditions. The first is the attitude of humility of which the Blessed Virgin was the prime example;[16] the second is her desire not to depart from what the Church and the saints hold. As long as she adheres to these guidelines, Teresa says that it is perfectly all right for her to tell her meditations to her daughters so that they can find guidance and consolation in the words of the Song.

Although Teresa comments on only eleven verses of the Song of Songs,[17] her *Meditaciones* can be considered an integral (not exhaustive) commentary on the Song, because it uses the biblical text in an orderly way to expound the essentials of the Carmelite's mystical teaching, specifically about the two kinds of mystical prayer (prayer of quiet and prayer of union), about the suspension of the faculties, about mystical union, about mystical death (*mors mystica*), and about suffering and service as the goal of the mystical path. A brief analysis will serve to provide the main lines, although not the rich detail of Teresa's interpretive skill.

"The kiss of the mouth" (Song 1:1) that is the subject of chapters 1.10–3.15 of the *Meditaciones* is a detailed consideration of the kiss as the symbol of the friendship and peace between God and the human soul, a friendship that extends even to the

---

[14] Teresa often mentions the need for experience for fruitful interpretation of the Song; see, e.g., *Meditationes*, ch. 4.1 (Steggink and de la Madre de Dios, eds., *Santa Teresa de Jesús*, 449; Kavanaugh and Rodriguez, trans., *Collected Works*, 242); ch. 4.7 (Steggink and de la Madre de Dios, eds., *Santa Teresa de Jesús*, 452; Kavanaugh and Rodriguez, trans., *Collected Works*, 246); ch. 5.4 (Steggink and de la Madre de Dios, eds., *Santa Teresa de Jesús*, 456; Kavanaugh and Rodriguez, trans., *Collected Works*, 249), and ch. 6.5 (Steggink and de la Madre de Dios, eds., *Santa Teresa de Jesús*, 459; Kavanaugh and Rodriguez, trans., *Collected Works*, 252).

[15] Steggink and de la Madre de Dios, eds., *Santa Teresa de Jesús*, 426; Kavanaugh and Rodriguez, trans., *Collected Works*, 219–220.

[16] On the Blessed Virgin as model for the humble *female* exegete, see *Meditaciones*, chapter 6.7 (Steggink and de la Madre de Dios, eds., *Santa Teresa de Jesús*, 460–461; Kavanaugh and Rodriguez, trans., *Collected Works*, 253). On Teresa's "hermeneutics of humility," see Slade, "Saint Teresa's *Meditaciones*," 27–43.

[17] Song of Songs 1:1 is the subject of *Meditaciones*, chapters 1–3. Song of Songs 1:2a is taken up in chapter 4, while chapter 5 deals with Song 2:3b. Song of Songs 2:4 is treated in chapter 6, and Song 2:5 is interpreted in chapter 7. In addition, six other verses come in for use (Song 2:6; 4:7; 4:9; 6:2; 6:9, and 8:4), mostly in chapters 5 and 6.

marital union of the Bride and the Bridegroom. Teresa defends the right of souls enkindled with true love for God to use the daring language of the Song: "But the one whom your love, Lord, has drawn out of himself, you will truly pardon if he says these words and also others, even though to say them is daring" (ch. 1.12).[18] Ecstasy is the essential language of the Song, as well as those who pray it. Chapter 2 is more prosaic, a long treatment of the various kinds of peace and friendship: nine forms of false peace (ch. 2.1–5); and several kinds of imperfect peace and friendship (ch. 2.16–30). It is only in chapter 3 that Teresa turns to the true "kiss of peace," that is, the union of our will with God, in which "there is no division between him and the soul, but one and the same will" (ch. 3.1).[19] This union of the kiss goes beyond the intellect: "The soul does not want to benefit by what the intellect teaches it, for this union between the Bride and the Bridegroom has taught it other things the intellect cannot attain to, and the soul tramples the intellect underfoot" (ch. 3.3).[20]

The second sensuous image from the Song that Teresa comments on is "the breasts that are more delightful than wine" (Song 1:1b), and that "give forth the most sweet fragrance" (Song 1:2a). For the Carmelite the two breasts are the two basic forms of mystical prayer, the prayer of quiet and the prayer of union, topics already discussed at length in her *Vida* (1562–1565) and here treated in chapter 4. The commentary on the breasts involves a threefold itinerary. First, the soul experiences the intoxication of the *wine*, which is identified with the prayer of quiet (ch. 4.2–3); next, it is "suspended in those divine arms [see Song 2:6], leaning on that sacred side and those divine breasts, [. . .] where it is sustained by the divine *milk* with which its Spouse is nourishing it" (ch. 4.4).[21] In the state of the suspension of the senses and the passive absorption of the milk of divine truths and virtues the soul can truly say, "Your breasts are better than wine." In the third stage, the direct experience of the *breasts* signifies the approach of the prayer of union (ch. 4.4–7), where the soul enjoys "tastes" (*gustos*) from God himself (another key motif in the Carmelite's mysticism). Teresa discourses on the stage of union by reiterating the image of the kiss of the mouth (Song 1:1) and citing Song 2:16: "My Beloved is mine and I am my Beloved's," as well as Song 6:2: "I look at my Beloved and my Beloved at me." The account of the prayer of union continues in chapter 5 with its exegesis

---

[18] Steggink and de la Madre de Dios, eds., *Santa Teresa de Jesús*, 427–428; Kavanaugh and Rodriguez, trans., *Collected Works*, 221.
[19] Steggink and de la Madre de Dios, eds., *Santa Teresa de Jesús*, 445; Kavanaugh and Rodriguez, trans., *Collected Works*, 236.
[20] Steggink and de la Madre de Dios, eds., *Santa Teresa de Jesús*, 445–446; Kavanaugh and Rodriguez, trans., *Collected Works*, 237.
[21] Steggink and de la Madre de Dios, eds., *Santa Teresa de Jesús*, 451; Kavanaugh and Rodriguez, trans., *Collected Works*, 244.

of Song 2:3b–4: "I sat down under the shadow of Him whom I desire and his fruit is sweet to my taste. The King brought me into his wine cellar and set charity in order in me."[22]

The long chapter 6[23] continues with the explanation of what it means for the soul to be led into the divine wine cellar and have God set its charity in order, while chapter 7[24] deals with Song 2:5: "Sustain me with flowers and surround me with apples, for I am dying of love," that is, the meaning of mystical death. Whereas in Teresa's earlier *Vida* ecstatic union with God had been the acme of the mystical path, in the *Meditaciones*, as well as in the later *Interior Castle (Moradas)* of 1577, the Carmelite alters her teaching to emphasize that the suffering of love, as well as service to others through the union of contemplation with action, are the true goals of the mystical life. After a treatment of the gifts that God gives the soul in the state of union (ch. 6.1–7), Teresa expounds on the ordering of charity that takes place through the action of will and love, not intellect (ch. 6.8–13). As the soul grows weak with love and is about to die, she begs her Beloved: "Sustain me with flowers; surround me with apples for I am dying with the sickness of love" (Song 2:5). The flowers signify the "great works" it wishes to perform "in the service of our Lord and its neighbor." Teresa goes on to say: "Martha [i.e., action] and Mary [i.e., contemplation] never fail to work almost together when the soul is in this state" (ch. 7.3).[25] Finally, the "apples" of the verse Teresa reads as the trials and persecutions that souls desire to undergo in the state of advanced union where they live under the "apple tree" of the cross of Christ (ch. 7.8; see Song 8:4). Teresa concludes by including her sisters in the task of her experiential hermeneutics: "Beseech his Majesty that I may understand through experience what has been said. Any sister who thinks she has some experience of these delights should praise the Lord and ask him for the last-mentioned works and trials so that the gain will not be just for herself" (ch. 7.10).[26]

---

22 Steggink and de la Madre de Dios, eds., *Santa Teresa de Jesús*, 453–457; Kavanaugh and Rodriguez, trans., *Collected Works*, 247–250. Chapter 5 contains both a reference to the shadow or obscurity of mystical consciousness and an account of the Trinitarian and Christological aspects of the prayer of union.

23 Steggink and de la Madre de Dios, eds., *Santa Teresa de Jesús*, 457–463; Kavanaugh and Rodriguez, trans., *Collected Works*, 250–255.

24 Steggink and de la Madre de Dios, eds., *Santa Teresa de Jesús*, 464–468; Kavanaugh and Rodriguez, trans., *Collected Works*, 256–260.

25 Steggink and de la Madre de Dios, eds., *Santa Teresa de Jesús*, 465; Kavanaugh and Rodriguez, trans., *Collected Works*, 257. On the union of Martha and Mary, see Culligan, "Mary and Martha Working Together."

26 Steggink and de la Madre de Dios, eds., *Santa Teresa de Jesús*, 468; Kavanaugh and Rodriguez, trans., *Collected Works*, 260.

2 Jeanne de Cambry

Teresa of Avila's *Meditaciones* only commented on a few verses of the Song of Songs; the little-known Augustinian nun of Tournai and later recluse at Lille, Jeanne de Cambry (1581–1639), treats almost every verse of the biblical song of love.[27] This interpretation does not present itself as a stand-alone scriptural commentary, but forms the basic content of books two to four of the four-book treatise called *Traicté de la ruine de l'amour propre et bastiment de l'amour divin*, which Jeanne worked on ca. 1604–1616. Copies of the French original (published 1622, 1627, and 1645) are rare, but the final three books were translated into English by the Recusant Benedictine nun, Dame Agnes More (1591–ca. 1650), a great-great granddaughter of St. Thomas More. This survives in a manuscript of 1691 and was published in 1992.[28] The treatise is structured according to the four seasons. Book 1 (winter) deals with asceticism and mortification (that is, the ruin of self-love) and does not use the Song of Songs. Book 2 (spring) begins the treatment of the mystical life and has two parts: Part I (chs. 1–9) deals with man as microcosm, while Part II (chs. 10–24) concerns love, annihilation, and the early stages of union with God, analyzed through an extensive interpretation of Song 1:1–5:1. Book 3 (summer) has twenty-one chapters on the "secret purgatory," that is, the mystical trials and tribulations of the soul, as interpreted through the verses of Song 5:1a–16. This book also has an extensive treatment of mystical annihilation, one of the basic themes of French seventeenth-century mysticism. Finally, Book 4 (autumn) features the fourth stage of perfection, "The Sacred Cabinet of the Most Pure Love of God," and contains twenty-nine chapters on the final stages of union. The first twenty chapters continue the exegesis of the Song of Songs, interpreting Song 6:1–8:14. Book 4, chapter 8, contains an important note on the nature of Jeanne's exegesis: "Inasmuch as the mystical Canticle of Solomon is full of divine wisdom which is understood by few secular persons and wholly unknown to worldlings, it is not permitted that everyone should read it [. . .]. In like manner it is with the secret and unknown ways of the soul that walks to God."[29] Once again, this commentator insists that the erotic verses of the Song, while dangerous to seculars, can be used by the devout to explain the secret and unknown ways that lead to union with God. It is important

---

27 Jeanne omits a few verses: vv. 3 and 6–16 of Song 1, and vv. 1–2 of Song 2. In the commentary on Song 3–8, she omits only two verses (Song 5:4 and 7:2).
28 The English version is Latz, ed., *Building of Divine Love*. For accounts of Jeanne de Cambry, see Droulers, "Cambry," 3:61–62.
29 Latz, ed., *Building of Divine Love*, 159.

to note, however, that Jeanne de Cambry does not exclude married layfolk from the devout souls who can profit from reading the Song of Songs.[30]

It is not possible here to review the details of Jeanne's extensive and rich reading of the Song, but a look at her interpretation of an important section of the book may provide a sampling of her exegesis. Annihilation, as noted above, was a major mystical theme for Jeanne and for most seventeenth-century mystics. The Augustinian nun's understanding of annihilation is not the total destruction of the soul and its powers, but the cancelling of fallen "self-love" (*amour propre*) and the natural operations of the soul through the action of divine love. Annihilation language is used throughout the work, but is especially strong in book 2, chapters 15–20, exegeting Song 2:13–3:5.[31] Chapter 15, for example, deals with the "Secret Annihilation of the Soul" through an exposition of Song 2:13–14. The verse "Arise, make haste, my love, my beautiful one," is read as God's "inviting his Spouse to elevate herself above herself, which means to forsake her own actions and operations, so that, by a transformation and beatifying love, she may elevate herself to a unitive contemplation of the secret and unknown perfections of the divinity."[32] This annihilation of her own operations permits God to work within her. It frees the soul from all "forms and images," so that "in a deified manner she sees, tastes, and knows in the divinity all that passes in the humanity [of Christ] united to the divinity." This happens by way of "an elevation of the most supreme part of the soul, wherein is the true portrait or image of the Sacred Trinity."[33] Chapter 16 follows with an exposition of Song 2:15–17, where Jeanne says that the soul in this "supereminent state" must avoid the "little foxes" of acts of vainglory and recognize the "truth of her own nothingness" in "profound humility"—again reflecting fundamental themes of contemporary French mysticism.[34] It is also noteworthy that chapter 18, exegeting Song 3:3–4a, the passage where the city watchmen find the soul, expands on her teaching on annihilation by specifying three forms of total emptying. The first is the naughting of the soul's own "amorous affection" for God.[35] It is not our own love for God that can attain him, but only the annihilation of our will that allows God's infinite will to act in us without us. The second annihilation is the annihilation of our understanding, which "is effected by a nudity and a for-

---

30 *Traicté*, book 4, chapter 29 (Latz, ed., *Building of Divine Love*, 207): "There are many souls and spiritual persons—both married persons and Religious persons—who are touched in so lively a way with this arrow of love that their lives are more angelical than human."
31 Latz, ed., *Building of Divine Love*, 41–59.
32 Latz, ed., *Building of Divine Love*, 42.
33 Latz, ed., *Building of Divine Love*, 43.
34 Latz, ed., *Building of Divine Love*, 44.
35 Latz, ed., *Building of Divine Love*, 52–54.

getting of all her own proper operations." The result is that "the understanding together with the memory and imaginative part come to flow or pass into the profound depths of their nothingness."[36] Finally, the third annihilation, which takes place in the center of the soul, is the recognition that the "flight of the spirit" has nothing to do with the soul's own activity, but is solely achieved by the divine power acting within it.[37]

3 Cecilia del Nacimiento

The decade after Jeanne de Cambry wrote her commentary, Cecilia del Nacimiento, the most important female Carmelite mystic of the generation after Teresa, composed two short commentary-treatises on verses from the Song of Songs.[38] Cecilia, who was influenced both by Teresa and John of the Cross, was a profound mystical poet.[39] Along with over a hundred poems, she wrote a number of tracts, such as the *Tratado de la unión del alma en Dios* (1602), the *Tratado de la transformación en Dios* (1603), and two personal accounts of God's favors to her in 1629 and 1633. At the command of her confessors, she wrote a *Glosa* on the verse *Dilectus meus mihi et ego illi* (Song 2:16) in 1634, and another in 1636 on the "sleep of the Bride" (Song 3:5; 5:2). Cecilia emphasized the importance of reading the Bible throughout her works: "Many times with a few words from the Sacred Scriptures, my soul feels these celestial sensations: sometimes a certain passage does it, sometimes another, and these words come at such a perfect time that they lift my soul up to God."[40]

Song of Songs 2:16 was long a favorite with mystics because of its emphasis on the mutuality of the love of Bride and Bridegroom—"My Beloved is to me and I to Him." According to Cecilia, "these words from the Song of Songs are what the soul says after she has handed over everything to God, when she does not love anything else outside Him, when all of her is His, and everything is His love" (*Gloss* I.2).[41] Then, God cannot deny Himself to her; her complete gift necessarily results in God transforming her into Himself: "And He has given my soul all of this so that she

---

[36] Latz, ed., *Building of Divine Love*, 52–53.
[37] Latz, ed., *Building of Divine Love*, 53.
[38] Cecilia's works were edited by Diaz Cerón, *Obras Completas*. There is a translation in Donnelly and Sider, trans., *Cecilia del Nacimiento*, where the *Glosses* on the Song of Songs are found (165–185).
[39] For an introduction to Cecilia, see McGinn, *Mysticism*, 360–369, and the literature cited there.
[40] From the *Second Account of God's Favors* 10 (Donnelley and Sider, trans., *Cecilia del Nacimiento*, 158).
[41] Donnelley and Sider, trans., *Cecilia del Nacimiento*, 166.

can give the same back to Him and be able to say, *et ego illi*" (*Gloss I*.4).[42] God gives Himself as Trinity (*Gloss I*.5–7), as Cecilia explains with the use of several other passages from the Song (5:10; 4:7; 2:14). The "game of love" (*ludus amoris*) involves a deep transformation in which "those qualities and conditions that are rooted and naturalized in her [...] must be expelled so that she can remain all pure and white" (*Gloss I*.9).[43] This ineffable experience is both Trinitarian and Christocentric, following the model of the Savior who gave his life for us (*Gloss I*.11 and 18). It is also Eucharistic. All souls are called to this transformation in the "center of the soul," an important Sanjuanist motif in Cecilia's mysticism (*Gloss I*.14). The Carmelite nun summarizes: "And with the soul making herself completely available to Him, He cannot help but be completely available to her. He is always the first one to love and He never stops, if she does not leave Him first" (*Gloss I*.15).[44]

Cecilia's second *Gloss* (*Gloss II*) on the Bride's sleep of love is primarily a reading of Song 3:5: "I adjure you, daughters of Jerusalem, by the gazelles and hinds of the fields, do not wake up the Beloved before she wishes." The nun explains: "That is why the soul who, lying awake on the divine chest of her Divine Spouse, begs her Beloved not to let the daughters of Jerusalem, that is, other souls, wake up his beloved spouse" (*Gloss II*.3).[45] Nothing earthly must be allowed to hinder the Bride's sleep of ecstasy. The "center of the soul" is held deep in God's center in a sleep that "makes all things belonging to this life seem like a dream and that marks the beginning of the eternal vigil" (*Gloss II*.3).[46] Again, the Trinitarian and Christological aspects of mystical union are emphasized, and Teresa of Avila's *Moradas* is referenced (*Gloss II*.11). Towards the end of the treatise (*Gloss II*.13) Cecilia brings up a theme found in many of her works: "the clear darkness that human understanding cannot comprehend."[47]

4 Marie de l'Incarnation

Marie de l'Incarnation (1599–1672), sometimes known as the "Teresa of the New World," is among the most important seventeenth-century female mystics.[48] Her

---

[42] Donnelley and Sider, trans., *Cecilia del Nacimiento*, 167.
[43] Donnelley and Sider, trans., *Cecilia del Nacimiento*, 169.
[44] Donnelley and Sider, trans., *Cecilia del Nacimiento*, 172.
[45] Donnelley and Sider, trans., *Cecilia del Nacimiento*, 177.
[46] Donnelley and Sider, trans., *Cecilia del Nacimiento*, 178.
[47] Donnelley and Sider, trans., *Cecilia del Nacimiento*, 182.
[48] On Marie de l'Incarnation as a mystic, see McGinn, *Persistence of Mysticism*, 308–321; Mali, *Mystic in the New World*.

mystical experiences began while she was still a young mother. After the death of her husband, she entered the Ursuline order at Tours in 1631 and in 1639 sailed for Quebec, where she spent the remainder of her life. The Song of Songs was important to her throughout her life. In the account of her spiritual progress called the *Relation de 1654* she tells about the origin of her brief *Entretien Spirituel sur l'Épouse des Cantiques* in 1635.[49] One of the nuns in the community had come across a book that cited Song 1:1 and asked Marie about the meaning of the "kiss of the mouth." Marie tells us: "Our mistress was there and had me bring a chair so that I could be more comfortable. Without further ado I began with the first word, which swept me along so that, no longer conscious of myself, I spoke for a long time, according as this loving action took hold of me. Finally, I became speechless, as though the Spirit of my Jesus wanted everything for Himself."[50] Like many female mystics, Marie claimed to have been given a miraculous understanding of Scripture.

The brief *Entretien Spirituel*, like Teresa's *Meditaciones* is not a full commentary, but focuses on eleven verses in a non-sequential order (Song 1:1; 3:4; 3:1; 2:3; 2:6; 2:4a; 2:4b; 3:5; 8:8–9; 6:1, and 8:14). The flavor of her reading can be seen in her comments on verses from chapter 2. Song 2:6 ("He places his left hand under my head and embraces me with his right") is read as the spiritual embrace of the "Bridegroom of blood" (Exod 4:25–26): "The arms of his holy affection are a thousand times more pressing than those of his body [. . .]. He puts 'his left hand under our head' to afflict us and baptize us in the baptism of his pain, and 'he embraces us with his right' to console us and to fill us with the delights of his grace."[51] Marie then interprets the famous text on the ordering charity (Song 2:4): "Why the ordering of charity? Is her charity out of order? No, because the order of charity is to love without order, and the measure of love is to love without measure. But she wishes to say that the Bridegroom has given her the love of his salvation before he gave her the love of the salvation of the neighbor, which is the true order of charity and justice."[52] Later she interprets "the Bride as a wall with bulwarks of silver and a door of planks of cedar wood" (Song 8:9) as two kinds of persons who work for the

---

[49] Marie's writings were edited by Jamet, *Écrits*. There is a partial translation by Mahoney, trans., *Marie de l'Incarnation*, which includes the whole *Relation de 1654* (41–178).
[50] *Relation de 1654*, VIII.xxx.14 (Jamet, *Écrits*, 2:289; Mahoney, trans., *Marie de l'Incarnation*, 101–102). The *Entretien Spiritual sur l'Épouse des Cantiques* can be found in Jamet, *Écrits*, 1:387–404. There is no English translation. For a study, see Mali, *Mystic in the New World*, 138–145. Marie's son, the Benedictine Claude Martin, used her notes to put the work together and publish it in 1682.
[51] *Entretian spiritual* (Jamet, *Écrits*, 1:400).
[52] *Entretian spiritual* (Jamet, *Écrits*, 1:400–401). Loving without order and without measure reflects Marie's knowledge of Bernard of Clairvaux's *De diligendo Deo*.

salvation of others: the wall signifying the preachers of the word of God, and the door as those who govern souls, such as prelates, pastors, and religious superiors.[53]

The central role of the Song of Songs in Marie de l'Incarnation's mysticism is also evident in the autobiographical account of her spiritual progress through thirteen states of prayer found in the *Relation de 1654*, despite the fact that the final state of Marie's mystical itinerary is not marriage to Jesus, but attaining his state of victimhood. The Ursuline employs nineteen verses from the Song across the work with the bulk of the citations coming in states six and seven (eight citations), which deal with erotic union with Christ, although the Song is also quoted five times in the account of victimhood in state thirteen.[54]

5 Jeanne Guyon

The last of the Early Modern female Song commentators to be considered is the lay mystic Jeanne Guyon (1648–1717), condemned as a Quietist in the 1690s.[55] Vilified by many, praised by others, Madame Guyon remains a bone of contention. Guyon is best known through her three-volume *Vie (Life)* that was not published until after her death. More accessible are two treatises on the mystical life, the *Torrents* of 1682 and the *Moyen Court (Short Way to Prayer)* of roughly the same time. Guyon was also a prodigious biblical commentator.[56] About 1684 she began to receive direct communications from God about the meaning of Scripture (see *Vie* II.21.1–3), which enabled her over the course of less than a year to write a twenty-volume commentary on the entire Bible, the first by a woman (over 8,000 pages!).[57] In contrast to the developing historical-critical understanding of the Bible in contemporary France, Guyon's exegesis is relentlessly spiritual—every verse and

---

53 *Entretian spiritual* (Jamet, *Écrits*, 1:402–403).
54 Marie uses Song 1:1 (twice); 1:2–3; 1:3 (three times); 1:6 (three times); 1:13; 2:4; 2:9; 2:14; 4:8; 5:1; 5:6; 5:14; 6:4; 8:1–2; 8:6 (three times), and 8:14. State six (Mahoney, trans., *Marie de l'Incarnation*, 74–80) cites Song 1:6; 8:1–2; 8:14 and 1:3; 5:1, and 2:9. State seven (ibid., 81–95) contains one general reference to the Song and a citation of Song 5:6. State thirteen (ibid., 156–178) cites Song 4:8; 1:3; 8:5; 8:6, and 7:6.
55 The literature on Madame Guyon is large, so here I only cite my treatment in McGinn, *Crisis of Mysticism*, 139–182, and 204–256 (chapters 3–4), where a good deal of the previous literature is noted.
56 On Guyon's exegesis, see Le Brun, "Madame Guyon et le Bible"; Le Brun, "Présupposés théoriques."
57 Guyon's *Explications* on the Bible were published posthumously by her Protestant disciple, Pierre Poiret, between 1713 and 1715, with twelve volumes on the Old Testament and eight on the New Testament.

every image is a message about the soul's progress to God. As with many spiritual interpreters, Guyon insisted on the mutual reciprocity of the outer text of the Bible and the inner text of the experience of the mystic. The only part of this vast scriptural enterprise published in her lifetime was the *Commentaire au Cantique des cantiques* put out at Lyons in 1688.[58] The commentary is the first interpretation by a woman to cover every verse of the Song. It can rightly be described as essential to understanding Guyon's mysticism.

Guyon's *Commentary* carefully follows the lush and shifting symbolism of the Song and is therefore not easy to summarize, but all the major features of her mysticism are found in the text. As with many commentators, she spends a good deal of time with the "kiss of the mouth" of Song 1:1,[59] seeing it as revealing a key element in her mystical teaching, the difference between union with God through the soul's three inner powers (memory, intellect, will), which is a mediated union with the three Persons of the Trinity, and the highest form of union, immediate union with God in the soul's essence, which is the kiss of the mouth. She says: "The essential union and the kiss on the mouth is the spiritual marriage, where there is a union of essence to essence and communication of substances and where God takes the soul for his Bride and unites with it, no longer personally or by any act or means, but immediately, reducing all into unity and possessing it in the unity itself."[60] Guyon reads a number of other verses of the Song as indicating the difference between union in the powers and essential union (see, e.g., the comments on Song 2:6; 2:8; 2:17; 3:5; 3:9; 4:2–3; 6:2; 6:4; 7:10, and 8:1). Furthermore, she identifies the essential union with bestowal of the "apostolic state," another important aspect of her teaching. "It is necessary to know," she says, "that God is all mouth, just as he is all word, and that the application of this divine mouth to the soul is the perfect pleasure and the consummation of the marriage [. . .]. It is what we can call the apostolic state, by which the soul is not only married, but also fertile" (Song 1:1).[61] The apostolic state, which Guyon claimed as her license for undertaking her controversial public teaching career, is also illustrated by her interpretation of a number of other verses of the Song.[62]

---

[58] The modern edition is by Morali, *Les Torrents et Commentaire*. The best English translation is in Guenin-Lelle and Mourad, trans., *Jeanne Guyon*, 99–180. For studies, see Lee, *Sacrifice and Delight*, 57–80; and McGinn, *Crisis of Mysticism*, 154, 176–182.
[59] Morali, ed., *Les Torrents et Commentaire*, 205–210; Guenin-Lelle and Mourad, trans., *Jeanne Guyon*, 99–103.
[60] Morali, ed., *Les Torrents et Commentaire*, 206; Guenin-Lelle and Mourad, trans., *Jeanne Guyon*, 100.
[61] Morali, ed., *Commentaire*, 207; Guenin-Lelle and Mourad, trans., *Jeanne Guyon*, 100.
[62] See Song 4:10–11 (Morali, ed., *Les Torrents et Commentaire*, 255–256; Guenin-Lelle and Mourad, trans., *Jeanne Guyon*, 139–140); Song 4:16 (Morali, ed., *Les Torrents et Commentaire*, 258; Guenin-Lelle and Mourad, trans., *Jeanne Guyon*, 148); Song 8:11 (Morali, ed., *Les Torrents et Commentaire*,

Essential union involves the soul's return to its origin in God, as Guyon explains in a number of comments (see, e.g., the remarks on Song 2:10; 3:4; 6:8, and 7:2). Does it also imply a loss of all difference between God and the soul, a form of indistinct union? Sometimes Guyon's language seems to suggest this, but a careful examination of several key passages shows that some distinction always remains. In the explanation of Song 1:1, for example, Guyon talks about essential union as being "totally complete, being made from all in all," using the famous example of "the drop of water that loses its material consistence when it is put in a barrel of wine." Although outwardly to the senses the water disappears, she says that the "being and its matter are always distinct," so that the soul can still be separated from God.[63] Many of the other images of the Song of Songs, such as the wound of love, the sleep of the Bride, and mystical death, are given insightful treatments in the *Commentaire*, too many to be cited here. As with so many of the seventeenth-century mystics, Madame Guyon insisted that the road to union was the way of annihilation, so annihilation and abandonment often occur in the *Commentaire*. Annihilation is achieved through sharing in the sufferings of Christ on the cross. Guyon explains this in commenting on Song 2:1, where the Bridegroom says, "I am the flower of the field and the lily of the valley." Guyon says that God takes the soul from the "well-flowered bed" (Song 1:15) and lays her with Christ on "the sorrowful bed of the cross." The Bridegroom then says, "I am the lily of the valley that only grows in annihilated souls, so that if you want me to draw you from your earth and take up life in you, you must be in the last stages of annihilation."[64]

6 Conclusion

A full study of the women who commented on the Song of Songs during the period 1566–1685 still remains to be written. This brief consideration of five of the most important of the commentators demonstrates, I hope, one important note: there is no *one* female approach to the biblical song of love. Male exegetes had little difficulty taking on the voice and persona of the Bride, because in the world of

---

300; Guenin-Lelle and Mourad, trans., *Jeanne Guyon*, 176), and especially Song 8:13–14 (Morali, ed., *Les Torrents et Commentaire*, 301–306; Guenin-Lelle and Mourad, trans., *Jeanne Guyon*, 177–180).

63 See *Commentaire* on Song 1:1 (Morali, ed., *Les Torrents et Commentaire*, 209; Guenin-Lelle and Mourad, trans., *Jeanne Guyon*, 102); see also the exposition of Song 7:10–11 (Morali, ed., *Les Torrents et Commentaire*, 290–291; Guenin-Lelle and Mourad, trans., *Jeanne Guyon*, 168).

64 *Commentaire* on Song 2:1 (Morali, ed., *Les Torrents et Commentaire*, 225–226; Guenin-Lelle and Mourad, trans., *Jeanne Guyon*, 115). For other appearances of the annihilation theme, see the comments on Song 1:8; 3:7; 4:8; 4:13; 5:6; 6:4; 6:8, and 6:10.

transcendent eros they could identify with her yearning desire for the Bridegroom expressed across the Song. How they expressed that identity was colored by their individual cultural and theological backgrounds, as well as their own states of mystical consciousness. The same can be said for each of these women commentators. They express a rich variety of modes of experiencing divine love, and the variety itself is integral to their message. Like the Bride, we may say of them, *Quid videbis in Sulamiten nisi choros castrorum* ("What will you see in the Sulamite but companies of camps")?[65]

Bibliography

Culligan, Kevin. "Mary and Martha Working Together: Teresa of Avila's *Meditations on the Song of Songs*." In *Seeing the Seeker: Explorations in the Discipline of Spirituality; Festschrift for Kees Waaijman*, edited by Hein Blommestijn, Charles Caspers, Rijcklof Hofman, Frits Mertens, and Peter Nissen, 315–329. Leuven: Peeters, 2008.

Diaz Cerón, José, ed. *Obras Completas de Cecilia del Nacimiento*. Madrid: Editorial de Espiritualidad, 1970.

Donnelly, Kevin, and Sandra Sider, eds. *Cecilia del Nacimiento: Journeys of a Mystic Soul in Poetry and Prose*. Toronto: Iter. Centre for Reformation and Renaissance Studies, 2012.

Droulers, Paul. "Cambry (Jeanne de) (1581–1639)." *Dictionnaire de Spiritualité ascétique et mystique* 3:61–62.

Guenin-Lelle, Dianne, and Ronney Mourad, eds. *Jeanne Guyon: Selected Writings*. New York: Paulist Press, 2012.

Hart, Mother Columba. *Hadewijch. The Complete Works*. New York: Paulist Press, 1980.

Jamet, Albert, ed. *Marie de l'Incarnation: Écrits spirituels et historiques*. 4 vols. Paris: Desclée de Brouwer, 1929–1939.

Kavanaugh, Kieran, and Otilio Rodriguez. *The Collected Works of Saint Teresa of Avila*. Vol. 2. Washington DC: ICS Publications, 1976–1985.

Latz, Dorothy L., ed. *The Building of Divine Love as Translated by Dame Agnes More: Transcribed from the 17th Century Manuscript*. Salzburg: Universität Salzburg. Institut für Anglistik und Amerikanistik, 1992.

Le Brun, Jacques. "Madame Guyon et le Bible." In *Madame Guyon*, edited by Joseph Beaude, 63–82. Grenoble: Jérôme Millon, 1997.

Le Brun, Jacques. "Présupposés théoriques de la lecture de la Bible: L'example de la Sainte Bible et Mme. Guyon." *RTP* 133 (2001): 287–302.

Lee, Bo Karen. *Sacrifice and Delight in the Mystical Theologies of Anna Maria van Schurman and Madame Jeanne Guyon*. Notre Dame: University of Notre Dame, 2014.

Mahoney, Irene. *Marie de l'Incarnation: Selected Writings*. New York: Paulist Press, 1989.

Mali, Anya. *Mystic in the New World: Marie de l'Incarnation (1599–1672)*. Leiden: Brill, 1996.

---

[65] Like many verses of the Song, the image is mysterious and elusive. The original Hebrew has been read as, "Why should you look upon the Shulammite as a dance before two armies?"

McGinn, Bernard. *The Crisis of Mysticism: Quietism in Seventeenth-Century Spain, Italy, and France.* New York: Crossroad-Herder, 2021.
McGinn, Bernard. "Hildegard of Bingen as Visionary and Exegete." In *Hildegard von Bingen in ihrem historischen Umfeld*, edited by Alfred Haverkamp, 321–350. Mainz: Philipp von Zabern, 2000.
McGinn, Bernard. "The Language of Love in Christian and Jewish Mysticism." In *Mysticism and Language*, edited by Steven T. Katz, 202–235. Oxford: Oxford University Press, 1992.
McGinn, Bernard. *Mysticism in the Golden Age of Spain.* New York: Crossroad, 2017.
McGinn, Bernard. "'One Word Will Contain Within Itself a Thousand Mysteries': Teresa of Avila, the First Woman Commentator on the Song of Songs." *Spiritus* 16 (2016): 21–40.
McGinn, Bernard. *The Persistence of Mysticism in Catholic Europe: France, Italy, and Germany (1500–1675).* New York: Crossroad, 2020.
McGinn, Bernard. "Women Interpreting the Song of Songs: 1150–1700." In *A Companion to the Song of Songs in the History of Spirituality*, edited by Timothy H. Robinson, 249–274. Brill's Companions to the Christian Tradition 98. Leiden: Brill, 2021.
McGinn, Bernard. "Women Reading the Song of Songs in the Christian tradition." In *Scriptural Exegesis: The Shapes of Culture and the Religious Imagination; Essays in Honor of Michael Fishbane*, edited by Deborah A. Green and Laura S. Lieber, 281–296. Oxford: Oxford University Press, 2009.
Morali, Claude. *Les Torrents et Commentaire au Cantique des cantiques de Salomon (1683–1684).* Grenoble: Jérôme Millon, 1992.
Slade, Carol. "Saint Teresa's *Meditaciones sobre los Cantares*: The Hermeneutics of Humility and Enjoyment." *Religion & Literature* 18 (1986): 27–43.
Steggink, Otger, and Efren de la Madre de Dios, eds. *Santa Teresa de Jesús: Obras Completas; Edicion Manual.* Madrid: BAC, 1986.

Timothy H. Robinson
Varieties of Reformed and Puritan Reception of the Song of Songs, 1550–1730

1 Introduction

When John Cotton's *A Brief Exposition with Practical Observations Upon the Whole Book of Canticles* was published posthumously in 1655, it became, in fact, the second published commentary the Puritan clergyman had authored on the Song of Songs. Cotton (1585–1652) was one of the most significant and influential figures in early New England Congregationalism, having been an established leader among English Nonconformists as vicar of St. Botolph's parish in Boston, Lincolnshire, where he preached a series of sermons on the Song of Songs in the early 1620s.[1] Those sermons were published in 1642 as *A Brief Exposition on the Whole Book of Canticles* after Cotton had fled the threat of persecution in England in 1633 to become the pastor of First Church of Boston, Massachusetts. In the 1642 version of his commentary, Cotton explained that the enigmatic Biblical work describes "the estate of the Church in the ages thereof, both Jewish and Christian, to this day."[2] Cotton's exposition was explicitly political, viewing the Song as historical and prophetic allegory and setting out his vision of a church purely reformed.

---

[1] Throughout this essay I refer to my subjects variously as "Reformed," "Protestant," "Puritan," or "nonconformist." There is a vast literature on the identity of various factions in English Protestantism during the sixteenth through eighteenth centuries and this essay is not the place to sort out the nuances of Puritan historiography. In general, "Protestant" or "Reformed" are broad terms that include all those members of the Church of England who split from Rome during the English Reformation of the sixteenth century, and, generally, reflected the Reformed theology of the Calvinian wing of the European Reformations. The terms "Puritan" and "nonconformist" identify groups who split from the Church of England—either voluntarily or forcibly—because they believed the reformation enacted by the Church of England had not gone far enough. They refused to "conform" with ecclesiastical authority and practice, largely in matters of church government and liturgical practices. Many clergy who remained within the Church of England, however, either bore Puritan leanings or produced theological writings that were congruent with and influential among England's and New England's Puritans. Thus, in this chapter, I use terminology broadly to identify distinctive Reformed theological emphases, while attempting, when appropriate, to identify the known status of specific figures.
[2] Cotton, *A Brief Exposition of the Whole Book*, title page.

Note: Some of this chapter is adapted from my previous work on Puritan reception of the Song, including the following: Hessel-Robinson, "Erotic Mysticism"; idem, *Reverend Edward Taylor*; Robinson, "Banquet of Love."

Cotton's interpretation of the Song as a prophetic allegory of the church's history and renewal fit squarely within the millennial visions of those Reformed Protestants, known popularly today as Puritans, who, resisting the Church of England as not being fully reformed, emigrated to New England to establish a "garden in the wilderness," or "a shining city upon a hill." Thus, it is strange that Ilana Pardes recently claimed "When the Puritans arrived on the shores of America in the seventeenth century, the Song of Songs was not among the biblical texts they projected onto new landscapes."[3] Pardes leaves Puritan treatments of the Song completely out of her otherwise excellent and interesting book on the history of Song reception. Perhaps the influence of Max Weber, who famously claimed that the Song "was for the most part simply ignored by the Puritans," continues to shape assumptions that the Puritans avoided the erotically charged language and imagery of the Song in their exhaustive engagement with the Bible.[4] In fact, though, immigrants to New England, like John Cotton, brought with them a fascination with the Song of Songs, or "Divine Canticle" as they knew it, along with an extensive tradition of applying it to Reformed and Puritan piety and politics. Some scholars have identified more than 30 commentaries and more than 50 paraphrases of the Song published in England alone between the sixteenth and eighteenth centuries.[5] In addition, individual sermons on the Song from this era are too numerous to count, liturgical and sacramental manuals, hymns, and personal diaries are filled with references and allusions to the Song, and many more commentaries and sermons appeared in New England during the seventeenth and eighteenth centuries. As one observer has put it, Puritan commentators shared their ancient and medieval predecessors' "preoccupation" with the Song of Songs.[6] Puritan interpreters agreed with the longer traditions of Christian Song reception that the work is to be interpreted as an allegory of the love between Christ and the church, inclusive of all its members.

Cotton insisted that approaching the Song as "historical prophecie or propheticall history" was the most profitable way to read the text, but acknowledged that multiple interpretations of the Song were valid and valuable, including more traditional readings that viewed it pertaining to Christ's relationship with the church or with the individual soul, and his later work incorporated a more personal and affective approach to the text.[7] While Cotton's historical-prophetic approach was not uncommon in the seventeenth century, other Puritan readings of the Song as

---

3 Pardes, *Song of Songs*, 172.
4 Weber, *Protestant Ethic*, 199–200 n. 97.
5 See Hammond, "Songs," 4.
6 Scheper, "Reformation Attitudes," 556.
7 Cotton, *A Brief Exposition*, 1642 version, 10. On Cotton's treatment of the Song, see Hammond, "Bride"; Sievers, "Refiguring"; Clarke, *Politics*, 123–124.

an allegory of love between Christ and the church or Christ and the individual soul were more common. John Collings (1623/1624–1690), an English nonconformist clergyman who produced a massive two volume commentary covering only the first two chapters of the Song, is more representative:

> I think I may further say, that there is no portion of Holy Writ so copiously as this, expressing the infinite, and the transcendent excellencies of the Lord Jesus Christ. None that more copiously instructs us, what he will be to us, or what we should be toward him, and consequently none more worthy of the pains of any who desires to Preach Christ.[8]

According to Collings, the Song permits readers to "see as much of Christ as can be seen of him on this side of Heaven."[9] In viewing Christ through the text of the Song, Puritan readers saw a portrait of beauty and desire to feed their spirits. Despite popular perceptions of Puritans as sexually repressed and embarrassed by the erotic contents of the work, they, like generations of readers before them, regarded the Song as the quintessential expression of intimacy between Christ and his people.[10]

In the rest of this article I will identify and examine three primary ways in which Reformed and Puritan readers during the sixteenth, seventeenth, and early eighteenth centuries received and appropriated the Song of Songs: as a historical-prophecy of church and state; as nurturing an erotic-affective spirituality; and as an archetypal poem that inspires readers to imitate it in their own devotional discipline of writing. In each of these three modes of reception, Puritan interpreters assumed what the long history of Christian reception of the Song had taught them: that the work is an allegory of divine love, describing the intimate relationship between Christ, the church, and the soul, and which is meant to kindle desire for Christ in its readers. Before turning to the three modes of Puritan reception, I will first examine one of the foundational reasons, besides their assumption of the allegorical nature of the poem, that Reformed readers so easily made the Song a crucial text for nurturing their spirituality: the assumption of the nuptial metaphor of the spiritual life.

---

8 Collings, *Intercourses*, 1:sig. A3r.
9 Collings, *Intercourses*, 2:30.
10 While, perhaps, not as extensively studied as other periods, traditions, or figures in the history of allegorical reception of the Song (e.g., Origen, the Cistercians, John of the Cross, etc.), Puritan reception has gained the attention of a number of scholars in the past half-century. For example, see Scheper, "Reformation Attitudes"; Hammond, "Songs," 56–109; Lewalski, *Protestant Poetics*, 59–69; Clarke, *Politics*; Schwanda, *Soul Recreation*; Hessel-Robinson, *Reverend Edward Taylor*, 27–70; Robinson, "Banquet of Love," 331–341.

2 The Nuptial Metaphor

An underlying foundation for the Song of Songs' appeal to Puritans was that they took for granted the centuries old trope of the "mystical marriage" between Christ and church or soul. Drawing upon various biblical passages such as Isa 54:5; Hos 2:19; Ps 45; Eph 5:32, and Rev 3:20, along with the Song of Songs, Reformed and Puritan interpreters regarded the metaphor of marriage as foundational for understanding the relationship between Christ and his people *and* as a fundamental image for the Christian spiritual life to which the Biblical canon bears witness throughout.[11] In his sermon *The Mysticall Match between Christ and His Church*, the influential English Puritan John Preston (1587–1628) begins with citations of Song 6:3 ("I am my beloved's and my beloved is mine") and Eph 5:32 ("This is a great mystery but I speake concerning Christ and concerning the Church"). These two verses serve as the foundation for Preston's development of the spiritual marriage metaphor which unfolds throughout the sermon. According to Preston, "The poynt out of these words is this, that, *There is a match between Christ and the Church:* and consequently, betweene Christ and every particular man that is a member of the true body of Christ; this is the great Mystery the Apostle tells us of in this place."[12] Thus, Preston establishes continuity in the reception of the reading pioneered by Origen that the Song explicates the relationship between both Christ and the church and Christ and the soul. The spiritual marriage metaphor underpins the sermon and Preston develops it by reflecting on the legal aspects of marriage, social understandings of marriage, and some personal perspectives on intimacy. While he never executes any sustained or systematic exegesis of either of the biblical passages upon which the sermon relies, Preston assumes the spiritual marriage metaphor as self-evident.

One reason the nuptial metaphor made sense to Reformed readers was their often-repeated conviction that God regularly accommodates to human understanding to illuminate mysteries too great for us to understand. Richard Sibbes (1577–1635), the popular English preacher influential on both sides of the Atlantic, asserted in his commentary on three chapters of the Song that it is "Out of mercy and pity" for humans that God's Spirit compares the deepest mysteries of divine-human communion to earthly things. "By stooping low to us," explained Sibbes, the Spirit raises us up to God.[13] Scripture renders the mystery of Christ's relationship to the church as a marriage "so that we might better see it in the glasse of a compari-

---

[11] For an overview of the spiritual marriage metaphor in Puritan spirituality, see Schwanda, *Soul Recreation*, 35–74.
[12] Preston, *Mysticall Match*, 1.
[13] Sibbes, *Bowels Opened*, 6.

son, which we cannot so directly conceive of as we may see the *sun* in water, whose beams we cannot so directly look upon."[14] Because marriage is the most "ardent" and pleasurable expression of human love—the "sweetest passage of our life"—according to Sibbes, it most fittingly and vividly represents the divine-human relationship and effectively nurtures communion between Christ and the soul.[15]

Almost one hundred years later, Jonathan Edwards (1703–1758), one of the greatest American theologians, often referred to as "the last Puritan," who preached 13 sermons on the Song and made many hundreds of references to it throughout his writings, mused that Solomon, "in his wisdom and great experience," had come to realize the "vanity" of all loves other than the love of God. Thus, states Edwards:

> God's Spirit made use of his loving inclination, joined with his musing philosophical disposition, and so directed and conducted it in this train of imagination as to represent the love that there is between Christ and his spouse. God saw it very needful and exceeding useful that there should be some such representation of it. The relation that there is between Christ and the church, we know, is very often compared to what there is between a man [and] his wife—yea, this similitude is abundantly insisted on almost everywhere in the Scripture—and a virtuous and pious and pure love between a man and his spouse is very much of an image of the love between Christ and the church.[16]

In another place Edwards stated the Song represents "the great love between Christ and his spouse the church, particularly adapted to the dispositions and holy affections of a true Christian's soul towards Christ, and representing his grace and marvelous love to and delight in his people."[17] Concomitantly, Edwards regarded earthly marriage as endowed with representational power, in its purest expressions illuminating the spiritual marriage to which the Scriptures bear witness: "The Holy Ghost mainly delighting in the marriage union as a representation, or similitude, of the union between Christ and his church, and marriage being instituted to that end, as the Apostle teaches in the latter end of the fifth [chapter] of Ephesians, therefore God would order the circumstances of marriage so as to render it the most lively image of this union."[18] Earlier, Collings more concisely summarized the importance of the marriage analogy in his Song commentary: "As the apostle makes use of the Ordinance of Marriage, to represent the mystical Union between Christ and the Church, Eph.5:32, So Christ is expressly called a Bridegroom, his Church,

---

14 Sibbes, *Bowels Opened*, 6.
15 Sibbes, *Bowels Opened*, 6.
16 Edwards, *Miscellanies*, 390. For an examination of Edwards's treatment of the Song, see Sweeney, *Edwards the Exegete*, 113–136.
17 Edwards, *Miscellanies*, 433.
18 Edwards, *Blank Bible*, 255.

and believing Soul in particular, the Bride."[19] The relationship between Christ and his people was, according to the title of a sermon by the eminent Boston Congregational minister Cotton Mather (1663–1728), a "glorious espousal."[20]

Adopting the nuptial metaphor and reading the Song of Songs against this backdrop, Puritan readers, far from rejecting its erotic language, embraced it as part of the analogy involving earthly marriage between women and men and spiritual marriage between soul/church and Christ. In fact, as one observer has noted, the marital, romantic, and erotic imagery employed in Puritan spiritual literature—sermons, diaries, commentaries, etc.—"grew lusher and more erotic" during the late seventeenth century and into the eighteenth century.[21] While Puritans appropriated the erotic and marital imagery for the spiritual life received from ancient and medieval sources, they were adopting language and imagery promulgated primarily by celibate monastic readers who shunned married life and the physical expression of erotic desires; Protestant readers, in contrast, with their understanding of married and family life as a conduit of grace, interpreted the Song through the range of their experience of marriage: erotic and romantic, covenantal, and domestic.[22] Thus, the enthusiastic Puritan embrace of the Song of Songs and its traditional/allegorical/erotic interpretation was a simultaneous embrace of the mystical marriage or nuptial metaphor for the spiritual life. And, while the Song of Songs was certainly a remarkable text illuminating this central metaphor for Puritans, they drew on passages throughout the canon to illuminate it.

3 Historical Prophetic Allegory

I have already introduced the historical-prophetic approach to the Song to which John Cotton gave expression in his early sermons on the Song. This approach, while common in seventeenth century England, had roots stretching back to Martin Luther (1483–1546), who thought of the Song as "an encomium of the political order" written by Solomon as a song of praise to God for establishing governments throughout history to maintain peace, justice, and order. The Song "deals with

---

[19] Collings, *Intercourses*, 1:29.
[20] Mather, *A Glorious Espousal*.
[21] Godbeer, "Love Raptures," 51.
[22] See Godbeer, "Love Raptures," 51–53. See also Porterfield, *Female Piety*, 14–30; Scheper, "Reformation Attitudes," 551–559. It should be noted, however, that much medieval monastic literature on the Song drew upon the idea that it was the premier representation of love between Christ and his beloveds because marriage and sexuality were the most intimate and complete expressions of love available to humans in this life.

matters of the loftiest and greatest kind, namely, with the divinely ordained governments," said Luther.[23] Rather than treating the stories of individual persons like other songs in the Bible, the Song of Songs narrates the story of God's whole people in order to relate how God preserves order and defends his kingdom against the devil's assaults.[24] While Luther's rather enigmatic approach to the Song did not make a major impact on the trajectories of Song interpretation, his proposal that the Song deals with sacred and secular history anticipated the Reformed historical-prophetic approach.

As historical allegory the Song was viewed as a historical and prophetic work in which the bridegroom in the text was identified as God and the bride as Israel or the church.[25] This approach helped the Reformed appropriate the Song in polemics against the Roman Catholic Church, and helped Puritans and other nonconformists to use it in polemics against the Church of England. The English clergyman Thomas Brightman (1562–1607) was one of the most prominent innovators of this approach. Brightman brought his Puritan convictions and his fascination with millennial speculation to the Song, Revelation, and Daniel, developing an eschatological hermeneutic in which he saw the Song as a prophetic history of the "church," covering the period between King David and Christ's second coming. To each of the literary units of the Song he assigned a corresponding historical period:

> The authority of this Song is declared in the Inscription. Then he [Solomon] prosecuteth his purpose in verse, which is wholly employed in describing the condition of the Church, as well as it was legall, from the time of David to the death of Christ, in the 3 first chapters and to the 6 verse of the 4 chapter. As also, as it was Evangelicall unto the Second Coming of Christ to the end of the book.[26]

Brightman found correspondence in the Song's details to a variety of historical figures, from Holy Roman Emperors to "Ecclesiasticall Teachers and Rulers," to various state churches in England, Ireland, Scotland, Geneva, Germany, Spain, and Sweden, as well as Anabaptists and others. For Brightman, the Song of Songs and Revelation speak to the same subject in different languages: the eschatological consummation of the Church's marriage to Christ, hinting that its time was drawing near.[27]

The English minister Nathanael Homes (1599–1678) shared Brightman's enthusiasm for apocalyptic texts and produced a great deal of eschatological material

---

23 Luther, "Lectures," 192.
24 See Luther, "Lectures," 192–195.
25 See Alexander, "Song of Songs."
26 Brightman, *A Commentary*, 980.
27 See Brightman, *A Commentary*, 124–125. The view that the Song was an abridged version of Revelation had medieval antecedents. On this, see Matter, *Voice*, 89.

throughout his life. Like Brightman and Cotton, Homes took the Song to be *"Prophetical* History or *Historical* Prophesie (after the manner of *Daniel's* Prophesying)" recording the state of the church "from *Solomons* time, down to the second coming of Christ."[28] Publishing his commentary in the early 1650s, Homes read the text as explaining the English civil wars of the previous decade and prophesying the end of Roman Catholicism in England: he viewed this as the literal sense of the Song.[29]

As already noted, John Cotton, also, saw the Song as a narrative and prophecy of the history of the Christian church. He depicted Solomon standing with his bride on a mountain surveying the history of "the church" from Solomon's time all the way to the final judgment: "As God led Moses to the top of Mount Pisgah, to behold all the places and situations of Israel: So he lifted up Solomons spirit to the mountaine of Activite (that I may so speake) where only all times to come are present, to behold the estate of the Church throughout the present, and all after ages."[30] Like Brightman and Homes, Cotton associated individual verses or passages in the Song with various time periods and figures. For Cotton, the opening chapter of the Song describes "the estate of the Church in the days, First of Solomon, verse 2–4. Secondly, of Solomon and Rehoboam, verse 5. Thirdly, of Rehoboam, verse 6–9."[31] Cotton explained that Song 1:4—"the King hath brought me into his chambers"—is a reference to places where God and Israel have enjoyed communion: "First, the Tabernacle of Gibeon. Secondly, the Arke at Jerusalem. Thirdly, the Temple."[32] With Brightman and Homes, Cotton associated the Song with Revelation. Connecting the concluding verse (8:14) of the Song ("Make haste my beloved") with Rev 20:20 ("Even so come Lord Jesus, come quickly"), Cotton said that each verse expresses the longing of the bride for her bridegroom to hasten home to her side.[33] For Cotton, the purpose of the Song was to nurture desire and preparation for the return of Christ in believers.

The events of the seventeenth century in church and society in England and New England, and the millenarian fervor in the air during that century seemed to invite Reformed commentators to seek out harbingers of current events in the Bible, and the Song of Songs was not excepted from their efforts.[34] However, the historical-prophetic approach eventually waned in favor of more traditional individual and ecclesiastical readings of the Song by Puritans who sought spiritual

---

28 Homes, *A Commentary*, A2.
29 See Clarke, *Politics*, 126.
30 Cotton, *A Brief Exposition of the Whole Book*, 13.
31 Cotton, *A Brief Exposition of the Whole Book*, 6.
32 Cotton, *A Brief Exposition of the Whole Book*, 20.
33 See Cotton, *A Brief Exposition of the Whole Book*, 263–264.
34 For more on this, see Alexander, "Song of Songs."

sustenance and nurture through more contemplative readings. In fact, a primary critique of the historical/prophetic interpretation was that it failed to highlight the spiritual relevance of the Song for believers in every age. As Presbyterian minister Robert Fleming (1660–1716) argued in critiquing Thomas Beverly's (d. 1702) commentary on the Song, Beverly had completely disregarded the Song's spiritual significance "since he leaves the spiritual sense thereof, and turns it wholly to Prophecy."[35] English Baptist minister John Gill (1697–1771), in his well-known work on the Song, argued that the historical-prophetic reading was misguided because it could only apply "to them that liveth at that time and not to others." Instead, Gill affirmed the traditional view that "every part of this song, the first as well as the last, is applicable to believers in all ages of the world."[36] Gill noted that the Song "has been useful to thousands who have had their spiritual senses exercised, for the comfort of their souls, faith, and their instruction in divine things."[37] Therefore, this should be the primary way readers approach the Song. Clarke has noted that by the late seventeenth century and early eighteenth the understanding of the Song as a "love story between Christ and the reader" had come to predominate Reformed and Puritan interpretation.[38] We now turn to that approach.

4 Erotic/Affective Interpretation

The interpretive approach to the Song of Songs that Clarke calls "a love story between Christ and the reader," might also be termed an "erotic/affective" interpretation. That is, Puritans viewed "true religion" as a warm, experiential "endeavor of the heart, an affair of the affections."[39] In the passionate and erotic language of the Song, they read a description of the fervent love affair they were called to have with their lord and savior.

The beauty of Christ was one aspect of an affective spirituality they drew upon the Song to express. Musing on the time of his conversion, Jonathan Edwards recounts how he would meditate on the "beauty and excellency" of Christ with the words of Song 2:1 in mind ("I am the rose of Sharon, the lilly of the valleys"):

---

[35] Fleming, *Mirrour*, sig. A4v.
[36] Gill, *An Exposition*, 16.
[37] Gill, *An Exposition*, 3.
[38] Clarke, *Politics*, 133.
[39] Sweeney, *Edwards the Exegete*, 132. Jonathan Edwards most famously rendered spirituality as such in his Treatise on *Religious Affections*.

> The words seemed to me, sweetly to represent, the loveliness and beauty of Jesus Christ. And the whole book of Canticles used to be pleasant to me; and I used to be much in reading it, about that time. And found, from time to time, an inward sweetness, that used, as it were, to carry me away in my contemplations [. . .][40]

Puritans often focused on Christ's spiritual beauty in physical terms. Christopher Jelinger (d. 1685) was a German Puritan who ministered in England. In his sermon on Song 2:1 Jelinger explained that the Song refers to Christ as a rose because the rose speaks to Christ's great beauty, which should be the object of contemplation for the desiring soul:

> O my soule, doe thou elevate and lift up thy selfe, and consider this ravishing and transcendent beauty of thy most deare and glorious Saviour, so as that no creature under the sun may be fairer and dearer in thine eies then he, who is fairer then all.[41]

The ways that the Song describes Christ's beauty make it the "most fragrant and precious of Scripture."[42]

In much Puritan treatment of the Song, Christ's beauty serves a seductive purpose, to stoke the soul's desire for Christ and draw it into union with him. Massachusetts pastor Edward Taylor (1642–1729), who produced numerous poetic meditations as preparation for celebrating the Lord's supper, many of which are based on verses from the Song of Songs, demonstrates this well in his treatment of the *waṣfs* of the Song.[43] Taylor composed lush descriptions of Christ's body, identifying a list of his attractive qualities. As the "chiefest among ten thousand" (Song 5:10) Christ is a king dwelling in a realm of glory beyond imagination, the thought of which stirs the poet's desire to join him there. The "bed of spices" which lodge in Christ's cheeks (Song 5:13) gives off a "Sweet beauty reeching in thy Countenance," and enthralling "amorous charms."[44] The strength of Christ's "legs like Marble Pillars" (Song 5:15) impress the poet.[45] Taylor confesses he is so smitten, "That all my heart and hearty Love most right / Leap thence and lodge [. . .] in thy heart."[46] Such is the wonder of Christ's beauty and strength that they cause the admiring soul to swoon. Speaking the words of Song 5:16 directly to Christ, Taylor declares

---

40 Edwards, "Personal Narrative," 793.
41 Jelinger, *Usefulnesse*, 16–21.
42 Jelinger, *Usefulnesse*, 1.
43 See Hessel-Robinson, "Language of the Feast," 90–113.
44 Taylor, *Preparatory Meditations* (PM). Citations will be to the individual poems by series, poem number, and line number. Here: *PM* 2.120:4–5.
45 Taylor, *PM* 2.123[b]:19–30.
46 Taylor, *PM* 2.123[b]:45–46.

"Thou altogether Lovely art, all Bright," telling him that "Thy Loveliness attracts all love to Thee."[47] Christ's beauty consumes the poet with desire for union with him.

English politician and mystic Francis Rous (1579–1659) provided one of the most extravagant examples of the allegorical/erotic interpretation of the Song in his treatise *The Mystical Marriage*. Rous's work is not a commentary on the Song of Songs per se, but rather an extended meditation on the nuptial metaphor punctuated throughout with verses from the Song. Alluding to Song 1:4 in his preface, Rous explains, "There is a chamber within us, and a bed of love in that chamber, wherein Christ meets and rests with the soul" into which nothing can enter to disturb the intimacy shared between Christ and the soul.[48] Rous's work draws on the Song's language to render one of the most erotically charged Puritan-era mystical reflections on the work, building around the central image of Christ and the soul communing in bed a mosaic of scriptural quotation and allusion. Like others, Rous also focuses on the beauty of Christ, urging his readers to do the same: "Fix [thine eye] upon him as upon the fairest of men, the perfection of spiritual beautie, the treasure of heavenly joy, the true object of most fervent love and inflamed affections."[49] Reversing the common condemnation of lust based on Jesus's words in Matt 5:28, Rous *encourages* his readers to "lust" after Christ, "for here it is a sin not to look that thou maist lust, and not to lust having looked."[50] Rous describes the pleasure experienced by the soul who comes into communion with Christ, the bridegroom of the Song, likening the wisdom and grace imparted by Christ to the soul as a kind of spiritual pillow talk: "There are some mysteries and secrets which thy husband will whisper into thee by his spirit in the bed of love."[51] After cataloging a list of criteria for evaluating the genuineness of an experience of encounter with Christ, Rous's prose erupts in a euphoric entreaty, asking Christ, his lover, to fill him with divine love:

> Yea, let thy spirit of love come so fully into my soul, that it stretch and enlarge her measure, and make her to grow from the measure in which she is, unto the measure in which she should be [. . .] Yea, let the measure sometime be not only full, but running over; even running over to a spiritual drunkenness [. . .] for these extasies and excesses of love, shall somewhat advance my ability of loving thee. For when my understanding, will, and affections, are all overflown, overcome, and amazed, then shall my wonder gaze on thee, and my very fainting shall be enflamed toward thee, and melt into thee.[52]

---

47 Taylor, *PM* 2.127:25–26.
48 See Rous, "Mystical Marriage," S2.
49 Rous, "Mystical Marriage," 687.
50 Rous, "Mystical Marriage," 687.
51 Rous, "Mystical Marriage," 712.
52 Rous, "Mystical Marriage," 736.

Bernard of Clairvaux's *Sermons on the Song of Songs* sound positively restrained compared to Rous's impassioned reveries on the experience of Christ mediated to him by the Song's imagery.

Not all Puritan commentary on the Song highlights the erotic tenor of its language quite so explicitly, of course. And, in the end, these authors were drawing on earthy marital and sexual imagery to point to a spiritual relationship. As Edwards noted of the nature of the Song of Songs: "it was a song of the most excellent subject, treating of the love, union, and communion between Christ and his spouse, of which marriage and conjugal love was but a shadow."[53] According to Edwards, the "most excellent" love depicted by the Song is the one between Christ and his bride, the church. In his sermon on Song 2:16, the English Presbyterian minister Thomas Watson (1620–1686) claimed "this *spiritual* union, brings in more astonishing delights and ravishments, than any other marriage-relation is capable of, the joy that flows from the mystical union, is, unspeakable and full of glory." For Watson, while earthly marriage can represent the spiritual marriage, what the Song speaks of is superior because "in other marriages, two make one flesh, but Christ and the believer make one spirit."[54]

Moreover, the longing for Christ expressed in much Puritan Song commentary and poetry in overtly erotic language was provisional. Or, perhaps it is better to say that it was anticipatory of something understood to be even greater than an ecstatic experience of communion with Christ in this life. Much Puritan treatment of the Song was eschatological, but not in the same manner as was the historical/prophetic approach. For Reformed and Puritan devotional writers the ultimate fulfillment of the desires they expressed was something reserved for the next life. The French Reformed theologian Theodore Beza (1519–1605), whose sermons on the Song were influential among English Puritans, reminded his readers that "the true consummation of this marriage is not in earth but in heaven."[55] Thomas Watson agreed: "The day of a Christians death, is the birth-day of his heavenly life; it is his Ascension day to glory; it is his marriage-day with Jesus Christ. After his funeral begins his marriage."[56] John Collings explained to his readers that the human experience on earth is meant to be a preparation for the heavenly marriage during which the bride can mature spiritually, making herself ready for union with the heavenly bridegroom: "Christ lets us live here, till we be of age, and in the mean while, is traveled to Heaven [. . .] and at that day he shall come, and take us into

---

[53] Edwards, *Notes on Scripture*, 92.
[54] Watson, *Shewing the Mystical Union*, 346–347. Emphasis added. On Watson's mysticism and treatment of the Song, see Schwanda, "Sweetnesse in Communion," 34–63.
[55] Beza, *Sermons*, 21.
[56] Watson, *Christian's Charter*, 88.

himself and the marriage of the Lambe will be complete."[57] Spiritual practices, like prayer, participation in the sacraments, and meditative reading of Scripture—especially the Song of Songs—are means by which believers can prepare for this consummation, but also stimulate their desire for it.

5 Poetic Paraphrases

As I have already noted, English readers of the Song produced a significant number of poetic paraphrases.[58] These renderings of the Song in meter and rhyme were themselves means of interpretation. Puritan readers recognized the genre of the Song as poetry as significant in its own right. Part of the Song's distinctiveness lay in its form as poetry or song; the text called for a hermeneutic suitable to that form. Further, Puritans understood poetry as especially effective in arousing spiritual affections, and writing poetry was recommended as a suitable devotional exercise.[59] Collings makes each of these observations, noting that the fact that the Song was composed as poetry signals its uniqueness among "most other books of Holy Writ," and suggests that composing and singing songs can "excite and inflame the affections."[60] He adds that "there is a secret virtue in *Poetry*, engaging Peoples hearts, and affections to attention."[61]

The Song of Songs and the Psalms were regarded as the most sublime expressions of poetry in the Bible, while David and Solomon, as their authors, were archetypal poets to be imitated, and the Song inspired Renaissance and Reformation era poets. The tradition of poetic paraphrase arose in reaction to the appropriation of the Song's lush, erotic language in secular love poetry and song, viewed by Puritans as a profane distortion of Sacred Scripture. Stanley Stewart argued that "the piously inclined poet saw verse paraphrases of the Bible as the logical answer" to what they regarded as the decadence of popular, secular love lyrics. Stewart contends that the proliferation of verse paraphrases of the Song resulted from a strong reaction to and competition with secular and courtly love poetry.[62] According to the poet William Baldwin (d. 1563) some saw only "wanton wurdes" in the Song and he argued that paraphrases served to "drive out of office the bawdy ballades

---

57 Collings, *A Cordial*, 89.
58 For more extensive treatment of this genre, see Stewart, *Enclosed Garden*; Flinker, *Song of Songs*; Hessel-Robinson, *Reverend Edward Taylor*, 64–68.
59 See, for example, Hambrick-Stowe, *New England Meditative Poetry*, 7–62.
60 Collings, *Intercourses*, 1:31.
61 Collings, *Intercourses*, 1:36.
62 Stewart, *Enclosed Garden*, 3.

of lecherous love that commonly are indited and sung of idle courtyers in princes and noblemens houses."[63] The London schoolmaster and writer John Wharton (ca. 1575–1578) distinguished between the profane nature of secular lyrics and the appropriate treatment of the Song's language and intention, warning in the preface to Jud Smith's paraphrase of the poem that readers would be disappointed if they picked up the work seeking something to stoke their lust:

> For surely if thou covet to hear anye old bable, as I may terme them or stale tales of
>
> > Chauser, or to learne how Acteon came by his horned head: if they mynde be fired to any such metamophorall toyes, this book is not apt nor fit for thy purpose.[64]

Wharton's warning is echoed in verse form in the preface to English clergyman John Horne's (d. 1676) paraphrase, *The Divine Wooer*:

> It was not my intent, strains to invent,
> Or witty phrases which some men count rich.
> 'Twas not thy lust to feed, while thou dost read,
> Nor yet to satisfie a vain fancy.
> But t'was thy Soul to win, from vice, and sin,
> And woo thee unto Bliss, that I writ this.[65]

One of the strategies for mitigating the "wantoness" of the Song's words in paraphrase was to preface sections with an explanation of the "argument" of each. The argument of the first song, according to Baldwin, is that the Church, Christ's spouse, has been delivered from "the corrupt kisses of fleshly pleasures and delytes," and having experienced "the pure fountayn of gods aboundant loue and mercy," now sings a song expressing how she is inflamed with desire for Christ's love.[66] Such instructions echoed warnings offered by Christian interpreters since Origen that one should take care not to mistake the erotic content of the Song for something it is not.

Another strategy was to incorporate doctrinal content into the texts.[67] Baldwin, for example, refers to original sin and the Reformed emphasis on grace as he embellishes the Song's first verse:

> The Kiss o Christe, which I of thee require
> Thy grace, thy peace, thy love (my Love) it is:

---

63 Baldwin, *Canticles*, preface, A.iiiv.
64 John Wharton in Smith, *A Misticall Devise*, preface, A.ii.
65 Horne, *Divine Wooer*, preface.
66 Baldwin, *Canticles*, sig.Avr.
67 On this and for further treatment of Baldwin's paraphrase, see Clarke, *Politics*, 15–18.

> Whiche while I lacke, thy fathers wrath and yre,
> Condemnesh me for my first fathers wisse.[68]

These excerpts illustrate the self-conscious manner in which religious poets competed with secular ones. Stewart noted how this interaction led many religious poets to adopt the language and patterns of secular lyrics in their adaptations of the Song, illustrated by Francis Quarles' (1592–1644) sonnets which paraphrased the biblical work. Quarles rendered the second verse of the Song's opening chapter—"let him kiss me with the kisses of his mouth, for your love is better than wine"—thusly:

> O that the bountie of those lips divine,
> Would seale their favours on these lips of mine;
> That by those welcome kisses I might see
> The mutuall love, betwixt my love and mee;
> For truer blisse, no worldly joye allowes,
> Then sacred Kisses, from so sweet a Spouse;
> With which, no earthly pleasures may compare:
> Rich Wines are not so delicate as thay're.[69]

Such imitations of secular forms sometimes actually served to highlight the erotic language of the Song, such as Baldwin's treatment of the *waṣf*s in Song 7:6–7. Despite the explanatory headings, Baldwin's treatment echoes the French tradition of "blason" which had developed a short time before, in which poets named parts of a woman's body as a suggestive erotic exercise:[70]

> Lyke thou art in stature to the tree,
> Of Palmes, for no wayght can let thee for to grow:
> And thy brestes are lyke as semeth me,
> To clusters of grapes, that rype hang doune below,
> O my Darlyng.[71]

The many English paraphrases of the Song that appeared in the sixteenth and seventeenth centuries ranged from virtually literal translations with extensive commentary, to flowery paraphrases like Quarles', to metrical versions intended for public singing. While these paraphrases were written to counter secular love poetry perceived as profane, they had the further effect of disseminating and emphasizing the traditional allegorical reading of the Song. They also highlighted the poetic nature of the Song of Songs and its spiritual value *as poetry*. Thus, as noted above, Puritans practiced poetry writing as a devotional discipline, along with diary-keep-

---

[68] Baldwin, *Canticles*, sig.Avr.
[69] Quarles, *Sion's Sonnets*, 123.
[70] See Flinker, *Song of Songs*, 55; Clarke, *Politics*, 17.
[71] Baldwin, *Canticles*.

ing, and spiritual autobiography. Writing served as a means of prayer and meditation. As Puritans sifted through the events of their lives, searching for evidence of God's work in their lives, recording their experiences facilitated their contemplative self-scrutiny. Writing also served as preparation for public worship. As Hambrick-Stowe notes, personal spiritual writing served as a "means of grace" for Puritans and they looked to the Bible, to David's Psalms and Solomon's Song, especially, for inspirational examples to emulate.[72]

6 Conclusion

Reformed and Puritan readers of the sixteenth through eighteenth centuries received the Song of Songs as centuries of their spiritual ancestors had, viewing it as an allegorical portrait of Christ's beauty and of the deep intimacy shared between Christ and his spouse, the church or the individual soul. Far from avoiding the erotic language and imagery of the Song, as many have assumed, Puritan readers embraced its sensual content as a description of Christ's great love for his people and as suitable for nurturing passion for Christ in his followers. As the influential Reformed minister Matthew Henry (1662–1714), whose commentary on the whole Bible remains in print today, alluding to an ancient dictum of Gregory the Great (540–604), wrote of the Song, "there are depths in it in which any elephant may swim," but pondering it will "excite the pious and devout affections in us; and the same truths that are plainly laid down in other scriptures when they are restated out of this come to the soul with a more pleasing power."[73]

Bibliography

Alexander, Philip. "The Song of Songs as Historical Allegory: Notes on the Development of an Exegetical Tradition." In *Targumic and Cognate Studies: Essays in Honor of Martin McNamara*, edited by Kevin Cathcart and Michael Maher, 14–29. Sheffield: Sheffield Academic Press, 1996.

Baldwin, William. *The Canticles or Balades of Salomon: Phraselyke Declared in English Metres*. London: 1549.

Beza, Theodore. *Master Bezae's Sermons Upon the First Three Chapters of the Canticle of Canticles*. London: 1598.

Brightman, Thomas. *A Commentary on the Canticles of the Song of Saloman*. London: 1644.

---

[72] See Hambrick-Stowe, *Practice of Piety*, 187–193.
[73] Henry, *An Exposition*, 820.

Clarke, Elizabeth. *Politics, Religion, and the Song of Songs in Seventeenth-Century England*. New York: Palgrave Macmillan, 2011.
Collings, John. *A Cordial for a Fainting Soule*. Vol. 2. London: 1650.
Collings, John. *The Intercourses of Divine Love Betwixt Christ and the Church, or The Particular Believing Soul*. 2 vols. London: 1683.
Cotton, John. *A Brief Exposition of the Whole Book of Canticles, or Song of Solomon*. London: 1642.
Cotton, John. *A Brief Exposition with Practical Observations upon the Whole Book of Canticles*. London: 1655.
Edwards, Jonathan. *Religious Affections*, edited by John E. Smith. Vol. 2 of *The Works of Jonathan Edwards*. New Haven, CT: Yale University Press, 1959.
Edwards, Jonathan *The Blank Bible: Part 1*, edited by Stephen J. Stein. Vol. 24 of *The Works of Jonathan Edwards*. New Haven, CT: Yale University Press, 2006.
Edwards, Jonathan. *The "Miscellanies," a-500*, edited by Thomas Schaefer. Vol 13 of *The Works of Jonathan Edwards*. New Haven, CT: Yale University Press, 1994.
Edwards, Jonathan. *Notes on Scripture*, edited by Stephen Stein. Vol. 15 of *The Works of Jonathan Edwards*. New Haven, CT: Yale University Press, 1998.
Edwards, Jonathan. "Personal Narrative." In *Letters and Personal Writings*, edited by George Claghorn, 790–804. Vol. 16 of *The Works of Jonathan Edwards*. New Haven, CT: Yale University Press, 1998.
Fleming, Robert. *The Mirrour of Divine Love Unvail'd, in a Poetical Paraphrase of the High and Mysterious Song of Solomon*. London: 1691.
Flinker, Noam. *The Song of Songs in English Renaissance Literature*. Cambridge, UK: D.S. Brewer, 2000.
Gill, John. *An Exposition of the Book of Solomon's Song, Commonly Called Canticles*. London: 1768.
Godbeer, Richard. "'Love Raptures': Marital, Romantic, and Erotic Images of Jesus Christ in Puritan New England, 1670–1730." In *A Shared Experience: Men, Women, and the History of Gender*, edited by Laura McCall and Donald Yacovone, 51–77. New York: New York University Press, 1998.
Hambrick-Stowe, Charles. *New England Meditative Poetry: Anne Bradstreet and Edward Taylor*. New York: Paulist Press, 1988.
Hambrick-Stowe, Charles. *The Practice of Piety: Puritan Devotional Disciplines in Seventeenth Century New England*. Chapel Hill, NC: University of North Carolina Press, 1982.
Hammond, Jeffrey A. "Songs from the Garden: Edward Taylor and the Canticles." PhD diss., Kent State University, 1979.
Hammond, Jeffrey A. "The Bride in Redemptive Time: John Cotton and the Canticles Controversy." *NEQ* 56 (1983): 78–102.
Henry, Matthew. *An Exposition of the Five Poetical Books of the Old Testament: Viz. Job, Psalms, Proverbs, Ecclesiastes, and Solomon's Song*. London: 1710.
Hessel-Robinson, Timothy. "Erotic Mysticism in Puritan Eucharistic Spirituality." *StSpir* 19 (2009): 93–112.
Hessel-Robinson, Timothy. "Language of the Feast: The Song of Songs in Edward Taylor's Eucharistic Theology." *Proceedings of the North American Academy of Liturgy* (2008): 90–113.
Hessel-Robinson, Timothy. *The Reverend Edward Taylor's Sacramental Meditations on the Song of Songs: The Erotic Devotion of an American Puritan*. Lewiston, NY: Edwin Mellen, 2012.
Homes, Nathanael. *A Commentary Literal or Historical, and Mystical or Spiritual on the Whole Book of Canticles*. London: 1652.
Horne, John. *The Divine Wooer: or A Poem Setting Forth the Love and the Loveliness of the Lord Jesus*. London: 1673.
Jelinger, Christopher. *The Usefulnesse and Excellency of Christ*. London: 1647.
Lewalski, Barbara Kiefer. *Protestant Poetics and the Seventeenth-Century Religious Lyric*. Princeton: Princeton University Press, 1979.

Luther, Martin. "Lectures on the Song of Solomon." In vol. 15 of *Luther's Works*, edited by Jaroslav Pelikan, 190–264. St. Louis: Concordia Publishing, 1972.

Mather, Cotton. *A Glorious Espousal*. Boston: 1719.

Matter, E. Ann. *The Voice of My Beloved: The Song of Songs in Western Medieval Christianity*. Philadelphia: University of Pennsylvania Press, 1990.

Pardes, Ilana. *The Song of Songs: A Biography*. Princeton, NJ: Princeton University Press, 2019.

Porterfield, Amanda. *Female Piety in Puritan New England: The Emergence of Religious Humanism*. New York: Oxford University Press, 1992.

Preston, John. *The Mysticall Match between Christ and His Church*. London: 1648.

Quarles, Francis. *Sion's Sonnets: Sung by Solomon the King and Periphras'd*. London: 1625.

Robinson, Timothy. "'The Banquet of Love': The Song of Songs in Reformed Sacramental Piety; 1586–1729." In *The Brill Companion to the Song of Songs in Christian Spirituality*, edited by Timothy Robinson, 327–357. Leiden: Brill, 2021.

Rous, Francis. "The Mystical Marriage, or Experimental Discoveries of the Heavenly Marriage between a Soul and Her Saviour." In *Treatises and Meditations Dedicated to the Saints, and to the Excellent Throughout the Three Nations*, edited by Francis Rous, 685–739. London: 1657.

Scheper, George. "Reformation Attitudes Toward Allegory and the Song of Songs." *PMLA* 89 (1974): 551–562.

Schwanda, Tom. *Soul Recreation: The Contemplative-Mystical Piety of Puritanism*. Eugene, OR: Pickwick Publications, 2012.

Schwanda, Tom. "'Sweetnesse in Communion with God': The Contemplative-Mystical Piety of Thomas Watson." *Journal for the History of Reformed Pietism* 1 (2015): 34–63.

Sibbes, Richard. "Bowels Opened: or, A Discovery of the Near and Dear Love, Union, and Communion Betwixt Christ and the Church." In vol. 2 of *The Complete Works of Richard Sibbes, D.D.*, edited by Alexander Grosart, 2–195. Edinburgh: James Nichol, 1862.

Sievers, Julie. "Refiguring the Song of Songs: John Cotton's 1655 Sermon and the Antinomian Controversy." NEQ76 (2003): 73–107.

Smith, Jud. *A Misticall Devise of the Spiritual and Godly Lover between Christ, the Spouse, and the Church or Congregation*. London: Henry Kirckham, 1575.

Stewart, Stanley. *The Enclosed Garden: The Tradition and the Image in Seventeenth-Century Poetry*. Madison, WI: University of Wisconsin Press, 1966.

Sweeney, Douglas. *Edwards the Exegete: Biblical Interpretation and Anglo-Protestant Culture on the Edge of the Enlightenment*. New York: Oxford University Press, 2016.

Taylor, Edward. *Edward Taylor's* God's Determinations *and* Preparatory Meditations*: A Critical Edition*, edited by Daniel Patterson. Kent, OH: Kent State University Press, 2003.

Watson, Thomas. "Shewing the Mystical Union Between Christ and the Saints." In *The Godly Man's Picture*, edited by Thomas Watson, 213–225. London: 1666.

Watson, Thomas. *The Christian's Charter: Shewing the Privileges of a Believer*. London: Ralph Smith, 1657.

Weber, Max. *The Protestant Ethic and the Spirit of Capitalism*, translated by Talcott Parsons. London: Routledge, 1992.

Yael Almog
The Song of Songs in Late Eighteenth-Century Germany
Theology and Desire

1 Introduction

This article will examine the cultural backdrop for the wide preoccupation with the Song of Songs in late eighteenth-century Germany, a period marked by the dawn of German Romanticism in philosophy, theology, and literature.[1] A rising interest in the Hebrew Bible fueled myriad translations of the Song by major late eighteenth-century German intellectuals, including the young Johann Wolfgang von Goethe (1749–1832), Johann Gottfried Herder (1744–1803), and Moses Mendelssohn (1729–1786). In postulating that these thinkers worked in proximity to each other, I will consider the Song's translations as a mirror of the period's polemics concerning biblical exegesis. This pertains especially to the period's debates on the Old Testament's aesthetic qualities. As recent scholarship has shown, considering the Bible as an aesthetic object during this period epitomized its reconceptualization as a cultural artifact of panhuman pertinence.[2] Using the example of the Song, the article will explore how discussions of the Hebrew Bible's aesthetic merits mobilized a new conception of humans and of humanity.

The article will contextualize the period's shifts in the conception of biblical exegesis by focusing on Herder's occupation with the Hebrew Bible. By juxtaposing Herder's preoccupation with the Song to Goethe's and Mendelssohn's respective translations of the text, I will situate the admiration of Hebrew aesthetics in the larger, polemical context of late eighteenth-century Germany. I shall then ask

---

[1] My approach to early Romanticism is informed by analyses of late eighteenth-century philosophy as reactionary to earlier eighteenth-century thought. As Frederick Beiser (*Romantic Imperative*, 4) writes, "the early romantics continued with, and indeed radicalized, the legacy of the Enlightenment." The reception of the Song of Songs will be explored as grounded in a transformative philosophical strand that straddled theology and aesthetics.
[2] As Jonathan Sheehan (*Enlightenment Bible*, 148–181) has shown, late eighteenth-century Germany featured a transformative approach that enabled the appropriation of the Bible for diverse agendas: aesthetic, pedagogic, and theological, among others. The proliferation of biblical translations, Sheehan argues, mobilized this transformation. Sheehan finds that the reception of theologian Robert Lowth's presentation of the Hebrew Bible as an aesthetic artifact was instrumental for this trend. Lowth allowed translators much liberty in exempting them from adhering to the text's original features, such as strict meter.

what specific elements of the Song were brought to the fore, or mobilized, in early German Romanticism. I will propose that the text's overt representation of human sexuality served to invest an egalitarian readership in a theological model that centers on the human experience.

A proponent of German Romanticism, Herder built on biblical exegesis to advance a radical rewriting of Enlightenment ideals. This rewriting entailed enhancing the presentation of theological exegesis as a transformative process focused on the reader.[3] In this regard, the emphasis on human reason was exchanged for the early Romantics' exploration of human features that were deemed equally important. The early Romantics redefined the human apparatus through a nonhierarchical positioning of reason and desire. Herder represents a far-reaching furthering of this trend onto a focus on human instincts and emotions. Concurrently, early Romantic philosophy, and Herder as its representative, reconceived the history of civilization in drawing a nonhierarchical relationship between different peoples, cultures, and historical eras. In this way, the admiration of ancient Greece, which permeated German classicism, gave way to the embracing of other peoples—including the ancient Hebrews.[4] Against the admiration of order and perfection, qualities associated with Greek cultural artifacts, salient contemporary thinkers praised aesthetic creations that consisted of unmediated expression of the impressions of the senses and of human desires.

By and large, the preoccupation with the Song of Songs mobilized the period's readings of the Bible through an aesthetic prism as a perspective that might revitalize theology. The crossing of theology into secular realms made the Song an epicenter of experimentation. The Song's explicit representation of human eroticism, which makes it exceptional in the biblical canon, played into the hands of authors who wished to celebrate human desire as central to theology. These hermeneuts explored the extent to which corporal imagery can be used as a spiritual token and investigated thereby the new societal functions of exegesis: functions that diverged from institutional theology.

2 Herder's Legacy

The German Romantics intervened in the enduring fascination with ancient nations as pillars of Germanic culture. In his *This Too a Philosophy of History for the Formation of Humanity* (*Auch eine Philosophie der Geschichte zur Bildung der*

---

[3] A view advanced in such works as Kant's *Religion within the Boundaries of Mere Reason* (*Die Religion innerhalb der Grenzen der bloßen Vernunft*, 1793).
[4] See Ilany, *In Search of the Hebrew People*; idem, "Between Ziona and Teutona."

Menschheit, 1774), Herder questioned what he termed the longstanding "idolatry" that the Greeks and Romans enjoyed in Europe.[5] Against this tendency, Herder portrayed civilization as a continuing chain that straddles diverse national cultures. Each link in the chain has a constitutive role for civilization. Thus, throughout his oeuvre, Herder referred to "the Orientals" (*die Morgenländer*) to denote national cultures whose contributions to civilization had been unjustly ignored. Among the Oriental peoples, Herder noted the importance of the ancient Hebrews, a people whose cultural activity gifted civilization the Old Testament.

The so-called discovery of the ancient Hebrews' contributions to civilization was entangled with a search for a new model of national identification.[6] A wave of poetic interest in biblical Hebrew poetry featured new literary texts that took on biblical themes by such popular poets as Friedrich Gottlieb Klopstock (1724–1803) and Salomon Gessner (1730–1788). The German Romantics operated in a new political climate: they opted to establish the unique nature of their people. They turned, correspondingly, to cultures that had previously been considered inferior. The ancient Hebrews made for a suitable national model. The cultural artifact identified with their nation, the Old Testament, was approachable as a part of the biblical canon. And at the same time that the Old Testament was widely read, it could also be treated as a lost cultural treasure: as a text whose comprehension had been impacted by the damaging influences of time and ill transmission.

Herder's thought vocalized this trend. Herder contended that the expression of passions is an authentic, untamed reminder of the natural, basic use of language that preceded the harmful influence of civilization. Several of his writings express critique of the Enlightenment presumption that society is improved through ongoing cultural activity.

Herder's salient, prize-winning essay *Treatise on the Origin of Language* (*Abhandlung über den Ursprung der Sprache*, 1772) represents this position. The *Treatise* advocates against the notion that Enlightenment society has perfected morality, education, and aesthetic expression. Enlightenment society sought to tame basic human impulses and desires. This resulted, in Herder's mind, in unnatural and restrained uses of language. His discussion of Hebrew takes the language as an exemplary primordial means of expression.

---

5 See Herder, "This Too a Philosophy of History," 341.
6 Ofri Ilany stresses the nationalist tendencies permeating the embrace of Hebrew by German thinkers who wished to distance themselves from Enlightenment values: "while rationalist philosophy and theology ridiculed the particular character of the Hebrew tradition, writers critical of the Enlightenment saw this very particularity as an inspiration, hoping indeed to save beleaguered Christianity through the national element of Hebrew poetry" (*In Search of the Hebrew People*, 146).

> Take the so-called divine first language, Hebrew, from which the greatest part of the world has inherited its letters: that it was in its beginning so livingly sounding, so unwritable, that it could only be written very incompletely, this is shown clearly by the whole structure of its grammar, by its so common confusions of similar letters, and of course most of all by the complete absence of its vowels. Whence comes the idiosyncrasy that its letters are only consonants, and that precisely those elements of words on which everything depends, the vowels, were originally not written at all? This way of writing, writing the inessential and omitting the essential, is so opposed to the course of sound reason that it would have to be unintelligible to grammarians, if grammarians were in the habit of understanding. With us the vowels are the first and most lively thing and the door hinges of language; with the Hebrews they are not written. Why? Because they could not be written. Their pronunciation was so lively and finely organized, their breath was so spiritual and ethereal, that it evaporated and could not be captured in letters.[7]

The inability to comprehend Biblical Hebrew's original rapport with readers is exemplary of the degeneration of the human senses. Westerners' ears are incapable of capturing differences in sound, pronunciation, and accentuation. Herder presented the ancient Hebrew nation as a powerful representative of this vital use of language. In citing Biblical Hebrew's so-called wild nature, Herder presented Hebrew poetry as an aesthetic model that bore significance for contemporary poetics in such early essays as his *On Recent German Literature* (*Über die neuere deutsche Literatur*, 1767).

Herder's praise of the ancient Hebrew nation supported not only his views on aesthetics but also his historiographical innovations. Herder advocated the idea that cultures—and, correspondingly, cultural artifacts—cannot be valued hierarchically. In his mind, cultures manifested values that corresponded with their specific time of conception. He unpacked this theory of cultural relativism in *This Too a Philosophy of History*. Modern individuals cannot postulate that they are morally or culturally superior to individuals of previous historical eras. Likewise, Westerners' attempts to declare themselves culturally advanced with their ostensibly moral and poetic innovations fall through. Herder postulated that to understand a foreign nation, one needs to attend to its cultural and historical norms. Critics have associated this idea with Herder's dictum from *This Too a Philosophy of History*: "feel yourself into everything."[8]

Praise of the Old Testament as an important cultural artifact necessitated, in Herder's time, further apologia. Like other advocates of the merits of biblical poetry, Herder had to address the association of the Old Testament with a religious group that had long been accused of its moral and cultural inferiority: the Jews. On

---

[7] Herder, "Treatise on the Origin of Language," 71.
[8] Herder, "This Too a Philosophy of History," 292.

the point of the Bible's transmission, Herder established that Jews' ongoing use of Hebrew in liturgical contexts corrupted the pure origins of Hebrew.[9]

Thus, *On the Spirit of Hebrew Poetry* (*Vom Geist der hebräischen Poesie*, 1783), Herder's most elaborated work on Biblical Hebrew's aesthetic merits, poses a distinction between the ancient Hebrews and Jews of later periods.[10] The discussion of Hebrew poetry takes the form of a Platonic dialogue between an audacious if curious student and an insightful teacher whose approach to Hebrew provokes the student's prejudices. The teacher seeks to refute the notion that Biblical Hebrew is inferior to ancient Greek and Latin.

On the Spirit of Hebrew Poetry presents Biblical Hebrew as a language of unique aesthetic merits. To achieve this, Herder wittingly addressed qualities of Hebrew that have given the language a dubious reputation. One such infamous quality is the partial lack of vowels that makes it impossible to know how the ancient language should be read.[11] Another ostensible fault is Hebrew's limited range of vocabulary.

On both points, Herder inverted the accusations against the language. He claimed that these features illustrate Hebrew's unique aesthetic merits rather than the language's ostensible weakness. In reference to the infamous lack of vowels in the language, Herder presented the inability to know how Biblical Hebrew should be read as a testimony to the language's exceptional nature. This showed, in Herder's mind, the seminal role of vowels in Hebrew. As we have already seen, Herder contended that the ancient speakers of the language were not able to register their speech in writing: their pronunciation was too lofty to do so. This depiction of Hebrew pronunciation animates an aesthetic preference. To Herder, poetry is meant to be heard. Hebrew poetry sets a model for oral transmission of poetic creation, as shown by the ostensible difficulty of capturing a language in writing.[12] Similarly, Biblical Hebrew's relatively small vocabulary highlights the dominance of verbs in the language. In Hebrew, nouns are often derived from verbs, as the teacher in Herder's dialogue points out. This quality makes the language, in Herder's eyes, foster constant movement. It follows that the language features a dynamic

---

9 See Herder, *On the Spirit of Hebrew Poetry*, 1:32.

10 Herder, *On the Spirit of Hebrew Poetry*.

11 A prevalent testimony to the discomfort that this quality of Hebrew provoked in Herder's time can be found in Goethe's biography. Goethe describes his endeavor to study Hebrew as an attempt that failed during the encounter with punctuation. The marking of vowels alerts readers to the mediated nature of their encounter with Hebrew. See Goethe, *Truth and Poetry*, 1:112.

12 As Tanvi Solanki ("Cultural Hierarchies and Vital Tones," 552) writes, Herder believed that "ancient cultures had strong communities due to the close affective bonds created by their musical, richly tonal languages, and their ritualized oral performances of epic poetry." As she shows (ibid., 554), Herder strove to improve his own readers by reminding them of poetry's oral origins, which are present, in his mind, in various cultural canons of foreign peoples.

flow that makes it especially suitable for the composition of powerful poetry. Herder's preoccupation with the Song of Songs demonstrates his ongoing attempt to conceptualize the aesthetics of Biblical Hebrew as a catalyst of a new theology, one that celebrates the human senses as integral to spiritual experiences and as central to biblical exegesis.

3 Translations of the Song of Songs in Early Romanticism: Herder and Goethe

In late eighteenth-century Germany, the Song attracted wide attention among individuals who represented diverging positions on the Enlightenment. The act of translating the Song was part and parcel of larger discussions on theology during that time. Herder was a great opponent of understanding the Bible allegorically. He advocated the reading of Scripture as a human text that was meant to address people in their language. Because of its overt engagement with corporal desire, the Song was an ideal example of this perspective. In declaring the Song exemplary of supreme poetry, Herder turned to specific elements of the text—aspects that supported his views on aesthetics, historiography, and intercultural interaction. These aspects pertained to the Song's poetic devices, particularly those that concerned hearing; to the Song's unfolding of eroticism; and to its corresponding exceptionality in the biblical canon.

Herder translated the Song twice (the manuscripts date to 1776 and 1778). The latter translation was included in the volume *Lieder der Liebe*, which purported to present the Orientals' cultural assets.[13]

Herder's translation of the Song manifests his praise of Hebrew's natural flow. In translating Song 2:8–9, Herder accentuated the sense of an enveloping plot. This is achieved through the allocation of action to separate lines:

> Stimme meines Lieben!
> Siehe, er kommt!
> Springt über die Berge,
> Hüpft über die Hügel.
> Wie ein Reh ist mein Lieber,
> wie ein flüchtiger Hirsch.

---

13 Herder's translations of the Song into German are reproduced in Baildam, *Paradisal Love*, 306–321, with awareness of Herder's scansion. Henceforth I will provide English translations of excerpts from Herder, Goethe, and Mendelssohn's respective translations of the Song.

> My beloved's voice!
> Look, he is coming!
> Jumps through the mountains,
> leaps through the hills.
> Like a deer is my beloved,
> Like a fleeting stag.[14]

The listeners are invited, in Herder's mind, to observe the Song's emerging images and stimulating narrative. The translation grounds his claim regarding the language's integral merits in vivid imagery and narratological veracity. Herder was attentive to the Hebrew syntax as well as to the rich choice of vocabulary. Moreover, the translation emulates the Hebrew sentence structure by instilling in the German the absence of the pronoun from the beloved's actions.

Herder's approach to the Song puts into practice his views on aesthetics and his notion of the Orientals as proponents of supreme aesthetic creation. Herder's translation demonstrates his view that readers should engage empathetically with the Bible by attending to the cultural climate of its authorship. Herder presumed that an interpreter's approach to a text builds on their understanding of the historical and societal norms of an era different from their own; similarly, the empathetic engagement with a text may reveal further truisms about history.

Herder's engagement with the background of the composition of the Hebrew Bible contrasted with Goethe's prism on the text. Though he expressed some interest in Jewish culture and Biblical Hebrew, Goethe commanded neither. Goethe instead approached the Song to substantiate a dissimilar aesthetic theory, one that promoted subjective perception of the text. He observed the text as a cultural artifact that encapsulates an aesthetic achievement through its poetic form. Goethe's translation demonstrates his statement that "many good translators" opt "to transmit transmissions further,"[15] for example, by reiterating the beauty of the transmitted text from their own perspective. His approach embodied a second strand of the early Romantic celebration of poetic representation of desire, one that was attuned to texts as eliciting interpreters' inventiveness.

Goethe considered the Song a most supreme instance of love poetry, and his exploration of the Song strove to experiment with textual representations of love.[16] The beauty of the Song was also available to the general reader in Goethe's mind. A main means of this accessibility was the existence of a prior translation that Goethe took as unsurpassed: the Luther translation (1545). Whereas Herder sought to offer

---

14 Baildam, *Paradisal Love*, 309.
15 Goethe, *Briefe und Aufsätze*, 155 (my translation).
16 See Sauter, "Writing (in) Love," especially 191. See also Bohnenkamp, "Goethe und das Hohe Lied."

an alternative to the Luther translation, Goethe opted to further what he saw as its merits.[17] Goethe's prose translation attempted to refine Luther's achievement, demonstrating Goethe's view that a particular cultural artifact sparks a coherent lineage of adaptations that capture its essence.

As his translation of Song 2:16–17 shows, Goethe's interpretation of the Song was far reaching:

> Mein Freund ist mein, ich sein, der unter Lilien weidet. Biss der Tag athmet, die Schatten fliehen, wende dich, sey gleich, mein Freund, einer Hinde, einem Rehbock, auf den Bergen Bether.[18]

> My friend is mine, I am his, who grazes among the lilies. Until the day breathes, the shadows flee, turn around, be like, my friend, a female deer, a roe deer, on the mountains of Bether.

The image of the male lover is constituted through a surprising reference to a female animal. Likewise, the "breathing" of the day is an original rendering of the Hebrew verb (פּוּחַ), in a phrase that can be readily interpreted as referring to the dawn. These choices, as well as the original distribution of the Song into new sections, mark Goethe's departure from the notion that translation should be loyal to the original and his attempt to present an innovative rendering of the Song.[19]

For both Herder and Goethe, the Song is of interest due to its centering on human desire. For Herder, this thematic epicenter elicits an inquiry into humanity's origins because these lie, in his opinion, in the veracity of expressive language. The interpreter (in this case, the translator) enters the shoes of the people who produced the original text. Goethe, in contrast, conceived the Song as an invitation for an exploration of individualistic poetic expression. In this venture, the biblical text is taken to encapsulate a poetic achievement. This achievement wears diverging forms in its different translations, maintaining, nonetheless, its unique poetic beauty. Standing at the center of the Song's imagery, desire prolongs this chain by provoking interpreters to take part in the text's creative rendering.

4 Mendelssohn's Theological Adaptation

The period's experimentations with biblical exegesis were met with mixed reactions among traditional readers of the Hebrew Bible. A germane representative of that reaction was Moses Mendelssohn: an observant Jew who was a leading propo-

---

17 See Baildam, *Paradisal Love*, 215–219.
18 The manuscript is from 1775; the text is published in Baildam, *Paradisal Love*, 328–332, here 329.
19 On Goethe's positioning of a translated text as a replacement of the original, see Bernofsky, *Foreign Words*, 191.

nent of Jewish emancipation. Mendelssohn's translation of the Song was emblematic of his larger efforts to translate select biblical texts into German. Those efforts express his mediation of the sudden enthusiasm about Hebrew's aesthetic merits and the Jewish circulation of Hebrew liturgy.

In a review of Herder's *Fragments on Recent German Literature*, Mendelssohn critiqued Herder's praises of Biblical Hebrew. Though Mendelssohn acknowledged Herder's celebration of the language as manifesting unrestrained linguistic expression, his diverging view of Biblical Hebrew poetry built on a starkly different approach to what good poetry entails. Countering Herder's intentions, Mendelssohn asked, "What do we want from poetry?" ("Was wollen wir mit der Poesie?").[20] According to Mendelssohn, poetry should aspire to represent the teleological progress of humankind. This stance on the societal and educational roles of aesthetic works objects to the attempt to trace a model of unrestrained poetic expression in the Hebrew Bible and to celebrate Hebrew poetics with this finding.

Two philosophical threads underpinned Mendelssohn's position. First, on a political level, Mendelssohn adhered to the notion of *Bildung* as instructive for both individuals and the nation. In this vein, his essay *On the Question: What Does 'To Enlighten' Mean? (Über die Frage: Was heißt aufklären?*, 1784) established that the longstanding improvement of a nation derives from cultural work that shows the nation's refinement to be embedded in its genuine and steady voice.[21]

Mendelssohn's ongoing philosophical work encapsulated a second, interrelated vector of resistance to Herder's idealized depiction of Hebrew. Mendelssohn's contributions to aesthetic theory granted him honorable standing in the German republic of letters. These early works postulated that striving for perfection is the ideal that should guide engagement with artwork. His essay *On Sentiments (Über die Empfindungen*, 1755)[22] thus established that attraction to beauty is integral to human nature. In his mind, the inclination toward perfection guides the human senses. It follows that an artwork's gradual unfolding conveys the feeling of perfection: the harmonious coexistence of all of its parts. Importantly, Mendelssohn viewed the relationship between art and nature as mimetic. Aesthetic artifacts are not a part of nature but are representative of nature. By witnessing mimesis, observers of art take advantage of artwork's supreme potential for refining human character. Herder's praise of ostensibly primordial poetics therefore met both political and metaphysical objections in Mendelssohn's thought.

---

20 Mendelssohn, *Gesammelte Schriften*, 3:307 (my translation).
21 See Mendelssohn, "On the Question," 314: "Culture in an external sense is called 'refinement.' Hail to the nation whose refinement is the effect of culture and enlightenment, whose external splendour and elegance is based upon an internal, solid genuineness."
22 In Mendelssohn, *Gesammelte Schriften*, 1:41–123.

Mendelssohn's Jewishness added a third dimension to his opposition to portrayals of Hebrew poetry as a universal asset rediscovered by contemporary readers. As we have seen, Herder distinguished Biblical Hebrew from Hebrew's later usages; the aesthetic assets embodied in the language pertained, in his mind, to the ancient Hebrew nation. Mendelssohn's religious devotion ruled out this distinction. Against it, Mendelssohn conceived Judaism as an ongoing, living tradition. He appealed to traditional Jewish circulation of Hebrew to establish that Jewish scholarship was aware of the language's merits. Thus, in a review of Lowth's celebrated account of the aesthetics of Hebrew poetry, Mendelssohn cited the work of Don Isaac Abrabanel as drawing on similar tenets.[23]

At the same time, Mendelssohn's examinations of Hebrew poetry, and particularly his act of translating the Song, marked his distinctive position as a Jew in the German-speaking republic of letters. His knowledge of Hebrew made him an apt candidate to take part in discussions on the Hebrew Bible, discussions that, as we have seen, fueled the period's philosophical examinations into human nature and the origins of civilization.

Mendelssohn showed awareness of the entanglement of those examinations with the aestheticization of the Hebrew Bible. He also attempted to intervene into this reciprocity. In the essay *On Lyric Poetry* (*Von der Lyrischen Poesie*, written in 1778 and published posthumously in 1810), Mendelssohn approached Hebrew poetry as representative of principles that defined, in his mind, the rapport of poetry with readers. The essay cites the ultimate ability of lyric poetry to come close to nature.[24] Mendelssohn established that the medial relation of poetry to reality is at the core of poetic creation. He postulated that an objective (or rational) representation of world phenomena should be the guiding thread in poetic creations.[25] Tellingly, Mendelssohn ended the essay with examples from Psalms, in his translation.[26] Using quotations from Pss 123, 126, 129, and 133, Mendelssohn wished to establish that the poet's subjective perception of reality is transmitted by digression or fragmentation. The biblical excerpts ultimately led him to conclude that poetry balances the state of confusion—which characterizes the subjective, affective conception of reality—with an overall objective understanding of world

---

23 See Mendelssohn, *Gesammelte Schriften*, 4:24.
24 See Mendelssohn, "Von der Lyrischen Poesie," 304.
25 For an analysis of this position and contextualization of the essay in contemporary aesthetic theory, see Scherpe, "Analogon Actionis und lyrisches System."
26 Weinberg ("Moses Mendelssohns Übersetzungen und Kommentare," 104) establishes that Mendelssohn's translation of Psalms for this essay marks an early instance of his emerging endeavor to translate select biblical texts into German.

phenomena. Mendelssohn's translation of the Song was a similar act of intervening into his period's proliferating discussions of biblical poetry in aesthetic theory.

5 Song of Songs: Mendelssohn's Faithful Endorsement

Mendelssohn's translation of the Song was printed in 1783, as part of a volume that continued his ongoing project of translating biblical books and commenting on them. The core of this project was a translation of the Five Books of Moses into German in Hebrew letters.

Mendelssohn's position as a translator was antithetical to that of the young Goethe. Mendelssohn's translation of the Song can be described as straightforward, and the translated text demonstrates his comprehensive knowledge of Hebrew. Mendelssohn built on this knowledge to register the language of the original text faithfully. He chose vocabulary that accorded with the literal understanding of the Hebrew words and transcribed proper names such as Kedar, Schelomo, Scharon, or Libanon methodically into German. Similarly, his translation imitates the Hebrew text's sentence structure. While Herder and Goethe chose original divisions of the Song, Mendelssohn followed the traditional division into eight chapters.

> Er küsse mich
> Küsse seines Mundes;
> Deine Liebe ist köstlicher als Wein
> Wie lieblich duften Deine Salben!
>
> He kisses me
> His mouth's kisses;
> Your love is finer than wine
> How nicely smell your oils![27]

Mendelssohn's conservative interpretation of vocabulary, reiteration of Hebrew sentence structure, and transcription of Hebrew proper names demonstrate his religiosity. A foremost proponent of Jewish emancipation, Mendelssohn often served as a mediator between the Prussian authorities and the Jewish community. This role permeated his engagement with his period's treatment of the Hebrew Bible as a cultural artifact stripped of traditional liturgical associations. His translation of the Song corresponds with his agenda to make the Hebrew Bible accessible

---

[27] The German translation is in Mendelssohn, *Gesammelte Schriften*, 15.1:239–252.

to Jewish individuals—Jewish youth in particular. His approach as a translator performs this loyalty to the Jewish sources.

These choices echo Mendelssohn's apologia on his translation of the Hebrew Bible. His decision to translate select biblical texts into German, which culminated in the translation of the Five Books of Moses into German in Hebrew letters, raised questions and objections in the Jewish community. As we have seen, in his exchange with Christian intellectuals, Mendelssohn stressed the tenets of traditional Jewish scholarship, which echo, according to his presentation, his contemporaries' attention, via the prism of aesthetic theory, to the unique traits of the Hebrew language. Likewise, in his correspondence with the Jewish community, Mendelssohn presented the ongoing traditional Jewish transmission of the Hebrew Bible as straddling translation (and other creative editorial strategies).

A main instance of this apologia is Mendelssohn's essay *Light for the Path* (אור לנתיבה, 1783),[28] the introduction to his biblical translation and interpretive commentary. The essay cites different means that Jewish interpreters have taken to avoid errors, on the one hand, and to make the Bible approachable to a large population of readers, on the other hand. To achieve the first goal, Jewish sages compared manuscripts while deciphering the meaning of words that might have been affected by scribal errors. The essay provides an overview of the history of translations of the Hebrew Bible into various languages, presenting biblical translation as a tradition that manifests Jewish sages' careful attempts to make the Jewish sources approachable to the Jewish population amidst changes in vernaculars that were comprehensible to Jews. Mendelssohn explained his own scholarly and ideological impetus and explicated his own commitment to *peshat* over *drash*, the literal meaning of the text over unapparent meanings. This is a guiding principle of Mendelssohn's commentary, just as much as it shapes his translation of the Song. Amidst exchange with Jewish leaders, which reflected the risk that his translations would be banned by prominent rabbis, Mendelssohn hinted that his engagement with the Hebrew text was far less risky to the Jewish community than other translations into German, which had been guided by and large by Christian interpretation.

Mendelssohn's translation of the Song into German exemplifies his mediation between Jewish transmission history and the cultural climate of his time. As the Song's rich corporal imagery was giving rise to myriad interpretations, Mendelssohn's adherence to the Bible's *peshat* embraced the Song as a text that has long-term, accepted standing in the Jewish canon. Ironically, it was exactly in the process of affirming the text's *literal* meanings that Mendelssohn reiterated, against his

---

[28] Mendelssohn, *Gesammelte Schriften*, 9.1:1–96, supplies the work's German translation.

Romantic contemporaries, the *allegorical* framing of the Song that insists that its imagery concerns the relationship of the human and the divine.

6 The Sensual Hebrews

What has the Song undergone through its adaptation by Herder and his immediate interlocutors? What aspects of the text—for example, tropes and literary devices— emerge as evocative of Romantic interest? The erotic nature of the Song has modulated much of the history of its reception, forcing its commentators to take a stance on whether it should be read allegorically. The Jewish tradition featured prohibitions on the recitation of the Song. Rabbi Akiva was famously said to forbid the singing of the Song in a celebratory fashion.

The reception of the Song by the early Romantics, and specifically by Herder, objected to an allegorical reading. Herder praised the Song exactly because of its overt eroticism. For Herder, the Song, with its vivid expression of sensual love, was a paragon of the Bible's humanness. The Song illustrated, in Herder's mind, the ancient Hebrews' untamed nature, expressed in their sensibilities and, more generally, in the merits of oral poetry.

Herder established that Hebrew poets addressed their audience skillfully. They excelled in appealing to their listeners' senses, as shown in their use of poetic devices that target hearing, such as alliteration, rhythm, and repetition. Such devices advertised the poets' verse to an audience that was characterized, according to Herder, by its enhanced sensibilities. Thus, Herder portrayed Hebrew poetry as supreme on two levels. First, it targeted a people whose sensibilities, and particularly their hearing, were uniquely sharp. Second, this nation featured a group of poets who had mastered the capacity to target an audience's senses through oral poetry.

As shown with the example of Herder's comments on Hebrew poetry, the celebration of spirituality as a means of enhancing human physicality attempted to rely on the Song's style. This reliance endorsed free, dynamic, and unmediated poetic expression and objected to the classist aesthetic models that praised order and perfection. In this way, the occupation of the German Romantics with the Song highlighted its dialogic and fragmented form. Both elements fueled an effort central to Romantic aesthetics and its philosophical backdrop. While the Romantics recognized that fractures and divisions are integral to social life, they ultimately sought to transgress them and strove for unity and wholeness.[29]

---

[29] See Beiser, *Romantic Imperative*, 3.

7 The Translatability of Scriptures

What is it about the Song that made it, in the course of history, into such a popular text in translation? The proliferating interest in the Song in late eighteenth-century Germany provides an exemplary case study for this question.

A recurrent public gesture, the translation of the Song mobilized the period's discussions on translation. In the late Enlightenment period, the German intellectual scene celebrated the ability of theological approaches to mobilize reading practices. One such approach attempted to trace the cultural and historical background that gave rise to the composition of the text. Herder was a main representative of this approach, an instance of his overall promotion of cultural relativism in historiography. In his analysis of Herder's translation of the Song, Ulrich Gaier references the notion of *Mentalübersetzung* ("mental translation") that Herder formulated in his reflections on the difficulty (or inability) of rendering Shakespearean writings into German.[30] Gaier locates this notion in Herder's view of the plurality of meanings of equivalent terms in the target language. The awareness of this plurality accompanies the translator's work.[31] With regard to the Song, Gaier finds that Herder's own translation employed this principle by way of referencing, through editorial means such as commentary, other possible translations.[32] Herder was committed to documenting the ostensible national spirit that reverberates in the original text, while registering, concurrently, the translator's attempt to penetrate that national spirit from within his cultural stance.

An alternative approach holds that a translation should capture a certain essence to be found in an original text without trying to register the text's historical context, lexical meanings, or specific literary devices. Correspondingly, Goethe's notion of translation permits translators to employ vocabulary and literary devices that are far from the original but that engage meritoriously the creativity and agency of the translator.

Mendelssohn's translation of the Song represents a third approach. His meticulous attempt to remain as close as possible to the origin limits the translator's interpretive prism. This confinement derives from the presumptions that tradition has disseminated the text faithfully and that the translator's vocation lies in facilitating that dissemination further by overcoming linguistic hurdles that emerge in certain historical moments. Mendelssohn's translation pedagogically intones the voice of

---

[30] See Gaier, "Lieder der Liebe," 328.
[31] See Gaier, "Lieder der Liebe," 328.
[32] See Gaier, "Lieder der Liebe," 329.

Jewish tradition. In so doing, his translation attempts to bring its audience to study the language of the original, rather than renounce it.

8 Desire and the Divine

Early German Romanticism gave rise to a new conception of the relationship of humans to the divine. Herder and his immediate interlocutors advanced a conception of religion as ingrained in the specific needs of human beings. It follows that the Bible should be perceived not as the word of God but rather as a text written to humans by humans. This endeavor raises additional questions with regard to the social roles of theological practices in general and of biblical exegesis in particular. Conceiving the Bible as tuned for human sensibility presents exegesis as a dynamic experience of exposing that sensibility. Readers are expected to trace the ways in which the text addresses the specific sensibilities of the audience for whom it was written. It follows that readers identify their own innermost traits as humans in the Bible.

The Song makes for an exemplary text for those exegetical principles. Its explicit engagement with human corporality makes the Song emblematic of the representation of human needs in a theological text. Building on this representation, the German Romantics used the Song to turn theology on its head. In their minds, the explicit occupation with human sensuality made the Song spiritually sublime, rather than questionable.

Bibliography

Baildam, John D. *Paradisal Love: Johann Gottfried Herder and the Song of Songs*. Sheffield: Sheffield Academic Press, 1999.
Beiser, Frederick. *The Romantic Imperative: The Concept of Early German Romanticism*. Boston, MA: Harvard University Press, 2006.
Bernofsky, Susan. *Foreign Words: Translator-Authors in the Age of Goethe*. Kritik: German Literary Theory and Cultural Studies. Detroit: Wayne State University Press, 2005.
Bohnenkamp, Anne. "Goethe und das Hohe Lied." In *Goethe und die Bibel: Tagungsband zum Symposium Goethe und die Bibel, Luzern, 22.–23.04.2005*, edited by Johannes Anderegg and Edith Anna Kunz, 89–110. Stuttgart: Deutsche Bibelgesellschaft, 2005.
Gaier, Ulrich. "Lieder der Liebe: Herders Hohelied-Interpretation." In *Perspectives on the Song of Songs/ Perspektiven der Hoheliedauslegung*, edited by Anselm C. Hagedorn, 317–337. BZAW 346. Berlin: de Gruyter, 2005.
Goethe, Johann Wolfgang von. *Briefe und Aufsätze aus den Jahren 1766 bis 1786*, edited by Adolf Schöll. Weimar: Landes-Industrie-Comptoir, 1857.

Goethe, Johann Wolfgang von. *Truth and Poetry: From My Own Life; or, The Autobiography of Goethe*, edited and translated by Parke Godwin. 4 vols. New York: G. P. Putnam, 1846–1847.

Herder, Johann Gottfried. *Ideen zur Philosophie der Geschichte der Menschheit*, edited by Martin Bollacher. Frankfurt a. M.: Deutscher Klassiker Verlag, 1989.

Herder, Johann Gottfried. *On the Spirit of Hebrew Poetry*, translated by James Marsch. 2 vols. Burlington, VT: Edward Smith, 1833.

Herder, Johann Gottfried. "This Too a Philosophy of History." In *Herder: Philosophical Writings*, edited and translated by Michael N. Forster, 272–358. Cambridge: Cambridge University Press, 2002.

Herder, Johann Gottfried. "Treatise on the Origin of Language." In *Herder: Philosophical Writings*, edited and translated by Michael N. Forster, 65–164. Cambridge: Cambridge University Press, 2002.

Herder, Johann Gottfried. "Über die neuere deutsche Literatur." In *Frühe Schriften, 1764–1772*, edited by Ulrich Gaier, 161–259. Frankfurt a. M.: Deutscher Klassiker Verlag, 1985.

Ilany, Ofri. "Between Ziona and Teutona: The Hebrew Model and the Beginning of German National Culture." *Historia* 28 (2012): 81–105. (Hebrew)

Ilany, Ofri. *In Search of the Hebrew People: Bible and Nation in the German Enlightenment*. Bloomington: Indiana University Press, 2018.

Kant, Immanuel. *Religion within the Boundaries of Mere Reason*, translated by Allen Wood and George Di Giovanni. Cambridge: Cambridge University Press, 1998.

Mendelssohn, Moses. "On the Question: What Does 'To Enlighten' Mean?" In *Philosophical Writings*, translated by Daniel Dahlstrom, 311–317. Cambridge: Cambridge University Press, 2012.

Mendelssohn, Moses. *Gesammelte Schriften: Jubiläumsausgabe*, edited by Ismar Elbogen, Julius Guttmann, Eugen Mittwoch, Fritz Bamberger, Haim Bar-Dayan, Simon Rawidowicz, and Alexander Altmann. Stuttgart: Frommann, 1971–2016.

Sauter, Caroline. "Writing (in) Love: Goethe's 'Buch Suleika' and the Biblical Song of Songs." *Publications of the English Goethe Society* 87 (2018): 188–203.

Scherpe, Klaus R. "Analogon Actionis und lyrisches System." *Poetica* 4 (1971): 32–59.

Sheehan, Jonathan. *The Enlightenment Bible: Translation, Scholarship, Culture*. Princeton: Princeton University Press, 2005.

Solanki, Tanvi. "Cultural Hierarchies and Vital Tones: Herder's Making of a German *Muttersprache*." *German Studies Review* 41 (2018): 551–565.

Weinberg, Werner. "Moses Mendelssohns Übersetzungen und Kommentare der Bibel." *ZRGG* 41 (1989): 97–118.

Elisabeth Birnbaum
The Song of Songs as a Drama
A Radical Change of Interpretation in the Eighteenth and Nineteenth Century

Introduction

Since late antiquity, many biblical scholars, whether they be Christian or Jewish, have favored an allegorical interpretation of the Song of Songs. But eighteenth- and nineteenth-century Europe saw a radical change in interpretation of the Song of Songs, brought about in large part by strong connections between the theological, intellectual, and cultural elites of the times.

Three main trends led to this new understanding:

1) The abandonment of traditional thinking and the primacy of human reason led to important changes in academic approaches. The scholastic method of deductive thinking had come to its results by relying on a long tradition of interpretation. But in the late eighteenth century, Protestant scholarship began to separate dogmatics from exegesis. The traditional approach was replaced by a new one, which relied only on the exegete's own senses, on his own critical rationality. The turn toward the senses, toward the obvious rather than the deduced meaning, and a new historical consciousness led to the development of the well-known historical-critical approach. Since then, the main interest of Protestant exegetes has lain in the original, historical setting of the text. This new understanding of history and historicity led to a focus on the Orient and its languages as the context for the Bible.[1] No longer did the faith of the church govern interpretive perspectives; instead, the time and place of the authors of the Bible was paramount. Exegetes felt empowered to develop totally new interpretations based on historical and linguistic knowledge rather than on spiritual traditions.

2) A new concept of marriage and love meant that sexuality, marriage, and love were united for the first time in history. Instead of marrying for dynastic reasons, more and more people married out of love. Marriage had always had to contain sexuality, but now marriage and sexuality also had to contain love. Suddenly, to marry each other meant to love each other. And to love each other meant to have

---

[1] See Polaschegg, *Der andere Orientalismus*, esp. 165–166.

the wish and the obligation to marry each other—and so a joyful (though not too permissive) sexuality was not only allowed but also inherent to the relationship.

In addition, the Reformation had eliminated the gap between the priesthood and married Christians. Protestant pastors were allowed to marry, and married people were allowed to be pastors. Thus, married couples were no longer considered less "holy" than clergy. However, this did not simply mean things were easier; it also meant new and higher demands. It meant that married people should not be less holy than the clergy; each and every married couple had to be virtuous and holy in an exemplary way.

3) A new enthusiasm for the Orient, part of the *Zeitgeist*,[2] led to a new perspective on the Hebrews, who were seen as a people of the ancient Orient. It is no wonder that Protestant exegetes were enthusiastic about the Orient—as many people at that time were.[3] The *Arabian Nights*, published in 1704–1717, inspired countless Europeans; travelogues of famous travelers to the Orient delighted aristocratic readers; and writers, musicians, and painters loved orientalist subjects.

Strikingly, Europeans looked at oriental culture with arrogance and admiration at the same time. There was a strange discrepancy between enthusiasm for the Orient and reservations about it. On the one hand, "orientals" were assumed to be ingenious and free from Western prudery[4] and thus were seen as a positive example of originality. Their behavior was said to be simple and undistorted, "given by nature." This view fit perfectly with the age's glorification of the natural, unaffected mind and Rousseau's concept of the "noble savage." The desire to return to a golden era or to paradise, a deep distrust of civilized culture, and high esteem for a natural, simple, and undistorted way of living—all were seen in the customs and traditions of the oriental peasant.[5] The concept of a people's "original" culture implied that the customs and traditions of the "oriental" Hebrews had remained

---

2 See Rhein, *Deutsche Orientmalerei*, 29–62.
3 Operas like *Die Entführung aus dem Serail* (W. A. Mozart); *Le Cadi dupé* (Chr. W. Gluck); and *Il turco in Italia* (G. Rossini) are only a few examples of the many works that were inspired by the Orient. Alla turca music was very fashionable during the Viennese classical period. In the visual arts, J. D. Ingres (who irritated visitors to salons in 1814 with a picture of a harem slave) and E. Delacroix created the first known works. Arabian literature inspired German poets to paraphrases, the most popular of which is J. W. v. Goethe's *Westöstlicher Divan*, a paraphrase of the Persian *Divan of Hafis*, which served as a sort of love code between Goethe and his beloved (much younger and platonic) friend Marianne Willemer. Knowledge about the Orient became a part of education.
4 See Böttcher, *Die ältesten Bühnendichtungen*, 24.
5 Besides, there was a general fascination with exotic subjects, especially of Egypt, which was driven inter alia by the affinity of the Freemasons for Egyptian culture, as can be seen, e.g., in Mozart's *Die Zauberflöte*. For an overview, see Rhein, *Deutsche Orientmalerei*, 29–62.

unchanged for nearly two thousand years.⁶ For Europeans, Hebrews reflected the spirit of ancient times, especially of the golden days of Solomon, and the wedding traditions of the contemporaneous rural population were supposed to be exactly the same as the wedding traditions of Solomon's day.⁷

Nevertheless, in addition to admiration there were also prejudice and contempt. The garden culture, the luxurious and exotic delights were admired but also regarded suspiciously. Luxury and decadence were opposed to the ideal of the simple way of life. Furthermore, the Orient, as the homeland of Islam, was seen as the origin of despotism and reactionary oppression. And regarding morals, so-called orientals were accused of being immoral, decadent, and excessive.⁸

Such was the context in which J. G. Herder (1744–1803) de-allegorized the Song of Songs, seeing it as a collection of love songs.⁹ But this was also the context for another interpretation of the Song of Songs that gained influence over the next hundred years: the drama theory.

1 Folk Drama, Not Folk Song

For Herder, the great collector of German *Volkslieder* (folk songs), the Song of Songs was a collection of songs of the simple people. Here, "love is sung as love has to be sung, simple, sweet, suave, pristine."¹⁰ Other exegetes shared this opinion; for example, K. Budde noted, "Anyway, most of it gushes unaffectedly out of the mouth of the simple people."¹¹ M. Jastrow enthused over the simplicity of the Song, which

---

6 E.g., Ewald, *Das Hohelied Salomo's*, 57, relies on eighteenth-century travel reports to "prove" the correspondence between Solomon and contemporaneous oriental habits and customs.
7 See, e.g., P. Haupt's description of sword dances to interpret Song 7:1–2: Haupt, *Biblische Liebeslieder*, 27–28; on problems of such equations, see Zakovich, *Das Hohelied*, 38–39.
8 See Konrad, "Von der 'Türkengefahr,'" esp. 24, 27–28, 35–36.
9 Relatedly, at this time many scholars had a specific view of the connection between poetics, language, and the characteristics of a people on the one hand and a certain understanding of genuineness on the other. The first is connected to Herder, for whom poetics was the native language of the human race, the elemental sound of language; language formed the customs of peoples. See Herder's *Über die Wirkung der Dichtkunst auf die Sitten der Völker in alten und neuen Zeiten*. His interest in *Volkslieder* ("folk songs," a term that Herder invented) was closely related. He focused on the Song of Songs, which he considered to be the "elemental sounds" of the Hebrew people. In 1778 he edited his *Lieder der Liebe* in Weimar.
10 Herder, *Lieder der Liebe*, 90: "Und zwar wird Liebe darinn gesungen, wie Liebe gesungen werden muß, einfältig, süß, zart, natürlich."
11 Budde, *Das Hohelied*, xx: "Das Meiste entquillt jedenfalls ungekünstelt dem Volksmunde."

had not been overlaid by the skillful hand of a poet. In his view, the Song of Songs was "the simplest kind of ballads scarcely touched by the polishing efforts of the selfconscious poet."[12]

J. F. Jacobi (1712–1791) developed his drama theory in 1771, specifically to counter the views of Herder, W. F. Hufnagel, J. F. Kleuker, W. M. L. de Wette, and others, who understood the Song of Songs as an anthology of songs. G. H. A. Ewald (1803–1875) became the most prominent advocate of the drama theory, dating the book to the preexilic period, which he viewed as the heyday of literature, a time when the Israelite people were free:

> The language of the book is virile and beautiful, most dense and short, just as one would expect in the heyday of literature. Where after the exile is a song of such ardent flight, of such great genuineness and creative power, in such an airy language as the Song of Songs? Do not all later ones show clear signs of a dull and elongated style of writing? And does not this one breathe the period of the free people through and through?[13]

The interpretation of the Song as a drama was highly regarded, dominating the interpretive landscape for nearly a hundred years (between ca. 1820 and 1920), not only in Germany but also in the United States and England. Christian commentators such as F. W. C. Umbreit (1820), Ewald (1826), B. Hirzel (1840), and E. F. Friedrich (1855) endorsed this view, as did rabbis like S. Herxheimer (1848) and L. Philippson (1848), who, as C. D. Ginsburg (1831–1914) stated, "by virtue of their high position and great learning, may be regarded as representing the view now generally entertained by the Jews respecting the Song of Songs."[14]

However, the drama theory was not as unanimously accepted as Ginsburg made it out to be. In 1850, F. Böttcher declared,

> We could be brief about the Song of Songs if we were to accept what H. Ewald [...] assumed from his point of view: "That the poem forms one unit and is in its way a sort of folksy drama or, better, a *Singspiel* [a singing game], can now be seen as proved." What we have quoted [above], from some of the newest publications, does not match this claim. Even in the 1940s,

---

12 Jastrow, *Song of Songs*, 13; see Rudolph, "Das Hohelied," 193.
13 Ewald, *Das Hohelied Salomo's*, 22: "Die Sprache des Buchs ist männlich und schön, höchst gedrängt und kurz und völlig so, wie man sie in der Blüthezeit der Literatur erwartet. Wo ist ein Lied nach dem Exil mit so feurigem Auffluge, mit solcher Originalität und schöpferischen Kraft, in so fliegend leichter Sprache, als das Hohelied? Zeigen nicht alle spätern die deutlichsten Spuren der matten und gedehnten Schreibart? und athmet dieses hingegen nicht die Periode des freien Volks durch und durch?"
14 Ginsburg, *Song of Songs*, 60.

one of the Halle Collegienheft [lecture notes] judged the Song to have some "dramatic spirit" but denied its dramatic form.[15]

Even supporters of the drama theory took the folksy origin of the Song for granted. Böttcher claimed the existence of old Hebrew folk plays and compared them with the folk plays of other peoples and countries:

> And for a long time, these folk plays were—like medieval mystery plays and even some plays of the seventeenth and eighteenth centuries—performed from memory and with unstudied, impromptu speeches, before the poetic art turned toward them and wrote lines and texts for them.[16]

According to Böttcher, Umbreit,[17] Ewald,[18] and C. F. Ammon[19] were the three most important representatives of the drama theory.

The coincidence of the two rising literary genres (drama and folk song) and the corresponding understanding of the Song is interesting. Perhaps it is no accident that Herder, who drew attention to the literary genre of folk song (he coined the term *Volkslied*) and saw it as an expression of a pristine culture, understood the Song as such a collection of folk songs, too. And perhaps it is also no accident that the new line of interpretation turned to the drama theory. The eighteenth century was the most important century for the development of German drama and drama theory. Prominent authors like G. E. Lessing (1729–1781), J. C. F. Schiller (1759–1805), and J. W. v. Goethe (1749–1832) redesigned and developed the genre with their plays and in part with their theoretical works, as for example in Lessing's important *Dramatheorie* of 1767.[20] Thus, in looking for an appropriate genre for the

---

15 Böttcher, *Die ältesten Bühnendichtungen*, xiv: "Ueber das Hohe Lied könnten wir hier kurz seyn, wenn sich annehmen liesse, was *H. Ewald* (Geschichte des V. Israel, III, 1, S. 174) von seinem Standpunkt aus versichert: 'Dass das Gedicht ein Ganzes ausmacht und der Kunst nach eine Art volksthümliches Dramas oder richtiger gesagt, ein Singspiel giebt, kann jetzt als bewiesen angesehen werden.' Was wir S. 2ff. aus neuesten Literaturerscheinungen angeführt haben, stimmt nicht zu dieser Behauptung. Und noch in einem Hallischen Collegienheft aus den 40er Jahren fanden wir dem H.L. zwar 'dramatisches Leben' zuerkannt, aber die 'dramatische Form' abgesprochen."
16 Böttcher, *Die ältesten Bühnendichtungen*, xii: "und lange sind diese Volksspiele (wie auch die mittelalterlichen Mysterien, und selbst manche Schauspielerstücke des 17. und 18. Jahrh.) mit blosen Reminiscenzen und kunstlosen Stegreifreden ausgeführt worden, ehe sich die poetische Kunst ihnen zuwandte und Verse und Texte dafür dichtete."
17 See Umbreit, *Lied der Liebe*.
18 See Ewald, *Das Hohelied Salomo's*.
19 See Ammon, *Salomo's verschmähte Liebe*.
20 See Lessing, *Hamburgische Dramaturgie*. Lessing, who relied on D. Diderot, argued for the separation of tragedies and comedies. According to him, tragedies should be reserved for the aristocracy, whereas comedies should belong to the bourgeoisie. His approach was innovative: royal persons within tragedies should be met with empathy not because they were kings but because they

Song of Songs, it was not difficult to think of drama, especially because the numerous dialogues and places mentioned pointed in this direction.

2 Historical, Not Allegorical

Understanding the Song of Songs as a drama means interpreting it nonallegorically.[21] The replacement of the scholastic method with (allegedly) more evident interpretations, and the ensuing separation of dogmatics from exegesis, accompanied by Luther's own ambivalent attitude toward allegory, made the nonallegorical approach acceptable. Uncovering the intention of the author became the new main goal of exegesis. And this intention could only be located in the literal sense of the text. The allegorical interpretation was explained as a later development with the explicit aim of providing theological value. Ewald rejoiced:

> And since they recognized that there was no reason at all for allegory in the Song, they rightly thought that the literal sense must be maintained. This principle, to search only for the intention of the author, the palladium of better exegesis, is the great and lasting benefit of that time, for which posterity must thank men such as J. D. Michaelis, Teller, Herder, and Eichhorn.[22]

As a consequence, the erotic relations between the lovers of the Song of Songs no longer had to reflect the relationship between God and his people or between Christ and his church.

But in being so read, it was no longer obvious to everybody what religious message there was in the book or why it had been included among the biblical books. The rejection of the allegorical understanding necessitated that the Song have some theological value, as otherwise it could (and did!) happen that exegetes would see no relevant meaning in the Song of Songs at all.

The question why the Song had became part of the Bible was answered in two ways.

---

were human. For an overview, see Hertel, "Dramentheorie," 63–66. On Lessing, see Ter-Nedden, *Lessings Trauerspiele*. As a young man, Schiller wrote a speech about the drama: *Die Schaubühne als eine moralische Anstalt betrachtet* (1784). Further reflections on drama by Schiller and Goethe can be found in the correspondence between the two; see Vollmer, ed., *Briefwechsel*, 1:344–351.

21 For a special form, see G. Wachter's interpretation of the Song as an allegorical *Singspiel*; Wachter, *Das Hohe Lied*.

22 Ewald, *Das Hohelied Salomo's*, 42: "Und da man einsah, daß in dem Liede gar kein Grund zur Allegorie sey, so glaubte man mit Recht den Wortsinn festhalten zu müssen. Dieser Grundsatz, nur den Sinn des Verfassers zu erforschen, das Palladium der bessern Exegese, ist der große und bleibende Gewinn, den jene Zeit errang, und für den die Nachwelt Männern, wie J. D. Michaelis, Teller, Herder, Eichhorn ewigen Dank zollen muß."

1) Hermeneutically, the Bible was now seen as historical national literature. The Song of Songs was written by Solomon, or at least attributed to him, and therefore was to be honored. Ewald claimed:

> Holy Scriptures were national scriptures in the eyes of their collectors, and from this perspective they could rightly include this Song after the exile, having been honored as Solomon's opus.[23]

As historical literature, biblical texts had to be historically true. A historical interpretation meant putting (or leaving) the Song in the context of 1Kgs 1–11, which was seen as a historically reliable report about Solomon. It was a case not of either allegorical or secular but of either allegorical or historical. The alternative to the interpretation of Solomon as God or Christ could only be to interpret Solomon as Solomon himself.[24]

The female lover in the Song of Songs was no longer God's people, the church, or the human soul but a historical, or at least real, woman connected to the time and place of King Solomon. Solomon, too, was no longer a symbol or a metaphor but the historical son of David, living in 1000 BCE. The text had to be connected to other "historical" aspects of him, not to ideas of "the true Solomon," that is, Christ.

Interestingly, no distinction was made between the ancient Orient and the Orient of the eighteenth century. Thus, Solomon was seen as the epitome of the oriental pasha, and his luxury fascinated people. It was natural that he should be the owner of a huge seraglio. But in so being, he did not fit into the seemingly simple and sensitive world of the Song of Songs, and he became the victim of divergent evaluations of the Orient. Thus, travel reports from the eighteenth century "proved" the lifestyle of Solomon and provided the Song with precise locations.

Positioning the Song as a historical, true drama also meant that its names, locations, and even expressions were taken literally. The male lover pastures a flock (1:7–8) and thus must be a shepherd. The girl has to guard the vineyards (1:6) thus must be a vintner, connected to the time and place of King Solomon. She was called the Shulammite (7:2) and thus must be from a village named Shulem. Ewald located the village near Bethlehem, at En-gedi, because Song 1:14 says, "My beloved is to me a cluster of henna blossoms in the vineyards of En-gedi." Ginsburg explained every detail of the book in this way. For example, he described the familiar situation of the woman as follows:

---

[23] Ewald, *Das Hohelied Salomo's*, 35: "Heilige Schriften waren den Sammlern offenbar Nationalschriften; und aus diesem Gesichtspunct konnte man nach dem Exil mit eben dem Recht dieses schon als Salomo's Werk geehrte Lied aufnehmen."
[24] See Wachter, *Das Hohe Lied*, 2.

> There was a family living at Shulem, consisting of a widowed mother, several sons, and one daughter, who maintained themselves by farming and pasturage. The brothers were particularly partial to their sister, and took her under their special care.[25]

Methodologically, the main issues were localization, dating, and the social classification of the protagonists. Unlike the allegorical interpretation, which explained the text in the context of theological and Christological dogmas, the historical interpretation and especially the drama theory put the text in a historical and dramatic setting. Scholars looked at as many hints as possible in the text in order to find the concrete historical events that the text seemed to report.

Even the question of authorship was decided according to the wording of the Song of Songs. Though Ewald, for example, did not see Solomon as the author of the Song, he claimed that the Song had to have been written not far from his time, around 920 BCE.[26] His main argument was Song 6:4, where the author mentions Tirza before Jerusalem. Thus, he conluded, the author must have seen Tirza as a more beautiful town than Jerusalem, which was only possible before its decline in 918 BCE.

2) To answer the problem arising from a nonallegorical understanding, scholars had to explain what theological value lay in the love song of a Hebrew king. The representatives of the drama theory found this value in the Song's ethical message. Ewald, for example, defended the Song rather apologetically when he asked, "And what is in the book that could make it unworthy to be next to the others? Does it not pursue an ethical idea? Where would vice be recommended?"[27] Afterward, he turned the tables and projected the discussion about the possible improprieties of the Song back onto the first centuries CE. Thus, he saw the allegorical understanding as the result of ignorance of the true design of the Song and as an attempt to conceal or mitigate its erotic contents. Allegory was nothing more than an explanation born of necessity[28] that should not be defended anymore.

Ewald conceded, though, that there were some aberrations in going from mere spiritual love to the other extreme of mere sensual love. In his view, Herder and others saw only expressions of emotions for their own sake in the Song and had

---

25 Ginsburg, *Song of Songs*, 4–5.
26 See Ewald, *Das Hohelied Salomo's*, 15.
27 Ewald, *Das Hohelied Salomo's*, 2: "Und was wäre in dem Buche, das es seiner Stelle neben den andern unwürdig machte? führt es nicht eine ethische Idee durch? wo wäre der Untugend darin das Wort geredet?"
28 See Ewald, *Das Hohelied Salomo's*, 34: "Und diese Noterklärung sollten wir noch in unserm reifern Zeitalter vertheidigen wollen?"

not considered the possibility that it might have an ethical tendency.²⁹ This conflict between allegorizers and literalists in Germany and England lasted, according to Ginsburg, until the 1830s.³⁰

3 Ethical, Not Indecent

The rejection of the allegorical understanding and the development of the "historical" understanding created new risks. The sensual and erotic language of the Song of Songs could easily endanger morality and transgress standards of public decency. Therefore, the main task of these exegetes was to defend the Song against charges of "immorality"—that is, interpretations that were too permissive and attempts to remove it from the Bible because of its alleged indecency.

One of Goethe's contemporaries, the Göttingen theologian J. D. Michaelis, for example, felt compelled to omit the Song from his Bible translation. He argued,

> The reason is not [. . .] that I deny King Solomon was the author of the Song—that I do not do. I think it is genuine and a poetically beautiful remnant of the antique. Instead, it is because the pictures of love seem to me to be such that I do not want to present them to my readers together with the Bible.³¹

As this argument shows, two things were crucial for the canonicity of a biblical book: the historical genuineness of authorship and/or the book's morality. If Solomon was in fact the author of the Song, one had to prove why it should be omitted from the Bible. The only reason to do so would be its immorality. Of course, the moral criterion that was laid on the Song was western European and Christian. The "other" was judged from this perspective. Thus, for example, according to Herder, Michaelis saw in the Song an oriental marriage "full of oriental love intrigues, intrigues d'amour, jealousy, ardor, quarrel, lustfulness."³² To avoid the resulting reluctance toward the Song's themes, representatives of the drama theory underlined the deep

---

29 See Ewald, *Das Hohelied Salomo's*, 43: "An eine ethische Tendenz dachte man nicht."
30 See Ginsburg, *Song of Songs*, 94; for a good overview of the pros and cons of the allegorical interpretation, see, e.g., 103.
31 Michaelis, *Deutsche Übersetzung*, xxiv: "Die Ursache ist nicht [. . .] daß ich es König Salomo abspreche, das thue ich nicht, sondern sehe es für ächt, noch dazu für ein poetisch schönes Ueberbleibsel des Alterthums an: sondern weil mir die Gemählde von Liebe so vorkommen, daß ich sie nicht gerne meinen Lesern zugleich mit der Bibel vorlegen möchte."
32 Herder, *Lieder der Liebe*, 97: "Er [Michaelis] dichtete eine glückliche Hypothese von einem Eheliede voll orientalischer Liebesränke, intrigues d'amour, Eifersucht, Brunst, Zank, Begier nach einer Nacht."

morality of the book. F. J. Delitzsch (1813–1890) conceded that physical love is an important theme in the Song but argued,

> one has to grip the Song of Songs with unwashed hands and to read it with very lecherous eyes to ignore the spiritual background of these sensual depictions. It is precisely this sensual and yet not sensual, this worldly and yet heavenly and wafting, this physical and yet sun-drenched and, so to speak, ethereal character of the Song of Songs that has made it, all along, a bantering riddle and the search for its solution a marvelous pleasure, which does not permit any fatigue.[33]

In loving each other virtuously, innocently, maritally, the two lovers supported and promoted the prevalent Protestant view of the holiness of marriage and love. They became proclaimers of Christian marriage as intended and created by God. And even more, as Ginsburg put it, "the importance of this Song is not to describe the chaste passion of conjugal love, but to *celebrate fidelity*."[34]

Thus, the Song of Songs "proved" to be a book of utmost virtue. The "celebrated Ewald showed in a masterly manner" the ethical message of the book: "This poem celebrates chaste, virtuous, and sincere love, which no splendour is able to dazzle, nor flattery to seduce." [35]

3.1 The Woman

First of all, for most interpreters, the woman of the Song had to be exceedingly virtuous. The consensus interpretation was that the heroine of the drama is a natural woman of the Hebrew people: pure, unaffected, and innocent. And—of course—she is espoused or married to her beloved. Even in her most passionate love she avoids any impression of shamelessness. She loves her beloved with true and unfaltering love. As Delitzsch wrote,

---

[33] Delitzsch, *Das Hohelied*, 156–157: "Man muß das Hohelied mit ungewaschenen Händen ergreifen und mit sehr geilen Augen lesen, wenn man den seelischen Hintergrund dieser sinnlichen Schilderungen nicht wahrnimmt. Eben dieses sinnliche und doch nicht sinnliche, dieses irdische und doch himmlisch und anwehende, dieses materielle und doch durchsonnte und so zu sagen ätherische Wesen des Hohenliedes hat es von jeher zu einem neckenden Räthsel und das Suchen nach seiner Lösung zu einem wundersamen Vergnügen gemacht, welches keine Ermüdung zulässt."
[34] Ginsburg, *Song of Songs*, 87 [emphasis original].
[35] Ginsburg, *Song of Songs*, 92: "Das ganze Lied ist ein Lobgesang auf die reine, schuldlose, treue Liebe, die kein Glanz blendet und keine Schmeichelei verstrickt"; cf. Ewald, *Das Hohelied Salomo's*, 1.

> The first moral trait in the character of the Shulammite is the essential feature of true love in general. True love loves the beloved exclusively not because of what he has but what he is.[36]

Delitzsch admired the beauty of the Shulammite as a moral value: "Her beauty is not only by nature, but vivid through virtue." However, he pointed out that the morals of the Old Testament were not yet on the same level as the New Testament's spirituality, though they were nevertheless superior to the merely feigned virtue of the "heathenish world": "The Shulammite is still nature and not yet spirit, but her naturalness is well educated in the fear of Jehovah, sanctified by Jehovah's grace."[37]

Delitzsch was not the only one to contrast the morality of the Old Testament with the morality of the New Testament, claiming the alleged superiority of the latter and the superiority of both in comparison to the heathen. Another widespread view of these times, now outdated, was the intellectual and social inferiority of women. A "good" woman was aware of her status and behaved accordingly. In Delitzsch's eyes, the virtuous woman of the Song was the "ideal bride," meaning that she was naive and submissive to her beloved:

> On the wedding day [. . .] she appears as the true ideal of a virtuous bride. Overwhelmed by the impression of the day she speaks but little, [. . .] yet she knows that she is no more her own master and wishes to be prepared for the pleasure of him who alone has her at his disposal.[38]

3.2 Solutions for the Permissive Parts

Though the interpreters of the Song of Songs did their best to highlight the virtue of the woman in the abovementioned ways, they still had to cope with the salacious words of the male voice of the Song. The permissive parts of the text seemed

---

[36] Delitzsch, *Das Hohelied*, 156: "Der erste sittliche Zug in Sulamith's Charakter ist der grundzug wahrer Liebe überhaupt. Die wahre Liebe liebt den Geliebten im ausschließlichen Sinne nicht um deswillen was er hat, sondern um deswillen was er ist."
[37] Delitzsch, *Das Hohelied*, 155: "Ihre Schönheit ist nicht blos natürlich, sondern sittlich lebendig. Das sittliche Leben ist nun zwar nicht neutestamentliches Geistleben aus Gott, welches zuletzt das Leibesleben in seine Gleiche verwandeln wird, aber es hat auch nicht den blosen Tugendschein, in welchem wie in der Heidenwelt, so überall in der Welt vielfach nur splendida vitia gleißen, die Sittlichkeit Sulamith's ist so wenig wesen- und werthlos als die alttestamentliche Sittlichkeit überhaupt, Sulamith ist noch Natur und nicht Geist, aber ihre Natürlichkeit ist wohlerzogen in der Furcht Jehova's, geheiligt durch die Gnade Jehova's."
[38] Delitzsch, *Das Hohelied*, 161: "Am Hochzeitstage, [. . .] erscheint sie als das wahre Ideal einer züchtigen Braut. Ueberwältigt vom Eindrucke des Tages spricht sie nur wenig, [. . .] aber sie weiß doch auch, daß sie nicht mehr über sich selbst zu gebieten hat und wünscht dem der allein über sie verfügt zum Genusse zubereitet zu werden."

to stand against a moral interpretation, and the Song had to be saved from any reproach that might make it an indecent book. Thus Jacobi, the pioneer of the so-called triangle hypothesis, named his 1771 commentary *The Song of Songs, Saved by a Simple and Unpretentious Explanation from Its Accusations*.[39]

3.2.1 The Love Triangle

According to Jacobi, the Song is a drama about a love triangle between Solomon, a young shepherd, and a young, beautiful but simple country girl. Ginsburg became an ardent advocate of this interpretation,[40] summing up Jacobi's theory as follows:

> Solomon was not the object of the Shulammite's affections, and [...] the beloved was a humble shepherd from whom the King endeavoured to separate her. [...] The pattern of this conjugal fidelity is the Shulammite, the heroine of the book. This humble woman was married to a shepherd. Solomon, being struck with her beauty, tempted her with the luxuries and splendour of his court to forsake her husband and enter the royal harem; but the Shulammite spurned all the allurements, and remained faithful to her humble husband.[41]

Ginsburg himself wrote a commentary on the Song of Songs and provided it with an extensive overview of the history of interpretation. There, he pointed out that even Ibn Ezra, the medieval Jewish exegete, came to the conclusion

> that the lovers are a *shepherd* and a *shepherdess*, and that *the king* is a *separate* and *distinct* person from the beloved shepherd. Thus he explains Ch. i. 4, "*I rejoice in* THEE (the shepherd) *more than if* THE KING *had brought me into his apartments.*"[42]

The most prominent exegete who favored the drama hypothesis was Ewald, who found in the Song an exciting story. In his eyes, the main theme of the Song is the praise of true love, set in historic guise by the author.

---

39 Jacobi, *Das durch eine leichte und ungekünstelte Erklärung von seinen Vorwürfen gerettete Hohelied*. Herder, too, was prompted by accusations against the Song of Songs; see Herder, *Lieder der Liebe*, 98: "jede Messe kommen neue glückliche Hypothesen, mystisch und arabisch, arabisch und mystisch. Die neue unanständiger, als die alte, [...] Ja, mehr als Einer hat Anlaß genommen, aus Gegelenheit dieses unschuldigen Buchs über den ganzen Kanon Erbrechungen zu sagen, die zu wiederholen mich die Muse bewahre."
40 Ginsburg, born Jewish in 1831 in Warsaw, converted to Christianity before his fifteenth birthday. He worked as a missionary to Jews in Liverpool and wrote his commentary on the Song in 1857, at the age of 26. See Ginsburg, *Song of Songs*, x.
41 Ginsburg, *Song of Songs*, 87–88.
42 Ginsburg, *Song of Songs*, 46 [emphasis original].

[The poet puts us] in a place where we see on the one side the court of Solomon with all its oriental glamour, and Solomon, whom everybody pays homage, is the tempter. On the other side we are to admire the gentle daughter of innocence. She shines from the first word to the last. And the author has made every effort to praise her appropriately and to raise a monument to her in her speeches. Shulamit (7:1) is the name of this heroine, a paragon of virtue and fidelity. She has grown up far away from city noise and court splendor, in a country town not far from Bethlehem, En-gedi (1:14). With a virtuous youth, her playmate and familiar from childhood, she has an affectionate association and finds herself in him. One day, she walks to a nice place near the town, and all of a sudden, she finds herself between approaching royal chariots. Timidly, she tries to move back, when the king sees this flower—and then, there is no return to her elders' home! She is taken away to the king's court, 6:11, 12; 1:4. Here, in the royal palace, the king starts one attack after the other; the king flatters her, begs her, even favors her over all beauties of his house in the presence of the other women. She, however, does not hear and always answers naively and at last with contempt: her friend is always in her mind. All happens in the presence of the other women; every speech is decent and pure; only the king drops some imprudent words. Thus, all arrows are fired in vain; after a few painful days, the king has to set her free, having acknowledged her unwavering faithfulness. Triumph is hers. She is a wall against vice and cunning, as she says herself (8:10). She seeks her glory only in saving her heart, like an inheritance (8:12). And there the book ends, since the idea of the poet has reached its consummation.

Thus, although some descriptions and expressions of love occur, the poet's religious idea, praising innocence, absorbs them and turns them into perfect harmony.[43]

---

43 Ewald, *Das Hohelied Salomo's*, 2–3: "Um solche Ideen im geschichtlichen Kleide zu schildern, zaubert uns der Dichter auf einen Schauplatz, wo wir auf der einen Seite den Hof des Solomo [sic] sehen mit aller morgenländischen Pracht, und Salomo selbst, dem alles huldigt, ist der Versucher. Von der andern Seite sollen wir eine zarte Tochter der Unschuld bewundern: sie glänzt vom ersten Wort bis zum letzten; und keine Mühe hat der Verfasser gespart, sie würdig zu loben und ihr in ihren Reden selbst ein Denkmahl zu errichten. Sulamit (7,1.) ist der Name dieser Heldin, ein Muster von Tugend und Treue. Sie ist erwachsen fern von Stadtgeräusch und Hofpracht, bei einer Landstadt nicht weit von Bethlehem, En-gedi 1,14. Mit einem tugendsamen Jüngling, ihrem Gespielen und Vertrauten von Kindheit an, seit einiger Zeit näher bekannt und sich in ihm findend, geht sie eines Tags auf einen anmuthigen Platz in der Umgegend, und unversehns geräth sie zwischen heraneilende königliche Wagen; scheu will sie sich zurückziehen, als der König die Blume sieht—und nun auch keine Umkehr wieder in das elterliche Haus! an den Hof des Königs wird sie gezogen 6,11.12. 1,4. Hier nun, im königlichen Pallast, folgt ein Angriff des Königs auf den andern; der König schmeichelt, bittet, zieht sie zuletzt gar allen Schönheiten seines Hauses in Gegenwart der Frauen vor: sie aber gibt kein Gehör und antwortet stets mit Einfalt und zuletzt mit Verachtung: ihr Freund bleibt ihr stets im Sinne. Alles geht indeß in Gegenwart der Frauen vor; alle Reden sind züchtig und lauter; nur dem Könige entfallen einige unachtsame Worte. So nun werden alle Pfeile vergeblich abgeschossen; nach einigen kummervollen Tagen, in denen der König ihre felsenfeste Treue erkannt hat, muß er sie frei geben: der Triumpf ist ihr; sie ist eine Mauer gegen Untugend und Schlauheit, wie sie selbst sagt 8,10; sie sucht ihren Ruhm nur darin, ihr reines Herz wie ihr Erbtheil zu bewahren 8,12., und damit schließt das Buch, da die idee des Dichters ihre Vollendung erreicht hat. So kommen denn wohl einige Schilderungen und Ausdrücke von Liebe vor: aber diese lös't die religiöse Idee des Dichters, die Unschuld zu preisen, in völlige Harmonie auf."

Song 1:4; 6:11–12 in particular are explained strictly scenically. The "I" that went to the garden is the Shulammite. Song 6:12, which causes difficulties for all exegetes, becomes the description of an abduction. Solomon is the villain, the "tempter." All the ostensibly permissive texts are assigned to him. Thus, interpreters were able to separate innocent and decent eroticism from flattering and impure lust. The two angles of understanding—the uncontrived and "natural" style of the Song on the one hand and the chastity of the main protagonists on the other—led to this division.[44] As Ewald argued,

> The king shows himself in his speeches as a mere flatterer who piles up sweet words without heart and vitality, his speeches are the pompous ones, especially near the end, where he does his utmost to persuade her; [. . .] Shulamit's friend, the absent, whom she nevertheless intrudes as speaking sometimes, talking rurally and suavely, much more affectionately and simply than the king.[45]

Ewald assigns the form of address "my friend" (1:10, 14, 15; 2:2, 10; 4:7; 6:4) to the king, "most beautiful of all women" to the choir (1:8; 5:9; 6:1), and "my sister, spouse" (2:10, 13, 14; 4:8–12; 5:1, 2, 4–6, 10, 16; 6:2, 3; 7:11, 12, 14) to the boyfriend.[46] So, for example, he assigns Song 4:1–7 to the king and Song 4:8–15 to the country boy:

> Who can fail to recognize that here (4:8–15) another person than in 4:1–7 must be speaking. Not only is there a new tone and the ceasing of flattery; the poet himself has clearly indicated the change of person by repeating the form of address: "my sister spouse" (highly adequate for the country boy, not for the king) in 8:9, 10, 11, 12; 5:1; whereas above in 4:1, 7, as everywhere where the king is speaking, [he repeats] the form of address, "my friend." The sense is: I save you from the greatest dangers, out of the caves of the lions and leopards of Lebanon; without fear you shall look down from the most dangerous hills.[47]

---

44 See Ewald, *Das Hohelied Salomo's*, 4; Ewald divided the book into four acts: 1:2–2:7; 2:8–3:5; 3:6–8:4; 8:5–14 (ibid., 5); he saw the book not as a drama in the strict sense of the word but as a "dramatic design."
45 Ewald, *Das Hohelied Salomo's*, 4: "Der König zeichnet sich selbst in seinen Reden als bloßen Schmeichler, der nur süße Worte häuft, ohne Herz und Kraft, seine Reden sind die schwülstigsten, vorzüglich am Ende, wo er alle Kräfte der Ueberredung anstrengt; Sulamit ist ängstlich und jungfräulich beschämt als Landmädchen am Hof, überall kindlich und streng, nur im Andenken an ihren Freund versunken; der Chor der Frauen am Hof wenig eingreifend und bescheiden; Sulamits Freund, der abwesende, den diese aber einigemahl redend einführt, ländlich und sanft, viel herzlicher und einfacher redend als der König."
46 See Ewald, *Das Hohelied Salomo's*, 7.
47 Ewald, *Das Hohelied Salomo's*, 117: "Wie kann man verkennen, daß hier (4,8–5,1.) eine ganz andere Person reden muß, als 4,1–7. Nicht bloß erhebt sich ein ganz anderer Ton und die bloße Schmeichelrede verschwindet; der Dichter selbst hat den Wechsel höchst klar angedeutet, indem hier stets die Anrede: meine Schwester Braut (sehr passend für den ländlichen Jüngling, nicht für den König) v. 8.9.10.11.12. 5,1., oben aber 4,1.7. wie überall, wo der König spricht, die Anrede: meine

The repetition of 4:1–7 in 6:4 is also turned against the king. It "proves" the hollowness of the king's love:

> We recognize the same flatterer; the poet makes the king repeat his previous speech (4:1–7), only more decorated, fuller, more urgent, mixed with new, elaborated, flattering words.[48]

Of Song 7:3 Ewald says, "It is true that this line is somewhat pompous. But one must not forget that the poet lets the king speak here."[49]

Another example highlights the difference from today's interpretations of "erotic" lines. Song 7:9 runs, "And your mouth like the best wine. It goes down smoothly for my beloved, gliding over lips and teeth." This line obviously caused problems, because it could easily be taken as indelicate. Thus, most exegetes went to great effort to make clear its "true design." Ewald solved the problem by making the king say these words.[50] Of course, he had to leave out some words:

> The indecent understanding that some interpreters find is proved by nothing. The sweet wine glides (like a speech) straight down and passes the lips of the sleeping woman, faintly inebriating [. . .]. In this context, the לְדוֹדִי [lĕ-dôdî, "for my beloved"] does not make sense at all, and I have no doubt that it is put here because of a very old scribal mistake from the following line.[51]

Of course, the triangle hypothesis must also explain the object of the Shulammite's loving words when she is alone with the king in his palace (e.g., in 1:2–7, 12–14, 16–17; 2:1, 3–7). Ewald and others developed a refined distribution of the text among the different protagonists. In the first scene, the Shulammite has only recently been brought into the royal seraglio and is still dressed in her country garments. While the king speaks alluringly to her, the Shulammite dismisses the praise and shifts it to her friend:

> the king arrives in time and tries to win her over with flattering promises (9–11). But Shulamit shows him, subtly but clearly, that her heart is averse to him and attached only to her friend

---

Freundin, wiederholt wird—Sinn: Ich rette dich aus den größten Gefahren, aus den Löwen- und Parderhöhlen des Libanon; ohne Furcht sollst du von den gefährlichsten Anhöhen herabschauen."
48 Ewald, *Das Hohelied Salomo's*, 127: "Wir erkennen ganz denselben Schmeichler; der Dichter läßt mit großer Kunst den König nur seine vorige Rede (4,1–7.) wiederholen, aber geschmückter, voller, dringender, mit neuen, ausgesuchten Schmeichelworten gemischt."
49 Ewald, *Das Hohelied Salomo's*, 135: "Es ist wahr, daß dieser Vers etwas schwülstig ist: aber man vergesse nicht, daß der Dichter den König reden läßt."
50 See Ewald, *Das Hohelied Salomo's*, 137.
51 Ewald, *Das Hohelied Salomo's*, 137: "der unanständige Sinn, den einige Ausleger hier finden, ist mit nichts zu beweisen. Der süße Wein gleitet [wie eine Rede] gerade hinunter und durchläuft die Lippen der Schlafenden, leicht berauschend [. . .]. In diesem Zusammenhange gibt aber לְדוֹדִי gar keinen Sinn; und ich zweifle nicht, daß es durch einen uralten Schreibfehler aus dem folgenden Verse hier eingesetzt ist."

at home (12–14). In vain the king repeats his flatteries (15): she applies the king's compliments to her friend and praises her happiness in rural simplicity (16–2:1).[52]

Ewald's explanation of Song 1:12 is similar:

> As long as the king was at his banquet, as long as he did not turn to the seraglio, to me; as long as the king was absent and his presence did not annoy me, my nard gave its fragrance, spread its sweet fragrance for me, which now, due to the arrival of the king, evaporates: I found myself well in the remembrance of my friend, whom she means by the fragrant nard.[53]

Another interpretation includes the woman's friend in Song 7:9. Böttcher, author of *Ausführliches Lehrbuch der hebräischen Sprache* (Extensive Textbook of the Hebrew Language), laid out the following dramatic composition:

> *Solomon (approaching with yearning desire):* I thought: I want to climb upward on the palm, touch its pendulous palm leaves! Would your breasts become like grapes of the vine *(pointing to the fruit basket)* and the fragrance of your breath like the fragrance of quinces *(handing her a wine goblet and trying to kiss her)* and your kissable lips like the most beautiful wine! *The female vintner (evading the king and going to kiss the entering shepherd):* It goes straight to my darling, sidling over his crimson lips.[54]

The Shulammite's response to the king's flattery in 4:1–7 and 6:4 is both exemplary and dismissive.[55] In the end, the rejected king leaves the Shulammite to her friend. On Song 8:10 ("I am a wall"), Ewald noted:

---

52 Ewald, *Das Hohelied Salomo's*, 53: "der König fällt zur rechten Zeit ein und will sie mit schmeichelndem Lobe und Versprechungen gewinnen (9–11.). Doch Sulamit zeigt ihm mit einer feinen Wendung, jedoch deutlich genug, ihr ihm abgeneigtes, nur dem heimathlichen Freunde zugewandtes Herz (12–14.). Vergeblich wiederholt der König seine Schmeichelworte (15.): sie bezieht das ihr vom König gemachte Lob auf ihren Freund und preist sich glücklich in der ländlichen Einfachheit [54] (16 –2,1.)."

53 Ewald, *Das Hohelied Salomo's*, 64: "So lang der König war an seiner Tafel, so lang er sich noch nicht hierher in das Frauengemach, zu mir, wandte, so lange der König abwesend war und seine Nähe mir nicht lästig wurde, gab meine Narde ihren Duft, verbreitete meine Narde mir süßen Duft, der nun durch des Königs Ankunft verfliegt: befand ich mich wohl im Andenken an meinen Freund, den sie unter der duftenden Narde versteht."

54 Böttcher, *Die ältesten Bühnendichtungen*, 48: "*Salomo (mit schmachtender Sehnsucht sich annähernd):* Ich dachte: will hinan auf die Palme, erfassen ihre Hangefedern! Und würden doch Deine Brüste wie Trauben der Rebe *(auf den Fruchtkorb deutend)* und der Ruch Deines Athems wie Quittenduft *(einen Becher Wein darbietend und einen Kuss versuchend)* und dein Kussmund wie schönster Wein! *Winzerin (indem sie dem König sich entzieht, und dem eintretenden Hirten einen Kuss zu bringen geht):* Der geht zu meinem Schatze den richtigen Weg, schleicht dessen Purpur-Lippen."

55 See Ewald, *Das Hohelied Salomo's*, 116–117.

[Shulamit's] unconquerable virtue broke the passion of the king, and what other choice did he have than to release her, who always despised the court, the splendor, the highest honor and who always turned her back to him?[56]

The flattering repetitive king on the one side, the sincerely loving shepherd and the unwavering and faithful country beauty on the other side. Ewald's use of this constellation, the product of a certain zeitgeist, influenced future reception that was a product of the same zeitgeist.[57] The love-triangle hypothesis was widely accepted in the eighteenth and nineteenth centuries. Ginsburg's overview mentions both Jewish and Christian exegetes who shared Ewald's interpretation. According to Ginsburg, the first Jewish interpreter "who recognised and elucidated the true design of this book"[58] was S. Löwisohn (1788–1821).[59] He was followed by Herxheimer and Philippson, two rabbis who "by virtue of their high position and great learning, may be regarded as representing the view now generally entertained by the Jews respecting the Song of Songs." [60]

Among Christian interpreters, Ginsburg mentions Jacobi, Ammon, and Umbreit, who before the "celebrated Ewald" showed the "true sense" of the book in a masterly way: "The little band, who struggled hard for the defence of the true design of this book, could now rejoice at the accession of a mighty leader to their ranks."[61] After 1840, more and more scholars accepted this view,[62] and Ginsburg joyfully states that after 1856, at the latest, "[i]n this opinion of the superiority of

---

56 Ewald, *Das Hohelied Salomo's*, 142: "ihre unüberwindliche Tugend brach die Leidenschaft des Königs, und was konnte ihm schon nach den vorher vom Dichter geschilderten Scenen übrig bleiben, als die ihn, den Hof, den Glanz, die höchste Ehre verschmähende, ihm stets abgewandte zu entlassen?"
57 It is not clear if Goethe shared this view. But interestingly, his translation of the Song excludes the two texts about Solomon: 3:7–11 and 8:10–14. The reasons are uncertain. T. Tillmann, e.g., denies that Goethe could have seen a shepherd as the beloved and would therefore have excluded Solomon. Nevertheless, he thinks that Goethe excluded this text because he didn't want to disturb the sense of "naive intimacy" with the exhibition of glory and pomp of the court (Tillmann, *Hermeneutik*, 223–224).
58 Ginsburg, *Song of Songs*, 59.
59 See Löwisohn, *Melizat-Jeshurun*.
60 Ginsburg, *Song of Songs*, 60.
61 Ginsburg, *Song of Songs*, 92.
62 Among Jewish exegetes, Ginsburg (*Song of Songs*, 101) mentions, e.g., S. Davidson (see Davidson, *Text of the Old Testament*, 806). Among Christian interpreters, Ginsburg (*Song of Songs*, 95) mentions Hirzel (*Das Lied der Lieder* [1840]), E. Meier (*Hohelied* [1854]), E. F. Friedrich (*Cantici* [1855]), and F. Hitzig (*Das Hohe Lied* [1856]), though the latter assumes two men and two women as protagonists. Delitzsch, *Das Hohelied*, rejected any attempt at allegorizing and preferred to regard the poem as celebrating the victory of virtuous love in humble life over the allures of royalty (see Ginsburg, *Song of Songs*, 96).

virtuous love to all the temptations of royalty, the Jew and the Christian, the Englishman and the German, are beginning to unite." [63]

3.2.2 The Unspoiled Oriental

The second widespread interpretation of the drama theory sees Solomon himself as the male lover of the Song. As a consequence, the permissive or flattering speeches must be defended and their morality and decency proved. One of the most prominent interpreters in this vein was Delitzsch, who in 1851 argued that Solomon was the author of a drama about the love between the king and a simple country girl. Delitzsch believed it was important that "[w]e expect to have depicted an occurrence of Solomon's life, but in a way that justifies the position within the canon that the poem has won and maintained."[64]

First, the woman had to be freed from any doubt regarding her reasons for loving a king. Delitzsch argued that

> in Solomon [she] loves not the king, but the man. [. . .] Accordingly, Shulamit loves Solomon: not his purple and his crown, but the whole of him, the person with this soul and this body that reflects this soul.[65]

Delitzsch divided the Song into six acts, each with its own place: act one (1:2–2:7) was set in the king's vine house, act two (2:8–3:5) in the house of the Shulammite and its surroundings, and so on.

In contrast to the triangle hypothesis, in Delitzsch's interpretation the intention of the king is pure and honorable, too. His words are not mere flattery, nor are the repetitions a sign of lack of emotion. When the king repeats the words of Song 4, which he had spoken at his wedding, in Song 6, it is an expression that nothing has changed between the two lovers.[66] His love is as innocent and chaste as hers. When he grazes among the lilies (Song 2:16), this is taken literally. It is a symbol of his

---

63 Ginsburg, *Song of Songs*, 101.
64 Delitzsch, *Das Hohelied*, 84: "Wir erwarten einen Vorgang aus Salomo's Leben dargestellt zu finden, so aber, daß die Stellung, die das Gedicht im Kanon gewonnen und behauptet hat, sich rechtfertigt."
65 Delitzsch, *Das Hohelied*, 156–157: "[Sie] liebt in Salomo nicht den König, sondern den Menschen. [. . .] So liebt Sulamith Salomo: nicht seinen Purpur und seine Krone, aber ihn ganz, die Person mit dieser Seele und diesem Leibe, der diese Seele wiederspiegelt."
66 See Delitzsch, *Das Hohelied*, 129.

enthusiasm for gardening. Thus, the king revels in the flowers of the garden, enjoys them, and gathers them.[67]

Delitzsch hurried to explain even the most intimate embraces as decent:

> Solomon holds Shulamit in his arms. Jubilant to have her as his own, he praises love as the most beautiful and most lovely of all joys. He does not mean the common carnal lust, because the reason for this praise of love is the matrimonial relationship that causes him such bliss.[68]

The country scenes of the Song, however, had to be explained in other ways. Why should a king act as a shepherd? Delitzsch answered the question by assuming a downward trajectory. Song 2:8–14, for example, he interpreted as follows:

> The king has descended from the throne of his power and glory to the childlikeness of his beloved; out of love, he has become the likes of her in his behavior, a shepherd for a shepherdess.[69]

However, this reading demonstrates that identifying Solomon with the male lover created a huge, hierarchical social and mental gap between the king and the woman. The Shulammite, according to this interpretation, is a country girl without much of a brain. Thus, Song 1:7 ("tell me [. . .] where you pasture your flock"), for example, is seen as her effort to get rid of her rivals and to be alone with Solomon,

> there, where she feels at home, in the meadows of the country. Now it is evening. Might he, whom her soul loves, tell her where he usually pastures his flocks, where he rests at noon, lest she, wandering near the flocks of his mates, appear like an unchaste harlot. The simple child of nature has no idea of the business of a king. Her naivete does not reach beyond a shepherd's occupation. She imagines the shepherd of people as a shepherd of sheep. The women of the palace consider themselves entitled to answer such a foolish question to the king.[70]

---

67 See Delitzsch, *Das Hohelied*, 127.
68 Delitzsch, *Das Hohelied*, 140: "Salomo hält Sulamith in seinen Armen. Selig, sie sein nennen zu können, preist er die Liebe als die schönste und lieblichste aller Wonnen. Er meint nicht die gemeine fleischliche Wollust, denn Anlaß zu dieser lobpreisenden Anrede an die Liebe ist das eheliche Verhältniß, in dem er sich so überglücklich fühlt."
69 Delitzsch, *Das Hohelied*, 100: "Der König ist von dem Throne seiner Macht und Herrlichkeit zur Kindlichkeit der Geliebten herabgestiegen, er ist aus Liebe in seinem Verhalten gegen sie ihres Gleichen geworden, der Hirtin ein Hirte."
70 Delitzsch, *Das Hohelied*, 91–92: "und zwar da wo sie sich heimisch fühlt, auf ländlicher Flur. Jetzt ist es Abend. Möchte der den ihre Seele liebt ihr sagen, wo er weiden, wo am Mittag zu lagern pflegt, damit sie nicht, bei den Heerden seiner Genossen umherschweifend, als eine unkeusche Dirne erscheine. Die Tochter des Landes hat keinen Begriff von dem Geschäfte eines Königs. Ueber den Beruf eines Hirten als den schönsten und höchsten reicht ihre Einfalt nicht hinaus. Sie denkt sich den Hirten der Völker als Hirten der Schafe. Auf eine so thörichte Frage an den König halten sich die Frauen des Hauses für befugt, selbst zu antworten."

Starting with Song 7:11, the lovers leave the town and go to the country. According to Delitzsch, this is because the woman is homesick and wants to show her homeland to her bridegroom.

Of course, the woman is not only humble and childlike but also chaste, pure, and virtuous. When in Song 2:6 she lies in her lover's arms and trembles in delight, her thoughts stay "full of childlike simple-mindedness within the circles of her humble parentage."[71] In Song 3, the fact that she sleeps alone in her bed is seen as proof of the ethical value of the Song. The girl was not intimate with the king before the wedding, and thus the Song does not depict common, sensual love in defiance of the divine order.[72] Even the seeking of the lover must be a dream, otherwise it would be not virtuous enough.[73]

Even after the wedding (seen in Song 3:6–11) the bride remains shy. Delitzsch's interpretation of Song 4:6 is unusual. The line is usually assigned to the male lover, but Delitzsch has the bride say it. She tries therewith to escape the too-ardent speeches of her bridegroom:

> The humble bride tries to evade the burning praise of love by uttering a wish to visit the mountain of myrrh and the hill of frankincense—presumably lonesome places in the royal palace area, where she intends to stay in the mood that suits the day, until nightfall calls her back to the king.[74]

The Shulammite's dancing in Song 7 is (compared to today's interpretations) totally desexualized as well:

> Her navel [...] is a circular bowl that never lacks spiced wine, i.e., as full of healthy freshness (see Prov 3:8) as that of spiced wine. [...] In such a way the daughters of Jerusalem praise Shulamit's beauty among themselves. They indulge in the purest feast for the eyes. Shulamit's dancing is the expression of her childlike mind. Her dancing in front of the daughters of Jerusalem, fulfilling their requests, is the expression of her humbleness; and the fact that her lovely beauty makes such a delightful impression on the daughters of Jerusalem, surpassing every loveliness and sublimity, is the consequence of the pure, chaste, and humble heart that beats within this beautiful body.[75]

---

71 Delitzsch, *Das Hohelied*, 94: "voll kindlicher Einfalt innerhalb des Kreises ihrer geringen Abkunft."
72 See Delitzsch, *Das Hohelied*, 99.
73 See Delitzsch, *Das Hohelied*, 103.
74 Delitzsch, *Das Hohelied*, 113: "Die demüthige Braut sucht den liebeglühenden Lobsprüchen auszuweichen, indem sie den Wunsch äußert, den Myrrhenberg und den Weihrauchhügel zu besuchen—wahrscheinlich einsame Plätze im Bereich des königlichen Palastes, wo sie in der diesem Tage entsprechenden Gemüthsstimmung zuzubringen gedenkt, bis das einbrechende Dunkel sie zum König zurückruft."
75 Delitzsch, *Das Hohelied*, 139: "Ihr Nabel, so weit er bei dem stärkeren Athmen der Tanzenden durch das Gewand hindurch sichtbar wird, ist eine kreißrunde Schale, der es nicht an Würzwein

Furthermore, Delitzsch understood Song 8:1–2 ("Oh that you were like a brother!") as a proof of the chaste love of the woman:

> Thus, the queen speaks the language of a child. Worldly splendor is not the homeland of her thoughts. And carnal lust is not the answer to her dreams. How else could she be so happy imagining Solomon to be her brother, whom she might kiss in public, who would teach her and to whom she would do good.[76]

Thus, the naïve country girl's attraction lies in foolish questions and childlike simplemindedness as well as in purity and virtue, and she is loved by Solomon exactly because of this, as Song 1:15 ("your eyes are doves") shows: Solomon praises her eyes, "which reflect her dovelike innocence."[77]

3.2.3 Conclusion

According to the common view of Song interpretations in the eighteenth and nineteenth centuries, the more permissive parts of Song of Songs were either spoken by the beloved and excused as cultural difference—the unaffected *Morgenländer* was declared to have a free, more relaxed attitude toward sexuality—but always in the innocent way of the noble savage and the couple in paradise; or, in the case of words deemed too indecent, they became flattery and blandishment in the mouth of Solomon, the "villain" of the piece. These words were rebuffed by the ethically unimpeachable lovers, which served to highlight the true love of the married couple even more.

---

fehlt, d.h. so voll Gesundheitsfrische (vgl. Spr. 3,8), wie jene von Würzwein. [. . .] So preisen die Töchter Jerusalems unter einander die Schönheit Sulamiths. Es ist die keuscheste Augenweide, in der sie schwelgen. Daß Sulamith tanzt, ist die Aeußerung ihres kindlichen Gemüths; daß sie vor den Töchtern jerusalems tanzt, den Bitten dieser willfahrend, die Aeußerung ihrer Demuth, und daß ihre liebliche Schönheit auf die Töchter Jerusalems einen so entzückenden, alles Liebliche und Erhabene überbietenden Eindruck macht, ist die Folge des in diesem schönen Leibe schlagenden reinen, züchtigen, demüthigen Herzens."

76 Delitzsch, *Das Hohelied*, 142: "So redet die Königin die Sprache eines Kindes. Die irdische Herrlichkeit ist nicht die Heimath ihrer Gedanken; auch ist Fleischeslust nicht das Ziel ihrer Wünsche. Wie könnte sie sonst in der Vorstellung, daß Salomo ihr Bruder wäre, den sie öffentlich küssen dürfe, der sie unterrichte und dem sie gütlich thue, sich so glücklich fühlen!"

77 Delitzsch, *Das Hohelied*, 93: "in denen sich ihre Taubeneinfalt spiegelt."

4 Impacts

4.1 The Seraglio and the Vineyard: A Parallel Prepared but Never Implemented

The drama hypothesis had several lasting impacts. It localized the book in a new way. Following the necessities of drama, each place mentioned in the Song became a real place. Often, exegetes tried to find those places in the land of the Bible itself. Herder mocked the exaggerated effort to localize every possible place:

> Hasselquist sought the closed garden [. . .], Pocock sought Solomon's sealed fountain [. . .] and d'Arvieur sought the sealed well [. . .], and they justly found them. It would be great if another was sent to seek the two gazelles and the round bowl and Solomon's wheat heap; they would find them, too.[78]

Nevertheless, Herder, like most exegetes of his time, also took a literal interpretation of some verses of the Song that today's interpreters see as metaphors—for example, pasturing among the lilies or the garden. Herder vehemently rejected an interpretation of the garden as a metaphor for the woman.[79]

The drama theory went one step further, introducing places not mentioned in the text. If the Song of Songs was a play, then each dialogue had to happen in a concrete setting. The book was seen as a succession of scenes. The most influential localization was the seraglio, which was introduced into the mental world of the Song. The supporters of the drama theory based their harem concept on the first verses of the Song, which mention a king and girls. They did not leave this to mere imagery but concretized it as "King Solomon" and "ladies of the harem." Furthermore, Solomon was identified with contemporary Muslim sultans, in either romanticized or demonized European distortion. The woman of the Song had been conducted or abducted into this royal place and either longed there for her absent lover or enjoyed the king's love in childlike obeisance. This concretization had a huge impact on later exegesis, and the harem continues to be indispensable for Song of Songs commentaries even today.

The key verses for current references to a harem are Song 8:11–12: "Solomon had a vineyard at Baal-hamon. [. . .] My vineyard is before me; you, O Solomon, may have

---

[78] Herder, *Lieder der Liebe*, 47: "Den verschlossenen Garten hat Hasselquist, [. . .] den versiegelten Brunnen Salomos Pocock, [. . .] und die versiegelte Wasserquelle d' Arvieur [. . .] gesucht, und wie es recht war, auch würklich gefunden. Es wäre gut, wenn noch eine Gesandtschaft ausgeschickt würde, die beiden Rehchen und den runden Becher und den Weizenhaufen Salomons zu suchen; sie würden es gleichfalls finden."

[79] See Herder, *Lieder der Liebe*, 32, 50.

the thousand." Most commentators see this vineyard, and especially the "thousand," as a metaphor for Solomon's harem and his thousand wives (with reference to 1Kgs 11), rather than a literal reference. This shift from literal to metaphorical came with the twentieth century and its focus on sexuality without moralizing tendencies. Instead of localizing each and every detail in realia, the metaphorical understanding of the book was renewed, not as allegorical but as metaphors for the body. Instead of locating the items of the Song of Songs geographically, they are now located on the body of the woman. For example, if the young man feeds among the lilies (Song 2:16), he savors the woman's womb. When he hurries to the cleft mountains (Song 2:17), these also are a synonym for her body. Since the woman obviously speaks about herself as a garden, each and every mention of a plant must be the woman, too. And of course, the vineyard of the woman is a synonym for the woman herself or her chastity.[80]

However, some relics of the eighteenth century remain, in particular the question of chastity and the harem of Solomon. According to recent exegetes, not only the vineyard of the woman in Song 1:6 and 8:12 but also the vineyard of Solomon must have something to do with women. Thus, the thousand silver coins become Solomon's harem, in which a thousand women live. G. Krinetzki describes Song 8:11–12 as

> the boasting song of a young man. [...] The vineyard means a royal harem full of blooming maids—a foil to the unique beloved, the vineyard of the young man, which surpasses the value of a harem.[81]

O. Keel in his commentary reflects on the name Baal-hamon ("Lord of multitude/turmoil") and concludes that it is only natural to think of a certain amount of turmoil in a harem of such size.[82] And Y. Zakovich states in regard to the "thousand" in Song 8:12, "The vineyard contains 1,000 vines according to the 1,000 women in Solomon's harem."[83]

Interestingly, scholars who favor the drama theory never take this key verse into account. Instead, they localize Solomon's vineyard exactly as they do the lilies or the mountain of myrrh or any the other location. It is simply a vineyard. And the "thousand" in Song 8:12 are seen as the same thousand silver coins mentioned in the previous verse. This is remarkable inasmuch as the vineyard of the woman is nevertheless seen metaphorically as a symbol of her chastity.

---

80 This last interpretation is found in eighteenth-century exegesis, too, but is mostly rejected.
81 Krinetzki, *Hoheslied*, 27: Song 8:11–12 is a "Prahllied eines Jünglings, verwandt mit 6,8–9. Der 'Weinberg' meint einen königlichen Harem voll 'blühender' Mädchen—ein Kontrastbild zu der einzig Geliebten, dem 'Weinberg' des jungen Mannes, d.h. der Geliebten, die den Wert eines Harems, symbolisiert durch die Einkünfte, die ein König wie Salomo aus einem guten Weinberg beziehen würde, unendlich übertrifft."
82 See Keel, *Das Hohelied*, 253–254.
83 Zakovich, *Das Hohelied*, 282.

The main interest in Solomon's vineyard lay in the question where exactly it was situated. Herder knew of a place named Hama near Balbeck, which is commonly called Aman and which seemed plausible to him.[84] Other scholars argued for Baal-gad,[85] Hammon in Asher,[86] or the Balamon mentioned in Jdt 8:3 LXX.[87] Ginsburg, following Rashi, localized the vineyard near Jerusalem and argued "בַּעַל הָמוֹן place of the multitude, because its beauties and charms attracted a multitude of people, thus presenting a greater temptation for the Shulammite."[88] According to Ginsburg, the "abandoning to the guardians" only shows that the vineyard was so huge that Solomon had to lease it out to a number of tenants.[89]

Neither Solomon's vineyard nor the "thousand" were seen as allusions to the harem. Instead, most interpreters in the eighteenth century, even those who supported the drama theory, understood Song 8:11–12 to be reckoning with richness. According to Herder, it is

> obviously a mocking story about the impact of guarding and saving. The king gets what he wanted, and everyone takes their own beyond the guardian's recompense. She keeps her vineyard on her own, so she says, so as not to be deceived or to pay a keeper's fee.[90]

Similarly, Ewald interpreted 8:11–12 as the Shulammite's mocking song, which she intones in remembrance of what has happened. She does not need custodians, as her own vineyard (i.e., her chastity) is in her own possession.[91] Thus, against a widespread opinion, Ewald took 8:10–14 not as fragments or appendices but as the triumphant ending of the book:

> For the consumption of the whole, at least [vv.] 8–12 are necessary: here, Solomon is finally clearly mentioned; the triumph of innocence, scorn and contempt for the king, these are shown in the brightest light right here at the end.[92]

---

84 See Herder, *Lieder der Liebe*, 87.
85 See Rosenmüller, *Handbuch*, 281.
86 See Ewald, *Das Hohelied Salomo's*, 150.
87 See Hitzig, "Das Hohe Lied," 104.
88 Ginsburg, *Song of Songs*, 190.
89 See Ginsburg, *Song of Songs*, 190.
90 Herder, *Lieder der Liebe*, 86: "Offenbar eine Spottgeschichte von dem, was aus dem Hüten und Wahren herauskommt. Der König bekommt, was er sich ausbedung, und jeder nimmt sich noch zum Hüterlohn das Seine. Sie wahret, spricht sie, ihren Weinberg selbst, so wird sie nicht betrogen und darf keinen Hüterlohn zollen."
91 See Ewald, *Das Hohelied Salomo's*, 148.
92 Ewald, *Das Hohelied Salomo's*, 151: "Zur Vollendung des Ganzen sind wenigstens [V.] 8–12. [sic] nothwendig: hier wird Salomo erst deutlich genannt; Sieg der Unschuld, Spott und Verachtung dem König, zeigt sich gerade hier am Ende im hellsten Lichte."

Ginsburg, too, understood these lines as a retrospective narration on the Shulammite's rejection of Solomon's wooing. He also included possession of the vineyard in Solomon's strategy:

> Having been obliged, when demanding her promised reward, to describe her virtue as an impregnable wall, the Shulammite now relates more circumstantially how she had resisted the attempt to gain her affections. Solomon had a large vineyard in Baal-hammon, which he offered to consign to her if she granted his request; but the Shulammite refused his offer, telling him he might keep his large estate to himself, for she was quite satisfied with her humble possession.[93]

Though Solomon's possession is so huge that he has to entrust it to guardians, "the Shulammite prefers to keep her little vineyard, and be with her beloved shepherd, rather than unfaithfully give him up for riches and honours." Thus, in Ginsburg's eyes Solomon is using his vineyard as an attempt at bribery that the woman rejects.

Delitzsch interpreted the lines the other way around: in his eyes, the woman stipulates a guardian's fee for her brothers. In this last chapter, the Shulammite thinks of her family, first of her little sister (8:8–10) and then of her brothers (8:11–12). She tells them of Solomon's huge vineyard, which he gave over to guards.

> She, too, has a vineyard in her possession. We know from 1:6; cf. 4:12–5:1: it is the entirety of all agreeable things from the abundance of her outer and inner gifts, that she is able to give to her beloved, her husband. The undiminished and undivided profit of this vineyard, the full thousand, belongs to nobody other than to you, Solomon, she says, addressing the king. But shall the faithful protectors of this vineyard go away empty-handed? Two hundred should be due to them for their faithful guarding. These protectors, who should also benefit from having made it possible that she become Solomon's possession as a pure virgin, are her brothers, the faithful guardians of her innocence.[94]

Others, like J. C. Velthusen, saw the verses as a sales negotiation between the brothers and Solomon: the brothers intend to sell their sister the Shulammite to Solomon as a concubine for a thousand silver coins. In the end, they get two hundred.[95]

---

93 Ginsburg, *Song of Songs*, 190.
94 Delitzsch, *Das Hohelied*, 152: "Auch sie hat einen Weinberg, der zu ihrer Verfügung steht; wir wissen schon aus 1,6. vgl. 4,12 bis 5,1.: es ist die Gesammtheit alles des Angenehmen, was sie dem Geliebten, dem Gatten aus der Fülle ihrer äußeren und inneren Gaben zu gewähren vermag. Der ungeschmälerte und ungetheilte Ertrag deses Weingartens, die vollen Tausend, gehören Niemand anders als dir, Salomo, sagt sie, nun zum Könige gewendet. Aber sollen die treuen Hüter dieses Weingartens ganz leer ausgehen? Zweihundert möchten doch ihnen gebühren für ihre treue Hütung. Diese Hüter, die auch etwas davon haben sollen, daß sie als reine Jungfrau Salomo's Eigenthum geworden ist, sind ihre Brüder, die treuen Wächter ihrer Unschuld."
95 See Velthusen, *Das Hohelied*, 521–523.

4.2 The Speech of the (Alledged) Brothers in Song 8:8–10

The second point that emerged from the tendency toward historicization and localization was the assumption that the woman's brothers safeguard her chastity in Song 8:8–10. The woman is often called "sister," mostly by her lover. This is always seen as a term of endearment. Only in 8:8–10, however, do followers of the drama theory assume literal brothers are speaking to the Shulammite. The young sister without breasts is the woman herself, whose chastity the brothers seek to preserve. This interpretation continues to be influential, and hardly anyone offers alternative interpretations.[96] This was not the case in the nineteenth century, however. Weißbach (1858) took the speaker to be the woman, laughing to scorn those who think they can conceal a woman's "blemish" (being neither tall nor beautiful and having no breasts at all) with riches and jewels (cedar wood and silver). In her eyes, this is as ridiculous as thinking it is possible to buy love.

> Anyone who tried to surround his sister, who lacks all personal charms, with a silver wall and a cedar door post, in order to present her like a castle with towers and doors, i.e., as a desirable possession, would expose himself to ridicule, just like someone who tried to buy love with all the wealth of his house.[97]

4.3 Impacts on Music and Art

As I have shown, the drama hypothesis was influenced by manifold hermeneutical, methodological, and religious and sociological trends and developments. Not least, it was inspired by the genre of drama itself. And in turn, the drama theory gave rise to new dramatic approaches. Since at least 1857, the story of the humble maid who rejects the alluring, rich king Solomon has inspired librettists and playwrights. The love triangle is prominent, for example, in plays like P. Heyse's *Die Weisheit Salomo's* (1886), J. B. Alexander's *King Solomon* (1899), and R. Woerner's *König Salomo* (1912) and as a side-subject in J. Kesselring's play *Mother of That Wisdom* (1933). The triangle has also been set to music, as in A. C. Mackenzie's oratorio *The Rose of Sharon* (1884), with a libretto by J. Bennett, or in the opera *Sulamith* (1906), by

---

96 But see Exum, *Song of Songs*, 44, 254–256, who sees the woman as the speaker of Song 8:8–10.
97 Weißbach, *Das Hohe Lied Salomo's*, 274: "wer seine aller persönlichen Reize entbehrende Schwester mit einem silbernen Mäuerchen und Cedern-Pföstchen umgeben wollte, um sie wie eine Festung mit Mauern und Thürmen oder Thoren, also als einen wünschenswerthen Besitz darzustellen, der würde sich gewiss ebenso lächerlich machen wie Jemand, der Liebe für alles Gut seines Hauses kaufen wollte."

S. Blumenthal and H. Lautensack, and especially in A. Rubinstein's and J. Rodenberg's *Sulamith* (1883).

The typical plot follows the Song of Songs: the Shulammite deplores her abduction into the seraglio. The daughters of Jerusalem are the ladies of the harem, who do not understand how a simple, poor country girl could refuse the riches of Solomon. Solomon tries to win her love but fails. The beloved shepherd obtains entry into the harem, and they escape. The guards of the town, however, pick them up and bring them back to the king. Finally, the king understands that the Shulammite will never love him, and so he lets her go. In most cases, the end of the play is Song 8:6 ("Strong as death is love").

Only a few musical plays depict Solomon as the beloved, but even then he must dress himself as a shepherd to win the girl's heart. Examples include the oratorio *Sulamith* by P. A. Klenau (1913); M. Brentano's drama *Sulamith: Balladen der Liebe* (1928); and W. Hiller's musical play *Schulamit: Ein erotisches Tryptichon* (1990). The peak of the "triangle" boom in literature and music occurred between 1880 and 1914. After World War I, the subject lost its attractiveness.

Though it took some time for exegesis to influence works of art, by the end of the nineteenth century the Song had become a favorite subject of both musical and nonmusical stage plays. The interlacing of culture, exegesis, and art are most impressively manifest in the story of this interpretation, which was enabled by the Romantics and itself influenced late-Romantic receptions of the book.

4.4 And the Harem?

To sum up, I have tried to point out that our cultural context has a deep impact on our biblical interpretation. But this also works the other way around: biblical interpretations influence our cultural context. They inspire artists whose works in turn inspire us to find new images that help us "explain" and perhaps adjust our present a bit. The drama theory was influential because it allowed the Song of Songs to become a metaphor, a role model of human love for eighteenth- and nineteenth-century people. The Song gave them an example of what it meant to love, in words and expressions that they could understand and that helped them form their own way of loving, if only as an unachievable ideal.

Today, the drama theory has very few supporters.[98] Most scholars prefer to see the Song of Songs as either a collection of songs or a poetic unity. Our knowledge of the ancient Orient does not allow us to equate the pashas of the eighteenth century

---

98 But see Hopf, *Liebesszenen*, who understands the Song as a dramatic text.

with the kings of Israel. And our understanding of the social hierarchy between man and woman has changed, too.

Nevertheless, there is hardly a commentator who does not mention Solomon's harem. The harem has survived. And one could ask, why?

Bibliography

Primary Sources (Eighteenth and Nineteenth Centuries)

Ammon, Christoph Friedrich. *Salomo's verschmähte Liebe oder die belohnte Treue: Ein Liebesgedicht aus dem Salomonischen Zeitalter*. Leipzig: Johann Ambrosius Barth, 1790.
Böttcher, Friedrich. *Die ältesten Bühnendichtungen: Der Debora-Gesang und das Hohe Lied dramatisch hergestellt und neu übersetzt*. Leipzig: Johann Ambrosius Barth, 1850.
Budde, Karl Ferdinand Reinhard. *Das Hohelied erklärt*. KHC 17. Tübingen: Mohr, 1898.
Davidson, Samuel. *The Text of the Old Testament: Considered with a Treatise on Sacred Interpretation, and a Brief Introduction to the Old Testament Books and the Apocrypha*. London: Longman's & Roberts, 1856.
Delitzsch, Franz Julius. *Das Hohelied: Untersucht und ausgelegt*. Leipzig: Dörffling und Franke, 1851.
Ewald, Georg Heinrich August. *Das Hohelied Salomo's: Übersetzt, mit Einleitung, Anmerkungen und einem Anhang über den Prediger*. Göttingen: Rudolph Deuerlich, 1826.
Friedrich, Ernst Ferdinand. *Quae Cantici Canticorum Salomonii esset poetica forma*. Königsberg: Borntraeger, 1855.
Ginsburg, Christian David. *The Song of Songs and Coheleth (Commonly Called the Book of Ecclesiastes): Translated from the Original Hebrew, with a Commentary, Historical and Critical*. 1857, 1861. The Library of Biblical Studies. Repr., New York: KTAV, 1970.
Haupt, Paul. *Biblische Liebeslieder: Das sogenannte Hohelied Salomos unter steter Berücksichtigung der Uebersetzungen Goethes und Herders im Versmasse der Urschrift verdeutscht und erklärt*. Leipzig: Hinrichs, 1908.
Herder, Johann Gottfried. *Lieder der Liebe: Die ältesten und schönsten aus dem Morgenlande*. Leipzig: Weygand, 1778.
Hirzel, Bernhard. *Das Lied der Lieder oder Sieg der Treue (Das hohe Lied): Übersetzt und erklärt*. Zürich: Ch. Beyel, 1840.
Hitzig, Ferdinand. "Das Hohe Lied." In vol. 16 of *Kurzgefasstes exegetisches Handbuch zum Alten Testament*, 1–106. Leipzig: Verlag s. Hirzel, 1855.
Jacobi, Johann Friedrich. *Das durch eine leichte und ungekünstelte Erklärung von seinen Vorwürfen gerettete Hohelied*. Celle, 1771.
Jastrow, Morris, Jr. *Song of Songs, Being a Collection of Love Lyrics of Ancient Palestine*. Philadelphia: Lippincott, 1921.
Löwisohn, Salomon. *Melizat-Jeshurun*. Vienna, 1816.
Meier, Ernst. *Das Hohelied in deutscher Übersetzung, Erklärung und kritischer Textausgabe*. Tübingen: Verlag der Buchhandlung zu Guttenberg, 1854.
Michaelis, Johann David. *Deutsche Übersetzung des Alten Testaments mit Anmerkungen für Ungelehrte*. Vol. 12. Göttingen: Vandenhoeck, 1785.

Rosenmüller, Ernst Friedrich Karl. *Handbuch der biblischen Alterthumskunde.* Vol. 1. Leipzig: Baumgärtnersche Buchhandlung, 1823.
Umbreit, Friedrich Wilhelm Karl. "Hohes Lied." In vol. 6 of *Herzog's Real-Encyklopädie für protestantische Theologie und Kirche,* edited by Johann Jakob Herzig, 206–220. Stuttgart: Rudolf Besser, 1856.
Umbreit, Friedrich Wilhelm Karl. *Lied der Liebe: Das älteste und schönste aus dem Morgenlande.* Göttingen: Vandenhoeck, 1820.
Velthusen, Johann Caspar. *Das Hohelied: begleitet mit einem vollständigen Commentar und historisch kritischen Untersuchungen von Johann Caspar Velthusen.* Braunschweig: Waisenhausbuchhandlung, 1786.
Vollmer, Wilhelm, ed. *Briefwechsel zwischen Schiller und Goethe.* 2 vols. in 1. Stuttgart: J. G. Cotta, 1881.
Wachter, Georg. *Das Hohe Lied des Salomo.* Memmingen: Hummel, 1722.
Weißbach, Friedrich Eduard. *Das Hohe Lied Salomo's: Erklärt, übersetzt und in seiner kunstreichen poetischen Form dargestellt.* Leipzig: T. O. Weigel, 1858.

Secondary Sources

Exum, Cheryl. *Song of Songs: A Commentary.* Louisville: Westminster John Knox, 2005.
Herder, Johann Gottfried. "Über die Wirkung der Dichtkunst auf die Sitten der Völker." In vol. 1 of *Abhandlungen der Baierischen Akademie über Gegenstände der schönen Wissenschaften,* 25–138. Munich: Strobl, 1781.
Hertel, Ralf. "Dramentheorie." In *Lexikon Literaturwissenschaft: Hundert Grundbegriffe,* edited by Gerhard Lauer and Christine Ruhrberg, 63–66. Stuttgart: Reclam, 2011.
Hopf, Matthias. *Liebesszenen: Eine literaturwissenschaftliche Studie zum Hohenlied als einem dramatisch-performativem Text.* Zürich: Theologischer Verlag Zürich, 2016.
Keel, Othmar. *Das Hohelied.* ZBKAT 18. Zürich: Theologischer Verlag Zürich, 1986.
Konrad, Felix. "Von der 'Türkengefahr' zu Exotismus und Orientalismus: Der Islam als Antithese Europas (1453–1914)?" In *Europäische Geschichte Online (EGO),* edited by Leibnitz-Institut für Europäische Geschichte (IEG). Mainz: 2010. Accessed March 16, 2021. http://www.ieg-ego.eu/konradf-2010-de.
Krinetzki, Günther. *Hoheslied.* NEchtB. Würzburg: Echter, 1980.
Polaschegg, Andrea. *Der andere Orientalismus: Regeln deutsch-morgenländischer Imagination im 19. Jahrhundert.* Berlin: de Gruyter, 2005.
Rhein, Karin. *Deutsche Orientmalerei in der zweiten Hälfte des 19. Jahrhunderts: Entwicklung und Charakteristika.* Berlin: Tenea, 2003.
Rudolph, Wilhelm. "Das Hohelied im Kanon." *ZAW* 59 (1942/1943): 189–199.
Ter-Nedden, Gisbert. *Lessings Trauerspiele.* Germanistische Abhandlungen 57. Stuttgart: J. B. Metzler, 1990.
Tillmann, Thomas. *Hermeneutik und Bibelexegese beim jungen Goethe.* Historia Hermeneutica: Series Studia 2. Berlin: de Gruyter, 2006.
Zakovich, Yair. *Das Hohelied.* HThKAT. Freiburg i. Br.: Herder, 2004.

Music and Literature Sources

Alexander, James B. *King Solomon: A Drama in Five Acts Relating to Incidents in the Life of the Wise King*. N.p., 1899.
Blumenthal, Sandro. *Sulamith: Lyrische Oper in zwei Aufzügen*. Text (relying on the Song of Songs) by Emil Mantels and Heinrich Lautensack. München: Dr. Heinrich Lewy, 1906.
Brentano, Manfred. *Sulamith: Balladen der Liebe*. Chemnitz: Dr. Käubler, 1928.
Heyse, Paul. *Die Weisheit Salomo's*. Berlin: W. Hertz, 1887.
Hiller, Wilfried. *Schulamit*. CD booklet. Mainz: Wergo Schallplatten, 1995.
Kesselring, Joseph. *Mother of That Wisdom: A Historical Play in Two Acts*. New York: Exposition Press, 1973 [1933].
Klenau, Paul von. *Sulamith: Nach den Worten der heiligen Schrift (übersetzt von Herder): Ein Opernakt in sechs Bildern*. Piano score by Heinrich Knappe. Wien: Universal-Edition, 1913.
Lessing, Gotthold Ephraim von. *Hamburgische Dramaturgie*. 2 vols. Hamburg: Cramer, n.d., ca. 1767–1768.
Mackenzie, Alexander C., and Joseph Bennett. *The Rose of Sharon: A Dramatic Oratorio, Founded on the Song of Solomon*. Piano score by Obadiah B. Brown. London: Novello Ewer & Co., 1884.
Rubinstein, Anton Grigorjewitsch, and Julius Rodenberg. *Sulamith: Ein biblisches Bühnenspiel in fünf Bildern*. Berlin: Ed. Bote u. G. Bock, n.d.
Woerner, Roman. *König Salomo*. Leipzig: Drugulin, 1912.

Caroline Sauter
Love and Language
The Song of Songs in Scholem and Rosenzweig

A very important, yet often overlooked chapter in the long and vibrant reception history of the Song of Songs is its significant role in German-Jewish thought in the early twentieth century, when thinkers such as Walter Benjamin, Gershom Scholem, Franz Rosenzweig, Hermann Cohen, or Martin Buber aim at establishing a new language theory, which emphatically takes the Jewish tradition and the Bible into account. The love language of the Song is a prime example of a language endeavoring to express what seems to be inexpressible through metaphor, allegory, and rhetoric. Since expression is a key concept in early twentieth century German-Jewish language theories, the Song of Songs gains new prominence in those circles, albeit in a sometimes hidden manner. In particular, it is a central reference in the works of two of its most eminent thinkers: Gershom Scholem (1897–1982) and Franz Rosenzweig (1886–1929).

While Scholem's translation of the Song and his reflections thereof are scattered throughout his early diaries and correspondence and remained unpublished during his lifetime, Rosenzweig's reading of the Song occupies the central chapter of his seminal *The Star of Redemption* and has received major scholarly attention. I will argue, however, that the Song is the centerpiece of both Scholem's and Rosenzweig's respective language theories, despite their different prominence. Both Scholem and Rosenzweig correlate their notions of love and language, and both employ the Song's metaphors in formulating and consolidating their own theories of language. Focusing on Rosenzweig's and Scholem's works, I will demonstrate that the Song and its reception is at the core of what could be called a "new thinking" of language that emerges in German-Jewish thought of the early twentieth century. Its most important feature is a novel conception of allegory.

In what follows, I will provide detailed close readings of the most noteworthy passages on the Song in Scholem's and Rosenzweig's oeuvre. My argument will proceed in two steps. First, I will look at Gershom Scholem's early engagement with the Song. Scholem translated the Song in 1916/17, at the age of 18, and reflected on it in his early diaries and correspondence with Walter Benjamin. In particular, the little sketch "Über das Hohe Lied" ("On the Song of Songs") from 1917 is pathbreaking for his early language philosophy. I will analyze Scholem's Song reception in theoretical terms, rather than comparing the Hebrew original to Scholem's German translation. The object of this section is therefore not to judge the quality of Scholem's translation, but rather, to provide an analysis of key concepts in

Scholem's reception of the Song of Songs—most importantly, his understanding of allegory and literalness—out of a close reading of his writings. Second, I will provide a close reading of the second book of the second part of Rosenzweig's *The Star of Redemption*. His chapter on the Song is the most striking display of what Rosenzweig himself calls his "speech-thinking" ("Sprachdenken")—a thinking of language which combines literature, theology, and philosophy. I will demonstrate that his conception of allegory, developed in his reading of the Song, facilitates an understanding of language as perpetual allegory, and introduces the language of love as a central topic for its interpretation. The conclusion will argue for the centrality of the Song in German-Jewish language philosophy of the twentieth century and beyond.[1]

1 Gershom Scholem: "On the Song of Songs" (1917)

On his nineteenth birthday in December 1916, Scholem's father printed Gerhard's (who did not call himself Gershom yet) translation of the biblical Song of Songs in his publishing house, under the title *Das Hohe Lied: Alt-Hebräische Liebeslyrik*, "The Song of Songs: Ancient Hebrew Love Poetry".[2] By choosing the subtitle "Ancient Hebrew Love Poetry" for his translation, Scholem highlights three aspects of the source text: the topic of love, the form of poetry, and the Hebrew language, all of which are interrelated in his early thought. In late 1916, the Song translation had occupied Scholem for quite a while already. In the summer of 1915, he had told Walter Benjamin about it. Later, he revised his first draft translation twice. After completing the translation, Scholem continued to reflect on the Song in a little sketch entitled "Über das Hohe Lied" ("On the Song of Songs") from May 1917,[3] as well as in numerous conversations with Benjamin and in

---

[1] The following section on Scholem draws in part on a previous publication of mine; see Sauter, "Hebrew, Jewishness, And Love," 151–178.
[2] This edition is reprinted in Gershom Scholem's early diaries. The diaries are henceforth quoted according to Gershom Scholem, *Tagebücher nebst Aufsätzen und Entwürfen bis 1923* (Kopp-Oberstebrink et al., eds.), vol. 1: *1913–1917* (in the following Tb I) and vol. 2: *1917–1923* (in the following Tb II). All translations from Scholem's diaries are my own; the German original will be given in the footnotes wherever necessary and appropriate. Scholem's German translation of the Song can be found in Tb I, 477–491.
[3] Scholem's "Über das Hohe Lied" ("On the Song of Songs") can be found in Tb II, 99–100. The text is dated "26.5.1917" in Scholem's own hand. He continued to revise his translation and completed a second version of the Song on May 19, 1917 (see Tb II, 17), but it remained unpublished, as did

their correspondence throughout 1916–1918. In fact, Benjamin was his most important interlocutor while Scholem worked on the Song, even if his friend had no knowledge whatsoever of the Hebrew language, was not familiar with biblical literature at all, and had only very little insight into what Scholem called "Jewish things." Yet the Song project—and the question of translation in general—was very much at the heart of their friendship from 1915 onwards: Scholem reports that in one of their very first encounters, Benjamin read four of his own *Fleurs du Mal* translations to Scholem, who in turn told him about his Song translation, "and he [Benjamin] replied that my project was much more difficult, and that his own work [on Baudelaire] was merely playing around ["Spielerei"]" (Tb I, 146–147).

It is therefore not surprising that Benjamin was the first person to read Scholem's final Song translation. Commenting on the second, revised version in a letter of July 1917, upon admitting his "ignorance" of both "the Song of Songs" and "of Hebrew," Benjamin writes:

> Your love for the Hebrew language can manifest itself in the medium of the German only as veneration for the essence of language and the word as such, only in applying a good and pure method. This means, however, that your work remains an apologetic one, because it does not express love and reverence for an object in its own sphere.[4]

Benjamin here formulates the challenge of translation in terms of love: translation, for Benjamin, means to "express love and reverence for an object in its own sphere." Scholem, who "experiences the Hebrew in the German" (Tb II, 87), as he himself puts it later in a diary entry, therefore fails to express his love for the Hebrew within the Hebrew's "own sphere." His declaration of love speaks a different language than its object. In this respect, Benjamin's critique of Scholem's Song translation is rather harsh and apodictic, but consistent: "Yet the German language is not as close to you as the Hebrew; therefore you are not *called* to be the translator of the Song of Songs." He adds, however: "I believe that in the end you will owe much more to this work of yours than to any other."[5]

These words appear to ring in Scholem's ears as he wrestles with another project of translating biblical poetry, about six months later: Lamentations. This new translation project is, in many ways, inseparable from his slightly earlier Song

---

the third version he worked on directly afterwards, despite his efforts to publish it in the Jewish student fraternity journal *Der Jüdische Wille* (*Zeitschrift des Kartells Jüdischer Verbindungen*); for details, see diary entries of May 20 and 24, 1917; Tb II, 19–20; 20–21.

4 Walter Benjamin to Gershom Scholem, July 17, 1917, in Walter Benjamin, *Gesammelte Briefe* (Gödde and Lonitz, eds.), vol. 1: *1910–1918* (in the following GB 1), 370–371 (my translation).
5 Benjamin, GB 1, 371 (my translation).

translation. In December 1917, after completing the translation of Lamentations, Scholem penned a diary entry, which reads like a belated response to Benjamin's critique of his German rendering of the Song. He admits that his translation of Lamentations is "entirely lacking the *German* language spirit," since "the power of Hebrew" affects him so deeply that he "cannot but experience the Hebrew in the German." Despite his perception of failure, however, Scholem goes on to note: "for *myself*, it remains a great deed: I have given to myself an account of my love."[6] Just like the Song translation, Scholem's Lamentations translation is a declaration of his love for the Hebrew language and for biblical poetry—written, however, in German, and hence, not in the same "sphere" as the object of his love.[7] It is therefore unsurprising that, in a lengthy letter to Scholem written in March 1918, Benjamin critiques the Lamentations translation in very similar terms as the earlier Song of Songs (again first admitting his "lack of relation to Hebrew scriptures," and his general "ignorance of Hebrew"): for him—and his wife—, Scholem's Lamentations are not "inspired by the German language."[8] This time, however, Scholem does not agree. He notes in his diary: "He [Benjamin] is wrong about the translation [of Lamentations], it is *completely* different from that of the Song of Songs" (Tb II, 167).

What then is the difference between the two translation projects? While both are concerned with biblical poetry, there are two key differences, in Scholem's view: first, their relation to Jewishness is different, and second, their understanding of allegory differs.

Concerning the aspect of Jewishness, Scholem himself was extremely critical of his own Song translation, even in its edited second and third versions, not primarily because of any linguistic flaws or shortcomings, but rather because he perceived a lack of Jewishness in them. In August 1916, he notes in his diary: "Now I know that my Song translation is entirely worthless [. . .]. So un-Jewish!" (Tb I, 380). And

---

[6] Tb II, 87: "Mich reißt die Macht des Hebräischen so hin, daß ich nicht [anders] kann, als auch im Deutschen das Hebräische zu erleben, und mag immerhin das mit Recht als Einwand gegen die letztlegitimierte Gültigkeit meiner Übersetzungen vorgebracht werden: dies völlige Fehlen des *deutschen* Sprachgeistes, den ich nur in der Umsetzung habe; so bleibt für *mich* dies doch immer eine große Tat: mir Rechenschaft abgelegt zu haben über meine Liebe." It is quite striking that love and lament (his translation of Lamentations) here seem to be closely interconnected. The same is true for Benjamin, Cohen, and Rosenzweig, and it might have to do with the fact that both love and lament are perceived as strong emotions at the limits of language, in which the possibility of linguistic expression is challenged.

[7] This is most probably why he planned to quit translating biblical poetry altogether after finishing the Lamentations project, see the diary entry dated Nov. 27, 1917 in Tb II, 84. Just a few days later, on Dec. 1, Scholem relates that he has completed Lamentations (Tb II, 87).

[8] Benjamin, GB 1, 443–444.

in a diary entry dated May 1917, he formulates three "fundamental objections" to his own second and third versions of the Song of Songs translation: "1.) The lack of dignity of the language; 2.) The assassination of the original's *severity* [. . .]; 3.) The lack of literalness."[9] He returns to these three objections in "On the Song of Songs," a short but very dense text written two days after his self-critique in the diary entry. This text is seminal for understanding the status of the Song in his early language theory, because it explains his concepts of literalness and allegory in the context of his understanding of Jewishness:

> Ancient Hebrew poetry, as much as any Jewish creation, is subject to the deep laws of teaching. The Song confirms that love is accessible to the Jew only where absolute greatness is achieved. [. . .] The Song does not concede in any way to the penultimate. Its severity stems from this fact. [. . .] Hebrew poetry obtains its unique greatness from the dignity of the language. The dignity of the language is that which is essentially untranslatable in any given language. It is *not* the style; rather, it constitutes another order, established by the union with *torah*. Only the traditional interpretation of the Song as allegory gives us an understanding of its inner greatness: the dignity was large enough to serve as a Symbolic Dwelling Place for *torah*, and for the Holy One of Israel. However, had the Song been penned with an allegoric intention, it would be very bad indeed, since it uses *every prohibited* means of allegory, whose greatness can only be extracted from its full literalness. The love of the Song is true love. [. . .] Veneration is the legitimate seal of linguistic dignity. The Song proves its veneration for the spiritual order of things in its perfect and pure metaphoricity.[10]

A specific understanding of "greatness" ("Größe") is at the heart of Scholem's understanding of the Song. He mentions the term "greatness" three times in the passage cited above: first, he claims that "love is accessible to the Jew only where absolute

---

9 Tb II, 20: "Fundamentaleinwände gegen meine zweite und dritte Übersetzung: 1.) Die Würdelosigkeit der Sprache; 2.) Die Ermordung der *Strenge* des Originals [. . .], 3.) Die mangelnde Wörtlichkeit."
10 Tb II, 99–100: "Die althebräische Dichtung unterliegt so tief wie irgend eine jüdische Schöpfung den tiefen Gesetzen der Lehre. Das Hohe Lied bildet die Bestätigung, daß nur, wo absolute Größe erreicht wird, die Liebe dem Juden zugängig ist. Das Hohe Lied konzediert dem Vorletzten nichts. Hieraus begründet sich seine Strenge. [. . .] Die hebräische Lyrik erhält ihre einzigartige Größe durch die Würde der Sprache. Die Würde der Sprache ist das, was an einer Sprache schlechthin unübersetzbar ist. Sie ist *nicht* der Stil, sondern macht vielmehr eine eigene Ordnung aus, die die Verbindung mit der Thora begründet. Die innere Größe des Hohen Liedes macht allein die traditionelle Deutung als Allegorie verständlich: Die Würde war groß genug, um der Thora und dem Heiligen Israels zum Symbolischen Wohnsitz zu dienen. Wäre aber in Wahrheit das Hohe Lied mit allegorischer Absicht gedichtet, wäre es sehr schlecht, denn es wendet *jedes verbotene* Mittel der Allegorie an, das seine Größe erst seiner vollen Wörtlichkeit entnimmt. Die Liebe des Hohen Liedes ist die wahrhafte Liebe. [. . .] Die Ehrfurcht ist das legitime Siegel der sprachlichen Würde. Das Hohe Lied erweist seine Ehrfurcht vor den geistigen Ordnungen der Dinge durch seine vollkommene und reine Metaphorik."

greatness is achieved," and views the Song as the poetic "confirmation" of this claim. Second, a specific greatness is unique to Hebrew poetry and to the Hebrew language: "Hebrew poetry obtains its unique greatness from the dignity of the language." And third, there is an "inner greatness" within the Song, which has to do with its traditional allegorical interpretation: "Only the traditional interpretation of the Song as allegory gives us an understanding of its inner greatness: the dignity was large enough to serve as a Symbolic Dwelling Place for *torah*, and for the Holy One of Israel" (Tb II, 99).

In order to understand Scholem's quite peculiar conception of greatness and its relation to the Song, we will have to understand the three related terms "severity" ("Strenge"), "dignity" ("Würde"), and "veneration" ("Ehrfurcht"), all of which were also at the heart of Scholem's self-critique, cited above. According to Scholem, "Ancient Hebrew poetry, as much as any Jewish creation, is subject to the deep laws of teaching. [...] The Song does not concede in any way to the penultimate. Its severity stems from this fact." (Tb II, 99) Severity is used here as both a poetic and an ethical term. As Hebrew poetry and as Jewish teaching alike, the Song is radical and uncompromising. It uses the full potential of poetic language *and* expresses the full rigor of teaching, and both together constitute its specific severity. Hence, the Song is not to be taken lightly—rather, it is the highest fulfillment, the fullest completion, and the ultimate perfection of the Hebrew language. Yet it is also the fullest rigor of a teaching, and of an ethic, which aims at "absolute greatness." Thus, when Scholem accuses his own Song translation of "assassinating the original's severity" (Tb II, 20), he is implying that his translation kills the radical perfection that the original both possesses and demands. In poetic terms, Scholem's translation does *not* express the fullness of the Hebrew original's poetic language and it is not equally powerful, because his translation is trying to accommodate German-language poetic conventions, both on a lexical and on a metric level—such as, for instance, a rearranging of words for the sake of iambic rhythms, or "the use of diminutive forms, which is completely foreign to the spirit of the Song."[11] In ethical terms, Scholem therefore dismisses his own translation of the Song as violent or even criminal (he is, after all, speaking of an "assassination"), instead of submitting to the lexical and metric severity of Hebrew poetry, which vouchsafes the poetic and ethical greatness of the Song in the original. The radical perfection of the (original) Song in both poetic and ethical terms is what Scholem calls its severity.

---

11 Tb II, 20–21: "Die Ermordung der *Strenge* des Originals in Wortfügungen und durch eine dem Kitsch sehr angenäherte Versifikation (die z.B. erlaubt, Worte des jambischen Rhythmus wegen umzustellen oder der Gebrauch von Diminutivformen, die dem Geist des Hohen Liedes fremd sind.)"

Scholem continues his argument by stating that "Hebrew poetry obtains its unique greatness from the dignity of the language" (Tb II, 99). Later, he remarks that "Hebrew has never left the epoch of its dignity," and thus "cannot express any vulgarities whatsoever" (Tb II, 100). It is linguistic dignity, rather than the Hebrew language itself, which he considers "essentially untranslatable in any given language." Hence, for Scholem, while Hebrew poetry per se is translatable, its dignity is not. This conception stems from the very important fact that, within the Song, the language's dignity "is *not* the style; rather, it constitutes another order, established by the union with *torah*" (Tb II, 99).

In his early work, Scholem has a very particular and emphatic understanding of *torah*: the term does not necessarily mean an empirical set of canonical texts, written in a certain language of origin, but rather the entire intellectual project of Judaism, based on transmission and tradition, as opposed to the "Jewish experience" that he strongly rejects.[12] In this sense, Scholem understands *torah* as the religious tradition of Judaism.[13] For him, *torah* "is not a law, just as Judaism is not a religion. *Torah* is the tradition of God and of divine things and the principle of the gradual recovery of truth" (Tb I, 433). Moreover, according to Scholem, the very word *torah* belongs to the religious sphere of Judaism, and therefore, it cannot be expressed in any other language but Hebrew, as we know from his slightly earlier Eliasberg critique.[14] According to a diary entry from November 1916, "there *is* no German term for *torah*" (Tb I, 433). Consequently, the untranslatable union with *torah* voices itself in the language of Hebrew poetry, and therefore also in the language of the Song—but only in the original. Hence, when Scholem criticizes his own Song translation for a "lack of dignity of the language," he is implying that it has lost the union with *torah* in this double sense: it has lost touch with both Jewish thinking and Hebrew poetry. The dignity of Hebrew poetry, and hence the "unique greatness" of the Song, goes back to the fact that it is a deeply Jewish form of expression. Therefore, he considers his attempt at translating the Song into German, following German-language poetic conventions and logic, as "un-Jewish." For Scholem, the dignity of the Song's language is its Jewishness, and the expression thereof in Hebrew poetry.

---

12 See Tb II, 303: "Erlebnis und Thora sind *absolute* Gegensätze."
13 In a letter, Scholem says that "torah is the epitome, the integral of the Jewish tradition" (quoted in German in Weidner, *Gershom Scholem*, 187). For instance, in his diaries Scholem calls Hermann Cohen's being ("Dasein") "Thora," since "it is worthy of being transmitted" (Tb II, 210). For further details on Scholem's conception of *torah*, see Weidner, *Gershom Scholem*, 188–191.
14 See Tb I, 496. Scholem's review of Eliasberg's Yiddish translations, which also entails a general theory of translation and a theory of Yiddish, appeared in January 1917, four months prior to his reflections "On the Song of Songs" from May 1917. For more details, see Sauter, "Hebrew, Jewishness, and Love," 158–167.

With this working definition of dignity, Scholem comes to the key part of his argument: he explains the specific "inner greatness" of the Song in relation to its allegorical interpretation.

> Only the traditional interpretation of the Song as allegory gives us an understanding of its inner greatness: the dignity was large enough to serve as a Symbolic Dwelling Place for *torah*, and for the Holy One of Israel. However, had the Song been penned with an allegoric intention, it would be very bad indeed, since it uses *every prohibited* means of allegory, whose greatness can only be extracted from its full literalness. (Tb II, 99)

In understanding and interpreting the Song as allegory, its dignity—namely, its essential, yet untranslatable Jewish aspect—comes full force: it is "large enough to serve as a Symbolic Dwelling Place for *torah*, and for the Holy One of Israel" (Tb II, 99). While the Song is, in its full literalness, truly erotic love poetry (a fact that is never denied, but always reinforced by Scholem), written in Biblical Hebrew, its dignity—which surpasses the literal scope—also encompasses another, unspeakable aspect of language: it provides refuge for the untranslatable and even unnamable foundations of the Jewish faith and the Hebrew language: *torah* and "the Holy One of Israel". Because of its dignity, the language of the Song possesses an unspoken, "symbolic" layer. This is the reason for its "inner greatness."

Scholem goes on to explain, however, that the Song was never meant to be an allegory: it has been *interpreted* as one, but it has not been written as one. On the contrary, the Song "would be very bad indeed," had it been penned with an allegoric intention, "since it uses *every prohibited* means of allegory, whose greatness can only be extracted from its full literalness" (Tb II, 99). According to Scholem, it is only in drawing on the full literalness of the Song's meaning—without any allegorical interpretation—that its greatness can be "extracted" from the (original) text. In other words, the Song possesses greatness in and of itself, literally, entirely regardless of its allegorical interpretation. The ability of the Song's language to add a surplus to the literal meaning, and thus to enhance literalness and accommodate unspoken and unspeakable elements, can be *understood* in considering the Song as allegory, but that does not mean that it *is* one. As an allegory, Scholem says, "it would be very bad indeed," simply because its allegorical qualities are so obvious. In contrast, the inner greatness found in the pure literalness of the Song is already so striking that no additional allegoric intention needs to be added to it.

This valorization of the literalness of the Song has to do with a sense of veneration in view of the Hebrew original. Scholem defines veneration it as follows: "Veneration is the spiritual relation to things, which sees them in their orders."[15] For Scholem, "the principle according to which the order of things is arranged" is

---

[15] Tb II, 99–100.

torah.[16] This connection again underlines the Jewish aspect of the source text. And interestingly, while Scholem is translating the Song and penning his essay "On the Song of Songs," he is simultaneously working on a specifically Jewish conception of love. In fact, this endeavor is running as a red thread throughout Scholem's early diaries, even if he generally understands love as the core principle of Christianity, while the core concept of Judaism for him is justice.[17] According to Scholem, goyish (or Christian) love disrupts and destroys the order of things, while Jewish love is based on *torah*, therefore it is an ordering principle. Especially within the realm of human erotic love—which is, after all, both the object and subject of the Song—, he frequently differentiates "Jewish love" from "goyish love," or "Christian love." For instance, in November 1917 he claims that "Jewish love—and I love in a Jewish way—is not like goyish love"[18] (Tb II, 75). The main difference in Scholem's stark contrasting of Jewish and goyish love is that Jewish love is spiritual and brings order, while goyish (or Christian) love is worldly and creates disorder:

> Love is the only spiritual order whose place is only and continually in the soul. Love is not in the world, yet all other orders are. Christian love, however, is also in the world. It creates disorder (Tb II, 76).

Applying this conception to the Song and its interpretation, a spiritual understanding of the Song would read the love expressed in it as Jewish love, removed from the world, and located within the soul, upholding and creating order, while a worldly reading would favor a Christian (or goyish) conception of love, located in the world, and bringing about disorder. This is, however, not to be taken as an argument for a purely allegorical interpretation of the Song and against (Christian, Protestant) conceptions such as Goethe's or Herder's, that view the Song as entirely human.[19] Rather, while its traditional allegorical interpretation in both Christianity and Judaism can give us insights into the very nature of the Song's language—namely, the fact that language goes beyond itself to entail an unspoken and unspeakable surplus—, it is still the Song's pure literalness as Ancient Hebrew love poetry (as the subtitle of Scholem's own Song translation has it) that guarantees its greatness.

---

16 Weidner (*Gershom Scholem*, 190) quotes a letter of Scholem's that defines *torah* as "das Prinzip, nach dem Ordnungen der Dinge gestaltet sind."
17 See Tb II, 359; Tb I, 404.
18 Moreover, Scholem frequently associates Christian love with magic ("Zauber"), defining magic as "the execution of an empirical action from a divine standpoint: the order of heaven becomes magic on earth" (Tb II, 75–76). Thus, the fundamental difference between Jewish and Christian love, for Scholem, is that "Jewish love does not do magic" (Tb II, 352).
19 For a detailed analysis of Herder's and Goethe's "literal" reception of the Song, see Sauter, „Writing in Love," 193–195, as well as Pardes, *Song of Songs*, 138–140. See also the contribution by Yael Almog in this volume.

Therefore, and quite counterintuitively, it is the rich imagery and the exorbitant metaphoricity of the Song which expresses its veneration for the spiritual and linguistic order of things, on a fully literal level.

The question of imagery and metaphor obviously is the key question when dealing with the Song. According to Scholem, it is by way of its images that veneration expresses itself in the Song, and vouchsafes its greatness and its truth:

> Any image that would confuse the (linguistic and spiritual) orders of a thing, would [...] speak against the greatness and the truth of the Songs, yet no word of this [...] compilation of fragments goes against the veneration of things, of their innate dignity.[20]

In other words, the very imagery of the Song, made up of words that are to be taken literally, is upholding the linguistic and spiritual order of things, whose very essence is dignity and veneration. This is what he states just before: "Veneration is the legitimate seal of linguistic dignity. The Song proves its veneration for the spiritual order of things in its perfect and pure metaphoricity" (Tb II, 100). If the Song's images or metaphors are "perfect and pure," they cannot confuse or destroy the spiritual order of things (as Christian or goyish love would), but rather, they support this order (as Jewish love does). This also means that any reading that would try to read something into the Song's "perfect and pure" metaphors must be flawed. Rather, their literal meaning is perfectly and purely enough to be able to accommodate elements of language that go beyond its verbal expression.

This is illustrated by a highly interesting choice of metaphor in Scholem's essay: the seal. According to Scholem, "veneration is the legitimate seal of linguistic dignity" (Tb II, 100). Scholem's choice of the seal metaphor is instructive, in so far as it relates back to the Song itself: he chooses a "perfect and pure" metaphor from the Song, in order to explain the merits of the Song's metaphoricity generally, and to address the notorious topic of the Song's puzzling and exuberant imagery. In the biblical source text, the seal is an eminent, often commented-on metaphor for the exclusive power of love. In fact, the one and only definition of love in the Song—which is, after all, "love poetry," in Scholem's own words—towards the end of the book, describes the strength, force, power, might, and fierceness of love and passion with images of death and cruelty, fire-flashes and flames:

> Set me as a seal upon your heart, a seal upon your arm; for love is strong as death, passion is cruel as the grave [*sheol*]. Its flashes are flashes of fire, a blazing flame [or, in another translation: a flame as fierce as the flame of *Yah*]. (Song 8:6; RSV; CJB)

---

[20] Tb II, 100: "Jedes Bild, das die (sprachlichen und geistigen) Ordnungen einer Sache verwirrte, würde [...] gegen die Größe, die Wahrheit der Lieder sprechen, aber kein Wort in der [...] Sammlung von Fragmenten widerstrebt der Ehrfurcht vor den Dingen, vor ihrer eingeborenen Würde."

Scholem himself translated this passage as follows:

> Gleich einem Siegel leg' mich auf dein Herz,
> Um deinen Arm gleich einem Siegelring,
> Denn stark wie der Tod ist die Liebe,
> Und hart wie die Hölle die Leidenschaft!
> Ihre Gluten sind Feuersgluten,
> Eine Flamme Gottes!
> (Tb II, 490)

Even poetic language seems to struggle when it comes to a definition of what love actually is. The only images that remain, the only image that seems to be a possible expression of the experience of love, is the ultimate, universal, and inescapable liminal experience in the human realm, the utter unknown—death. Death cannot, and can *never*, be put into words that are *not* figures of speech, since nobody can express her own experience of death, nor anyone else's. This verse from the Song of Songs interweaves love and death and God, the ultimate edges and limits of human verbal expression.

Why God? Does this verse mention God? It does (at least, in Scholem's translation), and it does not. One of the key points in the notorious discussion about the Song's canonicity has always been that it is one of only two books in the biblical canon (the other one being Esther) that does not literally talk about God. Hence, it is not, in a strict sense of the word, *theo-logical*, if we consider "theo-logy" to be "God-speech." The Song of Songs does not mention the very term "God"—except, possibly, in this verse, hidden and encrypted, by using a short form, *Yah*, of His unspeakable name, symbolized in the tetragrammaton *YHWH*.[21] In the Hebrew original, the term *Yah* is part of the same word that means "flame," so that the whole expression (*šalhæbætyāh*) could be translated as "the very flame of *Yah*," and the sentence then might possibly read: "Love is as strong as death—love's flashes are fire-flashes, the very flame of *Yah*." This seems to be the way Scholem understands it; accordingly, he translates *šalhæbætyāh* as "Eine Flamme Gottes!," "A flame of God!"

What connects God and love and death here is the image of flash, flame, and fire: an all-consuming, potentially dangerous, and powerfully violent element that easily gets out of control—and if it does, it is enormously destructive.[22] The power of love can only be described in terms of death: love is not stronger or more powerful than death. It is, simply, "as strong as" death. Just like the name of God, which is too

---

21 See Falk, *Song of Songs*, 131.
22 See Fishbane, *Song of Songs*, 209.

sacred to be pronounced,[23] the expression of love might be as dangerous, indeed as life-threatening, as pronouncing the ineffable name of God. Just like death and God, love faces us with a linguistic challenge: language will always fall short whenever we try to put love or death or God into words. Fire, flash, and flame, therefore, are not only images for the unimaginable, overwhelming force of love and death and God, but also for the threatening potential of their (attempted) verbal expression for language itself. This verse from the Song exemplifies powerfully that language will be confronted with the threatening fact of its own incompleteness whenever it tries to put love, or death, or God into words.

All this is alluded to by Scholem's choice of the seal metaphor. By referencing the seal, Scholem implicitly refers to the entire context of Song 8:6—the unspeakable name of God, the question of what can be expressed and what remains inexpressible, the (non-)theological nature of the Song, and of course the question of metaphor and allegory. This context finally brings us back to Scholem's previous argument: "Only the traditional interpretation of the Song as allegory is what gives us an understanding of its inner greatness: the dignity was large enough to serve as a Symbolic Dwelling Place for *torah*, and for the Holy One of Israel" (Tb II, 99). The Song's dignity—namely, its essential, yet untranslatable Jewish aspect—is "sealed" by the Song's metaphors. In Song 8:6, it is the metaphors of death, fire, and flame. Yet within its very metaphors—images made up of words—, the Song serves as a secret, "symbolic" dwelling place for *torah* and "the Holy One of Israel." In Song 8:6, this is true on a literal level: the metaphoric language possibly encompasses, literally, a short form (*Yah*) of the unspeakable name of God (*YHWH*). Hence, even the most fundamental inexpressible of Judaism, *YHWH*, can live and dwell within the Song's metaphors, as Scholem states above. While the name of God remains unspoken on a literal level, it is possibly alluded to in Song 8:6, and the metaphor of "a raging fire, a blazing flame, the flame of *Yah*" begs to be read allegorically, instead of literally. Yet the name of God is inscribed onto the literal level, not read into the allegorical one. Scholem himself translates the end of 8:6 rather surprisingly as "Eine Flamme Gottes!"—"a flame of God!," thus transcribing the secret hint ("*Yah*"), and rendering it, literally, as "God."

It is, however, still the traditional allegoric interpretation that gives us an understanding of the Song's inner greatness: only in allegory are we willing to acknowledge that language goes beyond itself. In the next section, we will see how Rosenzweig treats the idea of allegory or simile ("Gleichnis") in his reception of the Song.

---

23 See Schniedewind, "Calling God Names," 79.

2 Franz Rosenzweig: *The Star of Redemption* (1921)

For Franz Rosenzweig, the Song of Songs is literally at the center of his revolutionary intellectual enterprise, which he called the "new thinking"—in opposition to the "old thinking" of philosophical tradition. Rosenzweig's new model of philosophizing emphatically combines poetry, theology, and philosophy. Its culmination point is his seminal 1921 *Star of Redemption*, which has often been called the greatest work of modern Jewish philosophy.

It is telling that the biblical Song of Songs lies at the heart of Rosenzweig's *Star of Redemption*, which famously spans a cosmic scope "from death [. . .]" "[. . .] into life."[24] Indeed, Rosenzweig called the part of the *Star* that deals with the Song, its "Herzbuch": literally, its core-book, or even its very heart. The reading of the Song takes up the entire second book of the second part of the *Star*, and since the *Star* has a triadic structure, with three parts consisting of three books each, the Song is geometrically at the center of Rosenzweig's magnum opus. In other words, the whole system of the *Star* literally revolves around the Song as its centerpiece.

There seems to be a strong autobiographical moment to Rosenzweig's prominent placement of the Song in his work: namely, the passionate affair he had with Margit ("Gritli") Rosenstock, his friend's wife, while writing this specific portion of the *Star* from 1918 onwards.[25] The lovers seem to have shared an overwhelmingly intense physical and intellectual intimacy.[26] According to Paul Mendes-Flohr, Rosenzweig even "wrote a draft of his commentary on the Song while stretched out on his lover's bed, waiting for her to appear for an appointed tryst."[27] Therefore, Mendes-Flohr reads much of Rosenzweig's piercing analysis of the Song as a

---

24 The *Star*'s introduction begins with the words: "From Death, it is from death that all cognition of the All begins"; and its last part, *Gate*, literally ends with the two words "Into Life." Rosenzweig, *Star of Redemption*, 9, 173. For the German original, see Rosenzweig, *Der Stern der Erlösung*, 3 ("Vom Tode, von der Furcht des Todes, hebt alles Erkennen des All an."), 472 ("Ins Leben").
25 See Mendes-Flohr, "Between Sensual and Heavenly Love," 312. Rosenzweig's letters to Gritli are edited in Rosenzweig, *Die 'Gritli'-Briefe* (Rühle and Mayer, eds.). Gritli was not only *a* friend's, but *the* friend's wife: namely, Eugen Rosenstock's, the close friend whom Rosenzweig had the famous and decisive all-night discussion ("Nachtgespräch") with in 1913, that ended with his near-conversion to Christianity, and his emphatic re-turn to Judaism which would change his whole theological and philosophical perspective dramatically, and ignite the first sparks for the *Star*. On the friendship between Rosenzweig and Rosenstock (a converted Jew who had embraced his religious faith with extreme vigor and determination), see Mendes-Flohr, "Franz Rosenzweig and the German Philosophical Tradition," 4–7.
26 For a detailed description of the love affair and its intellectual significance for Rosenzweig, see Rühle, *Gott spricht die Sprache*, 48–50.
27 Mendes-Flohr, "Between Sensual and Heavenly Love," 312.

"love-letter" to Gritli, echoing a formulation that Rosenzweig himself coined.[28] In this reading, Rosenzweig endowed his own text on human and divine love with a secret sense that would be decipherable only for his lover. And in fact, he explicitly wrote to Gritli in October 1918: "This book II [of the *Star*] will not be difficult to read. Yet will anyone but you understand it?"[29]

Undeniable and important as the autobiographical background might be, there is more to Rosenzweig's reading of the Song than that. His commentary on the Song in the *Star of Redemption* is the most striking display of what he calls his "speech-thinking" ("Sprachdenken")—a thinking of language which combines poetry, theology, and philosophy, in order to capture, in Rosenzweig's terms, no less than the "cognition of the All."[30] This is as much a *literary* as a theological and a philosophical concern because the notion of "Gleichnis"—translated as "simile" or "analogy" or "allegory" in most English translations of the *Star*[31]—is at its very heart.

In his analysis of the Song, Rosenzweig concedes that the language of love is necessarily allegorical or simile-like ("gleichnishaft"), and he connects the literary question of allegory with the theological question of revelation via his idea of love. His theologico-philosophical theory of the language of love is developed out of his reading of the Song, in strong opposition to a so-called "worldly" and "objective" view he identifies here as Goethe's and Herder's:[32]

> Herder and Goethe claimed the Song as a collection of "worldly" love lyrics.[33] In this designation, "worldly" expresses no more and no less than that God does not love. And this was,

---

28 See Mendes-Flohr, "Between Sensual and Heavenly Love," 313. Rosenzweig calls "book II.2" "einen großen Brief."
29 Quoted in Rühle, *Gott spricht die Sprache*, 45: "Dieses Buch II wird gar nicht schwer zu lesen. Ob es dennoch noch jemand versteht außer dir?" (Oct. 3, 1918).
30 Rosenzweig, *Star of Redemption*, 9.
31 Barbara Galli, in her translation of the *Star*, strangely translates Rosenzweig's *Gleichnis* first as "simile" and then as "allegory," while William Hallo uses "analogy" or "simile" throughout. Myriam Bienenstock rightly points out the Jewish tradition of *mashal*, which seems to have a close connection with what Rosenzweig has in mind here—especially, because he is dealing with the Song of Songs, a text traditionally attributed to King Solomon, the "author" of three collections of biblical *mashalim* (Song of Songs, Proverbs, Ecclesiastes). See Bienenstock, "Die Sprache des *Hohelieds*," 271.
32 Ilana Pardes, in her "biography" of the *Song of Songs*, only devotes a very short chapter to Rosenzweig, reading him mostly as a critic of Enlightenment readings of the Song and an early precursor to Said's *Orientalism* (see Pardes, *Song of Songs*, 155–156).
33 I think that Rosenzweig slightly misunderstood Goethe's reading of the Song, equating Goethe's notion of this particular biblical text perhaps all too readily with Herder's. It is, of course, undeniable, that Goethe reads the Song as "oriental poetry" in the "notes and queries" to his *Divan*, just like Herder. But there is a crucial difference: while Herder rejects allegorical exegesis of the

after all, really the opinion. [...] The authentic love-relation of God to the individual soul was denied and the Song of Songs thereupon made out to be a "purely human" love lyric.[34]

Rosenzweig's problem with the nineteenth-century reading of the Song, that he saw most prominently exemplified in Goethe and Herder, is that, as he says, "'worldly' expresses no more and no less than that God does not love. And this was, after all, really the opinion."[35] Rosenzweig's own opinion is starkly different. In contrast to traditional allegorical readings in both Judaism and Christianity, Rosenzweig does not view the loving couple in the Song as an allegory for the love between God and the people of Israel, or the church, or the individual soul, or the Virgin Mary, but his argument works the other way around: rather than drawing conclusions on divine love from the image of human love, Rosenzweig says that "man loves *because* God loves and *as* God loves."[36] However, Rosenzweig does not deny the Song's literal, sensual, erotic meaning—on the contrary, he extols and celebrates it. But for him, the "relationship of the human to the divine, of the worldly to the spiritual, of the soul to revelation"[37] is inherent in *any* loving relationship on a human level, including erotic love. One could say, as Inken Rühle does, that this is a theomorphic, rather than anthropomorphic perspective.[38]

Out of this analysis of the Song, Rosenzweig presents a new conception of allegory, or simile ("Gleichnis"). Here is how Rosenzweig continues his argument:

> Love simply cannot be "purely human." It must speak, for there is simply no self-expression other than the language of love. And by speaking, love already becomes superhuman; for the sensuality of the word is brimful with its divine supersense. Like language itself, love is sensual-supersensual. To put it another way: simile ["Gleichnis"] is its very nature, and not merely its decorative accessory.[39]

Song altogether, Goethe incorporates the tradition of allegorical reading into his own poetry, thus endowing his love lyrics with a "second sense." In fact, I have demonstrated in my close reading of *The Book of Zuleika* and its paratexts that it was precisely the tradition of the Song's allegorical interpretation that is at the heart of Goethe's poetological appropriation of its lyrics. See Sauter, "Writing in Love," 188–204.
34 Rosenzweig, *Star of Redemption*, 200.
35 Rosenzweig, *Star of Redemption*, 200.
36 Rosenzweig, *Star of Redemption*, 199.
37 Rosenzweig, *Star of Redemption*, 199.
38 See Rühle, "Das Hohelied," 474.
39 Rosenzweig, *Star of Redemption*, 201, translation modified. I find it very unfortunate that Hallo translates *Sprache* as "speech" here (and not as "language")—apart from the fact that this passage contains an outright translation error (Hallo mysteriously translates "Sprache der Liebe" as "speech of life"). Rosenzweig's German original reads: "Die Liebe kann gar nicht 'rein menschlich' sein. Indem sie spricht—und sie muß sprechen, denn es gibt gar kein andres aus sich Heraussprechen als die Sprache der Liebe—indem sie also spricht, wird sie schon ein Übermenschliches; denn die

Rosenzweig states that "love simply cannot be 'purely human,'" because, as Inken Rühle has it, "divine love cannot find any other expression in the world than authentic worldly love."[40] Or, to paraphrase Paul Mendes-Flohr: "Human *eros* and divine *eros* coincide."[41] In this sense, the strict boundary between the sacred and the profane, that has been argued about for centuries in regard to the Song of Songs, is at least challenged, if not suspended altogether. Precisely *as* a profane text about erotic love, the Song is sacred insofar as divine love is analogous and homologous with mundane love—and, as Mendes-Flohr adds, "when that love is erotic, it *includes* the shape of the other's face, the aroma of the other's skin, the quality of his or her voice."[42] Rosenzweig does not look for a spiritual sense behind the profane meaning in the Song of Songs, but he rather detects God's touching the soul *within* the physical touch of a loving hand, and hears God's very own speech *within* the words of human love.

Love, Rosenzweig says "must speak, for there is simply no self-expression other than the language of love"[43]—in other words: Love and speech are inseparable. But the language of love is no ordinary language that would simply transmit information or—following Austin—"do things with words." Rather, so Rosenzweig continues, "by speaking, love already becomes superhuman; for the sensuality of the word is brimful with its divine supersense"[44]—and this is the case precisely because God's loving speech speaks *in* and *as* the words of human love.

For Rosenzweig, there is a potentiality in human language, and especially in the "language of love," that is brought about by language's and love's respective literariness: "Like language itself, love is sensual-supersensual. To put it another way: simile ['Gleichnis'] is its very essence, and not merely its decorative accessory."[45] Rosenzweig claims that language and love both are essentially "gleichnishaft": allegorical, or simile-like. He explicitly says that simile ("Gleichnis") is "more" than just rhetorical *ornatus* ("decorative accessory"): it rather is the essence ("Wesen"), the very nature of language and of love, and hence, of the language of love. And indeed, the language of love is figural: it is literature. As Julia Kristeva has remarked very insightfully in her *Tales of Love*, "the language of love is impossible, inadequate,

---

Sinnlichkeit des Wortes ist randvoll von seinem göttlichen Übersinn; die Liebe ist, wie die Sprache selbst, sinnlich-übersinnlich. Anders gesagt: das Gleichnis ist ihr nicht schmückendes Zubehör, sondern Wesen." (*Stern der Erlösung*, 224).

40 Rühle, "Das Hohelied," 474 (my translation).
41 Mendes-Flohr, "Between Sensual and Heavenly Love," 313.
42 Mendes-Flohr, "Between Sensual and Heavenly Love," 315.
43 Rosenzweig, *Star of Redemption*, 201.
44 Rosenzweig, *Star of Redemption*, 201.
45 Rosenzweig, *Star of Redemption*, 201.

immediately allusive when one would like it to be most straightforward; it is a flight of metaphors—it is literature."⁴⁶

For Rosenzweig, this literariness is not a sign of the defectiveness of language, as if language did not have the power to express itself fully without using similes, but, on the contrary, it is an essential quality of language. The essence of language, like the essence of love, is that the divine expresses itself *in* and *through* it, in and as *one and the same* language as human language. Thus, it endows human language not with a "sense," but rather with a "supersense," as he says, making it "superhuman" while remaining, at the same time, fully human. In other words, human love *is* divine love, and human language *is* divine language—and *not*. And this is made possible by language's essence as simile, as and in literature.

So far, we have seen that both language and love, and by extension the language of love, have an essentially literary quality. It is this literary quality which makes it possible for human love to be fully itself *and* fully not-itself at the same time (or, to put it differently, to be its own allegory): human love *is* divine love. For Rosenzweig,

> if [language] is truly simile ["Gleichnis"]—and therefore more than simile ["Gleichnis"]—then that which we hear as a living word in our I and which resounds toward us out of our Thou must also be "as it is written" in the great historical testament of revelation [. . .]. Once more we seek the word of man in the word of God.⁴⁷

Language is, as Rosenzweig says here, "truly simile—and therefore more than simile." What does this seemingly paradoxical statement mean? It means that language cannot be dismissed as being "only a simile."⁴⁸ Rather, it is truly and essentially simile, but precisely in its structure *as* simile and *because* of it, it is also truly and essentially "more" than itself, and therefore more than simile: namely, "the word of God" which speaks *in* and *as* "the word of man."⁴⁹ The fact that human language *itself* speaks "the word of God" makes it "more than simile," but at the same time, human language can only contain the word of God *because* it is simile. And this is what brings Rosenzweig back to the Song of Songs:

---

46 Kristeva, *Tales of Love*, 1.
47 Rosenzweig, *Star of Redemption*, 198, translation modified. The original reads: "Wenn Sprache mehr ist als nur ein Vergleich, wenn sie wahrhaft Gleichnis—und also mehr als Gleichnis—ist, so muß das, was wir in unserem Ich als lebendiges Wort vernehmen und was uns aus unserem Du lebendig entgegentönt, auch in dem großen historischen Zeugnis der Offenbarung [. . .] 'geschrieben stehn.' Wiederum suchen wir das Wort des Menschen im Wort Gottes." (*Stern der Erlösung*, 221).
48 Rosenzweig, *Star of Redemption*, 199 ("nur ein Gleichnis" in German; see *Stern der Erlösung*, 222).
49 Rosenzweig, *Star of Redemption*, 198.

> The analogue ["Gleichnis"] of love permeates as analogue all of revelation. It is the ever-recurring analogy of the prophets. But it is precisely meant to be more than analogy. And this it can be only when it appears without a "this means," without pointing, that is, to that of which it is supposed to be the analogy. Thus it is not enough that God's relationship to man is explained by the simile of the lover and the beloved. God's word must contain the relationship of lover to beloved directly; the significant, that is, without any pointing to the significate. And so we find it in the Song of Songs. Here it is no longer possible to see in that simile "only a simile." [. . .] The deeper meaning lodges here, precisely in the purely sensual sense, directly and not "merely" in simile.[50]

In contrast to traditional allegorical readings of the Song, Rosenzweig's conception does not try to detect a hidden meaning behind a literal one. Rather, the "deeper meaning" is "precisely *in* the purely sensual sense": it is one and the same, insofar as the sensual sense is purely and fully itself *and* not-itself at the same time. According to Rosenzweig, there is no "pointing towards" or "this means" in the Song; rather, human and divine language contain each other directly and immediately. In other words, the text does not contain *two* meanings, a literal and a spiritual sense, but the two—the human and the divine—are absolutely and completely and essentially *one*: they do not and cannot exist without one another.[51]

3 Conclusion

The biblical Song of Songs is, at the same time, one of the most powerful pieces of literature, and one of the most controversial and most often interpreted "sacred texts" in Western intellectual history. Its exuberant celebration of intimate erotic love with its unmatched poetic beauty and metaphoric richness, has shaped the imaginative tradition of Western literature like no other. And yet, in Jewish and Christian theology alike, attempts to sublimate its eroticism and to justify its place in the biblical canon, have also brought about a plethora of allegorical interpre-

---

[50] Rosenzweig, *Star of Redemption*, 199. The original reads: "Das Gleichnis der Liebe geht als Gleichnis durch die ganze Offenbarung hindurch. Es ist das immer wiederkehrende Gleichnis bei den Propheten. Aber es soll eben mehr sein als Gleichnis. Und das ist es erst, wenn es ohne ein 'das bedeutet,' ohne Hinweis also auf das, dessen Gleichnis es sein soll, auftritt. Es genügt also nicht, daß Gottes Verhältnis zum Menschen unter dem Gleichnis des Liebenden zur Geliebten dargestellt wird; es muß unmittelbar das Verhältnis des Liebenden zur Geliebten, das Bedeutende also ohne alle Hindeutung auf das Bedeutete, im Wort Gottes stehn. Und so finden wir es im Hohen Lied. Hier ist es nicht mehr möglich, in jedem Gleichnis 'nur ein Gleichnis' zu sehen. [. . .] Grade in dem rein sinnlichen Sinn, unmittelbar und nicht 'bloß' gleichnisweise, [steckt] die tiefere Bedeutung." (*Stern der Erlösung*, 221–222).
[51] See Rühle, *Das Hohelied*, 476.

tations. Thus, while the Song has shaped the development of our love literature as a genre, it has also modeled our understanding of the interpretation of "sacred texts." And it has shaped our understanding of one of the most fundamental, most powerful, and yet most mysterious human experiences: love. Throughout the ages, the biblical Song of Songs has prompted our thinking and talking and writing about love.

In Scholem's and Rosenzweig's reception of the Song of Songs, and in the larger context of early twentieth-century German-Jewish thought the connection between love and language is reinforced, and developed in view of the specifically Jewish aspect of the Hebrew source text, that both thinkers were intimately familiar with.

Scholem's contribution to the reception of the Song in twentieth-century thought is twofold: First, he highlights the Song's Jewishness and its rootedness in the Hebrew language and poetry. Scholem's ideas of severity, dignity, and veneration, that shape his conception of greatness in relation to the Song, are derived from the fact that the Song of Songs is a Jewish text, written in Hebrew poetry. This is important in so far as the literal reading of the Song in modern scholarship—particularly, in the wake of nineteenth-century Protestant scholarly interpretations—has tended to neglect the place of the Song in the cosmos of Jewish teaching, even though the aspect of Oriental culture became more and more important.[52] Second, however, Scholem maintains the value of its allegorical *interpretation*, even if the Song, for him, was never meant to be an allegory. While the Song's greatness is preserved on a literal level in the Hebrew and Jewish original, its traditional interpretation as allegory also reveals that language can accommodate much more than it says it does on a literal level.

Rosenzweig's reading also focuses on the potential of allegory for language: Rather than seeing an allegorical sense in a given linguistic entity, one and the same sense can be itself *and* not-itself simultaneously. Each of them is their own allegory. Therefore, the very structure of language, and of the language of love in particular, is allegorical. Allegory, however, is not meant as a literary genre in this case, or as a rhetorical trope, which would be part of the literary *ornatus* developed in classical rhetoric. Rather, it is a theory of allegory that takes allegory literally, as an "other-word" (*allos logos*). Viewed in this perspective, the words of love that the Song of Songs voices so beautifully and powerfully, are both fully and truly themselves and "other words" at the same time. And therefore, they are truly allegory, and more than allegory at once. Any loving, in this sense, is nothing but an allegory of loving.

---

52 See, for instance, Pardes, *Song of Songs*, 136–171 (chapter 4: "Modern Scholars and the Quest for the Literal Song").

This view of language may seem simple, but it is actually revolutionary. Viewing language as a non-closed entity that goes beyond its communicative function, connects Scholem's and Rosenzweig's thinking on the Song with Walter Benjamin's language theory, which in turn has been taken up by (for instance) French and American deconstructionists (Derrida, De Man) and developed further by contemporary thought on language within queer theory or postcolonial studies. Focusing on the "un-said," marginalized, excluded aspects of language, and trying to voice the unspeakable (such as love), is a pathbreaking contribution to the development of twentieth-century Western language theory.

Bibliography

Benjamin, Walter. *Gesammelte Briefe*. Vol. 1: *1910–1918*, edited by Christoph Gödde and Henri Lonitz. Frankfurt a. M.: Suhrkamp, 1995 [= GB 1].

Bienenstock, Myriam. "Die Sprache des *Hohelied*s: 'mehr als ein Gleichnis'? Zu Rosenzweigs *Stern der Erlösung*." *ZRGG* 69 (2017): 264–278.

Falk, Marcia. *The Song of Songs: Love Lyrics from the Bible*. Waltham: Brandeis University Press, 2004.

Fishbane, Michael. *Song of Songs: The Traditional Hebrew Text with the New JPS Translation*. The JPS Bible Commentary. Philadelphia: The Jewish Publication Society, 2015.

Kristeva, Julia. *Tales of Love*, translated by Leon Roudiez. New York: Columbia University Press, 1987.

Mendes-Flohr, Paul. "Between Sensual and Heavenly Love: Franz Rosenzweig's Reading of the Song of Songs." In *Scriptural Exegesis: The Shapes of Culture and the Religious Imagination; Essays in Honor of Michael Fishbane*, edited by Deborah A. Green and Laura S. Lieber, 310–319. Oxford: Oxford University Press, 2009.

Mendes-Flohr, Paul. "Franz Rosenzweig and the German Philosophical Tradition." In *The Philosophy of Franz Rosenzweig*, edited by Paul Mendes-Flohr, 1–19. London: University Press of New England, 1988.

Pardes, Ilana. *The Song of Songs: A Biography*. Princeton: Princeton University Press, 2019.

Rosenzweig, Franz. *Der Stern der Erlösung* [1921]. Frankfurt a. M.: Suhrkamp, 1988.

Rosenzweig, Franz. *Die "Gritli"-Briefe: Briefe an Margrit Rosenstock-Huessy*, edited by Inken Rühle and Reinhard Mayer. Tübingen: Bilam, 2002.

Rosenzweig, Franz. *The New Thinking: A Few Supplementary Notes to the* Star, edited and translated by Alan Udoff and Barbara Galli. Syracuse: Syracuse University Press, 1999.

Rosenzweig, Franz. *The Star of Redemption*, translated from the 2nd edition of 1930 by William W. Hallo. Notre Dame: Notre Dame University Press, 1985.

Rühle, Inken. "Das Hohelied—ein weltliches Liebeslied als Kernbuch der Offenbarung? Zur Bedeutung der Auslegungsgeschichte von *Schir haSchirim* im *Stern der Erlösung*." In *Rosenzweig als Leser: Kontextuelle Kommentare zum "Stern der Erlösung,"* edited by Martin Brasser, 453–479. Tübingen: Niemeyer, 2004.

Rühle, Inken. *Gott spricht die Sprache der Menschen: Franz Rosenzweig als jüdischer Theologe*. Tübingen: Bilam, 2004.

Sauter, Caroline. "Hebrew, Jewishness, and Love: Translation in Gershom Scholem's Early Work." *Naharaim* 9 (2015): 151–178.

Sauter, Caroline. "Writing in Love: Goethe's 'Buch Suleika' and the Biblical Song of Songs." *Publications of the English Goethe Society* 87 (2018): 188–203.

Schniedewind, William M. "Calling God Names: An Inner-biblical Approach to the Tetragrammaton." In *Scriptural Exegesis: The Shapes of Culture and the Religious Imagination; Essays in Honour of Michael Fishbane*, edited by Deborah A. Green and Laura S. Lieber, 74–87. Oxford: Oxford University Press, 2009.

Scholem, Gershom. *Tagebücher nebst Aufsätzen und Entwürfen bis 1923*. Vol 1: *1913–1917* [= Tb I]; Vol 2: *1917–1923* [= Tb II], edited by H. Kopp-Oberstebrink, K. Gründer and F. Niewöhner. Frankfurt a. M.: Jüdischer Verlag, 1995/2000.

Weidner, Daniel. *Gershom Scholem: Politisches, esoterisches und historiographisches Schreiben*. Paderborn: Fink, 2003.

Michaela C. Hastetter
"Black and Beautiful" (Song 1:5)
A Key Verse in the Exegesis of the Song of Songs from Origen to Dieter Salbert's *Schwarz—wie die Teppiche Salomos* (1971)

"I am black and beautiful"—the bride's self-declaration in Song of Songs 1:5 is a key verse both in the exegesis of the Song of Songs and in its setting to music across the centuries. Whether juxtaposed as equal attributes of the bride ("black and beautiful") or, from Jerome onward, presented as an antithesis (*nigra sum, sed formosa*, "I am black but beautiful"; Vulg. 1:4), this little verse provided the starting point for the exegetical dispute that unfolded between the Antiochene and Alexandrian schools of Christian theology in late antiquity. On the one hand, Origen, who was followed by the Alexandrian tradition of spiritual exegesis of Scripture, understood the blackness of the bride in a metaphorical, negative moral sense and thus elaborated a theology of *negritudo*, "blackness." On the other hand, Theodore of Mopsuestia took the blackness of the bride in a more literal, ethnic-historical sense and thus read the Song of Songs as a purely literal love song.

Throughout the centuries, the phrase *nigra sum, sed formosa* has been a popular subject for motets and masses drawing on the Song of Songs, and it also played a leading role in the twentieth century in the experimental piece *Schwarz—wie die Teppiche Salomos* for soprano and vibraphone by the German Lutheran composer Dieter Salbert (1932–2006), which premiered in 1971, with texts that have their source in Martin Luther's translation.[1] This article aims at a better understanding of the significance of blackness in Salbert's composition. It starts with a brief look at the spectrum of colors in the biblical Song of Songs (1) and then provides an overview of the main tendencies in the interpretation of the bride's blackness in patristic exegesis (2 and 3). This background allows for a theological approach to the study of Salbert's Song of Songs composition (4). The analysis of the work pays

---

[1] The piece had its premiere at the *4. Woche für Geistliche Musik der Gegenwart* in Saint Martin's Church in Kassel. See Salbert, *Schwarz*, 1 (quoted here and in the following after the pages of the score). The title means "Black—like the carpets of Solomon." In the biblical text, the use of masculine and feminine forms distinguishes the male "beloved" clearly from the female "beloved." To avoid ambiguity, in this article the female protagonist is usually referred to as "the bride," and the male protagonist as "the bridegroom."

Note: I thank Brian McNeil for translating this article (including all quotations) into English.

attention both to its relation to the biblical text and to its musical setting, using the method of structural analogy.[2]

1 Colors in the Song of Songs

It seems surprising that in the Song of Songs, where nature is associated with spring and summer, black is the first color mentioned, in 1:5. But it is not nature that is clothed in a black garment. Rather, the skin of the female protagonist is blackened; the following verse (1:6) explains that it has been burnt by the sun. There are several other color terms in the Song: The "fresh green" of 1:16 (or the "blossoming bed of green" in Luther's translation) is a vernal color ascribed to the bride and bridegroom's bed of love, and the complementary color purple is found on the seat of King Solomon's sedan chair (3:10). The lips of the bride are red in one of the descriptive songs (4:3), while the bridegroom appears in the colors "white and red" (5:10), but the locks of his hair are described as black like the color of ravens (5:11). With the exception of silver and gold, which are employed more as precious metals than as colors, the spectrum of colors in the Song of Songs ranges from words denoting black, to dark colored or dark brown, to green, red, and white. Red is common to both the bride and the bridegroom; only the hair of the man is black as a raven, while the bride is black and her skin dark brown. In the Hebrew text, the color white is reserved for the bridegroom until 6:10, at which point the bride appears in white beauty.

In its initial description of the bride's blackness, the Song of Songs parts company not only with the classical association of brides with the color white[3] but also with the biblical idea of color in the clothing of the exemplary woman, as in the description of the capable woman's white and red garment in Prov 31:22: "Linen and purple is her clothing." In the Song of Songs, however, the self-declaration "I am black" (1:5) does not refer to the choice of color in the woman's garments. Rather, the link between "black" and "I" (*shěchorah 'ani*) concerns something existential, since the translations of the Hebrew *shěchorah* and its *hapax legomenon* formation *shěcharhóret* (1:6)[4] are open to a broad range of interpretations. While the

---

2 See Hastetter, *"Horch!,"* 74–109.
3 See Marquardt, *Das Privatleben der Römer*, 43–44, with reference to Pliny the Elder, *Natural History* 8, 194 (brides with *tunica recta* in white and *flammeum nuptiale*, a veil in red), and other examples.
4 I am grateful to New Testament scholar Hans Werner Günther for drawing my attention to this. The transcription of the Hebrew text follows Reichert, *Das Hohelied Salomos*, 18.

Septuagint directly takes over the black color from the Hebrew text of 1:5, using Greek μέλαινά (retained in the Vulgate as *nigra*), Jerome's Latin translation alters the same Hebrew root for "black" (1:5) and "blackened" (1:6) with a sure sense of style, rendering 1:6 as *fusca sim quia decoloravit me sol*. Here, the color word *black* is lost and becomes, in a way that can be grasped semantically, a dark discoloration caused by the sun. Ernst Benz comments:

> *Fusca* is not directly black, but dark, sunburnt, blackish. Cicero employs this word to denote the color of the crows, which is gray-black, while Vergil employs it to describe the skin color of Amyntas, who was not black, but sunburnt. The adjective *fusca* thus leaves open the second interpretation, the allusion to the sunburnt complexion of the Jewish girl. [...] In that case, the text would not at all be speaking of an Ethiopian woman.[5]

The Hebrew *shĕchorah 'ani* (1:5) is open to a diversity of interpretations. It is only in the following verse (1:6) that an explanation is supplied: namely, that the bride's blackness is caused by the sun; but even this explanation leaves an opening for different interpretations.

From its very beginning, exegesis of the Song of Songs has taken a special interest in the bride's statement of 1:5. Her self-description as black in fact became the key to interpretative variations and was fundamentally determinative for Theodore of Mopsuestia's opposition to Origen.

2 Origen's Theology of *negritudo*

Origen's homilies on the Song of Songs[6] devote considerable space to the exegesis of blackness in 1:5–6.[7] Likewise, the Greek fragments of his commentary on the Song of Songs contain echoes of his theology of *negritudo*.[8] The surviving Latin version of his homilies presents the biblical verse that is our starting point with the variant *nigra sum et speciosa* (1:5).[9] He thus envisages an existential blackness of the bride on the basis of the biblical Hebrew color word *black*. He elaborates this

---

5 Benz, "Ich bin schwarz und schön," 227.
6 *Homiliae in Canticum* (*Hom. Cant.*). For a Latin/German edition, see Origenes, *Die Homilien und Fragmente zum Hohelied* (Fürst and Strutwolf, eds.), 61–137. For an English translation, see Origen, *Song of Songs* (Lawson, ed.), 265–305.
7 See Origen, *Hom. Cant.* I 5–6 (Lawson, trans., 274–279).
8 See Origen, *Fr. Cant.* 9 (on II 1,3–6; 1,51), 10 (on II 1,46–49), 11 (on II 2,21; 2,6–7), 12 (on II 2,16–19), and 13 (on II 3,1–12). For a Greek/German edition, see Origenes, *Die Homilien und Fragmente zum Hohelied* (Fürst and Strutwolf, eds.), 150–155. For an English translation, see Origen, *Song of Songs* (Lawson, ed.), 21–263.
9 See Origen, *Hom. Cant.* I 6 (Lawson, trans., 275).

theologically through four approaches, in keeping with the doctrine of the multiple meanings of Scripture.[10]

2.1 The Path from the Black to the White Bride: The Interpretation of *nigra* in the Moral Sense

In his first approach to Song 1:5, Origen puts forward a moral reading of the verse, beginning with the question how blackness without splendor is to be understood.[11] He relates the black (*nigra*) bride to the soul that has fallen into sin and has now done penance, becoming once again beautiful (*speciosa*) in the process of conversion. According to Origen, the perspective of this ascent is a transition from the black of sin to the splendid white light of the purified bride. He reads this out of the last chapter of the Song of Songs:

> She has repented of her sins, beauty is the gift conversion has bestowed; that is the reason she is hymned as beautiful. She is called black, however, because she has not yet been purged of every stain of sin, she has not yet been washed into salvation; nevertheless she does not stay dark—hued, she is becoming white. When, therefore, she arises towards greater things and begins to mount from lowly things to lofty, they say concerning her: Who is this that cometh up, having been washed white?[12]

The support of her beloved (*fratruelis/dilectus*, Vulg.) gives her soul the power that motivates her to this ascent; and in Origen's distribution of roles, the beloved is Christ.[13]

2.2 Moses's Black Wife as an Allegory of Christ and the Church: The Interpretation of *nigra* in the Allegorical-Mystical Sense

In his second approach, Origen interprets the *nigra* of the bride in the Song of Songs in relation to the black wife of Moses, a Cushite woman and the daughter of a Mid-

---

10 On the multiple meanings of scripture in Origen, see de Lubac, *Histoire et Esprit*, esp. 139–150.
11 See Origen, *Hom. Cant.* I 6 (Lawson, trans., 276).
12 Origen, *Hom. Cant.* I 6 (Lawson, trans., 276).
13 On the division of the Song of Songs into four roles (bride, bridegroom, maidens or friends of the bride, and companions of the bridegroom), see Origen, *Hom. Cant.* I 1. On *fratruelis* or *dilectus*, see Origenes, *Die Homilien*, 83 n. 44.

ianite priest (according to Num 12:1). Here, Origen begins by taking up the motif of penance, which allows the soul to become black and beautiful, whereas an unrepentant soul would be black and ugly:

> If you have repented, however, your soul will indeed be black [*nigra*] because of your old sins, but your penitence will give it something of what I may call an Ethiopian beauty. And having once made mention of an Ethiopian, I want to summon a Scriptural witness about this word too. Aron and Mary murmur against Moses, because Moses has an Ethiopian wife. Moses weds an Ethiopian wife, because his Law has passed over to the Ethiopian woman of our Song. [...] Moses cares nothing for their murmuring; He loves His Ethiopian woman.[14]

In the allegorical interpretation of Origen, Ethiopia becomes the image of the black but beautiful church of the gentiles, in contrast to Israel, which Christ, the new Moses, did not take as his wife. Origen's mystical understanding of blackness presents the beautiful black Queen of the South, who came from far away to hear the wisdom of Solomon (see Matt 12:42), as the principal witness (so to speak) to the missionary task of the church, the "black one is beautiful, for all she is called black," to sing "songs of a song," to "come from the borders of Ethiopia, from the ends of the earth, to hear the wisdom of the true Solomon"[15] [i.e. Christ].

Origen also employs the basic idea of the black church called together out of the gentile peoples in the allegorical interpretation in his commentary on the Song of Songs. In fragment 9 of book 2, on 1:5 (μέλαινά εἰμι ἐγὼ καὶ καλή), Origen interprets the black beauty as a self-statement of the church:

> But it is the church of the gentiles that says this to the souls from Israel, or rather from *Jerusalem*, confessing thereby that she is *black* [μέλαν] through not coming from luminous and enlightened fathers; and this is why she is exposed to the darkness [i.e., Kedar]. But she is *beautiful* because of the Word that she has received, and she resembles the *awnings of Solomon* that he possessed together with other things that he had acquired in his glory [see Matt 6:29].[16]

The acceptance of the Word—which is nothing other than a paraphrase of the acceptance of faith in Christ—constitutes for Origen the real reason why the church, as the bride of the Song of Songs, becomes white.

---

14 Origen, *Hom. Cant.* I 6 (Lawson, trans., 276–277). Origen likewise employs Zeph 3:10 and Ps 68:32 as OT evidence here.
15 Origen, *Hom. Cant.* I 6 (Lawson, trans., 277).
16 Origen, *Fr. Cant.* 9 (on II 1,3–6; 1,51); here and below, translations of Origen are the author's own, from the Greek.

2.3 Belief and Unbelief: The Transition from *nigra* to *fuscata*

In his further reflections on the black beautiful one and his search for reasons for her blackness, Origen finally touches on the relationship between belief and unbelief in the transition from the existential *nigra* (1:5) to the transformative *fuscata* (1:6). Instead of the blackness of sin, Origen now sees being sunburnt by the divine sun as the reason for the change of color:

> With full radiance His bright light has shone on me, and I am darkened [*fuscata*] by His heat. I have not indeed received His light into myself as it were fitting that I should, and as the Sun's own dignity required.[17]

Origen finally widens the spiritual meaning of *fuscata* to embrace the spectrum of unbelief, the refusal to believe, as a "crime" that, according to Rom 11:30–31, stands in the way of the "knowledge of Christ."[18]

2.4 The Colors of Christ as the Counterpart to the Blackness of the Bride

Taking black as a metaphor for sinfulness, Origen consistently interprets the *black and beautiful* bride of Song 1:5 as a reference to the sinful and penitent church. The principal colors of the Song of Songs are given a Christological connotation. The description of the colors of the bridegroom in 5:10, "My beloved is white and red," is unmistakably interpreted with reference to Christ in a fragment of Origen's commentary on the Song of Songs: "Yes, he is *white* because he is truly God, *red* because of the incarnation."[19]

The confession of Christ as truly God and human being is woven into this brief affirmation about the color combination, with which Origen embraces the totality of faith in Christ. And the precious stone in 5:14, which is hard to interpret, Origen expounds as a reference to Christ, writing of the sapphire "that is Christ."[20] For her part, the bride, ascending out of the blackness, has taken the path from 1:5 to 8:5, "Who is this who ascends, shimmering whitely, leaning [ἐπιστηριζομένη] on her beloved?"[21]—the path on which she has clothed herself in white, the color of

---

[17] Origen, *Hom. Cant.* I 6 (Lawson, trans., 278).
[18] See Origen, *Hom. Cant.* I 6 (Lawson, trans., 279).
[19] Origen, *Fr. Cant.* 50 (on IV–X).
[20] Origen, *Fr. Cant.* 53 (on IV–X).
[21] Origen, *Fr. Cant.* 83 (on IV–X), according to the old Greek version of Song 8:5 (with ἀναβαίνουσα λελευκανθισμένη).

Christ. Origen comments on this verse from the last chapter of the Song of Songs as follows:

> The ascent of the bride to the most-blessed dwellings is prophesied, when she has totally laid aside the darkness of wickedness and has put on the brightness of virtue, when she follows the Word and *is supported* [στηριζομένης] by him. This is why the heavenly powers marvel at the transformation of men to such greatness.[22]

2.5 Preliminary Conclusions

In his approaches to the interpretation of the bride's blackness in the Song of Songs, Origen avoids a literal reading and elaborates a multifaceted theology of *negritudo* that is influenced in the moral sense of Scripture by the Platonic schema of ascent, whereby the soul ascends in its process of conversion from blackness to whiteness and ultimately to the whiteness of Christ. He ascribes the correlation of the first Moses with the second Moses to the allegorical-mystical level of Scripture, in relation to the Ethiopian woman who prefigures the church of sinners, which shines in beautiful blackness when it is redeemed by Christ. Alongside this ecclesiological realism, the Alexandrian Origen posits a further accent by means of the next verse, 1:6, interpreting blackening by the sun as referring to the state of being touched by Christ when there is no response of faith. Origen contrasts the blackness of the bride to the white, red, and sapphire blue of the bridegroom, Christ; at the end of her ascent on the ladder of virtues, the bride appears in the color white, and she has laid aside all blackness.

3 The Black Bride in Theodore of Mopsuestia

3.1 A Courtship Song

Theodore of Mopsuestia's radically literal reading of Song 1:5 is the diametrical opposite of the Origenist interpretation that had left its mark on patristic theology up to that time. Theodore, an Antiochene, stylized Origen as his antipode and wrote an entire treatise entitled *In Opposition to the Allegorists*, in which he leveled vehement accusations against Origen.[23] He lamented the loss of the historical dimension and

---

22 Origen, *Fr. Cant.* 83 (on IV–X).
23 See Theodore of Mopsuestia, *Adversus allegoricos*. Fragments of the lost treatise are preserved in: Facundus, *Pro def.* III 6,13–14; X 1,29. For an English translation, see Theodore of Mopsuestia (McLeod, ed.), "In Opposition," 75–79.

the proximity of allegory to a pagan exegetical method that slips all too easily into the world of fables. A tardy echo of this anti-Origenist tendency can be seen in Henri de Lubac's book *Histoire et Esprit* (1950) on Origen's scriptural exegesis, and the Catholic Church held decisive reservations about the Alexandrian and his interpretation of sacred Scripture until the mid-twentieth century. In the first chapter of his book, de Lubac has assembled a whole litany, running to many pages, of accusations against Origen, across a spectrum from extravagances to oracular philosophy.[24] Origen is said to have gone too far with his allegorical exposition and to have interpreted Moses and Christ in a Platonic manner; the historicity of the sacred texts has been ruined, and speculations on speculations have falsified the truth of the biblical story. These accusations reflect something of the patristic dispute between the Alexandrian and the Antiochene schools. While the Alexandrian school followed Origen in assuming the multiple meanings of Scripture, the Antiochene school thought in a literal manner and took history as its starting point. It is unsurprising that the question of the exegesis the Song of Songs should have blazed up precisely at 1:5, in reference to the interpretation of the bride's blackness, since the openness of images, smells, and colors actually demands an interpretation.[25] Both in Origen and in Theodore of Mopsuestia, the interpretation of blackness played a central role in the development of an entire school's tradition.

It is precisely 1:5 that reveals the explosiveness of the literal interpretation of the Song of Songs in Theodore of Mopsuestia's commentary *In Canticum Canticorum*.[26] He understands the Song neither as a prophetic book nor as a book in keeping with historical traditions; rather, in his view, it can be understood only in light of the book of Kings. Theodore of Mopsuestia reads the blackness of the bride in Song 1:5 in light of 1Kgs 11:1, which recounts that "King Solomon loved not only the daughter of Pharaoh, but many other foreign women too" and then lists the nationalities of these women. Theodore reads the *nigra sum et bona* (Song 1:5) that underlies the Latin version of his brief commentary literally, as a reference to the dark skin color of the Egyptian daughter of Pharaoh, with whom King Solomon had a love relationship. Accordingly, for Theodore of Mopsuestia, it must be said that she was black and good. The emphasis on the goodness of the black daughter of Pharaoh was necessary because, as the Antiochene Theodore states, Jewish taste associated the "deformed color"[27] black with wickedness,

---

24 See de Lubac, *Histoire et Esprit*, 13–46.
25 In a similar vein to Jewish tradition, which interpreted the Song of Songs as an allegory of God's love for his people, the early church applied the metaphorical meaning of Scripture to Christ's nuptial love for the church.
26 See Theodore of Mopsuestia, *In Canticum*, 1.
27 Theodore of Mopsuestia, *In Canticum*, 1: *deformi colore*.

because it had the same nocturnal character as the people of Egypt, who were the descendants of Ham. The black skin color of the Egyptian daughter of Pharaoh whom Solomon wooed must therefore disgust the beautiful Hebrew women, since they saw it as ridiculous and inappropriate to a king's bride. Theodore's interpretation of the blackness of the king's bride primarily aims at explaining the jealous feelings of Hebrew women, who feel disregarded. Nonetheless, obviously, it also conveys ethnic stereotypes. His reconstruction of the story was that King Solomon built a house of gold, silver, and precious stones for the beautiful black Egyptian woman, and while she sat at table he delighted her with the love songs that he had composed especially for the occasion. It is here that Theodore of Mopsuestia sees the origin of the Song of Songs. For the first time in the Christian history of its interpretation, Theodore regards the Song of Songs as a secular bridal song with which King Solomon wooed the Egyptian daughter of Pharaoh to make her his bride.[28] The Acts of the Second Council of Constantinople in 553 rejected this exegesis as heretical, because the Antiochene had denied the divine inspiration in the Song of Songs.[29]

3.2 Preliminary Conclusions

In terms of scriptural hermeneutics, Origen and Theodore of Mopsuestia are not so very alien to one another, since both read the Song of Songs on the basis of the unity of Scripture, under the premise that Scripture is its own interpreter. With regard to Song 1:5, it is above all the book of Numbers and the letters of Paul that prompt Origen to undertake a soteriological explanation. Theodore of Mopsuestia draws on the book of Kings and thus arrives at an interpretation of Song 1:5 with an ethnic accent. The results could scarcely be more different: whereas Origen associates "black and beautiful" with the mystical path of the soul's ascent, which ultimately expands ecclesiologically, and sees the church as a whole symbolized in the beauti-

---

28 See Theodore of Mopsuestia, *In Canticum*, 1.
29 On this, see in detail Pelletier, *Lectures*, 322–325, with reference to Mansi, *Sacrorum Conciliorum*, col. IV, 202–203. New Testament scholar Marius Reiser observes, "Naturally, poetic texts, above all the Psalms and the Song of Songs, offered a fruitful field for drawing allegories. The Song of Songs was, however, seen by the head of the Antiochene school, Theodore of Mopsuestia, as a completely profane song of courtship of a bride. He did not find unanimous acceptance for this view even within his own school. Today, there is scarcely an exegete who would take a different view from Theodore. This, of course, prompts the question: How can one continue to regard this book as canonical, if one strictly rejects its allegorical interpretation?" (Reiser, *Bibelkritik*, 109; original in German).

ful black bride, Theodore of Mopsuestia thinks exclusively on the basis of dark skin color and interprets the Song of Songs as addressed to a specific black beauty from Egypt, the Pharaoh's daughter from the first book of Kings, whom Solomon wooed. In taking his starting point in Song 1:5, Theodore subsumes the entire Song of Songs under the genre of courtship songs.

4 A Path Toward the Interpretation of Dieter Salbert's Composition *Schwarz—wie die Teppiche Salomos*

The crucial question that arises at this point is where Dieter Salbert's composition can be located theologically. Is he more oriented to the allegorical interpretation of Origen and his followers, or is his music linked to a purely literal understanding along the lines of the Antiochene school, as epitomized by Theodore of Mopsuestia? After all, Salbert's composition *Schwarz—wie die Teppiche Salomos* is the only German-language setting of the Song of Songs in the twentieth century that has recourse in its title to Song 1:5.[30]

4.1 Title of the Work, Structure, and Selection of Texts

Salbert's *Schwarz—wie die Teppiche Salomos*, employs an abbreviated version of Song 1:5 in Luther's translation in its title. It is striking that his formulation of the title omits the self-statement of the bride ("I am") and puts the focus exclusively on the color black in comparison to the carpets of Solomon, the final comparison in 1:5.[31] Salbert's short composition, only a little longer than five minutes,[32] unfolds around the colors of the underlying poetic text. It is marked *Gefühlsbetont—mit Ausdruck* ("emotional—with expression")[33] and has four tempo units.

---

[30] On the evaluation of the entire corpus of settings of the Song of Songs in the twentieth century, see Hastetter, *"Horch!,"* 558–604.
[31] In Luther's translation, the entire verse reads, "Ich bin schwarz, aber gar lieblich, ihr Töchter von Jerusalem, wie die Hütten von Kedars, wie die Teppiche Salomos" ("I am black but very lovely, you daughters of Jerusalem, like the huts of Kedar, like the carpets of Solomon").
[32] See Salbert, *Schwarz*, 2: "Spieldauer: 5.10 Min."
[33] Salbert, *Schwarz*, 2.

Dieter Salbert, *Schwarz—wie die Teppiche Salomos*[34]	English translation
I	**I**
Tempi mehr zur Langsamkeit tendieren	**Tempi tending toward slowness**
Ich bin schwarz aber gar lieblich, ihr Töchter Jerusalems	I am black but very lovely, you daughters of Jerusalem
Wie die Hütten Kedars . . . schwarrr - - rrz wie die Teppiche Salomos. [Song 1:5]	like the huts of Kedar . . . blaccc - - kkk like the carpets of Solomon. [Song 1:5]
Sehet mich nicht an, daß ich so schwarz bin.	Do not see in me that I am so black.
Denn die Sonne hat mich so verbrannt.	For the sun has burnt me so.
Ich bin schwarrr - - - - rrz.	I am blaccc - - - - kkk.
II	**II**
schnell, möglichst geschlossen	**quick, *colla voce* as far as possible**
Des Nachts auf meinem Lager suchte ich den meine Seele liebt.	At night on my bed I sought him whom my soul loves.
Ich suchte, aber ich fand ihn nicht. [3:1]	I sought him, but I found him not. [3:1]
Ich beschwöre euch, ihr Töchter Jerusalems, findet ihr meinen Freund, so sagt ihm, daß ich vor Liebe krank bin. [5:8]	I adjure you, you daughters of Jerusalem, if you find my friend, then tell him that I am sick with love. [5:8]
Habt ihr nicht gesehn, den meine Seele liebt? [3:3]	Have you not seen him whom my soul loves? [3:3]
III	**III**
zögernd zerrissen	**hesitatingly disjointed**
Ich schlafe, aber mein Herz wacht.	I sleep, but my heart is awake.
Da ist die Stimme meines Freundes, der anklopft.	There is the voice of my friend, who is knocking.
Tue mir auf, liebe Freundin, meine Taube, denn mein Haupt ist voll Tau und meine Locken voll Nachttropfen. [5:2]	Open to me, dear friend, my dove, for my head is full of dew and my locks full of the drops of the night. [5:2]
Ich habe meinen Rock ausgezogen, wie soll ich ihn wieder anziehen. [5:3]	I have taken off my robe, how am I to put it on again. [5:3]
Da stand ich auf, daß ich meinem Freund auftäte. [5:5]	Then I got up, to open to my friend. [5:5]
IV	**IV**
verdichtend—rasante Abläufe	**solidifying—rapid sequences**
Mein Freund ist weiß und rot, auserkoren unter vielen Tausenden. [5:10]	My friend is white and red, chosen out of many thousands. [5:10]

---

34 The biblical references given in square brackets are not part of the score.

Ich bin schwarz, aber gar lieblich. [1:5]	I am black, but very lovely [1:5]
Sein Haupt ist das feinste Gold. [5:11]	His head is the finest gold. [5:11]
Habt ihr nicht gesehen, den meine Seele liebt? [3:3]	Have you not seen him whom my soul loves? [3:3]
Seine Augen sind wie Augen der Taube an den Wasserbächen. [5:12]	His eyes are like eyes of the dove at the brooks of water. [5:12]
Seine Lippen sind wie Rosen. [5:13]	His lips are like roses. [5:13]
Seine Hände sind wie goldene Becher voll Türki - - se . . .[35] [5:14]	His hands are like golden cups full of turquoi - - ses . . . [5:14]
Ich bin schwarrrz . . . [1:5]	I am blackkk . . . [1:5]
Seine Kehle ist süß und er ist ganz lieblich.	His throat is sweet and he is very lovely.
Ein solcher ist mein Freund, ihr Töchter Jerusalems. [5:16]	Such a one is my friend, you daughters of Jerusalem. [5:16]

Salbert has made his own selection of verses from the biblical Song of Songs, which he has assembled anew, partly repeating them and fusing them into a new unit of meaning. The framing movements I and IV play with the colors from the descriptive songs of the bride and bridegroom in the Song of Songs, while the two inner movements reflect the internal yearnings and emotional states of the bride until her beloved arrives. The deconstructed reconstruction of the text generates a logical sequence of action, which begins (I) with the self-presentation of the young woman in her blackness. She is consumed with nocturnal yearning for the beloved (II), until he knocks at her door (III), likewise in a nocturnal scene, and she opens the door to him. Their encounter (IV) is characterized by a rich contrast between the different colors, the beautiful blackness of the woman and the white and red of her friend. In her rapture of love, the black beloved finds ever new images to describe the light-skinned, blond beloved in his beauty, at the same time assuring herself of her own black loveliness.

The logical context of the four brief scenes at first sight suggests a literal understanding of the Song of Songs. The piece is developed from the perspective of the bride in black. Salbert's emphasis on the contrasting colors of the bride and the bridegroom is remarkable and seems contextually congruent with Theodore of Mopsuestia's literal interpretation, described from the perspective of the Egyptian daughter of Pharaoh: her beautiful blackness contrasts to the red and white of Solomon, son of the reddish-blond David with beautiful eyes (cf. 1Sam 16:12).

In Salbert's interpretation, however, one metaphor deviates from the underlying biblical text. The comparison of the hands of the king/friend to a precious stone

---

35 Song 5:14; Luther's translation has *goldene Ringe* ("golden rings").

(Song 5:14),³⁶ which Origen read as speaking of sapphire and Luther presented as "golden rings full of turquoises," Salbert transforms into "golden *cups* full of turquoises," moving undeniably beyond the original meaning. What can have prompted him to turn the golden rings or rolls into cups out of which turquoises flow? Perhaps he was thinking of the silver cup that Joseph, in Egypt, put into his youngest brother's sack of corn (Gen 44:2), although this would disregard the fact that that cup is described as silver. It would, of course, also be conceivable that the hands of the bridegroom, which are compared to a golden cup in Salbert's transformation of Song 5:14, are an allusion to the Last Supper and the eucharistic cup of wine in the hands of Jesus, which he gives to his disciples in order that they may drink from it. A eucharistic interpretation of the cup would also allow a direct parallel between the allegorical exegesis of Song 1:5 in Origen and the love scene in Salbert: Christ, who is wholly pure and divine (white), gives himself to his black bride, the church, even pouring out of his blood (red), in order to give her a share of his own pure white. In this interpretative variant, of course, the addition "full of turquoises" (Song 5:14) would be disruptive, because the blood or the wine in the cup should be associated instead with red. In Luther's version of the prophet Daniel's vision of the Son of Man, however, we do find the image of the turquoise as the expression of the body (Dan 10:6).³⁷ The eucharistic interpretation of the cup full of turquoises would therefore make sense, since Christ distributes his own self in the cup, in the eucharistic meal of body and blood, in order to become one body with those who receive him. Whether this was the intention of the composer, however, must remain an open question, for musical compositions bound to words cannot be interpreted exclusively on the basis of their textual constructions. Thus we must ask what the testimony of the notes, the musical language, tells us about Salbert's intention.

---

36 Klaus Reichert comments on the difficulty of translating this comparison: "*Rolls of gold*: it is unclear what exactly is meant, and the usual translation is 'rolls.' Perhaps rings or circlets are meant. Tarshish-stone: the original text has only Tarshish. No one knows what stone is meant; the name is often said to derive from Tartessus in Spain, a trading post of the Phoenicians. This was the tenth stone on Aaron's breastpiece. The following translations have been offered: 'chrysolite' (Septuagint), 'hyacinthus' (= amethyst? Vulgate), 'beryl' (Authorized Version), 'turquoise' (Luther, Mendelssohn, Herder), 'yellow stone' (Torczyner), 'chalcedony' (Buber), 'topaz' (HAL), 'garnet' (Keel); the Enzyklopädia Judaica gives the preference, on the basis of comparative sources (Onqelos, Targum), to 'aquamarine'" (Reichert, *Das Hohelied Salomos*, 116, original in German).

37 Turquoises are found in other passages in Luther's translation: in the throne vision of the prophet Ezekiel, who describes the appearance of the wheels in the throne-chariot as like a turquoise, all four wheels being one, as if one was inside the other (Ezek 1:14; 10:9); in Ezekiel's description of the jewelry in the garden of Eden (Ezek 28:13); and in the description of the priestly garments, where turquoise is always one of the decorative gems (Exod 28:20; 29:13).

4.2 The Composer's Self-Understanding

Schwarz—wie die Teppiche Salomos is one of Salbert's sacred vocal works[38] and technically also belongs to his experimental compositions. A comment that Salbert made about his basic approach as a composer. He documents the work's various stages of development and is helpful for understanding his experimental music:

> As a fourteen-year-old, I played hit songs on the piano in a smoke-filled pub in the suburbs. Later, I wrote songs for cabarets and comedies, and then the serious study of composition brought me onto a completely different track. Now it was a matter of confronting contemporary musical fads and their ideologies; and this had an influence on my compositions mostly in the sense of an undogmatic and above all a parodistic application. I found it interesting, for a time, to conduct musical statistics and to offer some pieces in which the postulates of directed music—for example, the emancipation of dissonance and din, and serial technique—were perhaps fulfilled to some extent. But this corset did not last long. I quickly found my way back to the free artistic use of sound, and I had learned a great deal. I found my place between the stools, and I omitted no opportunity to translate into music the insight that, for example, emotions are not in the least realities that lie outside music. They soon made their reappearance: the eternal qualities like rage, pain, pathos, serenity, irony, and sentiments. [...] From the mid-1970s, I was interested in the cathartic effect of music. The musical consequence was the confrontation with "trivial" elements in music. The trivial necessitates a widely differentiated acoustic field that is not its own, with atonal structures and free sequences that are also written down in graphic form; in short, a differentiated environment of which the trivial becomes an element. This dialectical relationship can be translated into music in a simultaneous juxtaposition, in a temporal succession of reciprocal effects, in mingling, interruption, or alienation. It is a play with communication, with the possibility of taking a text, an idea, a presentiment, or a memory and commenting on it musically, intensifying it, or parodying it. The music does everything with its specific—that is to say, "speechless," purely musical—means. Accordingly, I see the significance of my work as a composer in challenging hearers intellectually and supporting them emotionally—in the sense of a new humaneness in music.[39]

The graphic score of his *Schwarz—wie die Teppiche Salomos* comes from the period of transition from his rediscovered freedom as a composer to express emotions to his focus on the element of the trivial, frequently in a cross-fading technique that unites the ancient musical ideal of catharsis with postmodern collage techniques to form a synthesis. In addition, the composer wants the hearer not only to grasp

---

[38] Other such works include, e.g., *Theatralische Messe* (with texts from the liturgy and contemporaneous authors), *Stationen der Hoffnung—ein szenisches Oratorium* (with use of historic chants, including lyrics from Paul Gerhardt), *Shalom, Luther...* (based on Luther's choral *Eine feste Burg ist unser Gott*), *STIMMEN* (inter alia with quotes from the book of Job), *Die große Flut* (with texts from the book of Genesis), and *Klage und Vision* (with texts from the book of Lamentations); for more information, see https://musikverlag-zahoransky.de/edition-dieter-salbert/ (21.07.2021).
[39] Salbert, "Zitat" (original in German).

the emotional component of his music but also to be challenged intellectually by it. This may indicate that he has embedded in his music a deeper dimension that is not immediately perceptible.

4.3 The Language of the Music

In order to interpret Salbert's setting of the Song of Songs in relation to his understanding of Song 1:5, our investigation will focus primarily on the color components set to music in the framing movements I and IV. In general, we can say that there is a balanced relationship between language and music. In Salvert's composition, the color word that underlies the sound is itself subject to an artistic transformation when the color tone that determines the title, black (*schwarz*), is lengthened by multiplying the consonant *r*, apparently to play with a negative association of blackness:

schwarrr - - rrz (I, beginning)
schwarrr - - - - rrz (I, end)
schwarz (IV, beginning)
schwarrrz . . . (IV, middle)

The instruments in the work are the vibraphone (which can be alternated at certain points with xylophone, marimbaphone, or celesta)[40] and the soprano, which are related to each other as upper and lower voices, thereby evoking a kind of two-part work. Throughout the first movement, with Song 1:5 as the textual basis, the marimbaphone plays the lower B in a differentiated rhythm, evoking a monotonous soundscape as the ground. In the middle of the second notation system, the soprano inserts her self-revelation, "I am black," into the sustained B a semitone deeper, in B flat, with a sharp dissonance (see Figure 1). This is then contrasted musically with the antithesis "but very lovely" (Song 1:5), with which the soprano voice springs upward (C flat–D double flat–E flat–B), which then slumps in the following statement onto the bourdon note B. This is Salbert's comment on the blackness of the bride, which has already been indicated by the vibraphone, in combination with the dissonance caused by the entry of the soprano voice. He uses sounds to paint a monotony that is felt to be painful; but he paints her beauty with joie de vivre in a lively upward spring by the soprano, omitting the monotonous B. At the high point of the *"lieb-*lich," this appears as the lower voice in a distorted tritone constellation (B–F double flat).

The renewed hearing of the bride's self-revelation about her blackness (from Song 1:6) shapes the end of the first movement. The musical event is still perme-

---

[40] See the page on the explanation of the signs in Salbert, *Schwarz*, 1.

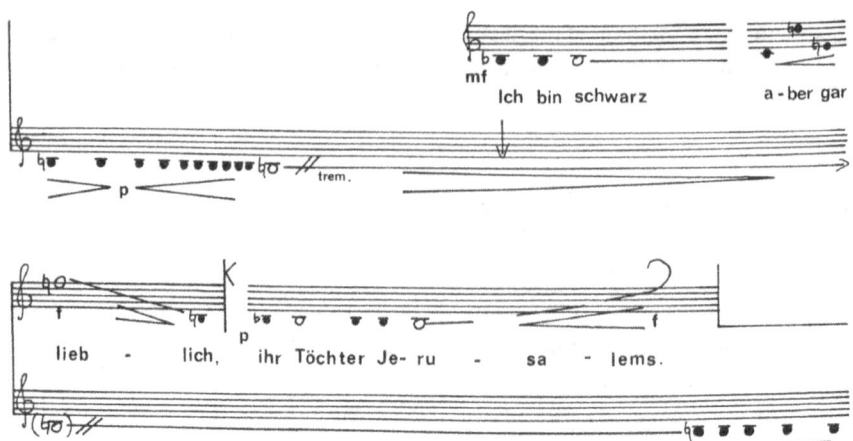

Figure 1: Movement I, first notation system and beginning of second notation system (Salbert, *Schwarz*, 2). Musikverlag Zimmermann. With kind permission of SCHOTT MUSIC, Mainz.

ated by the lower B in the manner of an organ pedal point, while the bride's song is broken open around her central note, B flat, with five cross-staff glissandi that resemble five open wounds (see Figure 2).

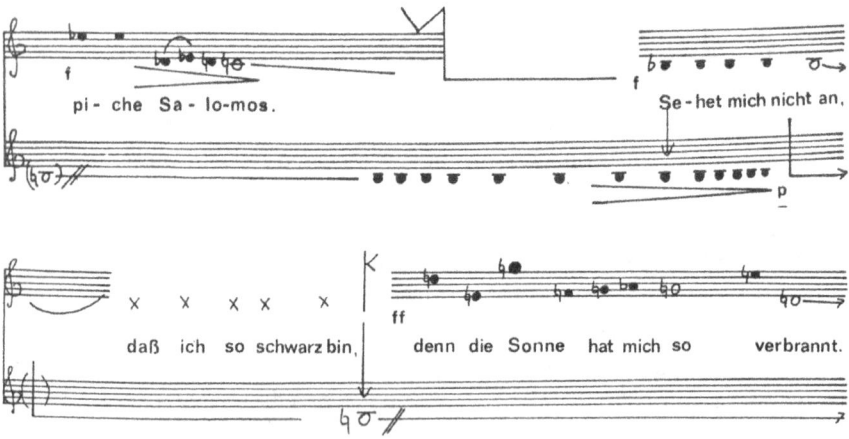

Figure 2: Movement I, page transition (Salbert, *Schwarz*, 2–3). Musikverlag Zimmermann. With kind permission of SCHOTT MUSIC, Mainz.

In the final phrase, the cross-staff glissandi of the bride around her central note, B flat, interrupt the "I am black" in the soprano with medium-length pauses that are posited in counterpoint to the vibraphone voice, which is now likewise interrupted with medium-length pauses (see Figure 3). This intones a painfully distorted song of lamentation that continually breaks off, similar to the intervals between the breaths when someone weeps intensely. The lamentation is cut off and peters out into a quiet whimpering. We hear nothing more about the beauty of the black beloved.

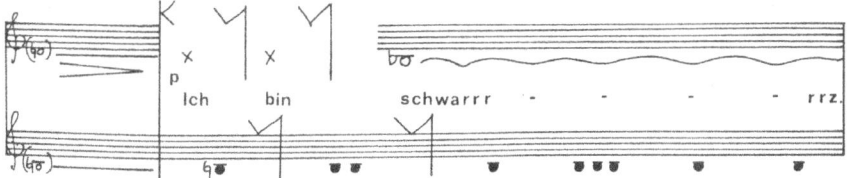

Figure 3: Movement I, second notation system (Salbert, *Schwarz*, 3). Musikverlag Zimmermann. With kind permission of SCHOTT MUSIC, Mainz.

If we compare the color constellations of the first movement with those of the fourth, in which this basic constellation from Song 1:5 ("I am black, but very lovely") is repeated note for note in the middle of the third notation system, we find a completely different initial situation, which introduces the description of the bridegroom from Song 5:10 ("My friend is white and red"). Eight rapid parallel beats on the marimbaphone (three diminished fifths: C–G flat, five octaves: D to high D) that continue in wide leaps, followed by an expansive cross-staff glissando and an anabatic line over almost three octaves, introduce the unaccompanied description of the friend in the soprano line, which appears musically in the loveliness-ductus as the antithesis to the blackness: E flat–E–G flat–high E flat–high E–F (see Figure 4).

Figure 4: Movement IV, first and second notation systems (Salbert, *Schwarz*, 7). Musikverlag Zimmermann. With kind permission of SCHOTT MUSIC, Mainz.

The fact that Salbert composed this work and performed it on the occasion of a weeklong contemporary spiritual music festival suggests a spiritual interpretation. The link between the cross-staff glissando and the striking anabatic line (G–high D flat) before the description of the friend as white and red could be interpreted along the lines of Origen's interpretation of the Christ-colors. This would result in the following depth dimension, which would indeed be a theological-intellectual challenge to the hearer:

Cross-staff glissando	*Anabatic line*	*"My friend is white and red" (Song 5:10)*
Jesus's death on the cross →	Jesus's resurrection →	The church's confession on the lips of the bride: "True God and true human being"

The final great color antithesis in IV comes on the last page in the second notation system, contrasting Song 5:14 with 1:5. The golden cups full of turquoises resound in an expanded loveliness-ductus with a completely free vibraphone accompaniment with a graphic notation,[41] in which Salbert combines free tone pitches with white clusters and small cross-staff glissandi (see Figure 5). In graphic terms, the form of the framed vibraphone voice, tapering from right to left, resembles a cup lying horizontally or a cornucopia opening out onto the blackness of the bride and is not to be repeated as often as wished—in other words, it resounds only once. Salbert makes a clear break immediately after this and presents the unaccompanied "Ich bin schwarrrz . . ." as a threefold cross-staff glissando in the soprano voice, which is no longer held fast on the tone pitch of the blackness, the lower B. The lonely monotony of the lower B is also done away with in the final variant of the bride's blackness. Her blackness has become the threefold glissando that continues and takes up the tone pitch of the turquoises in the cross-staff glissandi, after turquoises in full have been poured out of the cup in the bridegroom's hand.

The testimony of the notes suggests that these facts should lead us to think not so much of the eucharistic cup but rather of the event of baptism. The golden cup, graphically noted in a horizontal position, would be a metaphor for the vessel containing the baptismal water, from which in its reclining position turquoise-colored baptismal water streams forth, the threefold baptismal formula (three cross-staff glissandi in

---

41 See Salbert, *Schwarz*, 1 (the last noted term, "repeat as often as wished," does not apply here but is employed in other passages of the work):

freie Tonhöhen	Cluster ≙ weiße Tasten	Kreuzglissando	beliebig oft wiederholen
free tone pitch	cluster white	cross-staff glissando	repeat as often as wished

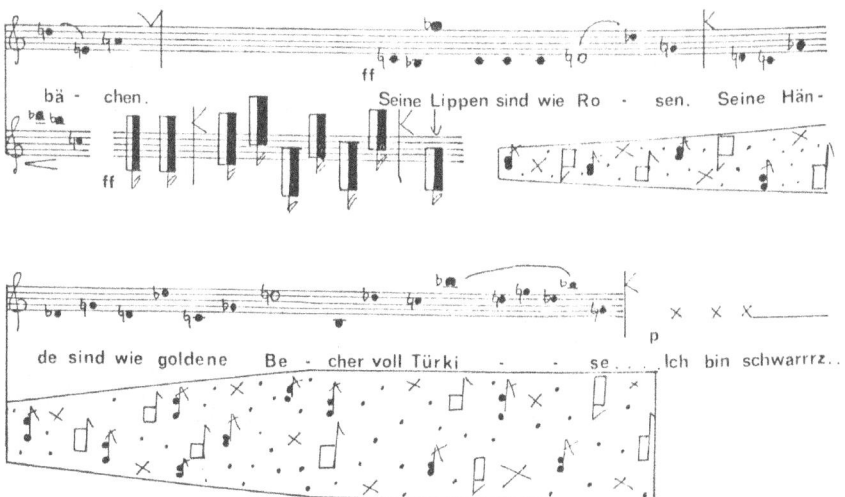

Figure 5: Movement IV, end of the first and beginning of the second notation system (Salbert, *Schwarz*, 8). Musikverlag Zimmermann. With kind permission of SCHOTT MUSIC, Mainz.

the soprano, corresponding to "in the name of the Father and the Son and the Holy Spirit") immersing the sinful black bride in the threefold life of the crucified love and thereby letting her become pure and white.[42] This reading would underline the fact that the graphic notation in this framing by the vibraphone is not to be repeated here as often as desired—and that in turn would be an allusion to the administering of baptism only once (cf. Eph 4:5). In this proposed spiritual interpretation, the bride's response to baptism would then be a new existence in Christ, in which her blackness has become cruciform in living out her faith in the triune God. In Romanesque church architecture, after baptism by immersion was no longer practiced, the "baptismal font" began to be formed "in the shape of a hollowed-out cylinder, but the font soon took on the form of a cup"[43] that might be made of stone or ore.

If we assume that Salbert's setting of the Song of Songs, like his composition on Job, also finds the depths of what it truly wants to say only in the compenetration of the secular and the spiritual,[44] then his composition has found a way to reconcile

---

[42] Thus, Salbert provides another example of an allegorical interpretation of Song 1:5, with the interpretation of black as sinful and white as redeemed by Christ. Origen's interpretation was widely received in German Protestantism, as is obvious, for example, in poem 4 of Gustav Jahn's poem collection *Das Hohelied: In Liedern* (see Jahn, *Das Hohelied*, 17–21).

[43] Wimmer, *Anleitung*, 82 (original in German).

[44] See Fromme, *Hiob-Rezeption*, 345. In Salbert's *Hiob* we find the biblical text interwoven with trivial components, giving the piece a parodistic touch and motivating recipients to their own reflections on the political background, as Fromme notes (ibid., 343).

the Antiochene literal reading of Song 1:5 (Theodore of Mopsuestia) with the Alexandrian spiritual reading (Origen). Externally, the arrangement of the text relates a love story that leads from the single woman's self-consideration as black but beautiful (in movement I) to her togetherness with the beloved, who is described as white and red, and culminating in the moment of self-acceptance, "I am black," as he pours out cups of turquoises as a metaphorical epitome of the act of love (in movement IV). In Salbert's text selection, the bride does not become white, but she is embraced with the wealth of love by the one who is white and red. And the cup, an element not found in the biblical text but whose form is noted graphically, seems to be a key element of the interpretation.

The eucharistic interpretation could not be verified in the music. Instead, I have examined the possibility of a soteriological-baptismal interpretation, for it is only after the cup full of turquoises has been poured out over the bride by the hands of the bridegroom that her blackness is set free in the music from the monotony of the lower B (vibraphone) in the dissonance with the lower B flat (soprano) and is brought with three cross-staff glissandi into the broad space of the love of the triune God. The graphical notation evokes patristic reminiscences: it seems to indicate that the black and formerly dissonant sound of the bride has become white and sonorous through baptism. Indeed, Salbert's music is "challenging intellectually" and "supporting emotionally—in the sense of a new humaneness in music."[45]

Bibliography

Benz, Ernst. "'Ich bin schwarz und schön' (Hohes Lied 1,5): Ein Beitrag des Origenes zur Theologie der negritudo." In *Wort und Religion: Kalima na Dini; Studien zur Afrikanistik, Missionswissenschaft, Religionswissenschaft; Ernst Damann zum 65. Geburtstag*, edited by Hans-Jürgen Greschat and Herrmann Jungraithmayr, 225–242. Stuttgart: Evangelischer Missionsverlag, 1969.

Die Bibel oder die ganze Heilige Schrift des Alten und Neuen Testaments nach der deutschen Übersetzung Martin Luthers. Stuttgart: Württembergische Bibelanstalt, 1968.

Facundus d'Hermiane. *Défense des Trois Chapitres (A Justinien)*, edited by J.-M. Clément and R. Vander Plaetse and translated by Anne Fraïsse-Bétoulières. Vol. 3. SC 478. Paris: Le Cerf, 2004.

Fromme, Daniel. *Die Hiob-Rezeption in der Musik des 20. Jahrhunderts: Zur Musikalisierung des Leidens*. Musik und Religion—Religion und Musik 3. Berlin: LIT-Verlag, 2016.

Hastetter, Michaela C. *"Horch! Mein Geliebter!" Die Wiederentdeckung der geistlichen Schriftauslegung in den Hoheliedvertonungen des 20. Jahrhunderts*. MThS.S 69. St. Ottilien: EOS Verlag, 2006.

Jahn, Gustav. *Das Hohelied: In Liedern*. Zweite Gesammtausgabe. Halle: Verlag von Richard Mühlmann, 1848.

---

45 Salbert, "Zitat" (original in German).

Lubac, Henri de. *Histoire et Esprit: L'intelligence de l'Écriture d'après Origène*. Theol(P) 16. Paris: Aubier, 1950.

Marquardt, Joachim. *Das Privatleben der Römer: Erster Theil*. Handbuch der Römischen Alterthümer 7. Roma: Verlag von S. Hizel, 1897.

Mansi, Johannes D. *Sacrorum Conciliorum nova et amplissima Collectio*. Vol. 9. Florence: Zatta, 1763.

Origenes. *Die Homilien und Fragmente zum Hohelied*, translated and edited by Alfons Fürst and Holger Strutwolf. Orig.WD 9/2. Berlin: de Gruyter, 2016.

Origen. *The Song of Songs: Commentary and Homilies*, edited and translated by R. P. Lawson. ACW 26. Westminster, MD: Newman Press, 1957.

Pelletier, Anne-Marie. *Lectures du Cantique des Cantiques: De l'énigme du sens aux figures du lecteur*. AnBib 121. Rome: Editrice Pontificio Istituto Biblico, 1989.

Reichert, Klaus, trans. *Das Hohelied Salomos: Zweisprachige Ausgabe*. Salzburg: Deutscher Taschenbuchverlag, 1996.

Reiser, Marius. *Bibelkritik und Auslegung der Heiligen Schrift: Beiträge zur Geschichte der biblischen Exegese und Hermeneutik*. Tübingen: Mohr Siebeck, 2007.

Salbert, Dieter. *Schwarz—wie die Teppiche Salomos*. Frankfurt am Main: Musikverlag Wilhelm Zimmermann, 1972.

Salbert, Dieter. "Zitat." Über den Komponisten Dieter Salbert. Musikverlag Zahoransky. Accessed April 9, 2021. https://musikverlag-zahoransky.de/dieter-salbert.

Theodore of Mopsuestia. *In Canticum Canticorum*. PG 66:699–700. Paris: J.-P. Migne, 1864.

Theodore of Mopsuestia. "In Opposition to the Allegorists." In *Theodore of Mopsuestia*, edited by Frederick G. McLeod, 75–79. ECF. London: Routledge, 2009.

Wimmer, Florian. *Anleitung zur Erforschung und Beschreibung der kirchlichen Kunstdenkmäler*, edited by Linzer Diözesan-Kunstverein. Linz: Joseph Feichtinger's Erben, 1863.

Ute Jung-Kaiser
"I Am Black *and* Comely"
Literal and/or Allegorical Interpretations in Theology, Music, and Image, Especially in the Present Time

שְׁחוֹרָה אֲנִי וְנָאוָה—the Hebrew statement from Song 1:5 is translated differently: the conjunction *and* appears in the Septuagint, the homilies of Origen, and many other translations. The replacement of the additive *and* with the limiting *but* is the result of early biblical exegetes who, despite the Greek's clear *melaina eimi (ego) kai kale*, chose *sed* instead of the additive *et* in the Latin translation: *Nigra sum* sed *formosa*.[1] On the one hand, the contrasting translation of the conjunction could signal racist prejudice ("ein rassistisches Vorurteil").[2] On the other hand, exegetes might "equate the aesthetic quality black with the ethical quality *bad* or *evil*,"[3] as did certain medieval interpreters. And as Ernst Benz pleads, we should not forget that *nigra* = *black* only appears in old-church medieval versions; the original text of the Vulgate reads not *nigra sum* but *fusca sum, sed pulchra*. *Fusca* is not specifically black but dark, tanned, blackish. This difference explains two theories: the lover is either "a real Ethiopian, a black woman who apologizes from the first word"—hence the limiting *but*—or "a Jewish girl who was tanned by the sun because she was forced by her siblings to look after the vineyards."[4]

The cultural-political significance of the appreciation of beauty in connection with the foreign/black/sacred is reflected in the way of how Song 1:5 is interpreted throughout the ages. There is no doubt that artistic works that adhere to the *and* are able to give greater weight to the immanent erotic tension between physical and culturally specific otherness and beauty (which is justified by it) than do those that obey the limiting *but*, because they let the incandescent synthesis between being "black" and being "great," which enhances this unique peculiarity, emerge all the more brilliantly. In view of the current debate on racism, which calls for social correction or reorientation toward people of different skin color, the discussion of this topic in the Song of Songs is particularly relevant.

---

1 See Mielke, *Nigra sum et formosa*, 79.
2 See Mielke, *Nigra sum et formosa*, 79.
3 Mielke, *Nigra sum et formosa*, 72. Following the editor's request, most of the foreign-language quotations have been translated into English.
4 Benz, "Ich bin schwarz und schön," 227.

Many modern musical and artistic interpretations of *nigra sum* are historically rooted; their vocabulary is based on either literal or allegorical guidelines, used unreflectively or purposefully. The nearly unmanageable variety of interpretations justifies the three-part conception of the present study: The first part presents a selection of significant cultural and religio-historical interpretations from past to present, which reveal thematic variations on being black. Two comparative aspects best illuminate this broad spectrum of interpretations: first, recourse to oriental cultures, which enables historical verification; and second, mystical interpretation of the color black in the Christian Middle Ages. The second part is devoted to settings in the twentieth and twenty-first centuries, which thematize and sound out the self-portrayal of the bride. The third part, finally, explains and reproduces a selection of fascinating visual representations.

The artistic images of the entire contribution—with the exceptions of the African film and the English novella—articulate less a plea that Black Lives Matter than that differences in the interpretation of *nigra* still exist today.

1 I Am Black: Interpretations in History and the Present

Figure 1: Advertising page from *La Noire de* . . . (1966), starring Mbissine Thérèse Diop.

The leading actress in the 1966 film *La Noire de* . . . (see Figure 1), Mbissine Thérèse Diop, is truly "black *and* beautiful."[5] She plays an African nanny who is taken by a French couple to Antibes; in the absence of French language skills, lonely and desperate, she kills herself, "using her own body, the only available weapon in the racist struggle."[6] An original African contribution, this documentary by Senegalese director Ousmane Sembène (1923–2007) was the subject of a retrospective at Locarno's 2019 film festival. The title of the retrospective, "Black Light," functioned as a program,[7] "a signum for exclusion and discrimination." But "Black Light" also refers to the "light at one end of the visible light scale that fluoresces some substances" and thus makes "something previously invisible recognizable" ("etwas vorher Unsichtbares erkennbar").[8]

Bivalent tributes to beautiful and beguiling African women can be found in the Bible as well, for example "Hagar, the Egyptian slave of Sarah, the seductive wife of the Egyptian Potiphar, and the most famous of all African women—if indeed she was an African woman—in the Bible in the view of the Middle Ages, the Queen of Sheba, and other African lovers of Solomon."[9] Another famous example is the Queen of Sheba. According the biblical account, she traveled to Jerusalem to visit King Solomon and to experience his much-vaunted wisdom (1Kgs 10), an encounter that the Ethiopian church considers a historical truth. Since in the Ethiopan church the queen bears the name Makeda, Andreas Mielke has posed the question whether she might be the Shulamit of the Song of Songs (= Makeda).[10] At the same time, Mielke notes that in the following text, 1Kgs 11, "immediately after the visit of the Queen of Sheba [. . .], Solomon [is reprimanded] for his 'lust for flesh,' which does not shy away from pagan women, including a daughter of the Egyptian pharaoh."[11] It is this bivalence that reveals why one of the illustrations in Hans Vintler's *Die Pluemen der Tugent* shows King Solomon in a compromising situation.

The severely damaged manuscript, which was probably created in Tyrol around 1411, was illustrated with sparingly colored pen and ink drawings. Accord-

---

[5] For the film and plot, see "La noire de—Ousmane Sembène—(1966) [Legendado em português]," https://youtu.be/YMDg2UAyXSs.
[6] Lueken, "Unübersehbare Unsichtbarkeiten," 9. See also Hug, "Vom alltäglichen Leben des Volkes," notably 90–95.
[7] Advertising text for the retrospective read, "The Locarno72 Retrospective intends to go beyond the concept of Black as identity or social issue to explore the imagery used by filmmakers who have tackled this question—historical and political—at different times and in different places"; Slater-Williams, "Locarno Film Festival 2019."
[8] Lueken, "Unübersehbare Unsichtbarkeiten," 9.
[9] Mielke, *Nigra sum et formosa*, 76.
[10] See Mielke, *Nigra sum et formosa*, 78.
[11] Mielke, *Nigra sum et formosa*, 79.

ing to commentators, the first part, including the ninth sheet (see Figure 2), is conceived differently than are those of the main part: its figures "are larger, rendered in immediate close view, drawn much more carefully in detail," although the proportions of heads and hands, which are too large, seem "a bit inconsistent." Striking are the "body-hugged," emphasizing the female breast, "the more voluminous, angular design."[12] The ninth sheet shows King Solomon in a reprehensible situation, following a dark-skinned woman who is worshipping an idol.[13] Since the black heathen woman is crowned like Solomon, only the Queen of Sheba can be meant.

Figure 2: Hans Vintler, *Die Pluemen der Tugent* (Tyrol? 1411). Colored pen drawing, manuscript. Innsbruck, Ferdinandeum, Dip., 877,9ʳ: "Solomon and Pagan (Queen of Sheba) Pray at the Idol Column." Österreichische Nationalbibliothek. See Frühmorgen-Voss et al., *Katalog der deutschsprachigen illustrierten Handschriften*, table 170.

---

12 Frühmorgen-Voss et al., *Katalog der deutschsprachigen illustrierten Handschriften*, 338–339.
13 According to Mielke, *Nigra sum et formosa*, 16.

The inscriptio, written in Gothic italics in the Bavarian-Austrian dialect, explains Solomon's denial of God in following the custom ("Sitte") and faith of the black pagan:

> Man vindt doch in der alten schrift, /
> so Salomon den tempel stift, /
> das in zwang ain schwarze haid[en]in. /
> Durch der selben willen verlos er sein sin, /
> das er gotes verlaugent [verleugnet] damit, /
> wenn er pett [/betet] di abgötter an nach irem sit [Sitte].[14]

This interpretation of the Ethiopian queen as a seductress could also be based on an old Jewish interpretation of the Song of Songs. According to Gerhard Maier, "the Targum relates the blackness to Israel, the apostasy of Israel, when they made the golden calf,"[15] and Pinchas Lapide confirms: "For Rashi, the greatest interpreter of the Middle Ages, this points to a statement by Israel that although it was tainted by the sin of the golden calf, it made up for it by accepting the Torah at Sinai."[16]

Likewise, the early Christian writer Origen (ca. 185–254) sees in the black bride "the church gathered from among the Gentiles" (*ecclesiae personam tenet ex gentibus congregatae*)[17]; he also makes Jewish references, but he turns them in a completely different direction: in his view, the daughters of Jerusalem, who despise the bride, represent "the synagogue, the Judaism, which sees its primacy over the gentiles in the election of the Fathers but is hostile to the Gospel."[18] The latter consider themselves genealogically superior to the pagan or the black bride as a representative of the "church gathered among the Gentiles." From an ecclesiological point of view, this levels the imbalance between the pagan church and the synagogue.[19] According to Origen, the Bride answers the Daughters of Jerusalem:

> I am indeed black, O daughters of Jerusalem, in that I cannot claim descent from famous men, neither have I received the enlightenment of Moses' Law. But I have my own beauty, all the same. For I me too there is that primal thing, the Image of God wherein I was created.[20] (Gen 1:27)

---

14 The passage reproduced here is the passage within the chapter "Von der lieb Karitas," 27–28 (vv. 818–828). A faithful textual transmission with detailed commentary can be found by von Zingerle.
15 Maier, *Das Hohelied*, 43.
16 Lapide, *Das Hohelied der Liebe*, 27.
17 Origen, *Commentarius in Canticum (Comm. Cant.)* II 1,3 (Fürst and Strutwolf, eds., 176; Lawson, trans., 92).
18 Benz, „Ich bin schwarz und schön," 229, summarizing Origen, *Comm. Cant.* II 1,3.
19 See Benz, "Ich bin schwarz und schön," 228.
20 Origenes, *Comm. Cant.* II 1,4 (Fürst and Strutwolf, eds., 178; Lawson, trans., 92). See Benz, "Ich bin schwarz und schön," 229.

This self-understanding also legitimizes the *and* in Origen's translation: "blackness" is not a contrast to but a part of beauty. According to Origen, the "church that comes of the Gentiles" (*ecclesia, quae ex gentibus uenit*),[21] which includes the most remote peoples on earth, also includes the Queen of Sheba, "who came from the ends of the earth."[22] If Solomon is considered a representative of Christ, then the Queen of Sheba stands for the church of pagans.

The depiction of the visit of the Queen of Sheba to Solomon in the so-called Verdun Altar (completed in 1181) also follows this interpretation (see Figure 3). The theologian Wernher († 1195), provost of the Klosterneuburg monastery, meticulously thought out the piece, which consists of many enameled panels, and commissioned it from the goldsmith Nikolaus (born in Verdun) for his monastery, which is near Vienna. The work's conception and its dedicatory inscription illuminate its didactic intention, according to which the New Testament is explained by the Old: The typology consistently implemented here "is a mode of interpretation that explains the New Testament through the Old, in that it depicts the exemplary nature of Old Testament people, actions, events, and institutions."[23]

The plaque depicting the visit of the Queen of Sheba to the wise King Solomon, as well as those of Abraham and the priest-king Melchizedek, address the desire of man for the highest knowledge and spiritual truth. As such, they illustrate analogous events in the New Testament, as when the three kings pay their respects to the holy child Jesus. Astonishingly, the artist shows a queen whose physiognomy seems quite European, though her skin is black, whereas her light-skinned companions have African facial features. The subscription and circumscription read:

> *Regina Saba. Misticat in donis regina fidem salemonis.*
>
> The Queen of Sheba. In the gifts, the Queen mysteriously hints at faith in Solomon.

At the top left is also shown "the virtue Misericordia (compassion), on the right Timor (fear, in this context meaning the fear of God), both of which fit well with offering gifts, and worship."[24]

---

[21] Origen, *Comm. Cant.* II 1,8 (Fürst and Strutwolf, eds., 178; Lawson, trans., 93).
[22] Origen, *Comm. Cant.* II 1,10 (Fürst and Strutwolf, eds., 180; Lawson, trans., 95). See Benz, "Ich bin schwarz und schön," 235.
[23] Röhrig, *Der Verduner Altar*, 49. See also ibid., 25–27, 55–56.
[24] Röhrig, *Der Verduner Altar*, 66.

Figure 3: Nicholas of Verdun, "Queen of Sheba with Solomon" (1181). Altar in Klosterneuburg, near Vienna. Floridus Röhrig, 65–66, Abb. 13: III/4. Cf. Hans-Joachim Kunst, *The African in European Art*, Bad Godesberg 1967, table 2.

Hans-Joachim Kunst, whose comments on the illustration are based on the studies of Floridus Röhrig, makes the following observation:

> This altarpiece was originally intended as panelling for a pulpit [. . .]. The enamel plates are arranged in such a way that the middle row contains scenes from the life of Christ in chronological order, and juxtaposed to each of these are two scenes from the Old Testament which prefigure it. This scene, the Queen of Sheba visiting King Solomon, and one depicting the meeting between Melchizedek and Abraham, are juxtaposed to the Adoration of the Magi. Scenes of the Old Testament are seen as prefigurations of those in the New. [. . .] On the Klosterneuburg enamel plate, the queen [. . .] is depicted as having a dark face. Her features, however, in accordance with the canons of classical antiquity, are of a European cast. Her followers, who are offering gifts in open caskets, have fair complexions; but it is noteworthy that the one who is standing has a widely arched forehead and short curly hair, the one who is kneeling has thick lips and a broad nose—all signs which mark them, if not as Africans, at

least as men of another race and above all as servants or slaves. How is this to be explained? [. . .] The classical European features made it clear to the observer that she was the wise king's equal.[25]

The Austrian composer Konrad Stekl (1901–1979) titled his hymnarium in three parts[26] *Der Verduner Altar*, op. 58 (1963), inspired by the piece's breathtaking beauty.[27] The editors of the published choral and piano score note:

> The impetus for the composition for [him] was the overwhelming sight of the magnificent altar of the monastery at Klosterneuburg. [. . .] Neuma[28] found in the Klosterneuburg abbey library are processed with all-interval scales into this modern choral work.[29]

The medieval veneration of the Queen of Sheba is reflected in a particularly attractive way in the military manual *Bellifortis* (originally 1402–1405, but with later revisions) by Conrad Kyeser, a major work of the Prague School of Illumination. The richly illustrated parchment primarily describes the martial arts around the turn of the fifteenth century. A sheet in the work's supplements shows the Queen of Sheba (see Figure 4). The full-page "costume design, with a haute and very modern-looking, slim elegance but with a very 'Gothic' posture,"[30] is signed with a six-line caption, whose first words are clearly oriented toward the Song of Songs (Song 1:5):

> *Sum regina Sabba, clarior ceteris et venusta.*
> *Pulchra sum et casta stat speculum picture sculptum.*

> I am the queen of Sheba, graceful and more famous than anyone else.
> I am beautiful and chaste, here is my picture, created by the artist.

This depiction makes the acceptance of the black and the cultic worship of black madonnas in the Middle Ages truly comprehensible. According to Mielke, "paradoxically, the encounter with the stranger (the Other) appears to be less [. . .] problematic in the Middle Ages [. . .], because the foreign was immediately adjacent and the unknown was very obvious and thus self-evident and almost commonplace."[31] But there, too, the tension between ethics and aesthetics is evident:

---

25 Kunst, *African in European Art*, 10–11. See also Kleinert, *Das Rätsel der Königin*; Damm, *Die Königin von Saba*.
26 Literally: "Ante Legem," "Sub Legem," "Sub Gratia."
27 See Stekl, *Der Verduner Altar*. See especially the piano score "Dialogue Saba and Salomo," 106–121. I do not know whether a recording of the piece exists.
28 Neuma are the first attempts to fix melodies in writing, they are only figurative gestures to indicate the melodic directional lines.
29 Opening comment by Wolfgang Suppan and Arthur Michl in Stekl, *Der Verduner Altar*.
30 Kyeser, *Bellifortis*, 90.
31 Mielke, *Nigra sum et formosa*, 11.

Figure 4: Conrad Kyeser, *The Queen of Sheba*. From the manuscript *Bellifortis*. Niedersächsische Staats- und Universitätsbibliothek Göttingen, 2 Cod. Ms. Philos. 63, Cim., fol. 122r. 24 x 32 cm.

The problem is old and gains importance for Middle High German literature, especially because of the contrast between biblical interpretation and secular literature. It is less the biblical exegetes, who struggled with "nigra sum, sed formosa," than the poets, who apparently granted the African women "nigra sum et formosa," who are interesting from a literary-historical point of view, especially with regard to discrimination against black Africans in later centuries.[32]

---

[32] Mielke, *Nigra sum et formosa*, 13.

Negative interpretations of black skin color in the Middle Ages are based on different sources, as Mielke points out:

> In biblical exegesis, Africans are understood either as descendants of Cain (blackness as Cain's mark) or as descendants of Noah's son Ham (blackness as curse). Rarely do quotations appear in a direct relationship to only one source; and indeed, since the beginning of Christian literature, biblical and ancient judgments and prejudices have flowed into each other not only once but again and again, in stereotypical form or in individual variation.[33]

This bivalence is latently perceptible and continues to this day. A significant example is the short story *The Black Madonna* (1958) by Muriel Spark (1918–2006).[34] It tells the story of Lou and Raymond, a childless couple living in a small town. Despite donations, social care, and helpfulness, Lou's desire to have children remains unfulfilled. When a black wooden statue of the madonna is given to the church, public worship booms. Lou venerates the black madonna, too, and pleads for its blessing, finally getting pregnant. But the child she gives birth to is black, and the drama takes its course: the child's skin color evokes social ostracism. Here, the ingenious conclusion proves that the radiance of the black madonna can be regarded as an alibi for antiracism.

The fusion of the madonna and the female lover of the Song of Songs seems to have been unproblematic to some medieval commentators. As early as the twelfth century, Rupert von Deutz and Honorius Augustodenensis provided the first mariological explanations of Mary as *sponsa* and *mater Dei*. Correspondences between Mary and the Song's bride appear on (anonymous) wooden printing boards from the fifteenth century (see Figure 5). Otto Clemen republished these in 1910 and provided them with helpful commentary. In his assessment, these are "primitive art":

> [The plants are] arbitrarily distributed over the soil. [. . .] The fact that the artist did not take nature as a model can also be seen from the strangely biased and non-free way in which he drew the rocks and ground elevations [. . .]. The figures are also removed from reality, they are ethereal, one might say: angelic-sexless (with the exception of the couple in picture 10b and the knights). Nevertheless, some positions and gestures are poignantly expressive. And the cycle of images as a whole is so imbued with innocence, tenderness and intimacy of feeling that it still captures the viewer, who lovingly sinks into the content.[35]

Even the banners on which the individual verses of the Song of Songs were displayed illustrate the exposed position of the bride. The scene on page x, which Otto Clemen helpfully describes and interprets, is impressive:

---

33 Mielke, *Nigra sum et formosa*, 72.
34 See Spark, *Black Madonna*, 34–51.
35 Clemen, *Canticum canticorum*, ix.

1b. In the middle, the bride travels as *Orans*[36] surrounded by rays, to the sky. [This is how the Assumption of Mary is always represented.] The words are put in her mouth: *Nigra sum, sed formosa, filie iherusalem, sicut tabernaculum cedar, sicut pellis salomonis* (1:4). [Rupert von Deutz explains this passage: "I'm black! Calls the bride. Because she was invented pregnant, she was initially despised in Joseph's and the relatives' eyes. But I am lovely! So she calls in view of her uninjured virginity.] The daughters of Jerusalem stammer adoringly: *Caput tuum ut carmelus, collum tuum sicut turris eburnea* [Song 7:5].[37]

The daughters of Jerusalem, who enrich the scenes on this and many other panels, act as witnesses and react via speech (in banners), comparable to the chorus in ancient tragedy. The bride is exalted as the bride of Christ, crowned and ascending to heaven. This scene is reminiscent of the *dealbata* scene of the loving soul (see below), who is elevated to the status of God's queen after her marriage to Christ.[38]

Figure 5: Woodblock printing (before 1465), anonymous. Scene with the bride as queen of heaven. Clemen, *Canticum canticorum*, x.

---

36 The Latin term denotes a figure found in early Christian art depicting an ancient prayer position, with arms raised and palms turned up.
37 Clemen, *Canticum canticorum*, x (and see n. 12).
38 See Clemen, *Canticum canticorum*, ix n. 10.

Blackness is no longer an issue; it is hidden in this early image, as it is in many recent examples.

1.1 First Comparative Aspect: Oriental Points of View

Hans-Peter Müller has tried to demonstrate how strongly the language of the Song of Songs is descriptive and opaquely "analogous" at the same time. In the double comparison "black as [. . .]" he sees the logical relationship between elements of the comparison expressly determined as an analogy:

> The combination of "primum comparationis" and "secundum comparationis" becomes stringent by explicitly naming a "tertium comparationis." [. . . If] the juxtaposition of the metaphorical and the material use of the metaphor "vineyard" [in the following stanza (1:6; cf. also 2:5 and 8:11–12) as "substitutive for the woman's body"] gives the girls in 1:6 the possibility of a careless suggestion, [. . . then basically] the shepherd's travesty (1:7–8) is to be thought of as a natural religious flight from civilization.[39]

When the bride explains, "my mother's children were angry with me; they made me the keeper of the vineyards; but my own vineyard I have not kept," she chooses the vineyard metaphor, which is related to the garden metaphor. The vineyard in 1:6 is both a literal reference and a "metaphor for beauty and physical stimuli."[40]

> [Even in the ancient Egyptian love poem, the] literary topos of [the beautiful girl as] "guardian of the vineyards" creates a wishful situation that allows the poet to "make the girl visible with new, unconventional traits" (Gerleman), i.e., to sing her real beauty—in love—triumphantly, through the contrast to the unloved "daughters of Jerusalem."[41]

Blackness, which in a figurative sense allows for the consideration of human weakness, can positively absorb allegorical interpretation. A beautiful proof appears in the postbiblical Hebrew poetry and illustrations of the medieval *Machsor Lipsiae*, the Jewish prayer book for the annual festivals. This manuscript, unquestionably the most precious of the University of Leipzig's library collection, addresses the willingness of God to forgive the repentant sinner[42] and to marry his people. It also depicts Israel as the bride of God:

---

39 Müller, *Vergleich und Metapher*, 14, 47; see also 29, 46.
40 Schreiner, ed., *Das Lied der Lieder*, 97.
41 Krinetzki, *Kommentar zum Hohenlied*, 71.
42 See the thirty-two illustrated pages from the *Machsor Lipsiae* in Schreiner, ed., *Das Lied der Lieder*, 107: "Im Tympanon des Tores ist ein Hirschbock zu sehen, der hier die Bereitschaft Gottes, dem reuigen Sünder zu verzeihen, andeuten soll." ("In the tympanum of the gate a deer buck can be seen, which indicates here the willingness of God to forgive the repentant sinner.")

The bride (with golden crown) and groom (with Jewish hat), sitting above the initial word under the arch with clover leaves, symbolize the community of Israel as the bride of God. According to another interpretation, the bridegroom is Israel and the bride is the Torah.[43]

The bride's blackness is illustrated first by the black goat-hair tents of a nomadic tribe in the Syro-Arabian desert and second by reference to the magnificent carpets/curtains inside Solomon's palace.

> I am black, [and] but comely, O ye daughters of Jerusalem, as the tents of Kedar, as the curtains of Solomon. (Song 1:5)

Even Origen acknowledged the "furs of Solomon" as an allusion to the black skins with which the tabernacle was covered (Exod 26:7–13):

> [. . .] if the Bride compares her beauty to the curtains of Solomon, she doubtless means the glory and beauty of those curtains which cover the tabernacle, which God hath pitched, and not man.[44]

Gerhard Maier also points out the identical words used for the "tent blankets" and the ceilings of the tabernacle (Exod 26:1–4; 36:8–20; Num 4:25), thus emphasizing the special nature of the comparison, which raises questions of religious history.[45] The Hebrew Bible scholar Othmar Keel asks (and answers) this question in a convincing manner. He even considers the "combination of the barren, exotic, frightening world of the Kedarenes with the equally exotic fascinating luxury of Solomon" to be an unusual qualification, because he interprets "the blackness of the speaker as terrible and fascinating at the same time, as mysteriously different." This is justified on the one hand by a Hittite ritual, "which regulated the relocation of the 'Black Goddess' from one temple to another," and on the other hand by the wife of Ahmose, the founder of the Eighteenth Dynasty of Egypt: Ahmose and his wife, "after their deaths, [became] the patron saints of the vast Theban necropolis. [. . .] Their blackness has] signals belonging to the realm of the very other, the divine. It is not the mortal Ahmes Nefertari, but a goddess, black as ebony"[46] (see Figure 6).

---

43 Schreiner, ed., *Das Lied der Lieder*, 105.
44 Origen, *Comm. Cant.* II 1,54 (Fürst and Strutwolf, eds., 198; Lawson, trans., 105). See also Benz, "Ich bin schwarz und schön," 229.
45 See Maier, *Das Hohelied*, 40–41.
46 Keel, *Das Hohelied*, 53–55.

Figure 6: Mural from an unknown Theban tomb, fourteenth/thirteenth century BCE. Drawing by Hildi Keel-Leu (reproduced here side by side) based on a photo of a representation of the deified queen Ahmose-Nefertari, New Kingdom, Twentieth Dynasty, 1152–1145 BD, from Thebes, Inherkau's tomb TT 359, at Deir el-Medina. Painted plaster. Inv.-No ÄM 2060. Photo by Lenka Peycock, Neues Museum Berlin, 2011. See Lhote, *Les chefs-d'œuvre de la peinture égyptienne*, 113.

On her head [Ahmose-Nefertari] wears the vulture head-dress of the goddess Mut, consort of the god Amun of Thebes, surmounted by a sun-disc and ostrich plumes. The cobra on her crown and the flail in her hand indicate her royal status. The lotus blossom was often held by deceased women, thought to be representing rebirth. The black colour of Ahmose-Nefertari's skin does not reflect her true coloration, but may symbolise regeneration.[47]

In addition to Keel, Klaus Reichert,[48] Martin Buber, Franz Rosenzweig,[49] and many others have taken over the self-confident depiction of the shepherdess as "black *and* beautiful." Joan B. Burton even draws a comparison with Theocritus's *Idyll*:

> Similarly, in Theocritus Idyll 10, the lovelorn reaper expresses admiration for a dark-complexioned woman (26–29):
>
> "Charming Bombyca, all call you the Syrian, lean and sun-scorched, and I alone, honey hued. Dark is the violet and the lettered hyacinth, yet in garlands these are accounted first."[50]

1.2 Second Comparative Aspect: Mystical Points of View

Origen proposed a mystical interpretation of the origin of black by interrelating two verses from the Song of Songs. First, he reads the defense of the bride against the daughters of Jerusalem in Song 1:6 ("Look not upon me, because I am black, because the sun hath looked upon me") as meaning that she was only *ex accidentibus* black. Rufinus (345–ca. 410) wrote, *Sol despexit me* ("the sun despised me"). The "blackness of the body," reinforced by sunlight, has nothing to do with the "blackness of the soul." Benz speaks of "a mysterious process of becoming black and white, whose 'mystery' Origen wants to reveal."[51] In order to legitimize his "unusually bold exegesis,"[52] According to Benz, Origen links two verses of the Song of Songs: first, the bride's apology in response to the mockery of the daughters of Jerusalem (see Song 1:6), and second, Song 8:5, which is based on the Latin translation by Rufinus: *Quae est illa quae ascendit* dealbata, *incumbens super fraternum suum?* ("Who is she that cometh up *dealbata* [become white], leaning on her brother?"; cf. KJV: "Who is this that cometh up from the wilderness, leaning upon her beloved?").

> This mental blackness is acquired not by birth but by omission. [. . .]. He who lazily turns away from the sun of righteousness becomes black; he who exposes himself to the sunbeam of justice is illuminated.[53]

---

47 Temple of Amenhotep I, http://www.deirelmedina.com/lenka/TempleAmenhotep.html.
48 See Reichert, *Das Hohelied Salomonis*, 17.
49 See Berlinghof, "Epilogue," v.
50 Burton, "Themes of Female Desire," 197.
51 Benz, "Ich bin schwarz und schön," 239.
52 Benz, "Ich bin schwarz und schön," 240.
53 Benz, "Ich bin schwarz und schön," 240, summarizing *Comm. Cant.* II 2,4 (Fürst and Strutwolf, eds., 200; Lawson, trans., 107).

So it is about the virtue of the Christian who struggles for his salvation. This legitimizes the reference to the] second verse (Song 8:5), see above. The people of Israel have not believed, but the black pagan, the church of the gentiles, has been irradiated by the light of the sun of righteousness.

> It is only through this ecclesiological interpretation that Origen transfers his "mystical" interpretation of the black bride to the individual soul, and here the black color is related to the state of sins. [. . . It is] basically a symbol of the state of the Christian par excellence. What Luther calls "simul iustus atque peccator," Origen calls "simul formosa atque nigra."[54]

This interpretation is echoed in certain *minnesongs* (songs of courtly love), especially the mystical poem *Christus und die minnende Seele* ("Christ and the Minning Soul"), in which the soul becomes worthy of its marriage to Christ only after a brutal purification process—*dealbata* (becoming white), as Rufinus commented.

2 Contemporary Settings

Not all the settings of the Song of Songs respect those verses that deal with the self-expression of the bride. They are not found in Krzysztof Penderecki's *Canticum Canticorum Salomonis* (1973), in Hermann Zilcher's free fantasy variations *Aus dem Hohelied Salomonis* (1918, op. 38), nor in Wilhelm Weismann's concerto *Sulamith* (1975), although the question-and-answer play between solo soprano, choir, and orchestra celebrated there (following the Vulgate, *Qualis est dilectus tuus*) would have legitimized such a reference. Helmut Bornefeld's *Canticum Canticorum* (1970) overwrites the second movement with "Schwarz bin und anmutig ich" ("Black and graceful I am") but leaves it—textless—to the duo of organ and drums, and Henning Frederichs, who also preferred an instrumental duo between oboe d'amore and organ for his *Shir ha-Shirim* (1998), spares said verses; the soloist has to breathe the selected passages into his instrument, which deliberately obscures the understanding of the same.

Hans Zender (1936–2019) composed his full-length work *Shir Hashirim* between 1992 and 1996. He chose an impressive cast: a large symphony orchestra, choir, and live electronics. His music seems irritating at times, since his microtonal, chromatically designed harmony works with unusual frequency mixtures: "the composition preceded Zender's preoccupation with chaos theory."[55] By choosing the Hebrew

---

54 Benz, "Ich bin schwarz und schön," 241, alluding to *Comm. Cant.* II 2,20 (Fürst and Strutwolf, eds., 208; Lawson, trans., 113).
55 Isabel Mundry, introduction to Zender, *Shir Hashirim*, 8.

title and giving an original translation of the Hebrew text into German, he locates his composition in the allegorical context of Judaism, which is also confirmed in the recording's notes: "It is a timeless allegory of the relationship between HaShem ('God') and the people of Israel, in terms of the love between a man and a woman."[56]

Each of the two protagonists is represented by a solo voice with accompanying instrument, chosen according to who is singing: (soft) flute accompanies the bride, (powerful) trombone the groom. The sung text allows the soprano to have a dialogical "conversation" with the solo flute.

In his oratorio *Canticum canticorum* (1900), Enrico Bossi (1861–1925) tried to establish the connection to the Jewish sources by assigning the bride a Hebrew chant and the chorale *Ecce panis angelorum*, based on the Gregorian sequence *Lauda Sion*, sung to the bridegroom (Christ). The orchestra opens the bride's solo with three motif sequences that anticipate the singer's insecurity. She adopts this questioning gesture, perhaps suffering and depressive, but this turns to certainty with the statement *sed formosa*, which is transfigured into a brightly shining C-major triad via a dominant climax.

> *Nigra sum, sed Formosa.* What an end, what true sentiment in this song of the bride! [. . .] The composer had a happy idea in various respects in introducing a very characteristic Hebrew melody in his cantata, a song that is variously used to signify the deviations of the Church that has lost faith and the rebellion of the enemies of Christ. This melody announces itself together with the words that explain its meaning and function: *Filii Matris, meae pugnaverunt contra me*. In this case, the members of the Church, who descend from the Jewish communion and wish to unite with Christ, are personified in the bride.[57]

The Hebrew chant, marked by vibrating emotion, a few excessive steps of seconds and low ambitus, provides the allegorical interpretation that those believers who come from the Jewish community and want to follow Christ must suffer.

Of the eight songs of Toivo Tulev's *Song of Songs* (2005), the fourth thematizes the phrase "I am black, but comely." Tulev was born in 1958 in Estonia. The influence of Gregorian singing and early polyphony in this work are noticeable; simple monodic passages alternate with a multivoiced choir that unlocks wide sound surfaces. Paul Hillier, who rehearsed the work for the recording, emphasizes the singableness of Tulev's compositional style:

> All of Tulev's music, it seems to me, "sings"—in the sense that to sing is to place yourself within a special condition. A word that is sung is no longer merely a word, but has become

---

56 Zender, *Shir Hashirim*, 16. See Hastetter, "*Horch!*," 348–445. The specific problem of being Black is not addressed.
57 Torchi, "Il cantico dei cantici di Bossi," 793.

enchanted, mesmerized by the fact of being sung. Singing is an expression of longing, of joy and pain mixed, of removal from the everyday world.[58]

The text is a collage created by the composer from various sources: the Song of Songs in both English (King James Version) and Latin (New Vulgate) translations, and two poems, *Cantico spiritual* ("Spiritual Canticle") and *Coplas del alma que pena por ver a Dios* ("Stanzas of the Soul that Suffers with Longing to See God"), by St. John of the Cross. Along with the original text in Spanish, the text uses selected passages of the English translation by Kieran Kavanaugh and Otilio Rodriguez.

These texts, expressing spiritual longing in the terminology of physical desire, seem perfect for the music—even though it may be odd to express it that way around. The words are in three languages—English, Latin, and Spanish. Tulev notes,

> The overlapping of languages works like a commentary, re-interpreting the original. When we aren't listening to our principal language the process of translating forms a kind of gap between the object and the new language, and this gap is filled with interpretation even while we are listening to it. The process of translation gives time for this and raises the activity above the normal.[59]

The premiere of Bernhard Foccroulle's *Nigra sum* for ancient organ, soprano voice, and cornetto took place in 2012. Foccroulle (b. 1953) declares the specially chosen *cornet à bouquin* a favorite instrument of Renaissance music and of the early baroque period, often considered the closest to human voice.[60]

The Latin text is sung—*Nigra sum sed formosa filiae Jerusalem*—but continues differently from Song 1:5–6, taking up formulations from 1:4 and 2:10–12:

> Therefore have I pleased the Lord / And he has brought me into his chamber / And said to me: arise my love and come.
>
> [interlude]
>
> For now the winter is past, the rain is over and gone, / The flowers have appeared in our land, / The time of pruning is come.[61]

The singer, it seems, has "pleased the Lord" because of her dark skin. The Lord's call ("arise my love"), the germination of plants, and the arrival of spring all aim at the climax, the act of love. The singing voice strives for tonally playful and orientalizing melismas (melodic embellishments). Gentle interjections, passages, or

---

58 Quoted after the booklet to Tulev, *By Night*.
59 Quoted after the booklet to Tulev, *By Night*.
60 Foccroulle, introduction to *Nigra sum*.
61 "Bernard Foccroulle—Nigra sum (2012)—Picard organ (1741) of Beaufays," https://youtu.be/mf1V-TH13LM.

answers from the cornetto, which are conducted partly in parallel, suggest a situation of conversation; the organ and cornetto partially anticipate or take over the fioritures (embellishments) of the singing voice. The dissonant frictions become suspended as they dissolve at the phrase's end. This work, too, reflects Foccroulle's global understanding of art, his trust in the culturally and ethnically connecting "capacité mystérieuse":

> Culture creates fundamental coherence across all of humanity, without denying differences. Art and culture have this mysterious capacity to express the identity of an era, a country or a great personality; but at the same time, they transcend this time, this nation, this individual and connect us with human beings living on the other side of the planet. [. . . Through art . . .] we can go to meet the other, his roots, his culture, his values. We can approach them in such a way that they touch us, and our fear of others turns into interest, recognition, perhaps admiration.[62]

The chamber-music work *Schwarz—wie die Teppiche Salomos* (Black—Like the Carpets of Solomon) for soprano and vibraphone (1971), by Dieter Salbert (1932–2006), is, like Foccroulle's, an independent composition.[63] The soprano falls below the introductory organ point by half a note, above the tremolo of the vibraphone, and the evocative sharpness of the minor second, the "I am black," is recited on a tone, in order to articulate the contradiction—"but comely"—in the *but* in two huge ninth jumps. The following sound repetitions of the vibraphone point to the singer's statement.

"I Am Black but Comely" is the first of five songs for soprano or mezzo soprano and piano with texts, edited and compiled by Julie Dalton-Williamson, in *From the Song of Songs* (1998) by Gary Bachlund (b. 1947). The original quotation of the Song of Songs (1:5) is followed by reflections by the lyricist Julie Dalton Williamson:

> I have stripped of my dress; / Must I put it on again?
> I have washed my feet; / Must I soil them again?
> Who am I, rising as the dawn? / Fair as the moon? / Clear as the sun?
> Terrible as an army with banners? / Tell me, you whom my soul loves,
> Where will you lead your flocks to graze? / Where will you rest at noon?[64]

---

62 Foccroulle: "[L]a culture crée une cohérance fondamentale à travers toute l'humanité, sans nier les differences. L'art et la culture ont cette capacité mystérieuse d'exprimer l'identité d'une époque, d'un pays ou d'une grande personnalité; mais en même temps, ils transcendent cette époque, cette nation, cet individu et nous relient à des êtres humains vivant de l'autre côté de la planète. [. . . Par l'art . . .] nous pouvons aller à la rencontre de l'autre, des ses racines, de sa culture, de ses valeurs. Nous pouvons les approcher de telle manière qu'elles nous touchent, et que notre peur de l'autre se transforme en intérêt, en reconnaissance, peut-être en admiration." Foccroulle and Delrock, *Entre passion et résistance*, 17, 101.
63 For this composition, see also the contribution of Michaela C. Hastetter in this volume.
64 Bachlund, "From the Song of Songs" (text from the score, ibid., 1–22).

Concrete reflections on nudity and metaphors that question the woman's identity follow the first three biblical verses: her beauty "rising as the dawn" and clarity "clear as the sun," and perhaps also reflections on their inconsistency, "terrible as an army." But despite all the reservations and fears, the concrete question follows: where is the lover to be found? The composer adds an oriental style to the piano accompaniment, with many embellishments that look improvisational, broken chords, and even pentatonic effects caused by the dominance of the black keys. The blackness almost seems to be figuratively thematic. Soft upward fifths on the horns support the gentleness and elegance of the singing voice, whose lyric passages and sequences alternate with the piano's descant. The questions of the middle section accentuate the dialogue between solo soprano and accompaniment.

Felicitas Kukuck (1914–2001) told translator Manfred Hausmann in 1969, "Now I will compose your Song of Songs, 'which is attributed to King Solomon.' In my estimation, it is the most beautiful adaptation of the wonderful Bible text."[65] In 1982 she published her *Vier Lieder für Sopran und Klavier nach Texten aus dem Hohelied Salomonis*, using texts from the hymn *Salomonis* according to Hausmann's translation. In the third song, *Die Wächterin* (Tanzlied): "Mag ich auch braun sein" ("The Guardian. [Dance Song]": "May I Also Be Brown"), the piano and vocals have different functions. The rhythmic and melodic patterns of the piano underline the dance style, while the singing voice exposes the "but beautiful" on the treble's high A flat and thus accentuates the supposed contrast between beauty and tanning. The voice repeats the same position during the ninth-jump to the "sun" and in the admission that she failed to guard her garden.

Kukuck has described her method of composing as "freitonal" ("free-tonal"). For her, "ein bestimmter Ausdruckswert" ("a specific expression value") is available at each interval.

> This must be appropriate to the semantic reference field of the word. Decreased and excessive intervals possess something painful. It is often claimed that the alterations cannot be heard. On the other hand, I am of the opinion that especially in the two-voicedness by certain continuations, for example resolutions or chromaticism, the alteration can be audible and thus the expressive value and the effect can be achieved.[66]

---

[65] Sprenger, *Felicitas Kukuck*, 125: "Jetzt will ich Ihr Lied der Lieder, 'das man dem König Salomo zuschreibt,' komponieren. Es ist für mein Gefühl die schönste Nachdichtung des wunderbaren Bibeltextes."

[66] Quoted after Philipp, "Dialogue with Felicitas Kukuck," 33: "[Ein bestimmter Ausdruckswert] muß dem semantischen Bereich des Wortes adäquat sein. Verminderte und übermäßige Intervalle besitzen etwas Schmerzhaftes. Oft wird behauptet, man könne die Alterationen nicht hören. Demgegenüber bin ich der Ansicht, daß gerade in der Zweistimmigkeit durch bestimmte Weit-

Nigra sum (1943),⁶⁷ a folk song-like movement in E minor by Pablo Casals (1876–1973) with a bar of 2/4, a simple piano accompaniment, and easy setting in two voices, is suitable for untrained singing voices. Its simplicity corresponds to the intended target group, namely, the Benedictines and friends of Monserrat, with whom Casals had maintained close contact since 1932.

> [At that time, he moved] out to the place of worship to personally rehearse his *Ave Maria*, composed for the pilgrimage of his home community on Montserrat, with the choir there. This beautiful occasion established a cordial relationship between Casals and the monks on Montserrat, whose quiet, devoted scholarly work he pays great respect to. He also expressed his friendly attitude to them by making a pilgrimage to them with his cello the next year and honoring them with a concert.⁶⁸

Montserrat, Casals confessed, "became my second home" ("wurde mein zweites Zuhause").⁶⁹ Núria Ballester called Casals's composition

> a moderate homorhythm and homophony, presenting the appearance of a melismatic chant of great religious function. [. . .] The loving woman, [. . .] identified with Our Lady of Montserrat given her dark complexion, [. . .] is the mystical personification of the Church being summoned by God.⁷⁰

The allegorical interpretation is based on Casals's close ties to the monastery. His deep religiosity, his unwavering belief in humanity, and his love for his homeland, Catalonia, were also triggers for his work. Quite fittingly, Robert Baldock opens his monograph on Casals with Casals's own words:

> Music must serve a purpose, it must be something larger than itself, a part of humanity, and that, indeed, is at the core of my argument with music of today—its lack of humanity. A musician is also a man, and more important than his music is his attitude to life. Nor can the two be separated.⁷¹

Casals's religiousness also transferred to his own game: when he celebrated Bach's *Sarabande of the C Minor Suite* at a concert in Zurich in the spring of 1942, one critic wrote that the performance was "as if an old, wise man were to read the most beautiful chapter of Scripture with deepest understanding."⁷² His "visionary"

---

erführungen, z.B. Auflösungen oder Chromatik die Alteration hörbar und damit der Ausdruckswert und die Wirkung erzielt werden kann."
67 "Pablo Casals—Nigra Sum (women's choir)," https://youtu.be/y_iVQBM05E8.
68 Von Tobel, *Pablo Casals*, 52.
69 Casals and Kahn, *Licht und Schatten auf einem langen Weg*, 70.
70 Quoted after Casals, introduction to *Cor*, 12–13.
71 Baldock, *Pablo Casals*. This quote precedes the complete work as a motto.
72 So the reviewer Ernst Isler, cited by von Tobel, *Pablo Casals*, 85: "Wie wenn ein alter, weiser Mann das schönste Kapitel der Heiligen Schrift mit tiefstem Verständnis lesen würde."

music-making opened up spiritual spaces of tolerance, humanity, and greatness. Casals's lived humanity is also reflected in his encounters with contemporaries.[73]

Such humanitarian interpretations of the Song of Songs explain why the American Michael Bussewitz-Quarm (b. 1971), a transgender woman, chose *Nigra sum* as a protest song—on the one hand to give "her fervent wish to spread knowledge and understanding of the transgender community" an "authoritative" voice and on the other to help "Syrians requiring humanitarian assistance."[74] Bussewitz-Quarm says,

> The history of *Nigra sum* dates back to the time of King Solomon. Some scholars believe the Songs of Solomon come from a Syrian wedding ritual, while others understand it as representing the "revival of life in nature." [She dedicates her work] to all refugees throughout the world and all who are lost. May you find peace and may this dark winter soon pass.[75]

The four-part a cappella movement is strictly choral, with few exceptions; floating dissonances are held and solved in the manner of early polyphony. The atmospheric choral work is opened by the solo tenor in a plagal church tone, which has a certain melancholiness; the association with antiphonal Gregorian singing seems intended. *Nigra sum* fades in several times in the following song, whose primary motif characterizes and ends in the final "Alleluia."

3 Contemporary Illustrations

Das Hohe Lied, with text following the Lutheran translation of the Bible and printed by hand in three colors, was published by Cranach Press in 1931. Harry Graf Kessler did the text arrangement, and graphic artist Eric Gill (1882–1940) designed and cut the woodcuts and initial letters. Gill had illustrated the Song of Songs for Golden Cockerell Press six years earlier, with eighteen woodcuts, but they were "marked

---

[73] See Corredor, *Gespräche mit Casals*, motto and 8, citing Romain Rolland: "Un seul grand homme qui deumeure humain sauve toujours, et pour tous, la foi dans l'humanité." ("One great man who, as a human being, always saves, and for all, faith in humanity"). Thomas Mann closed his letter to Corredor (dated March 1954) with the following words: "Das gebrechliche Menschengeschlecht hat Ehrenretter gebraucht wohl je und je. Ein solcher ist dieser Künstler—ein Ehrenretter der Menschheit. Mit Freuden bekenne ich, daß sein Dasein mir, wie Tausenden, ein Labsal ist." ("The frail human race has needed honor savers probably ever and ever. One such is this artist—an honorary savior of humanity. With joy I confess that his existence is to me, like thousands, a refreshment.")
[74] Bussewitz-Quarm, website, https://www.mbqstudio.com.
[75] "Nigra Sum—Michael Bussewitz-Quarm" (2017), introductory words to the score. See https://youtu.be/7o6p3lf4g1g.

by a 'cold eroticism' ['kalte Erotik'], as Kessler noted; in other words, they lacked any eroticism."[76]

> [But here, with a completely new approach,] the chain of song fragments became a sequence of nocturnal scenes, in the semi-darkness of which only the lovers gained their contours and a soul beyond the Song of Songs on their bodies.
>
> [... Kessler specified the "Gothic format," the coloring, the leaf size]. Under no circumstances should they be illustrations in the usual manner of woodcuts, i.e., with large areas of black and large areas of white [...]. They would leave no room for values, for shading, for the possibility of giving the two lovers a body and a soul.[77]

Since the first sheet is blackened and thus primarily outlines and shades stand out, the problem of "blackness" becomes irrelevant in this work. We see the naked young woman, floating in a seated posture in the middle of a forest of leaves, being handed a garment by two young women (see Figure 7). Whether the garment is revealing or concealing remains to be seen. "Through the psychology of dressing and undressing, the illustrations are deprived of the *nakedness* of the sexual; the naked figures are transformed into *nudes* by the act of change."[78]

American artist Debra Band illuminated the Song of Songs in 2005; the sixty-five illuminations incorporate traditional Jewish manuscript arts. In contrast to literal and allegorical interpretations, the artist says:

> I present my own interpretation of The Song of Songs. I treat the poems as a series of daydreams of a pair of lovers within a walled Garden. The garden imagery enables me to introduce iconography that relates to each of these two previously mutually exclusive readings at the same time. This fusion of the allegorical and the literal blossoms into a fuller emotional and spiritual realization of the passions expressed in these remarkable verses.[79]

She explains Song 1:5–8 as follows (see Figure 8):

> [the scene:] In the poem the woman defiantly asserts that while she is indeed sunburned—through no fault of her own—her lover will still love her. Images of clusters of grapes remind her that in spite of her imperfection she will always be desirable to her lover. Above the text, a cluster of grapes, which someone must have already picked at and tasted, hangs from its vine partly hidden by the double curtains, still full, still promising luscious juice. A mosaic of grapevines has lost a patch of its small tiles, but it remains shiny and colorful enough to fool the honeybee buzzing toward its tiles.[80]

---

76 Brinks, "Auf der Suche nach der Sinnlichkeit," 150.
77 Brinks, "Auf der Suche nach der Sinnlichkeit," 152, 154.
78 Brinks, "Auf der Suche nach der Sinnlichkeit," 154.
79 Band, *Song of Songs*, appendix, 218.
80 Band, *Song of Songs*, 8.

Figure 7: Woodcut from Eric Gill, *Das Hohe Lied*, 4. Leipzig: Cranach Press, 1931.

Figure 8: Illumination 3, "I Am Dark but Lovely," from *The Song of Songs: The Honeybee in the Garden*, illuminations and commentary by Debra Band. Philadelphia: Jewish Publication Society of America, 2005. Reproduced with permission from the artist.

[the interpretation:] [...] In spite of the moment of self-doubt, she remains confident that the apparent flaw will not prevent the union with her lover. [Here she compares the relationship between Israel and God....] Finally, Israel declares "I am black in this world and comely in the world to come," that is, after the dreamed-of-union with the divine beloved.[81]

Zeew (Ze'ev) Raban's illustrations in *Salomo: The Song of Songs* (1923) are just as idiosyncratic (see Figure 9). Raban (1890–1970) was a Polish Israeli, born Wolf Rawicki. His art is winningly beautiful but "eclectic":

The art of Zeev Raban was a synthesis of East (Byzantium and Persia) and West (neoclassicism and Jugendstil). The components of this formula are uniquely his own: idealization of reality, symmetrical metaphors, frontal and theatrical posing of narrow, elongated figures, processional structure, realism framed with Persian ornamentation of ancient arched stone windows, pseudo-pointillism, brilliant colors that recall stained glass, Byzantine mosaics, or precious gems.[82]

Figure 9: Illustration (clipping) from the front cover of Zeew Raban, *Salomo: The Song of Songs*. Berlin: Hasefer, 1923.

The Mayanot Gallery in Jerusalem published "the first Israeli catalogue of the work of Zeev Raban"[83] in April 1993, including his illustrations of the biblical books of Song of Songs (see Figure 9), Ruth, Esther, and Job and of the Passover Haggadah.

---

81 Band, *Song of Songs*, 9.
82 Ofrat, ed., *Zeev Raban*, 55–54.
83 Ofrat, ed., *Zeev Raban*, 55–54.

In these illustrations, Raban combined his different artistic preferences: a use of color suggesting stained glass windows, graphic decoration that recalls copper and stone carvings, the precision and detail of metal design, formal elements drawn from the design of jewelry, and more. [...] Yet of the handful of characteristics distinguishing this language, the most singular is the recurrent pairing of the lion and the gazelle. [...] Man as a lion, woman as a gazelle—Raban identified this syntax, both in the Song of Songs (Solomon and the Shulamite).[84]

The surrealist painter Arik Brauer (1929–2021) created particularly winning, color-saturated paintings of the Song of Songs, especially *Sulamith* and *Vereinigung* (2016). Art historian Kai Uwe Schierz calls Arik Brauer a "fantastic-realistic storyteller."[85] His visions depict dreamlike encounters and fantastic events with enigmatic people, surrounded by a great wealth of plants and figures. He illuminates his *Sulamith* (see Figure 10) in the same colors as the flower cups that frame her. Far behind her, a small naked man seems to be trying to plant a tree; small groups of people are arranged in a circle and seem to be discussing something; and in the background a very small flock of sheep with a shepherd enrich the ensemble. The second painting (see Figure 11) offers a kind of solution, combining black and white; the beautiful white-clad, dark-skinned woman has placed her right hand confidently on that of the man, who is facing her, dressed in black. The flower stalks held in their two left hands combine to create a flaming flower over their heads. The painter signed this picture, "What could be more beautiful than a flower of two roots with two colors."[86] Schierz notes:

> [This "fantastic painting" characterizes] a diffuse but atmospherically dense, color-saturated space, without a multitude of coordinates, without specific or temporal location, and with a wealth of figurative details that seem to float weightlessly in it. Although there are horizon lines that divide the image into a bottom and a top, earth and sky, a front and a back, everywhere soft transitions dominate.[87]

The artist himself designed his "fairy tales for adults" in order to draw attention to the beauty and artistic significance of the "wonderful," in accordance with the first surrealist manifesto of André Breton of 1924.[88] Following his understanding of the

---

84 Ofrat, ed., *Zeev Raban*, 46, 48.
85 Schierz, "Der Geschichtenerzähler," 15, 31.
86 Quote from Arik Brauer under the image reproduced in figure 11: "Was könnte schöner sein als eine Blüte aus zwei Wurzeln mit zwei Farben." Quoted after Schierz, "Der Geschichtenerzähler," 108.
87 Schierz, "Der Geschichtenerzähler," 27.
88 Schierz, "Der Geschichtenerzähler," 26.

Figure 10: Arik Brauer, *Sulamith*. "Seht mich nicht an, da ich so schwarz bin [Don't Look at Me because I'm So Black]" (2016). Oil on hardboard. 46 x 41 cm. WN 951. Reproduced with permission from the artist.

Bible, art, and culture, Brauer focuses above all on the Old Testament: "For me, the Bible is 'fantastic realism' in words, especially in the original text."[89]

The synthesis between black and white, dreamed up (and realized) in these two paintings, further legitimates—like most of the examples mentioned here—the perception of a liberated, species-unspecific, "race"-free concept of beauty, which is based on deep humanity. Hence, it also legitimates the conviction that skin color cannot and must not constitute a human criterion of differentiation; all human beings have the same dignity and value, and ultimately the *but* between the attributes *black* and *beautiful/comely/lovely* is to be read as an enrichment. But in order to avoid misinterpretation, we should replace the *but* with the connecting *and*.

---

[89] Brauer, *Die Farben meines Lebens,* 237: "Die Bibel ist für mich 'Phantastischer Realismus' in Worten, besonders im Originaltext."

Figure 11: Arik Brauer, *Vereinigung unter Palmen* [*Union under Palm Trees*] (2016). Oil on hardboard. 70 x 50 cm. WN 948. Reproduced with permission from the artist.

Bibliography

Bachlund, Gary. "From the Song of Songs." Complete score, 5 movements. IGB 136. 1998. https://imslp.org/wiki/From_the_Song_of_Songs_(Bachlund%2C_Gary).
Baldock, Robert. *Pablo Casals*. London: Gollancz, 1992.
Band, Debra. *The Song of Songs: The Honeybee in the Garden*, translated by Jewish Publication Society and David Band. Philadelphia: Jewish Publication Society, 2005.

Benz, Ernst. "'Ich bin schwarz und schön' (Hld 1,5): Ein Beitrag des Origenes zur Theologie der negritudo." In *Wort und Religion: Kalima na dini; Studien zur Afrikanistik, Missionswissenschaft, Religionswissenschaft*, edited by Hans-Jürgen Greschat and Hermann Jungraithmayr, 225–242. Stuttgart: Evangelischer Missionsverlag, 1969.

Berlinghof, Regine. „Epilogue." In *Das Hohelied: Der Gesang der Gesänge; The Song of Songs; Schir ha-Schirim*, by Otto Clemen, i–vi. Kelkheim: YingYang-Media-Verlag, 2005.

"Bernard Foccroulle—Nigra sum (2012)—Picard organ (1741) of Beaufays." Video direction by Philippe de Magnée. Extract of "Works for Historic Organs." https://youtu.be/mf1V-TH13LM. Retrieved 25.08.2020.

Brauer, Arik. *Die Farben meines Lebens: Erinnerungen*. Vienna: Amalthea, 2006.

Brinks, John Dieter. "Auf der Suche nach der Sinnlichkeit Kesslers und Gills Hohelied." In *Das Buch als Kunstwerk: Die Cranach Presse des Grafen Harry Kessler*, edited by John Dieter Brinks, 146–154. Laubach: Triton-Verlag, 2003.

Burton, Joan B. "Themes of Female Desire and Self-Assertion in the Song of Songs and Hellenistic Poetry." In *Perspectives on the Song of Songs: Perspektiven der Hoheliedauslegung*, edited by Anselm C. Hagedorn, 180–205. BZAW 346. Berlin: de Gruyter, 2005.

Casals, Pablo, and Albert E. Kahn. *Licht und Schatten auf einem langen Weg: Erinnerungen aufgezeichnet*, translated by Peter Baumann. Frankfurt: S. Fischer, 1971.

Casals, Pau. *Cor. Vol. 1*. Musical score. Barcelona: Editorial de Música Boileau, 2011.

Clemen, Otto. *Das Hohelied: Der Gesang der Gesänge; The Song of Songs; Schir ha-Schirim*. Kelkheim: YingYang-Media-Verlag, 2005. Reprint of *Canticum canticorum: Holztafeldruck von c. 1465*. Zwickau: F. Ullmann, 1910.

Corredor, José María. *Gespräche mit Casals*. Bern: Scherz, 1954.

Damm, Werner. *Die Königin von Saba: Kunst, Legende und Archäologie zwischen Morgenland und Abendland*. Stuttgart: Belser, 1988.

Foccroulle, Bernard. *Nigra sum pour soprano, cornetto et orgue*. Musical score. Paris: Lemonie, 2013.

Foccroulle, Bernhard, and Pierre Delrock. *Entre passion et résistance*. Brussels: Labor, 2004.

Frühmorgen-Voss, Hella, Norbert H. Ott, Ulrike Bodemann, and Gisela Fischer-Heetfeld. *Katalog der deutschsprachigen illustrierten Handschriften des Mittelalters 2*. Munich: Beck'sche Verlagsbuchhandlung, 1996.

Hastetter, Michaela. "*Horch! Mein Geliebter!*" *Die Wiederentdeckung der geistlichen Schriftauslegung in den Hoheliedvertonungen des 20. Jahrhunderts*. MthS.S 69. St. Ottilien: EOS Verlag, 2006.

Hug, Heinz. "'Vom alltäglichen Leben des Volkes und seiner Größe sprechen': Der Schriftsteller und Filmemacher Ousmane Sembène." In *Ousmane Sembène und die sengalesische Erzählliteratur*, by Papa Samba Diop, Elisa Fuchs, Heinz Hug, and János Riesz, 53–147. Munich: Edition Text und Kritik, 1994.

Keel, Othmar. *Das Hohelied*. ZBKAT 18. Zürich: Theologischer Verlag, 1992.

Kleinert, Ulfried. *Das Rätsel der Königin von Saba: Geschichte und Mythos*. Darmstadt: von Zabern, 2015.

Krinetzki, Günter. *Kommentar zum Hohenlied: Bildsprache und theologische Botschaft*. BBET 16. Frankfurt: Lang, 1981.

Kunst, Hans-Joachim. *The African in European Art*. Bad Godesberg: Inter Nationes, 1967.

Kyeser, Conrad. *The Queen of Sheba*. From the manuscript *Bellifortis*. Niedersächsische Staats- und Universitätsbibliothek Göttingen, 2 Cod. Ms. Philos. 63, Cim., fol. 122r., translated by Astrid Khoo. https://commons.wikimedia.org/wiki/File:BlackSheba-Text.jpg. Retrieved 16.07.2020.

Kyeser, Konrad. *Bellifortis*, translated by Götz Quarg. Düsseldorf: VDI-Verlag, 1967.

"La noire de—Ousmane Sembène—(1966) [Legendado em português]." https://youtu.be/YMDg2UAyXSs. Retrieved 14.07.2020.

Lam, Aboubacry Moussa. *L'Affaire des momies royales: La vérité sur la reine Ahmès-Nefertari*. Collection Préhistoire/Antiquité négro-africaine. Paris: Présence Africaine, 2000.

Lapide, Pinchas. *Das Hohelied der Liebe*. With woodcuts by HAP Grieshaber. Munich: Kösel, 1993.

Lhote, André. *Les chefs-d'œuvre de la peinture égyptienne*. Paris: Hachette, 1954.

Lueken, Verena. "Unübersehbare Unsichtbarkeiten." *Frankfurter Allgemeine Zeitung*, 16.8.2019.

Maier, Gerhard. *Das Hohelied, erklärt von Gerhard Maier*. WStB. Wuppertal: Brockhaus, 1991.

Mielke, Andreas. *Nigra sum et Formosa: Afrikanerinnen in der deutschen Literatur des Mittelalters*. Helfant Texte 11. Stuttgart: Helfant, 1992.

Müller, Hans-Peter. *Vergleich und Metapher im Hohenlied*. OBO 56. Göttingen: Vandenhoeck & Ruprecht, 1984.

"Nigra Sum—Michael Bussewitz-Quarm (2017)." Demo recording by Matt Curtis. https://youtu.be/7o6p3lf4g1g. Retrieved 02.09.2020.

Ofrat, Gideon, ed. *Zeev Raban*. Exhibition catalog. Jerusalem: Mayanot Gallery, 1993.

Origen. *Der Kommentar zum Hohelied*, edited and translated by Alfons Fürst and Holger Strutwolf. Orig.WD 9/1. Berlin: de Gruyter, 2016.

Origen. *The Song of Songs: Commentary and Homilies*, edited and translated by R. P. Lawson. ACW 26. Westminster, MD: Newman Press, 1957.

"Pablo Casals—Nigra Sum (women's choir)." https://youtu.be/y_iVQBM05E8. Retrieved 02.09.2020.

Philipp, Beate. "Dialogue with Felicitas Kukuck." In *Komponistinnen der Neuen Musik*, edited by Beate Philipp, 30–63. Kassel: Furore-Verlag, 1993.

Reichert, Klaus. *Das Hohelied Salomonis*. Salzburg: Residenzverlag, 1996.

Röhrig, Floridus. *Der Verduner Altar*. Vienna: Herold, 1955.

Schierz, Kai Uwe. "Der Geschichtenerzähler." In *Arik Brauer: Phantastisch-realistisch; Ein Lebenswerk*, edited by Kunsthalle Erfurt, 15–35. Halle: Mitteldeutscher Verlag, 2019.

Schreiner, Stefan, ed. *Das Lied der Lieder von Schelomo: Liebeslyrik aus dem alten Israel*. Bremen: Schünemann, 1982.

Slater-Williams, Josh. "Locarno Film Festival 2019: The Skinny's Highlights." The Skinny. August 29, 2019. https://www.theskinny.co.uk/festivals/international-festivals/highlights-72nd-locarno-film-festival-2019.

Spark, Muriel. "The Black Madonna." In *The Stories of Muriel Spark*, 34–51. London: Bodley Head, 1987.

Sprenger, Cordula. *Felicitas Kukuck als Komponistin von Solo- und Chorliedern*. Systematische Musikwissenschaft und Musikkulturen der Gegenwart 1. Marburg: Tectum-Verlag, 2008.

Stekl, Konrad. *Der Verduner Altar (op. 58)*. Piano score/Choral score. Vienna: Ludwig Krenn, 1962/1963.

The Temple of Amenhotep I. http://www.deirelmedina.com/lenka/TempleAmenhotep.html. Retrieved 12.06.2019.

Tobel, Rudolf von. *Pablo Casals*. Erlenbach: Rotapfel-Verlag, 1945.

Torchi, Luigi. "Il cantico dei cantici di Bossi." *Rivista musicale italiana* 7 (1900): 780–821.

Tulev, Toivo. *By Night (Songs—2005)*. Estnischer Philharmonischer Kammerchor. Conducted by Paul Hillier. Composite recording. Harmonia Mundi, 2006.

Zender, Hans. *Shir Hashirim*. Composite recording. Südwestrundfunk. Kairos Produktion, 2006. Compact disc.

Zingerle, Ignaz von. *Die pluemen der tugent des Hans Vintler*. Innsbruck: Wagner, 1874 (unfortunately without illustrations).

P. W. (Bill) Goodman
"The Time of Singing has Come"
The Lure of the Song of Songs for Today's Composers and Songwriters

1 Introduction

"Writing about music is like dancing about architecture—a really stupid thing to want to do!"[1] This warning about missing the point (attributed to Elvis Costello, amongst others), presumably also applies to speaking about music. Perhaps I should simply offer the reader or hearer some songs to listen to and leave it at that? However, some words are expected from a speaker or writer; so in addition to including online links to three songs,[2] I shall take the risk of offering some brief commentary on these contemporary appropriations of the biblical Song. In this I will highlight aspects of the biblical Song which they emphasise and also ways in which they differ from the biblical Song at the very points where they also closely resemble it.[3] Although the lyrics of these three songs are included here in full, actually hearing the songs in the course of reading this paper is crucial: the reader needs to ensure a means to play them.

2 "Rise Up My Love" (Howard Skempton)

In a career spanning more than fifty years, the English composer Howard Skempton (born 1947) has explored a variety of genres and styles. His interest in the Song of Songs is evident in four choral interpretations which he contributes to a recent album, one of which we now consider.

"Rise Up My Love"[4] is a far cry from the various experimental and abstract pieces through which Howard Skempton made his name in the 1970s.[5] In this and his three other choral interpretations of the Song of Songs found on the same

---

[1] Begbie, *Resounding Truth*, 14.
[2] See nn. 4, 15, and 24.
[3] An approach to comparison commended by Fox, "Rereading," 9.
[4] https://www.youtube.com/watch?v=kXbAMaY3fTQ.
[5] Details of the full range of Skempton's work can be found here: https://britishmusiccollection.org.uk/composer/howard-skempton.

https://doi.org/10.1515/9783110750799-024

album, harmony and a measured serenity are all pervasive. The passages he chooses from the biblical text (Song 2:10–14; 4:10; 6:2–3; 7:6, 10) convey no sense of discord between the lovers; nor do the sublime voices that sing them for us.[6] "Rise up my Love" presents Song 2:10–14, word-for-word, in the elegant cadences of the 1611 translation Authorised by King James.

> My beloved spake, and said unto me,
> Rise up, my love, my fair one, and come away.
> For, lo, the winter is past,
> the rain is over and gone;
> the flowers appear on the earth;
> the time of the singing of birds is come,
> and the voice of the turtle is heard in our land;
> the fig tree putteth forth her green figs,
> and the vines with the tender grape give a good smell.
> Arise, my love, my fair one, and come away.
> O my dove, that art in the clefts of the rock,
> in the secret places of the stairs,
> let me see thy countenance, let me hear thy voice;
> for sweet is thy voice, and thy countenance is comely.[7]

We hear the words of the man wooing the woman, enticing her to come out of her safe enclosure and be with him, so that they can revel in all the delights of springtime together.[8] In the Song of Songs each of the lovers caresses the other tenderly with words, seeking to touch the inner depths in this way; Skempton evokes something of that tenderness.[9] This musical arrangement involves a blend of male and female voices, which is quite appropriate: for here the biblical text offers the words of the man, conveyed to us through the voice of the woman—she is quoting what he has said to her (all presented in the words of the anonymous poet, whose gender is not known to us).[10]

---

[6] Skempton describes his turn towards writing liturgical choral pieces as a "coming home" which connected with memories of singing in school choirs; on this and his interest in setting established texts to music, see Fallas, "Conditions," 21.

[7] Skempton, "Rise Up My Love."

[8] In the biblical Song descriptions of natural landscape are repeatedly fused with those of the lovers' bodies and their experiences of erotic exploration: the invitation to travel becomes an invitation to intimacy. See Gray, "Come Be My Love," 372–373.

[9] See Garrett and House, *Song*, 163; Exum, *Song*, 13–14. Song 2:10–14 is the passage from the Song that has most entries in Dowling Long and Sawyer, *Bible in Music* (see Index, 329)—an indication of its attractiveness to a wide range of songwriters.

[10] The Royal Shakespeare Company's production (*Song of Songs: Movement, Text Passion*, performed at the Swan Theatre, 6.3.12) provided another example of the Song's male and female voic-

In the immediately preceding verses in the biblical passage, the woman describes the man approaching, leaping over the mountains and hills as if oblivious to any barrier; so one might imagine him arriving a bit breathless, perhaps even slightly sweaty and definitely high on adrenalin (not to mention testosterone)! But instead, the passion of the Song's young lovers is calmed into the controlled elegance of a Cambridge College choir singing in their chapel. The urgency in the succession of imperatives used by the man ("Rise up, come away [...] arise, come away [...] let me see thy countenance, let me hear thy voice") seems to be diminished in the slow, measured tempo and homophonic melody. The verse that immediately follows (Song 2:15) suddenly introduces an element of concern—about "little foxes" that might disturb and spoil the lovers' bliss; Skempton's piece concludes just before we reach that point.

Whose love is being celebrated here? Skempton's choral piece can be found in the context of an album entitled *My Beloved's Voice: Sacred Songs of Love*; the mention of "sacred" suggests the traditional allegorical understanding of the biblical Song depicting a relationship between God and human beings, be it Yahweh and Israel or Christ and the Church. In such an interpretation, parts of the biblical text where the man speaks (such as these verses which Skempton has chosen) represent the divine voice. Skempton's divine voice calls repeatedly but also gently, wooing the human lover with insistent pleas framed in elegant sounds.

Skempton gives an idealised vision of the beauty of love: inspiring, moving, and reassuring. His chosen medium and style produces a result which reflects the beauty of the biblical poetry and its exalted vision of love. But does that vision in the process become too understated, a little too respectable—perhaps in order to present a vision of human relationship with God which is sufficiently reverent and glorious in its *gravitas*?[11] Certainly Skempton's song ignores the tensions, demands and uncertainties which add complexity to love; the biblical Song does not ignore these, as we shall see elsewhere.[12]

---

es can blend, as the various actors sometimes took up and repeated each other's lines, along with an understated musical accompaniment from a classical ensemble.
11 Others have also wrestled with this tension; a famous medieval commentator found resolution in observing "an ardent love, blinded by its own excess to the majesty of the beloved. For what are the facts? He is the one at whose glance the earth trembles, and does she demand that he give her a kiss? Can she possibly be drunk?" Bernard of Clairvaux, *On the Song of Songs*, sermon 7,3 (Walsh, ed., 1:40).
12 Tensions in the lovers' relationship surface in various ways in the biblical Song. One example involves images of conflict, with both the man and the woman overwhelming each other and also surrendering to each other as "conquered conquerers." See Verde, "When the Warrior," 190–212.

3 "Dark I Am Yet Lovely" (Sinéad O'Connor)

Some of us remember Sinéad O'Connor's (born 1966) arrival on the popular music scene back in 1990, singing a passionate song of lost love (written by Prince), "Nothing Compares 2 U." After a journey through Christianity (which included ordination as a priest in an independent Catholic Church), Rastafarianism, and recently into Sufi Islam, O'Connor now also goes by a new name (Shuhada' Sadaqat), as well as her more familiar birth name, under which she continues to record and perform.[13] One song from her 2007 album, *Theology*,[14] entitled "Dark I am Yet Lovely,"[15] is full of references to the Song:

> Dark I am yet lovely as tents of Kedar
> As the pavilions of Solomon either
> Don't hate me because the sun has darkened me
> All my mother's sons were so angry with me
> They made me watch the vineyards
> My own things I did not guard
>
> On my bed at night I sought whom my soul loves
> Oh I sought I sought but I found him not
> So I ask U daughters of Jerusalem
> Where is my love? Oh tell me have U seen him?
>
> Majestic as Lebanon stately as cedars
> His mouth so delicious his fragrance so pleases
> Such is my beloved such is my darling
> And if U see him say my heart is pining
> For the kisses of his mouth and his flavours
> Oh the king had brought me into his chambers
> Say I delight in his love
> Say he's the one my soul was
>
> Vast floods can't quench love no matter what love did
> Rivers can't drown love no matter where love's hid
> So when U do find him out
> Bring him to my mother's house
> And into the chamber of her who conceived me
> Then will he know me and then will he see me
> Tell him that love isn't done
> Tell him don't leave me alone.[16]

---

13 O'Connor continues to see herself exercising a priestly role; see a recent interview with the Washington Post, https://www.youtube.com/watch?v=j88FRkAT0zE.
14 For more on O'Connor's *Theology* album, see Goodman, "Nothing Compares."
15 https://www.youtube.com/watch?v=7TWGwa6s49Q.
16 O'Connor, "Dark I Am."

O'Connor draws particularly on these passages from the Song of Songs:

> I am black and beautiful,
>   O daughters of Jerusalem,
> like the tents of Kedar,
>   like the curtains of Solomon.
> My mother's sons were angry with me;
>   they made me keeper of the vineyards,
>   but my own vineyard I have not kept.[17] (1:5–6)

> Upon my bed at night
>   I sought him whom my soul loves;
> I sought him, but found him not; (3:1)

> I adjure you, O daughters of Jerusalem,
>   if you find my beloved,
> tell him this:
>   I am faint with love. (5:8)

> Let him kiss me with the kisses of his mouth!
> [. . .]
>   The king has brought me into his chambers. [. . .] (1:2–4)

> I would lead you and bring you
>   into the house of my mother,
>   and into the chamber of the one who bore me. (8:2)

> Many waters cannot quench love,
>   neither can floods drown it. (8:7)

One of O'Connor's most striking musical gifts is her extraordinary voice. Hearing her sing "Dark I Am Yet Lovely" highlights one of the remarkable features of the biblical Song: the prominence of the woman's voice. "Here's a woman singing," as Kate Bush puts it in her own "Song of Solomon."[18] Female voices—mostly the woman, also a little from the daughters of Jerusalem—make up more than half of the biblical Song.[19] This is the only book in the Bible in which a woman's thoughts and words are so clearly predominant; in the poetry we see, feel, think and experience relationships from her point of view.[20]

O'Connor's vocal delivery might remind us of a word found seven times in the Song of Songs: *nepheš* (נֶפֶשׁ). Often translated "soul" in English bibles, *nepheš* has a wide range of meaning. The root word denotes "throat" or "neck," so *nepheš* some-

---

[17] Here and in the following, Bible references are taken from the NRSV.
[18] Bush, "Song of Solomon."
[19] This is not always evident in English translations, but is clearer in Hebrew, where gendered suffixes indicate whether a man or woman is being addressed.
[20] In what follows, I draw partly on my earlier article; see Goodman, *Nothing Compares*.

times signifies "breath," as a key sign of life and hence can refer to the person as a whole, their very "self" or "life"; it can also express "desire" for food, power or love.[21] For me, Sinéad O'Connor sings the Song of Songs with *nepheš*—her vocal expression, with its breathy, hungry, passionate intensity of longing conveys something suggestive of *nepheš*. For example, the woman in the Song describes herself as intoxicated with her lover's kisses (1:2) and "faint with love" (2:5; 5:8); O'Connor captures something of that inebriated "swooning" experience by the way her voice tails off as if breathless at the end of particular lines in the song.

How else does the medium convey the message? Something in the flow of O'Connor's melody and the swing of its rhythm suggests a waltz. A waltz conveys a certain lightness of spirit, or even euphoria. Part of the genius of the biblical Song's lyric poetry is in the way it goes beyond simply presenting the thoughts and feelings of its speakers, managing in addition to evoke those very feelings in the reader or hearer. One of those feelings is the delightful, light-headed sense of intoxication.[22]

Yet it takes two to waltz—and this seems to be a waltz for one. A feature of the biblical Song is its use of dialogue; the woman's voice predominates, but two voices are heard throughout. O'Connor's version gives us only the woman's voice; that sense of mutuality evident in the biblical text is missing. Indeed, the "he" of O'Connor's song seems to be not simply silent but actually absent: she sings to the daughters of Jerusalem about him, but does not address him directly. In the biblical text, the woman speaks regularly and directly to the man (1:16; 2:17; 4:16; 7:11–8:2; 8:5b–7, 14). His words are also heard, usually addressed directly to her (1:9–12, 15, 17; 2:14; 4:1–15; 5:1; 6:4–9; 7:1–9; 8:13). O'Connor's song is a monologue, not a duet. It raises obvious questions: where is he? Why are they separated? Does she not know where to find him? And is she speaking of a human lover or of a search for immediacy and intimacy in a relationship with God—or perhaps even both?[23]

---

[21] For *nepheš* as intense craving for food, see Pss 78:18; 107:9, 18; Prov 6:30; as craving for power and prosperity, see Pss 10:3; 35:25; Prov 13:2. In relational desire, it can refer to the familial (Gen 44:30), but is more often used of the sexual (as in Song 1:7; 3:1–4; Jer 2:24; Ezek 16:27). It depicts the "vital self" or true essence of a person in the repeated Deuteronomic call to love God with one's entire being (Deut 4:29; 6:5; 10:12; 30:2, 6, 10; Josh 22:5; 1Kgs 2:4; 8:48; 2Kgs 23:25).

[22] Francis Landy is one of a number who suggest the metaphor of dance in relation to the Song, although he chooses ballet. "The lovers pursue each other across the poem, elusive but in touch, changing roles, parting and converging. Thereby they partake in a rhythm, the shared pulse that is the subject of all erotic poetry. The Song consequently resembles the ritual courtship of dance; it would make good ballet." Landy, *Paradoxes of Paradise*, 57.

[23] Ellen Davis argues for a holistic understanding of human beings in which our religious capacity is linked with an awareness of our own sexuality: both involve desire to transcend the confines of the self for the sake of intimacy. "Human love always pushes towards transcendence. Profound

Looking at the verses from the biblical Song which O'Connor selects for her version, and those she chooses to omit, she seems to highlight some of the biblical Song's more uncomfortable themes. Drawing on its opening chapter for her opening verse, O'Connor presents the woman expressing concern that her dark skin may cause others to "hate me," as she remembers close family being "so angry with me" and revisits regrets about the past.[24] Then her lover is "sought and sought" but not found; the question "Where is my love? Oh tell me have U seen him?" is left unanswered—whereas in Song 3:1–4 the woman does eventually find him. The parallel passage in Song 5:2–8, where the woman experiences uncertainty, desire, loss, abuse, and despair, as her beloved calls but then goes missing, is evoked in O'Connor's next verse with "And if U see him say my heart is pining." O'Connor's closing verse brings a tone of assurance that "vast floods can't quench love, no matter what love did, / rivers can't drown love no matter where love's hid, / so when U do find him out, / bring him to my mother's house." Yet her closing line is a plea to "tell him don't leave me alone"—ending with the word "alone" poignantly indicates something unresolved; a sense of uncertainty and anxiety. The ups and downs, or ebb and flow, of an intimate relationship which are evident in the biblical Song are particularly strongly highlighted and emphasised in O'Connor's interpretation of it. Assurance and anxiety interweave in the experience of lovers.

4 "You Won't Relent" (Misty Edwards)

Finally, for an overt use of the biblical Song to express relationship with God, we turn to a contemporary Christian worship song: "You Won't Relent."[25] We hear it sung by its composer, Misty Edwards (born 1979), a worship leader at the International House of Prayer in Kansas City, accompanied by David Brymer.

> You won't relent until you have it all
> My heart is yours
> You won't relent until you have it all
> My heart is yours

---

delight in the other person whose soul seems to complete mine moves me some distance out of the self-absorption that seems to be the natural human condition." Davis, *Proverbs*, 248, cf. 233.

24 O'Connor's choice of "yet" (rather than the equally possible translation "and") in her song title might raise questions of any racial concerns implicit in the biblical text and subsequent understandings of it; helpful recent discussion of this can be found in Ausloos, "Between Exegetically Appropriate"; Biernot, "Black I Am." (Dowling Long and Sawyer, *Bible in Music*, mistakenly give the song title as "Dark I Am But Lovely" on the front cover and page 56.).

25 https://www.youtube.com/watch?v=kmRsT-tYdrg.

> I set you as a seal, upon my heart
> As a seal upon my arm
> For there is love
> That is strong as death
> Jealousy demanding as the grave
> And many waters can not quench this love
>
> You won't relent until you have it all
> My heart is yours
> You won't relent until you have it all
> My heart is yours
>
> Come be the fire inside of me
> Come be the flame upon my heart
> Come be the fire inside of me
> Until You and I are one
> Until You and I are one
>
> You won't relent until you have it all
> My heart is yours
> You won't relent until you have it all
> My heart is yours[26]

Edwards draws particularly on Song of Songs 8:6–7:

> Set me as a seal upon your heart,
>   as a seal upon your arm;
> for love is strong as death,
>   passion fierce as the grave.
> Its flashes are flashes of fire,
>   a raging flame.
> Many waters cannot quench love,
>   neither can floods drown it.
> If one offered for love
>   all the wealth of one's house,
>   it would be utterly scorned.

After the combined choir of Howard Skempton and then the solo voice of Sinéad O'Connor, here we find a duet, a male and a female voice, both speaking to another, an unnamed "you." The distinctive structure of alternating voices in itself may remind us of the Song of Songs.[27]

---

[26] Edwards, "You Won't Relent."

[27] J. S. Bach's Cantatas 49 and 140 also present intertwining duets, using lyrics from the Song of Songs. Bach reinterprets Jesus' wedding parables (Matt 22:1–14; 25:1–13) in the light of both the Song and Lutheran pietist themes; thus he depicts Christ searching for the bride, and giving her garments of righteousness. See Rogerson, "Use of the Song," 343–347, 350.

The male voice (David Brymer) addresses a "you" who is perceived as relentless and demanding, wanting everything—to which the singer responds apparently in calm submission: "my heart is yours." These lyrics are not directly linked with the Song of Songs; they might be suggestive of Ps 139:

> Where can I go from your spirit?
>   Or where can I flee from your presence?
> If I ascend to heaven, you are there;
>   if I make my bed in Sheol, you are there. (Ps 139:7–8)

This psalm presents imagery of a God one simply cannot get away from.[28] That impression of a God who insists on full attention is also suggested in "You Won't Relent" in the female lyric, with its emphasis on the phrase "jealousy demanding." A sense of holding nothing back is also conveyed by the sheer intensity in the way Edwards delivers her vocals in the middle of her song, as she soars up the scale and the full band kicks in, taking us from gentle, reflective ballad to visceral surge of rock music, with angst and exaltation interwoven in the passionate yearning for two to become one. There is no elegant understatement here, even though this song is clearly crafted and measured in its delivery.

In "You Won't Relent" it is the female voice which introduces key phrases from Song of Songs, taken from Song 8:6–7, the distinctive section widely acknowledged to be a high-point, its fervent crowning declaration. Here love is seen as an elemental power that will not be defeated, almost personified as a formidable character who refuses to rest once awoken. The poet intriguingly depicts love as *šalhebet-yāh* (שַׁלְהֶבֶתְיָה), perhaps a superlative, "mightiest flame," perhaps also a fleeting reference to the divine name, "flame of Yah." This is transformed in Edwards' lyric into a plea for the presence of the other, "Come be the fire inside of me," perhaps fusing "flame of Yah" with Pentecostal fire (Acts 2:3; cf. Luke 3:16; 24:32).[29]

Edwards also takes up the image of the seal, a tool and symbol which expressed the unique identity and commitment of its owner when impressed onto documents or clay. The biblical Hebrew indicates that it is the woman who is asking the man to set her as a seal on his heart and arm; she longs for her life to be fused with his in an inseparable bond of exclusive, mutual commitment. Misty Edwards' expresses a similar longing, but reverses the wording, turning that biblical plea ("set me as a

---

[28] This sense of God as one who cannot be evaded was later developed in a famous poem (by Francis Thompson) depicting God as "The Hound of Heaven," where the narrator is pursued by a divine love and a hand "outstretched caressingly."
[29] The allusions in Song 8:6–7 to Canaanite deities (Mot, Resheph, and Yam) suggest that a reference here to Israel's deity would not be inappropriate; see Mathys, "Solomon's Song," 132–138; Pope, *Song of Songs*, 668–669; Bergant, *Song of Songs*, 98–99.

seal upon your heart") into a promise that she will *set him* as a seal upon *her* heart and arm. One of the effects of this is to change assertiveness into responsiveness. A striking feature of the biblical Song is the woman's assertiveness, conveyed by the way she addresses the man with numerous imperatives, jussives, and cohortatives. We first encounter her through her opening exclamation: "Let him kiss me with the kisses of his mouth" (1:2), soon followed by the imperative "draw me after you" (1:4), "tell me" (1:7), later "turn my beloved" (2:17), "come, my beloved, let us go forth into the fields [. . .] let us go out early into the vineyards [. . .] there I will give you my love" (7:11–12), right through to the closing verse of the book, two final imperatives: "Make haste, my beloved and be like a gazelle or like a young stag upon the mountains of spices!" (8:14). Not to mention the way she goes out into the streets seeking him in chapters 3 and 5. Intermittently we also hear him calling to her with imperatives, such as those we noted earlier in Howard Skempton's piece (2:10–14; also 3:8; 5:2; 6:5). But it is her assertiveness that predominates in the biblical Song and is diminished in this contemporary appropriation of it.

The male-female duet in "You Won't Relent" also raises the question: who is speaking—and to whom? Are both these voices worshippers, addressing God? Or is one of them the divine voice—in which case, which one? Might she be the voice of God—taking her beloved worshipper to heart, receiving all the human worshipper gives? Or does the male vocal bring the voice of God, offering God's heart to a relentlessly desirous human? (In which case, the assertiveness of the woman in the biblical Song would be indicated here, after all.)[30] Could the male voice be the angel wrestling with a relentless, tenacious Jacob, who refuses to let go until receiving the fullness of divine blessing (cf. Gen 32:22–32)?[31]

Perhaps we should ask the writer what she means in this song—one of the differences between a contemporary text and ancient one is the possibility of doing that. I suspect that Misty Edwards would see both voices as those of the human worshipper. But even if it can be established, the significance of authorial intention is a contentious issue; when a text is released into the world (be it a song, a tweet, a paper, a book . . .), it takes on a life and power of its own, independent of whatever the author may have intended (an experience familiar to those of us who teach or preach!). For that matter, there is no mention in this contemporary song of any divine name—no address to "Lord" or "God" or "Jesus"; so it could even be heard as a couple of human lovers, expressing their feeling towards each other.

---

30 See the discussion in Carr, "Gender," especially 246.
31 The Song's linking of love, jealousy, and death/Sheol may be expressing their insatiability, relentless in their determination to have the loved one uniquely for themselves. "Lovers can never be satisfied, they will always want more. They seek a total, absolute experience." Assis, *Flashes of Fire*, 269. Cf. Bergant, *Song of Songs*, 98.

5 Conclusion

The Song of Songs' admirers down the centuries have been many and varied. Each of the recent songs we have considered highlight particular aspects of the biblical Song; yet such is the richness of that Song and its subject matter that even the three of them combined leave much still unsaid. We might summarise as follows:

Love is:
 . . . blissful serenity and harmony (Howard Skempton)
 . . . intoxication, longing, and anxiety (Sinéad O'Connor)
 . . . demanding, exclusive, self-surrender (Misty Edwards)
 . . . all of this—and more! (Song of Songs)

Bibliography

Ausloos, Hans. "Between Exegetically Appropriate and Politically Correct: Towards a Responsible Interpretation of the Song of Songs." In *The Song of Songs Afresh: Perspectives on a Biblical Love Poem*, edited by Stefan Fischer and Gavin Fernandes, 3–14. Sheffield: Sheffield Phoenix Press, 2019.

Assis, Eliyahu. *Flashes of Fire: A Literary Analysis of the Song of Songs*. LHBOTS 503. London: T&T Cark, 2009.

Begbie, Jeremy. *Resounding Truth: Christian Wisdom in the World of Music*. Grand Rapids, MI: Baker Academic, 2007.

Bergant, Dianne. *The Song of Songs*. Berit Olam. Collegeville, MN: Liturgical Press, 2001.

Bernard of Clairvaux. *On the Song of Songs*, edited and translated by Kilian Walsh. Vol. 1. Kalamazoo, MI: Cistercian Publications, 1977.

Biernot, David. "'Black I Am and Comely': Blackness and Whiteness as Part of Jewish Racial Discourses from Modern Times to Antiquity—and where is the Place of the Song of Songs in All This?" In *The Song of Songs Afresh: Perspectives on a Biblical Love Poem*, edited by Stefan Fischer and Gavin Fernandes, 15–43. Sheffield: Sheffield Phoenix Press, 2019.

Carr, David. "Gender and the Shaping of Desire in the Song of Songs." *JBL* 119 (2000): 233–248.

Davis, Ellen F. *Proverbs, Ecclesiastes and the Song of Songs*. Westminster Bible Companion. Louisville, KY: Westminster John Knox Press, 2000.

Dowling Long, Siobhán, and John F. A. Sawyer. *The Bible in Music: A Dictionary of Songs, Works and More*. Lanham, MD: Rowman & Littlefield, 2015.

Exum, J. Cheryl. *Song of Songs: A Commentary*. OTL. Louisville: Westminster John Knox Press, 2005.

Fallas, John. "Conditions of Immediacy: Howard Skempton Interview." *Tempo* 66 (2012): 13–28.

Fischer, Stefan, and Gavin Fernandes, eds. *The Song of Songs Afresh: Perspectives on a Biblical Love Poem*. Sheffield: Sheffield Phoenix Press, 2019.

Fox, Michael V. "Rereading 'The Song of Songs and the Ancient Egyptian Love Songs' Thirty Years Later." *WO* 46 (2016): 8–21.

Garrett, Duane A., and Paul R. House. *Song of Songs/Lamentations*. WBC 23B. Nashville, TN: Thomas Nelson, 2004.

Goodman, P. William. "Nothing Compares—Sinéad O'Connor's 'Theology,'" *Biblical Reception* 1 (2012): 213–232.

Gray, Erik. "Come Be My Love: The Song of Songs, 'Paradise Lost,' and the Tradition of the Invitation Poem." *PMLA* 128 (2013): 370–385.

Landy, Francis. *Paradoxes of Paradise: Identity and Difference in the Song of Songs*. Sheffield: Almond Press, 1983.

Mathys, Hans-Peter. "Solomon's Song 8:6–7: The Power of Love." In *The Song of Songs Afresh: Perspectives on a Biblical Love Poem*, edited by Stefan Fischer and Gavin Fernandes, 126–150. Sheffield: Sheffield Phoenix Press, 2019.

Pope, Marvin H. *Song of Songs*. AB. New York: Doubleday, 1977.

Rogerson, John M. "The Use of the Song of Songs in J. S. Bach's Church Cantatas." In *Biblical Studies / Cultural Studies: The Third Sheffield Colloquium*, edited by J. Cheryl Exum and Stephen D. Moore, 343–352. JSOTSup 266. Sheffield: Sheffield Academic Press, 1998.

Thomson, Francis. "The Hound of Heaven," ELCore.net, http://poetry.elcore.net/HoundOfHeavenInRtT.html [retrieved 20.05.2020].

Verde, Danilo. "When the Warrior Falls in Love: The Shaping and Reshaping of Masculinity in the Song of Songs." In *The Song of Songs Afresh: Perspectives on a Biblical Love Poem*, edited by Stefan Fischer and Gavin Fernandes, 190–212. Sheffield: Sheffield Phoenix Press, 2019.

Discography

Bush, Kate. "The Song of Solomon," from *The Director's Cut*. Fish People, 2011; previously *The Red Shoes*: EMI, 1993.

Edwards, Misty. "You Won't Relent," from *Relentless*. Forerunner, 2007.

O'Connor, Sinéad. "Dark I Am Yet Lovely," from *Theology*. Rubyworks, 2007.

Skempton, Howard. "Rise Up My Love," from *My Beloved's Voice: Sacred Songs of Love*. Signum Classics, 2014.

Song lyrics are quoted by kind permission of Forerunner Music (for Misty Edwards), Sinéad O'Connor's management team and Howard Skempton.

Appendix: Other Contemporary Music Related to the Song of Songs

Contemporary Classical

Hawes, Patrick. *Song of Songs*. Signum, 2009. Six songs by a contemporary English composer which draw on a selection of verses from the biblical Song, exploring the relationship of romantic and erotic love to spirituality.

Malone, Ryan. *Song of Songs*. 2012. An oratorio in two parts for chorus, soloists and string orchestra. It presents the full biblical text of the Song, using the New King James Version translation. https://www.youtube.com/watch?v=3yik3CvwvUw

My Beloved's Voice: Sacred Songs of Love. Signum Classics, 2014. Choir of Jesus College, Cambridge. Mark Williams, Director. This entire collection of choral works is inspired by the Song of Songs, with most of the contributions alluding to it. It includes three further pieces by Howard Skempton.

Pop/Rock

Bush, Kate. "The Song of Solomon," from *The Director's Cut*. Fish People, 2011; previously *The Red Shoes*, EMI, 1993. Celebrates human desire and sexuality, while also highlighting the prominence of the woman's voice, prompted by phrases from the biblical Song.

Contemporary Worship

Bennett, Morgan, Anna Blanc, and Farah Magnuson. "Waters Cannot Quench this Love." Impromptu worship from the International House of Prayer, Kansas City, involving gentle repetition of a single phrase from the Song of Songs. https://www.youtube.com/watch?v=ZoWFvgtNDcI

Miqedem. "Dodi Li," from *Miqedem (vol. 1)*. 2016. https://miqedem.bandcamp.com/album/miqedem-vol-i. A blend of eastern and western musical styles, with male and female voices repeatedly singing the biblical text of Song 2:16 and 3:2 in Hebrew.

Sinott, Jeremy, and Connie Sinott. "Come Away," from *Come Away My Beloved*. Rejoice Publishing and Productions, 2006. A worship album developed around references to the Song of Songs.

Smith, Martin. "Song of Solomon," from *Back to the Start*. GloWorks Ltd, 2015. Draws briefly on one image from the biblical Song, but is more focused on the felt needs of the worshipper to find intimacy with God.

Townend, Stuart. "Your Fragrance is Lovely," from *Personal Worship*. Kingsway Music, 1999. Phrases from the biblical Song, woven into a romantic worship song.

Contributors

Yael Almog (1982) is associate professor of German Literature at the School of Modern Languages and Cultures, Durham University, U.K.

Elisabeth Birnbaum (1969) has a PhD in Old Testament Studies and is director of the Austrian Catholic Bibelwerk, Austria.

Stefan Gasch (1974) is a researcher at the Department of musicology and performative studies, University of Music and Performing Arts Vienna, Austria.

P. W. (Bill) Goodman (1960) is director of Ongoing Ministerial Development in the Anglican Diocese of Sheffield, U.K.

Michaela Christine Hastetter (1971) is professor of Pastoral Theology and Religious Education at the Catholic University ITI, Trumau, Austria, Apl. professor at the Albert-Ludwigs University, Freiburg i.Br., Germany, and program head at the St. Ephrem Scientific Center for Orient and Occident Studies (STEP), Austria.

Uta Heil (1966) is professor of Church History at the Faculty of Protestant Theology, University of Vienna, Austria.

Ute Jung-Kaiser (1942) is professor emerita of Music Education at the University of Music and Performing Arts Frankfurt, Germany.

Tamar Kadari (1968) is a senior lecturer for Midrash and Aggadah at the Schechter Institute of Jewish Studies, Jerusalem, Israel.

Jonathan Kaplan (1976) is associate professor of Hebrew Bible and Ancient Judaism at the Department of Middle Eastern Studies, University of Texas at Austin, USA.

Rabea Kohnen (1980) is assistant professor of Older German Literature at the Department of German Studies, University of Vienna, Austria.

Gerhard Langer (1960) is professor of Jewish Studies at the Department of Jewish Studies, University of Vienna, Austria.

Hannah W. Matis (1981) is associate professor of Church History at Virginia Theological Seminary, USA.

Bernard McGinn (1937) is professor emeritus of Historical Theology and of the History of Christianity at the Divinity School, University of Chicago, USA.

Christopher Ocker (1958) is professor of the History of Christianity at San Francisco Theological Seminary, University of Redlands, USA, and professor of Medieval and Early Modern Studies at the Institute for Religion and Critical Inquiry, Australian Catholic University, Australia.

https://doi.org/10.1515/9783110750799-025

Timothy H. Robinson (1965) is associate professor of Spiritual Disciplines and Resources at Brite Divinity School Texas, USA.

Caroline Sauter (1984) is a lecturer in Comparative Literature at the Department of Comparative Literature, Goethe University, Frankfurt am Main, Germany.

Annette Schellenberg (1971) is professor of Old Testament at the Faculty of Protestant Theology, University of Vienna, Austria.

Ludger Schwienhorst-Schönberger (1957) is professor emeritus of Old Testament at the Faculty of Catholic Theology, University of Vienna, Austria.

Lieke Smits (1989) is a FWO Junior postdoctoral fellow at the Ruusbroec Institute of the University of Antwerp, Belgium.

Günter Stemberger (1940) is professor emeritus of Jewish Studies at the Department of Jewish Studies, University of Vienna, Austria.

Jonathan Vardi (1982) is a senior lecturer at the Hebrew Literature Department, Hebrew University of Jerusalem, Israel.

Erik Wade (1985) is assistant professor at the English and Creative Writing Department at the Oswego State University of New York, USA.

Elliot R. Wolfson (1956) is professor of Jewish Studies at the Department of Religious Studies, University of California, Santa Barbara, USA.

Ariel Zinder (1973) is a senior lecturer at the Department of Literature at Tel Aviv University, Israel.

Index

Hebrew Bible

Genesis
1:26	194
1:27	441
3	134
4:7	51
15:13	76
25:22	56
32:22–32	478
34:7	51
44:2	427
44:30	474
49:6–7	51

Exodus
1–10	80
2:15–21	96
2:15	44
4:25–26	323
11:4	74, 79, 84
12	80, 119
12:1–20	73–74
12:2	75–76, 82
14:31	118
15	38
15:1	120
15:2	84
15:18	75, 79–80, 84
15:25	84
17:9	51
18:4	44
19:17	81
20:1–2	132
20:15	38
24:7	75, 78–79, 81, 84
25:34	51
26:1–4	449
26:7–13	449
28:9–15	73
36:8–20	449
37:1	58
37:2	58

https://doi.org/10.1515/9783110750799-026

Numbers
4:25	449
12:1	96, 419
15:37–41	47
19:1–22	73
21:17	120

Deuteronomy
4:14	51
4:29	474
6:4–9	47
6:5	474
10:12	474
11:13–21	47
13:15	56
18:15	23
25:17–19	73
26	81
28:56	42
30:2, 6, 10	474
31:16	51
32:1	120
32:14	168
33:4	132

Joshua
1:8	123
10:12	120
22:5	474

Judges
5:1	120
5:4	75, 82, 84–85

1Samuel
2:1	120
16:12	426

2Samuel
6:19	167
22:1	120

1Kings
1–11	369
2:4	474

8:48	474
10	439
11	385, 439
11:1	422

2Kings
23:25	474

Ezra | 21
1:2	119
7:10	56

Nehemiah
10:1	44
11:23	44

Job | 21, 115
4:13	139

Psalms
10:3	474
27:8	187
35:25	474
41:5	192
42:7	193
45	184, 332
46:11	84
50:15	194
54:7	19
68:8	84
68:13	39
68:26	60
68:32	419
71	208
73	78
73:26	74, 77, 83
78:18	474
86:1	247
91:15	75, 81, 84
92:1	120
95:7	84
106:20	66
107:9	474
107:18	474
123	356
126	356

129	356
131	186
133	356
139	477
139:7–8	477

Proverbs — 12, 21, 181–182, 252

2:7	60
3:8	382
5:19	167
6:30	474
8	208
8:22	72
9	208
13:2	474
21:21	85
22:29	55
31:22	416

Ecclesiastes (Qoheleth) — 12, 72, 181–182, 252, 407

1:8	189
12:9	135

Song of Songs[1]

1	253, 298, 336
1:1–6:9	14
1:1–5:1	319
1:1–3:1	177
1:1–12	14
1:1–4	93
1:1	61, 63, 65, 133, 280, 287, 312, 316–317, 323–326
1:2–2:7	376, 380
1:2–17	4
1:2–7	377
1:2–4	298, 336, 473
1:2–3	13, 48–51, 297, 324
1:2	5, 7, 13, 24, 48–51, 65, 122, 132, 168, 253, 265, 287, 290–291, 316–317, 343, 474, 478
1:3	49, 267, 324
1:4	42, 46, 155–156, 267, 336, 339, 375–376, 447, 454, 478
1:5–8	459

---

1 For three passages in the Song, the verse numbering in the Vulgate differs from the verse numbering in the Hebrew tradition (Hebr. 1:2–17 = Vulg. 1:1–16; Hebr. 6:2–12 = Vulg. 6:1–11; Hebr. 7:3–14 = Vulg. 7:2–13). If not noted otherwise, this volume gives the verse numbering of the Hebrew tradition.

1:5–7	298
1:5–6	27, 417, 454, 473
1:5	3, 9–10, 89, 102, 186, 266, 294, 336, 415–434, 437, 444, 449, 455
1:6–9	336
1:6	3, 65, 324, 369, 385, 387, 416–417, 420–421, 429, 448, 451
1:7–8	27, 369, 448
1:7	26, 123, 188, 381, 474, 478
1:8	26, 42, 123, 155, 161, 326, 376
1:9–12	474
1:9–11	377
1:9	13
1:10	376
1:11	208
1:12–2:14	14
1:12–14	377–378
1:12	45, 229, 378
1:13	13, 324
1:14	303, 369, 375–376
1:15–16	213
1:15	326, 376, 378, 383, 474
1:16–2:1	378
1:16–17	229–230, 377
1:16	223, 416, 474
1:17	223, 474
2	249
2:1–2	297
2:1	326, 337–338, 377–378
2:2	224, 376
2:3–7	377
2:3–4	318
2:3	323, 316
2:4–5	28
2:4	46, 316, 323–324
2:5	119, 167, 316, 318, 448, 474
2:6	39, 229, 297, 316–317, 323, 325, 382
2:7–9	297
2:7	4, 28, 140
2:8–3:5	376, 380
2:8–14	381
2:8–13	119
2:8–9	352
2:8	75, 325
2:9	265, 324
2:10–14	470, 478
2:10–13	25, 119
2:10–12	454
2:10–11	208

2:10	13, 119, 303, 326, 376
2:12	119, 168
2:13–3:5	320
2:13–14	320
2:13	13, 376
2:14	81, 303, 322, 324, 376, 474
2:15–17	320
2:15	13, 119, 471
2:16–17	354
2:16	312–313, 317, 321, 340, 380, 385
2:17	17, 119, 168, 325, 385, 474, 478
3	18, 103, 382, 478
3:1–4	152, 474, 475
3:1	267, 323, 425, 473
3:3–4	320
3:4	13, 123, 323, 326
3:5	56, 140, 313, 321–323, 325
3:6–8:4	376
3:6–11	382
3:6	102, 171, 208–209
3:7–11	379
3:7	124, 326
3:8	478
3:9–10	58
3:9	57, 58, 325
3:10	58, 416
3:11	17–18, 26, 29, 42, 116, 206
4	244, 254, 257, 380
4:1–15	474
4:1–7	376, 377–378
4:1–6	255
4:1	124, 254, 303, 376
4:2–3	325
4:3	169, 416
4:4	47
4:6	169, 255–256, 382
4:7	208, 255, 291, 293, 301, 303, 316, 322, 376
4:8–15	376
4:8	26, 43–44, 118, 256, 303, 324, 326
4:9	48, 172–174, 256, 274, 277, 316
4:10–11	256, 325
4:10	470
4:11	118, 168
4:12–5:1	387
4:12–15	256, 271
4:12	247
4:13	326

4:16–5:1	18
4:16	19–20, 44, 257, 325, 474
4:17	229
5	245, 478
5:1–16	319
5:1	20, 25, 30, 242, 245, 324, 376, 474
5:2–8	475
5:2	3, 71–73, 77, 83, 85–86, 124, 156, 313, 321, 376, 425, 478
5:4–6	376
5:4	206, 319
5:5	206, 425
5:6–8	290–293, 295
5:6	206, 292–293, 324, 326
5:7	47, 207, 292
5:8	140, 145, 151, 205, 229, 292–293, 425, 473–474
5:9	291, 303, 376
5:10–16	118
5:10	122, 322, 338, 376, 416, 420, 425, 431–432
5:11	72, 416, 426
5:12	229, 426
5:13	338, 426
5:14	45, 118, 169, 324, 420, 426–427, 432
5:15	338
5:16	338, 376, 426
5:17	291, 303
6:1–8:14	319, 323
6:1	118, 323, 376
6:2–12	4
6:2–3	470
6:2	46, 316–317, 325, 376
6:3	56, 118, 332, 376
6:4–9	474
6:4	28, 102, 145, 160, 324–326, 370, 376–378
6:5	478
6:6–7	171
6:8	326
6:9	102, 316
6:10	145, 160–161, 171, 209, 296, 303, 326, 416
6:11–12	29, 376
6:11	291, 375
6:12	296, 303, 375–376
7	382
7:1–9	474
7:1–2	365
7:1	27, 375
7:2	44, 125, 303, 319, 326, 369
7:3–14	4

7:3	168, 377
7:4	56
7:5	44, 303, 447
7:6–7	343
7:6	119, 303, 324, 470
7:7–8	103
7:7	160, 291, 303
7:8	205
7:9	377–378
7:10–11	326
7:10	45, 50, 325, 470
7:11–8:2	474
7:11–12	478
7:11	376, 382
7:12	291, 376
7:13	125
7:14	24, 125, 376
8	418
8:1–2	24, 324, 383
8:1	126, 325
8:2	169, 473
8:3	56
8:4	56, 140, 316, 318
8:5–14	376
8:5–7	474
8:5	102, 324, 420–421, 451–452
8:6–7	476–477
8:6	141, 324, 389, 403–405
8:7	473
8:8–12	386
8:8–10	387–388
8:8–9	323
8:9	323, 376
8:10–14	379, 386
8:10	375–376, 378
8:11–12	9, 384–387, 448
8:11	325, 376
8:12	375–376, 385
8:13–14	326
8:13	126, 474
8:14	103, 145, 151, 168, 205, 287, 323–324, 336, 474, 478

Isaiah — 155
3:18–24	47
3:23	47
7:14	23

30:19	120
52:1–2	187
52:7	17
54:5–6	148
54:5	332
54:12	167
60:4	155

Jeremiah

2:2	39
2:24	474
9:21	190

Ezekiel

1:14	427
10:9	427
16	80
16:1–14	80
16:6	84
16:27	474
28:13	427

Daniel 335

10:6	427

Hosea

2:19	332
3:1	167
14:6	86

Micah

4:1–4	27
4:1	23

Zephaniah

3:10	419

Deuterocanonical Works

Sir 15:6	184
Sir 24:1–22	208
Sir 25:2	19
4Ezra 4:36–37	41

New Testament

Matthew
5:28	339
6:29	419
9:15	179
11:13	23
12:42	419
19:12	19
22:1–14	476
25:1–13	476

Mark
1:27	251

Luke
3:16	477
7:48	187
10	208
10:25–37	194
16:16	23
24:32	477

John
1:14	22
3:29	16, 179
4:34	22
5:1–9	205
17:4	22
20:19	19

Acts
2:3	477

Romans
10:15	17
11:30–31	420
12:3	192

1Corinthians
2:14	183
10:4	19, 247

2Corinthians
3:18 194
11:2 16

Galatians
3:11 17

Ephesians
2:20 247
5 333
5:32 332–333

Colossians
2:3 184

Philemon
3:14 19

Hebrews
7:27 22
9:2–3 22
9:12 22

1John
2:15–16 189

Revelation 335–336
1:13 41
3:20 41, 332
5:1 247
12 208
20:20 336

Patristic Literature

Apollinaris of Laodicea
Fragmenta in Canticum Canticorum 18

Apponius
In Cantica Canticorum
   I 19 108
   I 20–21 108

I 22–23	109
I 23–24	109

Athanasius of Alexandria
Epistulae festales
39	21–22

(Ps.-)Athanasius
Homilia in Canticum Canticorum	2, 18–21
Synopsis Scripturae Sacrae	2, 21–32

Beda Venerabilis
In Cantica Canticorum
I 1	109
I 5	109
I 7	108
VI	203, 218

Cyril of Alexandria
Anathema (ACO I 1,1)	31
Fragmenta in Canticum Canticorum	18
Second Letter to Nestorius (ACO I 1,1)	31
Third Letter to Nestorius (ACO I 1,1)	31

Didymus the Blind
Fragmentum in Cancticum Canticorum	18

Eusebius of Caesarea
Catena	22
Historia ecclesiastica	
6,22	12
6,32,2	13
Scholia in Canticum Canticorum	16

(Ps.-)Eusebius
Catena	16, 18

Facundus of Hermiane
Pro Defensione Trium Capitulorum	421

Gregory of Nyssa
In Canticum Canticorum homiliae XV	14–15

Hippolytus of Rome
Interpretatio Cantici Canticorum	12–13

Jerome

Epistula 33,4	13
Letter to Eustochium	204
De viris illustribus 61	12

(Ps.-)John Chrysostom

Synopsis Scripturae Sacrae	21

Methodius of Olympus

Symposium	12

Origen of Alexandria

In Canticum Canticorum (Libri II)	
Frag. (Philocalia 7,1)	13
Commentarius in Canticum (Libri X)	13–14, 221
Prologue 4	17, 58, 60
Prologue 4,1	23
I 4,1–30	109
II 1,1–57	95
II 1,3–6; 1,51 (frag. 9)	417, 419
II 1,3.4	441
II 1,8.10	442
II 1,46–49 (frag. 10)	417
II 1,51 (frag. 9)	417
II 1,54	449
II 2,4	451
II 2,6–7; 2,21 (frag. 11)	417
II 2,16–19 (frag. 12)	417
II 3,1–12 (frag. 13)	417
III 3,1–6	109
IV–X (frag. 50)	420
IV–X (frag. 53)	420
IV–X (frag. 83)	420–421
Homiliae in Canticum	13–15, 437
I 1	23, 418
I 5–6	417–420

Philo of Carpasia

Ennarratio in Canticum Canticorum	17–18

Procopius of Gaza

Epitome in Canticum Canticorum	18
Catena	18

Theodore of Mopsuestia
Adversus allegoricos   421
In Canticum Canticorum   422–423

Theodoret of Cyrus
Explanatio in Canticum Canticorum   16–17

Rabbinic Writings

Mishnah   49, 52, 121–124
m. 'Abod. Zar. 2:5   38, 41–42, 48, 50–51
m. Meg. 4:4   115
m. Ta'anit 4:8   38, 41–42, 45, 116
m. Šabb. 8:3   47–48
m. Yad. 3:5   38, 63–64, 115, 133

Tosefta   121
t. Ḥag. 2:3–4   38, 41
t. Ketub. 5:10   38, 41
t. Kip. 2:15   59
t. Sanh. 12:10   38, 64
t. Yad. 2:6   38

Babylonian Talmud   37, 121
b. B. Bat. 9b   85
b. Bek. 31b   46
b. Meg. 7a   63
b. Nid. 14b   124
b. Sanh.
    56ab   80–81
    90b   46
b. Yebam. 97a   46

Jerusalem Talmud (Palestinian Talmud)   3, 37–38, 41–52
y. 'Abod. Zar.
    2:5   51
    2:8, 41c   50
    2:8, 41c–d   42, 47–48
y. Ber.
    1:7, 3b   50
    2:1, 4b   45
    2:7, 5b–c   46
    4:5, 8d   47–48
    9:1, 13a   44

y. Ḥag. 2:1, 77b	42
y. Ḥal. 4:8, 60a	43
y. Ketub. 5:13, 30b	42
y. Meg. 1:13, 72b	44
y. Moʿed Qaṭ. 3:7, 83c	45
y. Peʾah 7:4, 20b	45
y. Sanh.	
4:2, 22a	46
11:6, 30a	50
y. Šabb.	
6, 8b	47
8:3, 11b	47
y. Šeb. 6:1, 36d	43
y. Šeqal.	
2:7, 47a	45
6:1, 49c	45
y. Soṭah 8:3, 22d	45
y. Sukkah 4:8, 54d	44
y. Taʾan. 4:10–11, 67b	42

Targumim

	131, 156, 427
Second Targum of Esther	120
Targum Onqelos	117, 427
Targum Pseudo-Jonathan	117
Targum Ruth	120
Targum Song of Songs	V, 3–4, 60, 115–126, 441
1:2	122
1:8	123
3:4	123
3:7	124
4:1	124
4:2–3	124
4:4	124
4:11	118
5:2	86–87, 124
5:10	122
5:12	124
5:14	118
6:2	124
6:4	124
6:5	124–125
6:7–9	121
6:7	121
6:9	125
6:12	125
7:2	125

7:3	125
7:14	126
8:1	126
8:13	126

Other Texts

'Abot de Rabbi Nathan I:1	63
Agadath Shir ha-Shirim / Shir ha-Shirim Zuta	55, 133
Exodus Rabbah	
2.5	73
19.5	80
Genesis Rabbah 77.1	75
Lamentations Rabbah	117
Leviticus Rabbah	
19.1	72
31.4	119
Massekhet Soferim 10–21	118
Megillat Antiokhos	121
Mekilta	118
Beshallaḥ 7	119
Shirata	
1	120
3	118
Mekilta de Rabbi Ishmael	38–39, 43
Pisḥa	
5	80
14	43, 58
Beshallaḥ	
5	47
7	43
Shirata	
6	47
Baḥodesh	
1	42, 45
8	47
9	38–39
Mekilta de Rabbi Shimon bar Yoḥai	81
Beshallaḥ 24:2	47
Midrash Tehillim (Midrash on Psalms)	
19:7	123
Midrash Shir ha-Shirim (Song of Songs Rabbah)	3, 4, 37, 45, 55–67, 87
1:1.7, 8	72
1:1.11	60
1:2.1	60
1:4	155
1:6.3	65

1:8	135
1:12	133
1:13	132
1:14.3	86
1:15.2, 4	81
2:2.6	86
2:8.1	75
2:8–13	119
3:9.1–3:10.4	59
3:9.2	57–58
4:1.2	81
5:2.2	83–87
7:10.1	46
8:6.3	86
Midrash Shir ha-Shirim (Greenhut)	55
Pesiqta de Rab Kahana	3, 37, 45
5	119
5.6	73–83, 85, 86
5.7	72, 74–76
5.9	119
Pesiqta Rabbati 15	73, 119
Seder Eliyahu Rabbah	116
Sipre Deuteronomy	38
301	81
305	42

Anonymous Works/Works not Related to One Person

Acta Conciliorum Oecumenicorum (ACO)	
Concilium Universale Ephesenum	31
Concilium Universale Constantinopolitanum	16
Antiphoner of Compiègne	208
Apostolic Constitutions	30
Ascendam in palmam	205
Bible moralisée	267–268, 271
Biblica pauperium	7, 267, 269
Bibliotheca Veterum Patrum	16
Canterbury Glosses	91–97
Homiliae Dominicales et Festivales (Admont)	199–210
Lehre der liebenden Gotteserkenntnis	6, 215, 221–227

Leiden Glosses	92, 107–110
Life of Saint Mary of Egypt	3, 89–110
Machsor Lipsiae	448
Pseudo-Clementines	30
Rothschild Canticles	277–278
Schöppenchronik	226
Speculum virginum	200
St. Trudperter Hohelied	6, 200, 203, 221, 312
Thoofkijn van devotien	272

Persons

Abrabanel, Isaac	356
Abraham ibn Daud	166
Abraham ibn Ezra	159–160, 374
Abu Nuwas	166
Abu al-Walid Marwan ibn Janah	172–173
Aelfric of Eynsham	99, 107
Agnes of Poitou	204
Agricola, Alexander	291, 293, 297, 306
Ahmose Nefertari	449–451
Ahmose I	449
Alamire, Petrus (Petrus Imhoff)	7, 288–289, 292
Alan of Lille	245
Alcuin of York	203–204, 287
Alexander Jannaeus (Yannay)	121
Alexander, James B.	388
Alexander, Philip	116–117, 120
Alliaco, Petrus de see d'Ailly, Pierre	
Alterman, Nathan	167
Ambrose of Milan	177, 228
Ammon, Christoph Friedrich	367, 379
Amoraim (amoraic)	2–3, 37, 40, 45, 47, 50–52, 55, 60, 62, 64, 131
Angela of Foligno	312
Anne of Bohemia and Hungary	299
Anne of Brittany	295
Anselm of Laon	252
Apollinaris of Laodicea	18, 21
Apponius	92–93, 108–109
Aristobulus II	121

Aristotle	250
Arnold of Bonneval	179
Arnulf of Louvain	280
Athanasius of Alexandria	2, 11, 16, 18–22, 26–27, 30–32
Augustine of Hippo	177, 187, 231–232
Bach, Johann Sebastian	457, 476
Bachlund, Gary	455
Bakhtin, Mikhail	232
Baldock, Robert	457
Baldwin, William	341–343
Ballester, Núria	457
Band, Debra	459, 461
Banez, Domingo	315
Barbireau, Jacobus	291, 297–298, 306
Bauldeweyn, Noel	290–291, 299–302, 307–308
Bavière, Isabeau de	241
Beatrice of Nazareth	312
Beatrix of Hungary and Bohemia	297
Beda Venerabilis	92–94, 96, 107–109, 203, 210, 216, 218, 220, 287
Ben Azzai	42
Ben Zoma	42
Benedict XVI	190
Benjamin, Walter	9, 393–396, 412
Bennett, Joseph	388
Benz, Ernst	417, 437, 451
Bernard of Clairvaux	5, 177–196, 199, 202, 210, 221, 224–225, 231–232, 265, 279–281, 287, 316, 323, 340, 471
Beverly, Thomas	337
Beza, Theodore	340
Blumenthal, Sandro	389
Bob Dylan	129
Boethius	243
Bornefeld, Helmut	452
Bossi, Enrico	453
Böttcher, Friedrich	366–367, 378
Brauer, Arik	463–465
Braun, Johann Wilhelm	222
Brentano, Manfred	389
Breton, André	463
Brightman, Thomas	335–336
Brun of Schönebeck	6, 215, 226–234
Bruno of Segni	179
Brymer, David	475, 477
Buber, Martin	393, 451
Budde, Karl Ferdinand Reinhard	365
Burstyn, Shai	288

Bush, Kate	473
Bussewitz-Quarm, Michael	458
Calix of Rome	12
Casals, Pablo	457–458
Cassiodor (Roman Statesman)	17
Catherine of Bologna	313
Catherine of Genoa	313
Catherine of Siena	313
Cecilia del Nacimiento	7, 313–314, 321–322
Champion, Nicolas	300, 302
Charles V	288–289, 299
Charles VI	241
Chiu, Remi	288
Cicero	417
Clare of Assisi	312
Clemen, Otto	446
Clemens non Papa, Jacobus	290
Cochlaeius, Johannes	244
Cohen, Gerson	155
Cohen, Hermann	393, 396, 399
Collings, John	331, 333, 340–341
Compère, Loyset	291–294, 306–307
Corbin, Henry	133
Costello, Elvis	469
Cotton, John	329–330, 334, 336
Cuno of Regensberg	205
Cyril of Alexandria	18, 31
Cyril of Scythopolis	97–98
Cyrus the Great	119–120, 124
Dahlenburg, Jane Elizabeth	288
d'Ailly, Pierre (Petrus de Alliaco)	6, 241–260
Dalton-Williamson, Julie	455
Damasus (Pope)	14
Davidson, Samuel	379
De Man, Paul	412
Defoe, Daniel	153
Delacroix, Eugène	364
Delitzsch, Franz Julius	372–373, 379–383, 387
Denys the Carthusian	244
Derrida, Jacques	136, 412
Dhuoda of Septimania	311
Diderot, Denis	367
Didymus the Blind	18
Diop, Mbissine Thérèse	438–439

Dolezel, Lubomir	153–154
Dunash ben Labrat	170
Edwards, Jonathan	333, 337, 340
Edwards, Misty	10, 475–479
Eichhorn, Johann Gottfried	368
Eleazar bi-Rabbi Qillir	133
Eliasberg, Alexander	399
Elisha ben Abuyah	42
Epiphanius of Salamis	17
Epiphanius Scholasticus	17
Eusebius of Caesarea	12–13, 16, 22
Ewald, Georg Heinrich August	365–370, 372, 374, 376–379, 386
Falkenburg, Reindert	271–272
Ferdinand I	299
Ferraige, Jacques	313
Févin, Antoine de	291, 295, 300, 302, 307
Fischer, Arwed	227
Flavius Josephus	121
Fleming, Robert	337
Foccroulle, Bernhard	454–455
Forestier, Mathurin	300, 302
François I	298
Frederichs, Henning	452
Frederick the Wise of Saxony	289
Freehof, Solomon	138–139
Friedrich, Ernst Ferdinand	366, 379
Fugger the Elder, Raymund	299–303
Fugger, Jakob ("the rich")	302
Gaon, Saadiah	129
Gascongne, Matthieu	290–291, 298–299, 308
Gerhardt, Paul	428
Gerson, Jean	242–243
Gertrude the Great	312
Gessner, Salomon	349
Ghiselin, Johannes	291, 293–294, 306
Gill, Eric	458, 460
Gill, John	337
Ginsburg, Christian David	366, 369, 371–372, 374, 379, 386–387
Gluck, Christoph Willibald	364
Godfrey of Admont	201–202
Goethe, Johann Wolfgang von	8, 347, 351–354, 357, 360, 364, 367–368, 371, 379, 401, 406–407
Goscelin of Saint-Bertin	96, 101
Gregory of Nyssa	2, 11, 14–15, 21, 93, 109, 180, 210

Gregory the Great	177, 203, 344
Guyon, Jeanne	7, 313, 324–326
Hadewijch of Antwerp	312
Hadrian of Canterbury	3–4, 89–110
Haimo of Auxerre	216, 219–220
Hasday ibn Shaprut	170
Hasmoneans / Hashmonay	117, 120–122
Hasselquist, Fredrik	384
Haupt, Josef	222
Hausmann, Manfred	456
Hellinck, Lupus	290, 307
Heloise of the Paraclete	311
Henry III	215
Henry IV	215
Henry VIII	289, 295
Henry, Matthew	344
Herder, Johann Gottfried	8, 71, 347–357, 359–361, 365–368, 370–371, 374–384, 386, 401, 406–407, 427
Herrad of Hohenbourg	200
Herxheimer, Salomon	366, 379
Heyse, Paul	388
Hildegard of Bingen	200, 202, 205, 311–312
Hiller, Wilfried	389
Hillier, Paul	453
Hippolytus of Rome	2, 11–14, 17, 30
Hirzel, Bernhard	366, 379
Hitzig, Ferdinand	379
Homes, Nathanael	335–336
Honorius of Autun / Augustodunensis	179, 227–228, 287, 446
Horne, John	342
Hrabanus Maurus	200, 203, 216
Hrotswitha (of Gandersheim)	311
Hufnagel, Wilhelm Friedrich	366
Hyrcanus II	121
Imhoff, Petrus *see Alamire, Petrus*	
Ingres, Jean-Auguste-Dominique	364
Irimbert of Admont	200–201, 205, 222
Irmingart of Admont	200
Isaac ibn Ghiyyat	152
Isaac ibn Sahula	133
Isaac, Heinrich	291, 295–296, 298, 306
Isidore of Seville	101
Jacobi, Johann Friedrich	366, 374, 379
Jahn, Gustav	433

Jastrow, Marcus	365
Jeanne de Cambry	7, 313, 319–321
Jelinger, Christopher	338
Jerome	12–14, 95–96, 177, 204, 210, 251, 255–256, 415, 417
Jesus Christ	20, 96, 185, 225, 242, 251, 259, 267, 279, 312, 323–324, 331, 338–340, 427, 432, 442, 478
John Chrysostom	16, 21
John Hyrcanus	121
John Moschus	97–98
John of Germanicia	16
John of Mantua	203
John of the Cross	321, 331, 454
Joseph ibn Hasday	170
Josephus *see Flavius Josephus*	
Josquin Desprez	288, 291, 296–297, 300–302, 306–308
Juana of Castile	296
Julian of Norwich	313
Kant, Immanuel	348
Karaites	122
Katherine of Aragon	295
Kavanaugh, Kieran	314, 454
Kesselring, Joseph	388
Kessler, Harry Graf	458–459
Klenau, Paul August von	389
Klenkok, Johannes	250
Kleuker, Johann Friedrich	366
Klopstock, Friedrich Gottlieb	349
Kristeva, Julia	232, 408–409
Kukuck, Felicitas	456
Kunst, Hans-Joachim	443
Kyeser, Conrad	444–445
Lambrecht of Regensburg	274
Lantins, Arnold de	290
Lapide, Pinchas	441
Lautensack, Heinrich	389
Lawrence of Durham	179
Le Petit, Ninon	300
Leclercq, Jean	5, 178–179, 199
Leeu, Gerard	272, 274–275
Leo X	289
Lessing, Gotthold Ephraim	367
Levi bar Nezira	45
Lieberman, Saul	40, 62, 133
Lombard, Peter	242, 251
Lorris, Guillaume de	241

Louis I	299
Louis XII	295
Löwisohn, Solomon	379
Lowth, Robert	347, 356
Lubac, Henri de	244, 422
Luther, Martin	184, 334–335, 353–354, 368, 415–416, 424, 426–428, 452
Mackenzie, Alexander C.	388
Macrina (the Younger)	311
Maimonides, Moses	81
Manchicourt, Pierre de	290
Mandelbaum, Bernard	73
Mann, Thomas	458
Marbrianus de Orto	297, 300, 302, 307
Marcion of Sinope	30
Margaret of Austria	288–290, 292–294, 299, 302
Mariamne I	121
Mariana de San José	313
Marie de l'Incarnation	7, 313–314, 322–324
Markell of Ancyra	19
Martin, Claude	323
Mary (mother of Jesus)	6–7, 24–25, 30, 180, 203–204, 206–210, 214, 224–226, 228, 231–234, 245, 265–266, 269, 271, 287, 289, 291, 295, 299–302, 304, 408, 446–447
Mary of Egypt	3, 89–110
Mary of Hungary	299
Mather, Cotton	334
Matilda of Tuscany	203
Matitiah (High Priest)	121
Maximilian I	289, 292, 295–297
Maximus the Confessor	98
Mechthild of Hackeborn	312
Mechthild of Magdeburg	312
Meier, Ernst	379
Meister Eckhart	182, 232
Mendelssohn, Moses	8, 347, 352, 354–360, 427
Methodius of Olympus	12
Meun, Jean de	241
Michaelis, Johann David	368, 371
Michelangelo	282
Michl, Arthur	444
Mielke, Andreas	439, 444, 446
Migne, Jacques Paul	101, 201
Monica (Saint)	311
Montfaucon, Bernard de	19, 21
Montreuil, Jean de	241

Morales, Cristóbal de	290
More, Agnes	319
More, Thomas	319
Mouton, Jean	300, 302, 307
Mozart, Wolfgang Amadeus	364
Nebuchadnezzar	86, 124
Nestorius	31
Nicholas of Lyra	244, 252
Nicholas of Verdun	442–443
Nietzsche, Friedrich	190
Nilus of Ancyra	18
O'Connor, Sinéad	10, 472–476, 479
Ohly, Friedrich	219, 222–225
Olympias (Deaconess)	14
Origen of Alexandria	2, 9, 11, 13–15, 17, 21, 32, 58, 60, 92–95, 109, 132, 150, 177, 180–181, 221, 265, 287, 311, 331–332, 342, 415–435, 434, 437, 441–442, 449, 451–452
Ovid	259
Palestrina, Giovanni Pierluigi da	288, 290
Paschasius Radbertus	203–204
Paul	16–17, 178, 192, 194, 423
Paul de Saint-Sacrament	313
Paul of Naples	97–98
Penderecki, Krzysztof	452
Peregrinus of Hirsau	200
Perpetua of Carthage	311
Peter Damian	204
Petrucci, Ottaviano	288, 292
Pez, Bernard	201
Philip the Fair	288, 296–297
Philippson, Ludwig	366, 379
Philo of Carpasia	2, 17–18, 30
Phinot, Dominique	290
Pierre de la Rue	290, 297, 300, 302, 306–307
Pizan, Christine de	241
Pliny the Elder	416
Poiret, Pierre	324
Porete, Marguerite	312
Preston, John	332
Prince (Musician)	472
Procopius of Gaza	18
Pseudo-Dionysius the Areopagite	180

Quarles, Francis	343
Queen of Sheba	7, 266, 439–440, 442–445
Raban, Zeew	462–463
Rabban Gamliel	61, 63–64
Rabbi Abba	44
Rabbi Abbahu	84
Rabbi Abun	47
Rabbi Abun bar Hiyya	48
Rabbi Akiva	40, 42, 63–64, 81, 115, 133, 138–139, 311, 359
Rabbi Azariah	132
Rabbi Bibi	58
Rabbi Eleazar ben Rabbi Tsadok	42
Rabbi Eliezer	40, 72
Rabbi Hama bar Uqba	50–51
Rabbi Hiyya	44
Rabbi Hiyya bar Abba	74, 77, 83
Rabbi Hiyyah bar Ada	46
Rabbi Hunia	84
Rabbi Isaac	44, 51, 65
Rabbi Ishmael	38, 40, 42–45, 47–51, 58, 80
Rabbi Joshua	48–49, 50–51
Rabbi Joshua ben Levi	85, 132
Rabbi Judah	48
Rabbi Judah bar Rabbi Shimon	132
Rabbi Justus	43–44
Rabbi La (Hela/Ela)	51
Rabbi Levi	75, 81, 84
Rabbi Mana	48
Rabbi Nahman	75
Rabbi Natan	61, 63
Rabbi Nehemia	76
Rabbi Shimon	44, 46–47, 81
Rabbi Shimon ben Laqish	46
Rabbi Tanhuma	51, 58, 84
Rabbi Yannai	44, 46, 75, 81–82, 84
Rabbi Yasa	84
Rabbi Yehoshua	72
Rabbi Yehoshua ben Levi	85, 132
Rabbi Yehoshua from Sikhnin	75, 81, 84
Rabbi Yehudah	75
Rabbi Yehudah ben Rabbi Ilai	57–59
Rabbi Yehudah ben Rabbi Simon	60–62
Rabbi Yitzhak	60, 62–63
Rabbi Yohanan	44, 46, 50, 155
Rabbi Yohanan ben Tortah	46
Rabbi Yohanan ben Zakkai	42

Rabbi Yose	74, 79
Rabbi Yudan	44, 84
Raoul of Laon	252
Rashi	136–137, 152, 254, 386, 441
Rav Periri	45
Rawicki, Wolf	462
Regilind of Admont	200
Reichert, Klaus	427, 451
Rem, Bernhard	301
Rembrandt	282
Resh Lakish	46, 84
Richafort, Jean	300
Richard (Abbot of Préaux)	179
Ricoeur, Paul	247
Robert of Tombelaine	203
Rodenberg, Julius	389
Rodriguez, Otilio	454
Röhrig, Floridus	443
Romanet of Savoy, Marguerite	313
Rosenstock, Eugen	405
Rosenstock, Margit (Gritli)	405–406
Rosenzweig, Franz	9, 393–413, 451
Rossini, Gioachino	364
Rous, Francis	339–340
Rousseau, Jean-Jacques	364
Rubinstein, Anton Grigorjewitsch	389
Rufinus of Aquileia	13, 451–452
Rupert of Deutz	179, 202, 204–210, 222, 225, 265, 279, 287, 446–447
Saadiah Gaon	129
Salbert, Dieter	9, 415–434, 455
Samuel Ha-Nagid (Ismail ibn Naghrila)	166–170, 172–174
Schiller, Johann Christoph Friedrich	367–368
Scholem, Gershom	9, 393–413
Sembène, Ousmane	439
Shimon bar Abba	50
Shimon bar Nezira	45
Sibbes, Richard	332–333
Simeon the Righteous	125
Skempton, Howard	10, 469–471, 476, 478–479
Smith, Jud	342
Solomon	7, 9, 15–16, 22, 27, 29, 57–63, 65, 71–72, 116, 120, 122, 124, 133, 135–138, 171, 181, 206, 214, 228, 233, 245, 248, 252, 254, 258, 266, 319, 333–336, 341, 344, 365, 369–371, 374–376, 378–381, 383–390, 406, 415–416, 419, 422–426, 439–443, 449, 455–456, 458, 463, 472–473

Solomon ibn Gabirol	145–151, 153, 157, 162, 170–172
Sophronius (of Jerusalem)	97–98
Spangenberg, Wolfhart	226
Spark, Muriel	446
Stekl, Konrad	444
Stenzl, Jürg	7, 288
Stewart, Stanley	341, 343
Suppan, Wolfgang	444
Suso, Henry	182
Tannaim (tannaitic)	2, 37–52, 55, 58, 60, 62–64, 130
Tauler, Johannes	182
Taylor, Edward	338
Teller, Wilhelm Abraham	368
Teresa of Avila	7, 313–319, 321–323
Theocritus	451
Theodore of Mopsuestia	9, 15–16, 214, 415, 417, 421–424, 426, 434
Theodore of Tarsus	3–4, 89–92, 95–99, 107
Theodoret of Cyrus	2, 16–17, 21, 23, 92–93, 109
Thérache, Pierre de	300, 302
Thompson, Francis	477
Tulev, Toivo	453–454
Umbreit, Friedrich Wilhelm Carl	366–367, 379
Velthusen, Johann Caspar	387
Venerable Bede *see Beda Venerabilis*	
Veny d'Arbouze, Marguerite de	313
Vernazza, Battistina	313
Vintler, Hans	439–440
Virgil	259, 417
Vourda, Laurentius de	300
Watson, Thomas	340
Weber, Max	330
Weerbeke, Gaspar van	291, 293–295, 307
Weismann, Wilhelm	452
Weißbach, Friedrich Eduard	388
Wernher (Provost of Klosterneuburg)	442
Wette, Wilhelm Martin Leberecht de	366
Wharton, John	342
Willemer, Marianne	364
Williram of Ebersberg	6, 215–221, 226, 233
Williram of Saint-Thierry	180
Woerner, Roman	388
Wolfram of Eschenbach	228

Yanguas, Diego de	315
Zender, Hans	452
Zilcher, Hermann	452
Zosimus	98–100, 102–107

www.ingramcontent.com/pod-product-compliance
Lightning Source LLC
Chambersburg PA
CBHW051533230426
43669CB00015B/2580